A NEW HISTORY OF BRITISH SHIPPING

A NEW HISTORY OF BRITISH SHIPPING

Ronald Hope

JOHN MURRAY

First published in 1990
by John Murray (Publishers) Ltd
50 Albemarle Street, London W1X 4BD

British Library Cataloguing in Publication Data
Hope, Ronald, *1921–*
A new history of British merchant shipping.
1. Great Britain. Merchant shipping, history
I. Title
387.50941

ISBN 0–7195–4799–7

Typeset by Butler & Tanner Ltd
Printed and bound in Great Britain by
Butler & Tanner Ltd, Frome and London

Contents

Abbreviations used in Notes:
EHR = *Economic History Review*
JTH = *Journal of Transport History*
MM = *Mariner's Mirror*
IJNA = *International Journal of Nautical Archaeology and Underwater Exploration*

Illustrations

For illustration credits please see the Author's Prologue.

Tables and Charts

For
Marion

Prologue

When Marcus Samuel founded the Shell Transport and Trading Company, one-time owners and operators of the world's largest tanker fleet, he adopted a seashell, and subsequently the scallop shell, as a trademark. As a boy in London I lived where the Saxons sailed up the Heathwall Brook from Nine Elms to found Clapham. In the marshlands between Heathwall Brook and the Thames was St Patrick's Island or Patrick's Ait, later corrupted to Battersea, where perhaps the Celtic saint came to convert the heathen. On St James's Day each year some of the young converted begged for pennies, sitting on the pavement alongside a few flowers in a jam jar with a scallop shell for collecting box.

I like to think that some tenuous link exists between Marcus Samuel's choice of an emblem and the children's use of the scallop shell and all those British pilgrims who used to set out by sea for Santiago de Compostela, and beyond Compostela to the eastern Mediterranean. After Jerusalem and Rome, Compostela – St James of the Field of the Star – was and remains Christendom's most important target for pilgrimage. Tradition has it that a bishop was guided to this spot by a star in 835 and there found the bones of the apostle James. Why St James's emblem should be the scallop shell is not clear. No other saint has a specific badge of pilgrimage, but those who journeyed to Compostela commonly bought the shells there and attached them to their cloaks.

The pilgrims would have landed at either Corunna or Pontevedra, both about thirty miles from the shrine. At Pontevedra, uniquely, there is a church built to the blessed Virgin as Pilgrim, and the Virgin wears a scallop shell on her hat. Is it possible that there are connections, through this scallop shell, with the tin trade and the eastern Mediterranean, and thus with Aphrodite, patroness of seafaring, who was born of the sea foam and, in Botticelli's painting at least, stands upon a scallop shell? Sir Mortimer Wheeler envisaged some such 'thin connecting thread' and in many places the Virgin superseded Aphrodite or Venus. The Virgin, with the planet Venus, remains Stella Maris, star of the sea.

Ideas, unlike goods, do not pay freight, though in shipping history they have often proved important cargo. However, it is not the purpose of this work to advance hypotheses. Between 1874 and 1876 W. S. Lindsay published his *History of Merchant Shipping and Ancient Commerce* in four fat volumes. Originally what I had in mind was to mark the centenary of Lindsay's great work by publishing a new history of merchant shipping, modifying Lindsay where necessary in the light of recent scholarship and bringing him up to date. In particular, I hoped to do for my time what Lindsay had done for his, for he was particularly good on the 19th century, and both of us had spent our working lives in shipping.

As it turned out, I was too busy between 1974 and 1976 and for some years thereafter, playing my own small part in this long history, to write a book of this description. It was in those years that the Marine Society, the Seafarers Education Service and a number of other societies were brought together, and I was intimately associated with all of them. Retirement has provided opportunity and 1988, after all, proves no bad date on which to end this chronicle. It is just 400 years since the English defeated the might of Spain and began their maritime rise. And it is just 100 years since the British Empire celebrated Queen Victoria's Golden Jubilee, the time at which maritime decline, at least in a relative sense, may be said to have set in.

As Dr P. N. Davies and Dr Sheila Marriner have pointed out, in an article which appeared in the *Journal of Transport History* in March 1988, much useful material on maritime history has been published in recent years, but it has included 'no general synthesis of existing work'. I hope that this book approaches to the general synthesis that has been called for. Some may not approve of my manner of presentation, which is not thematic as was the late Ralph Davis's great study of shipping in the 17th and 18th centuries. Instead, I have tried to keep all my balls in the air for relatively short periods of time, so that the reader will see what things were happening together. He will not often find matter out of context in these pages and I hope they are all the better for that.

I acknowledge with gratitude the help and encouragement of the Leverhulme Trust and the honour the Trustees accorded me by appointing me an Emeritus Fellow. I am indebted to the Council of the Marine Society for their practical support of the book and to my former colleagues in the Society for many kindnesses. To Lord Briggs and John Bamborough I am grateful for a cheerful faith in me. G.J. Bonwick made helpful comments on an early draft of the last five chapters; and Dr Gordon Jackson pointed to some recent books and papers which had eluded me, as did two anonymous but learned readers of a first manuscript. To my old mentor, Professor Sir Henry Phelps Brown, and to Mrs Sheila Hopkins and Lord Jay, I am indebted for the price index which, updated to 1988, I have used in making estimates of the present value of past amounts. For two voyages to sea I offer warm thanks to P & O Containers and the Harrison Line and to their Directors and staffs. For looking out books and journals I thank the staff of the National Library of Scotland. My debt to those books and journals and to their authors – not least to Professors K. R. Andrews, R. Davis, F. E. Hyde, S. G. Sturmey and R. W. Unger, to Dr P. N. Davies and to G. V. Scammell – will be obvious from the pages of this work, though none is responsible for what I have written.

For the illustrations I am grateful to that excellent marine artist Peter Knox and to the Marine Society for Nos 2–9 inclusive and for No. 15; to A. G. Credland, Keeper of Maritime History, and the Hull City Council for No. 1; to former seafarer and Japanese prisoner-of-war A. H. Joyce for Nos 12, 13, 14, 20, 22, 23, 27 and 28, Nos 23 and 27 being his original paintings; to marine artist L. J. Pearce and the Marine Society for No. 10; to Captain J. de Coverly for No. 11; to professional seafarer and skilled model-maker R. A. Wilson for Nos 16 and 21; to F. G. G. Carr, CB, CBE, and Captain F. Bell of the Cutty Sark Maritime Trust for No. 17; to S. Cock and the St Ives Museum for No. 18; to the Tyne and Wear Museums Service for Nos 19 and 25; and to P & O for Nos 29, 30 and 32.

As publishers, John Grey Murray and his colleagues have been exemplary. Last but not least, this work would never have been completed had it not been for the sympathetic understanding and quiet persistence of my wife.

Ronald Hope
Doune
31st December 1989

600 years of sail

Late 13th-century cog

A single square sail provides the motive power

1450: earliest three-masted ship

A lateen sail is fitted on the mizen mast, a square sail and a square topsail on the main mast, and a square foresail on the foremast. A spritsail is shown under the bowsprit.

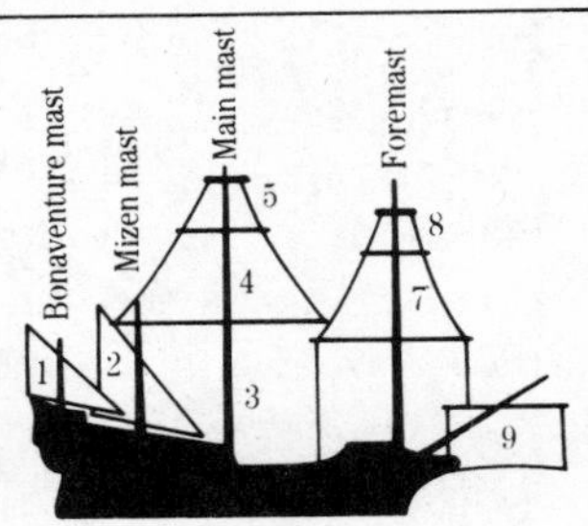

1600: most advanced ship

Sails: 1. Bonaventure. 2. Mizen (1 and 2 being lateen sails). 3. Mainsail 4. Main topsail. 5. Main topgallant. 6. Foresail 7. Fore topsail. 8. Fore topgallant 9. Spritsail

18th-century London barge

A spritsail (the pole is set diagonally across a fore and aft sail) has replaced the original square sail, and a sail is also set from the forestay. Leeboards are fitted, flat boards which can be let down on either side of the vessel. The one on the lee side is lowered when sailing.

18th-century hoy

The single mast supports a gaff sail (the gaff is the spar which extends the upper portion or head of the fore and aft sail). It also sets two head sails and sometimes a square topsail.

1770 – 1850: packet schooner

Fore and aft sails on both main and foremast are surmounted by square topsails.

1820 – 1910: merchant schooner

The topsail schooner with both topsail and flying topgallant sail, the rest of the sails being fore and aft.

1800 – 1840: three-masted barque

Sails: spanker, topsail and topgallant on the mizen; mainsail, main topsail and main topgallant on the main; foresail, fore topsail and fore topgallant on the foremast; and jib.

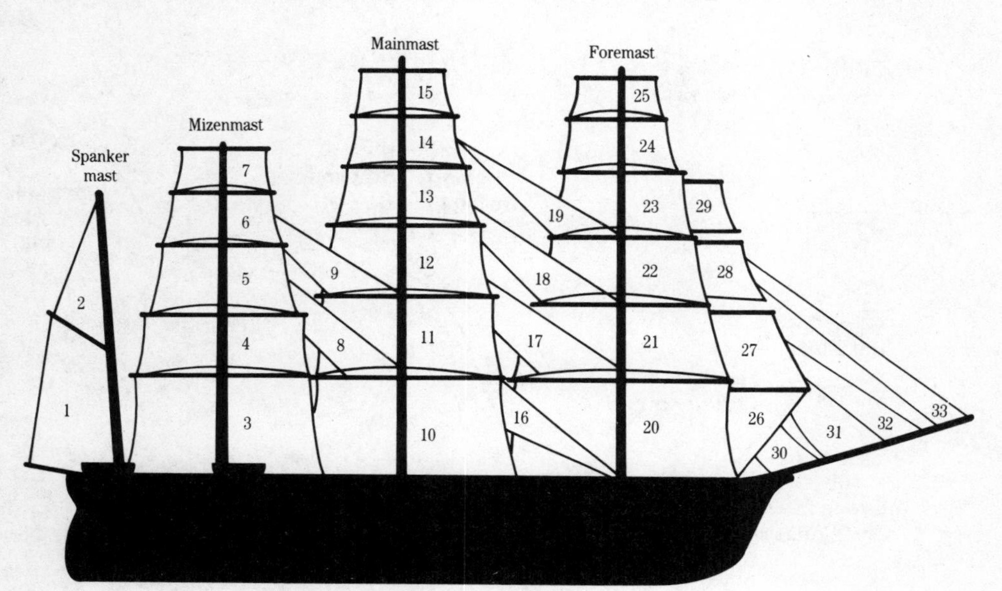

1870 – 1905: four-masted barque

Sails: 1. Spanker. 2. Jigger topsail. 3. Mizen crojack. 4. Mizen lower topsail. 5. Mizen upper topsail. 6. Mizen topgallant. 7. Mizen royal. 8. Mizen topmast staysail. 9. Mizen topgallant staysail. 10. Mainsail. 11. Main lower topsail. 12. Main upper topsail. 13. Main topgallant. 14. Main royal. 15. Main skysail. 16. Main staysail. 17. Main topmast staysail. 18. Main topgallant staysail. 19. Main royal staysail. 20. Foresail. 21. Fore lower topsail. 22. Fore upper topsail. 23. Fore topgallant. 24. Fore royal. 25. Fore skysail. 26. Lower studding sail. 27. Lower topsail studding sail. 28. Upper topsail studding sail. 29. Upper studding sail. 30. Fore staysail. 31. Fore topmast staysail. 32. Jib 33. Flying jib (After Landström)

British Seafaring 600 – 1600

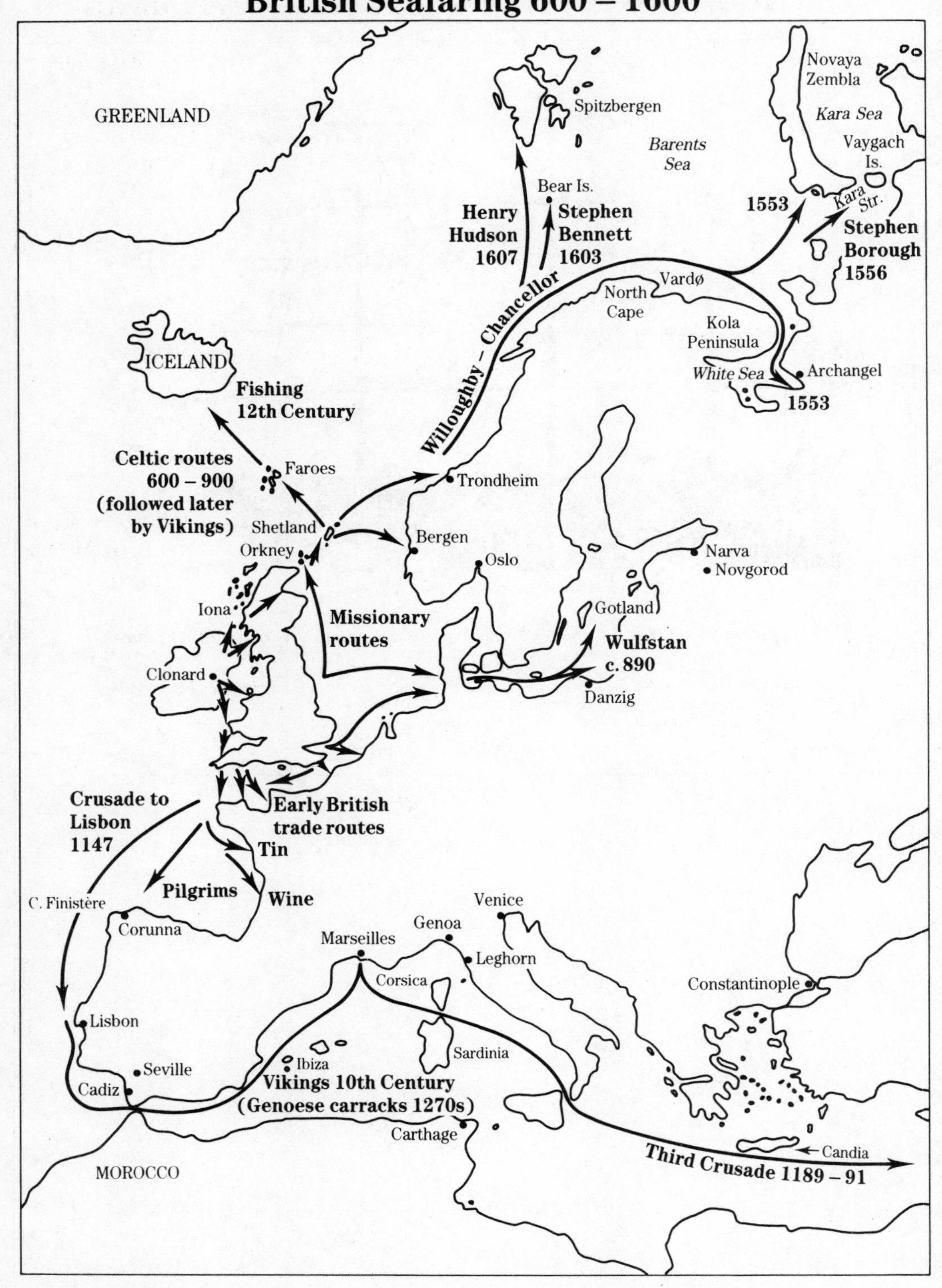

The British in North America and the Caribbean 1497 – 1655

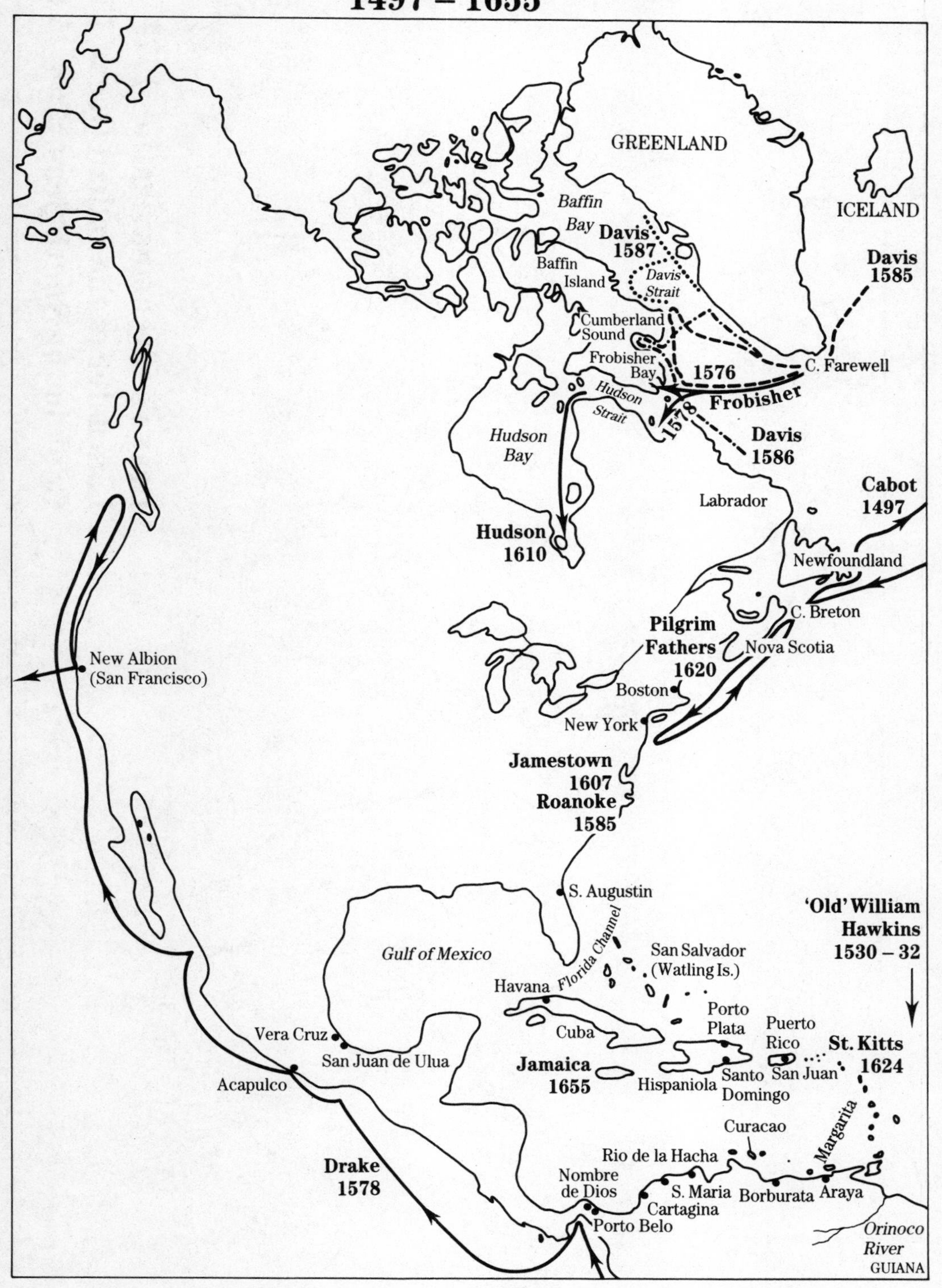

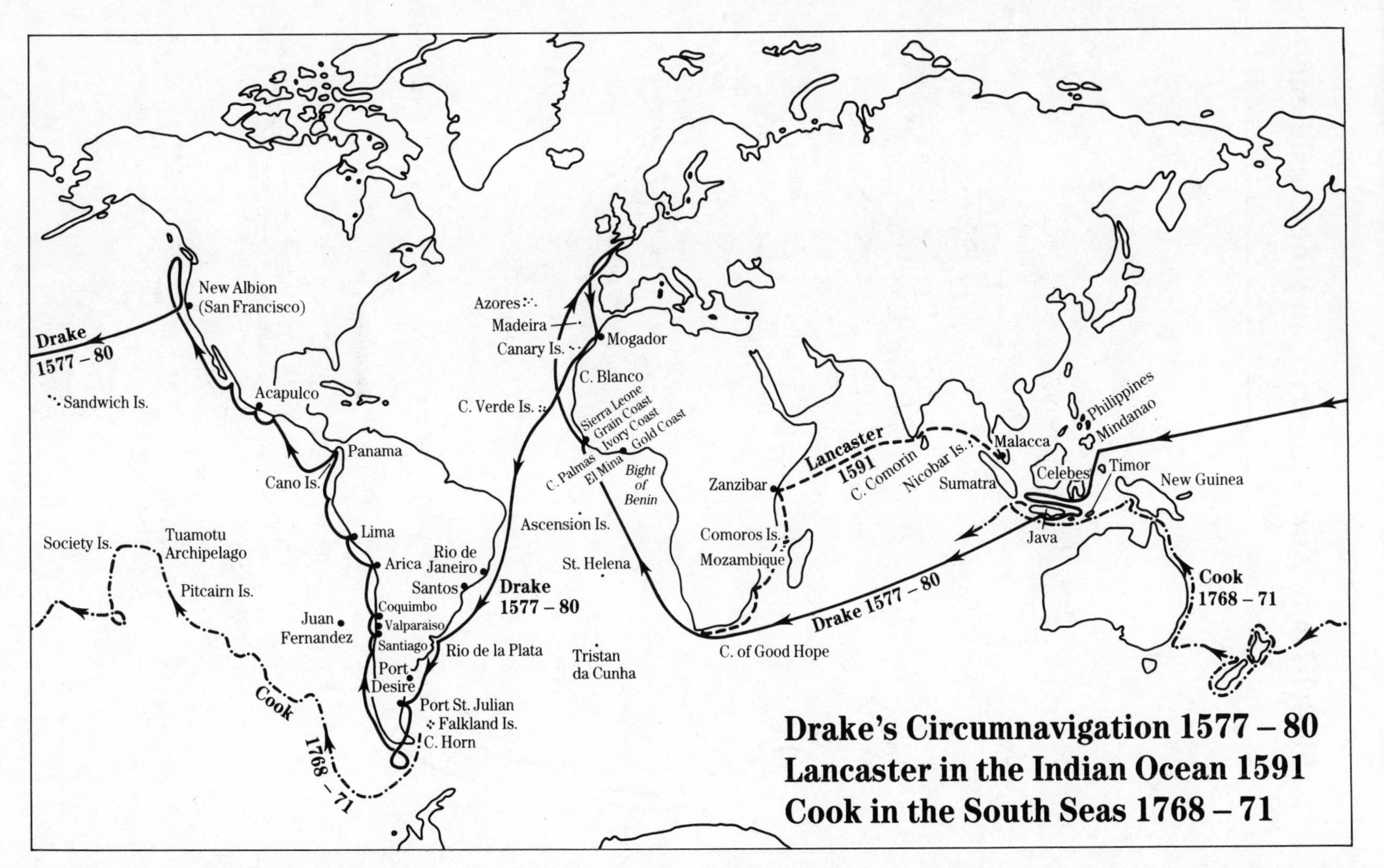

Drake's Circumnavigation 1577 – 80
Lancaster in the Indian Ocean 1591
Cook in the South Seas 1768 – 71

I

THE BEGINNINGS OF BRITISH SHIPPING

3000 BC–1400 AD

It is not our conquests, but our commerce;
it is not our swords, but our sails,
that first spread the English name . . .
over and about the world.

—Lewis Roberts
The Treasure of Traffike
(London 1641)

1

The Coming of Sail
(3000 BC–300 AD)

The first farmers arrived in Britain from France about 3000 BC and brought their livestock with them. The nature of their boats is unknown but in fine weather the prehistoric dugout canoe, hollowed from the substantial trunk of a forest tree and anything up to fifty feet long and five feet wide, would be adequate for the purpose.

In having to transfer their livestock across the English Channel, these immigrants to Britain may have made significant improvements to the boat. If they did, we have no evidence of them. It can be said, however, that those who then or subsequently improved the boat were the most skilful, enterprising and intelligent men of their time and the boat was the most significant of all man's inventions.

Boats and ships are ways of moving goods and people. They thus help to solve the economic problem of so distributing scarce resources as to increase the satisfactions of men and women. If goods unobtainable at home are sought abroad this normally becomes the basis for trade, though such goods may also be obtained by the exchange of gifts or by the use of force.

The peaceful interchange of goods by sea in British waters becomes apparent from the time of the first farmers onwards, even though Britain remained in the Stone Age for at least another thousand years. Such exchanges were made, for instance, in the finer types of flint and stone used for making axes, adzes and other tools, most of them tools essential to boatbuilding. Tools dating from this time and originating in northern Ireland have been found in Sittingbourne in Kent; stone axes from the Lake District have been discovered in the Isle of Man; Prescelly stone from south Wales travelled as far as Antrim in Ireland; Antrim flint crossed the water to Scotland; and a Welsh axe has been found in Jersey.[1] Voyages to obtain such goods need never have been made out of sight of land and dugout canoes would have sufficed for the purpose.

Not long before 2000 BC bronze, an alloy of copper and tin, was being manufactured in the eastern Mediterranean. A growth in trade became necessary in consequence of such manufactures because only in very few parts of Europe are copper and tin ores found reasonably close together. To save transport costs flint axe-heads had been roughly fashioned near the sources of the raw material. Metallic ores, similarly, were smelted as closely as possible to outcrops or mines and the metal was usually traded in the form of ingots. This meant that the knowledge of metal-working spread gradually as new sources were discovered. From Iberia or France the new techniques spread to Britain. Copper was in use in Britain soon after 1700 BC and bronze by 1500 BC. By this time tin had been discovered in Cornwall and was being exploited.

What, if anything, this new knowledge had to do with the mysterious megalithic peoples we do not know. They take their name from the large stone or megalithic tombs which they left behind them, and they appeared along all the seaboards of Western Europe, including those of the British Isles, less than a thousand years after the first British farmers. These tombs, however, are empty of copper and bronze objects. Perhaps the megalithic peoples were missionaries who blazed a trail, as the Irish saints did in later centuries, or perhaps they were colonists and craftsmen with skills other than metalworking to sell. Whatever the truth may prove to be, there seem to be connections between the art of these megalithic peoples and early art in the eastern Mediterranean.

If the megalithic connection remains a mystery, contact between Britain and the Mediterranean in the early Bronze Age cannot be denied and its inspiration appears to have been a trade in tin. How was such contact made?

From seals discovered at Knossus and dating from this period it is known that the Minoan inhabitants of Crete were familiar with the use of sail. The subsequently close relations between the Minoan and the Mycenaean cultures are also well established. Could Mediterranean sailors, Minoan or perhaps Greek (for it is too early for them to have been Phoenician), have sailed round the Iberian peninsula to Britain, doing some ocean navigation on the way, as early as 1500 BC or at any time in the thousand years thereafter?

Technically the achievement is practicable. The seaworthiness of extremely primitive craft has been amply demonstrated by the small-boat navigators of modern times; both the Atlantic and Pacific oceans have been crossed by log rafts, and the Atlantic by a reed raft. By 1500 BC the sailors of the eastern Mediterranean knew something of navigation by sun and stars, and the sounding-rod or long pole was in use even if the lead and line was not. Once it had been established, by land or coastal navigation, that Ushant lay north of Finistère, seafarers sailing on the direct route would not need to worry that they were a few days out of soundings or beyond the 100-fathom line; and while voyaging round the British Isles and the English Channel they would be in soundings most of the time. Even with no more than a simple square sail of the kind used by the Egyptian ship which went to the land of Punt about 1500 BC – and to suppose any more complicated rig would be unwarranted – a vessel could sail from Cornwall to Finistère and back again, since the prevailing winds come from the west. Throughout most of the Bronze Age, say from 1500 to 600 BC, the weather in western waters appears to have been kinder than it is today and Bronze Age navigators would have ventured abroad only in summer. Conditions were set fair for long-distance communication, and most writers interested in the subject seem to have assumed that in the early Bronze Age it was all plain sailing.

But, given that it was practicable, was it probable? Rock carvings of what may be boats, dating from this period, are to be seen near Dublin and in Brittany. If they are boats, there is no indication that they were sailing boats.

According to legend St Sampson, when travelling from Wales to Brittany in medieval times, put his boat in a cart to cross the tip of Cornwall, and this was no new custom. The distribution of prehistoric settlements in Britain makes it clear that the navigators of the frail craft of the Bronze Age preferred to avoid dangerous headlands and overland portage was probably common. The terminals of the transpeninsular route across Cornwall were at Harlyn Bay and Penzance – the road between them was followed perhaps by St Sampson – and there were similar overland routes between Milford Haven and Cardigan in Wales, Glenluce and Stranraer in Scotland, and Lochgilphead and Crinan also in Scotland. All this suggests hand-propelled craft operating over relatively short distances. A journey from Ireland to Brittany would be broken in Pembrokeshire and Cornwall.

The modern seafarer likes to stand out to sea, well away from the land, but it was not so in ancient times. That in the early Bronze Age there were maritime links between Spain and Britain and between Britain and Scandinavia has been established by archaeological findings, but it does not follow that these sailors sailed the ocean sea routes. It is more likely that the early travellers from Portugal and Galicia would coast along to the mouth of the river Loire, but would scarcely have the pluck to venture round the Pointe du Raz, still less to venture near the rocky reefs of Ushant. The significance of Brittany, Cornwall and Pembrokeshire in early seafaring is probably that they were barriers to coastal navigation.

It may still be argued that superior Mediterranean seafarers did what the seafarers of north-west Europe did not dare to do, but the evidence is nowhere apparent. Centuries later the Mediterranean seaman did not much like what lay beyond the Straits of Gibraltar, and he was never one for crossing the open ocean if he could avoid it. The probability is that British knowledge of metal-working came by way of the well-established overland routes which were later followed by the Greek tin trade. In the Bronze Age, crossing France along the river highways, hazardous as it was, may well have been considered much safer than crossing the Bay of Biscay.

One mighty effort made by British seafarers prior to the Bronze Age, however, can scarcely be questioned, though it has been demonstrated that dugout canoes would have sufficed for the task accomplished. It was in the second millennium BC that the bluestones on Salisbury Plain were transported from the Prescelly mountains in Pembrokeshire. Since there were no wheeled vehicles in Britain at the time it would seem that the bluestones must have been transported by water most of the way. Once across the Bristol Channel they went, no doubt, up the river Avon rather than round Land's End, but even so the minimum journey by sea would have been longer than that famous route from Tyre to Joppa along which the Phoenicians, some seven hundred years later, towed rafts of cedarwood for the building of King Solomon's temple.

Cedarwood floats and the navigational problem facing the Phoenicians was simple. The Stone Age seamen of Britain, on the other hand, faced formidable problems. One solution would have been to carry each bluestone on three dugout canoes which were lashed together, each canoe perhaps 35 feet long, 4 feet wide and 2 feet deep.[2] Such dugouts would not have been exceptionally large for the period and the remains of larger ones have been found. Whatever solution the ancient Britons found, the stones stand at Stonehenge as a monument to the craftsmen of that time.

Once the knowledge of metal-working had arrived in Britain, and gold, tin and copper had been discovered there, the subsequent trade in and around the country must have been largely of a maritime nature. It is from this period that clear evidence emerges of a significant advance in British boatbuilding.

On the foreshore at North Ferriby, some seven miles upstream from Hull, the remains of boats dating from about 1500 BC have been discovered and these boats are the oldest plank-built boats in the world other than those of similar date found in Egypt.[3] The largest of these boats would have been some 54 feet in length and 8.5 feet in the beam. The basic parts of one of them consisted of a very large keel-plank in two pieces, scarfed or joined together, to which was attached on each side a rather thinner plank. A number of cross-bars ran across these three planks and fitted into slots in cleats. The cleats had been left standing above the thickness of the planks when the shipwrights had adzed them out. Although such a boat may have worked only in the Humber estuary and the remains offer no evidence of the use of sail, it looks as if earlier than 1500 BC Britons went to sea not merely in dugouts but in wooden craft that were considerably more sophisticated.

By the later years of the second millennium, say between 1200 and 1000 BC, vessels existed of a size and quality sufficient to transport bulk materials across the English Channel. It would also appear that by this time shipping was operated by specialist carriers. The evidence for this statement was found in the sea, near Dover and at Salcombe in Devon, in the shape of two cargoes of Continental artefacts, axe-heads, chisels, dagger blades and spearheads among them.[4] Since some goods of British manufacture – the Pile type of flanged axe, for example[5] – also appear in Denmark at this time, we may suppose that a regional system of trade existed and some of it may have been in British hands.

Some of the legends upon which Homer based the story of the wanderings of Ulysses appear to date from a period before 1200 BC, and it would seem from these that there must have been some Greek or Minoan exploration of the Western Mediterranean by sailing ships before this time. Homer had perhaps heard something of the Straits of Gibraltar and the distant north, for the enchantress Circe gave Ulysses a fair wind to 'the deep-flowing river of ocean and the frontiers of the world, where the fog-bound Cimmerians live in the city of perpetual mist'. This might sound like some foreigner's view of Britain if the next sentence did not take us farther north still for, 'when the bright sun climbs the sky and puts the stars to flight, no ray from him can penetrate to them, nor can he see them as he drops from heaven and sinks once more to earth, for dreadful night has spread her mantle over the heads of that unhappy folk'. Since no ships of Homer's time or before would venture into the Arctic night, this passage was perhaps inspired by some traveller's tale that has been transmogrified in the retelling along the largely overland routes by which amber moved from the Baltic area to the Mediterranean.

Although some of the Homeric material may date from earlier times, the stories probably took their present form in the 8th century BC, and internal evidence – like the reference to the 'river of ocean' – makes it probable that incorporated in them are snippets of information current at the time. In the 8th century both Greeks and Phoenicians were exploring the western Mediterranean and it is from somewhat later than this time that we can date the earliest evidence of the use of sail beyond Gibraltar.

The date at which the Phoenicians of Tyre founded Carthage is uncertain, but it is believed to be later than the legendary founding ascribed to princess Dido in 814–813 BC, and it may have been over a century later. Classical references to the Isles of the Blest that lay beyond Algiers are similarly post-8th century. Excavated material in Utica, 700 or more miles east of Gibraltar and traditionally the oldest Phoenician foundation, is not older than the 7th century BC[6] and archaeology thus confirms what may be deduced from literary sources. By this time a settlement at the mouth of the river Plym, twelve miles south of the ore-bearing rocks of Dartmoor, where the ores of tin, copper, silver and gold could all be found, had been a port for a hundred years, trading with Brittany and south-west France or northern Spain or both.[7]

The Greek historian Herodotus, who flourished about 450 BC, tells us that Colaeus of Samos brought a rich cargo from Tartessos about 650 BC. This early centre of the metal trade is commonly thought to have been near the mouth of the river Guadalquivir or the mouth of the river Huelva, both of them running into the Gulf of Cadiz on the Atlantic side of southern Spain, probably predating the Carthaginian Gades, which settlement, on or near the site of modern Cadiz, prospered from about the middle of the 6th century.

According to Herodotus, too, some Phoenician sailors may have circumnavigated Africa about 600 BC. Whatever the truth concerning this voyage by way of the Red Sea, it is quite clear that the Carthaginians were sailing beyond the Straits of Gibraltar from this time on. There may have been some contact with the north-west tip of Spain, in the region of Santiago de Compostela, but further north than this archaeology does not take us.

It is from about this period – say 500 BC – that the exploratory voyages of Hanno and Himilco appear to date, though the sources of our information spring from a much later era. Hanno, who may have ventured as far south as the Gulf of Guinea, need not detain us, but for those interested in early British seafaring the voyage of Himilco is of particular significance since Himilco apparently sailed north from the Straits of Gibraltar. He is the first to have done so who is still remembered by name.

A single reference in Pliny apart, our only authority for Himilco's voyage is a Latin poetaster named Avienus who was writing in the 4th century AD, though his sources are supposed to date from the 4th and 2nd centuries BC. In his *Ora Maritima* Avienus relates how Himilco sailed north until he reached a high headland called Oestrymnis, which may have been in Brittany. Here he appears to have met traders in metals who could cross to Ireland in two days in skin-covered boats. Himilco himself seems to have learned nothing directly of Cornish tin, and he laid great stress on the tedium and dangers of navigation in this part of the world, an area where, according to him, one might be paralysed for weeks or even months by flat calms. His own voyage seems to have taken more than four months and, even for those times, he appears to have experienced unusual weather in the Bay of Biscay. There is certainly no indication in this account of Himilco's voyage or elsewhere that the Phoenicians established any direct trade with Britain in tin. Such trade as existed was carried on by intermediaries, perhaps from Spain, perhaps from Brittany, and probably from Britain, since that was where the tin came from.

The commercial empire based on Carthage flourished from about 550 to 200 BC and near the beginning of this period the Carthaginians were successful in excluding the Greeks from the Atlantic. It is not surprising, therefore, that to Plato, who lived from 427 to 347 BC, all that existed beyond the Straits of Gibraltar belonged to the realm of myth. However, Pytheas, a Greek sailor from Marseilles, voyaged off western Europe in about 320 BC, though it is unlikely that he sailed out of the Mediterranean round Iberia. The reason for relating Pytheas's voyage to this period is that Aristotle does not mention it but his pupil Dicaerchus does. Our main authority for the details of the voyage is Strabo who did not write his *Geography* until the 1st century AD and who considered that Pytheas was an arrant liar.

As an indication of Pytheas's lack of veracity Strabo quotes him as saying that Kent was some days' sail from France, but here something would depend on the prevailing winds and from where in France Pytheas sailed. Strabo's main case against Pytheas rests on his remarks concerning Thule and the 'curdled' sea. Pytheas seems to have heard of an island – the place which he called Thule – which was a six-day voyage from Britain, and this place was but one day's voyaging from the 'curdled' sea, something which was neither sea nor land nor air but a blend of all three and quite impassable.

Anyone who has been to Iceland, and from Iceland across the Denmark Strait to the ice-barrier, may feel that he knows what Pytheas was talking about. But Thule need not have been Iceland. Norway, too, may have appeared an island to sailors who had not fully explored its coasts, and pack ice in the fjords may have been the curdled sea. Shetland or Orkney are other possibilities. Whatever the exact location, Pytheas indicates in other ways that he had learned something of life in the far north.

All this may seem a far cry from British merchant shipping, but from this brief account of Greek and Phoenician exploration two points of significance emerge. First, it would appear that sail had come to north-west Europe, probably by the 6th century BC when Himilco entered these waters, and certainly by the 4th century BC when Pytheas followed him. Second, such trading and long distance voyaging as was regularly carried on in these north-west seas was carried on not by Mediterranean seafarers but by those who lived in north-west Europe. There is no hint in such classical literature as has survived that any Greek of Pytheas's time or thereafter attempted to follow his example and make a sea voyage to Britain, but there is ample evidence that the overland route to and from Marseilles grew and flourished from about 300 BC to 50 BC. The evidence indicates that the seafaring traders of north-west Europe during this period – and they may well have been of the same stock – operated largely from Brittany and Ireland. It was they who traded regularly to Ictis (or Mictis), the island off the south coast of England which was mentioned by the historian Timaeus, who died about 256 BC. This island – which could have been St Michael's Mount, or, perhaps, Mount Batten in Plymouth Sound – was joined to the mainland at low tide, and it was here that the inhabitants of Cornwall traded their tin ore which, extracted from the earth, was hammered 'into pieces like dice'.[8] Early Iron Age jewellery dating from the 5th and 6th centuries BC, made locally but in the style of the Basque regions, and an Etruscan-style bronze figurine and a bronze figure wearing Hellenistic armour, dating from the 3rd and 2nd centuries BC and probably made in Italy, have all been found at Mount Batten.[9]

Marseilles had been founded as a Greek trading centre about 600 BC and from this centre Greek influence spread gradually across France and into Britain. This influence was the inspiration of the so-called La Tène culture by way of which the Iron Age came to Britain. By this time the overland trade in tin was well-established and, if it was not introduced earlier or independently discovered (as the use of leather sails in Julius Caesar's time suggests it may have been), it is at this time that sail could have been introduced from the Mediterranean by way of the river traffic. Sail would have aided the cross-Channel paddlers whenever the wind was favourable, and if sail was inspired from the Mediterranean the 5th or 6th century BC seems the most likely period for its introduction, at least in the south of Britain.

A boat discovered on the banks of the river Ancholme in Brigg, Lincolnshire, nine miles south of South Ferriby, dates from about 500 BC and appears to be in the tradition of the Ferriby boats of a thousand years earlier, with still no evidence of the use of sail. This further British plank-built boat pre-dates by some 300 years the earliest plank-built boat found on the Continent, the so-called Als boat or war canoe which was propelled by paddles and used no sail. Since there is clear literary evidence of the use of sail in British waters at least 750 years earlier than there is any evidence of sail being used in Scandinavian waters, and still earlier archaeological evidence of trading links emanating from the British Isles, it seems likely that sail in northern waters arrived from the south, though the Scandinavians appear to have hit upon an original method of boat construction – the clinker-built boat – which was to prove useful in northern waters some centuries later than the period now under consideration.

By 55 BC, the time when the Romans invaded the country, Gallic influence was powerful in Britain and wine was already an important article of commerce. The Belgic princes of Britain went to their graves with a generous supply of wine stored in Roman amphorae,[10] and by their time it is clear that a number of different local craft plied on the waterways and along the coast. For two of these Julius Caesar himself provides the evidence.

'Things were ... far from well with us', wrote Caesar in his *War Commentaries* of one of his campaigns in Spain; and among the things that were not well was an inability to repair the bridges across a river. 'I therefore directed the troops', Caesar continued, 'to build a number of boats, modelled on some that I had once seen in Britain. The keels and ribs were made of light timber, the rest of the hull was of wickerwork covered with hides.'

From the wording of this account it is clear that Caesar had encountered skin-covered vessels while in Britain and that, so far as he was aware, they were confined to British waters. From his reference to keels it is probable that he was referring to sea-going craft and not to river coracles, and from this and other literary evidence it may be inferred that the home of these craft was further west than Kent.

In his *Natural History*, written during the 1st century AD, by which time England was absorbed into the framework of Roman provincial administration,[11] Pliny also makes reference to these British curragh-like vessels. Pliny is the writer who records that, according to Timaeus, it was on Ictis that tin was bought, and Timaeus said further that the Britons sailed there in boats of osier covered with sewn hides. In another place Pliny states categorically that in his time boats in British waters were made of wickerwork covered with hides. A 3rd-century historian records that 'the sea which separates Ireland from Britain is rough and stormy throughout the year; it is navigable for a few days only; they voyage in small boats of pliant twigs, covered with the skins of oxen. During the time they are at sea, the voyagers abstain from food.'

A gold model of one of these British boats, probably dating from Pliny's time, was discovered at Broighter, County Derry, in Ireland in

1896. This model is complete with mast, eight seats, what appear to be eight rowlocks on each side, and a steering oar on the port quarter. As modelled, the vessel is a bit broad in the beam and not particularly graceful but the real thing may have differed little from the Irish curraghs seen on Ireland's west coast in recent times, vessels which might be as much as twenty feet long.

If the curragh ever had root in any part of England, it was perhaps replaced by the plank-built boat when iron tools arrived. Caesar certainly gives a graphic description of such wooden vessels built by the Veneti, who were, he says, 'by far the most powerful (people) on the coast of Brittany'. The Veneti possessed a large fleet which plied between their own ports and Britain. 'They knew more about the handling of ships and the science of navigation', wrote Caesar, 'than anyone else thereabouts; and their control of the few scattered harbours which afford refuge from those violent storms so characteristic of the open sea enabled them to levy tolls on nearly all who used those waters.' Who, one wonders, were in a position to defy the Veneti by not submitting to their imposition of tolls? Presumably those who were thus powerful came from Britain or the Low Countries since the Veneti themselves were the most powerful people on the coast of Brittany, and only the Britons had alternative harbours at hand. Rivalry between the sailors of Brittany and those of Cornwall was familiar enough a thousand and more years later.

The Veneti ships described by Caesar were highly sophisticated and could have been developed to this point only after many centuries. Since the Veneti had command of the seaboard, Caesar himself built warships on the Loire, recruited seamen and pilots, and drafted rowers from Transalpine Gaul. But because of their local knowledge and their practical seamanship the advantages seemed to be all on the side of the Veneti. Caesar tried to capture their towns from the land, but their naval resources were such that 'as soon as a position became untenable they concentrated a whole fleet of ships, evacuated the place, and withdrew to neighbouring strongholds'. At sea Caesar was also handicapped. The Veneti had greater skill and better seaboats. Their vessels, wrote Caesar,

> were relatively flat-bottomed, and could therefore ride in the shallows or on an ebb tide. With their unusually tall prows and sterns they could weather high seas in a gale of wind; and the hulls, made entirely of oak, were capable of standing up to any amount of rough handling. The cross timbers consisted of beams a foot thick, fastened with iron bolts as thick as a man's thumb, and iron chains instead of ropes were used to secure the anchors. Their sails were made of raw hides or thinly dressed leather, due possibly to the absence of flax and ignorance of its uses, but more probably to a mistaken belief that canvas

> was unequal to the violence of the Atlantic gales and unsuitable for manoeuvring vessels of that burden.

Such ships may sound to some like a forerunner of the medieval cog. Certainly they betoken a technological advance peculiar to the English Channel. The ships were presumably 'carvel'-built, plank against plank, or so keen an observer as Caesar would have remarked upon the difference between Roman and Gallic practice. Moreover, unlike the oared galleys which Caesar had built or the oared Viking ships of later times, these sailing vessels, with their one square sail, were not primarily warships but fishing vessels or merchantmen. Their advantage in combat lay, as Caesar pointed out, first in their solidity and bulk, which rendered them safe against ramming, second in their height out of the water, which placed them beyond the reach of Roman missiles and grappling irons, and third in their seaworthiness in these dangerous, tidal waters. The Romans' sole advantage, apart from the device described below, lay in the speed and manoeuvrability given to their ships by the use of oars, particularly in periods of calm.

Two hundred and twenty Gallic ships appeared to do battle with Caesar's fleet and, even after Caesar's carpenters had built turrets on their galleys (as in the 13th century AD the Norsemen fitted 'castles' on their longships to combat the cog), the high poops of the Veneti ships still overtopped them. Nevertheless, Caesar defeated them because

> our men had prepared one device that proved most useful – sharp-pointed hooks fixed into the end of long poles, not unlike siege-hooks in appearance. These instruments gripped the halyards, which were drawn taut and then snapped by rowing hard ahead. As soon as the halyards were cut, the yard-arms naturally collapsed: and since the Gallic ships relied exclusively upon their rigging, they came to an immediate standstill once this was gone.

The Veneti were sailors, not soldiers, and when the ships were immobilised by a dead calm Caesar vanquished them all, very few of the Veneti managing to reach the shore. Sixteen hundred years later Sir Francis Drake was luckier with his western ocean weather and the ram, grapple and board tactics of the Mediterranean were at last superseded.

In his account of the Gallic wars Caesar tells us that the Veneti had recalled every one of their ships to do battle with the Romans and the Romans annihilated both ships and men. The trade in which the Veneti had engaged was principally with the south of England and since, in ways unspecified, the Britons had helped the Gauls in the wars, they became Caesar's next target. The men of Kent and Sussex chose not to meet Caesar at sea. Either they were not great sea-fighters or they had taken heed of the fate of the Veneti. Warned by 'some traders' of the Roman plans, they made ready to receive the enemy ashore. Much the same thing happened more than a thousand years later when William the Conqueror crossed to England.

At the time of the Roman invasion the population of Britain was probably not more than 400,000. Relatively powerful though it was, the entire Veneti merchant marine would scarcely have provided the crew for a battleship in World War II – say, the *Prince of Wales*'s 1612 men. Even in 54 BC, when Caesar returned to Britain with 800 ships (of not more than 50 tons each on average) and five legions, totalling perhaps 27,000 men and 2000 cavalry, his entire force would scarcely have filled the *Queen Mary* and the *Queen Elizabeth* when they were trooping in that same war. Given such figures, the trade carried on by sea cannot have been other than small scale. Nevertheless, it would have been of significance both to those involved in it, and to the communities they served.

When the Veneti were defeated this trade did not cease. Relatively rich English merchants were to be found in the south of the country,[12] and from the merchant fleet of Roman Britain parts of three vessels have survived in London. These vessels all yield evidence of a local tradition of shipbuilding, albeit with Gallic influences.

The so-called Blackfriars ship dating from the 2nd century AD was some 55 feet long and of 22 feet beam, built of oak, with massive floor timbers and relatively slender side frames. To the outside of the frames broad strakes or longitudinal planks had been nailed carvel-fashion. The bottom of the ship was flat, enabling it to sit upright on the river or sea-bed at low tide. Nails up to twenty-nine inches long were used, and the ship was probably propelled by a single square sail. The internal depth indicated that it was decked and provided with a hatch over a hold abaft the mast. On its last voyage this vessel had carried building stone from near Maidstone in Kent, down the Medway and up the Thames, and it was probably sunk in a collision. One authority sees in it a distinct Celtic tradition, different from both Scandinavian and Mediterranean models, a basic form from which the medieval cog could have developed.[13]

The New Guy's House boat, discovered on the site of Guy's Hospital, is of similar age but seems to have been a small, flat-bottomed river barge, carvel-built and also constructed of oak. In construction it had much in common with the Blackfriars ship though there were some differences.[14]

The third vessel was discovered on the site of County Hall and was similarly of oak and carvel-built, about 60 feet long and 16 feet wide. Along the centre of the keel were numerous five-inch wooden pins or trenails, possibly to secure a protective false keel below the true keel. The strakes were three inches high near the keel, thinning to two inches at the sides, fixed to one another and to the keel by draw-tongued joints. Very little metal was used in the construction, but a few joints were strengthened by large-headed iron nails.[15] The mast was ten inches in diameter, and the ship is believed to have dated from about 300 AD.

By this time the Roman Britons had long maintained a lighthouse at Dover, and the character of British trade had undergone some changes. Between 500 and 200 BC there had been a vigorous trade in tin between Cornwall and the mouths of the rivers Loire and Gironde, the tin then travelling overland across Gaul to the Mediterranean. To Cornish tin, lead and silver from the Mendips and gold from Ireland were added.[16]

As the Bronze Age turned into the Iron Age the demand for tin declined and with it the trade to Cornwall. Tacitus wrote: 'Britain yields gold, silver and other metals, to make it worth conquering. Ocean, too, has its pearls, but they are dusky and mottled.' Tacitus was not convinced of the value of British pearls, and he does not mention tin specifically among the metals. Martial makes a fleeting reference to a 'barbaric' basket which had been imported from Britain, subsequently claiming this art of basket-making as Roman in origin. Strabo, our only other authority on British trade in Roman times, records that Britain produced 'corn, cattle, gold, silver and iron, which things are brought thence, and also skins, and slaves, and dogs sagacious in hunting; the Celts use these, as well as their native dogs, for the purposes of war'. The order in which these British exports are recorded is not necessarily significant, but again there is no mention of tin.

With the decline of the tin trade and the concentration of Roman power in the south-east, ports in this latter area became important, London pre-eminent among them. According to one modern writer of repute the river Thames in Roman times was

> lined with cargo-ships, in size and shape not unlike the Thames barges of today, though with rather more freeboard and rarely with more than a single mast. In their holds are the great two-handled jars, filled with oil and wine, that may almost be said to have stood, commercially, as a symbol of Mediterranean civilisation *in partibus*. Here and there is a cargo of Gaulish pottery, such as that which, some time in the second century, was overwhelmed in the Thames estuary off Whitstable, where Samian dishes are still dragged up from time to time in the nets of fishermen. Occasionally a ship comes from Gaul or Italy bearing works of art, wrought in bronze or marble, such as the colossal statue of Hadrian now in the British Museum, or the marble river-god (in the London Museum). More rarely a galley, with oars and sail, sweeps up-river from the

> Channel Fleet, or brings some Roman official to the island. And at the wharves the merchant ships are loading for the return voyage with cargoes of corn, of skins, or of gangs of chained hillmen impressed as slaves or soldiers for the Continent.[17]

Certain reservations notwithstanding, this passage – the last sentence of which clearly derives from Strabo – is less fanciful than some other descriptions of early seafaring. The scale of this trade was still small, of course, and it would not be carried on throughout the year. London also had its ups and downs during the four centuries of Roman domination and its trade was by no means regular. Nevertheless, there is archaeological or literary evidence for trade in all the commodities mentioned. The imports consisted of luxury items for the ruling classes: 'ivory bracelets and necklaces, amber, vessels of glass, and small wares' from 'Keltica', so Strabo tells us; to these the archaeological record adds small pipe-clay figurines of deities and red-glazed pottery from Gaul and Germany, metal jugs, candelabra and other fittings from Italy and, above all, oil and wine. Nearly 2000 years later, into the 1960s, the General Steam Navigation Company (long since fully absorbed into P & O) still traded in wine and other French products on the very site by Tower Bridge which the merchants of Roman England must have used.

Two statements in the above quotation, however, must be questioned: there is no evidence for the existence of two-masted vessels in north-west Europe at this time, though they were to be found in the Mediterranean; and the suggestion that ships may have come direct to the Thames from Italy is probably mistaken. Strabo makes no mention of direct sailing from Italy: according to him the passages in common use began from the mouths of the rivers Rhine, Seine, Loire and Garonne, and thus it remained for more than a thousand years.

Some trade extended to the north of England. South Shields (Arbeia) was a flourishing port in the 3rd and 4th centuries, with supplies being trans-shipped into lighters to be taken upstream. Carlisle and Corbridge were also active ports, and a votive slab discovered at Bowness-on-Solway in Cumbria, near the western extremity of the defensive wall against the Picts, makes reference to some trading exercise, perhaps by sea. The suggestion, however, that at this time 'vast' quantities of goods passed across Roman frontiers into Scotland could be misleading.[18]

How much of this British trade was in the hands of British merchants and seafarers is unknown. It may be that such trade in Roman times was largely in foreign hands, though shipbuilding was clearly an industry on the Thames and native seafaring continued in the west. Indeed, if they had not done so already by the time of Pytheas, the skin-boats of the Celtic Sea were shortly to venture far into the Atlantic.

Notes

1. S. Piggott, *Scotland before History* (1958), London, pp. 32–3. *See also* G. Clark, 'Traffic in Stone Axe and Adze Blades' (1965), EHR, 2nd Series, Vol. XVIII, No. 1.
2. R. Atkinson, *Stonehenge* (1956), London, pp. 106–8.
3. B. Greenhill, *Archaeology of the Boat* (1976), London, p. 21.
4. K. Muckelroy, 'Middle Bronze Age Trade between Britain and Europe: a maritime perspective' (1981), *Proceedings of the Prehistoric Society*, Vol. 47, p. 275ff.
5. J. Clark, *Prehistoric Europe* (1952), London, p. 257.
6. W. Culican, *The First Merchant Venturers* (1966), London, p. 108ff.
7. B. Cunliffe: see *The Independent*, 13th February, 1989.
8. J. Thomson, *History of Ancient Geography* (1948), Cambridge, p. 145. *See also* A. Jamieson (ed.), *A People of the Sea: The Maritime History of the Channel Islands* (1986), London, '1. The First Eight Thousand Years,' by B. Cunliffe; *and* I. Maxwell, 'The Location of Ictis' (1972), *Journal of the Royal Institution of Cornwall*, pp. 293–319.
9. B. Cunliffe, report cited.
10. T. Powell, *The Celts* (1958), London, p. 111.
11. P. Salway, *The Frontier People of Roman Britain* (1965), Cambridge, p. 1.
12. *Ib.*, p. 38.
13. P. Marsden, 'A boat of the Roman period found at Bruges, Belgium, in 1899, and related types' (1976), IJNA, Vol. 5, No. 1. Also: P. Marsden, 'The County Hall ship, London' (1974), IJNA, Vol. 3, No.1.
14. G. Bass (ed.), *A History of Seafaring based on Underwater Archaeology* (1972), London, pp. 121–2.
15. London Museum Catalogue No. 3, *London in Roman Times* (1946), London, p. 152.
16. J. Clark, *op. cit.*, p. 277.
17. London Museum Catalogue No. 3, p. 156.
18. Salway, *op. cit.*, particularly pp. 25, 61 and 212.

2

Celts, Saxons and Vikings

(300–1100)

To Strabo the world was an island surrounded by sea and it was possible to circumnavigate it. However, those who had tried to do this had turned back, he wrote, 'not because of any continent that stood in their way and hindered their further advance, in as much as the sea continued open as before, but because of their destitution and loneliness'.

Strabo was writing of Mediterranean seafarers. Around the Irish Sea, on the other hand, there were seafarers who were not unduly dismayed by 'destitution and loneliness' because they were all too familiar with both. Of all those who used the seas off the west coast of Europe in the so-called 'dark ages' the Vikings have received the most attention. But the Celts traded at sea, voyaged far into the Atlantic, and pioneered true oceanic navigation centuries before the Norsemen ventured outside the sheltered waters of the Baltic Sea or their coastal fjords, centuries even before the Norsemen used sail.

The Romans, who scarcely occupied Brittany and Cornwall and who only Romanised Wales at a rather late date in their occupation of Britain, never conquered Ireland at all. Since they were not a seafaring people, they avoided the coast where they could and, although forced to police the English Channel, particularly in the region of the Straits of Dover, they left the ancient sea-lanes between France, Cornwall, Ireland and the north alone.

According to Irish tradition the first Irish fleet made an expedition overseas in 222 AD and well before the end of that century the southern Irish were settling on the coasts of Cornwall and south Wales. The Cornish tin mines, which appear to have been little worked for more than 200 years, were then re-opened and trade gradually extended.

In the 3rd and 4th centuries AD the Roman Britons built a series of watchtowers on Anglesey, in north Wales and on both sides of the Bristol Channel. At the mouth of the river Severn they seem to have maintained a flotilla to ward off Irish attacks,[1] and the vessels are likely to have been fast, light, oared galleys provided with side rudders, vessels which had to put into the coast at night because they had nowhere for men to sleep.

Roman cargo vessels, on the other hand, were slow and hard to handle. Such ships were double-ended and, on the larger ones, the stern was higher than the bow. They carried a single square sail though, in the Mediterranean at least, some carried an artemon as well, a small square sail slung under the bow which was set as a headsail to aid steering. By the 3rd century a small triangular sail, used in fair weather to help drive the ship, may have been set above the mainsail.[2]

The officials and landowners of the Empire were principally interested in the spices, wines and silks which such ships brought from France, Germany and Spain. In the 4th century the export of bronze, iron and gold beyond the Imperial frontier was forbidden; indeed, anticipating the mercantilists of later centuries, a law of 374 AD stated that efforts should be made to regain by trade such gold as had passed into the hands of 'barbarians'. A little later, wine, olive oil and – perhaps significantly – the plans of ships were added to the banned list.

Like many of the restrictive laws of later centuries, the Roman laws failed in effect. A large number of bronze and other objects of late Roman provincial origin arrived in Ireland in the 4th century and hoards of late Imperial coins have been discovered in both Galway and central Ireland. The sites of similar finds extend along the western maritime route to Scotland and the Norwegian coast. Southward this Celtic trade, if that is what these finds imply, seems to have stretched to western Gaul and Spain, where Corunna in Galicia was known as Portus Britanniae. The Celts were probably the first to cross the Bay of Biscay directly.[3]

Just as Hull and South Shields appear to have been maintained in Roman Britain as centres for maritime trade with the Picts of Scotland, so Chester may have been a centre for similar trade with the Irish. But in the last days of the Empire, if the 'barbarians' wanted goods that the Empire produced, they had to seek them in their own ships, and one writer who has made a detailed study of the northern seas in this period concludes that the 'rise of maritime strength in the Atlantic was the direct result of Rome's own commercial iron curtain'.[4] That this Atlantic traffic of the 4th and 5th centuries was small scale, essentially separate from that of the Mediterranean, and almost certainly in British and Irish hands, is indicated by the use of silver, iron and even female slaves as the means of exchange. Gold was not used as a currency.[5]

Some time in the second quarter of the 5th century – probably about 440 AD when Britain seceded from the Empire – the Roman fleet in the English Channel ceased to exist. These were disturbed times and some of the skills of the Romano-British shipwrights may then have disappeared. Both before and after this date the Irish continued to raid and trade with the western coasts of Britain, and Niall of the Nine Hostages, who was responsible for the capture of the young St Patrick, even extended his raids as far as the Isle of Wight.[6] One result of the upheavals of the time was Celtic settlement in both Brittany and Galicia. This colonisation began from south Britain in the middle of the 5th century and continued to the early 7th century, with peak phases at the beginning of the period and again in the middle of the 6th century. In the second peak period the population of Devon and Cornwall seems to have been particularly involved, probably pressed by the Saxon immigrants to Wessex.[7]

The result was that for a time fewer goods were exchanged but such exchanges did not cease altogether. St Patrick himself took passage in a merchant ship to Gaul when he escaped from his slavery in northern Ireland; and after ordination he returned by ship to Britain to visit his family before making one more return trip to Auxerre, after which, in 431–2, he set sail for Ireland and his Christian work. Indeed a whole stream of west British and Irish saints appear to have studied at the monastery of Lérins on the Mediterranean.[8]

It is in this period, round about 500 AD, that 'King' Arthur may have lived. Geoffrey of Monmouth's *History of the Kings of Britain*, which was written after the Norman Conquest, can scarcely be accepted as fact, but his suggestion that Arthur subdued both Ireland and Iceland and was promised tribute by the King of Gotland and the King of the Orkneys is at least indicative of some knowledge of Iceland and the Baltic well before the Vikings sailed the oceans. Geoffrey even suggests that a later king added these territories plus Norway and Denmark to his dominions.[9]

Whatever the credibility of all this, the Irish saints were certainly venturing into the Atlantic at this time, and one of the most interesting of the Irish sagas is that of St Brendan. To discover exactly where St Brendan went is no simple problem, but there can be little doubt that those lands 'where is ever day and never night' are north of the British Isles; and from references to westward sailing, land which 'began to move', bubbling cauldrons, and other volcanic and seismic activity,[10] it seems highly probable that something was known of Iceland. It has even been argued that St Brendan discovered the Vinland of the Vikings some 500 years before the Vikings did so themselves but, if he did venture thus far, America proved of no economic importance until the voyage of Columbus, 500 years later even than the Viking voyages of discovery.

St Brendan is believed to have made one series of voyages from about 519 to 524 and another from 525 to 527. On the first series he sailed in curraghs, the skin-boats of the Irish which were still the commonest ships in the Irish Sea, and in one account we are told that the saint and his companions used iron tools to prepare a very light vessel of the Irish kind, with wickerwork sides and ribs covered with cowhide tanned in oak bark, and tarred at the joints. Into this craft they put provisions for forty days, butter enough to dress any hides used to repair damage to the boat, and 'all utensils necessary for the use of the crew'.[11]

The accounts vary, but it is possible that the curraghs built for St Brendan, who was born in Kerry, the home of the best curraghs, were capable of carrying twenty people and may have been constructed from as many as thirty hides. St Columba and St Cormac, who followed St Brendan upon the seas, also used curraghs, and the former was accompanied by twelve companions on his first voyage to Iona in 563. The latter, who was one of St Columba's disciples, made at least one voyage in skin-covered boats into the Arctic, though not by intent, when he ran before a southerly gale for fourteen days. At the end of this ordeal he encountered some dreadful stinging creatures which were, it has been conjectured, the formidable mosquitoes to be met with in summer in Greenland.[12]

But although the curragh was cheap and eminently seaworthy, it was not the only type of vessel sailing the western ocean in the middle of the 6th century. Ships have always been built to serve particular purposes, either peaceful or warlike, and shipbuilders have never been confined to a single method of working. From Adamnan's *Life of St Columba* we learn that the Irish at this time were building a number of different types of vessel, and St Brendan, upon the advice of his foster-mother, is said to have made his second voyage in wooden ships.

From the hoards of coins and other archaeological evidence it has been argued that by the middle of the 6th century a maritime trade, at least partly in the hands of a Celtic thalassocracy, linked Spain, Atlantic Gaul, Ireland, Scotland, England and Scandinavia,[13] and all this at a time when the Scandinavians had not yet adopted sail. Irish bronze balls and Celtic pins dating from the 7th and 8th centuries have been discovered in Iceland, and Irish names are found there in some coastal localities. The Irish monk Dicuil, whose *Liber de Mensures Orbis Terrae* was written about AD 825, identified Pytheas's Thule with Iceland and indicates that Irishmen were settled there at least thirty years before the coming of the Vikings in 860. The Icelandic and Norwegian sagas tell the same story.[14] In the Icelandic summer, we are told by Dicuil, a man could see perfectly well to remove lice from his shirt at midnight, and one day's sailing northward was the frozen sea.[15]

Some slight indications of the size of the maritime traffic in the Irish Sea can be gleaned from written sources. Thus from Cormac's *Glossary*, compiled in the 9th century, it appears that Niall's grandson had a fleet of fifty curraghs running between Ireland and Scotland, but these vessels were not apparently very sturdy for one day the whole fleet was caught in a great tidal whirlpool near Rathlin Island and there were no survivors. Again, when the fugitive Irish chieftain Lughaid MacCon was offered help for an invasion of Ireland by a Scottish king, we are told that the number of small craft supplemental to the ships, galleys and barks requisitioned to carry the invading hosts across the sea was so great that there was a 'continuous bridge of curraghs' between Ireland and Scotland.[16] In 729, according to the Annals of Tigernach, 150 Pictish ships were wrecked off the headlands of Ross Cuisini.

This mention of Pictish vessels serves to illustrate that not all traffic in the Irish Sea was in Irish hands. Ireland itself remained economically primitive. Although there was some development in native craftsmanship in gold, the production of leather goods, the weaving of coarse cloth and perhaps the beginnings of linen manufacture, there was only one true urban centre, Cashel in Tipperary, stronghold of the kings of Munster, and the exchange of goods still seems to have been carried on without the use of money. However, the Irish monastic establishments like Armagh, Clonmacnois and Glendalough – some of them containing as many as 3000 monks and students apart from large secular populations – fulfilled many of the functions of towns, and by the 8th century, Carmen Fair, near Wexford, and Telton Fair, near Dublin, were attracting a large number of visitors each year.[17]

Much of the trade may have been in the hands of Gaulish merchants and, further north, the Picts may have traded to the coasts of Norway. Trade was no Irish monopoly, but in the 6th and 7th centuries the Irish pioneered the distant sea voyaging which set an example to the Norsemen and subsequently inspired many voyages of discovery.

It has been suggested that the Irish monks and traders who went north and west were guided by the geese which migrate annually between Ireland (and other parts of Great Britain) and Iceland.

> These noisy and conspicuous birds, the brent geese, white-fronted geese, barnacle-geese and grey-lags, wintered in their tens of thousands in Northern Ireland, and in the Shannon Estuary (which St Brendan knew). But ten days or a fortnight after the Spring equinox they begin to leave. A large flock rises, and one long skein after another disappears over the northern horizon. A week or so later another flock departs in the same way, honking as they fly, and in four or five weeks' time the marshes are deserted – all have disappeared. They are on their way to summer breeding places in Iceland and Greenland.[18]

It is obvious from the Irish sagas that the Irish mariners were keen observers of the ways of birds. Flying along a direct route the geese reach Iceland in less than twenty-four hours, whereas seamen in curraghs would take close on a week in fair weather – the period reported by Pytheas in 300 BC. Even so, the seamen might set a course by the northward migration and keep to it by watching successive skeins of birds pass overhead. The birds migrate at times which would set convenient limits to summer voyaging.

It may also have been bird migration which first tempted seafarers across the Bay of Biscay. In these days of electronic aids and mechanically-propelled vessels the seafarer does not need to be as observant of nature as once he was, and the modern seafarer often travels too fast to observe it. But there is no doubt that the seafarers of old took careful note of all natural happenings. From time immemorial birds had been of service to them. Four or five hundred years after the voyagings of the Irish monks the Vikings sent up ravens to sight land, just as Noah had done in Old Testament times, and Columbus, like his predecessors, was well aware that land was usually not far off if birds were sighted at sea. In northern waters sailors observed where the Greenland whale and the bottle-nosed whale fed, not only for whaling purposes but so that they might know where they were on other occasions, and they watched the variations in the phenomena known as the Northern Lights in the expectation of learning something that would be of use to them.

From their observations of the sun at noon and the Great Bear at night these seafarers would have a shrewd idea of how far north or south they were. Above all, long experience would tell them something of the behaviour of the winds. It has been said of the 8th-century voyage of Floki the Viking, for example, that he went out before a south-east wind knowing full well that it would turn east before long and take him towards the islands which were his goal. Viking journeys to the east coast of Britain would be made when the depression track was to the north of the British Isles.[19]

Original discovery might result from accident – as when the Viking Gunbjorn was blown off his course to Iceland in 876 and sighted Cape Farewell – but these early navigators knew enough about the sea and sky to go over the same route again, and such knowledge, with a few simple navigational aids like the magnetic compass, was sufficient in the eyes of many mariners right down to modern times.

In this northern seafaring the distances from island to island are not immense. The layman contemplating an Atlantic voyage is apt to think of a journey of some 3000 miles out of sight of land, and so the Atlantic crossing can be. But the distance from Ireland to Iceland is only 600 miles and sailing from Malin Head on any bearing between 15 and 45 degrees west of north will bring a ship within sight of Iceland's mountains and into soundings within six days, given a following wind. 'And the steersman would know that if he came near to Rockall he must be too far to the west, or if near to St Kilda he would be too much to the east.'[20] Even from a curragh the mountains of south-east Iceland would be visible on a clear day as much as ninety miles away.

The other distances involved are shorter still: from the Butt of Lewis to Iceland, 400 miles; from the Shetlands to the Faroes, 200 miles; from the Shetlands to Norway, 200 miles; from the Faroes to Iceland, 250 miles; and so on. In good weather and with favourable winds the mariner need never be much more than a day out of sight of land.

This is not, of course, to underestimate the achievements of these Celtic seamen. The north Atlantic can be as rough and treacherous in summer as in winter, and good weather could never be taken for granted on these ocean voyages, however weatherwise the mariner. The western world owes much to the intrepidity of these British seafarers, and the Vikings were not the least in their debt.

In the first half of the 8th century the Moors overran Spain and southern France and trade between these regions and Ireland largely disappeared. Contacts with Scotland and Norway continued, however, and it was along these routes that the Vikings of western Norway began to move. Some of this early penetration was peaceful – at times the Vikings seem to have been traders and purchasers of land rather than raiders – and by the end of the 9th century Norsemen were established in Iceland, the Faroes, the Shetlands, the Orkneys, the Isle of Man and along the coast of Ireland. After 860 there was a great mingling of Celts and Norsemen in Ireland and a revival of trade with England and France. For a couple of hundred years there was considerable economic development in Ireland, a process to which both Norse and Irish contributed, for although there were some mainly Norse communities on the coast, they did not always have the upper hand, and by the middle of the 10th century there had been much intermarriage.

The overland trade routes between the Baltic and the East by way of Russia, which seem to have been blocked round about the middle of the 9th century, were reopened between 870 and 880 and an influx of silver served to stimulate trade in the northern seas. More gold and cloth began to flow into England from Ireland. About the year 900 there is evidence that wine was being imported into Ireland once again. When attacked by the Irish king Muirchertach Leathercloaks in 941, Dublin, a Norse stronghold, was surrounded by a wall and rich enough to pay him tribute in gold, coloured mantles and foodstuffs. Similarly, when the Irish captured Limerick in 968 they found jewels, gold, silver and fine oriental silk cloth, and its commerce continued after the conquest for the city or, rather, fortified camp paid an annual tribute to its conquerors of 365 tuns of wine.

By this time the maritime initiative in the Irish Sea was with the Irish Norse rather than with the Irish themselves and the skin-boat or curragh, like the sailing ship in the early 20th century, had become economically outmoded. Integrated into Irish life as they were, the Norsemen exported Irish honey, wheat, timber, hides, leather goods and red and blue cloth in knarrs, wooden cargo vessels of Scandinavian design, and brought back luxury items. From Iceland they imported furs, a coarse woollen cloth used for sails, sheepskin coats and falcons. There was also a trade in slaves, both to Iceland and to France.[21] It may be hazarded, however, that the traffic was busiest on the routes from Belfast to the Clyde and from Belfast and Dublin to the Mersey and Anglesey, routes which have remained the most significant to the present day. Apart from oatmeal and a little salmon, salt and iron, Scotland did not have much to export, but there were healthy trading links between the Irish Norse and the Danes of York until the fall of the Danish kingdom of York in 954, when Chester began to grow in importance, a mint being established there. In part this was due to the export of Nantwich salt. By the year 1000 Cardiff, Swansea, Bristol and Totnes were also significant ports on the west coast of Britain, and in that year it was the Anglo-Saxon penny that King Sitric III of Dublin took as his model when he minted the first Irish coins.

Until recent times the historians of maritime affairs have been pre-eminently naval historians and the impression often given is that British shipping began with Alfred the Great who built a navy to defend his country against the maritime Vikings. Indeed the general reader could be forgiven for concluding that it had never occurred to the Anglo-Saxons to go to sea, that Alfred had to wait until he saw a Viking ship before the idea of building one came to him, and that these sea-raiders from Denmark had evolved ocean-going ships by themselves some centuries before the inhabitants of England thought of crossing the North Sea.

This scenario is not very convincing, but the Vikings have long enjoyed excellent publicity agents. Even in the past generation it has been suggested that the Anglo-Saxons rowed down the coast of the Low Countries and thence across to England,[22] and it seems to be assumed from such statements that they learned nothing about sailing for centuries afterwards. Respected archaeologists have said that the Sutton Hoo find 'proves that Nordic and Anglo-Saxon boat-building followed much the same structural lines, and passed through more or less the same stages.'[23] But the Sutton Hoo ship proves nothing of the kind.

To show that the Anglo-Saxons were experienced seamen one need look no further than their poetry. The 'riddles' found in the Exeter Book, given to Exeter Cathedral by Leofric, Bishop of Devon and Cornwall and Chancellor to Edward the Confessor, abound in references to the sea and these references must have been widely understood and appreciated. Two of the riddles describe storms at sea, one an anchor, another a ship, and yet another an iceberg which 'stove in the ship's sides, relentless and ravaging'.[24] Where did these seafarers meet icebergs? It is true that William Cowper wrote a poem to commemorate the appearance of an iceberg in the North Sea in the 18th century, and it is probable that both the 8th and the 18th centuries were relatively cold in Britain. Nevertheless, icebergs were not typical of European seas and even to come across growlers or drift ice the Anglo-Saxon seafarer must have voyaged fairly far north.

These riddles and the poem called *The Seafarer* were probably written down in the 8th century but may well relate to an earlier tradition. The spokesman in *The Seafarer* is certainly no novice in the ways of the sea. He tells of his sufferings but admits the sea's fascination; he is contemptuous of the soft ways of the landsman and yearns to set forth on another voyage. 'I can utter a true song about myself, tell of my travels, how in toilsome days I often suffered a time of hardship ... dread was the rolling of the waves. There the hard night-watch at the boat's prow was often my task, when it tosses by the cliffs. Afflicted with cold, my feet were fettered by frost ... The man who fares most prosperously on land knows not how I, careworn, have spent a winter as an exile on the ice-cold sea ...'

This will be recognised by the professional seafarer as an authentic voice. It is typical of plaints uttered by British seafarers down the ages. And equally typical is the passage that follows: 'And yet my heart is now restless in my breast, my mind is with the sea-flood over the whale's domain ...' It was not only in the veins of Celts and Vikings that sea water flowed. Laurence Binyon's sailor, John Winter, who ached to ship out when winter came to Deptford, could well have been of Saxon origin.

It is clear from the Sutton Hoo discovery that by the first half of the 7th century the unseaworthy boat discovered at Nydam in Denmark, and dating from the 4th century, had developed into a boat, some 89 feet long and 15 feet wide amidships, which was rowed by 38 oarsmen. But this was a boat of the Angles, a people who derived from the Baltic, and it is not in this direction that the origins of Saxon vessels are to be sought.

In the less well organised society that succeeded the break-up of the Roman Empire harbours turned back into beaches, quays disappeared and trade declined. Simpler and smaller vessels were required and it became necessary to build them more economically. The clinker-build of the Scandinavians, with its use of light planks and more easily worked timber, offered the necessary savings and southern shipwrights began to adopt Scandinavian methods. At the same time, the wooden barrel, which was known to the later Romans but had perhaps been invented in Spain as the wine trade developed there,[25] could be stowed in a ship more economically than the Roman amphora and thus better use could be made of such space as was available.[26]

Archaeology cannot determine whether an artefact originating in one place which is found in another place arrived as a result of trade or came some other way, perhaps as loot or from an exchange of gifts. However, in consequence of what one cautious writer describes as 'pre-market exchange mechanisms', goods are known to have arrived in East Anglia and Kent from the Rhine between 500 and 600, and in Sussex from the Seine between 600 and 640.[27] By the 8th century, if not before, goods from the Seine were reaching Southampton, English cloaks were of good repute on the Continent,[28] and Charlemagne was complaining to Offa of Mercia that Saxon traders in France were attempting to pass themselves off as pilgrims in order to avoid tolls.[29] At the same time the Frisians were carrying goods to a number of European countries, including England where they established depots in London and York. When the Vikings attacked Friesland in and after 810 these traders migrated south.

Such trade was not a continuous activity and its scale was small, with ships carrying no more than seven or eight tons of cargo. The British well-to-do exchanged wool, metals and slaves for luxuries that their estates could not provide, and salt was a commodity necessary to rich and poor alike.

According to Sidonius, who lived in 5th-century Gaul, Saxon vessels carried sails,[30] and a Romano-Celtic tradition of shipbuilding persisted. In the 8th or 9th century a quay was established once more just downstream from London Bridge and the remains of a contemporary vessel found there appear to relate to the hulk or *hulc*, a representation of which has been found on a 9th-century Anglo-Saxon coin.[31] The hulk, a vessel which had rounded ends and no keel and was built differently from Scandinavian craft, has been described as like a hollowed-out banana. It was an effective carrier of cargo and easy to beach. With its two side-rudders and a mast stepped well forward, it had much in common with the Celtic sailing ships.[32]

The Graveney boat, discovered in Kent and dating within a year or two of 895, also derives from a southern tradition of boatbuilding, but with its raked stem is more reminiscent of the cog, a vessel used in both England and the Low Countries. The cog was a double-ended vessel which could not be beached but which lay dry at low tide.[33]

In the Anglo-Saxon riddle about the iceberg we do not learn whether the ship was carvel-built in the Celtic fashion or clinker-built on the Scandinavian model or was a mixture of both. But we are told that it had many ribs and that in its midst was a 'mouth' or hold which was 'useful to men'. The ship could have been a large fishing vessel but was more probably a merchant ship (though it might have served as both) because, apart from an indication that there was some deck planking, the description hints that the cargo may have contained more than fish: 'it brings to the people provision in plenty, bears food within it, and each year yields to men a gift of which men, rich and poor, make use'. The reference to each year could imply that it made one annual trading voyage in the summer months, which was the custom of most merchantmen for centuries to come.

In Saxon Britain there was undoubtedly a diversity of ships and a diversity of sailors, some fishing offshore, some whaling, some coasting, and some venturing abroad. That sails were in general use on the east coast, as on the west coast, by 700 is indicated by the information which relates to this period that St Ives awaited a favourable wind to take him from Northumbria to Brittany, that St Wilfrid sailed directly across the North Sea to Frisia and that St Willibrord was sailing about the North Sea endeavouring to convert the heathen Dane.[34] Indeed it is possible that the saints brought sail to the warlike Danes across the North Sea as they brought sail to Norway from the Irish Sea.

Southern ships of the early 9th century are alluded to in Bishop Rimbert's *Vita Anskarii* in which a voyage from Cologne to Frisia is described. That these ships were well in advance of northern ships, at least in comfort, is indicated by the choice made by King Harald of Denmark. Travelling north in Anskar's company, Harald chose a southern vessel for his purpose and ordered two cabins to be suitably prepared for him and his companion.[35] At this time the 9th-century Osberg and Gokstad ships, excavated along Oslo fjord, were still essentially vessels for use in the Baltic rather than in the North Sea and the knarr, a Viking cargo-vessel which by the second half of the century could carry thirty people, together with their cattle, fodder, goods and furniture, west to Iceland or south to Britain, might have short half-decks at bow and stern and a fully-integrated keel, but it was never, so far as we are aware, provided with cabins.

'Unambitious optimism', the Celtic Iris Murdoch has written in another context, is 'part of the Anglo-Saxon tradition.' Although familiar enough with the sea, the Saxons, like the Veneti of Roman times, built no warships until, at the end of the 9th century, King Alfred, in response to the Viking attacks, built some new ships of his own contrivance, 'neither after the Frisian design nor after the Danish, but as it seemed to himself that they could be most serviceable.'[36] Like the Veneti ships, these vessels stood high out of the water; but they proved no more successful against the Vikings than the Veneti ships proved against the Romans. However, from such ferment was born the vessel known as the keel. Developed perhaps on the east coast by the Angles, the keel was clinker-built and provided with a keel, which made it sail better and faster than a hulk in open waters. Its stem and stern were raked and, length to breadth, its ratio was about 4:1. Its oars were used largely for manoevring it in harbour. By the year 1000 it was the common large vessel alternative to the hulk built in England and toll records show that it was used in the 11th century to carry wine in barrels from the Continent to London.[37]

Aelfric's class reader, written at the end of the 10th century, tells us much about the life of his times. Among Aelfric's acquaintances are monks, farmers, hunters, fishermen, saltworkers and merchants. The fisherman admits that he is too much of a coward to go deepsea fishing – 'I prefer to catch fish which I can kill and not fish which can kill me' – but he admires the courage of those who hunt the whale. The trader is a boastful character, fit enough in his own estimation to be an alderman and necessary 'to the king, to the wealthy folk and to everyone else.' He trades abroad, selling his cargo in distant lands and buying commodities not known at home – 'purple garments and silks, gems and gold, cleverly made suits of armour, spices, wine and oil, ivory and brass, copper and tin, sulphur and many other things.' He transports all these, he says, with much danger, though the copper and tin no doubt came from other parts of Britain. 'Sometimes I endure shipwreck and the loss of all my goods, not to mention the risk of losing my life.' In consequence, he confesses, he sells these goods at a price much higher than that which he has paid for them.[38]

King Alfred himself (849–899) is testimony to the voyage of the merchant Wulfstan, whose name suggests that he was Saxon. Wulfstan sailed into the Baltic where he traded his goods with the warlike people who lived near the mouth of the Polish river Vistula. Their horses, he reported, were a particularly worthwhile purchase.[39]

Not content with his trading contacts with Germany, France, Italy, Flanders and Frisia, most of them made just across the narrow seas to such ports as Quentovic (the modern Étaples), Rouen and Amiens, King Alfred was obviously interested in developing contacts with Scandinavia and the Baltic. By about 900, according to the saga of Egil, dried fish and furs were being sent to England – perhaps to East Anglia – from western Norway in return for wheat, cloth and metals. English bronzework dating from this period has been discovered on the west coast of Norway, while Grimsby hoards of the 10th century indicate a trade with the eastern Baltic.

By 911 the Danes had secured land in eastern England and in Normandy. At this time they were voyaging as far south as the Mediterranean and were continuing trading patterns pioneered by the Frisians. By the end of the century Viking attacks were no longer the piracy of independent freebooters but raids organised as part of an overall political strategy, and the Vikings were turning their new type of vessel, the Viking longship, to commercial advantage. Greenland was colonised, initially from Iceland, in 986, and from Greenland the Vikings proceeded to North America (Vinland) where at least two Scots, a man and a woman, went ashore with the Viking leader Karlsefani. Those who were in this vessel were eventually shipwrecked in Ireland.[40]

In England trade had become by this time a road to honour, for King Athelstan (924–939) had enacted that if any merchant or mariner successfully accomplished three voyages on the high seas with a ship and cargo of his own, he should henceforth be advanced to the dignity of a thane and become entitled to all the privileges attaching to this rank.[41] When, more than half a century before King Sitric III of Dublin, the Duke of Normandy first coined money at Rouen, he too modelled his pennies on an Anglo-Saxon one. The importance attached to trade by both Vikings and Saxons is indicated by the treaty made between Olaf Tryggvasson and Ethelred the Unready in 991 whereby Olaf agreed that his men would not molest Anglo-Saxon or foreign ships in English ports, nor English ships in foreign ports.[42]

By the end of the 10th century pilgrims were voyaging not merely to Santiago de Compostela but to the Holy Land. Dried cod or stockfish was being imported from Iceland, and grain was moving by sea from Poland to the Low Countries. Flemish merchants were buying wool in London and bringing Rhineland millstones with them.[43] British tin, copper and lead was finding its way to Germany, fine English cloth reached Regensburg on the Danube, there was a colony of Saxon merchants established at Hedeby, a Viking town in Denmark, and other English merchants held a privileged position in Pavia in Italy where they bought silks, spices and other oriental luxuries. Economically the north-west region was united by a silver coinage deriving from England and

Germany, and a higher proportion of the population was living in towns. Such centres as London, Dublin, Cologne, Hedeby and Novgorod were already cities in the later medieval sense. None of this progress would have been possible had no improvements been made to the most complex machine of the early medieval world, the ship.

The scale of this activity, however, was almost certainly less than that of Roman times. In 54 BC Caesar had conquered Britain with 500 ships and 20,000 men. By the year 1005 the population is thought to have grown to nearly one million from the 400,000 of Caesar's time. England was divided into 310 districts and each district was supposed to pay for the building and upkeep of one naval vessel of 60 oars and its crew. Theoretically, therefore, the naval defence forces might muster as many as 18,000 men. However, a few years later Canute was able to conquer the country with no more than 240 ships manned, in all probability, by fewer than 10,000 men. Even allowing for the fact that in the previous quarter of a century the Saxons had paid £240,000 to Danish invaders, and had thus been weakened economically, it does not suggest that trade was of great significance.

Under William the Conqueror and his successor England entered upon a period of economic stagnation. British trading ships, in so far as they had existed before the Conquest, grew fewer, and German, Frisian and Flemish merchants seized such opportunities as there were to maintain and develop a commerce which was to culminate in the power of the Hanseatic League. In the Bayeux Tapestry, which tells the story of the Norman Conquest, the ships illustrated seem to differ little from the 9th-century Gokstad ship, which was a one-masted, double-ended clinker built vessel measuring 79 feet long, 16.8 feet wide and 6.8 feet deep amidships. The Bayeux Tapestry ships may have been a little deeper, and the sheer or upward slope at bow and stern may have been more accentuated, though such differences could be attributable to the foibles of the sempstresses. This Tapestry, which is now believed to have been embroidered by English lay women within ten years of the event, may not have represented the most advanced ships of their day. However, there is one interesting difference between the Saxon and the Norman ships seen on the Tapestry. In the words of one authority, the Saxon ships 'nearly all show that the line of the uppermost strake, which carries the oar-ports, instead of being continuous from bow to stern as in the Norman vessels, was broken amidships, abreast of the mast, leaving the central portion of the ship without oar-ports.'[44] This may suggest that whoever instructed the needlewomen, whoever designed the tapestry – possibly Bishop Odo, William the Conqueror's half-brother, who was in the fighting – knew that the Saxon ships were different. They might have been the recently developed keel, a ship which operated with few oars, a ship which was much more dependent upon its sail than the Norman longship. They might also have been like the ship with a 'mouth' which is described in the Anglo-Saxon riddle. It is highly probable that they were requisitioned merchantmen since they were taking Harold on a trip to France.

Notes

1. A. Lewis, *The Northern Seas* (1958), Princeton, New Jersey, pp. 17–19.
2. R. Unger, *The Ship in the Medieval Economy, 600–1600* (1980), London, pp. 34–5.
3. V. Childe, *Prehistoric Communities of the British Isles* (1940), Edinburgh, p. 130.
4. Lewis, *op. cit.*, p. 43.
5. T. Powell, *The Celts* (1958), London, p. 102.
6. J. Bury, *Life of St Patrick* (1905), London, pp. 25–6.
7. Powell, *op. cit.*, p. 179.
8. Bury, *op. cit.*, pp. 38–9.
9. Geoffrey of Monmouth, *History of the Kings of Britain* (1963), London, pp. 194, 238–9.
10. J. O'Meara, *The Voyage of St Brendan* (1976), Ireland, pp. 5 and 18.
11. *Ib.*, p. 8.
12. E. Taylor, *The Haven-Finding Art* (1956), London, p. 69.
13. Lewis, *op. cit.*, p. 110.
14. G. Jones, *The Norse Atlantic Saga* (1964), London, pp. 9–10.
15. A. Courtauld, *From the Ends of the Earth* (1958), Oxford, pp. 25–6.
16. J. Hornell, *Water Transport* (1946), Cambridge, p. 142.
17. Lewis, *op. cit.*, pp. 134–5.
18. Taylor, *op. cit.*, p. 76.
19. C. Burland, 'By Weather to Wineland' (1950), MM, Vol. 36, pp. 81–2.
20. Taylor, *op. cit.*, p. 75.
21. Lewis, *op. cit.*, pp. 336–8.
22. D. Phillips-Birt, *The History of Seamanship* (1971), London, p. 101.
23. A. W. Brøgge & H. Shetelig, *The Viking Ships: Their Ancestry and Evolution* (1951), London, p. 52.
24. R. Gordon, *Anglo-Saxon Poetry* (1954), London, p. 300.
25. P. Marsden, *Roman London* (1980), London, p. 69.
26. Unger, *op. cit.*, pp. 42, 51–2.
27. R. Hodges, 'The Hamwih pottery: the local and imported wares from 30 years' excavations at Middle Saxon Southampton and their European context' (1981), Southampton Archaeological Committee Report 2, CBA Research Report 37, p. 93.
28. T. Lloyd, *The English Wool Trade in the Middle Ages* (1977), Cambridge, p. 1.
29. D. Whitelock, *English Historical Documents I* (1955), London; R. Hodges, *Dark Age Economics: The origins of towns and trade, AD 600–1000* (1982), London, pp. 32, 87–9 and 90.

30. Lewis, *op. cit.*, p. 48.
31. L. Miller, 'New Fresh Wharf 2, the Saxon and early medieval waterfronts' (1977), *The London Archaeologist*, 3(2), pp. 47–55; S. McGrail (ed), *The Archaeology of Medieval Ships and Harbours in Northern Europe* (1979), BAR International Series, 66: 5. 'The Medieval Ships of London', by P. Marsden, p. 86; V. Fenwick, 'A new Anglo-Saxon ship' (1983), IJNA, vol. 12, No. 2; J. Fletcher, 'The date of the Graveney boat' (1984), IJNA, vol. 13, No. 2, p. 151.
32. Unger, *op. cit.*, pp. 58, 61–2.
33. P. Cameron, 'Saxons, sea and sail' (1982), IJNA, vol. 11, No. 4, p. 325; S. McGrail, *Ancient Boats* (1983), Princes Risborough, p. 50.
34. Whitelock, *op. cit.*, pp. 713–14.
35. C. Robinson (trs.), *Anskar: The Apostle of the North* (1921), London, p. 43.
36. G. Garmonsway (trs.), *The Anglo-Saxon Chronicle* (1953), London, p. 90.
37. Unger, *op. cit.*, pp. 76–8.
38. G. Golding, *Records and Songs of Saxon Times* (1932), London, p. 74.
39. J. Bosworth, *A Description of Europe and the Voyages of Othere and Wulfstan by King Alfred the Great* (1855), London, p. 20ff.
40. Jones, *op. cit.*, pp. 189–90.
41. B. Thorpe, *Ancient Laws and Institutes of England* (1840), London, p. 81.
42. Whitelock, *op. cit.*, p. 401.
43. M. Thomas, *A Survey of English Economic History*, 3rd ed. (1967), London, p. 19. See also *The Independent*, 23.2.1989.
44. R. & R. C. Anderson, *The Sailing Ship: Six Thousand Years of History* (1926), London, p. 46.

3

Medieval Ships and Trade
(1100–1400)

The Britain of the 12th century had something in common with Australia in the 19th century. Wool was said to be 'half the wealth of the whole land' and it contributed nearly all the country's foreign earnings. A thriving export trade in wool, from all parts of Britain and Ireland to Flanders, existed by the reign of Henry I (1100–1135). By the end of the 12th century fine quality English wool fetched higher prices than any wool in Europe, and it was indispensable to the growing cloth industry in such cities as Ypres and Ghent.[1] By the 13th century British wool was also important to the cloth-workers of Florence.[2] Towards the end of that century over 25,000 sacks of wool, each sack weighing 364 pounds, were being exported each year, with Boston as the leading export port, followed by London, Hull, Southampton, Lynn (King's Lynn from the time of Henry VIII), Newcastle upon Tyne, Ipswich and Sandwich.[3] In the boom years of the first half of the 14th century, before the Black Death of 1349 and into the early years of the Hundred Years War (1337–1453), raw wool exports increased to 35–44,000 sacks a year,[4] and this represented wool shorn from more than 10 million sheep. In the last third of the 14th century exports declined to less than half this amount.

English cloth, too, was of good repute, the centre of the industry lying at first in the towns of the East Anglian plain, though no town of any size was without its branch of the industry. Fine light English worsteds were popular for summer wear then as now. 'Stamfords' were well known in Genoa by 1200,[5] and 'Lincoln scarlet' – along, no doubt, with Robin Hood's Lincoln green – was among the most highly priced cloths in a tariff of tolls in Venice in 1265.[6] At home and abroad these cloths of many colours were much in demand in privileged households.

In the course of the 13th century the fulling-mill, which used water-power, dispersed the industry to the countryside, where the labour was also cheaper, and thus moved its centre of gravity from the flat east to the upland west. By the 14th century demand was no longer for 'Stamfords' and 'Lincolns' but for 'Cotswolds', 'Mendips' and 'Kendals'.

The production and export of English cloth was rising before the Black

Death. After the setback then suffered, exports began to increase again and by the end of the 14th century some 40,000 broadcloths or their equivalent, each measuring 24 yards by 1·5 or 2 yards, were being exported annually.[7] Since 4·5 broadcloths used the amount of wool that would fill a sack, this figure was equivalent to the export of a further 9000 sacks of wool, in addition to the 15,000 sacks which were then being exported, and wool in the form of cloth was, of course, more valuable. Wool exported as cloth did not make up for the contraction in the volume of wool exports, but the total volume of wool and cloth exports had not dropped faster than population and the combined value may well have been higher than it was previously.

Apart from wool and the developing trade in cloth, England still exported tin, sold either as rods or blocks of pure ore or made up into pewter vessels, the latter being an essentially English manufacture. Some tin was carried by Italian vessels as far as Asia Minor. In 1380–1 Genoese and Catalan merchants together shipped some 350,000 pounds. In the 14th century, however, it is unlikely that the annual value of such exports exceeded £10,000.[8] Fowey in Cornwall derived its importance from the tin trade and in the reign of Edward III (1327–1377) Fowey was said to furnish more seamen to the king's fleet than London.[9] Lead was also mined in several parts of the country and some of it went to supply roofs and gutters for foreign castles and abbeys. On one occasion 100 cartloads of lead were shipped from Newcastle upon Tyne to Rouen for the roofing of Clairvaux and on another 241 cartloads were despatched to the same destination from York.[10] Grain was exported from Lynn and from the Severn valley, often round the coast, but also abroad. Salt and dried fish was exported from Yarmouth and elsewhere, for even at the time of the Domesday survey a city like Oxford expected to be supplied with salt herring, carried up-river by boat. Hides, meat and dairy produce also featured among exports at times, but the quantities were of little significance.

From the late 12th century onwards English and Scottish coalmines were developed and exports from the Tyne grew rapidly during the reign of Edward III. Sea-coal Lane, still to be found near Ludgate Circus in London, was there in 1253, the coal being unloaded presumably at the foot of the lane at a wharf in the Fleet river. But foreigners appreciated the new fuel more than did the English and for a time its use in the city of London was prohibited while the queen resided there because 'it might prove pernicious for her health'.[11] The French exchanged corn for coal at Newcastle – the earliest example of a trade in 'coal out, corn home', which was to be the backbone of British tramp shipping in the half-century prior to 1939. By 1377 more than forty ships were employed in the Tyneside coal trade, exporting something like 7000 tons a year, mainly to the Low Countries.[12]

Among imports, wine was pre-eminent. The thin English wine could not compete with the flood of French wine which was imported into a richer England from the middle of the 12th century onwards. By the first third of the 14th century English imports accounted for something like one-quarter of the total exports from Bordeaux and amounted to about 20,000 tuns a year. The equivalent of 40 million bottles of wine for a population of four million people, these imports suggest that the better off male might have drunk a bottle or two a day. After the Hundred Years War started in 1337, wine prices rose and imports from Bordeaux fell, though some compensation came from an increase in imports of Spanish wine.

Second in importance among British imports were raw materials required by the woollen industry, principally dyes and the substances which fixed dyes – alum and wood ash, the latter also being used in soap manufacture. Some dyes were home-produced from lichens, barks and madder, but woad, which produced or helped to produce the blues, violets, greens and blacks, was an import of such consequence that it became the subject of the first national customs duty of which there is clear evidence, a duty which contributed substantially to the exchequer of Richard I (1189–1199). Woad came from Picardy by way of Amiens and the Somme and from areas further south. Like Mexico's cochineal, which subsequently replaced it, the brilliant scarlet dye called kermes or 'grain' derived from the dried bodies of an insect which looked like grain. Found on a species of oak, kermes came from Spain, Portugal and the Barbary coast. Brazil, a cheaper red dye more often used for dyeing leather, was believed to come from the East. Imported saffron provided a yellow dye. Alum, the mordant used solely for scarlet dyes, came from the Gulf of Smyrna and the Black Sea. Wood ash, on the other hand, was imported from the Baltic.[13]

Although salt was produced at Nantwich, near Chester, and also on the east coast of England and elsewhere, such was the demand in medieval Britain that it was an important import and over two-thirds of these imports came from the Bay of Bourgneuf in the neighbourhood of Nantes.[14] From northern Spain came iron, supplemented from the 14th century onwards by increasing amounts of Swedish iron. From Iberia, too, came quicksilver, olive oil, soap, wax, fine leather, figs, dates, raisins, almonds, licorice, sugar, rice, and occasionally oranges and lemons, both of these latter being expensive luxuries. Mediterranean fruits also came from Italy, and Italian merchants had such other luxury goods to sell as silks, cloth of gold, currants from Greece, sweet wines from the Levant, and all the riches of the East: pepper, cinnamon, cloves, ginger and other spices; rubies, emeralds, ivory and sandalwood; rare dyes; and cotton and muslin. Such trade was not yet in the hands of the English.

Across the narrow seas from Flanders came fresh vegetables, as well as fine cloths, some of them made from English wool; and in times of war with Spain, goods from the Mediterranean would be bought there. Steel imports, originating in Westphalia and France, were also of some significance.[15]

Baltic timber in the shape of boards and rafters is an almost universal item in medieval building accounts. Also from Norway and the Baltic came other forest products: masts, spars and oars, wood ash, tar and pitch. Wax for candles, fish and whale oil, and costly furs like sable, marten and ermine, were other northern imports. These goods arrived largely through London and ports on the east coast. Eleven ships of German and Frisian origin driven into Scarborough by storm in 1293 had among their cargo 20,060 boards, 99 barrels of pitch, 261 casks of wood ash, 45 barrels of butter, 22 lasts of seal blubber and oil, 23 lasts of herrings in barrels, 52 lasts and 19 dickers of hides and skins of oxen, horses, goats, seals, calves and lambs, 500 hare skins, 15½ bundles of popel and strandelin (kinds of fur), 2800 stockfish or dried cod, a piece of wax, 300 bowstaves and four young goshawks.[16] A last of hides comprised 20 dickers and a dicker ten hides. For such goods wool, cloth and corn would be taken in exchange.

As Norman influence grew in Ireland the slave trade came to an end since the entire population became the king's subjects. From about 1175 to 1250 the Irish Sea region was part of a vibrant and growing economy and Ireland exported grain both to Gascony and to England and fish came to rival hides in commercial importance. Wine was imported, particularly through Waterford. After the middle of the 13th century, however, there was some decline in Irish prosperity.[17]

The population of England grew rapidly in the 12th and 13th centuries from the roughly one million inhabitants at the time of the Norman Conquest to perhaps four million just before the Black Death of 1349. Thereafter it fell rapidly and at the end of the 14th century was about 2·3 million.[18] Governments were also growing more powerful in the 12th and 13th centuries; the fulling-mill was of such significance that its introduction has been described as an industrial revolution; and the ship was being improved. These factors, reacting one upon another, resulted in a quickening of economic activity and a growth of trade, though the initial impetus was only partly British.

The so-called Billingsgate tolls of the early 11th century are the first English source to identify specific groups of alien traders. Those mentioned are men of northern France, the Low Countries and probably the Rhineland, but there is no mention of Frisians or Vikings. The merchants of Cologne seem to have established a foothold in London by the year 1000.[19] In 1157 Henry II allowed them to open a 'factory' or 'kontor' in London and these German merchants subsequently became identified – from about 1241 – with the Hanseatic League, an association of German merchants in a number of German towns, including Lübeck, Bremen and Hamburg. The Hanse controlled the lucrative herring fishery in the Baltic and thus, in the 13th century, had almost complete control of the Baltic and Scandinavian trades. The London kontor was one of four great Hanseatic kontors, the others being in Bruges, Bergen and Novgorod, and the league were the first to develop a shipping system which was as complex as that of the Romans.

By the early 13th century some churchmen were conceding that the merchant's calling was a necessary and justifiable one, and by the early 14th century English merchants and ships were also trading to the Baltic, those from the north-east coast, at least, competing on equal terms with Hanseatic merchants.[20] Competition came, too, from the Dutch, who were seeking their share of the profitable Baltic grain trade to Bruges, a trade in which the cost of transport was almost half the price of the grain.[21] Since the Germans tried to exclude the Dutch from the herring fishing grounds off the Baltic coast of Denmark, the Dutch began increasingly to exploit the resources of the North Sea and developed, late in the century, new techniques of barrelling and pickling the herring. The fish were gutted as soon as they were caught, salted, and placed in barrels in layers, head to tail. Each layer was then separated by salt and the filled barrel was tightly sealed.[22] The North Sea herring were inferior to those of the Baltic but were more plentiful and they sold more widely.[23]

Mediterranean seamen never had much taste for the western ocean and they seem never to have ventured to the east coast of Britain. Although Italian merchants were resident in England from the early 13th century, it was not until the 1270s that Genoese carracks opened a direct sea route from the Mediterranean to north-west Europe, and they then began to exchange alum for English wool. The first organised voyage of Venetian galleys to north-west Europe was in 1314, and there is no record of their presence in England before an ill-fated voyage to Southampton in 1319. Before 1270 Flemish merchants had handled the bulk of English wool exports. By 1275 the English were handling about one-third of the trade, the Italians one-quarter, and German and French merchants much of the rest. In the early 1270s at least 327 Englishmen obtained licences to export wool,[24] and by the 14th century English merchants had the capability of handling the bulk of the nation's wool exports. As well as venturing into the Baltic, English ships were by this time taking a predominant place in the Gascon wine trade, though they still played only a small part in the trade to Iberia.

One of the factors in these changes was the government's need for dependable revenues, and trade was an obvious source. The Billingsgate tolls listed a number of goods on which taxes were imposed and by 1203 a customs duty on wool exports was well established, London in that year paying some £836, Boston £780 and Southampton £712.[25] In 1275 this duty was established at half a mark or 6s. 8d. per sack. In 1303 a 'new custom', as distinct from what now became the 'ancient custom' of 1275, increased the duty to be paid by aliens who exported wool to 10s, and in 1347 differential customs duties were also imposed on exports of English cloth, though the Hanseatic merchants successfully resisted payment.[26]

In the first forty years of the 14th century the Staple was established, a fixed point through which most raw wool had to be exported, with a Company of English merchants dominating the trade. London became the chief wool port and Calais the Staple town, though there were times when the Staple was established elsewhere. In proportion to the value of cloth, when compared with wool, the customs duties did not bear so hard on cloth. The result was that a further boost was given to the English cloth trade. Although the export of wool came to be largely in English hands, the export of cloth was not. Despite periodic outbursts against foreign traders, Germans and Italians established a valuable stake in the growing export of English cloth, and alien trade continued to be a substantial component of English overseas commerce for the rest of the Middle Ages, sometimes larger even than it had been in the early 14th century.[27]

To meet the demand for the carriage of bulk cargoes – wool, wine, grain and fish – the shipbuilders of northern Europe built vessels suitable for the task. Ships became bigger and deeper and there was a five-fold increase in carrying capacity between 1000 and 1250. By 1250 northern ships were as good as those of the Mediterranean though the northern economy still lagged behind.[28]

As we have seen, there was already a diversity of vessels even as early as the 6th century, and by the 10th century the hulk, the cog, the keel and the knarr were only the more important cargo carriers in northern seas. The experts are not always agreed on the origins of particular vessels, and the same name is used down the years for vessels which grew to become quite different vehicles. It is therefore difficult to give a clear picture of the development of shipping in the Middle Ages.

The Viking cargo-vessel, the knarr, in which America was discovered, is said by one writer to have been replaced by the buss; while another seems to believe that the cog was of Scandinavian origin.[29] The consensus is that the cog, which began as a small flat-bottomed coaster in the 10th century or earlier, was developed by the Germans, perhaps out of the Rhine, and had become by 1400 a ship of 200 tons or more, 90 or more feet long and 30 or more feet in the beam. Taken over by the Hanse, their sailors did not sail the cog through the entrance to the Baltic Sea until the middle of the 13th century, where it presumably replaced the knarr. The cog was built either without a keel or with a simple keel-plank from which stem and stern posts, straight but angled, rose sharply and in a straight line, the ship having a high freeboard. The bottom-planking was laid flush or edge to edge, the steep sides being clinker-built from the turn of the bilge.[30] A bowsprit, or spar, at the bow, appeared in the 13th century and a small square sail slung under it helped the vessel to move to windward. Superstructures or 'castles' were added fore and aft for purposes of defence, and a topcastle added to the mast. At the stern a windlass was used to raise sail and haul the anchor. The cog of this ilk dominated the northern carrying trade, particularly from the Baltic, for about 150 years.

The round-bottomed hulk grew as large as the cog in the course of the 14th century and after 1380, in the view of one authority, shipbuilders merged the cog and hulk into one composite design which cut costs.[31] Certainly by the end of the 14th century almost all large carriers were referred to as cogs. This composite vessel continued to be of shell construction, that is, the frames were inserted after the skin or shell of planking had been completed, and this method of building limited the size which could be achieved.

Sometime during the 12th or 13th century the stern rudder was introduced, all earlier ships having a steering oar or oars, a single oar being commonly, though not invariably, lashed to the starboard quarter – the 'steering board' from which the word starboard is derived. A carving upon the font in Winchester Cathedral, which is believed to date from about 1180, is commonly cited as the earliest known example of a ship with a stern rudder, though others suggest that this carving represents a steering oar set rather further aft than usual. However this may be, there is no argument about the seal of Ipswich, which has been traced back to 1200, for there the sternpost gudgeons are clearly shown.[32] With a stern rudder the ship could answer better to the helmsman, for a side rudder could be lifted clear of the water and become useless if the vessel heeled over. The area of the sail could also by this time be varied by tying up the canvas in a bundle with the aid of reef points or by adding or removing an extra piece known as a bonnet at the bottom of the sail.[33]

As with other new ideas, it took time for the stern rudder to be adopted universally. Documents from the 13th century distinguish between different types of steering gear in merchantmen and it is significant that ships with the stern rudder paid higher port dues – twice as much as other ships, for example, at Torksey in Lincolnshire.[34] From the customs dues payable in London and Ipswich it is also clear that vessels were divided into a number of classes, the largest being those with a 'scalter', a word variously spelt but one which seems to have meant some permanent form of shelter or cabin accommodation.[35]

Other vessels in common use included balingers and barges, these terms sometimes being used in conjunction with the term 'nef' or 'nave' in the Anglo-Castilian trade. Balingers were usually smaller than barges, being mostly between 40 and 60 tons, though sometimes as small as 16 tons. Barges were mostly under 100 tons but could be as large as 200 tons.[36] The Thames barge and the Tyne and Humber keels were still commercially viable in the years before World War II, and one or two are still used in youth training. Through them we have some contact with the shipping of the Middle Ages. The Tyne keel is a double-ended undecked lighter, but the Humber keel is decked fore and aft with large hatchcovers amidships and therefore much better suited to voyages at sea. Sixty-two feet overall and 15·5 feet in the beam, the Humber keel is propelled by one primitive square sail hoisted on a mast amidships and carries a load of about 100 tons. She seems practically identical with a description which has been preserved of an ancient ship discovered near the river Rother in Sussex in 1822. This vessel may have been employed to carry stone to the site of Bodiam Castle in 1386 and it seems reasonable to suppose that she may have been a medieval English coaster.[37]

By the end of the 13th century the size of ships was usually stated in tuns or tons, referring to the number of wine casks or tuns of wine they could carry, though the reckoning of tonnage was confused. The ton was originally 20 true hundreds – 20 hundredweights – and thus 2000 pounds. As such it reappears as the tun of wine, a measure based on the weight of one cubic foot of liquid which constituted a wine-bushel. Eight wine-bushels of 1000 ounces or $62\frac{1}{2}$ pounds each constituted a hogshead or quarter of a tun, and four hogsheads or 32 wine-bushels made a tun. Taking waste space into account a tun of wine, which was also 252 gallons, occupied about 40 cubic feet, and this became the dry-cargo ton, a space occupied by four quarters of wheat which also weighed approximately 2000 pounds.[38]

By 1300 some of the largest vessels, with crews of up to 30 men, were as much as 240 tons burden (tons burden being roughly equivalent to modern net tonnage), but these were exceptional. The average English merchantman was under 100 tons burden and the forecastle, still of course a fighting castle, featured only in the larger ships. Smaller ships were built without any erection forward, though the after castle had been extended to provide cabin accommodation. By this time, too, merchantmen were carrying a ship's boat amidships.

In the 11th century Edward the Confessor, instead of maintaining a fleet himself, planned a similar result by offering certain of the Channel ports privileges in return for an obligation to provide a specified number of ships when required. These ports – the so-called Cinque Ports of Sandwich, Dover, Hythe, Romney and Hastings, and Winchelsea and Rye – reached the peak of their power in the 13th century, when they were supposed, at their own cost, to supply the Crown with 57 ships for 15 days a year, each ship to be manned at the rate of 21 men and a boy. In 1244 the first of several seamen's hospitals was built at Sandwich.[39]

However, it soon became apparent that it was insufficient for the purposes of defence to put the keeping of the seas out to contract. The first occasion after the Norman Conquest when a larger fleet was required than could be supplied by the Cinque Ports was Richard I's Crusade in 1189. This fleet numbered more than 100 vessels and the ships had to be purchased or hired in all the ports of England, Normandy and Poitou. In the next century the king owned some galleys, a number of them roomy enough to serve also as merchantmen, and these latter he would charter out when opportunity offered. In 1232, for example, John Blancboilly paid the king 50 marks a year for the use of the royal ship *Queen* and, provided he kept it in good condition, he could trade with it where he liked.[40] In 1297 Edward I raised a fleet of 305 ships with a complement of about 5800 sailors.

By the middle of the 14th century, by which time most of the Cinque Ports were silting up, the king kept 40 or 50 ships of his own at Rotherhithe and Ratcliff, not far from the Tower of London, but these were by no means sufficient for either naval operations or the transport of troops without the impressment of English merchantmen or the chartering of foreigners. In 1347, ten years into the Hundred Years War, Edward III mustered 738 ships, over twice as many as Edward I, and about 15,000 sailors.[41] Throughout the Hundred Years War merchantmen remained the backbone of the navy, but impressment, embargoes on free movement and inadequate compensation all played havoc with their normal trades and profits and complaints were frequently voiced.

Despite the decline of some of the Cinque Ports, Dover remained the chief port for passenger traffic to the Continent and as early as 1312 there existed a gild of ferry-ships, the members of which served the passage in rotation. The charge for a man's passage to Wissant had been 2d and to Calais 3d but in 1314 complaints were heard of higher prices with 'new and young men' charging as much as 12d (perhaps £20 in 1988 prices). The passage for horses cost 18d or even 3s, and there were complaints that the ferries were overloaded, 40 or 50 horses being put aboard a ship fit to carry only 24. Such a ship must have been at least the size of the County Hall vessel of AD 300, that is, 60 feet long and 16 feet wide.

As Romney, Winchelsea and Hythe declined, other ports grew in importance. The Cinque Ports themselves had carried on a running feud with Yarmouth – one of their barges being attacked by three from Yarmouth in 1297, for example, when the Cinque Ports' barge had been looking out for pirates from Calais[42] – and a less serious one with Poole. On the east coast, in addition to Yarmouth, Scarborough and Whitby attracted merchants from Flanders, Norway, Germany, France and Scotland, merchants who came to buy herrings when they appeared off the coast in late summer. This coast was busy with both foreign and home trade and, in addition to Hull and Newcastle upon Tyne, Dunwich, Boston, Lynn and Ipswich were all ports of significance. It has been estimated that in 1346 more than 200 vessels were owned along the east coast between Berwick and the Thames.[43] Fifty years later it was alleged that there were 300 ships from England in the Baltic port of Danzig at one time, though this seems improbable.[44]

Sandwich still flourished in Kent, as well as Dover, and on the south coast there was Southampton in addition to Poole and Dartmouth. In the west Chester and Bristol remained major ports, though King John had recognised already that the site of Liverpool promised well. London, however, remained pre-eminent, a city which at the close of the Middle Ages could compare with any in Christendom.

Some elements of order were being introduced into maritime affairs by this time. From 1154 to 1453 the vineyards of Gascony and the port of Bordeaux were in British hands and wine from Bordeaux was a rapidly expanding trade in the 13th century. It was for the regulation of this trade that the Judgements of Oléron were drawn up, Oléron being an island about the size of Jersey which lies a mile or two off the French coast just south of La Rochelle. There a maritime court is said to have been held and the body of maritime law established became gradually more widely accepted in northern waters.

The Judgements of Oléron stress the importance of the crew. Master and crew messed together, having very much the same status, and it was as necessary for the master to consult the crew before sailing as it had been in the days of St Paul; if he failed to accept the majority view he was held responsible if the ship were lost by storm. If the master were involved in a dispute with a member of the crew the matter was to be decided by a free vote, and the master was held responsible for any loss or damage if he did not abide by the decision. If there were a storm and the question of jettisoning part of the cargo or tackle arose, at least one-third of the crew had to agree to the action taken.

In the event of shipwreck seafarers were required to help in the work of salvage, but in return they were entitled to both reward and their fare home; if necessary, the master could raise the cash for this on the security of the salved goods. When a ship arrived in port the master had to show the merchants the ropes and tackle with which he prepared to hoist the wine casks or other cargo; if he failed to do so, he was responsible for any damage caused by a rope breaking.[45]

There are many other provisions in the Judgements, ranging from the perquisites to which seafarers were entitled in particular trades to the decapitation of a pilot who ran a ship ashore and had no means of making amends, but enough has been said to indicate that here were the beginnings in northern seas of that maritime code which, subject though it is to continual modification, has since become accepted throughout the world. The Judgements of Oléron, which were possibly codified in the 12th century by Richard Cœur de Lion, were certainly accepted in England by the 14th century, and they became the basis of codes adopted in many German, Dutch and Flemish ports.

It would be premature to suppose from this that life at sea in medieval times was anything but uncertain. In the 13th century the masters of all ships were licensed to annoy the king's enemies, and thus was the privateer born. From the end of the century letters of marque could be issued and such letters authorised any party injured upon the sea to take reprisals. But the distinction between privateer and pirate was a fine one and on one occasion Henry III found it necessary to hang indiscriminately some thirty seafarers who might have been either.[46] Some of the barbarous punishments proposed in the Judgements of Oléron for those who connived at shipwreck or the murder of seamen indicate that the control of such crimes was largely impracticable. There was also much uncertainty in international relations. The provision of a 'safe conduct' by Edward III for foreign merchant shipping on passage from Spain to Flanders did not prevent the capture of such ships by English sailors, nor did it prevent the bringing of such captured ships into an English port.[47] A generation later, in 1379, a Portuguese ship was arrested and detained in England while inquiries were made in Bristol concerning the attitude of the Portuguese. On this occasion the Bristol authorities replied that they had examined many of their citizens trading to Lisbon and these had reported that for two years past they had been treated there as friends.[48]

Merchantmen adopted the convoy system for self-protection, electing one of their number as commander for the voyage. In times of trouble the ships also carried soldiers. The wine fleet then sailed as one, as did fleets bound for other destinations. In the 13th century the cog was adapted for fighting purposes and became, by the later 14th century, the only warship of any consequence. Once governments became committed to the control of shipping, they took a greater interest in both shipping and shipbuilding, and began to fix load limits, first for pilgrims and then for cargo, thus having to develop rules for measuring the capacity of ships.[49] In 1368 Edward III decreed that English and Gascon ships should be loaded with wines before foreign ships were loaded, and in 1381 and 1382 the first Navigation Acts – unenforceable though they were – made it illegal to charter foreign ships if English ships were available.

The effects of war on the wine trade may be illustrated by the rise in freight rates from Bordeaux to London between 1320 and 1350, when they rose from about 8s. to 13s. 4d. a tun. At the beginning of the 14th century every port in England engaged directly in the wine trade but, with the general decline which overtook English shipping in the later 14th century, ports on the east coast became less involved while the relative importance of Bristol increased.[50] Many of these wine-traders possessed their own ships and it was in this trade that the largest ships – a few of them over 200 tons – were used.

Some of these ships sailed round from Bristol to Plymouth and elsewhere to pick up pilgrims bound for St James of Compostela and a poem from this period, preserved at Trinity College, Cambridge, provides a graphic picture of both the sailors and their passengers. 'Men may leave all games when they sail to St James', the poet tells us, for their troubles often begin at sea. He goes on to explain that, whether they sail from Sandwich, Winchelsea or Bristol, many of them are likely to be seasick and wish that they were dead before they have been long on the water.

> And some would ask for salted toast,
> For they could eat nor boiled nor roast;

A man as soon could pay their keep
For two days as for one.

The sailors find the sufferings of the pilgrims amusing and enjoy their food meanwhile. Eventually, the shipmaster calls the carpenter, tells him to bring his gear, and orders him to make cabins 'here and there' and many small compartments. A sack of straw, he suggests, will come in handy, for some of the pilgrims will have to sleep in their cloaks and will appreciate any extra warmth. However, 'I would as soon have been in a wood without meat or drink', recalls one of the voyagers,

For when 'twas time to go to bed
The pump was close beside our head,
And better that a man were dead
Than smell the stink of that.

On this verse John Masefield, sailor and poet laureate, commented, 'The water which leaks into a tight wooden ship generally rots in the bilges. The smell of this rotten water is abominable, but the presence of the smell indicates that the leak is inconsiderable.' The verse also records an early use of the pump, the clearance of water being effected earlier by 'winding balles', consisting of a windlass and buckets.[51]

By the early 14th century Bristol ships and others from the west country, often hired by London merchants, were venturing further south into areas where hitherto Spanish vessels had predominated. By the end of the century they were sometimes engaged in quite complex voyages touching several countries on the English Channel and the Atlantic routes and venturing into the Mediterranean and to North Africa.[52]

Geoffrey Chaucer knew all about English merchant shipping in the 14th century for, the son of a wine merchant, he spent his youth where the Walbrook flowed into the Thames. In adult life he travelled widely. He translated a treatise on the astrolabe for his son and, more important still, from 1374 to 1386 he lived above London's Aldgate while he was working in the Custom House as Comptroller of the Customs and Subsidy of Wools, Skins and Leather and, from 1382, Comptroller of the Petty Customs as well.

Chaucer's merchant, who wore a Flemish beaver hat upon his head, was particularly anxious that the seas between East Anglia and the Low Countries should be kept clear of pirates. But the 'shipman', who came from the west – 'for aught I know, he came from Dartmouth town' –

. . . knew well all the havens as they were,
From Gotland to the Cape of Finistère,

And every creek in Brittany and Spain.
His sailing barge was called the 'Maudelayne'.

Weather-beaten and tough, the shipman proved good company, and none knew more than he about tides, currents and phases of the moon. He was particularly familiar with the wine trade, and was not over-scrupulous in his dealings with his charterers –

Full many a draught of wine had he withdrawn
As, homeward-bound from France, the merchant slept –

but he was prepared to do battle with pirates, and he gave no quarter. None was his equal in pilotage, Chaucer assures us, and he could take a vessel safely as far south as Carthage, nearly 1000 miles east of Gibraltar.

Such skills did not go unrewarded. According to the 'Inquisition taken at Queenborow',[53] in 1375, for the round voyage from London to Bordeaux, the ordinary mariner received 8s. plus the cost of the freight on a tun of wine, which would have more than doubled his earnings; for the round voyage to any port on the south coast of Ireland he received 10s. plus the freight on 30 hides; for a round voyage in the Newcastle coal trade the payment was 4s. and free space for two quarters of coal; and for a voyage to Scone in Scotland he had 8s. and the freight of a last of herring between three men. These were minimum wages. On the larger ships the owner was expected to provide, in addition, meat three times a week, and every evening bread with a relish in the shape of cheese, onions, sardines or other fish. The wages of the crew were a first charge on the ship. Occasionally an owner would engage a crew 'on shares' or as partners in his trading venture.

It is difficult to assess the real or annual value of such payments. In the service of the Crown the 14th-century seaman received 3d a day, usually with a bonus of 6d a week in addition. At the same time a mason, the best-paid type of artisan, could look for no more than 3d a day without food or 4d if he were a master mason.[54] The seaman's pay was above that of the common labourer but he may not have earned it so regularly. At 1988 prices the seaman may have earned some £600 for six months at sea and the master at least twice this amount. In 1390 a parliamentary petition deplored the exorbitant wages demanded by seamen; no doubt there had been a marked rise in such demands after the Black Death.

Details exist of a shipment of corn from Yorkshire to London in 1351. The voyage from Hull apparently took 30 days despite the distribution among the crews of 40d 'that they might haste the more rapidly and might take more care over looking after the foodstuffs'. Perhaps even then some seafarers believed, as they did later on in the days of long-distance sailing, that 'more days' meant 'more dollars' for, in addition to their somewhat modest incentive bonus, the ordinary sailors were paid 3d a day and the masters 6d. Two of the ships in this little fleet of four had crews of 12 men, the other two having crews of ten.[55]

Navigation was undertaken by the master or mate, and a clerk or purser would probably keep the ship's books and look after stores. In addition to these there would be a handful of 'mariners of the poop', including a boatswain, and the 'mariners before the mast'. Larger vessels would carry 'pages', cabin-boys and servants, including a cook. Discipline of a kind was enforced by fines and such punishments as ducking in the sea from the yardarm.

The seaman's work was seasonal but the season was gradually extended. None of the Hanseatic ships was allowed to put to sea between Martinmas (November 11th) and Candlemas (February 2nd) except those loaded with herring, cod or beer, which were allowed to sail at a later date to take advantage of the winter market. In the anonymous Scandinavian *King's Mirror,* a treatise written about the middle of the 13th century in the form of a dialogue between father and son, we read: 'If you are preparing to carry on trade beyond the seas and you sail your own ship, have it thoroughly coated with tar in the autumn and, if possible, keep it tarred all winter. But if the ship is placed on timbers too late to be coated in the autumn, tar it when spring opens and let it dry thoroughly afterwards. Always buy shares in good vessels or in none at all. Keep your ship attractive, for then capable men will join you, and it will be well manned. Be sure to have your ship ready when summer begins and do your travelling while the season is best. Keep reliable tackle on shipboard at all times, and never remain out at sea in late autumn if you can avoid it'.[56]

Although Chaucer's shipman must have relied largely on a well-stored memory, by the 14th century he had available to him both tide tables and books of sailing directions, guides which would give him much information about the depth of water in different areas and the type of 'ground' or bottom which he might expect to find sticking to his tallow when he cast his lead. The lead and line can be used as well in fog or darkness as in the light of day, and in the 13th and 14th centuries it was the means by which the course was discovered.

The attraction exerted on iron bodies by a naturally occurring mineral – lodestone or magnetite – appears to have been known to the Chinese and to the Greeks in ancient times, and there have been suggestions that the Arabs used magnets floating upon a bowl of water before Europeans did. But there is no definite evidence of the lodestone or magnetic compass being used for the purpose of navigation before 1200. The Englishman Alexander Neckam, writing at this time, described the sailor's use of the magnetised needle,[57] but innovations were not adopted rapidly in medieval times and there is little evidence for the general use of the compass in merchant ships until much later.

Charts were not yet used by northern seafarers, but the sand-glass makes its appearance in the inventories of English ships from 1295 onwards[58] and was used for setting and keeping the watch. As far as he could the medieval sailor kept within sight of land and sailed from 'view to view' or from one landmark to another. For short voyages, says the *King's Mirror,* 'one has to make sure of fair winds to last a day or two only, which is not difficult for men who understand the weather.' On long voyages, too, careful account was taken of the weather before the voyage was embarked upon though the hazards were obviously greater and, in the event, a voyage might prove unexpectedly long. A journey across the Bay of Biscay, for example, could take several months and finish in quite the wrong place, and a voyage to Iceland might not succeed at all. In 1307 there is a record that even a voyage from Ireland to the coast of Cumberland could, on occasion, take as long as two months.[59]

Whenever the sun shone or the stars came out, however, navigators would have more than a shrewd idea of their latitude or distance north of the equator because of the midday 'height' of the sun and the position of the stars in the different seasons. By the 13th century Norsemen used sunstones, perhaps devices for indicating the position of the sun even in cloudy conditions.[60] Further south the astrolabe was in use and as early as 1292–5 Robert the Englishman, at Montpellier, compiled tables which gave the daily declination of the sun from the celestial equator, thus facilitating accurate observations for latitude.[61] It is also probable that the medieval seaman, like those who were to follow him, could form a tolerably accurate estimate of the speed of his vessel by observing some flotsam or bubbles floating past.

Some hazards at sea were not wholly natural. Wrecks were frequent, and such catastrophes might be aided by coast-dwellers. In the legal sense wreck occurred only when no one survived the loss of a ship, and so this did not foster survival. Those who lived on the coast cared little for the claims of merchants and not infrequently they resisted any attempt to enforce the law. In 1315, when the *Santa Maria* of Fuenterrabia, laden with goods for Gascony to the value of £2200, was wrecked off Dungeness the goods were carried off by the men of Winchelsea, Rye and Romney and, when the warden of the Cinque Ports tried to hold an inquiry, the men of these towns assembled in arms and prevented him from doing so.[62] Again, in 1363, four great ships, evidently on their way from England since they were carrying wool, cloth, tin and other goods to the alleged value of £70,000, were wrecked off Plymouth and the cargo was stolen by the local inhabitants.[63]

From the beginning of the 13th century the national records are also full of complaints of piracy by or at the expense of British ships, the notorious William de Marcis, for example, making his headquarters on Lundy Island. It is not to be wondered at that Chaucer's shipman gave short shrift to those who attacked him at sea, sending them home 'by water' to 'every land'.

St Nicholas, patron saint of seafarers, was a popular subject among the decorators of medieval English churches and the seafarer was in need of his intercession. Storms were a greater peril even than pirates, wreckers ashore and seafarers from rival ports. If report be true Edward I, when a young prince, was once brought to his knees by a storm at sea, being granted his life only after promising the Virgin that he would found a Cistercian monastery.

The Virgin, represented by the planet Venus (the evening star and *stella maris*, still the symbol of the Roman Catholic organisation which ministers to seafarers), was thought of as a lantern shining for voyagers on a sea of evil. To help each other seafarers used lanterns and lights both on their ships and on shore. As in Roman times, there were now lights at the entrances of Dover and Calais harbours. At times in the 13th century lights were maintained at the entrance to Yarmouth, and between 1314 and 1328 an octagonal lighthouse 35 feet high was built at St Catherine's, on the Isle of Wight.[64]

Clearly, the medieval seafarer did not navigate wholly by guess and by God. He was hard and resourceful and as skilled in the arts of navigation as many a shipmaster in the last days of sail. By Chaucer's time British merchant seamen had developed the one-masted ship with its square sail about as far as it was capable of development. To north and south they knew all the waters between the Arctic Circle and Morocco, while to east and west they were familiar with the sea between Iceland and Finland. Although they lived at a time of some recession, it was as cheap to import timber from the Baltic to southern England as it was to bring it from the Midlands. In every English port of any consequence there was a body of merchants engaged primarily, though seldom wholly, in overseas trade, and some of these were the most notable citizens of their day. William of Doncaster, for example, was much concerned with the importation of Bordeaux wines, traded frequently to Ireland, and exported wool from Chester and elsewhere, sending some in 1309 across country to Ipswich and thence to Flanders. Besides being a shipowner, he was an army contractor and government official. In the city of London, Gilbert Maghfeld, who was an ironmonger and merchant operating largely on credit, was said to be worth about £1200,[65] perhaps £4·5 million in modern currency. London was a prosperous city and, although trade had its ups and downs, then as now, both merchants and seafarers were equipped to take further steps forward.

Notes

1. T.H. Lloyd, *The English Wool Trade in the Middle Ages* (1977), Cambridge, pp. 1–6.
2. M.W. Thomas, *A Survey of English Economic History,* 3rd edn. (1967), London, pp. 60–1.
3. J.L. Bolton, *The Medieval English Economy, 1150–1500* (1980), London, p. 175.
4. Lloyd, *op. cit.,* p. 310.
5. Bolton, *op. cit.,* p. 153.
6. A.L. Poole (ed), *Medieval England* (1958), Oxford, p. 229.
7. E.M. Carus-Wilson & O. Coleman, *England's Export Trade 1275–1547* (1963), Oxford, pp. 138–9.
8. Bolton, *op. cit.,* p. 294.
9. A.L. Salzman, *English Trade in the Middle Ages* (1931), Oxford, p. 281.
10. Poole, *op. cit.,* p. 230.
11. W.S. Lindsay, *History of Merchant Shipping* Vol. I. (1876), London, p. 410.
12. Salzman, *op. cit.,* p. 282.
13. E.M. Carus-Wilson, *Medieval Merchant Venturers* (1954), London, pp. 216–21.
14. W.R. Childs, *Anglo-Castilian Trade in the Later Middle Ages* (1978), Manchester, p. 123.
15. Bolton, *op. cit.,* p. 280.
16. Salzman, *op. cit.,* pp. 362–3; *see also* J. C. Davies, 'Shipping and Trade in Newcastle-upon-Tyne, 1294–1296' (1953), *Archaeologia Aeliana,* 4th Series, Vol. XXXI, p. 175 ff.
17. J.T. Maple, *The Irish Sea Region, 850–1254 AD* (1985), University of Kansas.
18. Bolton, *op. cit.,* p. 51; R. Hodges, *Dark Age Economics: The origins of towns and trade, AD 600–1000* (1982), London, p. 164.
19. N.S.B. Gras, *The Early English Customs System* (1918), Cambridge, p. 154; also *The Independent,* 20.10.1988.
20. J.C. Davies, *op. cit.,* p. 188.
21. R.W. Unger, *The Ship in the Medieval Economy, 600–1600* (1980), London, pp. 166–9.
22. Bolton, *op. cit.,* p. 276.
23. G.V. Scammell, *The World Encompassed: The first European Marine Empires* (1981), London, p. 376.
24. Lloyd, *op. cit.,* p. 50.

25. E. A. Carson, 'Customs History and Records of Trade and Shipping' (1972), MM, Vol. 58, No. 4, pp. 447–8.
26. T. H. Lloyd, *Alien Merchants in England in the High Middle Ages* (1982), Brighton, Sussex, pp. 204–9; also N. S. B. Gras, *op. cit.*, pp. 53–72.
27. *Ib.*, pp. 208–9.
28. Unger, *op. cit.*, p. 139.
29. Unger, *op. cit.*, pp. 133–8. R. Moreken, 'Longships, Knarrs and Cogs' (1988), MM, Vol. 74, No. 4, p. 391 ff.
30. A. McGowan, *Tiller and Whipstaff: The Development of the Sailing Ship, 1400–1700* (1981), London, p. 6.
31. Unger, *op. cit.*, pp. 168–9.
32. R. & R. C. Anderson, *The Sailing Ship: Six Thousand Years of History* (1926), London, p. 58.
33. Poole, *op. cit.*, p. 175.
34. Salzman, *op. cit.*, p. 354.
35. *Ib.*, pp. 226–7.
36. J. W. Sherborne, 'English Barges and Balingers in the late Fourteenth Century' (1977), MM. Vol. 63, No. 2, pp. 109–14.
37. Anderson, *op. cit.*, pp. 49–50.
38. D. Burwash, *English Merchant Shipping 1460–1540* (1947), Toronto, p. 88 ff. *Also* McGowan, *op. cit.*, p. 32.
39. T. J. Runyan, 'Ships and Mariners in Later Medieval England' (1977), *Journal of British Studies*, Vol. XVI, No. 2, p. 16.
40. Poole, *op. cit.*, p. 177.
41. Runyan, *op. cit.*, p. 4. *See also* J. W. Sherborne, 'The English Navy, Shipping and Manpower, 1369–1389' (1967), *Past & Present*, No. 37, pp. 163–75.
42. Salzman, *op. cit.*, pp. 270–1.
43. G. V. Scammell, 'English Merchant Shipping at the End of the Middle Ages' (1961), EHR, 2nd Series, Vol. XIII, No. 3, p. 327. *See also* B. Waites, 'The Medieval Ports and Trade of North-East Yorkshire' (1977), MM, Vol. 63, No. 2; and J. C. Davies, 'Shipping and Trade in Newcastle-upon-Tyne, 1294–1296' (1953), *Archaeologia Aeliana*, 4th Series, Vol. XXXI, p. 175 ff.
44. G. D. Ramsay, *English Overseas Trade during the Centuries of Emergence* (1957), London, p. 98.
45. T. Twiss (ed.), *The Black Book of the Admiralty*, Vol. 1 (1871), London, p. 89.
46. Lindsay, *op. cit.*, p. 395.
47. *Ib.*, p. 420.
48. Salzman, *op. cit.*, p. 263.
49. Unger, *op. cit.*, p. 151.
50. M. K. James, *Studies in the Medieval Wine Trade* (1971), Oxford.
51. Salzman, *op. cit.*, p. 231.
52. Childs, *op. cit.*, p. 149.
53. See *The Black Book of the Admiralty*, p. 133 ff.
54. C. E. Fayle, *A Short History of the World's Shipping Industry* (1933), London, pp. 113–14.
55. Salzman, *op. cit.*, pp. 216–17.
56. G. J. Marcus, 'The Navigation of the Norsemen' (1953), MM, Vol. 39, pp. 115–16.
57. E. Power & M. Postan (eds.), *Studies in English Trade in the Fifteenth Century*, p. 160.

58. E. Taylor, *The Haven-Finding Art* (1956), London, p. 140.
59. Salzman, *op. cit.*, p. 246.
60. B. E. Gelsinger, 'Lodestone and Sunstone in Medieval Iceland' (1970), MM, Vol. 56, No. 2, pp. 219–26. *See also* Marcus, *op. cit.*, p. 120.
61. Burwash, *op. cit.*, p. 4.
62. Salzman, *op. cit.*, p. 254.
63. *Ib.*, p. 251.
64. W. C. Hassall, *How They Lived 55 BC–1485* (1962), Oxford, p. 90.
65. James, *op. cit.*, p. 212.

II

THE RISE OF BRITISH SHIPPING

1400–1890

4

Merchant Adventurers (1400–1498)

Round about 1435 a long polemical poem, *The Libel of English Policy,* was written to demonstrate the central importance to England of her command of the seas. The poem suggested that England's wool provided her economic strength, and that her possible control of traffic passing through the Straits of Dover gave her geographic strength. The poet, a true descendant of Chaucer's merchant, is much concerned with the command of the seas between England and the Netherlands and between England and France, waters in which English ships had long played a significant role, but he also surveys at length the trade from more distant places and suggests that England's commercial power can be extended in these directions. A powerful England at sea, he points out, would have other nations – the Flemings and Spaniards; even the Venetians and Genoese – at its mercy:

> Cherish merchandise, keep the admiralty.
> That we be masters of the narrow sea.

The *Libel* presaged the protectionist and mercantilist policies of centuries to come, but the power necessary to implement such policies did not yet exist.

That power was to come, in part, from the development in the 15th century of the full-rigged, three-masted ship, a marriage of Mediterranean and Atlantic ideas which gave rise to an invention which opened up the world and served merchants and governments for a period of more than 400 years.

This new type of vessel began, probably in the first quarter of the 15th century, when Mediterranean or Atlantic coast shipbuilders constructed the hull of a cog, not in the clinker-built way, where the frames were inserted after the shell of planking had been built, but by the skeleton method, where the framework was built and the hull planks, laid edge to edge carvel-fashion, were fixed to that framework. The ship thus built was stronger and, size for size, took less timber. It could also be built bigger than clinker-built vessels.

Into the new hull the builders stepped first two and then three masts. To the square mainsail a lateen or triangular sail was added, a sail of the type used for centuries by seamen in the eastern Mediterranean. This sail was affixed to a small mizen mast behind the mainmast. It helped with the steering, and it helped the ship to cover more ground to windward. Another two-masted experiment was to fit a foremast in front of the mainmast, each of these masts being fitted with a square sail. This proved less efficient. Finally, the three-masted ship was deemed best for many purposes. The main driving power came from the square sail on the mainmast, to the lower part of which extra power could be added by lacing on a bonnet. A foremast carried a smaller square sail. The mizen mast carried a lateen sail. All the masts were supported by stays and shrouds.

The ship thus provided was called a carrack. The carrack was a vessel broad in the beam and deep in the hull, with the keel twice as long as the ship was wide, while the length on deck was three times the breadth of the ship.

During the course of the 15th century the carrack increased in size. The average size of ships hired by the English king grew from about 80 tons to 120 tons between 1410 and 1450, though not all such ships would be carracks. The size had increased further by 1470, round about which time a spritsail was added on the underside of the bowsprit and a topsail was added above the mainsail on the mainmast. The topsail tended to lift the ship out of the water and the spritsail tended to pull it down. Together they added to the driving power. The other sails also tended to grow larger.[1]

The carrack, or something like it, might prove to be the deepsea ship of the future, but it was not the only or even the main vessel used by British sailors in the 15th century. More than forty names given to types of vessel are recorded and sometimes, to make confusion worse confounded, the same names are used to describe quite different vessels.

The balinger continued to be used for fishing and for trade to France and may, indeed, have originated as a whaling boat in the Bay of Biscay. In the course of the 15th century it added a second mast to its mainmast but it had ceased to be a seafaring craft by Elizabethan times.

Barge and bark are words that appear to have had a common origin but they were applied, unfortunately for the purposes of clarity, to a number of different vessels. Generally larger than balingers, sea-going barges were numerous among the merchant ships impressed by the Crown in the first half of the 15th century, but tended to become fewer as the century wore on. Although mentioned in the trade from Scotland and with the Low Countries, the barge, like the balinger, was found most frequently in western ports. A typical size was 60 to 80 tons, though as early as 1392 a Dartmouth barge carried a cargo of 150 tons from Seville to London and a few were bigger still. During the 15th century some of these vessels developed from possessing one mast to possessing three, with two bonnets on the main course and one on the foresail, while some also set a sail under the bowsprit.[2]

In the early part of the century one English cog was said to carry 185 tuns of wine home from Bordeaux, and a cog of Fowey in the middle of the century was of 240 tons burden. By this time the larger cogs and barges may not have differed very much. Some time within the next hundred years – it is not known exactly when – their control system was improved by the addition of a whipstaff to the tiller. In larger ships the tiller, which guided the rudder, went through an opening in the stern and the helmsman could not be seen on deck. There was thus a problem of communication. To solve this the bottom of a heavy pole was fastened to the forward end of the tiller and this pole projected through a hole to the deck above. The pole or whipstaff pivoted in a greased leather washer or grommet. With this innovation in common use by the end of the 16th century, the helmsman could stand on the deck above and could push the top of the whipstaff to one side or the other, moving the tiller in the opposite direction. In this position the helmsman could see the sails again and hear instructions.[3]

By the middle of the 15th century the caravel or carvel had been introduced into English waters from Portugal. It was usually, though not invariably, lateen-rigged and was at first smaller and more slender than the balinger. In this form it was favoured as a messenger and scout in naval operations and as a raiding vessel by pirates. It may have developed into the pinnace, a vessel of about 30 tons much used in the following century, though the pinnace has also been associated with the spinace, a decked vessel of from 10 to 40 tons which traded across the Channel and to Spain. In another incarnation the carvel is said to have developed into a beamier 150–200 ton ship with three masts in the second half of the 15th century. Its name, at least, makes a clear reference to its method of construction.[4]

Another vessel in 15th-century use was the picard, similar in size to the spinace. The picard sailed in the Irish trade, brought fish to market and was used as a lighter; it was widely distributed in British waters. In addition to the picard there was the crayer, of 25 to 50 tons, much used in the cross-Channel trades, though it has also been described as a river boat. The crayer was provided with a comparatively complex sail plan, carrying a topsail and perhaps even a studding sail, a narrow supplementary sail run out on a short boom beyond the outer edge of another sail to increase the lateral spread of square sails.[5]

The keels still sailed from Newcastle and the Humber, while on the Norfolk Broads and in the Thames estuary the wherry, a vessel measuring 22·5 by 4·5 feet, was used to carry light merchandise and passengers. In 1464 English smacks appear at Chichester.[6]

In addition the British were using the Dutch dogger, a vessel of from 40 to 100 tons which had been engaged in the North Sea and Icelandic fisheries from British ports since the previous century; and by the end of the 15th century the English were also sailing the Dutch hoy, a vessel of 36 to 50 tons which they used in their trade with the Low Countries. Sturdily built and economical in both rig and manning, the hoy became a maritime maid of all work for some 300 years.

The picture is a complex one. Ships and ship sizes changed in response to economic pressures and defence requirements. At the end of the 15th century the carracks and galleys of the Mediterranean were still the giants of the maritime world, but the Dutch had by this time built up a fleet of 300 herring busses, a vessel of which mention is first made in 1415, ranging in size from 40 to 160 tons.[7] In Britain shipbuilders were busy borrowing foreign ideas and equipment and were eventually to build vessels which were better adapted than most others to the conquest of the world's oceans. But merchants also bought shipping from the Baltic in the first half of the century, and there are records indicating that citizens of London, Newcastle and Southampton all bought vessels in the Low Countries in the 1470s.[8] For reasons of security, and to cut unit costs, ships moved towards larger sizes in the early 15th century, but the smaller and faster ship came into its own again, at least in the Anglo-Castilian trade, once the English Channel became safer in the latter part of the century.[9]

By the second half of the century many merchantmen carried more than one mast. The *Margaret Cely,* though only 60–70 tons burden, carried three masts, as did the 'new carvel' built for Sir John Howard at the beginning of Edward IV's reign.[10] The 'castles' at stem and stern had become an integral part of the ship, with the forecastle noticeably the higher of the two. The mainmast was fitted with a stalwart fighting top and was supported by elaborate rigging coming down abaft amidships while, to give greater strength, there were many more forestays and backstays than there had been in earlier ships. The ship's galley by this time was provided with a permanent hearth, and the new methods of construction provided a stronger base for ship-borne artillery, which was rapidly improving and gave European seafarers their great advantage in other parts of the world.

There was no sudden break with tradition and the old was built alongside the new, as it was in those later times when steam ousted sail. But a new and thrusting merchant class was arising in England, a class given encouragement by the Tudor monarchs since they needed the revenue that merchants could provide. At times the monarch also needed these merchants' ships, together with their crews, to carry troops overseas or to fight at sea. Merchants, shipowners and seafarers might complain, as they did in 1413, about the monarch's 'vainglorious' impressment of ships to make up his fleet for the invasion of France, and no doubt they did not relish paying duties which in 1421 alone amounted to more than £50,000.[11] But it could not have been all loss. If things went well, returns on shipping soon covered any initial outlay, sometimes within a year, and in most cases ships did arrive safely and the risks involved were worth taking. William Canynges the younger of Bristol, one of the foremost shipowners of his age, with a fleet worth £3800 in the 1460s (perhaps £1·5 million at 1988 prices), boasts on his tomb that he once supplied to Edward IV, who was described as the 'Merchant King', no less than 2670 tons of shipping. Since he and his family built St Mary Redcliffe, the church in Bristol which houses his tomb, it is unlikely that he did it for nothing.

Henry VII tried to encourage shipowners. In his Navigation Acts he returned to the policy first attempted in the reign of Richard II. His Act of 1485 forbade the import of wine from Gascony other than in English, Irish or Welsh ships, and four years later the prohibition was extended to the import of woad. Furthermore, no foreign ships were to be used by English merchants if English ones were available. Such legislation was still not particularly effective but Henry VII also negotiated commercial treaties, took an active interest in exploration and offered a bounty where ships were built that exceeded 140 tons.

At the end of the 14th century cabins had had to be specially constructed in a ship for the future Henry IV, just as they were for the 2100 pilgrims who voyaged to Compostela in 1445.[12] But by the end of the 15th century merchant ships normally possessed at least a few permanent cabins, no doubt allotted to officers and to merchants or their factors. The ordinary sailor had to furnish his own bed, a portable straw-filled pallet which must have been much the same as the 'donkey's breakfast' of the early 20th-century mariner. Since being put in the hold or under hatches was a punishment, the sailors clearly did not live amidships. In all probability they lived under the forecastle, as they did later. On going ashore the sailor had to leave his chest and his bed as security against his return.

The laws of Oléron, which were accepted as the basis for maritime law both in the English court of Admiralty and in the various local courts which exercised a maritime jurisdiction, prescribed the rights and duties of only three ranks in a ship's crew – the master, the lodesman (pilot or navigator) and the common mariner. There were, of course, others on board. The *Margaret Cely,* which was typical of a common class of 15th-century merchant ship, carried among the crew, in addition to a master, a purser, a boatswain, a cook and a ship's boy. In 1485 one of the Cely family noted a payment of 2s to the 'bottswayne and his mate', and there was sometimes a master's mate. The lodesman too might have his helpers. In one Bristol ship a quartermaster was promoted to master of another ship and his training had been such as to make him a competent pilot and commander. If there were a captain – as there usually was on an expedition – he was not the shipmaster but an official who exercised a general control in matters of defence, administration and policy. The pinnace belonging to Howard's carvel had a 'cockswayne', and a steward supervised the meat and drink. The crew would be completed by the ordinary mariners and a cat, the latter serving as ratcatcher.

From all this it would seem that by the end of the 15th century the typical crew of an English merchantman – master, mate, quartermasters, boatswain, boatswain's mate, purser, cook, steward, perhaps an apprentice or ship's boy, and other 'hands' – was little different, in name at least, from that carried by small vessels in the last days of sail, except that the crews of some ships, numbering perhaps from 20 to 30 in a 100-ton ship and more in bigger ships, could be disproportionately large when there was a need for rowers.

Ashore at least five seamen's gilds had been established by the 15th century, at Lynn, York, Hull, Bristol and Newcastle upon Tyne. Only two of them have ordinances which indicate any attempt to maintain standards of seamanship,[13] and the system of training then and for long afterwards was unsatisfactory. Arrangements for apprenticeship varied widely. Not until the 20th century was a City livery company for seafarers established in London and by that time indentured apprenticeship was in shipping company hands. The 15th-century seamen's gild had mainly friendly society functions and began ashore that interest in and compassion for the sailor which after the Napoleonic Wars was carried on by the missionary societies. The gild or fraternity at Bristol, for example, was formed in 1445 because 'the craft of mariners is so adventurous that, daily being in their voyages sore vexed, troubled, diseased and distressed, the which (by) good means of prayers and good works might be graciously comforted'.[14] The gild was supported by a levy on each master mariner who, on arrival in port, had to pay 4d a tun on his cargo. This money went to support a priest and twelve poor sailors whose duty it was to pray daily for all merchants and mariners 'passing and labouring on the seas'. As one versifier wrote in 1418:

> The wise man his son forbade
> ... the shipman's craft for peril of [being] dead.

Whether the mariner labouring on the sea was normally as full of religious observances as the Bristol seamen's gild is another matter. There is no evidence that the religious ritual observed in Spanish ships of the day was also observed in British ships, and probably many seafarers never thought upon God until their end was nigh, as is suggested by the 15th-century tale of Beryn:

> For fifteen days the tempest was so strong
> That one man after another (wishing to survive)
> Confessed and made vows that he might remain alive,
> Some to see the sepulchre and some some other place,
> To such an holy sentence, for help and e'en for grace,
> Some to fast and do penance, and some to deeds of alms.

Distinctions between employer and employed were gradually becoming well established, though the employee might have a share in the profits and sometimes even a voice in management. The three basic systems of reward were often combined or refined: the first was a share in the profits and derived from the Rhodian or Mediterranean sea law which predated by more than 1500 years the laws of Oléron; the second was a wage, paid usually by the voyage, but also by the month or by the distance travelled; the third was a claim on a proportion of the cargo space. In the Cely accounts part of the wage was paid on finishing the outward leg of a voyage, providing capital which might be spent on goods to bring home, and the rest was paid on the return to England.

The Howard and Cely accounts indicate that salted meat, salt or smoked fish and bread and beer were the staple foods when the ship was at sea, varied by eggs, butter, fresh vegetables, raisins, figs and other modest luxuries when the ship was in port. Voyages were normally of short duration for ships continued to cling to the shores. On its way from London to Bordeaux in 1486 the *Margaret Cely* took on fresh provisions at Plymouth, La Rochelle, the Ile de Rhé and Blaye. The privations of sea life were not always what they were to become in later centuries. Ship's biscuits were not unknown, for by the end of the 15th century there were complaints in Southampton that bakers were monopolising their supply, but the *Margaret Cely* picked up bread wherever she could.

According to an entry by Fra Mauro on his map of 1458, Baltic seamen sailed to Iceland 'neither with chart nor with compass', but in the accounts of John Starlying, clerk to the king's ships in the reign of Henry IV, mention is made frequently of sailing-needles and compasses. There is no record of direct passages from Britain to Iceland or even across the Bay of Biscay in the pre-compass era, and the gradual adoption of the compass must have greatly facilitated both oceanic navigation and the construction of charts. With the aid of the compass the Mediterranean had been mapped accurately in the 14th century, but comparable charts of northern seas did not begin to appear until a century or more later. The evidence suggests that the use of the compass spread northwards from the south, and the author of *The Libel of English Policy* informs us quite unambiguously that the sailors of Bristol and neighbouring ports were navigating to Iceland 'by needle and by stone' by 1423. A properly marked compass card was, indeed, in use by Chaucer's time for Chaucer tells us that 'shipmen reckon their parts in 32'.

The 'Dutchman's log' is reckoned to be almost any object thrown overboard to help in the estimation of the ship's speed. As late as the early 20th century it might still be the ashes from the galley fire. The Dutchman's log used in conjunction with the sand-glass, or half-hour glass, could measure the distance travelled and, if the length and duration of a particular tack or course were calculable, deduced or dead (ded) reckoning became possible. By 1480 seagoing craft of all descriptions in Britain were commonly provided with lead and line, sand-glasses and compasses,[15] and dead-reckoning had been raised to the level of a fine art.

Next in the navigator's armoury came the astrolabe, quadrant and cross-staff, all forerunners of the sextant, and all used to measure the elevation of heavenly bodies above the horizon. With their use latitude could be estimated, but merchant seamen adopted them only gradually. Even Vasco da Gama, when he wished to take an observation of the sun with his new mariners' astrolabe, went ashore to do so. Although learned men knew that a difference of one hour between the local times of the passing of the same position of the heavenly bodies along the celestial equator meant a difference of 15 degrees longitude in the observer's position on the earth's surface, no timepiece sufficiently accurate for use at sea was to become available until the 18th century. Between the 15th and 18th centuries dead-reckoning had to suffice.

The first known pilot book or rutter in English dates from the middle of the 15th century, though it had earlier origins, and it appears to be independent of a contemporary German *Seebuch*.[16] The author is unknown but the extant manuscript is the work of William Ebesham, a scribe of Edward IV's reign. Assuming that the reader is familiar with the general aspect of the British coast, the writer proceeds to give him the tides, currents and soundings, together with the bearings of a number of prominent headlands and instructions for avoiding certain well-known shoals and rocks. Different chapters deal with the coast from Berwick-upon-Tweed to Land's End, the coasts of France and Spain from Saint-Malo to the Straits of Gibraltar, the seas and coasts in the west of Britain, including a course about Ireland, soundings and types of bottom to be found in the English Channel, and two direct routes across the Bay of Biscay.

Part of the latter reads, in modernised form, as follows: 'You come out of Spain and you are at Cape Finistère. Then steer north, north-east. When your dead-reckoning suggests that you are two-thirds the way across, and if you are bound to the Severn estuary, you must steer north by east till you come into soundings. If soundings are 100 fathoms, or else 80, then steer north until you sound 72 fathoms and pick up fair grey sand. That is the ridge that lies between Cape Clear and Scilly. From there go north till you come into soundings of ooze, and then follow your course east-north-east or else east by north ... If you reckon you have crossed the Bay and you are bound for the Channel, steer north, north-east and by north until you come into soundings of 100 fathoms. Then steer north-east until you come into 80 fathoms. If the ground is streamy, you are between Ushant and Scilly at the entrance to the Channel. Continue on your course until you strike 60 fathoms, then steer north-east ...'[17]

This sophisticated treatise obviously owes much to earlier pilots. The effect of the moon upon tides was known and there were certain rule-of-thumb guides to high tide. In local waters highly specialised pilots or lodesmen were to be found, bearing heavy responsibilities and not infrequently sued in Chancery or in the Court of Admiralty for failure to fulfil contracts. Indeed the Admiralty undertook of its own accord to prevent unqualified men from practising navigation.

In addition to pilot books, charts were coming into use. Traverse tables appear in a Genoese manuscript dating from 1390, and these gave the length of each course for all thirty-two points of the compass. As charts developed they were covered with a network of lines which helped the pilot to lay a course and served as a substitute for the modern use of parallel rulers and the printed compass rose.

One important consequence of the improvement in ships in the 15th century and of the development of means of navigating with some accuracy in bad weather – a consequence which has been little remarked but one which was essential to oceanic discovery and world-wide trading – was the gradual extension of the sailing season. An act of the Scots

Parliament of 1466 forbade sailings between October 28th and February 2nd, and the ballad of 'Sir Patrick Spens', probably composed in this period, reflects the typical mariner's fear of winter voyaging:

> Be it wind, be it wet, be it hail, be it sleet,
> Our ship must sail the foam . . .

An active shipmaster in Scotland might get in two trips a year to Norway, or one to Bordeaux and one to Danzig, but no one attempted two trips a year to the Baltic.[18] About 1444, however, a Venetian merchant in London took delivery of goods discharged from two galleys – 162 bales of woad, 10 bales of pepper, 8 bales of sandalwood, 40 butts of currants, 70 bales of dates and 48 pieces of Tartary silk – and these goods were brought ashore on December 29th.[19] Although sailing was still largely seasonal, contrary winds might keep ships at sea well into the winter. The chances of survival in such conditions had improved considerably.

The scale of British foreign trade remained small. Its value in the middle of the 15th century has been estimated at some £3 million, half of this being exports and the other half imports. Some 50 per cent of this trade was in the hands of native merchants. The proportion handled by the Hansards was rising from, perhaps, 10 to 20 per cent, and that handled by Italians and other aliens declining from, perhaps, 40 to 30 per cent.[20] British trade per head of population was less than one-fiftieth of what it is today though, unlike many modern imports, those of the 15th century could not be produced at home.

In the first half of the century wool exports declined from about 14,000 sacks a year, worth some £80,000, to round about 10,000 sacks, worth rather more than £50,000, at which level they continued, broadly speaking, until the end of the century. At the same time the export of broadcloths rose from some 40,000, worth about £75,000, to nearer 50,000, worth £90,000, but the expansion was not maintained and dropped to about 40,000 again.[21]

With the exceptions of wool destined for Italy and of wool of poor quality, wool continued to be shipped to Calais by the Merchants of the Staple, of whom there were over 300, mostly in London, though the wool itself was also shipped from Boston, Ipswich, Hull and sometimes Sandwich.

Wool for export was packed in 'sarplars', most containing two sacks, and canvas was used as a covering, large quantities of canvas and packthread being bought at Calais. After the weighing and sealing of sarplars, the merchant was supposed to pay customs and other dues, though credit was normally allowed. The sarplars were then stowed on ships under the direction of officials.[22] All merchants divided their wool among several ships to lessen the risk of loss and normally from five to eleven merchants would have consignments on each ship. In 1478 the wool fleet from London, sailing in July, comprised 38 ships carrying 1160½ sacks, 12 cloves of wool and 268,227 wool-fells or sheepskins. The next big wool fleet sailed the following spring. Three years later, in November 1481, Richard Cely, a merchant stapler operating in London and Calais, split his consignment of 11,500 sheepskins between six ships, *Mary* of London, *Christopher* of Rainham, *Thomas* of Maidstone, *Mary Grace* of London, *Michael* of Hull and *Thomas* of Newhithe.

Part of Cely's shipment consisted of summer fells, part were winter fells, and the rest was Cotswold wool. Each sack of wool might realise from £3 to £9, according to quality, with an average price of £6–7 a sack and an average profit of £2–3 a sack.[23] Freight from London to Calais was 6s. 8d. the sarplar plus a penny for 'premage' or primage, now a percentage addition to the freight paid to the owners or charterers of a vessel, but then a customary allowance made by a shipper to the master and crew for the loading and care of the cargo. Before the ship sailed a 'searcher' came aboard and compared the lading with the cockets or ship's documents, which he then marked and gave to the purser with a bill of discharge. For this he took a fee which varied with the nationality of the ship, and sometimes he would delay the sailing of the ship to secure a tip (*pot de vin*) from the merchants.[24]

On arrival at Calais port dues of 4d a sack and 2d a hundred fells were payable, after which the wool was landed and taken to a warehouse. There the officials of the Staple would compare it with the particulars on the cocket, reweigh it, and test the quality of the wool. In 1417 English merchants are to be found complaining that although their cockets are in order and the wool is out of their hands from the time it is weighed in England until it is reweighed at Calais, they are nevertheless accused of smuggling more than is marked on their cockets. One writer has suggested that the wool may have got wet.[25]

There are other references to smuggling, and about 1450 smuggling was alleged to be one of the causes of the decay of the Calais staple. But the English government's insistence that wool be paid for in gold or silver was a more important factor in this decline, and the future lay not with the Merchants of the Staple but with the rival Fellowship of the Merchant Adventurers.

By a series of charters granted between 1404 and 1408 legal recognition and a corporate status were conferred upon three companies of English merchants trading abroad. Two of these, which did not flourish, embraced merchants trading to Norway and to the Baltic. The third, embracing merchants trading to the Low Countries, did flourish, and came to be regarded as the principal Company of the Merchant Adventurers. In London the Mercers, or dealers in textile fabrics, naturally predominated in this Company, and it was in the Mercers' hall that exporters met and convoys were arranged.[26]

These Merchant Adventurers traded largely in English cloth, by now England's most valuable export. Complaint was made that whereas in the days of Edward III the revenues of the Calais staple reached £68,000, they were down by 1449 to under £12,000. Although economic decline was general in the third quarter of the 15th century and cloth exports did not boom until the end of the century, the trade carried on by the Adventurers with the Low Countries, mainly through Antwerp, had become by far the most important trade in English hands. In return for English cloth they received linen, Delft pottery and a great many cheap consumer goods like lamps, copper kettles, drinking glasses, pepper-grinders and scissors, though it is also on record that London exported such other consumer goods as basins, plates, saucepans and daggers, and leather products like buckets, bottles and bellows. From abroad English merchants also bought fish – herring, eels, cod, ling and mackerel – and vegetables. One cargo brought to London in 1420 included 180 ells of linen, 250 barrels of onions, 275 bunches of garlic, 300 cabbages and 20 sacks of onion seed.[27] By the end of the century the looms of Bruges and Ypres, sustained by English wool for more than 200 years, were being put out of action, at least in part, by imports of English cloth.[28]

To the north and in the Rhine hinterland trade remained largely in the hands of Hanseatic merchants who turned increasingly to England for cloth. Their interests clashed with those of a small group of merchants from Lynn, Hull and Boston who wanted to handle the cloth trade to the Baltic themselves.[29] At the beginning of the 15th century English merchants in Danzig complained of ill-treatment and imprisonment and in 1402 an English settlement in Bergen was wiped out by Hanseatic pirates. For most of the 15th century the English were shut out of the Baltic and had little trade with Norway. The municipal records of the east coast towns contain a number of references, mostly indirect, to the existence of a group of merchants who traded to the Baltic in the 15th century and who were distinct from the London merchants, but these references disappear by the 1470s.[30]

The English kings of the time could not do without the services of the Hanseatic merchants. In 1430 Henry VI forbade his subjects to go to any port in Scandinavia other than Bergen, a prohibition which remained in force, at least nominally, as late as 1507. In 1436 Henry VI confirmed the Hanse's privileges, as did Edward IV in 1463, the League helping him to regain the throne in 1471. In 1474 the Treaty of Utrecht between England and the League restored to the merchants of both parties their full trading privileges, and it was agreed on both sides to exact no customs or similar dues that had not been in force for at least 100 years. The Steelyard, where the steelyard balance was used on a site which now accommodates London's Cannon Street station, was leased to the League, and Hanseatic merchants returned to Lynn, Boston and Hull, ports from which they had withdrawn. But trouble came again less than twenty years later. In 1493 the London mob attacked the Steelyard, broke down the great door, beat the merchants, and would have burned the place down had they not been dispersed. The Hanse retorted by refusing to allow the English to trade in Prussia. These German merchants, however, were too useful for even the powerful Henry VII to complete the breach.

Wars disrupted trade, as always. During the 15th century England was often at war with France. Further disruption came when the dukes of Burgundy sought to unite the Low Countries – Flanders, Holland, Zeeland and Brabant. Markets in the Baltic were disturbed by wars. In the North Sea something approaching a state of war existed between English sailors and those of the Hanseatic ports, and some who had formerly traded to the Baltic now turned pirate. The cessation of the Bergen trade sent others to Iceland and Greenland[31] despite the King of Denmark's claim that Henry VI's prohibition regarding Scandinavia extended to his Icelandic dependency.

To increase their supplies of salt, used for the preservation of fish and meat, the Hanse had extended their own trade to the Bay of Bourgneuf in central France, and in consequence some of their ships sailed through waters which the English considered very much their own. In May 1449 Robert Winnington from Devon, on the lookout with his English privateers for a squadron of Breton ships, met with a fleet of a hundred vessels, Flemish, Dutch and Hanseatic, on its way to the Bourgneuf saltworks. 'I came aboard the Admiral', Winnington testified, 'and bade them strike (surrender) in the King's name of England, but they bade me shit in the King's name of England.' Incensed by this, and despite high odds against him, Winnington captured the whole fleet.[32] From the Isle of Wight he subsequently released the Dutch and Flemish vessels but made a prize of the Hanseatic booty. English merchants were made to bear the cost of the capture later on, but this did not save the Hanseatic salt fleet from further attack in 1458.

Piracy pure and simple was common. In 1422 the Earl of Warwick gained some £10,000 by piracy and by plundering a fleet of Genoese merchantmen bound for Lübeck.[33] In 1477 Bartholomew Couper, a London merchant, took 400 pilgrims bound for Santiago de Compostela aboard his ship *Mary* of London, 320 tons, when she was in Ireland. He was subsequently taken by Irish pirates alleged to number 800 and sailing in three vessels.[34]

Matters were further complicated by the taking of reprisals after the issue of letters of marque. A few years before Robert Winnington's capture of the salt fleet John Hamshire and Henry May, gentlemen, with 29 others, merchants and mariners, were attacked by 20 Breton ships when aboard the *Clement* of Hamyl. The Bretons took 2000 marks' worth of property, excluding the ship's rudder, sail, bonnets, cables, anchors, cords, ropes, wood, candles and victuals which they also seized, and, leaving some of the ship's company in their shirts and others 'mother naked', they abandoned them to their fate in a disabled ship in bad weather. Having sued without success for two years in the courts of the Duke of Brittany, John Hamshire and Henry May sought and gained, two years prior to the Winnington expedition, letters of marque against the Bretons for their damages and losses.[35]

Early in the 15th century Harry Pay of Poole and John Hawley of Dartmouth, men of the Drake mould, made their names dreaded by the king's enemies in France and by the merchants of Genoa and Castile. During the breakdown of central government under Henry VI matters took a turn for the worse and the gallants of Fowey and elsewhere became the terror of peaceful merchants, for these pirates had powerful support from the country gentry – Courteneys, Trevelyans and others in Cornwall, for example – who are to be found on the one hand as receivers of stolen property and on the other as commissioners to inquire into piracies.[36]

As yet the state was not very powerful. In 1406 the safeguard of the sea was entrusted to merchants and shipowners who were given tonnage and poundage (subsidies from the wine duties and customs dues on other goods) and a grant from the wool subsidy, but this did not prove very effective. Another plan in 1442 to protect trade in the Channel was short-lived. In 1474 the Society of the Staple unsuccessfully claimed an allowance of over £2600 which it was said had been expended on securing the safe passage of wool to Calais, the king having failed to provide the necessary protection.[37] Punitive expeditions were sometimes sent by the Crown to clear the seas, and one favourite device was to grant pardon to all but the ringleaders to encourage followers to betray them. Later in the century the most troublesome freebooters were offered pardons if they took employment in the royal service. Not until the reign of Henry VII did a real Royal Navy begin to take shape, and as late as 1490 we find an instance of private bargaining for protection when a number of London and other English merchants offered Francis Catayen £200 to protect their ships across the North Sea and back with a Genoese carrack and 150 men. This story is preserved because the merchants subsequently endeavoured to defraud Catayen.

Pirates and privateering notwithstanding, some trade survived. In the first half of the 15th century the wine trade from Bordeaux was fairly stable, but imports, at round about 12,000 tuns a year, were lower than they had been in the 14th century. They fell still further, to some 5000 tuns, when war broke out again in 1449, and although there was some revival in the 1460s, only at the very end of the century did imports again reach 10,000 tuns. The loss of Gascony to the French in 1453 proved a fatal blow to what remained of Gascon enterprise in England and during the troubled years of the mid-15th century other aliens, notably Bretons and, later, Spaniards, absorbed much of this carrying trade. The reduction in volume led to increased quantities of Greek and Iberian wines being imported into Britain in the second half of the century. The crews of merchant ships were nearly doubled in size in the war years and freight rates from Bordeaux to London remained high, round about 23s a tun, compared with 8s in 1320.[38]

Trade between England and Castile, on the other hand, increased rapidly in the 15th century. In exchange for cloth, of which England offered at least a dozen types in twenty or more shades, the Spaniards supplied wool, oil and dyes, as well as iron ore, wine, leather and various foodstuffs. The value of the goods brought to England by Spanish merchants in 1483–4 was about £14,000 and they took in return English goods to much the same value. Of every five ships in the trade by this time, two were English.[39]

In 1438–9 Venetian galleys brought to London almonds, currants, dates, figs, oranges, pomegranates, raisins, sugar, cinnamon, green ginger, other drugs and spices, sweet wine and over 1000 hundredweights of pepper; and two of these galleys could load 10 per cent of England's total cloth exports for the return journey. The malmsey wine they brought from Crete was so popular that people even in the north of England could assume that it was in a butt of malmsey that the king disposed of a troublesome brother. Genoese carracks carried raw materials, particularly alum, for the cloth industry, as well as other Mediterranean and eastern products. Florentine galleys were also involved in the trade, all these vessels calling at Seville or Cadiz on their way north. Whichever port they used in England for unloading their goods, London was the headquarters of the Italian merchants and there was a colony of 50 or 60 of them there in the mid-15th century. The Lucchese firm of Felice da Fagnano and Company, which traded to London in the 1440s, imported rich damasks, satins, velvets and cloth of gold.[40] Banking was essentially an Italian monopoly at this time, the use of credit was ubiquitous, and the Italians had developed the bill of exchange.

The author of *The Libel of English Policy* had hoped that more of the most lucrative trades would fall into English hands and in some degree this was happening. In 1465 some 30 per cent of the ships entering the port of London were English and this proportion had risen to 40 per cent by 1519.[41] A similar story can be told of Southampton, a port of call for the great Mediterranean ships, for here English ship entries gradually increased until they outnumbered foreign entries; at the same time the English vessels here and round to Bristol greatly extended the scope of their trade.

Friendly relations had long existed between England and Portugal. John of Gaunt (1340–99), a son of Edward III, uncle of Richard II and father of Henry IV, as well as patron of Geoffrey Chaucer, was also father-in-law to John I of Portugal and thus grandfather of Henry (1394–1460), the very English-looking prince who was dubbed 'the Navigator' by a 19th-century English scholar, and who was responsible for the discovery of the Azores and the opening of the route to the Gulf of Guinea. A first cargo of gold and slaves was brought from West Africa in 1441.[42] By way of another daughter John of Gaunt was also father-in-law to a king of Castile and relations between England and Spain were gradually strengthened.

These were only tentative steps towards an extension of English trade into the Mediterranean. In 1412 there is evidence that English vessels were at Ibiza and Genoa though the Genoese thwarted an attempt at this time to trade direct.[43] In 1446 Robert Sturmy of Bristol obtained a licence to send 40 sacks of wool and 100 ingots of tin in the *Cog Anne* through the Straits of Morocco to Pisa for sale in Florence. The ship, which had a crew of 37, also carried 160 pilgrims bound for Joppa (Jaffa) in the Holy Land. There the ship loaded pepper, ginger and other exotic goods for the return journey, but was subsequently lost in a storm off Greece.

Sturmy was not daunted. Eleven years later he obtained a licence for his ship *Katherine Sturmy*, employed the previous year in carrying pilgrims to Compostela, to ship 6000 cloths (worth about £40,000), 600 sarplars of wool (worth £7000 or more), plus tin, lead and wheat, to the Levant, and on this occasion he decided to sail in her. It is indicative both of the risks involved in shipping at this time and of the profits to be made from a successful voyage that on the eve of sailing, in June 1457, Sturmy made his will and enjoined that, if his ship came home, his legacies should be doubled. In the event, the Genoese ensured that neither Sturmy nor his ship came home, and the Genoese community in London was eventually fined £6000 to cover the losses.[44]

Three years after the fateful voyage of the *Cog Anne*, John Taverner of Hull built one of the largest merchant vessels of the period, received a licence to take on board wool, tin, hides and any other merchandise, whether the property of English or foreign merchants, for carriage to Italy, provided he paid the duty charged to aliens.[45] Twenty years later, Edward IV – who in 1478 and again in 1482 sent one of his own great ships south with a cargo of wool and cloth – was making various commercial treaties to liberalise trade and these encouraged English shipowners to embark upon more distant voyages. By the reign of Richard III English merchants had extended their operations to the point of applying for the appointment of an English consul at Pisa, and by 1490 Henry VII was proposing, in conjunction with the Florentines, to establish a staple for English wool there.[46]

Throughout the reigns of Edward IV and Henry VII there are scattered references to English ships venturing into the Mediterranean, some as far as Constantinople, Chios and Candia (Crete). Prospective profits outweighed the risks involved and for the first time the shipowner, as distinct from the merchant, evolves as a wealthy and influential citizen.

After London, Bristol ranked with York as the most notable of English cities. William Canynges, the shipowner who claimed to have provided Edward IV with 2670 tons of shipping on one occasion, employed 800 men at sea and another 100 ashore. He was a fellow burgess with Robert Sturmy and five times mayor of Bristol. His ten ships included vessels of 400, 500 and even 900 tons burden, though the latter was quite exceptional and far above the average for the period. In 1467, during his mayoralty, the Society of Merchant Adventurers of Bristol was founded with the object of establishing a kind of private navigation act by the terms of which none of the fellowship would send goods on a ship freighted by a non-member, and in foreign ports preference would be given to Bristol ships whenever possible.[47] Canynges was not unique. William of Worcester, himself a Bristol man, tells us some six years after Canynges' death that Thomas Strange owned about twelve ships and John Godeman several more, the two together accounting at that time for rather more than half Bristol's trade, leaving aside the trade with Ireland which was largely in Irish hands.[48]

This wealth – like that of many west country ports – had originated in the exchange of cloth for wine in Gascony, but trade with southern Ireland was also important. Limerick was already a prosperous city, possessing ships of its own of 200 tons, and Galway was the centre of the Irish pilgrim traffic to Compostela, more Irish than Bristol ships being engaged in this trade. Bristol had close links with Waterford and Kinsale, though they were not always harmonious. In 1449, for example, the *Mary* of Bristol, while on a fishing expedition, captured a 55-ton Spanish vessel carrying wine, iron and salt worth £160, but men from Kinsale subsequently took the *Mary*, killing three of her crew in the process.[49] Ireland imported perry and beer as well as wine, alum and leather goods, and exported hides, tallow, lard, wax, oak, linen, wool, horses, hawks, wheat in some years, occasionally butter, and, on one occasion at least, bacon.

Herring of Slegoth and salmon of Bame
Has made in Bristol many a rich man.

This couplet is quoted for the instruction of merchants in a 15th-century commercial handbook, and herring was a common breakfast dish, the white herring, fresh or salted, and the red herring or kipper both being priced in the Bristol customs accounts at £3 the last of 12,000 fish. More rarely seen were seals, valued at 2s. 6d. each and reputed fit only for the digestion of mariners. Whalemeat was 2s. the barrel and porpoise or 'sea pig' 5s., the tongue of the latter being such a delicacy that, in giving the Bishop of London the right to all porpoises brought ashore on his land, Henry I reserved the tongues for himself.

Some Bristol ships fished. Some sailed simply to Ireland and back. But others sailed on long and complex courses, visiting first Bordeaux or Lisbon and thence to Ireland; or sailing by way of Ireland and Brittany to Flanders, returning by way of London and Southampton; or even penetrating the Baltic as far as Danzig, and calling on the way back at Hull, Grimsby and Sandwich; or setting out for Bordeaux in the winter, and crossing the ocean to Iceland and back in the summer.

English and Irish mariners were no strangers in Icelandic and Greenland waters but links had been weakened in the latter half of the 14th century, as they were between Iceland and Norway. At the beginning of the 15th century, however, a direct trade between England's east coast ports and Iceland was re-opened, a reaction in part to the Hanse's attempted closure of the Baltic and Bergen to English ships. Corn, beer and cloth from England were welcomed in Iceland, and the prices paid by the English for stockfish were generally regarded as fair.[50]

The two-masted vessel carved on a stall-end in St Nicholas' Chapel in Lynn – now in the Victoria and Albert Museum – dates from this time and by 1424, the year in which Bristol mariners entered the trade, Lynn had a recognised body of Iceland merchants. Altogether, nineteen ships were licensed to trade to Iceland in 1443, while in 1451 even so small a port as Walberswick sent thirteen vessels to fish in northern, including Icelandic, waters. English fishing doggers were greatly superior to those of the Icelanders themselves, who were short of good timber, and one dogger, with a crew of about nine men, could carry 15 lasts – 15 or more tons – of cod, ling and halibut, valued at nearly £100.[51]

For more than sixty years the bulk of the Icelandic trade remained in English hands, and English fishermen probably caught more fish in Icelandic waters than did the Icelanders. After a visit there in 1477, Christopher Columbus is said to have written an account which describes how the English came with merchandise, particularly from Bristol. William Canynges traded there and lost a ship in one venture.

The cargo carried in Canynge's ship, worth about £500, comprised barrels of wheat and meal, butter, honey, wine, malt and beer; such hardware as pots, pans, knives, copper kettles, swords, nails, horseshoes and combs used in weaving, for there were few metallic ores to be found in Iceland; wood, pitch, tar, wax and salt; such wearing apparel as hats, caps, shoes, girdles, gloves and purses; needles, thread, pins, yarn for fishing nets, and paper; and, of course lengths of linen and woollen cloth, the latter being worth at least one-third of the value of the entire cargo.

The Icelandic trader might bring back hides, fish oil, or the cheap native cloth, but the chief merchandise was stockfish, three fish to the pair of women's shoes, fifteen fish for a firkin of honey, and so on. The total value of these return cargoes of fish might be anything up to £1000 when sold at home.

The trading ships left for Iceland between February and April, operated their market there during the summer months, returned home between July and September, and then went, perhaps, to Bordeaux for the vintage.[52]

England's commercial ascendancy over Iceland declined in the second half of the 15th century because of Hanseatic rivalry abroad and the granting of too many licences for the trade at home. By the 1480s competition was becoming intense and Bristol seamen were already casting round in the north Atlantic for new pastures. John Jay, a relative of William of Worcester, joined with others in 1480 to despatch two ships from Bristol to seek the 'Island of Brasylle'. It was not the only venture of its kind and, if all of them proved unsuccessful commercially, it is not equally certain that they proved unsuccessful geographically. It was a true instinct and not just chance that took John Cabot and his infant son Sebastian to Bristol in the 1490s.

Henry VII had missed his opportunity to back Columbus, but the young Sebastian Cabot, who was to exert a considerable influence on the development of British shipping, was able to observe the excitement – as it were 'a thing more divine than human'[53] – which was caused at Henry VII's court by the news of Columbus's discovery. Shortly before Columbus set foot on the mainland of South America, the Cabots discovered the mainland of North America.[54]

Apart from fish in the waters of the New Found Land, the discovery of North America in 1497 did not appear to offer much but unfamiliar birds and wild cats. The practical Henry VII and his practical English merchants could not work up much enthusiasm for wild cat schemes. In the 15th century the English had tried and largely failed to break into the Baltic. They had extended their trade to Spain and made slight incursions into the Mediterranean. And they had crossed the north Atlantic. But English maritime domination was to be found only across the North Sea and the English Channel, where there was a quick return on capital and a low degree of risk.

Notes

1. A. McGowan, *Tiller and Whipstaff: The Development of the Sailing Ship, 1400–1700* (1981), London, pp. 6–14. *See also*, R. W. Unger, *The Ship in the Medieval Economy, 600–1600* (1980), London, pp. 216–17 and p. 225.
2. D. Burwash, *English Merchant Shipping, 1460–1540* (1947), Toronto, pp. 102–7 and 115–16.
3. McGowan, *op. cit.*, pp. 40–41.
4. W. R. Childs, *Anglo-Castilian Trade in the Later Middle Ages* (1978), Manchester, pp. 158–9; McGowan, *op. cit.*, p. 35; Unger, *op. cit.*, p. 204 and p. 212.
5. Burwash, *op. cit.*, p. 122. E. Power & M. Postan (eds.), *Studies in English Trade in the Fifteenth Century* (1933), London, p. 239.
6. Burwash, *op. cit.*, pp. 136–41.
7. G. V. Scammell, *The World Encompassed: The first European marine empires* (1981), London, p. 376.
8. G. V. Scammell, 'Shipowning in England circa 1450–1550' (1962), *Transactions of the Royal Historical Society*, 5th series, Vol. 12.
9. W. R. Childs, *op. cit.*, pp. 159–61.
10. Burwash, *op. cit.*, p. 87.
11. W. S. Lindsay, *History of Merchant Shipping*, Vol. 1 (1876), London, p. 441 and p. 452.
12. J. J. Keevil, *Medicine and the Navy*, Vol. 1, 1200–1649 (1957), London, p. 29.
13. Burwash, *op. cit.*, p. 29.
14. A. L. Salzman, *English Trade in the Middle Ages* (1931), Oxford, p. 241.
15. G. J. Marcus, 'The First English Voyages to Iceland (1956)', MM, Vol. 42, p. 5.

16. Burwash, *op. cit.*, p. 24.
17. Marcus, *op. cit.*, p. 23.
18. S. G. E. Lythe, *Scottish Trade with the Baltic, 1550–1650* (1955), Dundee, p. 73.
19. Salzman, *op. cit.*, p. 108.
20. J. L. Bolton, *The Medieval English Economy, 1150–1500* (1980), London, p. 307.
21. *For more precise figures see* E. M. Carus-Wilson & O. Coleman, *England's Export Trade 1275–1547* (1963), Oxford, pp. 122–3 and 138–9. *See also* T. H. Lloyd, *The English Wool Trade in the Middle Ages* (1977), Cambridge, p. 310.
22. Salzman, *op. cit.*, p. 312.
23. Power & Postan, *op. cit.*, p. 42.
24. *Ib.*, p. 12.
25. Salzman, *op. cit.*, p. 315.
26. M. W. Thomas (ed.), *A Survey of English Economic History*, 3rd Ed. (1967), London, p. 87.
27. N. S. B. Gras, *The Early English Customs System* (1918), Cambridge, p. 117. *See also* Salzman, *op. cit.*, p. 359.
28. M. J. Stephenson, 'Wool Yields in the Medieval Economy' (1988), EHR, 2nd Series, Vol. XLI, No. 3, p. 368 ff.
29. Bolton, *op. cit.*, p. 308.
30. *See:* R. Davis, *The Trade and Shipping of Hull 1500–1700* (1964), EY Local History Series: No. 17, East Yorkshire Local History Society; and G. V. Scammell, 'English Merchant Shipping at the End of the Middle Ages: some East Coast Evidence' (1961), EHR, 2nd Series, Vol. XIII, No. 3.
31. Power & Postan, *op. cit.*, pp. 151–2. *See also* G. Jones, *The Norse Atlantic Saga* (1964), London, p. 3.
32. Salzman, *op. cit.*, pp. 274–5.
33. Lindsay, *op. cit.*, p. 454.
34. Salzman, *op. cit.*, p. 228.
35. *Ib.*, p. 261.
36. *Ib.*, pp. 255–6.
37. *Ib.*, p. 272.
38. M. K. James, *Studies in the Medieval Wine Trade* (1971), Oxford, pp. 151–3.
39. W. R. Childs, *Anglo-Castilian Trade in the Later Middle Ages* (1978), Manchester, pp. 6–7, p. 63, p. 83 and p. 157.
40. Bolton, *op. cit.*, p. 347.
41. Burwash, *op. cit.*, p. 148.
42. S. E. Morison, *Portuguese Voyages to America in the Fifteenth Century* (1940), Harvard University Press, p. 11.
43. Power & Postan, *op. cit.*, p. 99.
44. *Ib.*, p. 225. *Also* Salzman, *op. cit.*, pp. 438–9.
45. Lindsay, *op. cit.*, p. 455.
46. T. H. Lloyd, *op. cit.*, p. 287.
47. Salzman, *op. cit.*, p. 278. *See also* E. M. Carus-Wilson, *The Merchant Adventurers of Bristol in the Fifteenth Century* (1962), Bristol.
48. Power & Postan, *op. cit.*, p. 239.
49. *Ib.*, p. 193.
50. Marcus, *op. cit.*, pp. 316–17.
51. E. M. Carus-Wilson, *Medieval Merchant Venturers* (1954), London, pp. 125–27.

52. Power & Postan, *op. cit.*, pp. 174–5.
53. R. Hakluyt, *The Principal Navigations, Voyages, Traffiques and Discoveries of the English Nation*, Vol. V (1927), London, p. 86.
54. For further discussion see K. R. Andrews, N. P. Canny & P. E. H. Hair (eds.) *The Westward Enterprise: English activities in Ireland, the Atlantic and America 1480–1650* (1978) Liverpool: 'Bristol and America 1480–1631', by Patrick McGrath, pp. 81–102.

5

England Outward Bound

(1498–1552)

On July 25th 1498 Pedro de Ayala, who had been sent to England by Ferdinand and Isabella of Spain to secure the alliance of Henry VII against France, wrote to his masters as follows:

> I think your Highnesses have already heard that the King of England has equipped a fleet in order to discover certain islands and continents which he was informed some people from Bristol, who manned a few ships for the same purpose last year, had found. I have seen the map which the discoverer has made, who is another Genoese like Columbus, and who has been in Seville and Lisbon asking assistance for his discoveries. The people of Bristol have, for the last seven years, sent out every year two, three or four light ships in search of the island of Brasil and the seven cities, according to the fancy of this Genoese. The King determined to send out ships because, the year before, they brought certain news that they found land.... I have seen on a chart the direction they took and the distance they sailed; and I think that what they found, or what they are in search of, is what your Highnesses already possess.[1]

To the Spaniards this was the nub of the matter. In 1493 a papal bull had drawn an imaginary line from north to south 100 leagues west of the Azores and Cape Verde Islands and provided that the land and sea beyond that line should be a Spanish sphere of exploration. By the treaty of Tordesillas, signed between the Spanish and Portuguese in 1494 – and sanctioned by the Pope in 1506 – the boundary line was moved 270 leagues further west, confirming to the Portuguese not only the true route to India but most of the south Atlantic and, as appeared on its discovery in 1500, the land of Brazil.[2] The Pope was involved because he alone could authorise missions to the heathen. It is not certain, however, that Henry VII knew anything of these arrangements, and they were never taken very seriously by that part of the western world which was soon to break with Rome.

By 1490 Bristol merchants shared the Spanish and Portuguese knowledge of the Atlantic islands already discovered. They were trading with Madeira, probably trading with the Canaries and possibly trading with the Azores.[3] As Ayala indicates, they were also making voyages to discover land to the west of the British Isles; an English project for trading in Africa was under discussion; and by their association with Iceland the English knew already of the existence of Greenland, had probably visited it, and had heard of Markland and Vinland.

John Cabot was the Genoese to whom Ayala referred. Although probably born in Genoa, he had become a citizen of Venice and it was in that city that his son Sebastian was born, perhaps about 1481. In 1493 John Cabot may have been in Valencia when Columbus passed through fresh from the Indies,[4] and it is possible that he brought the news of the discovery of the New World to the Court of Henry VII. Since he had also been in the Near East and to Mecca and was familiar with the writings of Marco Polo, as well as being an expert in the spice trade, he may even have had his doubts about Columbus's claim to have arrived in China. In Lisbon and Seville, where Ayala tells us that he had sought aid for his prospective discoveries, Cabot would have talked to Bristol men – like Robert Thorne the Elder who was keenly interested in the advance of navigation and cosmography – and learned of their discovery of the New Found Land. It was then that he must have decided that the exploration from Bristol gave promise of a new trade route, and England became his obvious base.

Thus in 1496, three years after Columbus's discovery of the West Indies, Cabot and his sons, Ludovico, Sebastian and Sancio, received, in association with their English colleagues, letters patent from Henry VII to seek out 'regions or provinces of heathens and infidels' eastwards, westwards or northwards. One-fifth of any net profits were to go to the King.[5]

Henry VII was willing to concede to other nations any discoveries which they had made, and his subjects did not immediately seek any fight with fellow Europeans. They did, however, seek a slice of the cake, which, as they rightly thought, was big enough for everyone. If privateering was subsequently forced upon them it was partly because the Portuguese and Spaniards declared that the English could not trade in territories which these nations claimed, a declaration which was novel at the time.

The richest slices of cake were thought to lie in the east, and once the earth was generally recognised as round the east was the principal target even when ships sailed north, south and west. One eye was also kept on the possibilities of colonisation, partly because a colony might prove a staging post on the way to the east, and partly because colonies themselves offered prospects of profit to the mother country.

After an abortive attempt in 1496, John Cabot and 18 or 20 others set out in 1497 to become the first Europeans to be credited with the discovery of the American mainland. Vikings had preceded them – at least to Newfoundland – and Celts may have done so. So, no doubt, had Bristol seafarers in the years immediately prior to 1496. But Columbus had still not reached the mainland, and it was not until two years later that one of Vasco da Gama's squadron arrived in the Tagus with the news that the sea route to India had been discovered.

Cabot and his companions – including two Bristol merchants who may have been Robert Thorne the Elder and Hugh Elyot – sailed in the *Matthew*. After fifty-two days at sea they reached what may have been Cape Breton Island and took formal possession of it in the King's name. Then they sailed along Nova Scotia and beyond for some 900 miles before turning north to discover two small islands and Newfoundland. They saw no natives, though there were signs of them, but they thought they were in north-east Asia. They arrived back in Bristol on 6th August and for about ten days John Cabot was the lion of London. The King gave him £10 'to have a good time with', granted him an annual pension of £20, and promised him ten ships on his next voyage.

The following year the king provided one ship and the merchants of Bristol and London four more. This was the fleet to which Ayala referred. What happened is uncertain but John Cabot did not return, nor did any spices. There was no sixty-fold return on capital invested, as there proved to be on da Gama's voyage, and there is no further reference in England to the discovery of Cipango or Asia across the Atlantic.

The Spanish authorities believed that in this year – the year in which Columbus himself touched for the first time, probably in Venezuela, the main continent of South America – some English seafarers coasted south through the Spanish islands into the Caribbean and, since Cabot's ships were provisioned for a year, it is possible that part of his fleet did this and continued their voyage into 1499. The fact that there were no quick returns, however, was discouraging.[6]

João Fernandes and João Gonsalves, exporters of goods from Bristol to Lisbon, were aware of all that was going on at this time. Fernandes was an Azorean *llabrador* or small landowner, a merchant who had hopes of raising finance in Portugal for an expedition which would explore the northern seas. He was disappointed in this aim because a man of greater influence got in first. This was Gaspar Corte Real, a nobleman of the Portuguese court who also owned property in the Azores. In May 1500 King Manoel of Portugal issued a comprehensive grant for discovery to Real, who sailed first to the east coast of Greenland, where he was stopped by ice, and then round Cape Farewell to the west coast, after which he returned to Lisbon. João Fernandes may have sailed on this expedition but he was otherwise engaged when, in 1501, Real sailed again to the west coast of Greenland and, being stopped by ice there too, crossed the Davis Strait to America. In 1502 his brother, Miguel, went to look for him and in 1503 a further Portuguese expedition went to look for both. After that the Portuguese gave up their search for another passage though they began to exploit the Newfoundland fishery, as the English were doing already and as the Bretons and French were to do later.

The Portuguese had better outlets for their capital in the sea route to India and were limited in any westward exploration by their agreement with the Spaniards. These factors, together with English familiarity with the northern seas, explain why, before the end of 1500, Fernandes was seeking partners in Bristol to explore further for a northern passage to the spice islands. In 1501 Henry VII granted a patent for discovery to João Fernandes, Francisco Fernandes and João Gonsalves, described as squires of the Azores, and Richard Warde, Thomas Asshehurst and John Thomas, merchants of Bristol. This patent did not supersede the Cabot patent of 1496, which had been inherited by John's sons and their partners, for each syndicate was authorised to draw benefit from its own discoveries.

The new syndicate made voyages from Bristol in both 1501 and 1502, probably to Greenland, then known as the land of the *llabrador* or Azorean landowner, and perhaps to modern Labrador, to which the name seems to have been transferred from Greenland about 1566, possibly by Sir Humphrey Gilbert. It appears that three Eskimos were brought back to London on one of these voyages, and the King was pleased by the discovery of open water in the Davis Strait which gave promise of a north-west passage to Asia round the New Found Land.

It is possible that in this same year Robert Thorne the Elder, who became Mayor of Bristol later on, and Hugh Elyot made an American voyage on the Cabot patent. However this may be, the two syndicates seem to have united forces at the end of the sailing season for in December 1502 the King issued a new patent to João Gonsalves, Francisco Fernandes, Thomas Asshehurst and Hugh Elyot, and to their heirs and deputies. This prohibited them from entering lands first discovered by the King of Portugal or other friendly princes and in the possession of such princes, thus giving early expression to the doctrine which the English upheld, namely the doctrine of effective occupation.

The new Company of Adventurers to the New Found Land made voyages across the Atlantic in each of the three years that followed, probably exploring southwards as well as northwards since they brought back 'popinjays' or parrots. In these same years English merchants and the English court were being fed, by English seafarers serving at sea with the

Spaniards, with further information on the new Spanish discoveries. After Isabella's death in 1504 Englishmen seem to have had little difficulty in making their way to Mexico and the West Indies so long as they sailed under the Spanish flag and appeared sound on matters of religion.[7]

Unless financial success followed quickly upon such voyages further capital was not forthcoming. Not until 1509 did Sebastian Cabot, with two ships, make another voyage of exploration to the north-west, a voyage which convinced him that he had discovered a north-west passage through the Hudson Strait.[8] When he returned to England, however, he found that in his absence Henry VII had died and that Henry VIII, his successor, had other preoccupations.

It was not that Henry VIII was uninterested in discovery and the sea, for he appreciated the value of a merchant navy both as a source of supply and as a means of defence, but his sights were set on targets nearer home. By 1512 his vessels, no longer commandeered indiscriminately but hired for specific purposes, were engaged in what proved, so far as England was concerned, the last of the medieval sea-fights. This action took place off Brest in the course of Henry's first French war, and the *Regent* and the *Cordelière* grappled and fought it out side by side, hundreds of men being killed and both ships lost through fire. Shortly afterwards Henry VIII began to place heavy guns in his ships and thus changed the course of naval warfare. Skilful sailing was essential to the effective use of gunnery, and the English, though not noted for their book-learning, were already unsurpassed as practical seamen. Skilful sailing and effective gunnery together were to establish English supremacy at sea.

In the meantime, Sebastian Cabot, unsupported by the new king, transferred in 1512 to the service of Spain and lived in that country for most of the next thirty-six years. However, he did not relinquish his English contacts. Indeed, he proceeded to play a potentially dangerous game, and it may be that the Spaniards were willing to employ him because in their employment he was less of a threat to Spanish interests,

With Cabot abroad, the English made at least one more attempt to find a north-west passage. In 1517 an expedition set out under the command of John Rastell, brother-in-law to Sir Thomas More and a London printer who was interested in cosmology. Unhappily, it never sailed beyond Cork.[9]

Throughout this time Robert Thorne the Elder and his partners, succeeded by Robert Thorne the Younger and his brother Nicholas, were carrying on their trading business with the ports of Andalusia and building up their business connections through Spain with the Canary Islands and the West Indies. They often stayed in Seville and shipped goods in Spanish vessels in which they may have held shares. They remained in touch with Cabot, and the Thornes' factor Thomas Tison was said to be the first Englishman to live in the West Indies.

After Magellan's expedition set sail in 1519, with a Bristol man as gunner aboard Magellan's ship, Sebastian Cabot, although at this time Pilot-Major of Spain, returned to London to try to negotiate with Wolsey and Henry VIII the command of another English expedition across the Atlantic. This may have been done with the knowledge of Charles V, of Spain and the Holy Roman Empire, who was then in alliance with the English king,[10] but Cabot's subsequent behaviour suggests that not all his dealings were known to Charles. The London merchants thought his proposition too risky and so Cabot tried to bring the Venetians in as partners with the promise of showing Venice 'a passage whereby she would obtain great profit, which is the truth, for I have discovered it'. While these negotiations were proceeding the surviving ship of the Magellan expedition arrived home, in September 1522, with the news of a south-west passage through the Straits of Magellan, and Cabot must have thought it wise to break off negotiations which had proved fruitless, partly for fear that his Spanish employer might regard his actions as treasonable but also because the results of the Magellan expedition offered new opportunities.

In 1524 Cabot was appointed chief of a company under Spanish protection to prosecute trade with the Moluccas through the Straits of Magellan. In the following year there was further talk in England of another exploratory expedition but this came to nothing. Instead, Robert Thorne the Younger, who was resident in Spain at the time, took a venture in Cabot's expedition, largely so that two English friends of his might sail with the fleet and bring him reports.[11] In the event the reports were only of exploration of the Rio de la Plata area of South America because, in consequence of internal dissension, the expedition went no further.

Thorne remained convinced that a shorter route to the spice islands would be found in the north-west and in 1527 he tried to promote a further voyage of discovery. In consequence the King sent out two vessels, *Samson* and *Mary Gilford*, under the command of John Rut. In the region of 63°N this expedition met with dangerous quantities of ice, *Samson* was probably lost, and *Mary Gilford* may have returned home by way of the West Indies.[12] Thereafter, although the English did not lose sight of the possibility of finding a north-west passage, nearly fifty years were to pass before determined efforts in that direction were made again. In 1534, two years after the death of Robert Thorne the Younger, who died worth

£17,000 (perhaps £3.6 million at 1988 prices), Jacques Cartier explored the river St Lawrence for the French, and in 1536 an English gentleman of fortune, Robert More, led an expedition of 120 men, including 30 gentlemen, to the north-west. More's venture ended in disaster off Newfoundland, and a further expedition proposed for 1541 came to nothing.

Fishing off both Newfoundland and Iceland, however, continued, Bristol men fishing in the former seas and east coast men fishing in the latter. For the year 1528 we have an accurate estimate of the scale of the Icelandic fishery, which remained in English hands. Some 149 ships sailed for Iceland from English east coast ports: 32 from Dunwich, Walberswick, Southwold, Easton and Covehithe; 30 from Yarmouth; 30 from Cley, Blakeney and Cromer; 14 from Harwich, Ipswich, Manningtree, Dedham, Sudbury and Colchester; 10 from Lynn; 6 from Aldeburgh, Sizewell and Thorpe; 4 from Boston; 3 from Woodbridge; and 8 from London. These vessels ranged from 30 to 100 tons in size, with crews of nine or more, and it was customary for them to rendezvous at some point on the east coast before the end of April and to proceed together along the Scottish coast and thence through the Pentland Firth or between the Orkney and Shetland islands. In time of war with Scotland they were given some protection.[13]

On arrival off Iceland fishing for cod and ling was carried on throughout the summer or until the holds were full. The salting of the fish proceeded with the fishing and each vessel would bring home upwards of fifteen lasts of stockfish. The return voyage was made before the end of September with the same precautions as on the outward passage, and the stinking fish found a ready sale in England in October and November. It was a rough trade carried on by rough men. James V of Scotland complained a few years later that the fishermen were in the habit of capturing Scotsmen on their way north to serve as slaves during the season.

In the Middle Ages Bristol had had the foremost share in this Icelandic trade but now, in consequence of their enhanced knowledge, Bristol fishermen preferred the Newfoundland banks which, although further away, produced more fish. There is no mention of Bristol ships going to Iceland during the reign of Henry VIII or his two successors.

Throughout this time Henry VIII had tried to keep the peace with Spain and up to about 1536, when his divorced wife Catherine of Aragon died, he had succeeded. Trade with Spain developed and in 1530 Henry allowed his subjects trading to Spain to form a Company or Gild of St George. Trade with Portugal was also developing. There was nothing odd, therefore, about William Hawkins' voyages to Brazil between 1530 and 1532. Hawkins, who had been born in the last decade of the previous century, was a merchant who exported cloth and tin from the west country. Back to England his ships brought fish, wine and salt, with occasional consignments of oil, wood, sugar, soap and pepper. A new cargo, being transhipped in Portugal, was Brazil wood, the material which yielded a useful red dye. So abundant was it in Portugal's new south American possession that it had provided the colony with a name.

According to Richard Hakluyt, 'old' William – whose son John was to become more widely known – went three times to Brazil in his ship *Paul* of Plymouth, of 250 tons. On the first voyage he touched at the river Sestos in modern Liberia and from there sailed to Brazil where he traded for unspecified local commodities which presumably included Brazil wood. On the second voyage he left Martin Cockeram, a Plymouth man, as hostage to the natives in exchange for their chief who wished to witness the delights of civilisation. Although the chief died on the way back, Cockeram was released when the ship arrived in Brazil for the third time.

There may have been further expeditions in the years that followed for in 1540 the *Paul* was away for eight months and returned with a hundredweight of elephants' tusks and 92 tons of Brazil wood. In 1540, too, John Phillips sailed from Portsmouth to the New World in the *Barbara* of London, being arrested on his return for piracy. On the outward leg of his voyage he had captured two small Spanish ships and he took another in Santo Domingo which was laden with hides and sugar. He sailed this latter ship home instead of the leaky *Barbara*. From Southampton the merchants Robert Renegar and Thomas Borey engaged in the Brazil wood trade, and in 1542 Robert Thorne's brother Nicholas sent one of his ships from Southampton into the Mediterranean with a part-cargo of Brazil wood.[14]

By this time both the Portuguese and the Spaniards had discovered the lucrative possibilities inherent in the slave trade and were endeavouring with greater determination to restrict trade with their overseas possessions to their own vessels. Slavery was nothing new in Spain, for expeditions had been made to the Canary Islands in the 14th century to round up natives to work on sugar plantations. The importation of negro slaves into the West Indies was formally licensed by Charles V in 1517. He granted the right to one of his favourite courtiers and thus began the *Asiento*, a licence which for two centuries was to be a prize in European wars. By 1540 10,000 negroes a year were being imported into the West Indies alone. By the end of the 16th century some 900,000 had probably been shipped to the West Indies and more again to Mexico and South America.[15] Forty per cent of those transported were said to die on the transatlantic passage.[16]

In 1540 the English had no part in the slave trade and in the following year the Portuguese sent fighting ships to the Brazil coast to protect their interests. For the moment English mercantile development seemed thwarted in all directions.

The significance of shipping and trade, however, was by no means underestimated. An Act of Parliament for 'the maintenance of the Navy of England' was passed in 1540 and the preamble set out the reasons for maintaining shipping in some detail. First, ships were 'profitable, requisite, necessary and commodious' for trade and communication. Second, they were a means of defence and offence in time of war, and helped to keep the country secure. Third, they provided a livelihood, not merely for seafarers and their families, but for all those who catered to ships and seafarers. Shipping at the time, the preamble indicated, was suffering from a slump and in consequence, 'the towns, villages and inhabitations near adjoining unto the sea coasts are utterly fallen in ruin and decay'. To help in the revival of shipping the Act offered certain advantages in the form of lower freights to foreigners shipping in English vessels.

This act had little effect and piracy proved more profitable than pious aspirations. The first comprehensive act against piracy had been passed in 1535[17] and it permitted the Admiralty Court to pass sentence of death on pirates and to deprive them of the benefit of clergy. But within ten years of the act – in Henry VIII's last French war of 1544–6 – piracy of certain kinds again became respectable in the form of privateering, being legalised by the issue of letters of marque. By this time the letter of marque had become somewhat more sophisticated than it had been a century earlier, now becoming a commission issued to a private shipowner by a belligerent state authorising him to employ his vessel as a warship. Privateering thus became big business with considerable commercial possibilities. Whenever other business flagged the Hawkins family, for example, found employment in equipping or patronising privateers and, since the family had close links with the Huguenot privateers of La Rochelle, the ethics of any particular operation were not always obvious to the outsider.

In Southampton Robert Reneger played the kind of role played in Plymouth by William Hawkins. Like Hawkins, he wanted to extend beyond the medieval trade boundaries and send his ships overseas. Like Hawkins, he abandoned the Brazil trade for privateering when war came along, obtaining letters of marque against the French after entering into a recognisance not to attack the subjects of the King of Spain. Reneger and his son John, however, did not abide by these rules. In 1545, with four ships and a pinnace, they captured off St Vincent a Spanish treasure-ship homeward bound from Hispaniola, the second largest of the West

Indian islands. Such a prize – foreshadowing the later exploits of Francis Drake – furnished an object lesson in the wealth of the Spanish Indies which the seafarers of southern England never forgot, for the gold, pearls and other cargo of this treasure-ship were worth the dazzling sum of 29,315 ducats.

England almost went to war with Spain over this incident. Reneger asserted that he had only secured just reprisal for the confiscation of a prize of his in Spain, but the Spaniards declared that he was a known pirate and proceeded to arrest all English merchants and ships in their waters. It was some months before these ships and merchants were released, and in the meantime the Spaniards complained that Reneger was swaggering at the English court as though he had done a meritorious deed.[18] The fact was that privateers were encouraged or restrained according to prevailing political conditions.

By this time French privateers were already active in the Caribbean and French vessels had penetrated the Indian Ocean in the wake of the Portuguese.

Portuguese trade to the East was conducted through the India House in Lisbon, a public monopoly operated by the Crown. The Portuguese had taken Goa in 1510, reached the Moluccas by 1513 and discovered Japan, by accident when a party of would-be China traders were blown there by a typhoon, in 1543. The essence of this new trade was pepper, largely purchased in Malabar, and it was a trade which employed relatively few ships.

The other major system of trade to Europe which was rapidly being established was one which employed many more ships and seamen. By the 1540s Spanish loot from Peru had arrived in Europe, silver-mining had started in Mexico, and a Spanish colonial society was being established in the Caribbean based on sugar plantations cultivated by imported negro slaves. In 1543 the merchant houses of Seville trading to America were legally incorporated in a powerful merchant gild, the Consulado, though the gild was operated under close government control.[19]

In 1545 Henry VIII mustered a fleet against the French. It is said to have consisted of 56 royal ships (one of them the *Mary Rose*), 25 hired galleys, 60 privateers and 40 merchantmen – 181 ships in all. The Crown fleet amounted to 12,455 tons inclusive of *Henry Grâce à Dieu* or *Great Harry*, a ship of 1000 tons and the biggest to that date to have been built in England, though James IV of Scotland had rigged an even greater ship, *Great Michael*, in 1512. The *Great Harry* had three decks and four masts, exclusive of a bowsprit and spritsail yard, and the mainmast was 75 feet high, but the other vessels were endowed with more modest equipment, varying from 450 to 40 tons in size and with crews of 300 to 32 men.[20] The seamen, many of whom were merchant seamen pressed to serve, were paid 6s 8d (an angel) per month, and in this war they suffered from the plague.[21] Nothing like the Italian quarantine rules of the time were deemed necessary and the final muster indicated that only two-thirds of the 12,000 men mustered ten days earlier were still healthy. The king proceeded to demobilise the fleet and shortly before his death in 1547 the war ended.

However, Henry VIII had achieved something. A navy had been created and by the institution in 1546 of the Navy Board the king had established a means of organising it. Like his father, he paid a bounty – of 4s. or 5s. a ton – if large merchant ships were built, and he established regular surveys of ships and a ship census.[22]

There was also a movement towards the better buoying and lighting of the coasts and estuaries. The Corporation of Trinity House, which probably had earlier origins, had been granted a charter in 1514, and two other Trinity Houses had been formed in Hull and Newcastle upon Tyne, but in 1547 the Corporation was reorganised and became more effective. As well as the supervision of lighthouses, buoys and beacons, its duties now included the examination, licensing and regulation of pilots and the settlement of disputes between officers and sailors in the merchant service. It sought to raise the standard of seamanship and to reduce the number of wrecks due to the ignorance of mariners.[23]

Twenty years earlier an English translation of Pierre Garcie's *Grand Routier* had appeared. This was an advance on the 15th-century pilot book, and its contents included detailed descriptions, profiles of headlands similar to those given today, information on calculating tides and phases of the moon, a diagram for telling the time by the pole star, and a copy of the laws of Oléron. It went through at least six English printings and was added to as it was republished.

Artefacts found on the ill-fated *Mary Rose*, which had been refitted in 1536, included a slate protractor, a pair of dividers and a pocket sundial which served as a wristwatch.[24] But as an indication of what the master might by this time carry with him we have an inventory supplied by John Aborough, master of the *Michael* of Barnstaple, in 1533. This included two compasses worth 10s; a balestow or cross-staff, a quadrant, a lodestone and a running-glass (sand-glass) worth 26s 8d; a rutter (pilot book) in English which it had taken him eighteen months to compile, together with a Castilian rutter and a 'reportery' (perhaps a seaman's manual) in Portuguese for which he wanted 40s; and a map in glass which cost 6s 8d. He also carried a card or chart for the Levant, a lute and a gospel. It is possible that on some voyages pilots were employed and expected to provide their own navigational equipment, for in 1539 there is a record of Richard Hall of Ratcliff in London being shipped as master for a voyage to Malaga and the owner promised him 5s over and above his wages 'for the pricking of a card in the said voyage', that is, for working out the ship's course and marking it on a chart.[25]

By this time gunnery at sea had become of prime importance. The *Mary Rose*, which had been built in 1509 and capsized in 1545, may have been the first English ship to have gun ports below the upper deck. While the Dutch went on developing merchant ships like the buss, the English were developing the warship, which was becoming increasingly distinct from the trading vessel. By the 1540s the planking of ships in clinker fashion was no longer considered for warships of any consequence because it was inadequate for the carriage of heavy guns. Except for some smaller types, clinker-building methods also died out in merchant shipbuilding.

The carrack was improved into the galleon at this time, probably in Spain in the second quarter of the 16th century, though within a few years it was to be found in the service of Portugal, Genoa, Venice and England as well. Warships normally carried four masts, a bonaventure mast with a lateen sail, in addition to the foremast, mainmast and mizen. The foremast in such a ship would carry a topsail as well as the course or bottom sail. The mainmast would carry a topgallant sail as well as a topsail and course. There would also be a lateen topsail on the mizen in a four-masted ship. The rig included a spritsail. The keel was from two to three times the breadth of the ship. As a warship this type of vessel was supreme until 1588 when it was outmoded by another form of galleon developed in England. The galleon dominated long-distance trade routes to the end of the 16th century and became a manoeuvrable and seaworthy vessel which required only an adequate method of steering it to reach the limits of its development. Oak was favoured for the building of such ships, and an innovation of the period was the use of pillars to add support to the deck beams.[26]

From discoveries made aboard the *Mary Rose* much has been learned of the 16th-century seaman and his life.[27] He wore shoes of leather or canvas, woollen hose, baggy knee breeches, probably a sleeveless leather jerkin and a knitted woollen hat. He might carry a wooden comb and an embroidered leather purse, and he took with him a palliasse and a seaman's chest. He played gambling games involving dice, dominoes and backgammon. He might also play the fiddle, the tabor pipe or the shawm, and some of the sailors on board carried a bosun's call as the duty bosun's mate still did in World War II. He poured his drink from leather bottles and while near harbour might eat fresh pork, beef, mutton or venison. The official ration was a pound of biscuit and a pound of meat on each of four days a week, with dried fish and cheese instead of meat on the other three days. He supplemented the salt provisions by fishing when occasion offered, and drank a lot of beer. Peas, prunes, herbs and spices also entered into his diet.

The barber-surgeon's equipment included wooden ointment jars, ceramic medicine flagons, flasks for drugs, razors, a pewter bleeding bowl, a urethral syringe, a chafing dish, a small charcoal brazier and a wooden mallet. Men wounded in battle, as we learn from John Hawkins, were placed in the hold so that their cries would not demoralise those still fighting.

Privateering had increased the efficiency of individual fighting units and the battle quality of English ships and seamen grew rapidly superior to those of Spain. English ships, though smaller than those of Iberia, were better designed and easier to handle and could sail closer to the wind. The next fifty years were to witness a great enhancement of English power and the growth of considerable ambitions for trade. Achievement up to 1550, however was modest, and the English merchant marine was still of small significance.

Although, by contemporary standards, much wealth was invested in shipping in England, there was little surplus capital as yet to invest in risky long-distance voyages. The story of the great voyages of discovery is often told but it always needs to be remembered that by far the great majority of merchantmen sailed on short, unspectacular voyages, carrying unspectacular commodities. After 1500 the new Atlantic seaboard market grew slowly, shifting northwards from Iberia to Flanders, first to Bruges, and then by 1550 to Antwerp, which became the centre of all European trade and finance.[28] The first consignment of eastern spices had reached the Portuguese factory in Antwerp in 1501 and Antwerp quickly became a major centre for their distribution to north-west Europe. These spices and the silver of America flowed through Portugal and Spain into the hands of government creditors, largely Italian and German bankers, and thus created an expansion of trade throughout Europe. One of the side effects was some weakening of the Italian city states and the annual galley fleets to England and the Low Countries ceased to be profitable. Organised sailings came to an end in 1532.[29] Another effect was to give a new importance to England's position and, in particular, to that of London.

London was England's one substantial commercial city. Although it bore no comparison with Venice, it ranked in significance with Verona or Zurich, and the first half of the 16th century witnessed a meteoric rise in its cloth exports, a consequent accretion to the power of the London merchants, and a vast strengthening of the London–Antwerp commercial axis.[30] Although England's wool exports had declined to 5000 sacks by this time, London's cloth exports had nearly trebled, rising from some 49,000 short cloths in 1500 to nearly 133,000 in 1550.[31] By this latter date London was handling about 90 per cent of this trade or twice its proportion a century earlier. Marine insurance and the use of agents was becoming increasingly common. In 1548, for example, Thomas Cavalchanti, John Gyralde and their company in London insured a ship going with cloth from Southampton to Messina, the assurers being content, according to the document, 'that this writing be of as much force and strength as the best that ever was made or might be made in this Lombard Street of London'. Appended to this document were the names of nine underwriters who set their names against various amounts of money.[32]

The great ships of the Baltic cities now became rare visitors to Hull and the ports of East Anglia as the merchants of the Hanse, like other aliens, concentrated increasingly on London. Big ships disappeared from the east coast. The average coal shipment from Newcastle upon Tyne seems to have halved in size between 1465 and 1552, and the biggest ship in Newcastle in 1544 was only 160 tons, compared with at least two of 250–300 tons in 1465. The average size of the 240 or more ships owned between Berwick and the Thames was only 40 tons,[33] and not many of them traded overseas. Between 1537 and 1542, when an average of 100 English ships a year paid toll in the Zeeland anchorages that served Antwerp and Bergen-op-Zoom, only two came from Hull though the number increased subsequently.[34]

By this time a small but rapidly growing number of Scottish craft from Kirkcaldy, Dysart, Pittenweem and Anstruther were delivering coal down the east coast, and 70 or so east coast vessels were trading to Scotland, though only a handful of these sailed from London.[35] The Scots also fished and exported hides to the Baltic. The Clyde had trading contacts with the Baltic and the Low Countries, as well as with Ireland and England, but the main Scottish ports, apart from those on the east Fifeshire coast, were Leith and Dundee.[36]

The relative importance at this time and for long afterwards of both coastal trading and of the fishing industry should not be overlooked, though the vessels employed were mostly small. In the North Sea herring fishery alone well over 200 vessels were normally engaged, half of them from the Cinque ports and half from the east coast.

In Bristol, where the high hopes raised by the North American discoveries had not been fulfilled, ground had been lost to London by the middle of the 16th century. The Newfoundland fishery was not developed at this time to the extent that might have been anticipated, and for sixty years the city played only a minor part in the voyages of exploration.[37]

In the Levant conditions for English traders deteriorated after 1538 because of Turkish depredations and the weakening of the Italian republics.[38] One of the last English voyages to this area before 1575 was probably made at this time by Roger Bodenham who sailed from Tilbury in the bark *Aucher*, owned by Sir Anthony Aucher. In Crete Bodenham was refused a Turkish safe-conduct and only narrowly escaped capture by Turkish galleys when he ventured as far as Chios.

English trade to the North African coast, on the other hand, made some progress in this period. James Alday, who had once been servant to Sebastian Cabot, lay claim to having 'invented' the Moroccan trade, and there were Spanish merchants among the promoters of the early English voyages. Henry Ostrich, who had married one of Cabot's daughters, was involved, as were Thomas Wyndham and Sir John Luttrell, both of them distinguished naval commanders.

In 1551 two ships, one of them *Lion* of London, were sent to Morocco. The following year three ships were sent, *Lion*, *Buttolfe* and a Portuguese caravel bought in Wales. In 14 days the little fleet sailed from Bristol to Safi, a port from which the Portuguese had been driven out in 1541. From Safi they went to Agadir, another port from which the Portuguese had been driven out, and there they stayed for three months. Linen, woollen cloth, coral, amber, jet, probably munitions and other goods were exchanged for sugar, molasses, dates and almonds. None of the crew died of sickness but on the return voyage *Lion* sprang a serious leak and had to put in at Lanzarote in the Canaries where seventy chests of sugar were unloaded and some of the crew went ashore. These seafarers were attacked, several being killed, and the ship only just escaped destruction at the hands of the Portuguese fleet.

From then on the Barbary trade became a recognised line of business, with Jewish intermediaries arranging the exchange of cloth, ironmongery and other goods for the sugar which was much prized in England. The Portuguese opposed the development of this trade but within twenty years it had become more valuable than the trade with Portugal itself.[39]

Notes

1. J. Williamson (ed), *The Cabot Voyages and Bristol Discovery under Henry VII* (1962), Cambridge, p. 238.
2. J. H. Parry, *The Spanish Seaborne Empire* (1966), London, pp. 46–7.
3. G. V. Scammell, 'The English in the Atlantic Islands, c. 1450–1650', (1986), MM, Vol. 72, No. 3, p. 299.
4. Williamson, *op. cit.*, p. 40.
5. Williamson, *op. cit.*, pp. 51–2.
6. Williamson, *op. cit.*, pp. 109–10.
7. J. Williamson, *Maritime Enterprise 1485–1558* (1913), Oxford, p. 228.
8. Williamson (ed) (1962), *op. cit.*, p. 165.
9. E. Dodge, *Northwest by Sea* (1961), New York, pp. 28–9.
10. Williamson (ed) (1962), *op. cit.*, p. 150.
11. R. Hakluyt, *The Principal Navigations, Voyages, Traffiques and Discoveries of the English Nation*, Vol. 1 (1927), London, p. 218.
12. Dodge, *op. cit.*, p. 30.
13. M. Oppenheim, *A History of the Administration of the Royal Navy and of Merchant Shipping in Relation to the Navy from 1509 to 1660 with an Introduction treating of the Preceding Period* (1896, reprinted 1988), London, p. 89.
14. J. Williamson, *Sir John Hawkins, The Time and the Man* (1927), Oxford, p. 14.
15. D. Mannix, *Black Cargoes* (1963), London, pp. 4–5.
16. G. V. Scammell, *The World Encompassed: the first European marine empires* (1981), London, p. 256.
17. H. C. Hunter, *How England got its Merchant Marine, 1066–1766* (1935), New York, p. 46.
18. Williamson (1913), *op. cit.*, p. 272.
19. Parry, *op. cit.*, pp. 117–25.
20. W. S. Lindsay, *History of Merchant Shipping*, Vol. II (1876), London, pp. 96, 98 and 557–8.
21. J. Keevil, *Medicine and the Navy, Vol. I, 1200–1649* (1957), London, pp. 63 and 99–100.
22. Burwash, *op. cit.*, p. 17; Oppenheim, *op cit*, pp. 42–88.
23. Hunter, *op. cit.*, p. 41.
24. E. Bradford, *The Story of the Mary Rose* (1982), London, p. 146.
25. Burwash, *op. cit.*, pp. 32–3; pp. 19–20.
26. A. McGowan, *Tiller and Whipstaff: the Development of the Sailing Ship, 1400–1700* (1981), London, pp. 20–30.
27. M. Rule, *The Mary Rose: The Excavation and Raising of Henry VIII's Flagship* (1982), London.
28. M. W. Thomas (ed), *A Survey of English Economic History*, 3rd ed. (1967), p. 113.
29. J. H. Parry, *The Age of Reconnaissance* (1963), London, pp. 47–52.
30. D. C. Coleman, *The Economy of England 1450–1750* (1977), Oxford, pp. 48–51.
31. E. M. Carus-Wilson (ed), *Essays in Economic History* (1954), London, p. 153.
32. L. F. Salzman, *English Trade in the Middle Ages* (1931), Oxford, p. 270.
33. G. V. Scammell, 'English Merchant Shipping at the End of the Middle Ages: some East Coast Evidence' (1961), EHR, 2nd series, Vol. XIII, No. 3.

34. R. Davis, *The Trade and Shipping of Hull 1500–1700* (1961). EY Local History Series: No. 17. East Yorkshire Local History Society, p. 5.
35. *Ib*; p. 4; Oppenheim, *op. cit.*, p. 89.
36. S. G. E. Lythe, *Scottish Trade with the Baltic, 1550–1650* (1955), Dundee, p. 75.
37. K. R. Andrews, N. P. Canny & P. E. H. Hair (eds), *The Westward Enterprise: English activities in Ireland, the Atlantic and America 1480–1650* (1978), Liverpool: 'Bristol and America 1480–1631' by Patrick McGrath, pp. 92–3.
38. G. Ramsay, *English Overseas Trade during the Centuries of Emergence* (1957), London, p. 38.
39. T. Willan, *Studies in Elizabethan Foreign Trade* (1959), Manchester, pp. 95–100.

6

Voyages North and South
(1552–1569)

In consequence of the voyages of discovery the first half of the 16th century had proved a period of remarkable prosperity and economic expansion for Europe, witnessing an upsurge in population and the rapid growth of towns. During this period the English cloth trade to Antwerp prospered. The fleet of the Merchant Adventurers arrived twice a year in the Zeeland anchorages, and the English merchant colony in Antwerp numbered more than 300.[1] If contemporary evidence can be relied upon, English exports to Antwerp were worth more than £1 million, most of this sum being made up by the value of finished and unfinished cloths. The 40,000 finished cloths fetched some £300,000. The 80,000 unfinished cloths, which were dyed and finished in the Antwerp region, fetched twice that sum. From Antwerp and Bruges the cloth found its way into central Europe. The Italians depended on it in their trade with Turkey and Alexandria, and for the Easterlings, the German merchants in the Baltic, it was essential to their trade with Russia, Poland and other Baltic states. The English sellers made gross profits of 25 per cent, which yielded a sum that was not far short of Queen Elizabeth's total revenue.[2]

However, after the middle of the century Europe suffered increasingly from governmental mismanagement of its finances and from the effects of war. Antwerp suffered a catastrophic collapse in its cloth market and ceased to be a satisfactory staple town. For this reason it became imperative for the English to discover new markets for their cloth. Not unaffected by all this, and also suffering from Dutch competition, the Hanseatic League was in decline. In 1552 the merchants of the Steelyard in London were made subject to the same dues and regulations as other aliens.[3] The times were propitious for a new English thrust into the Baltic.

In 1549, fifteen years before the English merchants were driven out of Antwerp altogether, Sebastian Cabot had been invited back to England. His advice was to be sought on the opening of new trades, and one of the moving spirits was the shipowner John Dudley, who was briefly Duke of Northumberland and a prominent member of Edward VI's council.

Cabot recommended an expedition to the north-east with the purpose of discovering yet another route to the Indies and, with this in view, he obtained a re-issue of the Cabot patent of 1496.[4] When the proposed expedition to the north-east came in prospect a year or two later, Richard Chancellor, who had sailed to the Levant on a voyage sponsored by Cabot, was appointed Pilot Major. Chancellor had already worked closely with John Dee, the mathematician, and was well known as a student of navigation who had improved the navigational instruments then in use. To lead the expedition Sir Hugh Willoughby, a soldier, was selected from a crowd of eager applicants to be Captain-General.

To discover a north-east passage to the Indies three vessels were fitted out by a group of London business men and financiers who raised a total of £6000 in shares of £25 each. The vessels were *Edward Bonaventure* (160 tons), *Bona Esperanza* (120 tons) and *Bona Confidentia* (90 tons), each ship being equipped with a pinnace and a boat. Chancellor sailed aboard *Bonaventure*, together with Stephen Borough as sailing-master, Borough's younger brother William (who became Comptroller of the navy in Queen Elizabeth's reign), and a ship's company which totalled 47, ten of them passengers. In *Bona Esperanza* were Sir Hugh Willoughby and 34 others, inclusive of six merchants. In *Bona Confidentia* were Captain Cornelius Durforth and 31 men, inclusive of three merchants.

The keels of these ships were sheathed in lead – the first metal sheathing used in England – to protect them against teredos or ship-worms, and Cabot framed a set of rules to govern conduct during the prospective voyage to Cathay or China.[5]

These rules were justly regarded as models of good sense and they influenced the rules which were to govern many future expeditions. A log book was to be kept, containing the courses steered and observations of the wind, weather and tides, the daily altitude of the sun at noon, and the position of the moon and stars. The captain was also to record the 'names of the people of every island, with the commodities and incommodities of the same, their natures, qualities and dispositions, the site of the same, and what things they are most desirous of, and what commodities they will most willingly part with, and what metals they have in hills, mountains, streams, or rivers, in or under the earth.'

Morning and evening prayers were to be read daily, and no 'blasphemy, swearing, lewd talk, dicing, card-playing, or other devilish games' were to be permitted. The cook or steward was to give weekly or even more frequently an exact account of the victuals used such as 'flesh, fish, biscuits, meat, bread', as also of 'beer, wine, oil or vinegar'. Economy was enjoined, and no liquor was to be spilt in the ballast, 'nor filthiness to be left with(in) board: the cook room and all other places to be kept clean for the better health of the company'. The sick were to be relieved and comforted, and 'every manner of person, without respect, to bear another's burden'. The men were to be provided with the Company's livery, but this uniform was to be worn only when the captain 'shall see cause to muster or show them in good array'.

No person was to engage in private trade until the Company's interests were satisfied. 'In dealing with strangers all must be careful not to enter into any discussion about religion.' People could be enticed on board to provide useful information, and it was recommended to make them drunk if possible, but no violence was to be used.

No better planned nor better equipped expedition had ever left England. The ships were provisioned for 15 months and Willoughby had powers to press men if required. In July 1553, later in the year than was sensible, the fleet set course for North Cape, armed with a letter from Edward VI addressed to all rulers and eulogising the benefits of trade. All areas beyond the Danish outpost of Vardø, about 150 miles east of North Cape in modern Norway, were at this time unknown. After discovering the Arctic island Novaya Zemlya, some 500 miles further east between 70° and 80°N, Willoughby, who had been separated by storm from *Bonaventure*, wintered with *Bona Esperanza* and *Bona Confidentia* on the river Arzina 'near unto Kegor' in Lapland. Through ignorance of how to cope with an Arctic winter everyone on board these ships perished.

Richard Chancellor, in *Bonaventure*, waited at Vardø for a week for the other two ships and then proceeded into the White Sea, anchoring at the mouth of the river Dvina. Reaching Nenokso, twenty-five miles west of St Nicholas and somewhat further from St Michael or Archangel, he proceeded to Moscow, picking up a few words of the Russian language on the way. In Moscow he so impressed Ivan IV ('the Terrible') by his tact and dignified behaviour that the tsar gave him a letter for the English sovereign inviting Englishmen to trade with Muscovy and promising his protection. Chancellor returned home in 1554, having been robbed on the way by Flemish pirates, and recommended trade with Russia.

In February 1555, by which time 'Bloody' Mary was on the throne and married to Philip II of Spain, a charter was granted to the Russia Company and Cabot was made a governor for life. It was the first fully incorporated joint-stock company in England. In a regulated company, like the Merchant Adventurers, the members traded either individually or in partnership with their own capital, the company itself not engaging in trade. The joint-stock company traded as an entity and the members did not, or were not supposed to, trade individually within the area of the company's monopoly. That the Russia Company was given a monopoly was the natural reward accorded to pioneers of a new branch of trade and, since its purpose was to open a northern passage to Asia, it was given a monopoly of all exploration and new trade north of British latitudes, including the north-west. Of the 201 members the majority were London merchants. They included some Staplers and many Merchant Adventurers, as well as those who had pioneered the new voyages to Barbary, the Guinea coast and the West Indies.

Fresh capital was raised by a call on members to finance Chancellor's second voyage, to be made with *Edward Bonaventure* and a ship named for the two monarchs, *Philip and Mary*. A letter for the tsar, written in Greek, Polish and Italian, was furnished by the monarchs, and King Philip, by giving his full countenance and support to these voyages, tacitly admitted that in his view the papal division of the globe did not extend to the Arctic regions. The path was thus prepared, though it was many years before it was trodden, for the retreat of Spain from an untenable position to the more reasonable one of maintaining her monopoly in lands already colonised by Spaniards.

A London agent or factor bought and sold the Company's goods in London. Since Russia was economically less advanced than England, largely manufactured goods – fully dyed and dressed cloth, copper sheets and metalware from England and wine, sugar, spices, fruits, paper and metalware from abroad – were loaded for the second expedition, to be exchanged for fish oil, potash, wax, furs, hemp, flax and ropes. The north-east passage was not planned to be an alternative to the Baltic route to Russia, which was still difficult of access, but this is what for a time it became, as it did again in World War II; and, as on that later occasion, it helped further to undermine the position of the Germans.

This northern route presented great difficulties and dangers. The physical conditions were dominated by its length, its northern direction and its termination in a port which was icebound from autumn to spring. The ships could only hope to make one round voyage a year. According to a timetable proposed by William Borough, the ships should leave the Thames at the beginning of May and reach St Nicholas at the end of that month. They should then stay for thirty days, leave at the end of June and reach London by 10th August. If all the Russian goods were not ready by the end of June 'one good ship or two' should remain at St Nicholas until mid-August.[6] In fact, the ships usually seem to have left St Nicholas for the return voyage later than Borough recommended, rarely earlier than the last week in July, arriving in England in September or October.

The tsar welcomed the second expedition, hoping that this trade might prove a source of arms, and that England might supply the skilled workers and professional men who were sorely needed in Russia. He granted the company a monopoly of English trade and the right to trade anywhere in Russia without the payment of duty.[7] In Moscow the merchants were granted a house, with the right to buy a house in Vologda and in Colmogro, both great marts between Moscow and the coast, and to build a warehouse on Rose Island in the Dvina opposite St Nicholas.[8]

While these two voyages were being made to the north, other English seafarers, financed in part by the same merchants, were once more pushing southwards. In his voyages twenty years earlier William Hawkins had not turned the corner at Cape Palmas to sail towards the Bight of Benin because at Cape Palmas the coast turns east, and even a little north of east, and the wind blows almost continuously from the west, the Guinea current flowing from the same direction. All this makes it extremely difficult for a sailing vessel to retrace her course from any point on the Gold or Ivory Coasts. Now, however, began those voyages which gave rise to a saying whose truth was proven on this first occasion:

> Beware and take care of the Bight of Benin;
> Few come out, though many go in.

In 1553 a syndicate of London Adventurers prepared a Guinea expedition under the command of Thomas Wyndham, who was well acquainted with William Hawkins, and secured as pilot a renegade Portuguese Jew named Antonio Anes Pinteado who was a native of Oporto. The French had entered this trade already and a French surgeon was enlisted for Wyndham's expedition. To seek a cargo of 'grains', which were something of the nature of pepper, Wyndham insisted on going further east than the 'whoreson jew' advised and in consequence died of a fever. Two-thirds of the crew of Wyndham's ship *Lion* also died, and those who survived took passage home in her companion vessel *Primrose*, leaving their merchants behind up-country. Pinteado himself died on the homeward passage and scarcely 40 of the 140 men who went on this expedition returned. Throughout history, however, dead sailors have proved no liability and, since 150 pounds of gold had been secured on the Gold Coast, the voyage was a success and the commercial possibilities of the Guinea coast had been proven.

In 1554 – the year in which Chancellor returned from Moscow, and also the year in which old William Hawkins died, leaving behind his sons William and John – a strong syndicate was formed to send out a new Guinea expedition. Sir George Barnes, Sir John Yorke, Anthony

Hickman, Edward Castlyn and Thomas Locke were among the financiers, and John Locke, Thomas's brother, was put in command. John, like his brother, was primarily a merchant and had just returned from a pilgrimage to Jerusalem. With him on this expedition sailed the 15-year-old Martin Frobisher, nephew to Sir John Yorke and already a survivor from Wyndham's expedition of the previous year.

Five vessels were prepared this time – *John Evangelist* (170 tons), *Trinity* (140 tons), *Bartholomew* (90 tons), and two pinnaces, one of which foundered before clearing the English coast.[9] The other four ships made calls on the Gold, Ivory and Grain Coasts, returning with 400 pounds of gold (worth about £20,000 or £3 million at 1988 prices), 250 tusks and a large quantity of 'grains'.

Unsurprisingly, such success evoked a protest from the Portuguese government, which considered West Africa its province, and the English Privy Council (under Mary) proceeded to forbid further voyages to Guinea, at least on paper. Despite the Roman Catholic character of their government, however, the London merchants made it clear that they were not tolerating any restrictions on trade, whatever the Pope may have decreed. 'We be merchants', they replied to the Portuguese protest,

> who, by common usage of the world do use traffic in all places of the world, as well Asia and Africa as Europa, and have never been restrained from resort to any places... And following this our accustomed usage we have of late resorted to sundry places both towards the south and north parts of the world, in both which we find the governors and the people of the places well willing to receive us friendly and gently. Amongst other places, our factors did about two years past resort to sundry places where we found several princes or governors, and with them trafficked, exchanging merchandise and from them returned quietly, thinking without offence we might use there (where we found no resistance) the same liberty that we use and do find in all other places of the world.[10]

By this time, as one Venetian observer remarked, a number of Merchant Adventurers and Staplers were each worth from £50–60,000; and one traditionalist wrote of the Merchant Adventurers in 1554: 'To such a pride are those kind of men become ... as, contrary to nature and all God's forbode, the merchant is now become the prince, and who needeth aid at their hands shall so pass therein as he shall feel the tyranny they have...'[11]

In March 1555 there is record of a further voyage to Morocco in which Sir John Yorke, one of the promoters of the Locke expedition, was involved. The *Grace of God* of London was chartered and freighted at £3 a ton. Dates were loaded in Morocco to the account of John Gardener, another City merchant involved, and the charter party indicates that some charterers were trading on their own account while others were in partnership.[12] This voyage proved a prosperous one.

Queen Mary and the Privy Council notwithstanding, another successful Guinea voyage was also embarked upon in this year. This time, William Towerson, yet another London merchant, sailed from Newport in the Isle of Wight on 30th September in command of *Hart* (60 tons) and *Hind*. Towerson succeeded in making a better homeward passage than did his predecessors. By 13th February he was clear of Cape Palmas, having passed the whole of the Gold and Ivory Coasts in nine days, for he had discovered from experience that from 2am until 8am in the morning the wind blew off the shore from the north-north-east although all the rest of the time it was at south-west. On 14th May 1556 both ships anchored safely in Bristol. Towerson did not lose a man in either crew and, although he does not reveal the total cargo secured, the daily reckoning indicates about 130 pounds of gold and some 50 tusks. Considering the modest investment, the return must have been excellent.[13]

Towerson followed this voyage with another in 1556–7, securing clearance this time by lavish bribery and after claiming that he was sailing only for the Barbary coast. Curiously, on his third voyage, which started in January 1558 before Queen Elizabeth came to the throne, he employed two royal ships – *Minion* (300 tons) and *Tiger* – as well as the privately-owned *Christopher*. *Minion* had four masts, with lateen sails on her two mizens, and was the ship in which Sir John Hawkins was to be found later at San Juan de Ulua. On this occasion *Tiger* had to be abandoned in mid-ocean on the homeward passage because her men were too weak to handle her. The other two vessels staggered into Portsmouth in October with no more than 12 men on their feet.

The Africans could not satisfy the European thirst for gold and between them the French and English had somewhat overdone the Guinea trade. Towerson's third voyage was less profitable than his previous two. Nevertheless, it had been made clear to the Portuguese that they could not keep this trade entirely to themselves and the English began to wonder if the Spaniards were not in the same case.

In the meantime the Russia trade continued. In April 1556, the month before Towerson returned from his second voyage to Guinea, the Russia Company despatched three ships northwards. Stephen Borough sailed as master of the pinnace *Searchthrift*, which carried a crew of ten and could float in five feet of water. Borough was sent to explore east of the White Sea and he reached Vaigach Island before pack ice drove him back to winter at Colmogro. He recorded that 'the good old gentleman Master Cabota' went down to Gravesend to see them off and at the farewell dance in the local inn 'entered into the dance himself amongst the rest of the young and lusty company'. Cabot, aged about 82, died in the following year.

In company with *Searchthrift* were *Edward Bonaventure* and *Philip and Mary* carrying 'extraordinary masters and sailors to bring home the two ships which were frozen in Lappia'. These, of course, were Willoughby's ships *Bona Confidentia* and *Bona Esperanza* which were salvaged on this voyage only to be lost on the passage home. *Bonaventure*, too, was wrecked on the Scottish coast during a furious gale and Chancellor lost his life in his successful exertions to save Osep Napea, the Russian ambassador who was accompanying him back to England. Much valuable cargo was lost either in the sea or from pillage 'by the rude and ravenous people' of Scotland.

Despite the heavy losses suffered by this expedition, four more ships were despatched to Russia in May 1557, two of them – *John Evangelist* and *Trinity* – being vessels which had been to Guinea in 1554. A letter written by the Company to its agents on this occasion provides much information:

> You shall understand we have freighted for the parts of Russia four good ships to be laden there by you and your order: That is to say, the *Primrose* of the burden of 240 tons, Master under God John Buckland: the *John Evangelist*, of 170 tons, Master under God Laurence Roundal: the *Anne* of London, of the burden of 160 tons, Master under God David Philly: and the *Trinity* of London of the burden of 140 tons, Master under God John Robins . . . You shall receive, God willing, out of the said good ships, God sending them in safety for the use of the Company, these kind of wares following, all marked with the general mark of the Company as follows. 25 fardles [bundles] containing 207 sorting clothes, one fine violet in grain, and one scarlet, and 40 cottons for wrappers, beginning with number 1, and ending with number 52. The sorting clothes may cost the first peny £5. 9s. the cloth, one with the other. The fine violet £18.6s.6d. The scarlet £17.13s.6d., the cottons at £9.10s. the pack, accounting 7 cottons for a pack. More 500 pieces of Hampshire kersies [coarse narrow cloth woven from long wool], that is 400 watchets, 43 blues, 53 reds, 15 greens, 5 ginger colours, and 2 yellows which cost the first peny £4.6s. the piece, and three packs containing 21 cottons at £9.10s. the pack, and part of the clothes is measured by Arshines. More 9 barrels of pewter of Thomas Hasel's making, etc. Also the wares be packed and laden as is aforesaid, as by an invoice in every ship more plainly may appear. So that when it shall please God to send the said good ships to you in safety, you are to receive our said goods, and to procure the sales to our most advantage either for ready money, time or barter: having consideration that you do make good debts, and give such time, if you give any, as you may employ and return the same against the next voyage;

> and also foreseeing that you barter to a profit, and for such wares as be here most vendible, as wax, tallow, train oil [which might be derived from whales, seals or even walrusses], hemp and flax. Of furs we desire no great plenty, because they be dead wares. And as for felts we will in no wise you send any. And whereas you have provided tar, and as we suppose, some hemp ready bought, our advice is that in no wise you send any of them hither unwrought because our freight is £4 a ton or little less; which is so dear as it would not bear the charges: and therefore we have sent you 7 ropemakers, as by copies of covenants here inclosed shall appear; whom we will you set to work with all expedition in making of cables and ropes of all sorts. . .

The Company was not interested in such bulky commodities as masts, tar, hemp or feathers because these were cheaper to import from Danzig and other Baltic sources, from which area freight rates were lower. In addition to the ropemakers they sent a skinner to choose mink and other valuable skins, and ten Company apprentices to be aptly employed, 'some to keep accounts, some to buy and sell by your order and commission, and some to send abroad into the notable cities of the country for understanding and knowledge'. They also requested a thorough examination of the woollen cloth, leather and metal markets, together with dyes used in the leather and cloth trades, so that they could judge exactly what would sell and what was worth buying.[14]

To finance this expedition there was a further call for money, the four ships being chartered from private owners though the owners of at least three of them were members of the Company. Osep Napea returned to Russia with presents for the tsar aboard *Primrose* and a commercial treaty was concluded which continued in force for over 300 years.[15]

The Russia Company had failed to find a north-east passage, though it continued to search for a profitable route to the east along the rivers of Russia and into Persia. In 1558, the year in which Elizabeth I came to the throne of England, the Russians acquired Narva, thus securing for themselves a port on the Baltic. This made a considerable impact on the trade. English shipowners outside the Russia Company were already trying to break the company's monopoly and by 1564 six such 'interlopers' from east coast ports were trading to Narva. In 1566 a bill was passed confirming the Company's privileges and extending them to Narva though, at the same time, provincial merchants from Newcastle upon Tyne, York, Hull and Boston were admitted to the company.[16]

In arguing its case the Company emphasised its services to navigation, pointing out that it employed a man 'learned in cosmography', at a salary of £20 a year, to teach its mariners and retained in its service a number of skilled pilots and masters. In the year in which the bill was passed the

Company complained that the ships returning from St Nicholas were not fully laden, though the cordage made under the direction of English craftsmen was now perfectly acceptable. (It rapidly came to be accepted as the best.) In the following year the company began to trade to Narva as well as to St Nicholas; indeed, in indication of the greater significance of Narva, it sent ships loading 1300 tons to the Baltic port and ships loading only 800 tons to the White Sea. Two of the total were to load for Spain and Portugal, one for Rouen, and the rest for London.[17] As the years passed the Russia Company sustained some considerable losses, but not so many as to drive it out of business. Until the 1580s its joint-stock organisation remained unique.

Despite the new initiatives of the 1550s England still ranked low among the maritime nations. With, perhaps, 50,000 tons of merchant shipping of all kinds (less than the capacity of two modern containerships), England probably possessed a smaller fleet than Hamburg, Lübeck, France, Venice or even Ragusa and Genoa, and she still lagged well behind the Dutch, Spaniards and Portuguese. By this time over 1000 Dutch ships entered the Baltic each year to fetch timber, corn and hemp, while English ships entering the Baltic numbered no more than fifty.[18] Such shipping as there was in England continued to be employed almost wholly on the coast, in the fisheries and across to the near Continent, and the fleets employed in trades north and south were meagre in the extreme by comparison with those of other maritime powers.

The government of the new queen, however, pursued the policies in support of shipping of her Protestant predecessors. Although the Navigation Acts which were then on the Statute Book were repealed, a more sweeping system of preferential duties was instituted, bounties on the building of ships were paid more regularly, and a new statute prescribed that no timber was to be cut down for iron smelting within fourteen miles of the coast. Within five years Henry VII's Navigation Act was re-established, coastwise trade was restricted to English ships and, to support the fishing fleets, it was decreed that Wednesdays and Saturdays were to be observed as fish-eating days.[19]

Relations with Spain had remained cordial until Elizabeth came to the throne, the English trading mainly to the ports of Andalusia, at Seville and Cadiz, and particularly to San Lucar at the mouth of the Guadalquivir, where they had chartered privileges and an English church. They also did business on the Biscay coast, from which area iron was exported to England, while Vigo Bay was used as a place of assembly and for the victualling and repair of ships on any expedition, whether mercantile or piratical. The Spanish colony of Canary Island was open to the English and there Anthony Hickman and Edward Castlyn, who had helped to finance John Locke's Guinea expedition of 1554, had established a regular business.[20]

By this time there was also a resident English factor in Morocco, and in 1559 we find *John Evangelist*, which was in Russia two years previously, and *Mary Martin* in this trade, with tin, sword blades, long lances, oars, iron and kerseys being exchanged for gold, copper, sugar, dates, gum arabic, amber, wax, dressed skins and horses.[21] In 1561 an English ship sailed for Morocco with books in Hebrew for Moroccan Jews in addition to the exports previously listed. As trade with the Low Countries declined, the Moroccan trade increased and merchants who had previously imported sugar from Antwerp now imported it direct. By 1566 the Moroccan trade – almost wholly in London hands – was about as important as that with Portugal, annual imports being valued officially at something between £6000 and £10,000.[22]

In 1561, Elizabeth, who made no pretence of acknowledging the king of Portugal's right to limit her subjects' trading areas, regularised the Guinea trade. The old Guinea syndicate renewed its operations and in June it entered into an indenture for the use of four royal ships. The expedition was dogged by misfortune but still traded at a profit, the Crown's share being paid to Benjamin Gonson, Treasurer to the Navy.[23]

The following year 30-year-old John Hawkins, the younger son of old William Hawkins and son-in-law to Benjamin Gonson, made his first slaving voyage. Bred to the sea, and probably learning his seamanship in his teens in the trade to the Canaries, John, with his brother William, had inherited from his father a fleet of merchantmen and privateers, together with some exclusive knowledge about trade and navigation. It was Pedro de Ponte, a Spanish merchant living in Tenerife, who suggested to him the feasibility of a trade in slaves. His father-in-law interested Thomas Lodge, a governor of the Russia Company and a member of the Grocers Company, and two other well-known entrepreneurs, Alderman Lionel Ducket and Sir William Winter.[24] In October 1562 Hawkins sailed with fewer than 100 men in three ships, *Solomon* (120 tons), *Swallow* (30 tons) and *Jonas*, a bark of 40 tons. Pedro de Ponte supplied a Spanish pilot and arranged for a group of Spaniards in Hispaniola to buy his wares.[25]

Hawkins knew that it was healthier not to overcrowd his ships with crew and this voyage was free of illness. But his ships must have been crowded when he crossed the Atlantic with more than 300 slaves, even though he augmented his fleet with a Portuguese vessel which appears to have been chartered. In his own words he acquired the slaves 'partly by the sword and partly by other means',[26] and exchanged them in

Hispaniola for hides, sugar, ginger, pearls and precious metals. Some of his cargo went for sale in Portugal, where it was seized by the authorities because of his venture into Guinea, the Portuguese choosing to regard him as a pirate though this was far from Hawkins' own view. A further vessel which he had chartered in Hispaniola was seized in Cadiz and, unsuccessfully, he tried to recover the cargo by going to Spain himself. Since he had been a freeman of Plymouth when, only eight years previously, the borough had feasted Queen Mary's bridegroom King Philip of Spain, Hawkins could claim that his desire was to serve his 'old master',[27] even though his old master had been rejected as a suitor by Hawkins' new queen. That he was not permitted to do so was largely because the king thought he had the situation in France in hand and therefore had less need to appease the English. Despite his losses and his disappointment, Hawkins still showed a handsome profit on the voyage.

Although one historian in modern times has said that 'hardly anyone, except possibly Montaigne, saw anything wrong in the slave trade',[28] this statement is difficult to substantiate. The pragmatists and advocates of expediency have always been in conflict with the warm-hearted humanists, not infrequently within the same human mind. Queen Isabella of Spain, for example, forbade the enslavement of Indians, though not apparently until it proved unprofitable.[29] Queen Elizabeth, too, declared that enslavement was detestable and that the trade in Africans would call down vengeance from heaven upon the undertakers, though she changed her tune when Hawkins showed her his profit and loss account and took a share in his next voyage.[30] Drake gave a slave his freedom and, with no equivocation, the Spaniard Bartolomé de Alborney attacked the injustice and immorality of the slave trade in 1573.[31] Only a few years after Hawkins' first slaving voyage the Parlement of Guienne declared: 'La France, mère de Liberté, ne permet aucuns esclaves',[32] and Francesco Carletti, a trader born in Florence, wrote in 1591 that the slave trade seemed to him 'an inhuman traffic unworthy of a professed and pious Christian'. Carletti described it as making a profit 'out of human flesh and blood'.[33] Thirty years after Carletti, when offered slaves for sale by a Gambian ruler, Richard Jobson, an Englishman, replied: 'We are a people who do not deal in any such commodities, neither do we buy or sell one another, or any that have our own shapes.'[34] Hawkins, however, had no such qualms.

In May 1563, while Hawkins was planning his second voyage, Martin Frobisher brought five French prizes into Plymouth and shortly afterwards, with Thomas Cobham, captured the *Catherine*, a vessel with tapestries on board for King Philip. On this occasion he was sent to gaol for his pains.[35] It remained difficult to know where to draw the line between piracy and privateering. The mayor of Dover and other leading inhabitants of that city were said to have captured over 600 French prizes in 1563, which was legitimate at that time since England was at war with France. But they also appear to have plundered sixty Spanish vessels, and even English vessels were not safe.[36] William Hawkins, John's elder brother, was joint owner with Thomas Stukeley of a privateer and, despite the war with France, was arranging an Anglo-French expedition to Florida until his partner revealed the scheme to the Spanish ambassador.[37]

Another Guinea expedition took place in this year, arousing further Portuguese opposition,[38] and in January 1564, the year in which the Spaniards conquered the Philippines, Philip excluded all English traders from the ports of the Low Countries and gave orders for the arrest of every English vessel in his harbours. Hawkins and the Queen were therefore well aware of the risks they took when the second slaving expedition set out.

Hawkins did not sail again from Plymouth until October 1564. This time the expedition comprised the Queen's great but defective ship *Jesus of Lübeck* (700 tons), so called from the port from which the Queen had purchased her, *Solomon* (now enlarged to 140 tons), *Tiger* (50 tons) and the pinnace *Swallow* (30 tons), the two smaller craft being suitable for entering rivers on the Guinea coast. The crews numbered 80, 35, 20 and 15 respectively, a total of 150, which was subsequently increased to 170 by the gentlemen adventurers and their servants.

Twelve and a half tons of ships' biscuit provided basic carbohydrate. In addition the fleet was provided with 120 barrels of meal, 40 hogsheads of beef, 20 quarters of beans and peas, 80 flitches of bacon, 6 lasts of stockfish and 12 hundredweight of ling. For drink there was 40 tons of beer, 35 tons of cider and 40 butts of malmsey; at £6 a butt, the malmsey was a drink for gentlemen. Among the miscellaneous items were a tun of oil, a pipe of vinegar, a hogshead of honey and a quarter of aniseed. For the feeding of 50 negroes only 120 quarters of beans and peas are mentioned. There are also estimates for 'cotts' – perhaps bunks in the hold – and for shirts and shoes for negroes. The total cost of the expedition, exclusive of the capital value of the ships, the value of any cargo carried and sundry disbursements not listed, appeared to be £4990.[39]

At Ferrol Hawkins issued the sailing orders which became a tradition in the British navy: 'Serve God daily [i.e. conduct daily prayers], love one another, preserve your victuals, beware of fire and keep good company [i.e. the fleet should keep together].'

In Tenerife Hawkins held a conference with Pedro de Ponte. Off Sierra Leone he stopped at Sambula Island where he spent several days going ashore each day to burn the villages and seize the inhabitants.[40] At Bymba he lost seven sailors to gain ten slaves; but eventually he filled his holds with some 400 negroes, sailing for the West Indies on 29th January 1565.

It proved to be a long crossing for the ships were becalmed for twenty-eight days, and at Margarita, a large island off Venezuela, he failed to secure a Spanish pilot. The Spanish king's interdict on trading by foreign vessels had by this time reached the New World. At Borburata, near modern Puerto Cabello, the Spaniards refused to trade until Hawkins pointed out that he wished to be of service to Spain, and then an argument over duty ensued. Not until Hawkins landed with 100 sailors armed with 'bows, arrows, harquebusses and pikes' did trade proceed, and subsequently the Spanish governor was sent back to Spain as a prisoner for submitting to Hawkins in this way.

Round about this time Hawkins sampled the potato in Venezuela and took on fresh meat and hides in Curaçao. He then proceeded to Rio de la Hacha where, after he had again landed with 100 men, he was granted a licence to trade on fair terms. Most or all of the slaves were now sold, together with other goods, and he obtained gold, silver, pearls, other jewels and very cheap hides in exchange. He hoped to exchange some of the treasure for sugar and more hides in Hispaniola but, through ignorance of the area, he missed Hispaniola, Santa Cruz and Havana. To reach Florida he secured a French pilot, and there he found a French colony whose immediate necessities he relieved, leaving his own fleet at risk of being short. Hoping to please both English and Spaniards, he also offered to bring the French colonists home, but they refused, only to suffer annihilation at the hands of the Spaniards later in the year.

From Florida the expedition sailed north to the Newfoundland banks, where fresh fish was obtained, and thence returned home, where the ships arrived on 20th September 1565. Only twenty men had died, including the seven killed at Bymba. Lord Pembroke and his colleagues in the Privy Council cleared 60 per cent profit, and the Queen was paid £500 for the wear and tear to her ship alone. Hawkins returned a comparatively wealthy man.

But the rough had to be taken with the smooth. A rival expedition led by David Cartel had set out at the same time as Hawkins, comprising *Merlin* and two other ships, *John the Baptist* and *Minion*, contributed by the Queen. *Merlin* blew up and Cartel then joined Hawkins until the two quarrelled at the Cape Verde Islands. Cartel met strong opposition from the Portuguese and it appears that *John the Baptist* was taken and her crew interned. As Hawkins returned home, William and George Winter also tried their hand by sending out *Mary Fortune* (70 tons), but she was sunk by the Portuguese and most of her crew drowned.

De Silva, the Spanish ambassador, endeavoured to obtain the prohibition in England of both slaving and 'piracy' but, although lip-service was paid by the English government to his demands, the effects were minimal. Martin Frobisher, who had been cruising in the Channel in *Mary Flower* in 1565, gave security the following year not to go to sea without a licence, but he solved the problem by obtaining a commission from Cardinal Châtillon, the Huguenot leader, to capture ships which were enemies to the French.[41] George Fenner was prohibited from slaving in consequence of de Silva's vigilance but he sailed from Plymouth on 10th December 1566 all the same.

By this time all merchantmen were at least partially armed and Fenner's largest vessel, *Castle of Comfort* (150 tons), was a private warship with a crew of 70. *Mayflower* and *George*, a pinnace, sailed with her, the owners being merchants, one of whom was engaged in the Barbary coast trade. The three ships sailed to trade on the Guinea coast but had no success there, for by this time even the Azores were growing too hot for Englishmen. An Anglo-French adventure in this same year – seven French and sixteen English ships, probably pirates and freebooters, led by Peyrot de Monluc – met with Portuguese opposition at Funchal and returned when their leader was killed.

John Hawkins had various meetings with the Spanish ambassador in 1566 to discuss his possible service to Spain, for example in the Mediterranean, and he signed a bond to send no ships to the Spanish Indies. His brother William gave no such undertaking and, of course, the bond signed by John did not rule out an expedition to the Guinea coast. Both brothers must have been part-owners in yet another 1566 expedition which had sailed a few weeks before Fenner's. This expedition was under the command of Captain John Lovell, and the ships were *Paul* (200 tons), *Solomon*, *Pasco* (40 tons) and *Swallow*. Francis Drake, aged 24 and a kinsman of the Hawkins brothers, was of the company.

According to the Portuguese, Lovell arrived at Cape Verde late in 1566 with four ships and some pinnaces and there took a Portuguese trader carrying negroes, wax, ivory and other commodities. In February 1567 he took another ship in sight of Santiago in the Cape Verde Islands, killed some of the crew and set the rest onshore, and thus acquired a further 15,000 ducats-worth of sugar and negroes. At the same time he was said to have taken a Lisbon ship bound for Brazil worth 2000 ducats, and before leaving the vicinity, he made a final capture worth 5000 ducats. Both *Solomon* and *Swallow* had been in John Hawkins' fleet on his first two slaving expeditions but, while *Solomon* presumably was not, *Swallow* must have been John Hawkins' own ship. In fulfilment of his bond, therefore, *Swallow* now returned home from the Guinea coast laden with ivory and other commodities, while Lovell's other ships crossed to the West Indies, probably touching at Margarita, Borburata and Curaçao before being defrauded of payment for their slaves at Rio de la Hacha. They seem to have returned to England sometime in 1567.

The ill-fated Anglo-French adventure of 1566 had been planned to look for gold in Africa. Involved in this expedition were two Portuguese, Antonio Luis and Andre Homen, the latter also being known as Gaspar Caleira, and after de Monluc's failure these two came to England to sell the idea of finding gold in Africa to the English. Hawkins appears to have made this the excuse for his next venture.

Hawkins swore to the Spanish ambassador that his ships would not sail for prohibited places, but de Silva grew suspicious when the ships loaded quantities of beans, the usual food for slaves, as well as fine cloths and linens. The Hawkins brothers invested £2000; William Winter was probably involved, and so were the Queen and other members of the Privy Council.

On 30th July 1567 the Queen's warships *Jesus of Lübeck* and *Minion* left London for Plymouth. At Plymouth the Hawkins' fleet was ready: *William and John* (150 tons), with Thomas Bolton captain and James Raunse master; *Swallow*, possibly a new *Swallow* of 100 tons; *Judith* (50 tons); and *Angel* (33 tons). As the squadron was finally organised Hawkins sailed in *Jesus* with Robert Barrett of Saltash as master. Although he was only in his twenties, Barrett acted as Hawkins' second-in-command for the whole force in all matters of action, taking charge of most of the landing parties necessary in the course of the expedition. Drake was at first on board *Jesus* but later in the voyage obtained command, first of a captured Portuguese caravel, and then of *Judith*. The captain of *Minion* was Thomas Hampton, and among the others were William Clarke, a merchant representing the interests of London investors, George Fitzwilliam, who had sailed with Hawkins in 1564 and was deep in his confidence, and Captain Edward Dudley, a soldier. Among the cargo were linen, woollens, cottons and taffetas, tin, arm rings and swords.

During this year the Queen, having failed three years earlier, tried to renegotiate the English trading arrangements with the Portuguese. The English stance was made clear by her principal adviser, William Cecil. 'If the Pope's authority and gift be alleged', Cecil instructed, 'to answer that the same is unknown to us. If they allege prescription, possession must go before: the King of Portugal hath neither conquered Ethiopia nor keepeth possession, nor yet useth authority there or receiveth any tribute.' Unsurprisingly, the negotiations did not prove a success.

While Hawkins was making his preparations in Plymouth in August 1567, seven Spanish warships sailed into Plymouth Sound on a trumpery excuse and giving no salute. Hawkins fired on them and was subsequently reprimanded – an action which proved to tie his hands later on at San Juan de Ulua. After this, the proposed guides for this expedition in search of gold, Luis and Homen, alias Caleira, decided that it was expedient to disappear from the Plymouth scene and went off to France.[42]

It was at this point that Hawkins suggested to the Queen and Cecil that the voyage should become a slaving voyage and they now concurred. The six ships sailed on 2nd October. Four days later de Silva, whose intelligence service must have been good, remonstrated: 'Your mariners rob my master's ships on the sea, and trade where they are forbidden to go; they plunder our people in the streets of your towns; they attack our vessels in your very harbours, and take our prisoners from them; your preachers insult my master from their pulpits, and when we apply for justice we are answered with threats.'[43]

'During the voyage out of the said fleet,' wrote a seaman aboard Hawkins' ship *Jesus*, 'when night fell and the new watch began to come on deck and the hourglass was turned, everybody on board the ship would assemble round the mainmast, kneeling bareheaded, and the quartermaster would begin praying, and everyone would recite the psalms of David, Our Father, and the Creed, in the English tongue.' Another witness added that the quartermaster compelled attendance with a rope's end.[44]

But it was not all prayers. According to John Hartop, who was of the company, Hawkins made a deal with three African chieftains and the 'three kings drove seven thousands negroes into the sea at low tide, at the point of land, where they were all drowned in the ooze except for five hundred which we took and carried thence for traffic in the West Indies.'[45] Prior to this Hawkins had impressed a Portuguese caravel, *Gratia Dei*, which had been captured by the French, and put Drake in command. Later, the French captain was reinstated and another of the French ships on the Guinea coast joined him. In February 1568 the fleet sailed west.

The ships were allowed to revictual at Margarita and they sailed for Borburata on 9th April. At Borburata there was unofficial trading over a period of two months and Hawkins then sailed for Curaçao and Rio de la Hacha. Drake, now in command of *Judith*, had gone ahead and seized a Spanish ship. Hawkins, a stickler for the letter of the law, would not have done this even though he had a score to settle with Miguel de Castellanos, the King's Treasurer at Rio de la Hacha, who had defrauded

Drake and Lovell's expedition of the previous year. When Hawkins arrived he negotiated by force a licence to trade, made compensation for property which his men had destroyed, and disposed of 250 slaves and other goods.

After further trading, Hawkins' fleet – particularly the *Jesus* – suffered damage in a gale and he had to put in to San Juan de Ulua, near modern Vera Cruz, on the Mexican coast to refit. Two days later the annual Spanish treasure fleet arrived from Seville carrying Don Martin Enríquez, the new Viceroy.

The story of the subsequent Spanish treachery has been frequently told. Drake escaped in *Judith* and Hawkins got away, with some of his fleet's treasure, in *Minion*. Only 15 of his crew are said to have survived to reach Plymouth in January 1569, five days after Drake.[46] Robert Barrett, master of the *Jesus*, was subsequently burnt at the stake in Seville market place.[47] Financially disastrous, this expedition marked a turning point in English relations with Spain.

Notes

1. G. Ramsay, *English Overseas Trade during the Centuries of Emergence* (1957), London, pp. 17–19.
2. D. B. Quinn & A. N. Ryan, *England's Sea Empire, 1550–1642* (1983), London, p. 24.
3. L. F. Salzman, *English Foreign Trade in the Middle Ages* (1931), Oxford, p. 337.
4. G. Causton & A. Keene, *The Early Chartered Companies* (1896), London, p. 196.
5. R. Hakluyt, *The Principal Navigations, Voyages, Traffiques and Discoveries of the English Nation*, Vol. 1 (1927), London, pp. 267–8.
6. Hakluyt, *op. cit.*, Vol. II, pp. 247–8.
7. Hakluyt, *op. cit.*, Vol. I, pp. 313–18.
8. T. Willan, *The Early History of the Russia Company* (1956), Manchester, pp. 10–14.
9. Hakluyt, *op. cit.*, Vol. IV, p. 47.
10. J. Williamson, *Maritime Enterprise 1485–1558* (1913), Oxford, p. 289.
11. *Ib.*, pp. 140–1.
12. T. Willan, *Studies in Elizabethan Foreign Trade* (1959), Manchester, pp. 102–3.
13. Williamson, *op. cit.*, pp. 293–5.
14. Hakluyt, *op. cit.*, Vol. II, p. 267; Vol. I, p. 356; Vol. I, p. 380 ff.
15. W. S. Lindsay, *History of Merchant Shipping*, Vol. II (1876), London, pp. 82–3.
16. *See* R. Davis, *The Trade and Shipping of Hull 1500–1700* (1961), EY Local History Series: No. 17, East Yorkshire Local History Society, pp. 7–8.
17. Willan (1956), *op. cit.*, pp. 78–80.
18. R. Davis, *The Rise of the English Shipping Industry in the Seventeenth and Eighteenth Centuries* (1962), London, pp. 1–2.
19. H. C. Hunter, *How England got its Merchant Marine, 1066–1766* (1935), New York, pp. 67–8.

20. J. Williamson, *Sir John Hawkins, the Time and the Man* (1927), Oxford, p. 51.
21. Willan (1959), *op. cit.*, pp. 104–7.
22. *Ib.*, pp. 108–9.
23. Williamson (1927), *op. cit.*, p. 54.
24. G. Dow, *Slave Ships and Slaving* (1927), Salem, Mass., p. 19.
25. Williamson (1927), *op. cit.*, p. 81.
26. D. P. Mannix & M. Cowley, *Black Cargoes* (1963), London, p. 21.
27. Williamson (1927), *op. cit.*, p. 168.
28. A. L. Rowse, *The Expansion of Elizabethan England* (1955), London, p. 174.
29. J. H. Parry, *The Spanish Seaborne Empire* (1966), London, p. 21; J. Williamson (ed), *The Cabot Voyages and Bristol Discovery under Henry VII* (1962), Cambridge, p. 53; S. E. Morison, *Christopher Columbus, Mariner* (1956), London, pp. 130–1.
30. Mannix, *op. cit.*, p. 22.
31. G. V. Scammell, *The World Encompassed: The first European marine empires, c. 800–1650* (1981), London, p. 257.
32. Williamson (1927), *op. cit.*, p. 80.
33. F. Carletti, *My Voyage Around the World* (1965), London, p. 13.
34. R. Jobson, *The Golden Trade* (1623), London; (C. Kingsley, ed., reprinted, no date, Teignmouth).
35. Rowse, *op. cit.*, p. 256.
36. Lindsay, *op. cit.*, Vol. II, p. 116.
37. Williamson (1927), *op. cit.*, p. 96.
38. *Ib.*, p. 56.
39. *Ib.*, pp. 94–5.
40. Mannix, *op. cit.*, p. 22.
41. Williamson (1927), *op. cit.*, pp. 124–6.
42. *Ib.*, pp. 132–6 and p. 162.
43. Lindsay, *op. cit.*, p. 128.
44. Williamson (1927), *op. cit.*, p. 148.
45. Mannix, *op. cit.*, p. 23.
46. J. Williamson, *The Age of Drake* (1952), London, pp. 81–93.
47. Rowse, *op. cit.*, p. 176.

7

The Glitter of Gold

(1569–1581)

For more than a century after the defeat at San Juan de Ulua the English abandoned the slave trade. With the contemporary fall of Antwerp as a trading centre the English were deprived of a stable foreign outlet for their exports. Envy of the rich trades of the Iberian empires and the new situation in the Low Countries drove English ships further afield and into privateering.

As civil war began again in France La Rochelle emerged as a base for the Huguenot cause. In the Netherlands Dutch rebels against Philip II took to the sea and their roving squadrons of 'sea-beggars' joined forces with the privateers from La Rochelle. Some English shipmasters took commissions from the leaders of both to plunder the shipping of the Catholic French and Spaniards. Spain's trade to the north virtually ceased, while her ships on the Atlantic and in the Caribbean became increasingly subject to plunder. Collaboration between Dutch, French and English expeditions became common.[1]

In 1567 King Philip had appointed the Duke of Alba captain-general in the Netherlands with instructions to suppress Protestantism and separatism. When John Hawkins arrived back in Plymouth from his disastrous third slaving voyage he found that King Philip's ships, carrying pay for Alba's troops, had been brought into Plymouth by English privateers operating under the flag of William of Orange, leader of the Dutch rebels. To compensate in part for her losses in the West Indies, which included the loss of her capital ship *Jesus of Lübeck*, Queen Elizabeth commandeered the treasure in the Spanish vessels as a 'loan'.[2] Spanish reprisals for this action included the seizure of English ships, the sequestering of their cargoes and the imprisonment of their crews. To this, Elizabeth responded by ordering the imprisonment of every Spaniard in England and the arrest of every vessel in her ports or in the Channel owned by any of Philip's subjects.

The situation was more than a little complicated. Martin Frobisher, who had been sent to prison in 1563 for taking a Spanish ship and who in 1565 was sailing with a Huguenot licence, by 1569 was among those sailing with a commission from William of Orange. In that year he was sent back to prison for the piracy of a French vessel. Other ships were still sailing under the Huguenot flag and these included *Castle of Comfort*, a vessel jointly owned by William Hawkins and Richard Grenville, which had sailed in Fenner's unsuccessful expedition to the Guinea coast in 1566. Still other ships carried English letters of marque, and piracy was also rife. In 1568 one seafarer gave testimony that French pirates had seized his ship off Belle Isle, between Newfoundland and Labrador, and 'with great torture and pain wound a rope about this jurat's head and the residue of his company's heads and wrested the same to confess where more money remained'. He thought 'they would have wrung his eyes out of his head.'[3]

Several times in these years, when the situation became intolerable, the government sent out a squadron to clear the seas of pirates but such expeditions had little success. In the West Indies the Spaniards complained that 'for every two ships that come hither from Spain [and there were about sixty a year[4]], twenty corsairs appear,' though this was, no doubt, an exaggeration. The Hawkins brothers and their partners were not over-scrupulous in the ways in which they compensated themselves for losses suffered in the West Indies, and Plymouth, Dover and Mede Hole in the Isle of Wight, an anchorage used by English, Dutch and French alike, become emporia for goods taken at sea. As the cold war between Spain and England hotted up, these havens became substitutes for Antwerp and Seville, and spices, wines, saffron, oil, soap and woad taken from Spanish, French and Portuguese ships were sold at all of them.[5]

One consequence of the changing political situation was a new turn in Hamburg's history. In 1567 the Merchant Adventurers of London agreed with the city's senate that an English factory or trading establishment should be set up there for ten years.[6] A little later the English strengthened their trading links with the Baltic by way of Elbing, the modern Polish Elblag, and the Russia Company continued to explore down the Russian rivers in an effort to establish a trade with Persia. For a brief period, between 1570 and 1572, Ivan revoked the Company's privileges because he had failed to establish a defensive and offensive alliance with Elizabeth. 'We thought you had been ruler over your land', he wrote to the Queen. 'But now we perceive that there be other men that do rule, and not men but bowers [knaves] and merchants, the which seek not the wealth and honour of our majesties, but they seek their own profit of merchandise.'[7]

This fit of pique, however, did not last, and the Russia Company's privileges were restored on payment of half customs duties. Trade to St Nicholas and to Narva continued though interlopers tried to encroach upon it, as they also did in the trade to Hamburg.[8]

From 1570 onwards a number of influences were at work to strengthen English connections with the Mediterranean. In 1571 Rome, Venice and Spain together defeated the Turks decisively at Lepanto but the Turco-Venetian war, of which this battle was part, weakened the hold of Venice on seaborne traffic through the Mediterranean. The English gradually extended their sphere to the Adriatic and, in the 1580s, to Turkey.[9] The Moroccan trade continued and, after 1573, the English began to trade to Leghorn as that port was developed by the Dukes of Tuscany. After 1575 it became possible to import currants directly from the Greek islands, a trade which had long been a Florentine preserve,[10] and two agents were sent by London merchants to Constantinople itself.

In May 1570 Queen Elizabeth was excommunicated. Catholic risings were being plotted in England, and William Cecil (who became Lord Burghley in the following year) considered it politic to forbid Hawkins to sail on any further slaving voyage. Undaunted, Hawkins proposed that he should take his ships to attack the homeward-bound treasure fleet as it returned to Spain from Vera Cruz. This proposal was not pursued though, in the winter of 1570–71, in a further effort to recoup their losses, the Hawkins brothers sent Drake to sea and on this occasion he despoiled Venta de las Cruces.[11]

The following summer, with Burghley's connivance, Hawkins pretended to espouse the Catholic cause to get those of his men who had been captured back from Spanish prisons. For the service of King Philip he offered sixteen ships, of which *Christopher*, a vessel of 500 tons, carrying a crew of 250 and provided with 50 guns, may have been a Hanse or Flemish prize, and two or three others may have been hired. All told these ships totalled 3170 tons, were manned by 1585 crew and carried 406 guns. This fleet was one-fifth bigger than the fleet which William Canynges claimed to have supplied to the king a century earlier. It gives some indication of Hawkins' power, and his fleet probably occupied a place in the first Elizabeth's shipping analogous to that occupied by P&O at the beginning of the second Elizabeth's reign, though the conditions of the time were, of course, very different.

After what was obviously a show of strength, the English prisoners in Seville were released and John Hawkins, by now a member of the English Parliament, was forgiven his transgressions in the Spanish Indies and granted a patent of Spanish nobility. In the meantime Burghley had uncovered the Romish plot in England: there was no English rising against the Queen, and no Spanish invasion to place Mary Queen of Scots upon the English throne.

Later in this year, 1571, Drake made a rapid voyage of reconnaissance in the 25-ton *Swan*, burnt a ship in Cartagena and brought the owner back for ransom. Corsairs or privateers – with crews composed of English, French or Flemish seamen – commanded the Channel and were disrupting trade, including the staple English wool trade to the Netherlands. In response to the frustrations of what might be described as the legitimate English merchant community, in March 1572 a commission was issued to John Hawkins and George Winter to repair to the coasts of Kent, Sussex, Southampton and the Isle of Wight to order all those 'commonly called freebooters', which included the Dutch sea-beggars, to avoid English harbours on pain of forfeiture of ships and goods. Furthermore, all Englishmen were to leave the service of freebooters, and English pirates, both men and ships, were to be arrested. That Hawkins should be involved indicates the ambivalence of this gesture.

In December 1572 the *Primrose*, then in the Solent, was probably not unique in having a Frenchman, Captain Valeton, in command, a Cornishman as sailing-master and a boatswain who came from Southampton.[12] In this vessel a number of London merchants had shipped cloth and other goods for Vianna and Caminha in Portugal but the ship fell foul of the Spanish trade embargo which had been occasioned by Queen Elizabeth's seizure of Spanish treasure in Plymouth after the loss of *Jesus of Lübeck*. At Vigo 'all cruelty and torments' were used against the factors and they were 'laden with chains and irons'.[13]

Financed by Hawkins and others, Drake sailed again that winter with *Swan* and *Pasco* and took treasure worth £40,000, perhaps £5.6 million at 1988 prices, though half went to the syndicate's French partners.[14] Following the massacre of St Bartholomew in 1572 Richelieu lay siege to La Rochelle and Hawkins' ships were involved in an unsuccessful English and French attempt to relieve the beleaguered city.[15]

Hawkins was frequently involved in litigation and an interesting light is shed on the privateering business by a court case which he brought in 1574 against George Stoderd and eight other London men who formed an underwriting syndicate. Captain Valeton, the French rover who had been in command of *Primrose*, had brought into Plymouth the *Esperance* of Havre which belonged to a Rouen merchant, Fernando de Quintanadoine. The conditions of the time had led to a practice by which the owners of goods passing through the Channel insured them in London – another step in the mercantile progress of England – and in this case the ship and a cargo of Barbary sugar had been insured with Stoderd and company for £200. If an insured ship was taken and a claim made, the underwriters would contact men influential in the seaports – in this case Hawkins – to see if they could ransom the vessel and its cargo at a price below their value. Two parties, the privateers and the intermediary, thus made a profit on every capture, the merchants paid a regular toll in the shape of premiums, and the underwriters lost part but not all of the sum insured for. The underwriters gained, of course, where ships reached their destinations safely.

The intermediaries exploited their local influence, bringing pressure to bear on the privateers to accept low sums for their prizes. In the case of the *Esperance* John Hawkins stated in his bill of complaint that he had made a verbal agreement – 'our word our bond' is the motto of the modern Baltic Exchange, one of the institutions which grew out of such verbal arrangements – with Stoderd and company at the Royal Exchange. By this agreement he had undertaken to redeem any ships in which they were interested in return for his expenses and a reasonable fee. Aware that the ship was insured for £200, he had redeemed it for £65 and then delivered both ship and cargo to Quintanadoine's factor. Thereafter the defendants in the lawsuit had refused to pay anything to Hawkins and he prayed in court for redress.[16]

Hawkins had been prevented by the Privy Council from visiting the Netherlands just prior to the massacre of St Bartholomew, but one of those who made a visit at this time was Sir Humphrey Gilbert, stepbrother to Walter Raleigh. Six years earlier Gilbert had drafted his still unpublished *Discourse to prove a Passage by the North-West to Cathaia and the East Indies*. For four years, from 1566 to 1570, he had been otherwise engaged in Ireland (for which services he was knighted) and his interest in a north-west passage had been left in abeyance, but from 1570 onwards the subject must have been much discussed once more in Court and in maritime circles. Gilbert considered that the discovery of a north-west passage was reserved for the English, who had most to gain from it. To the argument that if such a passage existed it would have been discovered already by the navigators of Spain and Portugal, he replied that it was not in their interest to find it. He repeats a tale that the King of Portugal gave the Emperor Charles V 350,000 crowns to leave the discovery unattempted and remarks, 'It is to be thought that the King of Portugal would not have given the Emperor such sums of money for eggs in moonshine'. The pilots of these nations, he claimed, were now forbidden on pain of death to explore to the north-west lest they 'should beat the bush, and other men catch the birds'.

That there was even then some contact between England and the New World despite Spanish prohibitions seems evident from a report on Vera Cruz in Mexico – from the neighbourhood of which Drake and Hawkins had been driven four years earlier – by a merchant named Henry Hawks.

Hawks must have been trading to Vera Cruz at the time of the San Juan de Ulua affair for he wrote in 1572 of five years' observation of the prevalent yellow fever and malaria. 'This town,' he wrote, 'is inclined to many kinds of diseases, by reason of the great heat, and a certain gnat or fly which they call a musquito, which biteth both men and women in their sleep; and as soon as they are bitten, incontinently the flesh swelleth as though they had been bitten by some venomous worm. Many there are that die of this annoyance.' Hakluyt commissioned this report, which he included in his great account of English voyages, but it aroused no interest in the medical profession then or subsequently. Mosquito-borne diseases continued unchecked for another 300 years.[17]

By 1573 Richard Grenville, in conjunction with William Hawkins, Piers Edgcumbe and others, was thinking too of finding a southern route to eastern Asia through the Straits of Magellan. His plans were for a voyage to find the postulated Terra Australis – thought to be essential in the southern hemisphere as a counterbalance to the land masses of the north – and also to find the western end of a north-west passage. Both these projects were to remain on the maritime agenda until Captain Cook's time. In presenting his plan, Grenville set forth a complete programme of colonial empire with all the usual anticipated benefits: an increase in shipping; the spreading of God's word; a market for manufactured goods; the discovery of gold; and colonial settlement. In 1574 Elizabeth refused to Grenville the licence which she granted to Drake only three years later.[18]

In that year, 1574, John Noble took a ship to the Caribbean and the crew of 28 were all killed by the Spaniards with the exception of two boys who were sent to the galleys for life. Shortly afterwards, Gilbert Horsley appeared off the American coast and collected a handsome profit. In 1576 Andrew Barker, a Bristol merchant who had had a ship and cargo confiscated in the Canary Islands on the grounds of heresy, sought his own redress in the Caribbean. Unfortunately for him, mutineers made off with his valuable haul, though their skiff capsized in a storm, while the Spaniards captured and decapitated Barker. Also in 1576 John Oxenham, who had been with Drake four years earlier, led an expedition to the Isthmus of Panama with a view to holding it against the Spaniards with the aid of the rebellious Cimaroons but he was caught and subsequently hanged.[19]

Not without difficulty, trade proceeded in other parts of the known world. In 1575, the year in which English agents had been sent to Constantinople, imports from Morocco were valued officially at £28,639.[20] But the following year there is evidence of problems in the trade for an

Admiralty examination tells us that, homeward bound from Barbary, the *Antelope* of London was captured by a Frenchman of Havre. The French demanded that the crew admit that the cargo was Portuguese. Not obtaining a voluntary statement to that effect, they hanged the purser, whereupon the rest of the crew made the required admission.[21] Such problems notwithstanding, English trade to the Mediterranean, and through the Mediterranean to Turkey, was the most important event in Elizabethan commercial strategy between the opening of the Russian trade and the founding of the East India Company.[22]

As a member of the Russia Company, Sir Francis Walsingham, Queen Elizabeth's Principal Secretary from 1573 to 1590, was close to those London merchants most concerned with the drive for eastern trade. The Dutch were by this time trying to encroach upon the Russian trade and, in 1576, the Company made another attempt to expand its activities by the discovery of a north-east passage.

The vessel sent on this expedition was baffled once more by the great accumulation of ice in the Kara Strait beteen Novaya Zemlya and Vaigach Island, and the only result of the voyage was that it led to some further fishing. In addition to fish oil, the Company's ships now proceeded to bring home salmon from this area in the Barents Sea. In a good season the catch could amount to 10,000 fish.[23]

Independently of Humphrey Gilbert, Martin Frobisher and Michael Locke (or Lok) now put before the governors of the Russia Company their own project for the discovery of a north-west passage. To obtain geographical information they had consulted the historian Richard Willis, together with the literary executor of Richard Eden. Twenty years earlier, the latter had published his translation of the *Decades of the New Worlde* by Peter Martyr and this book contained a map which showed parts of North America. The map, supposedly drawn from material supplied by Nicolo and Antonio Zeno, who were said to have made a voyage into the Western Ocean in the late 14th century in the service of 'a northern chieftain', contained great errors but appeared to have some basis in fact.[24]

In consequence of the approach made by Frobisher and Locke, Dr John Dee, who became the official geographical and mathematical adviser to the Russia Company after the death of Sebastian Cabot, wrote out advanced instructions on the use of instruments of navigation and 'the rules of geometry and cosmography'. Others with whom the expedition was discussed included Richard Hakluyt, Stephen Borough (the most experienced of the Arctic explorers) and his brother William, now Comptroller of the Navy. William drew up a chart of rhumb lines on which to plot new discoveries.

It was at this juncture that Humphrey Gilbert became associated with Michael Locke, no doubt because they had common interests, and in the following year George Gascoigne, a poet who was related to Frobisher, called on Gilbert and came away with a copy of his *Discourse to prove a Passage by the North-West to Cathaia and the East Indies* which he proceeded to publish without Gilbert's consent.[25]

The outcome of all this ferment was Martin Frobisher's first voyage to the north-west. Influential supporters – who may have included Lord Burghley, Walsingham, Robert Dudley Earl of Leicester and the Earl of Warwick, with all of whom Frobisher, his prison sentences notwithstanding, was well acquainted – subscribed £875, plus £1205.11s.8d which was spent on victuals and equipment.[26] On this occasion the Queen, who also knew Frobisher well, subscribed only her good wishes.

In 1576 Frobisher sailed in command of *Gabriel* (20 tons), *Michael* (25 tons) and a pinnace of 7 tons, a Lilliputian fleet even by the standards of the time. After rounding the southern point of Greenland, he sailed up the coast and crossed over to Baffin Island where he took one of the westward-looking openings in the hope that this might prove to be the looked-for passage. Failing to discover any open passage, Frobisher loaded a piece of black ore which he thought might contain gold and sailed for home.

In London Michael Locke took Frobisher's ore to three different and reliable London assayers, each of whom told him that the stone contained no gold. But Locke persevered, for he had lost £738 on this expedition, and eventually he found an Italian assayer, John Baptista Agnello, who told him what he wanted to hear. Although Walsingham was not convinced that gold had been found, Locke had no difficulty in financing a second voyage.

In March 1577 the Crown granted a charter to Locke, Frobisher and their backers to form the Cathay Company, Locke being appointed Governor for life and Frobisher High Admiral. This time the Queen contributed £1000 and the 200-ton *Aid*, subscriptions for this voyage amounting in all to £5150.[27] Aboard *Aid* were 64 mariners, and in company with her sailed *Michael*, with 16 mariners, and *Gabriel*, with 13. Altogether 143 people sailed in the three ships, inclusive of 36 officers and gentlemen, 14 'mynars and fynars', and Jonas Schutz, a German assayer friend of Agnello's who was taken along as the expert. Stores included 30 tons of coal, presumably to be used by the miners and finers.

Outward bound, Frobisher met with 'three sail of English, fishermen from Iceland, bound homeward, by whom we wrote our letters unto our friends in England', a practice which was to be followed by ships outward bound on long voyages for nearly 300 years. On 20th August, in Canada, the ships loaded a full cargo – 200 tons – of the ore which Schutz assured Frobisher was rich. Frobisher then 'annexed' the country.

Frobisher's arrival back home inspired a boom of a kind new to the commercial world. Bernard Cranich, a German mining expert, declared his expectations of a good yield from the ore and people rushed to invest. 'This country', it was declared, 'no doubt promiseth good hope of great commodity and riches, if it may be well discovered.'[29]

Frobisher on this second voyage had sailed aboard the 200-ton *Aid* and as the trade routes lengthened merchant ships serving such routes grew bigger. Between 1560 and 1577 the number of English ships between 100 and 200 tons increased from 72 to 120 and the number of ships over 200 tons increased from 6 to 15.[30] On the other hand, despite the building at this time of the 950-ton *Triumph* at a cost of some £4000,[31] big warships of 800 to 1000 tons were falling out of favour with the English for, as Walter Raleigh wrote, they were less serviceable, more costly, seldom used, and very deep in the water. A ship of 600 tons could carry as many guns as a vessel twice the size and it was more manoeuvrable.[32] Henceforward middle-sized galleons described as 'race-built', relatively fast and weatherly ships, became the mainstay of the royal fleet, and they were armed increasingly with culverin, which were lighter than cannon, quicker to fire, longer in range and had less recoil. Of this ilk was the 500-ton *Revenge*, completed in the year of Frobisher's arrival with his promising ore, a ship which was to serve as Drake's flagship in 1588 and which Grenville was to command in his last legendary fight.

It was in the heady atmosphere of Frobisher's arrival in London that the Queen granted to Drake the licence which she had refused to Grenville. To Drake's sailors it was intimated that his ships were going to Alexandria, but those at court were aware that Drake's real task was to investigate a route to the east beyond America, to investigate the possibilities of colonisation in South America, and perhaps to seek a western entrance to a north-west passage.[33]

The full list of Drake's promoters has never been recovered but they probably included the Queen, the Earl of Leicester, Walsingham, Sir Christopher Hatton, Sir William Winter, John Hawkins, and his father-in-law Benjamin Gonson (whom Hawkins was to succeed as Treasurer of the Navy in the following year). Drake sailed at the end of the year, on 13th December 1577, on the voyage which was to become famous as his circumnavigation. It is indicative of the improvement in shipbuilding that his ships were ready to sail in mid-winter.

With a promise of gold, the only commodity (apart from silver) which was of much interest to sovereigns, Queen Elizabeth invested £1350 in Frobisher's third voyage of 1578. This time 15 ships set sail, ranging from the 400-ton *Thomas Allen* to the little *Moon*, smaller even than the veterans *Michael* and *Gabriel*. John Rashleigh's ship *Francis of Fowey* carried forty-one miners. One hundred and twenty prospective colonists were also of the party, complete with a fort built in sections to be assembled for wintering, an early example of prefabricated building.

On this voyage Frobisher penetrated the Hudson Strait and a clergyman named Wolfall, who was with the fleet, celebrated the first communion service of the English church in the New World. It is doubtful whether his prayers were answered for some forty men died of scurvy, exposure and various accidents, no colony was established, and the ore which had aroused so much interest proved to be valueless for it was not only gold that glittered. The Queen had burnt her fingers and it was not long before Frobisher's wife and children were in want. Michael Locke was ruined and thrown into a debtors' prison.[34] The speculators had had enough of the north-west passage.

It was in this same summer of 1578 that Humphrey Gilbert was given letters patent. Subsequent to the publication in 1576 of his *Discourse* – which had proved an advertisement for Frobisher's Company of Cathay – Gilbert had put up a project to seize the fishing fleets of Spain, Portugal and France during the fishing season off Newfoundland. The ships numbered over 300 and the tonnage was estimated at 7000. Another plan of Gilbert's was to capture the Spanish treasure fleet and plant an English colony in the West Indies.

Gilbert's letters patent empowered him for six years 'to discover search find out and view such remote heathen and barbarous lands, countries and territories not actually possessed of any Christian prince or people as to him . . . shall seem good. And the same to have hold occupy and enjoy to him his heirs and assigns for ever.'[35] In November 1578, after various vicissitudes, Gilbert sailed with seven ships. Henry Knollys, who was associated with him but did not sail with him, had engaged in various acts of piracy, and there were many pirates among Gilbert's crews. *Anne Aucher* was the Admiral's ship, with Gilbert in command and Henry Pelly as master. *Falcon*, a royal ship, was commanded by Walter Raleigh, with the Portuguese Simon Fernandez as master. Together the ships carried 122 guns and 409 men and they were victualled for a year.

Thomas Churchyard's verse of this period may well refer to Gilbert:

> But such that seek for fame in foreign place,
> Forsake great ease and wealth where they are bred,

Are special men, and do deserve more grace
Than all the rest, whatever may be said;
Leave wife and friends to try the tumbling seas,
Make open sale of life and all they have,
Are men that may both prince and country please,
Who shall of right be honoured to their grave.

Gilbert's fleet returned home five months later, having suffered losses and achieved little. Gilbert himself was dominated by the idea of establishing a colony but he displayed 'a certain incapacity or unwillingness to prevent his men seizing foreign merchant vessels'.[36]

In 1578 the Queen had finally abrogated all the ancient immunities of the Hanseatic merchants and in 1579 the Eastland Company, described as 'the Fellowship of Eastland Merchants', received its first charter, the prime mover being Sir Edward Osborne. The term 'Eastland' referred to land beyond the river Vistula but the Eastland Company was given sole trading rights through the Skagerrak in Norway, Sweden, Poland, Lithuania (with the exception of the port of Narva which was reserved to the Russia Company), Prussia and Pomerania, from the river Oder eastwards to Danzig, Elbing and Königsberg.[37] There were no pirates in the Baltic and private venturers were grieved by the establishment of the new company; interloping became common, as it was already in the Russian trade.

In March 1580 Gilbert sent *Squirrel*, a tiny frigate of only 8 tons, across the Atlantic. The vessel probably made a landfall in New England but was back home before the end of June.[38] This was a remarkable feat of seamanship but its immediate economic importance was insignificant. A certain John Walker also went to the American coast about this time and brought back 300 stolen hides and reported the discovery of a silver mine. In this year Gilbert renounced to John Dee any rights he had to discover a passage north of 50 degrees.[39]

To the north-east yet one more attempt was made to discover a passage to Cathay. Arthur Pet, who had sailed with Chancellor, took the 40-ton *George*, and Charles Jackman, one of Frobisher's veteran pilots, had command of the 20-ton *William*, which was lost on returning from the Kara Sea.[40] In the same year the contacts made earlier in Constantinople bore fruit when Murad III issued a charter allowing the English to trade on the same terms as other European traders, though the French ambassador subsequently persuaded the Sultan to revoke this charter.[41]

The great maritime event of 1580, however, was Drake's return in September from his circumnavigation of the world. The expedition had been furnished more than adequately with every kind of provision, and Drake did not forget those things which might serve to delight or impress.

His furniture was sumptuous; his table utensils were of silver;[42] and he carried both musicians and painters, the latter to paint pictures of the coasts he visited. His chief surgeon was killed, but Drake and his officers understood the use of 'lotions, emplaisters and unguents', and – like other Elizabethan commanders – he took every opportunity to provide his men with fresh supplies. Only after April 1579 did sickness appear, and he had then been sixty-eight days out of sight of land. Drake also carried skilled craftsmen so that he was able to careen and repair his ship at any time.

Aboard the 160-ton *Golden Hind* Drake passed through the Magellan Straits in 16 days, thus making the shortest passage of the century, for Magellan himself had taken 37 days and Cavendish and Richard Hawkins were to take 49 and 46 days respectively. Off Panama on the west side of the continent his success was ensured by the glitter of real gold when he captured the richly laden treasure ship *Nuestra Señora de la Concepción*, nicknamed *Cacafuego* (Shitfire). 'We found in her great riches', it was reported, 'as jewels and precious stones, thirteen chests full of reals of plate, four score pound weight of gold, and six and twenty ton of silver.'[43] Drake, who invariably released his prisoners, took the view that, if the King of Spain would not permit trade in the Atlantic, then he must suffer depredations in both oceans. He also intended to recover what his cousin had lost at San Juan de Ulua ten years previously.

But loot was not his only aim. When he concluded that he would not be able to return home the way he had come, he went as far north as British Columbia looking for a western entrance to the north-west passage, and found good anchorage near San Francisco where he saw that a fortified post might be established to act as dockyard, refuge and entrepôt, a half-way house, if it proved practicable to establish trade with the east by this route. San Francisco came at last to be used in this way by the American Cape-Horners in the China trade in the 19th century.

From the west coast Drake eventually made a prosperous voyage across to the Moluccas, crossed the Indian Ocean, and thus returned to Plymouth round the Cape of Good Hope. He was the first English commander to cross the Pacific and to cross the Indian Ocean and he returned home to become the most popular hero of the first Elizabethan age.

Drake's astonishingly valuable plunder, probably approximating to £16 million at 1988 prices, excited the general public but the authorities, while not uninterested in his immediate financial success, also attached importance to the verbal agreement he had made with the Sultan of Ternate in the Spice Islands. This agreement allowed the English to break into the Portuguese monopoly of the spice trade. Immediately, comprehensive strategic plans began to be drawn up. Drake was to return to the East Indies, Henry Knollys would winter in the region of the Magellan Straits and join Drake in the Moluccas after plundering Spanish ships as much as possible. Gilbert was to go with six ships to Cuba and establish a base from which to raid the Spanish treasure fleets in the Atlantic. Frobisher was to renew his attempt to find a north-west passage and link up with Drake by that route.[44] However, other events intervened and, although within twenty years they were to lead to the establishment of the East India Company, the only immediate outcome of all these general plans was Edward Fenton's voyage of 1582.

Notes

1. K. R. Andrews, *The Spanish Caribbean: Trade and Plunder 1530–1630* (1978), New Haven and London, pp. 97 and 136; *also* K. R. Andrews, N. P. Canny & P. E. H. Hair (eds.), *The Westward Enterprise* (1978), Liverpool, p. 117.
2. W. S. Lindsay, *History of Merchant Shipping*, Vol. II (1876), London, pp. 133–4.
3. T. Willan, *Studies in Elizabethan Foreign Trade* (1959), Manchester, p. 14.
4. J. H. Parry, *The Spanish Seaborne Empire* (1966), London, p. 123.
5. J. Williamson, *Sir John Hawkins, the Time and the Man* (1927), Oxford, pp. 258–9.
6. G. Ramsay, *English Overseas Trade during the Centuries of Emergence* (1957), London, p. 215.
7. T. Willan, *The Early History of the Russia Company* (1956), Manchester, pp. 116–7.
8. *Ib.*, pp. 45–6.
9. R. Davis, *The Rise of the English Shipping Industry in the Seventeenth and Eighteenth Centuries* (1962), London, p. 5.
10. Ramsay, *op. cit.*, pp. 39–40.
11. A. Rowse, *The Expansion of Elizabethan England* (1955), London, p. 179.
12. Williamson, *op. cit.*, pp. 240–89.
13. Willan (1959), *op. cit.*, p. 26.
14. Rowse, *op. cit.*, p. 180.
15. Williamson, *op. cit.*, p. 277.
16. *Ib.*, pp. 290–1.
17. R. Hakluyt, *The Principal Navigations, Voyages, Traffiques and Discoveries of the English Nation*, Vol. VI (1927), London, p. 280.
18. Rowse, *op. cit.*, pp. 181–2.
19. *Ib.*, p. 180.
20. Willan (1959), *op. cit.*, p. 113.
21. Williamson, *op. cit.*, p. 140.
22. K. R. Andrews, *Trade, Plunder and Settlement* (1984), Cambridge, p. 93.
23. G. Causton & A. Keene, *The Early Chartered Companies* (1896), London, pp. 39–40.
24. E. Dodge, *Northwest by Sea* (1961), New York, pp. 68–9.
25. *Ib.*, pp. 66–7.
26. M. Frobisher, *The Three Voyages* (1847), pp. ix–xi.
27. *Ib.*, pp. ix–x and xii.
28. *Ib.*, pp. 105–7.

29. *Ib.*, p. 233.
30. Davis, *op. cit.*, p. 7.
31. M. Oppenheim. *A History of the Administration of the Royal Navy and of Merchant Shipping in Relation to the Navy from 1509 to 1660 with an Introduction treating of the Preceding Period* (1896, reprinted 1988), London, p. 128.
32. W. Raleigh, *Works*, Vol. VIII (1829), Oxford, pp. 337–8.
33. Andrews (1984), *op. cit.*, p. 141ff; N. Crouse, *In Quest of the Western Ocean* (1928), p. 118.
34. Dodge, *op. cit.*, p. 83.
35. H. Gilbert, *The Voyages and Colonising Enterprises of Sir Humphrey Gilbert* (1940), London, p. 35.
36. *Ib.*, pp. 47–8.
37. Causton & Keene, *op. cit.*, p. 61.
38. Gilbert, *op. cit.*, p. 50.
39. *Ib.*, p. 52.
40. Dodge, *op. cit.*, p. 41.
41. M. Epstein, *The Early History of the Levant Company* (1908), London, p. 11.
42. F. Drake, *The World Encompassed* (1628), London, p. 8.
43. Rowse, *op. cit.*, p. 183.
44. Gilbert, *op. cit.*, p. 53.

8

The Profits of Privateering (1581–1588)

In 1580, on the death of King Henry of Portugal, Philip II of Spain, who had a claim through his wife, seized Henry's kingdom. Spain now held the entire Iberian peninsula together with Sicily, Naples, Sardinia, the Duchy of Milan and the area which is now Belgium and Holland. Spain also held the Portuguese settlements in Africa, the whole of the East Indies and, in Philip's view, all of the Americas. Although Spanish control of this vast empire did not compare with British control of its similarly sized empire when at its peak, the relative power of Spain at this time was enormous. From shipments of silver alone, Philip received as his 'Royal Fifth' some two million ducats a year, or something in excess of £500,000. After 1580 Philip was in a more powerful position than ever before to hinder England's claim to share in the new discoveries and their associated trade, and henceforward the struggle between the two powers was intensified.

In November of this year a group of London merchants sent the *Minion* on a trading voyage to Brazil. The purser, Thomas Grigges, spoke Portuguese and had been in Brazil in the *Elizabeth*, a ship which had accompanied Drake in 1577 but which returned home at that time from the Magellan Straits. *Minion* did not prove a happy ship and the master, Stephen Hare, was accused of favouring the sale of his own goods. In June 1581 the ship sailed north-east from Santos to Bahia, and there three seamen complained that they were being inadequately fed and they deserted the ship. As a result of the complaints, Richard Eareswicke, a factor, was removed from his job. 'For his punishment', we are told, 'according to the order of the sea, he was bound to the main mast with a base chamber about his neck for the space of half a quarter of an hour'. It scarcely seems a harsh punishment, and Thomas Grigges, who was also dismissed from his post, escaped even a proposed ducking at the yard-arm. Eventually, the ship appears to have returned home with a part-cargo of sugar.[1]

Commercial ventures of greater significance arose from the issue in 1581 of a charter – for seven years in the first instance – to the Levant

Company. Denmark's growing power in the Baltic had confined the Russia Company's trade to the northern route once more[2] and, since the voyages to Persia down the Russian rivers had never proved remunerative and return cargoes from St Nicholas proved inadequate, it became more important than ever to establish a route to the east.

Sir Edward Osborne, who had despatched the agents to Constantinople in 1575 and been prominent in the formation of the Eastland Company in 1579, became Governor of the new Levant Company, and prominent within it were Richard Staper and the Barbary merchants. It was agreed that only the twelve members should trade. They were to send shipping yearly and the commodities to be sold included 'all sorts of cloth and kerseys, dyed and dressed to the best proof, tin, lead and black cony skins'. The imports were to include oils, indigo (which came second in value to sugar in the Barbary trade and was a better dye than woad), raw silk, spices, drugs, currants, Cretan wines, cotton wool and yarns, grograms (a material made of silk and mohair), chamblotte (a material which included camels' hair), carpets, alum, aniseed and brimstone.[3]

Fourteen ships totalling 2250 tons traded to Zante and Candia in this year, their crews numbering 510 men. The ships were: *Merchant Royal* (350 tons, 60 crew), *Primrose* (300 tons, 60 crew), *Suzanne* (300 tons, 50 crew), *Edward Bonaventure* (250 tons, 50 crew), *Providence* (200 tons, 40 crew), *Ascension* (180 tons, 35 crew), *George Bonaventure* (150 tons, 35 crew), *Charity* (140 tons, 30 crew), *Toby of Harwich* (140 tons, 28 crew), *Harry of London* (120 tons, 26 crew), *Gift of God* (120 tons, 24 crew), *Thomas Bonaventure* (100 tons, 25 crew), *White Hind* (100 tons, 25 crew), and *Christ* (100 tons, 22 crew). Two years later there is a record of an English merchantman going beyond Zante and Candia and arriving in Constantinople.[4]

Merchant Royal and *Edward Bonaventure* were ships that were fully comparable with the Queen's warships of medium rank. Such vessels were of a size and fighting capacity previously unknown among English merchantmen and they were symptomatic of new developments in the English merchant fleet which, in the ten years that had passed since 1572, had increased in tonnage from 50,000 to 67,000 tons. Both vessels were to fight against the Armada in 1588.

Drake's circumnavigation was followed up in 1582 by a voyage commanded by John Hawkins' brother-in-law, Edward Fenton. This voyage was intended to obtain a footing in the East Indies and to penetrate China, where Fenton was to leave an agent to learn the language and act as factor. Leicester invested £2200. Drake invested both his bark *Francis* and a large sum of money. Among the other backers were the Russia merchants.

Two large ships, the galleon *Leicester* and *Edward Bonaventure*, the latter returned from Candia, were 'deeply laden' with goods for trade and these, together with *Francis* and the pinnace *Elizabeth*, made up the fleet. A third William Hawkins, grandson to the old man now dead and son to John's brother William, was second-in-command, and the young John Drake, who had been among the circumnavigators, was of the company. Since Sir Francis Drake, Fenton and their associated sea-captains were 'great favourers of scholars', Richard Madox, a young Fellow of All Souls College, Oxford, was appointed chaplain of Leicester's ship. Wisely, the Queen did not invest, for it proved to be a divided force. Quarrelling among themselves, the commanders hung about off the coast of Guinea while their men died of fever, and eventually they returned from South America having achieved nothing.

At the end of this same year the second William Hawkins, now a man over 60, sailed with John Hawkins' only son, Richard, a youth of about 21, as his vice-admiral with *Primrose* of London (300 tons), *Minion* (180 tons), the bark *Hastings* (100 tons), two other ships of 100 tons, both belonging to Sir Francis Drake, and a pinnace of 80 tons. This fleet, which was intended to go through the Straits of Magellan, appears to have sailed to Santiago in the Cape Verde Islands where many of the men were murdered. From there it sailed to the West Indies where Hawkins appears to have traded discreetly and profitably. He dredged for pearls at Margarita and visited Puerto Rico before returning to Plymouth in November 1583.[5]

On the whole these were not profitable times. Further disruption was being caused in the English Channel and the North Sea by privateers now acting under letters of marque issued by Don Antonio, pretender to the throne of Portugal, and at one time William Borough, Drake and Carew Raleigh were all involved in trying to clear them. Piracy was an automatic response to a shipping slump and in 1582 the ships of an English woman owner, Agnes Cowly, were attacked in the Channel by English pirates, both her sons being killed. Scottish ships were also attacked. At this time Culross in Fife was one of the thriving Scottish ports, trading in coal and salt to Veere and elsewhere in the Netherlands. In 1582 King James of Scotland complained to Elizabeth that 'the spoils committed lately by English pirates on merchants and adventurers of this nation . . . so generally grieve the people as they cry out, and pitifully complain thereof, and these hurts have most often fallen on the most honest sort and best affected, amongst which number this [bearer] and sundry other of his fellows are commended to me by persons of good quality and credit.'[6] On this occasion some compensation was paid.

It is in such circumstances as these that propaganda for American colonisation becomes overt. Humphrey Gilbert was still following up his charter of 1578 for new discoveries and to settle a colony, and he now gathered together five ships, the largest being made available by his step-brother Walter Raleigh. In April 1583 Christopher Carleill, Walsingham's stepson and commander of the *Tiger* in the Russia Company's trading season of the previous year, published a piece of promotional literature entitled 'A brief and summary discourse upon the intended voyage to the hithermost parts of America'. He contended that the existing trade with the Continent and Africa was precarious and decayed, and that trade with Russia had 'cost the [Russia] Company above four score thousand pounds before it could be brought to any profitable reckoning' and was still 'ticklish'. It was uncertain because of the annual nature of the voyage, the cost of ambassadors (a cost borne by the Company), Dutch competition, the possibility of interference from the king of Denmark and the nature of the Russian emperor and his dealings.[7] Fleets were sent twice a year to Spain and Portugal but there was always the possibility that these might be seized,[8] while in Algiers seamen were being held to ransom. Carleill stressed the rapidity of the Atlantic passage, and considered that the natural commodities deriving from America – fish, timber, cordage, furs, wine, wax, honey, oil (if olives were planted), and probably salt and other minerals – were prospectively a more rewarding investment than the Russian trade.

At this time in England there was speculation in land which was forcing the price up and this rise in prices inspired still other proposals for the conquest and settlement of North America. In 1578 Richard Hakluyt the elder, lawyer cousin to his voyage-collecting namesake, had stressed the value of colonies as a source of raw materials and new products which would serve as bases for new manufactures, and suggested that colonies would also provide new and exclusive markets for English manufacturers. Anthony Parkhurst, who had sailed to North America with John Hawkins, stressed the value of cheap food for the English people. Colonies would provide bases for use against Spain, though the English Catholics were also much interested in colonies as a means of escaping from repression at home. Indeed between 6th June 1582 and 28th February 1583 Gilbert assigned at least 8.5 million acres on the mainland and seven islands off the coast of North America to Catholics who were to make their own way to this promised land. Such negotiations must have had the prior approval of at least some members of the government, and they probably thought that it was a good idea to rid themselves of the Catholics in this way.[9] From the proceeds of such sales Gilbert tried to finance his expedition.

In November 1582 the exploitation of the commercial privileges under Gilbert's patent was assigned to a mercantile corporation called 'The Merchant Adventurers with Sir Humphrey Gilbert' which was to have its headquarters in Southampton. Despite powerful propaganda among them the merchants of London and Bristol held aloof from Gilbert's proposals, with the result that the expedition was under-capitalised.

Gilbert sailed in June 1583 with a substantial stock of goods for trade and 260 men, some of them craftsmen. He also took Morris dancers and musicians. The Admiral's ship was *Delight* (120 tons), and in company with her were *Swallow* (40 tons), *Golden Hind* (40 tons), *Squirrel* (10 tons) and the bark *Raleigh* (200 tons), though the latter put back to Plymouth after only two days at sea.[10] The first port of call was St John's, Newfoundland.

By this time the Newfoundland fishery was a century old and a reasonable, if informal, international organisation had been established. English, French, Basques and Portuguese all fished off Newfoundland but, if Hakluyt the elder were to be believed, the English had the best ships, 'and therefore gave the law to the rest, being in the bays the protectors of others, for which it was then, and has been of old, a custom to make them some sort of acknowledgement as Admirals, such as a boatload of salt, for guarding them from pirates and other violent intruders, who often drive them from the good harbours'. In fact, the English were not always admirals, for the captains took this office in turn.[11] The fishermen indeed appear to have organised themselves both amicably and effectively prior to Gilbert's arrival on the scene. They chose a new admiral each week and the admiral and the masters adjudicated on disputes and established a round of social visits from ship to ship. Ashore, the drying of the fish was carried on systematically, and the fishermen had established a garden in which raspberries and wild roses grew and in which they planted peas when they arrived in May, harvesting them in August.[12] When Gilbert arrived there were 36 ships within St John's harbour, 20 of them being Portuguese or Spanish.

Swallow, crewed largely by pirates, had already taken a 'Newlander' which allowed her crew on board, 'whom they rifled of tackle, sails, cables, victuals, and the men of their apparel: not sparing by torture (winding cords about their heads) to draw out else what they thought good'.[13] Since in August of the previous year Henry Oughtred, a prominent Southampton merchant who may have had money in the Gilbert venture, had sent out his own ship *Susan Fortune* and one of Sir John

Perrot's, *Popinjay*, both heavily armed, to take prizes off Newfoundland, and these had seized and robbed three Portuguese vessels, it is scarcely surprising that the fishing fleet in St John's did not welcome Gilbert with open arms. However, he sailed in without opposition and, perhaps because they thought it politic, the Portuguese plied him with fresh fish, wines, marmalade and 'most fine rusk or biscuit, sweet oils and sundry delicacies'.[14]

After he had formally taken possession of Newfoundland for himself under the Crown of England, Gilbert sent the *Swallow* home, filled with sick seamen, and sailed to the mainland with the remainder of his fleet. *Delight* foundered on the way, with the loss of over eighty men, sixteen survivors getting away to Newfoundland in the ship's boat where they lived on peas and berries until they were picked up by a whaler from St Jean de Luz.

Golden Hind and the diminutive pinnace *Squirrel* sailed for home, Gilbert aboard *Squirrel*. As the two ships approached Ireland they ran into bad weather and the men aboard *Golden Hind* pleaded with Gilbert to join the larger ship, but he remained where he was, reading a book and remarking, 'We are as near to heaven on sea as on land'. That was the last seen of him, for the *Squirrel* was lost in the storm.

In November 1583 Sir George Peckham, a Roman Catholic who had been involved with Gilbert in the assignation of land in North America to English Catholics, published a treatise entitled 'A true report of the late discoveries' which was prefaced by ten commendatory poems, including poems by Sir Francis Drake, John Hawkins, Martin Frobisher, Anthony Parkhurst and Arthur Hawkins. Thomas Churchyard's lines quoted above, are echoed by Drake:

> Who seeks by worthy deeds to gain renown for hire,
> Whose heart, whose hand, whose purse is pressed, to purchase his desire,
> If any such there be that thirsteth after Fame,
> Lo, here a means to win himself an everlasting name.
> Who seeks by gain and wealth to advance his house and blood,
> Whose care is great, whose toil no less, whose hope is all for good,
> If anyone there be that covets such a trade,
> Lo, here the plot for commonwealth and private gain is made.
> He that for virtue's sake will venture far and near,
> Whose zeal is strong, whose practice truth, whose faith is void of fear,
> If any such there be, inflamed with holy care,
> Here may he find a ready means his purpose to declare:
> So that, for each degree, this treatise doth unfold
> The path to Fame, the proof of zeal, and way to purchase gold.

These verses are interesting for what they tell us of Elizabethan motivation and the character of those who participated in this expansion of a nation. Arthur Hawkins wrote:

> My friends, if at the Exchange a man should go and tell
> That such and such commodities he had to sell
> Whereof we stood in need, and scarcely to be found,
> Whereby a quick return with profit would redound,
> I doubt not ere I passed but you would crave the sight
> Of these commended wares – and buy them if you might.
> You are proferred at this time fair grapes to make your wine,
> The pleasant fruits of Spain, the figs and orange fine,
> The speckled Russian furs that Easterlings us send,
> The rosin, pitch and deals that Dansk and Denmark lend;
> The metal here is shown that with a quenchless fire
> Inflames our thirsting hearts unstaunchèd in desire –
> A bargain you may have; 'tis put into your hands.
> Of all commodities you have from other lands –
> And at so easy price you cannot choose but gain –
> A trifle is the most, together with your pain.
> But what is that some say? Our Englishmen give ear
> Only to gain? God shield it should be true I hear.
> If we religious be, let's rig our ships with speed
> And carry Christ to these poor souls that stand in need.
> Why pause ye thereupon? The freight will quit the charge,
> For what is done for God doth find reward full large.

One other voyage of 1583 deserves mention. As we have seen, *Edward Bonaventure*, which had been in Crete in 1581, sailed with Fenton on the abortive voyage of 1582. In 1583 *Merchant Royal*, also in Crete in 1581, was sent on a trading voyage to Olinda in Brazil – where, of course, the English were still interlopers – and stayed six months, leaving three factors behind to sell goods remaining unsold. One of them probably died, and the other two were subsequently accused of having belonged to Fenton's company and thus having been involved in his seizure of spoil and the sinking of a Spanish ship.[15] Profitable trade was clearly not easy where merchants could not establish a safe depot.

In 1584 Ivan IV of Russia died and although his son Theodor, probably through his brother-in-law Boris Godunov, granted new privileges to the Russia Company, no mention was made of a monopoly, nor of trade with Persia.[16] English interlopers apart, both Dutch and French now had a share in this trade.

Trading in Morocco, too, still had its problems. According to Hakluyt, if ships trading to Morocco were driven upon the Spanish coast at this time their goods were confiscated and the crews were 'thrust ... into the Inquisition' on a charge of bringing 'armour, munitions and forbidden merchandise to strengthen the Infidels against these parts of Christendom'.[17]

Although the north European cloth trade of the Merchant Adventurers continued with a substantial measure of success,[18] some capitalists, faced with the contemporary difficulties, thought that profits could also be made in privateering. In 1584 prize goods, indeed, proved to be worth more in Plymouth than was foreign trade[19].

After Gilbert's death Walter Raleigh, who had been involved financially in the expedition of 1583, became the prime mover in the attempt at American colonisation, a project which appealed particularly to the gentry. Raleigh at this time was the reigning favourite at Elizabeth's Court – he was knighted in 1585 – and for the purpose of urging on the Queen the wisdom of western expansion and discovery he persuaded Hakluyt the younger to compile his most influential work, the 'Discourse on Western Planting'. It persuaded the Queen in 1584 to grant to Raleigh patent powers which were almost identical to those which had been granted to Gilbert, except that the Newfoundland fishery was excluded. It has been noted already that Gilbert had made over to Dee in 1580 his rights to land above 50°N and in 1583 Dee seems to have made over his assignment to Adrian Gilbert, Humphrey's brother, and to John Davis, who was a neighbour of the Gilberts in Devon. Raleigh obtained a wider grant in 1584 which led to John Davis's series of brilliant voyages in further search of the north-west passage, while Raleigh himself concentrated on colonisation in the warmer climates farther south.[20]

By 1584, the year in which William of Orange was assassinated, the old amity between Spain and England was clearly ended and it was in the interests of England to keep as quiet as possible about Raleigh's north American ambitions, and hence there was little printed publicity. However, in 1584 Raleigh sent out a couple of west country barks, one under the command of Philip Amadas and the other under the command of Arthur Barlowe, with the Azorean Portuguese Simon Fernandez as pilot. Fernandez had served in Gilbert's expedition of 1578 and had probably taken the tiny *Squirrel* across to New England in 1580. The new expedition took the southerly course across the north Atlantic and probably landed in Puerto Rico. One short-term objective was to facilitate privateering by the establishment of a mainland base in north America from which the Spanish Indies and the fleets coming from them might be attacked more effectively,[21] and the expedition leaders appear to have brought back favourable reports of the north Carolina coast, suggesting that fish, game and valuable timber were to be found there. Thomas Hariot, a scholar who had taught Raleigh navigation, was on this voyage and he brought back with him two Indians, Manteo and Wanchese, who taught him Algonkian as he taught them English.

In the following year the Barbary Company was established, with a collective licence issued to the Earl of Leicester, one other member of the nobility, and some forty London merchants.[22] England's first agent, Henry Roberts, arrived in Morocco in September and stayed there for three years. It was a move indicative of England's growing strength.

More direct moves against Spain were made on three other fronts, moves which grew into one concentrated effort.

In 1585 Drake was sent to the West Indies, raiding Vigo on the way and subsequently taking Santo Domingo and Cartagena. Sir Richard Grenville, cousin to Walter Raleigh, together with Ralph Lane, and accompanied by Simon Fernandez and Philip Amadas, also undertook to set up the first permanent settlement in America on Raleigh's behalf. And Bernard Drake of Ashe was ordered to Newfoundland to round up the Spanish fishing fleet and bring it to west country ports.

Drake's appearance off Santo Domingo in the summer of 1585 was, in effect, Elizabeth's declaration of war on Spain; and to take the Spanish fleet was one part, if not the major part, of Drake's design. He had gathered round him a fleet of twenty-five ships, among them the Queen's ships *Elizabeth Bonaventure* (600 tons) and *Aid* (250 tons). The rest were all private ships, the largest being the galleon *Leicester* (400 tons), which had been Fenton's flagship in 1582. The London contingent included *Primrose*, and the rest of the fleet were mainly west country vessels. Drake's flag was hoisted in *Elizabeth Bonaventure* and his flag-captain was Thomas Fenner, one of the most daring and experienced officers of his time. Martin Frobisher was vice-admiral and flew his flag in *Primrose*. Francis Knollys, the Queen's cousin and Leicester's brother-in-law, was a rear-admiral in *Leicester*. Captain Edward Winter, son of Sir William, commanded *Aid*, and Christopher Carleill was lieutenant-general commanding the land forces. Thomas Drake, the admiral's youngest brother, commanded Sir Francis's ship *Thomas Drake*. Tom Moone, one of the oldest and most devoted followers of Drake's corsair days, commanded *Francis*, another of Drake's ships. Among others whom he had trained on his voyage round the world were George Fortescue, commanding the bark *Bonner*, John Martyn in the bark *Benjamin*, Edward Careless, described by Hakluyt as an excellent mathematician and engineer, in *Hope*, and Richard Hawkins with his first command as captain of the galliot *Duck*. The whole force, including soldiers, sailors, Italians, French, Portuguese and one Castilian, some of them impressed, numbered 2300 men.[23]

Raleigh was authorised by the Queen to name his newly-discovered territories in America 'Virginia' in her honour, and she put her ship *Tiger* (160 tons) at his disposal and empowered him to obtain gunpowder from the Tower of London worth £400. Sir Francis Walsingham was a prominent adventurer in the Grenville voyage, and Raleigh himself contributed at least one ship, *Roebuck* (140 tons), which had been at sea earlier in the year searching for prizes with which to enlarge his fleet. *Waterhound* of Brill was probably seized for this purpose and renamed, her master and pilot, who were probably French, apparently being taken unwillingly on the voyage. Seven ships departed in April, Grenville in *Tiger*, with Fernandez as master, John Clark in *Roebuck*, George Raymond in *Lion* of Chichester (100 tons), Thomas Cavendish in *Elizabeth* (50 tons) and probably Arthur Barlowe in *Dorothy* (50 tons). The other ships were two pinnaces. The fleet carried about 600 people altogether, perhaps 300 or 400 of them colonists.[24]

The Spaniards had already established settlements in Florida to deny the coast of eastern north America to any other nation and they had destroyed a French colony there in 1565 after Hawkins had passed that way. Grenville stopped at a small island off Puerto Rico where a pinnace was built to replace one lost by storm. After this Grenville and Cavendish, in *Tiger* and *Elizabeth*, left this area, took a couple of prizes, loaded some salt after parleying with Spaniards, did some other trade, and eventually sailed with five vessels on 29th May, trading further with Spaniards at Puerto la Plata in Hispaniola.

In coasting up the American coast *Tiger* had all her corn, salt, meal, rice, biscuit and other provisions damaged or destroyed by salt water, which was a serious blow to the prospective colony. The latter, they decided, should be established on Roanoke Island in latitude 36°, 40 miles north of Cape Hatteras and on the latitude of Gibraltar, for Raleigh's 'Virginia' was mostly in what is now North Carolina. Ralph Lane was left behind with a number of men, Grenville's plan being to return home for fresh provisions. Off Bermuda, Grenville captured the 300 or 400 ton *Santa Maria* and her rich cargo of gold, silver, pearls, sugar, ginger, hides, cochineal and ivory. He brought this prize home in October and the rewards of privateering more than paid for the whole expedition.

The previous year, after a failure of the Spanish corn crop, Philip of Spain had offered English merchants special inducements to carry supplies of corn to Spain. However, with reports of the activities of Drake and Grenville coming in, Philip arrested these English merchantmen when the ships began to arrive in number and imprisoned their crews. This move aroused tremendous resentment in England and, although the ships were soon released, the English thereafter regarded all Spanish vessels as fair game.[25]

When news arrived that English shipping had been arrested in Spain, the Queen ordered Bernard Drake, who, under orders from Raleigh, had been preparing *Golden Royal* (110 tons) to head a further squadron to sail for Virginia, to sail for Newfoundland instead to warn English fishermen there not to take their catch to Spain and to seize what Spanish vessels he could. Bernard Drake and his men took a Portuguese prize and a Brazilman on the way to Newfoundland and then rounded up seventeen Spanish fishing vessels. Off Newfoundland they met with *Lion* and *Dorothy* of Grenville's fleet and, joining forces with these two ships, they engaged in further privateering on their way home.[26]

While all this was going on John Davis, a scientific navigator of the first calibre, was renewing the search for a north-west passage. In 1585 Adrian Gilbert arranged for him to take command of *Sunshine* (60 tons) and *Moonshine* (35 tons), the capital being put up by London and West country merchants, and particularly by William Sanderson of the Fishmongers Company, a highly successful merchant adventurer and a patron of geographical studies who was related to the Gilberts and Raleighs by marriage.[27] From this voyage Davis returned home after exploring some distance up the Cumberland Sound and reported to Walsingham that he had discovered a large new island likely to yield worthwhile trade in fur and leather. He had also concluded that a north-west passage probably existed.

In May 1586 Davis sailed on his second voyage to the north-west, finding his finance largely in Devonshire. His fleet was a little larger than in the previous year for, in addition to *Sunshine* and *Moonshine*, he sailed with *Mermaid*, 120 tons, and *North Star*, a pinnace of 10 tons. *Sunshine* and *North Star* were sent up the east coast of Greenland while Davis himself, with the other two ships, proceeded up the Davis Strait. He found the mosquitoes troublesome but the Eskimos friendly. *North Star* was lost and *Mermaid* was sent home because of sickness. Davis, in *Moonshine*, sailed along the coast of Labrador and caught and salted cod, but the voyage lost money and the western merchants withdrew their support.

In 1587 Davis sailed once more with three vessels. Two of them went fishing and returned home after sixteen days on the grounds but Davis, in his own ship, *Sunshine*, sailed north to the record latitude of 72°12′N.

On this third voyage Davis kept a traverse book which was an improvement on earlier systems and established the form for entering the necessary information in the log book. He did much else to advance navigational practice and was one of the developers of the back staff, which replaced the cross staff for observing the height of the sun. The back staff was more accurate than its forerunners, and easier to use since the sun did not have to be looked at directly. As genial and considerate as he was honest and conscientious, Davis was a commander of steady purpose who had little in common with the contemporary pirate. But he brought home no easy returns and as commercial ventures his voyages were a failure.

Drake arrived back in England in July 1586, shortly after Davis had sailed on his second voyage. On this occasion Sir Francis had proved considerably less successful than had been hoped. The key project which he seems to have had in mind was the capture of Cartagena, as a preliminary to the crossing of the Isthmus and the garrisoning of Panama.[28] However, although he took and sacked both Santo Domingo and Cartagena, he could not hold onto them. He had lost 500 men, largely from malaria, and he no longer had the necessary strength.[29] At the beginning of April the fleet sailed for home and on 19th June Frobisher, in *Primrose*, removed the unrelieved Lane and his colonists from Roanoke. Sugar cane and banana plants had been introduced to the colony from Puerto Rico, and Thomas Hariot had reported that flax, hemp, timber products and other exports (including the gum of the native sassafras, a slender, aromatic tree, which it was thought might help patients suffering from syphilis) might be produced in America, but further supplies and settlement were essential for success.[30] Lane brought with him back to England the first tobacco and Raleigh introduced the custom of smoking. Raleigh also planted the first European potato on his estate near Cork.[31]

As it turned out, it was unfortunate that Lane decided to leave with Frobisher, for a supply ship arrived shortly afterwards and this was but a forerunner of a large expedition for which Grenville had made preparations in Bideford. This expedition, comprising two large vessels and four or five smaller ones, the total force numbering some 400 men, had probably sailed in early May. The ships took prizes on the outward voyage and arrived at Roanoke about a fortnight after the supply ship had departed. When he discovered that Lane and the colonists had left, Grenville took the half measure of leaving behind only fifteen to eighteen men with supplies which might last for two years. Grenville arrived home shortly after Drake, having taken a further prize on the way but also losing thirty-four men through sickness.[32]

The week before Drake's return home in July Thomas Cavendish had sailed from Plymouth. The provision for this venture, which was to achieve the third circumnavigation of the world, was modest, comprising

Cavendish's own ship, the 120-ton *Desire*, and two further vessels of 60 and 40 tons. The total complement was 123 and the ships were victualled for two years.

In August 1586 John Hawkins put to sea in the hope of intercepting the homecoming East Indian carracks and the treasure ships from the West Indies. By October, however, his fleet of some eighteen ships was back in England, having missed both the Portuguese and the Spanish fleets. The latter alone had brought to Europe gold and other goods worth £2.5 million. One of the serious economic problems of the time was that Spanish bullion was creating inflation and ships were becoming more expensive to maintain at sea. Sailor's pay, which Henry VIII had raised from 5s to 6s 8d a month in the last war of his reign, now had to be raised to 10s a month.[33]

In 1587, 'intending to persevere in the planting of his country of Virginia',[34] Raleigh sent out a new contingent of colonists, comprising some 100 men and 17 women under John White as governor, White sailing as admiral in *Lion*, with Simón Fernandez as master. With them they had a flyboat and a pinnace. Before Grenville's return it had been intended that White's colony would supplement Lane's community on Roanoke Island with a second settlement further north which was to establish a city of Raleigh on Chesapeake Bay.[35] After Grenville's return it was decided to reinforce the small community that he had left behind him but, on arrival, with the exception of the bones of one of them, they found no trace of these men. However, a further 110 settlers were left on Roanoke Island, each of whom had been promised 500 acres of land, and on 18th August a granddaughter, christened Virginia Dare, was born to White in the New World.

Having gathered 'all the corn [maize], peas, pumpions and tobacco that we found ripe', White himself returned to England in the flyboat with the task of finding and speeding further supplies, but this task proved more than he could achieve, and the Roanoke colony was doomed. Raleigh and his backers had probably laid out about £30,000 and, even though some return would have come from privateering, pioneer colonisation was proving an expensive business.

It was privateering which offered the best prospects of a quick profit. In July 1587 Alvaro Flores had sailed for Spain from Havana with over 100 vessels and on board these vessels there is estimated to have been some £19 millions-worth of plate, jewels and merchandise.[36] This fleet arrived safely in Europe but by the time White returned from Roanoke the picture at home was dominated by Drake's attack on Cadiz. By 1587, the year in which Mary Queen of Scots was executed, Philip II, now old and

Fig. 1. SEAFARERS' INCOMES, 1375–1987, AT 1988 PRICES

Average annual peacetime incomes for deepsea seafarers at 1988 prices; in addition food is supplied at sea throughout. Broadly speaking, seafarers' earnings appear to have increased 15-fold in real terms since late medieval times.

DATE	AB	NOTES	MASTER	NOTES
	1988 PRICES £S PER ANNUM	CONTEMPORARY RATES	1988 PRICES £S PER ANNUM	CONTEMPORARY RATES
1375	680	2d.–3d. a day. Six months work a year assumed.	1400	6d. a day. Six months work a year assumed.
1500	680	Henry VII paid 1s. a week to shipkeepers and 1s. 3d. a week on active service. Six months work a year assumed. Victualling was said to cost as much as pay.	1750	Henry VII paid 3s. 4d. a week plus victuals. Six months work a year assumed.
1585	725	Sir John Hawkins' figure of £6. 10s. p.a.	2900	Sir John Hawkins' figure of £26. 1s. 8d. p.a.
1650	900	24s. a month. Twice this figure in wartime.	3000	c. £60 p.a. plus perquisites. Twice this figure in East Indiaman or Levanter plus perquisites.
1750	900	c. £14 p.a. Three times this figure in wartime.	4500	c. £72 p.a. Twice this figure in East Indiaman plus perquisites.
1800	800	c. £18 p.a. (£21 p.a. in East Indiaman). Perhaps 6 times this figure in a slaver in wartime.	4500	But the master of an East Indiaman could earn £4–5000 per voyage in wartime (say £100–120,000 at 1988 prices). However, he 'bought' his ship for £8–10,000. A packet service captain received £104 p.a. basic but might make this up to £1000 p.a. (= £2500–24,000 at 1988 prices).
1815	850	c. £33 p.a. 35s. a month in Far East trade; 55s. to United States; 60s. to Baltic.		
1860	1100	45s. a month in Far East trade; 60s. to United States; 50s. to Baltic.	4000	Master in Baltic trade £84 p.a. basic, but a crack clipper master might earn £1000 p.a. (£30,000 at 1988 prices).

1890	1200	AB 50s. and fireman 55s. per month.	8000	£180 p.a. foreign-going; £240 p.a. Black Sea; £300 p.a. Far East.
1906	1600	AB £3 per month in sail and £4 per month in steam.		
1910	2500	AB £5. 10s. per month (cargo); £6 p.m. (passenger); £7 p.m. (coast).	10,000	Master of a 4000-ton steamer £264 p.a.
1916	2350	AB £8. 10s. per month; fireman £10 p.m. Wartime inflation accounts for fall.		
1925	2600	AB £10 per month.		
1932	3800	AB £9. 2s. per month. Deflation 1925–32 accounts for rise in real income.	10,200	Master of a 10,000-ton steamer £288 p.a.
1939	3600	£9. 12s. 6d. per month basic.		
1943	5000	£24 per month including war risk bonus.		
1947	4200	£24 per month after 4 years. Excludes overtime.		
1962	4200	£44. 10s. p.m. for AB with seniority pay. Excludes overtime.	13,300	£1680 p.a. = masters' basic income on average vessel.
1975	5600 (basic) 10,200 (with overtime)	£35. 05 per week (basic); £63. 22 p.w. (average earnings); 52 days leave a year.	28,000	£9214 average earnings; 122 days leave a year.
1979	5000 (basic) 9500 (with overtime)	£50.90 p.w. (basic); £97.43 p.w. (average earnings); 60 days leave a year.	23,500	£12,433 average earnings; 131 days leave a year.
1987	5300 (basic) 10,650 (with overtime)	£95.00 p.w. (basic); £191.19 p.w. (average earnings); 68 days leave a year.	27,000	£25,000 + 145 days leave a year.

(*Sources:* Sir John Hawkins; M. Oppenheim, *A History of the Administration of the Royal Navy* . . .; G. V. Scammell, 'Manning the English Merchant Service in the Sixteenth Century'; J. Press, 'Wages in the merchant navy, 1815–54'; General Council of British Shipping for 1975, 1979 and 1987. Other sources are indicated in the text.)

desperate, had decided to defeat the English fleet and perhaps invade Kent. Elizabeth despatched Drake to disrupt his preparations.

Drake had sailed on 2nd April in command of 23 vessels, inclusive of 4 galleons and 2 pinnaces belonging to the Queen, the venture being financed on a joint-stock basis. In Cadiz harbour Drake destroyed 37 ships by his own account and 24 according to the Spaniards.[37] Whatever the true figure, the blow to the gathering Armada was considerable. Later, off the Azores, he captured the great carrack *San Felipe*, homeward bound from the Indian Ocean and laden with luxury goods worth £114,000, more than double the cost of Drake's whole expedition. Drake's total haul for the voyage amounted to £140,000 (nearly £11 million in 1988 prices), of which the Queen took £40,000, the London merchants £40,000 and Drake £17,000, the remainder going to other adventurers.[38] From these amounts expenses had to be deducted but the profit remained immense.

By this time privateering had become of considerable economic significance, as significant in Elizabeth I's economy as automobile production in Elizabeth II's. If £50,000 is taken as the proceeds of Grenville's West Indian prizes, inclusive of *Santa Maria*, in the voyage of 1585, the division of the spoils would be: £2500 in cash to the Customs; £5000 in kind (one-tenth) to the Admiral; about £14,000 to be divided among the crews; about £14,000 to the owners; and £14,000 to the victuallers. To keep the seven vessels at sea for six months would have cost £3–4000 and, if only one pinnace were lost, the capital loss would not exceed £200 out of an investment in ships of some £2000. The hired ships would need to be repaired and made good at some unknown cost, probably not exceeding £500, and wages and stores for those left with Ralph Lane might have cost from £3–5000. The total investment might thus be of the order of £7–10,000 and the adventurers, if owners and victuallers formed a single syndicate, as seems likely, might clear a profit of £20,000 or some 200 per cent.[39] The commander of such an expedition could purloin some of the most valuable booty and minimise his receipts, making more for himself and less for his backers. This analysis, of course, is of a profitable expedition and by no means every expedition was as profitable as this one.

Other figures are available which indicate the value of certain branches of what may be described as legitimate trade. The Russia Company in 1587, for example, officially imported goods valued at £13,530.13s.4d, though the true value was perhaps twice this sum.[40] Imports from Morocco in 1588 were officially valued at £36,573 and had increased more than three-fold in twenty years.[41] In 1589 Sir Edward Holmden, later Master of the Grocers Company, imported goods from Venice and Zante which were officially valued at £8069 and he was said to be responsible for more than half the total imports from those areas.[42] Despite the embargo, trade to the Guinea coast continued and the first Guinea Company, recognised by Don Antonio, pretender to the Portuguese throne (deemed by Elizabeth to be King of Portugal), was established in 1588. This trade, however, was not considerable.

The traditional short sea trades to the Continent were worth, perhaps, £1 million a year. From the figures above, it would appear that the value of the long-distance trades did not yet exceed £100,000 a year. While this is twice the value of Grenville's haul, it is considerably less than the value of the goods which Drake secured from the *San Felipe*.

Invasion from Spain had been expected in England before Drake sailed in 1587, but reprisals became ever more imminent after his success and on 9th October orders were issued to prevent shipping in English ports from sailing. This stopped Grenville from sending seven or eight ships to Roanoke, for the authorities decreed that they might be required at home for the purposes of defence. Nevertheless, in April 1588 two small vessels, *Brave*, a bark of 30 tons, and *Roe*, a pinnace of 25 tons, left Bideford with instructions from Grenville to make a call at the colony, but Captain Arthur Facy of *Brave* was intent on privateering or piracy and the proposed call was abandoned by both vessels. There were other privateering voyages in 1588 but no ships put in at Roanoke and both Grenville and Raleigh proved to have other preoccupations.[43]

In Elizabeth I's reign up to 1588, 29 new ships of war had been built and the other royal ships had been re-modelled, the high upper works and decks being cut down and the ships made much lower in accordance with new designs prepared by such leading shipwrights as Peter Pett and Matthew Baker. The Duke of Medina Sidonia, who led the Spanish Armada, and his officers were surprised by the sailing qualities of these English galleons. They were also unprepared for the quality of their armament. By Elizabeth's reign England was in the forefront of the iron armaments industry with eight foundries producing guns famous for their cheapness and reliability.[44] To fire these guns, well-mounted on shipboard carriages unlike some of the Spanish heavy pieces, the English also had better gunners. Both in weight of broadside, effective ship to ship, and in speed and manoeuvrability, particularly to windward, the English were superior to the Spaniards and could thus dictate the tactics of any sea-battle.[45]

Not everything was perfect, of course, for there was much chicanery. Of Sir William Winter's ships, the *Edward* had been wholly and *Mary Fortune* mainly built of government timber, and the Queen and her subjects paid about twice what they should have done for the royal ships. These royal ships were by now easily distinguished from ordinary merchantmen, and had become the type of ship from which all major western warships were derived until the middle of the 19th century. Captains took bribes to let men off service, and kept back arms and wages; pursers stole provisions and made false entries; cooks sold victuals; and boatswains removed rigging and cordage.[46] Provisioning remained poor and, as in the stormy summer of 1588, ships had to keep at sea for long periods after they had exhausted their supplies. Even so, the English sailor was better fed than the Spaniard, and John Hawkins, who was knighted by Howard, together with Martin Frobisher and others, in the course of the running battle with the Armada, increased the proficiency of the fighting fleet by reducing the number in the crew. Hawkins' ratio for warships was one sailor to two tons of shipping. In merchantmen it might be as low as one sailor to eight tons, or even thirteen tons, of shipping,[47] but before 1582 warships had carried one sailor for every 1.5 tons of shipping.

The Portuguese and Spanish merchant fleets together were said to total 250,000 tons, four times that of the English fleet.[48] Nevertheless, to the Armada of 128 ships England was able to oppose 197 ships, though the total English tonnage was far smaller, and the number of men involved on the Spanish side, at nearly 30,000, was roughly twice the number of Englishmen.[49]

Part of the Armada was sighted off the Scilly Isles on 29th July 1588 and there was action off Portland on 2nd August. Both fleets were becalmed off the Sussex Downs on 5th August and they anchored off the Calais roads the following day. Medina Sidonia's ships were in an exposed and dangerous position, and when the fleet set sail it spread out for miles downwind far beyond Calais. Drake caught up with the Admiral off Gravelines on 8th August and the English fleet attacked *San Martin*, Medina Sidonia's flagship. With the wind in the west and shoals between Dunkirk and Ostend to the south, Medina Sidonia could only gather up his force and continue sailing northwards. The decisive battle had been won though the English did not realise it and lacked the ammunition to finish the job. Off the Scottish coast the English broke off the action and demoralised groups of the Armada were driven to and fro by storms in the north Atlantic.[50]

Of the 30,000 who set out from Lisbon only some 10,000 returned to Spain, and not all of these survived for long. Probably no more than 1500 died in battle; more than half perished through sickness, starvation and disease; a further 6000 died in shipwrecks; and another 1000 appear to have been murdered in Ireland. So far as the English were concerned, fewer than 100 men died in battle, though another 6 or 7000 may have died from disease.[51] Philip lost almost half his fleet if ships seriously damaged are included, most of these losses being due to the hazards of the sea. The English lost no ships and the ships suffered little damage.[52]

Thomas Cavendish returned home from his circumnavigation of the world to find that the great battle with Spain had been fought and won. It had cost Elizabeth £160,000 and the war chest of £300,000 amassed by Lord Burghley now stood empty. But the cost to Philip of Spain was nearer £3 million[53] and, although the war was to continue until 1604, Spanish power had received a mortal blow.

Notes

1. T. Willan, *Studies in Elizabethan Foreign Trade* (1959), Manchester, pp. 5–8.
2. T. Willan, *The Early History of the Russia Company* (1956), Manchester, p. 180.
3. M. Epstein, *The Early History of the Levant Company* (1908), London, p. 18n.
4. Epstein, *op. cit.*, p. 14.
5. *Further English Voyages to Spanish America, 1583–1594* (1951), London, p. xviii.
6. F. E. Dyer, *The Life of Admiral Sir John Narborough* (1931), London, p. 134.
7. Willan (1956), *op. cit.*, p. 181.
8. H. Gilbert, *The Voyages and Colonising Enterprises of Sir Humphrey Gilbert* (1940), London (The Hakluyt Society), pp. 351–4.
9. *Ib.*, p. 72.
10. K. R. Andrews, *Trade, Plunder and Settlement* (1984), Cambridge, p. 195.
11. Gilbert, *op. cit.*, p. 85. *See also* G. T. Gell, *English Enterprise in Newfoundland 1577–1660* (1969), Toronto.
12. Gilbert, *op. cit.*, pp. 401–2 and p. 86.
13. *Ib.*, p. 399.
14. *Ib.*, pp. 401–2.
15. Willan (1959), *op. cit.*, p. 9.
16. Willan (1956), *op. cit.*, p. 165.
17. *Ib.*, p. 179.
18. D. B. Quinn & A. N. Ryan, *England's Sea Empire, 1550–1642* (1983), London, p. 145.
19. Willan (1959), *op. cit.*, pp. 81–2.
20. Gilbert, *op. cit.*, p. 99.
21. D. B. Quinn (ed), *The Roanoke Voyages 1584–1590*, Vol. I (1955), London (The Hakluyt Society), p. 6.
22. Willan (1959), *op. cit.*, p. 185.
23. *Further English Voyages to Spanish America, 1583–1594* (1951), London, p. xxxv, p. 227.
24. Quinn, *op. cit.*, pp. 120–1.
25. A. Rowse, *The Expansion of Elizabethan England* (1955), London, p. 260.
26. Quinn, *op. cit.*, pp. 159–72.
27. J. Davis, *The Voyages and Works of John Davis, The Navigator* (1880), London (The Hakluyt Society), p. xi. ff.

28. Quinn, *op. cit.*, pp. 250–1.
29. J. Keevil, *Medicine and the Navy, Vol. I, 1200–1649* (1957), London, p. 94.
30. Quinn, *op. cit.*, p. 325.
31. W. Raleigh, *The Discovery of the Large, Rich and Beautiful Empire of Guiana* (1595), London (The Hakluyt Society, 1848), p. xxxii.
32. Quinn, *op. cit.*, p. 469.
33. M. Oppenheim, *A History of the Administration of the Royal Navy* ... (1896, reprinted 1988), London, p. 134.
34. R. Hakluyt, *The Principal Navigation, Voyages, Traffiques and Discoveries of the English Nation*, Vol. VI (1927), London, pp. 196ff.
35. Quinn, *op. cit.*, p. 497.
36. *Further English Voyages to Spanish America, 1583–1594* (1951), London, p. xviii.
37. J. Williamson, *The Age of Drake* (1952), London, p. 298.
38. *Ib.*, p. 302.
39. K. R. Andrews, *Elizabethan Privateering* (1964), Cambridge, pp. 73–4, pp. 124–49, p. 192.
40. Willan (1956), *op. cit.*, p. 182.
41. Willan (1959), *op. cit.*, p. 278.
42. *Ib.*, pp. 193–4.
43. Quinn, *op. cit.*, p. 554.
44. P. Padfield, *Armada* (1988), London, p. 89.
45. T. Glasgow, Jr, 'Gorga's Seafight' (1973), MM, Vol. 59, No. 2, pp. 180–1.
46. Rowse, *op. cit.*, p. 254.
47. G. V. Scammell, 'Manning the English Merchant Service in the Sixteenth Century' (1970), MM, Vol. 56, No. 2, pp. 131–2.
48. G. Jackson, *The History and Archaeology of Ports* (1903), Kingswood, Tadworth, Surrey, p. 22.
49. G. V. Scammell, *The World Encompassed: The first European marine empires* (1981), London, p. 469; D. A. Thomas, *The Illustrated Armada Book* (1988), London, p. 92; p. 210.
50. Padfield, *op. cit.*, pp. 143–73.
51. Thomas, *op. cit.*, pp. 210–11.
52. Padfield, *op. cit.*, p. 191.
53. Andrews (1984), *op. cit.*, p. 231.

9

The East at Last (1588–1603)

In 1589, the year in which the second William Hawkins died and Sir John Hawkins was granted a year's leave from his duties as Treasurer of the Navy, Richard Hakluyt the younger published the first edition of *The Principal Navigations, Voyages, Traffiques and Discoveries of the English nation, made by Sea or over Land to the most remote and farthest distant Quarters of the earth at any time within the compass of these 1500 years*. It was a seminal work, and Hakluyt's lectures, publications and advice made him as politically influential in promoting overseas expansion as Queen Elizabeth's closest counsellors.

The Spaniards already maintained a reader in navigation who instructed and examined all those who commanded ships to the Indies. Hakluyt saw the need for a nautical college or university, and Drake offered to put up half the cost of a lecturer's salary, but Hakluyt in this respect was before his time. Other than in the fields of naval architecture and marine engineering, it was not until well after World War II that the British merchant navy had any dealings with universities or universities with the merchant navy.

Hakluyt was more successful in achieving his other aims. In his *Voyages* are printed many papers of careful instruction for factors and merchants going abroad, one of them by his cousin and namesake, *Remembrances for a Factor at Constantinople*, which contains a reasoned defence of the practical study of birds and beasts, flowers and trees, and their properties and uses. 'If this care had not been heretofore in our ancestors', wrote Richard Hakluyt the elder, 'then had our life been savage now; for then we had not had wheat nor rye, peas nor beans, barley nor oats, pear nor apple, vine nor many other profitable and pleasant plants, bull nor cow, sheep nor swine, horse nor mare, cock nor hen, nor a number of other things that we enjoy, without which our life were to be said barbarous: for these things and a thousand that we use more the first inhabitors of this Island found not here.'[1] By way of further example he cites the latest importations of strange commodities.

In the same year, 1589, *The marchants avizo* was written for the guidance of factors, who were recommended to 'be not greedy nor in lust after that which is both displeasant unto God, hurtful to thy body, an enemy to thy soul, and a shortener of thy life, which is Wine, Wealth and Women'. With sound 16th-century philosophy it was strongly implied that godliness was a valuable aid to material prosperity. The work included instruction in letter-writing (recommending brevity), bills of lading, bills of exchange and policies of assurance. The first letter announced, appropriately enough, that the ship in which the factor was travelling had been driven into the wrong port.[2]

Although English exports made some recovery towards the end of the 16th century, commerce-raiding rather than commerce itself became, for a time, the chief way in which the English endeavoured to accumulate capital. In the three years following the defeat of the Armada at least 236 English vessels went privateering, most of them merchantmen converted for this purpose, and at least 299 prizes, together worth about £400,000, were captured. The value of prizes thus exceeded £100,000 a year and was equivalent to or in excess of the pre-war trade with Iberia. Privateering accounted, perhaps, for 10–15 per cent of England's total imports.[3] The capital accumulated by such London merchants as Sir John Watts, Sir Thomas Myddelton and Paul Bayning played no small part in the subsequent launching of the East India Company and the foundation of England's first American colonies. Not all privateering expeditions succeeded in capturing a Portuguese carrack loaded with treasure, but an analysis of 271 such expeditions made between 1589 and 1591 suggests that an average profit of at least 60 per cent was made on the fixed capital invested.[4] For a year or two the value of captured prizes may have amounted to as much as four per cent of the Elizabethan national income. On the other hand, the war took its toll of ships, legitimate trade and seamen's lives and much of the economic gain may have been illusory. Social costs seldom enter into the calculations of individual businessmen. The seaman's life aboard a privateer was usually nasty, brutish and short, and the drunken sailor, 'stinking of pitch and poor-john' (stockfish) as Beaumont and Fletcher described him, was already a byword. Nevertheless, privateering was popular with many seamen, evoking much crude patriotism, mixed with godliness and greed.

Innumerable expeditions, great and small, sailed from England: small men and local gentry, leading London merchants, influential courtiers and the Queen herself, all invested in privateering ventures. In 1589 the Privy Council issued a formal decree justifying the confiscation of any ship which carried munitions or victuals to the enemy, and all vessels passing through the English Channel were liable to be stopped unless they could show a pass from the Lord Admiral. In July Norris and Drake intercepted off the mouth of the Tagus a convoy of some sixty Hansa ships laden with goods from the Baltic.[5] As a riposte to the attack by the Armada it was not very effective, but it cost the Hanseatic cities dear in terms of men and capital, and Drake brought back 150 ordnance while his prizes sold for £30,000. Over the next two years sugar worth at least £100,000 was captured by English privateers and sugar was cheaper in London than it was in the West Indies. This prize sugar created a new consumption habit.

In 1589 a number of ventures were also made overseas to the West Indies, Brazil and further south, including John Chidley's expedition which was intended to pass into the Pacific Ocean, though only two ships reached the Magellan Straits, Chidley died, and very few of his company survived to reach home again.

John Davis was this year at sea, not in the north-west, but with the Earl of Cumberland's squadron – which included *Victory*, one of the royal ships – off the Azores. They had an unenviable time, being kept from home by contrary winds and suffering severe deprivation until the end of the year. They were so short of water that

> raindrops were so carefully saved, that so near as we could, not one was lost in all our ship ... Some licked with their tongues (like dogs) the boards under foot, the sides, rails and masts of the ship. Others that were more ingenious, fastened girdles or ropes about the masts, daubing tallow betwixt them and the mast (that the rain might not run down between), in such sort that those ropes or girdles hanging lower on the one side than on the other, a spout of leather was fastened to the lowest part of them that all the raindrops that came running down the mast might meet together at that place and there be received.[6]

No more than five ships came from St Nicholas in 1589, and only three in 1591. Masts, tar and hemp would not bear the freight costs and wax imports were declining with the decay of the Russian woods from which they came. Cordage and cables, together with oil, skins and high quality furs were the main imports, though the Company was also happy to receive about forty tons of good quality caviare a year, some of which was re-exported to Turkey where it was regarded as an aphrodisiac.

In 1590 it was reported that the Levant or Turkey Company had employed nineteen ships in five years and made twenty-seven voyages but less than £12,000 had been paid in customs. 'Factories' were established at Constantinople, Smyrna and Aleppo, and English cloth was exchanged for currants, malmsey and raw cotton,[7] but the ships were always at hazard. In 1590, in the Straits of Gibraltar, ten of the homeward-bound ships were attacked by Spanish galleys each of which was strongly armed and manned by crews numbering 300. After a stiff fight lasting six hours all the galleys were put to flight badly damaged and with the loss of many men, the English apparently suffering no losses at all.[8]

Stouter and larger vessels had had to be built for this trade, which by 1600 had expanded to employ over 1000 sailors, and in the 1590s there was a boom in the construction of large ships. Raleigh remarks upon the great improvement in English shipbuilding which he had witnessed, instancing among other innovations the chain pump, brought into use by Hawkins, 'which takes up twice as much water as the ordinary did'. In 1590 Hawkins had the cookroom of his flagship *Mary Rose* removed from the hold to the upper deck, 'as well for the better stowing of her victuals as also for better preserving her whole company in health during that voyage being bound to the southwards'. The normal practice had been to build a hearth of some fifty bricks in the hold above the wet ballast to reduce the risk of fire, and one result was that the ballast became contaminated and was a health hazard. This, however was an isolated change and cookrooms or galleys were still to be found in the hold in the 18th century. A patent log was invented by Humphrey Cole at this time but it does not appear to have superseded the ordinary log line. Other improvements were more readily adopted, a better method of striking topmasts, for example, and a system of sheathing by double planks having a layer of pitch and oakum or hemp between them.[9] Tackle for handling anchors improved and anchors increased in weight and cables in length relative to the size of ships. Raleigh's *Ark Royal,* 800 tons, had three anchors at the bow, each one ton in weight, together with a sheet anchor of 1.1 tons, her cables being 15 and 17 inches in circumference and 100 fathoms in length. Sanitary arrangements were rudimentary, usually consisting of open boxes slung over the rail, precarious perches which sailors were reluctant to use in bad weather.[10]

The use of more highly developed oceanic vessels, combined with high standards of seamanship, led to an extended use of English vessels in the Mediterranean, and they were able to offer such competitive freight rates that on occasion even the Venetians employed them.[11] Barbary corsairs were a constant threat and were often bought off with gifts amounting in all to as much as £2000 a year,[12] though there were also English piracies against the Papists, including French ships and those from Ragusa, the modern Dubrovnik, some of whose ships had been commandeered for the Armada. The net effect of these operations was to bring down the price of Eastern commodities in England and English taste grew more refined.

The Guinea Company made a lucrative venture in 1590, exchanging linen and woollen goods, ironware, glass beads and hawks' bells for ivory and palm-oil, but in all this time the colony on Roanoke Island had not been revisited. In the autumn after the defeat of the Armada Raleigh and Grenville were busy elsewhere, convoying troops to Ireland and keeping guard at the western approaches. After that they went to Ireland to inspect their properties in Munster. Upon his return to England Raleigh put under way a further attempt to relieve the Roanoke settlement, having made a tripartite agreement between himself, White and others associated with the City of Raleigh venture, and Thomas Smythe who headed a group of nineteen business associates. The greatest of the privateering entrepreneurs, John Watts, prepared *Hopewell* (140 tons), *Little John* (100 tons) and *John Evangelist*, a pinnace, and they received permission to sail provided they called at Roanoke. White sailed in *Hopewell*. Two other vessels, *Moonlight* (80 tons) and *Conclude*, a pinnace, also intended to make the call. When the promised call was made at Roanoke, however, it was found that the settlers had left and, as far as could be judged from the evidence, they had left voluntarily.[13] This proved to be the end of English colonisation for more than a decade.

Despite a number of prizes, 1590 was a disappointing year in the campaign at sea. In June, Frobisher had gone with a squadron to the Azores, and Hawkins had made for the Spanish coast, but English plans for a blockade came to nothing, and the Spanish fleet was not intercepted. On his own return from sea in 1590 Drake, whose father had been an ardent lay preacher, wrote to Burghley that he had no good news to report: 'And thus God's infallible word is performed, in that the Holy Ghost said, Paul doth plant, Apollos doth water, but God giveth the increase; for I may boldly say unto your lordship I was very well provided, both of shipping, victual, furniture and a quiet and sufficient company; but seeing this hath been the good pleasure of God, I do content myself and hold all to come for the best.' Elizabeth was neither pleased nor impressed. 'God's death!' she exclaimed. 'This fool went out a soldier and is come home a divine.'[14]

It was in this year that Drake, Hawkins and others set up the Chatham Chest, a fund for the relief of sick and aged mariners, which functioned well to begin with though it afterwards fell victim to corruption. To finance this first venture in national insurance, sixpence a month was deducted from the wages of the able seamen serving in the fleet. Two years later Hawkins was to found at his own expense an almshouse for 'poor decayed' mariners and shipwrights which was called Sir John Hawkins' Hospital, a foundation which still survives.

In 1591 the privateers set sail once more, Raleigh joining John Watts' syndicate. The prizes which this syndicate brought home were officially valued at £31,380, and £14,740 (less some £2500 net costs) was divided as profit among the investors. It was of this result that Raleigh wrote contemptuously, 'A small return, we might have gotten more to have sent them a-fishing'.[15]

Grenville sailed as second in command of a squadron of about fifteen vessels sent to intercept a Spanish treasure fleet off the Azores. When fifty-three Spanish vessels approached to protect their treasure ships, the English retreated, but Grenville was delayed and cut off. Undaunted, he attempted to run his ship, *Revenge*, through the Spanish line. The epic story has been told often, and is celebrated in verse. After fifteen hours of hand-to-hand combat against fifteen Spanish galleons and a force of 5000 men, the *Revenge*, with a crew of 190, was captured, and a few days later the wounded Grenville died on board the Spanish flagship. *Revenge* proved to be the only royal ship lost during the entire course of the war with Spain.

On 26th August, a fortnight before Grenville's last fight, Thomas Cavendish, into whose family Hakluyt had married, sailed again from Plymouth for the South Seas with John Davis as his second-in-command, hoping to be at least as successful as he had been in his circumnavigation. His fleet consisted of the galleon *Leicester, Roebuck, Desire* (the ship in which he had sailed round the world), *Black Pinnace* and the bark *Daintie* owned by Davis and Adrian Gilbert, the total force numbering about 400 men. He intended to return to the East Indies by way of the Magellan Straits and to explore the north Pacific once more for a western entrance to a north-west passage. However, the ships were kept for some weeks in the doldrums and, with no access to fresh food, scurvy became rampant. In April 1592 they were still within the Magellan Straits with men dying of cold and hunger. All the ships except *Desire* were lost without trace and Cavendish with them. Aboard *Desire,* Davis managed to check the scurvy with scurvy grass gathered at Port Desire in Patagonia.[16] He also discovered the still disputed Falkland Islands, which were rediscovered the following year by Richard Hawkins. Of those who sailed in *Desire* only eighteen of seventy-six survived to reach home, and as the ship approached the Irish Sea only five men were capable of work. The ship was run ashore in Bantry Bay on 11th June 1593.

Equally unfortunate was James Lancaster's voyage of 1591, also intended for the East Indies but terminating disastrously. The narrative by Edmund Barker has a sufficiently descriptive sub-title:

A voyage with three tall ships – the *Penelope*, Admiral; the *Merchant Royal*, Vice-Admiral; and the *Edward Bonaventure*, Rear-Admiral – to the East Indies; by the Cape of Buona Speranza, to Quitangone, near Mozambique, to the Isles of Comoro and Zanzibar, on the backside of Africa, and beyond Cape Comori in India, to the Isles of Nicubar and of Gomes Pulo, within two leagues of Sumatra, to the Islands of Pulo Pinaom, and thence to the mainland of Malacca, begun by Mr George Raymond in the year 1591, and performed by Mr James Lancaster, and written from the mouth of Edmund Barker, of Ipswich, his lieutenant, in said voyage, by Mr Richard Hakluyt.

Those who survived were brought home from the West Indies by a French ship, landing in Europe in May 1594. Lancaster had accumulated a fund of useful knowledge which was to prove of great value to the East India Company a few years later.[17] For the moment, however, it was largely through the Levant Company that England imported eastern products and its monopoly was extended in 1592 to the overland route to India as well as to the whole of the eastern Mediterranean.

Raleigh fell from favour in 1592 when the birth of a son betrayed to the Queen his marriage to Elizabeth Throckmorton, and he and his wife were imprisoned in the Tower of London. He bought their release with part of his share of the profits from a privateering voyage in which he had invested, but he never regained his ascendancy at court.

The privateering voyage from which Raleigh made enough to secure his release – as distinct from his disappointing ventures of the previous year – was one on which Sir John Borough captured the fabulously rich Portuguese carrack *Madre de Dios*, said to be the largest ship afloat, with a booty worth perhaps £500,000, though so much disappeared after her capture that a mere £140,000 remained for the investors. Of this latter total the Queen, who was a shareholder to the extent of some 10 per cent, eventually took about half.[18] Inspired by this capture, and no doubt financed by some of the profits made, Richard Hawkins, son of Sir John, planned a voyage into the South Seas. He was not the leader his father had been, but he was a man of considerable intellect and he provided a fascinating account of his adventures and his reflections upon them.

Hawkins sailed from Plymouth on 12th June 1593 aboard the *Dainty* (300 tons), a vessel which Queen Elizabeth had renamed since she did not like its original name, *Repentance*. In company with him were *Hawk* and *Fancy*. For his 164 men he had to search lodgings and ale-houses

for some would be ever taking their leave and never depart: some drink themselves so drunk that except they were carried aboard, they of themselves were not able to go one step; others, knowing the necessity of the time, feigned themselves sick; others to be indebted to their hosts, and forced me to ransom

> them, one his chest, another his sword, another his shirts, another his card and instruments for sea; and others, to benefit themselves of the imprest [advance of wages] given them, absented themselves, making a lewd living in deceiving all whose money they could lay hold of, which is a scandal too rife among our seamen.

It took him, his friends and the justices of the peace two days to round up his crews.[19]

To aid the keeping of good discipline at sea, Hawkins decreed that in every ship there should be a 'palmer of ferula' to be kept by someone who had been caught swearing. 'He who had the palmer should give to every other that he took swearing, in the palm of the hand, a palmada with it, and the ferula. And whosoever at the time of evening or morning prayer was found to have the palmer should have three blows given him by the captain or master; and that he should be still bound to free himself by taking another or else to run in danger of continuing the penalty.' It seems unlikely but within three days, apparently, no oaths were to be heard.[20]

For wear when night watches were kept, Hawkins provided one cloak or 'rug-gown' for every two men, and these cloaks, soaked in water or urine, were to be used to dowse a fire, for Hawkins was very conscious of the great danger of fire on board.[21]

In Hawkins' view, after teaching the Dutch and others the value of good discipline at sea, the English had been overtaken by those who had learned from them. The Spaniards sought to imitate English methods, but they did not look after their sailors – mostly 'Allmaynes, Flemmings, or strangers' – and subjected them to military despotism.[22]

One trouble with the English was that too often the command of a vessel was given to inexperienced friends or relatives. The good commander, suggested Hawkins, should be possessed of 'a sharp wit, a good sea business, knowledge in navigation' and experience of command.[23] On man management he commented:

> My meaning is not that the captain or governor should be tied to the actual toil, or intermeddle with all officers, for that were to bind him to impossibilities, to diminish and abuse his authority, and to deprive the other officers of their esteems, and of that that belongeth to them, which were a great absurdity; but my opinion is that he should be more than superficially instructed and practised in the employments. Yea, I am verily persuaded that the more absolute authority any commander giveth to his under officers, being worth of it, the sweeter is the command and the more respected and beloved the commander.

Except in an emergency situation, he suggests that orders should be passed by way of the officers and that they should be given the orders, preferably written down, in confidence unless the occasion required a public announcement.[24]

For coastal navigation, Hawkins pointed out, it was important that the mariner should know how 'to cast his tides, and to know how they set from point to point, with the difference of these in the Channel from those on shore'. Experience had taught him that by attention to such detail a vessel working down Channel might gain great advantage.[25]

Before he sailed, Richard Hawkins had learned of the failure and death of Cavendish, but nothing had been heard of Davis, who had reached Bantry Bay the day before. His account of his own voyage is full of interesting observations. He comments that Madeira and the Canaries are fertile and rich in sugar and wine, but that the Cape Verde islands are unhealthy.[26] He describes the plantain as 'very tender like butter, but no conserve is better, nor of a more pleasing taste'; and coconuts are 'of the fashion of a hazel nut' but 'as big as an ordinary bowl'.[27]

Although ocean currents could set a ship off course, Hawkins concluded that faulty navigation, and particularly the inability of sailors to determine longitude, was the major reason why ships coming from India and looking out for the Azores might suddenly sight Spain and vice versa.[28]

Scurvy appeared on board when the vessels were within four degrees of the equator:

> In twenty years since I have used the sea, I dare take upon me to give account of ten thousand men consumed with this disease. That which I have seen most fruitful for this sickness is sour oranges and lemons, and a water which amongst others (for my particular provision) I carried to the sea, called Dr Stevens his water, of which, for that his virtue was not then well known unto me, I carried but little, and it took end quickly, but gave health to those that used it.[29]

When Hawkins arrived in Santos he wrote to the governor in Latin and sent his captain, who spoke a little Spanish, ashore with a piece of crimson velvet and other gifts. He said that he was bound for the East Indies but had been forced to Santos by contrary winds. The governor refused to trade, but allowed him ashore with a flag of truce and sixteen well-armed men to collect 200–300 oranges and lemons, which 'was what we principally sought for', and a few hens. A little later he tells us that he made fresh water from sea water by distilling it.[30]

Hawkins stopped at an island now called Saint Anna Island where he found the herb purslane in great quantity and served it as a salad, with oil and vinegar, as a cure for the scurvy.[31] Even so he lost half his company and he burned the *Hawk*. Later he took a 300-ton Portuguese ship, but released her after taking some of her provisions. In a storm he was deserted by the *Fancy* and comments that the Spaniards would punish such desertion.[32]

In the Magellan Straits Hawkins reports on the bird-life and speculates upon the possibility of the Celts having discovered South America before the Spaniards arrived: the birds

> are of divers sorts, and in great plenty, as penguins, wild ducks, gulls and gannets; of the principal we purposed to make provisions, and those were the penguins, which in Welsh, as I have been informed, signifieth a white head. From which derivation and many other Welsh denominations given by the Indians, or their predecessors, some do infer that America was first peopled with Welshmen, and Montezuma, King, or rather emperor, of Mexico, did recount unto the Spaniards, at their first coming, that his ancestors came from a far country and were white people. Which, conferred with an ancient chronicle that I have read many years since, may be conjectured to be a Prince of Wales, who many hundred years since, with certain ships, sailed to the westwards with intent to make new discoveries. He was never after heard of.[33]

After entering the Pacific, Hawkins reports that the beef began to give out but, preserved in pickle, was still as good as the day they set sail from England – it was well worth the extra expense. In Lima, in the house of his captor Don Beltram de Castro, he also ate pork preserved in the same way which was four years old and which was still good.[34]

After refreshing themselves at an island off Chile, probably Juan Fernandez, Hawkins and his men privateered off Valparaiso. One of his Spanish prisoners confessed that he, the prisoner, had lain in watch with a hundred men ready to catch Hawkins with balsa wood rafts had the English relaxed their watch. Hawkins comments that he feared the enemy less than the local wine, for drunken men were easy prey:

> and though I am not old, in comparison of other ancient men, I can remember Spanish wine rarely to be found in this kingdom. Then hot burning fevers were not known in England, and men lived many more years. But since the Spanish sacks have become common in our taverns, which, for conservation, is mingled with lime in its making, our nation complaineth of calenturas, of the stone, the dropsy, and infinite other diseases, not heard of before this wine came in frequent use, or but very seldom. To confirm which my belief, I have heard one of our learnedst physicians affirm that he thought there died more persons in England of drinking wine and using hot spices in their meats and drinks than of all other diseases.[35]

On leaving the coast of Chile, Hawkins tells us, his men demanded one-third of the gold that had been taken, and this was their due. He regrets that many Elizabethan commanders defrauded their men. 'I have known ships worth two hundred thousand pounds, and better, clean swept of their principal riches, nothing but the bare bulk being left unsacked ... yet all winked at and unpunished.' His father insisted, he went on, that any commander who took a ship should produce the bill of lading and bring it back to England for examination. If it went adrift, prisoners were examined on the subject of the cargo and a captain was punished if he could not render a proper account. 'I am witness', he concludes, 'and avow that this course did redound much to the benefit of the general stock: to the satisfaction of Her Majesty and Council, the justification of his government, and the content of his followers.'[36]

Unfortunately for Hawkins, the Spaniards on the Pacific coast had been alerted by the activities of Drake and Cavendish and were more prepared for action. Between the treasure ports and Panama there was never any bad weather and Hawkins found his opponents had a larger sail area and lighter spars than the *Dainty* so that in any light breeze they could catch him. Six vessels went out from Callao to seek Hawkins to the south and they found him off Cañete in Peru. He escaped on this occasion but a week or two later, in June 1594, with 1300 men against his 75, he was forced to surrender in the Bay of Atacames. When the *Dainty* was taken, the ship was on the point of sinking, Hawkins himself was lying helpless with six wounds, and fewer than twenty of his men were still alive. It was the insubordination of his men that had kept Hawkins in the danger area, but when the battle came they fought for three days against overwhelming odds. Hawkins himself was not set free by the Spaniards until 1602.[37]

While Richard Hawkins was sailing to South America John Davis was engaged in writing *The Seaman's Secrets*, a book which was published in 1594. Its contents were described as follows: 'wherein is taught the three kindes of Sayling, Horizontall, Paradoxall, and sayling upon a great Circle: also an Horizontall Tyde Table for the easie finding of the ebbing and flowing of the Tydes, with a Regiment newly calculated for the Finding of the Declination of the Sunne and many other most necessary rules and instruments not heretofore set forth by any'. Having already greatly improved the back staff, Davis now provided the second original manual of navigation in English. The first, William Bourne's *The Regiment of the Sea*, had appeared in 1577 as a supplement to Richard Eden's translation of a work by Martin Cortes. Davis's object was to furnish a practical guide for the sailor, imparting such scientific knowledge as was necessary for the comprehension of the art of navigation. Davis claimed that in this art the English were not matched by any other nation, and his book ran through eight editions between 1594 and 1647.

In 1594 it is recorded that the searcher of Ipswich inspected the cargo of some shipping bound from London to Hamburg that had put in at Harwich. It was found to consist of merchandise on which duty had not been paid, but for his pains the searcher was threatened with legal action and worse by the owners of the goods who were stated to be men of great wealth, and the searcher had to apply to the Lord Treasurer for support in his detention of the contraband. In such smuggling trade tin was second to none as an export which evaded customs and some three-quarters of the tin mined went abroad, much of it still to the market at Lyons which had been used for some 3000 years and from which it was shipped to Marseilles and other Mediterranean ports.

Over the next few years a number of expeditions in line with those made earlier were despatched to the New World though the efforts made were uncoordinated. In October 1594 Captain James Lancaster, who had been home less than six months, made a voyage with three ships – *Consent* (240 tons), *Solomon* (170 tons) and *Virgin* (60 tons) – and a galley-frigate from London to Olinda in Brazil. He was said to have occupied Pernambuco, the port of Olinda, for thirty days despite its being strongly fortified and manned and despite repeated attacks after he had taken it. He took twenty-nine prizes, including a rich Indian carrack, and brought home no fewer than fifteen ships laden with loot. John Watts and Paul Bayning were among the London merchants who financed this voyage which was described in the official account as 'well governed and prosperous'.[38]

A month later, in November 1594, Robert Dudley, afterwards Earl of Warwick, set out from London with four vessels, apparently fitted out at his own expense. These were *Bear* or *Peregrine* (200–300 tons), *Bear's Whelp* (80 tons) and two small pinnaces, *Earwig* and *Frisking*. On their way down Channel, just past the Needles, they met a Scottish fleet bound from Bordeaux and Dudley was given a hogshead of wine.[39] One motive for the expedition was to capture Spanish prizes but of the four vessels only *Bear* proved to cross the Atlantic, where Dudley laid claim to Trinidad in the Queen's name, though it was not until 1802 that this claim became a reality. Dudley also looked for gold but was forced to admit that 'all is not gold that glittereth'.[40] After taking a prize, he ran up the coast to Florida and Virginia, crossed to the Azores and fought a further Spanish ship, arriving home in May 1595.

In the early spring of 1595 Sir Walter Raleigh, still in disgrace with the Queen, tried to recover his former position by organising another expedition from the west country. The previous year he had sent Captain Jacob Whiddon out to collect useful information and now set out himself to discover the legendary city of Manoa ruled by El Dorado, the gilded one. He arrived in Trinidad only ten days after Dudley had left it, and proceeded to look for Manoa in modern Guyana, from which country he brought home some ore samples. He sold linen to the Spaniards at Puerto de los Hispaniola and intended to call at Virginia but was prevented from so doing by bad weather.

Raleigh hoped that Guyana would prove as rich for the English as Peru had proved for the Spaniards and in consequence let his pen run away with him when he came to write his account of *The Discovery of the Large, Rich and Beautiful Empire of Guiana*.[41] 'Guiana is a country', he asserted, 'that yet hath her maidenhead, never sacked, turned nor wrought, the face of the earth hath not been torn, nor the virtue and salt of the soil spent by manurance, the graves have not been opened for gold, the mines not broken with sledges, nor their images pulled down out of their temples.'[42] But the virgin Queen was not impressed and the intelligence he brought did not arouse the interest he anticipated. Many of his statements were regarded as fabulous and his recommendations regarding possession as chimerical. The failure of Drake and Hawkins in the following year did nothing to increase enthusiasm.

The second expedition to leave England in the spring of 1595 sailed from Plymouth on 12th March. Captain Amyas Preston and Captain George Sommers took 'two tall ships', *Ascension* and *Gift*, but there were others in company. By 21st June, after sacking a number of Spanish settlements, they were anchored off Hispaniola but suffered great sickness with 'flux of the bellie' or dysentery. They met up with Raleigh but lost him again, and eventually returned home in September without having achieved anything of significance.[43]

Furnished by the Queen with six ships – *Defiance, Garland, Hope, Bonaventure, Adventure* and *Foresight* – and having collected twenty-one other vessels, Drake and Hawkins also sailed for the West Indies from Plymouth on 28th August 1595. The company numbered some 2500, and Hugh Platt, who was subsequently knighted by James I, advised Drake on the victualling of the fleet. At this time it was common for such expeditions to carry for the sailors only dried fish, bacon, cheese, butter, dried peas, beer, vinegar, oil, hops, bread and large quantities of biscuit. On Platt's advice Drake carried 'a cheap, fresh and lasting victual, called by the name of macaroni amongst the Italians' which it was thought would be useful when fresh food ran out. He also advised them to carry their essences of spices and flowers, which were used for flavouring syrups, juleps and conserves, not in the form of essential oils which might grow mouldy, but as powders.

Despite all such precautions, John Hawkins fell sick at the Virgin Islands on 6th November and, after an illness of six days, died at San Juan in Puerto Rico. He was reported to be worth £10,000.[44]

The fleet then sailed off Curaçao, attacking where it could, but sickness increased. Two days after Christmas the company reached the Nombre de Dios river and on New Year's Eve attacked and burned the port. It was here, on 15th January 1596, that Drake first began to keep to his cabin in the flagship *Garland*. He lingered for a fortnight but the dysentery slowly gained on him and on 28th January it was recorded that 'at 4 of the clock in the morning our General Sir Francis Drake departed this life, having been extremely sick of the flux, which began the night before to stop on him'. That same day Drake was buried at sea and the fleet attacked Puerto Bello.

At a muster on 6th February only 2000 of the original 2500 men were still alive and many of these were sick. As ships were sunk, their crews were removed to make up the complements of the remaining vessels. In May they sailed for home and more of the sailors died after their arrival in Plymouth.[45]

In 1596 Captain Laurence Keymis, who was with Raleigh on the first expedition to Guiana, led another expedition to that area which set out in January and returned in June. In December Leonard Berrie sailed a pinnace westwards for Raleigh, returning six months later. Also in 1596 the Earl of Cumberland fitted out eleven ships at his own expense and, having plundered the Canaries, attacked and captured San Juan in Puerto Rico. The fate which had befallen Drake and Hawkins in these waters now overtook Cumberland's ships. After about forty days in Puerto Rico, the bloody flux and other diseases carried off such numbers of his men that he was forced to return to England with, as it was said, 'more glory than wealth'.[46]

Another fleet under the Earl of Essex was operating off Cadiz and the Azores in 1596–7. John Davis was almost certainly employed in it, but it is notable chiefly for marking the Navy's official introduction of hammocks, which lessened the risk of fire created by the erection of bunks and were generally thought to be more hygienic. At the beginning of 1597 the *Bear, Whelp* and one other vessel made an ill-starred voyage of which there is little record under the command of Captain Benjamin Wood. It was intended for 'China' but did not round the Cape of Good Hope.[47]

The post-Armada decade was not a sparkling one. Privateering had attracted many men to the sea who were willing to sail for their victuals and a prospect of prize money and they were not always fully employed. Indeed in 1597 an Act was passed 'against Lewd and Wandering Persons pretending themselves to be Soldiers or Mariners'.[48] Nevertheless, the lesser predators helped to weaken Spain's grip on the West Indies and strengthened the merchant marine. Elizabethan statesmen were right to see ships and seamen as the key to mercantile wealth and power, and during the long war with Spain the English captured well over 1000 prizes, thus augmenting their fleet.[49]

The regular arrest by the English of Hanse ships trading to Iberia brought about the expulsion of English traders in Germany. In response, in 1597, the English closed the Steelyard, the Hanse's London base. Members of the Eastland Company, however, continued to trade in the Baltic, mostly exchanging dyed and dressed cloth for naval stores with the merchants of Danzig, Elbing and Könisberg.[50] The export of Polish grain to western Europe, largely in Dutch vessels, had enriched this area.

The Barbary Company's charter having expired, the Morocco trade was thrown open and after 1597 English merchants traded to this area either individually or in partnership. English trade came increasingly into English hands. In the rise of both England and Holland, and the relative decline of Spain and Portugal, one factor of significance was a growing shortage of timber in the Mediterranean and hence a decline of shipbuilding.[51] On the north-west coast of Europe the Dutch and the English were much better placed to secure timber and naval stores economically.

In 1597 Howard led an expedition which sacked Cadiz, but King Philip's armadas of 1596, 1597 and 1598 were directed against Flanders rather than against England. Sustained both by the herring fishery and by the grain trade from the Baltic, the Dutch were by this time well in advance of the English in maritime commercial development. They had sent interlopers to the West Indies already and, by 1599, were importing salt from the Caribbean, loading it at the great natural salt pan at the western end of the Araya peninsula which lies between La Margarita and Cumaná.[52] The year previously, at the suggestion of the Earl of Essex and as a navigator of distinction, John Davis had taken service with the Dutch. He was employed as chief pilot in the second Dutch voyage to the East Indies, returning to England in June 1600,[53] in time to pilot the Lancaster expedition described below.

In September 1599 some £30,000 had been promised by more than a hundred London merchants 'to set forth a voyage this present year to the East Indies and other the islands and countries thereabouts and there to make trade',[54] Richard Staper being prominent among those involved.

On 31st December 1599 a Royal Charter was granted for 'all oceanic regions not already bespoke' and this marked the birth of the East India Company together with England's entry into unrestricted trade world wide. Penalties were to be imposed on interlopers, though the Company itself could grant licences to outsiders 'to trade to the East Indies', and naval forces of 'six good ships and six pinnaces with 500 mariners' were to guard the Company's vessels unless they were required for the Royal Navy. The Company started with more capital than had been promised originally, for £72,000 was subscribed altogether in shares of £50 each. In 1600, to mark this auspicious event, Elizabeth sent John Mildenhall as Envoy to the Great Moghul by the overland route from Constantinople.

The following year began what the subsequent account described as 'The first voyage made to East India by Master James Lancaster (now Knight) for the merchants of London, anno 1600, with four tall ships, (to wit) the *Dragon*, the *Hector*, the *Ascension*, and *Susan*, and a victualler called the *Guest*'. The expedition sailed from Woolwich on the 13th February 1601, with some 500 men. The General, James Lancaster, was on board the *Red Dragon* and Davis was his Pilot Major. The *Dragon* had been bought for £3700 from the Earl of Cumberland, having been previously called *Malice Scourge*, and she was a first-rate man-of-war of 600 tons with a crew of 202 men. John Middleton was on board the vice-admiral, *Hector* (300 tons), with a crew of 108 men. *Ascension*, commanded by William Brand, was a vessel of 260 tons, with a crew of 82 men; and *Susan* (240 tons), under John Heyward, had 88 men. These three ships were all substantial Levanters. The victualler was 130 tons. 'These ships they furnished with men, victuals and munitions for twentie monethes, and sent in them, in merchandise and Spanish money, to the value of seven and twentie thousand pounds: all the rest of their stocks was spent and consumed about the shippes and other necessaries appertayning to them, with money lent to the mariners and saylers beforehand that went upon the voyage.'[55] Ironware, tin, lead, broadcloth, Devonshire kerseys and gold formed the bulk of the cargoes carried, and Lancaster's instructions were to obtain agreements for free trade in the East Indies and to exchange his outward cargo for pepper and spices at the greatest profit possible. He was also to try to buy small quantities of musk, ambergris, wax, camphor, opium, silk and precious stones.

Seven months were taken to reach Table Bay in South Africa, an unusually long time, much of it being spent in the doldrums to the north of the equator. More than a hundred men died of scurvy in the smaller vessels, but Lancaster had no trouble in *Red Dragon* and he attributed this to giving each man three spoonfuls of lemon juice each morning and not allowing the ship's company any solid food until midday. The lemon juice had been preserved by Hugh Platt.[56]

The fleet anchored in Table Bay while the sick men recovered on shore. Before sailing again, 1000 sheep and 42 oxen were obtained from the natives to provision the ships, one piece of iron eight inches in length being exchanged for a sheep and two pieces for an ox. In the Indian Ocean the ships watered at several islands and at one of them thirteen died from drinking impure water. They were more than a year out from London when they reached Achin in northern Sumatra.

To the King of Achin Lancaster presented a letter and gifts from Queen Elizabeth, and a treaty was signed granting free entry, trade which was free of customs, assistance against dangers, justice, freedom from arrest and freedom of conscience. The merchants then tried to buy pepper but there was not much to be had.[57]

Lancaster then cruised in the Malacca Strait and took a 900-ton Portuguese carrack. She was carrying 600 passengers and a rich cargo from Bengal to Malacca. The English transferred 950 packages of calico and pintado (painted cotton) to their own ships and then left the carrack to continue her voyage while they sailed back to Achin. The ship which had been partly loaded with pepper was then completed with calico and sent home. One of the other ships obtained a full cargo of pepper and cloves at another Sumatran port and also sailed for home.

Red Dragon and *Hector*, with the remainder of the carrack's cargo, then sailed east to Bantam in Java where the Dutch had ousted the Portuguese in 1596. Lancaster was warmly welcomed by the Bantamese and the Dutch, and the ruler of Bantam told Lancaster that the English could trade there without hindrance. Chinese merchants were already well established in Bantam, as elsewhere in Malaysia and Indonesia.

Within five weeks, the remaining goods brought out from London were exchanged for 276 bags of pepper and the two ships were fully loaded. Within five years of the closing of the Hanseatic Steelyard in London, Lancaster had left three merchants and eight men to establish an English trading station in Bantam, and he also sent a pinnace with merchants and men to the Moluccas to found a factory there. His two ships then sailed for home on 21st February 1603, arriving in the Thames on 11th September.

Lancaster's four ships had returned with over a million pounds worth of pepper, giving a return of 95 per cent to the merchants who had invested in them. Having successfully opened English trade to the East at last, Lancaster, who was knighted on his return, retired from the sea to become a director of the East India Company.

Notes

1. R. Hakluyt, *The Principal Navigations, Voyages, Traffiques and Discoveries of the English Nation,* Vol. III (1927), London, p. 99.
2. T. Willan, *Studies in Elizabethan Foreign Trade* (1959), Manchester, pp. 18–19.
3. K. R. Andrews, *Elizabethan Privateering* (1964), Cambridge, pp. 32–4 and 124–8.
4. K. R. Andrews, *Trade, Plunder and Settlement* (1984), Cambridge, pp. 249–51.
5. G. Ramsay, *English Overseas Trade during the Centuries of Emergence* (1957), London, p. 111.
6. J. Pinkerton, *A General Collection of the Best and Most Interesting Voyages and Travels in All Parts of the World* (1808), London, p. 815 (Cumberland's Voyage to the Azores.)
7. Ramsay, *op. cit.*, p. 41.
8. G. Causton and A. Keene, *The Early Chartered Companies* (1896), London, p. 72.
9. M. Oppenheim, *A History of the Administration of the Royal Navy* . . . (1896, reprinted 1988), London, pp. 126–8.
10. J. H. Parry, *The Age of Reconnaissance* (1963), London, pp. 74–6.
11. Ramsay, *op. cit.*, p. 72.
12. Causton & Keene, *op. cit.*, p. 72.
13. D. Quinn (ed), *The Roanoke Voyages 1584–1590,* 2 vols (1955), London (The Hakluyt Society), p. 557; pp. 579–80; p. 594.
14. J. Williamson, *Sir John Hawkins, the Time and the Man* (1927), Oxford, pp. 460–1.
15. Quinn, *op. cit.*, p. 598.
16. J. Keevil, *Medicine and the Navy, Vol. I, 1200–1649* (1957), London, pp. 98–9.
17. C. Markham (ed), *The Voyages of Sir James Lancaster, Kt to the East Indies* (1877), London (The Hakluyt Society), p. 4.
18. Andrews (1964), *op. cit.*, p. 73.
19. R. Hawkins, *The Observations of Sir Richard Hawkins, Knt, in his voyage into the South Sea in 1593* (reprinted from the edition of 1622) (1847), London (The Hakluyt Society), p. 26.
20. *Ib.*, pp. 65–6.
21. *Ib.*, p. 63.
22. *Ib.*, p. 195.
23. *Ib.*, p. 18.
24. *Ib.*, pp. 187–9.
25. *Ib.*, p. 23.
26. *Ib.*, p. 45.
27. *Ib.*, pp. 49–50.
28. *Ib.*, pp. 54–5.
29. *Ib.*, p. 60.
30. *Ib.*, pp. 77–82.
31. *Ib.*, p. 86.
32. *Ib.*, pp. 102–3.
33. *Ib.*, p. 111.
34. *Ib.*, p. 143.
35. *Ib.*, p. 153.
36. *Ib.*, pp. 162–7.
37. J. Williamson, *The Age of Drake* (1952), London, p. 350.
38. Markham, *op. cit.*, p. 4.

39. G. Warner (ed), *The Voyage of Robert Dudley afterwards styled Earl of Warwick and Leicester and Duke of Northumberland to the West Indies, 1594–5* (1899), London (The Hakluyt Society), p. 4.
40. *Ib.*, p. xxvii.
41. W. Raleigh, *The Discovery of the Large, Rich and Beautiful Enpire of Guiana* (1595), London (The Hakluyt Society, 1848).
42. *Ib.*, p. 73.
43. K. R. Andrews, *English Privateering Voyages to the West Indies, 1588–1595* (1959), Cambridge (The Hakluyt Society), pp. 381 ff.
44. G. V. Scammell, 'Shipowning in the Economy and Politics of Early Modern England' (1972), *The Historical Journal,* Vol. XV, p. 405.
45. Keevil, *op. cit.*, pp. 108–9.
46. *Ib.*, pp. 109–10.
47. Warner, *op. cit.*, p. xxii.
48. H. C. Hunter, *How England got its Merchant Marine, 1066–1776* (1935), New York, p. 75.
49. Andrews (1984), *op. cit.*, pp. 258–9.
50. R. W. K. Hinton, *The Eastland Trade and the Common Weal in the Seventeenth Century* (1959), Cambridge, p. vii and p. 162.
51. R. W. Unger, *The Ship in the Medieval Economy* (1980), London, p. 270.
52. K. R. Andrews, *The Spanish Caribbean* (1978), New Haven and London, pp. 174–7.
53. J. Davis, *The Voyages and Works of John Davis, The Navigator* (1880), London (The Hakluyt Society), p. lxii.
54. H. Stevens, *The Dawn of British Trade to the East Indies* (1886), London, p. 5.
55. Markham, *op. cit.*, p. 57.
56. *Ib.*, p. 62.
57. *Ib.*, pp. 83–4.

10

Seeds of Empire
(1603–1649)

With the short sea trades across to the Continent in mind Queen Elizabeth's Lord Treasurer, Burghley, had declared that one hoy 'will bring as much in one year as ten merchant ships are wont to bring from other places in two years'.[1] Unlike some of the merchants in the City of London and most of the seafarers in the west country, Lord Burghley and his mistress were little Englanders who, while welcoming a quick and high return on capital invested, had little time for distant trading and gave scant support to overseas colonisation. When the Queen died in 1603 England's foreign trade was still very modest, and not one colony abroad had been established.

James I and Charles I, who succeeded Elizabeth on the throne, were even less supportive of their merchants and seafarers. Although by the outbreak of the Civil War England had a battle fleet second to none, most of the royal ships were too slow to deal with Moorish pirates or Dunkirk privateers, and this was what mattered to the commercial shipowners.[2] In the time of these two monarchs it was the Dutch who were in the ascendant.

Recognised by the Spaniards as an independent nation in 1609, the United Provinces, later known as the Dutch Republic, were already the principal carriers on the Atlantic coasts of Europe, and within some ten years of Elizabeth's death had become as pre-eminent on the world's oceans as Venice had once been in the Mediterranean. The blocking of the river Scheldt by the sea-beggars had shifted the focus of economic activity from Antwerp to Amsterdam and finance and trade now burgeoned round the shores of the Zuider Zee.

From the 15th century onwards the Dutch had developed one bulk carrier after another, the line beginning perhaps with the herring buss, which had been evolved to enable a larger net to be worked and to make fishing possible in more distant waters. By the 16th century the buss could carry home more than 200 tons of fish and, although the average load decreased thereafter to about 100 tons, the buss came to dominate the herring industry. Out of the fishing season the buss would be used as a cargo vessel.

By the end of the 15th century the Dutch had also developed the hoeker for catching cod, and this vessel was fitted with a 'bun' amidships, a chamber which kept the filleted cod fresher in salt water. The hoeker, without the bun, was also used as a general carrier when not fishing.

Other Dutch vessels included the buyscarveel, basically a fully-decked buss introduced about 1550, and the boier or boyer, which was widely used by 1575. The early boiers, mostly between 50 and 130 tons, were two-masted and fitted with an early form of ketch rig, namely a square spritsail, a square mainsail and a square topsail on the main mast, and a lateen mizen, though this rig was sometimes modified to economise crew and maximise profits. The boier was built for the grain trade and for work in the North Sea.

By the end of the 16th century the boier had been widely replaced by the vlieboot, anglicised to flyboat, broad in the beam, shallow-draughted and built with a high square stern. Above the lateen mizen a square topsail was added. The vlieboot was usually less than 100 tons and largely used in coastwise trading.

About 1600 the vlieboot was superseded in many bulk trades by the fluyt, to which the English word flyboat became attached. The major achievement of Dutch ship designers, the fluyt was to have an enormous influence on shipbuilding, particularly in England. The herring buss had had a length to beam ratio of near 4:1. By 1610 the length to beam ratio of the fluyt had become 6:1 and the vessel – little more than a floating hold with a flat bottom and near vertical stem and sternpost – was designed to carry a maximum amount of cargo. Bluff-bowed and fully-decked, the fluyt carried virtually no upperworks at the forward end. Aft there was a narrow poop above a rounded stern. One square sail was carried on the foremast and two on the main mast. The lateen mizen also carried a square mizen topsail, and there was a spritsail under the bowsprit. The early fluyts were about 150 tons, but the size increased rapidly to 200 tons and some were built to exceed 400 tons. They sailed well.[3]

In the 17th century the English remained devoted to the armed merchantman and, while this could compete with the Dutch in the Mediterranean and in the dangerous trade to the East Indies, other trades were largely lost to the cheaper and more convenient 'flyboats'. From Archangel to the Garonne trade was best served by Dutch vessels of from 200 to 500 tons, largely unarmed ships built for stowage, cheaply built and cheaply operated. These were the ships that carried wine, salt, fish, grain, timber; weighty naval supplies like pitch, tar, hemp and flax; and such metals as lead, tin, iron and copper. North of the Straits of Gibraltar port-to-port trade was largely in Dutch hands, as were the North Sea fisheries for herring and cod and the 'Greenland' or Spitzbergen whale fishery. The big Dutch ships also operated from the Garonne to the Levant, the Canaries, Madeira and Guinea.[4]

Usurping the position of the declining Hanseatic League in the Baltic Sea, the Dutch came close to eliminating English competition as well as gaining a near monopoly on Baltic timber and other essentials of naval construction. With low interest rates and ships built for one-third of the cost of English ships, the Dutch controlled over 1000 ships by 1600 and, according to one authority, round about three times as many, plus a further 3000 fishing craft, albeit many of them very small, by 1610. Until the middle of the 17th century England received the bulk of her imports in Dutch ships.[5]

The twin pillars on which Dutch prosperity rested were the grain trade from the Baltic and the North Sea fisheries. The shipment of grain from the Baltic to the Low Countries had begun by the 14th century and remained important down to the industrial revolution. By the first half of the 17th century Amsterdam possessed great granaries for storage purposes and grain exports averaged some 150,000 tons a year. The western Mediterranean was usually short of grain at this time and between 1600 and 1625 there was a vigorous trade between the Baltic and the Mediterranean. Grain exports peaked at 220,000 tons in 1618 and in the second quarter of the century, Dutch exports of grain to the Mediterranean declined and few contracts for delivery further south than Portugal were secured. The grain was mostly exchanged for salt, much used in the fishing industry, and in the period from 1625 to 1650 French salt tended to replace that from Iberia. Silver was also used in the exchange of commodities with the Baltic. After these came such commodities as wine and herring from the west exchanged for forest products from the east, Danzig (modern Gdansk) being Amsterdam's principal trading partner. Between 1550 and 1650 the Dutch accounted for nearly two-thirds of all the passages recorded through the Skagerrak,[6] and over 1200 Dutch vessels were engaged each year in the Baltic. The number of English ships entering the Baltic each year had doubled in the last half of the 16th century but between 1604 and 1624 they still averaged only about 100 a year.[7]

Extending their operations overseas, Dutch smugglers had begun to appear off Brazil at about the time Philip launched his Armada against England, and the first Dutch slaver recorded in the West Indies appeared off Trinidad in 1606. In 1621 the Dutch West India Company received its charter, and after 1630 Dutch traders, in addition to being the carriers of Spanish and Portuguese products in the Old World, became the carriers of the colonial trade of Spain and Portugal in the New World. Amsterdam became a market for logwood, cochineal, cacao and tobacco, for Peruvian silver and Brazilian sugar and gold, just as it was a market for Eastern silk, cloves and pepper. Between 1630 and 1640 the Dutch also became the principal suppliers of slaves to the New World, settled in New Amsterdam (now New York), and seized Curaçao, Saba, St Martin and St Eustatius. They so weakened Spain that the English, French, Scots and Danes were subsequently able to establish colonies in a long string from Newfoundland to Barbados.[8]

In the east the Dutch very largely destroyed Portugal's empire, for the Dutch forces were more numerous, better trained, better led and better disciplined. By 1603 the Dutch had sent fifteen expeditions to the Far East against England's one. Portugal's dealings in spice foundered and by the mid-16th century a Portuguese reformer could write, 'The empire in the east is like a ship that is sinking. Everybody shouts we are foundering, but nobody pumps the water out.'[9] It was the Dutch who named and described Cape Horn in 1616 and it was the Dutch who discovered Australia, though systematic exploration was left to Captain Cook.

The former alliance between Dutch and English now changed, especially at sea, into jealousy, resentment and conflict. National pride was increasingly reinforced by England's growing economic interests in the outer world, and English insistence upon deference to their flag, a major cause of the first Dutch war, was symptomatic of an intensifying nationalism which continually fired effort to win a share in the rich trades and vast lands which the explorers had conjured up.

'The Dutch', wrote Raleigh in 1603 in a document presented to King James I,

> have as many ships and vessels as eleven Kingdoms of Christendom have, let England be one. They build every year near one thousand ships, although all their native commodities do not require one hundred ships to carry them away at once. Yet, although we have all things of our own in abundance for the increase in traffic, timber to build ships, and commodities of our own to lade about one thousand ships and vessels at once (beside the great fishing), and as fast as they make their voyage might relade again; yet our ships and mariners decline, and traffic and merchants daily decay.

Raleigh was exaggerating outrageously but he was representative of those with imperial ambitions. Shipbuilding materials were not abundant in England, though English oak was unsurpassed for ship timber. To complete the most famous warship of the 17th century, *Sovereign of the*

Seas (launched 1637), which proved to be the forerunner of the ships of the line for the next two centuries, Phineas Pett had to bring oak from Northumberland to Woolwich, and suitable oaks were so scarce that saplings were pinned into curves for use 100 years later. Ship timber had been imported from the Baltic for four centuries and in 1634 the first cargo of masts from New England was brought into the Thames.[10] The Dutch were no better off so far as timber was concerned but, with a more advanced financial and business community and the hinterland of Europe as a market, they were better able to marshall their resources.

The City of London was making progress but it still had far to go. The establishment of the chartered companies had increased its importance because the London merchants were close to government and could lobby more easily for privileges. They had secured much of the trade once in the hands of foreigners and the average annual figure for the export of cloths from London by foreign merchants had fallen from 60,000 in the 1540s to 5000 by the 1610s.[11] But the last boom in traditional broadcloth exports early in the reign of James I petered out in the turmoil of European markets at the beginning of the Thirty Years War (1618–48) and the future was to lie with the so-called 'new draperies', introduced into Norwich and Essex by refugees from the Low Countries at the end of the 16th century. The new draperies had become as important as the old by 1620.[12]

England's neutrality during the Thirty Years War helped English ships to compete with the Dutch despite their higher unit costs, for the lightly armed Dutch fluyt suffered greatly at the hands of Dunkirk privateers.[13] Trade picked up with Spain and Portugal after peace was made with Spain by James I in 1604,[14] and by 1625 the Merchant Adventurers had regained and held much of their old grip on the cloth trade. In 1622 the Dutch were prohibited from trading to England in Baltic commodities and from 1624–42 the Eastland Company exported an average of 32,000 cloths a year.[15]

Although some of the Eastland Company's trade was carried on from Hull and Ipswich, there were already complaints that, with nearly half of the kingdom's trade in its hands, London was too important; but London ships had constantly to battle with interlopers from the English outports, especially in trades where merchants in the outports did not need to invest too heavily to compete. The west country ports from Dorset to Bristol contested with London shipping interests for control of the Newfoundland fisheries and in their summer voyaging some of the west country ship-masters earned enough to live in comfort all winter, a few even keeping carriages.[16]

Newcastle upon Tyne was well placed for trade with north-west Europe though most of her coal shipments went south to London. According to Mistress Quickly, when Falstaff promised to marry her, he was 'sitting in my Dolphin chamber, at the round table by a sea-coal fire.' In the second half of the 16th century Newcastle's annual shipments of coal had quadrupled to 140,000 tons. By 1634 they were over 400,000 tons.[17] Four-fifths of the total was carried round the English coast, the rest going to the Continent in foreign vessels. These coal exports were heavily taxed and the tax was higher if the cargo was carried in foreign ships. Nevertheless, the merchants of Newcastle remained content at this time to leave the management of the coal export trade to foreign 'hostmen'. Hanseatic ships still carried coal to Flanders, and the French came in fleets of fifty ships to carry it to France.[18] By 1615, however, over 400 English vessels were also engaged in the coal trade, one half of them supplying London,[19] and the ships used grew gradually bigger. In 1606 the average coal cargo imported into London was 73 tons; by 1638 it had doubled to 139 tons.[20]

Newcastle also exported lead, and the Newcastle Adventurers sent wool to the Low Countries, substituting coarse cloth when the export of wool was forbidden in 1618. Other exports included grindstones, salt and the skins of lambs, sheep and rabbits, cargoes being delivered to all ports between Danzig and Rouen, but chiefly to Emden, Hamburg, Elbing and the ports of the Low Countries. Imports included pitch, tar, flax, hemp, ropes, timber and rye from Norway and the Baltic, with all except the rye being used in the mines as well as in the building of keels and colliers. From the Low Countries came alum, madder, spinning-wheels, soap, pins, needles, frying pans, stone pots and glass, together with such re-exports as ginger, aniseed, raisins, prunes and figs.[21] Hops were imported from France and fish from Scotland.

Given the conditions of the time, Hull was a busy port, exporting cloth, lead and sometimes corn, the cloth going as far north as Vardø and as far south as Bordeaux. Timber and tar were brought in from Norway and Danzig, ashes for use in the manufacture of soap from Danzig and Copenhagen, iron, canvas, gunpowder and clapboard from Elbing, salt and fish from Scotland, wine, vinegar and resin from Bordeaux, and cargoes similar to those described above from the Low Countries. By the end of the 16th century Boston's former glory as a wool-exporting port had diminished, but cloth was exported from Ipswich, corn from King's Lynn and corn and kippers from Yarmouth.[22]

There were other provincial ports exporting minerals, cloth and agricultural products, but England remained primarily an agricultural country, importing from Antwerp, Middelburg or Rotterdam many of the manufactured goods it required, among them glass, paper, canvas, linen, pins and pans. For the textile industry dyes, mordants, oil, woolcards and flax were imported; timber was imported for shipbuilding, housebuilding and barrel-making; hops were imported for beer; and salt was imported for curing fish. Fish, fruit and spices were the chief imported foods and wine remained, as it had been since the pre-Roman era, the most important single import.

Such changes in English trade as had taken place in the second half of the 16th century resulted from efforts to break away from the old established routes to find new markets for both old and new products. Although the new trades with Russia, Africa, America, the Levant and the East Indies did not yet contribute much to the total volume of England's foreign trade, they did represent a new dynamic in the country's commerce, and joint stock organisation, involving the establishment of great trading companies, helped to solve the problem of finance.

Expansion was aided by the development of both fishing and the coal trade, for these were great employers of ships and seamen. By 1614 the East Anglian ports alone employed over 100 vessels in the Iceland fishery besides a great number of smaller craft in the North Sea. By this time, too, over 200 ships from Devon, Cornwall and Dorset were fishing for cod on the Newfoundland Banks, a six-fold increase in 40 years. By mid-century there were more ships still, perhaps twice the number. As Sir William Monson said of fish at this time: 'True it is that there is no commodity in the world of so great bulk and small value, or that can set so many ships of burden at work. As for example, a mean merchant may freight his ship of 250 tons with fish that will not cost above £1600, that 40 merchants cannot do of richer and better commodities'.

Newfoundland dried cod had initiated a trade which was to last for 400 years. It was already well organised. The charter-party was the cornerstone of an elaborate edifice of safeguards – partnership, marine insurance, loans – designed to ensure the investor of the maximum control and a minimum risk. In the west country a small fishing ship could be hired for as little as £16 a month. A large London vessel might cost more than ten times as much.[23] Even at the end of the 19th century a cargo of salt might still be carried from Biscay to Newfoundland in a brig of 180 tons, there to be used to cure cod. Salt cod would be loaded by this same vessel for Leghorn or other Mediterranean ports, and from these ports wine and oil would be brought back to England. Carrying salt cod was a stinking business and as an item of diet it was familiar to merchant seamen as late as the 1920s when one wrote: 'Most Fridays, for breakfast, we had boiled salt fish. It was taken out of the storeroom on Thursday and hung on deck so that the fresh ocean breezes might dispel the more noxious fumes. The mere mention of salt fish still induces in me a feeling of nausea.'[24]

Although there was some subsequent revival, the trade of the Russia Company was practically extinguished by 1615 and within twenty years of Elizabeth's death it became impossible to maintain the joint-stock structure. The tsar complained that the English were re-exporting Russian corn to Turkey, Russia's enemy, and were also supplying Turkey with arms, and it was true that the English had sold Russian tallow and cables to the Turks. But the deepseated problem in the trade was not political so much as geographical. The opening of the Russian port of Narva in the Baltic had made the route to the far north too expensive and interloping too easy, and trading by way of the Levant proved more profitable. In Arctic waters the Company's ships often turned to fishing and whaling or to hunting the walrus when other trade did not fill their holds.

Many of the Russia merchants, however, had other commercial interests and so were still in a position to finance further Arctic exploration. It was the great Russia merchant Francis Cherry who financed the voyage made in 1603 by Stephen Bennet which resulted in the discovery of Bear Island (Björnöya) in latitude 74° north. Bennet named it Cherry Island and thereafter Cherry's ships and others hunted walrus there. Four years later, Henry Hudson, also financed by Russia Company merchants, sighted Spitzbergen between 76° and 81° north and reported numerous whales and walrus. Although neither the English nor the Dutch were able to go whaling at this date without the help of fishermen from the Basque country, both were to the fore at this time in the whaling business, though English whaling petered out in the 1650s.[25]

There was still an interest in finding a passage to the east in northern waters. In 1602, with finance supplied by the East India Company, George Waymouth looked unsuccessfully for a north-west passage. In 1609 Henry Hudson discovered the Hudson river and what was to become New York harbour, and the following year he entered Hudson Bay. In 1612 a Northwest Passage Company was incorporated under the personal patronage of Prince Henry and the search was continued intermittently until Luke Fox of Hull and Thomas James of Bristol made the last attempts for many years in 1631–2. Although there was little direct result from these further voyages of exploration, they led in the second half of the 17th century to the fur trade and the formation of the Hudson Bay Company.

In the meantime permanent colonial settlement began in America. In her negotiations with Spain in 1600 Elizabeth I stipulated for recognition of the doctrine that only effective occupation could give a valid title to new lands and that the rest were open and free to all-comers. When the Spaniards would not agree the Queen ended negotiations. But the success of the privateers had weakened Spain both at sea and in Europe. Although there was no mention of the colonial issue when peace with Spain was made in 1604, after Elizabeth's death, the English interpreted the treaty to mean that trade to the East Indies was free and that North America and the West Indies unoccupied by Spain were open to colonisation.

By 1603, the year in which he gave warning of Dutch maritime power, Sir Walter Raleigh was out of favour and no longer of political importance. After the accession of James I in that year, Raleigh's enemies arranged for his arrest – he was accused with others of plotting to dethrone the new Scottish king of England – and he remained incarcerated in the Tower of London for thirteen years. Although not pardoned, he was then released to make one last (and unsuccessful) voyage to the Orinoco and unjustly condemned to death on his return, being executed in 1618. With all the bravura of the Elizabethan seafarer, he commented in his last hours: 'The world is itself but a larger prison, out of which some are daily selected for execution'.

Shortly before Raleigh's imprisonment in the Tower, inspired by French and Dutch successes in that field, English merchants had re-entered the West Indian trade after a lapse of thirty years. By this time, despite the new king's aversion to the habit, smoking was widespread, and by 1610 tobacco imports, largely from Venezuela, were valued at more than £60,000 a year.[26] James I declared an end to privateering when peace was made but, even if this was too much to hope for, in the new conditions of the time the import and sale of tobacco became a more reliable way of making money.

At this same time, in 1602–3, Raleigh had sanctioned further exploration of the North American coast under the terms of his charter from Queen Elizabeth and a couple of cargoes of sassafras, useful it was now thought for the cure of the plague as well as of the French pox, had been brought back. On his subsequent imprisonment, Raleigh's charter rights reverted to the King, who then granted a further charter in 1606 to a curious double joint-stock company consisting, on the one hand, of London merchants and, on the other hand, of merchants from Plymouth, Bristol and Exeter. It was the London half of the company which financed a fleet, under Christopher Newport as admiral, which at last established the first permanent English colony in the New World. On their arrival in Chesapeake Bay the new colonists were told that there were still seven of the original English settlers at Roanoke alive among the Indians, 'four men, two boys and one maid'. The girl could have been Virginia Dare, the first child born in America of English parents. However, nothing further was heard of these settlers and they probably died at Indian hands.

Newport's fleet consisted of *Susan Constant* (120 tons), *Godspeed* (40 tons) and the pinnace *Discovery,* and in 1607 the admiral chose a site on the James River, emptying into Chesapeake Bay, which became Jamestown. Perhaps only the indomitable Captain John Smith saved the young colony from extinction, for the settlers included too many useless 'gentlemen'. The double joint-stock company was replaced by the Virginia Company in 1609 and in 1617, three years after one of the colonists had married the Indian princess Pocahontas, tobacco was grown profitably in Virginia for the first time, though this was not the end of the colony's troubles. In 1623 the Privy Council took the management of the colony into its own hands,[27] and shortly afterwards about 1000 bondsmen or indentured servants began to arrive in Virginia annually.[28]

By this time the better organised Pilgrims, aided by the plague which had been brought to the local Indians by Europeans, had arrived further north in the *Mayflower* (180 tons) to establish what became a self-governing colony in Plymouth harbour. In the thirty years that followed the settlement at Jamestown other small settlements were established along the coast to the north, in Massachusetts, Maryland and Rhode Island, and in the 1620s settlement began in the West Indies, the original one being made in St Kitts in 1624. By 1632 there were further settlements in Barbados, Nevis, Antigua and Monserrat.

These first colonists were almost entirely dependent on England for clothes, leather goods, other manufactures, salt, beer and wine, and to the West Indies food too was carried, either from England or from Ireland. The workforce consisted largely of young, white indentured servants, many of them Irish. Though Maurice Thompson, a London merchant, took sixty negroes to St Kitts in 1626, the English slave trade had scarcely begun. The cash-crop was tobacco but until after mid-century all this trade was small. In 1635 the whole tobacco crop of Virginia and Maryland could have been loaded into one large contemporary ship, and the other commodities which the northern colonists might supply came more cheaply from the Baltic.

From the peace of 1604 until conflict was renewed in 1624 trade between England and Spain revived, wine being the chief import, principally in this period 'sack' from Malaga and the Canaries. Olive oil came from southern Spain, oranges and lemons from Seville, and raisins from Malaga and Alicante. The products of Spanish America – cochineal, indigo and logwood – were also imported by way of Cadiz but tonnages were small. From the area round Bilbao iron was exported to England's western ports, together with growing cargoes of Spanish wool bound for the cloth industries around Bristol and Exeter. Because the west of England was much engaged in these trades any attempt by London interests to commit them to a regulated company was violently opposed and the trades to both Spain and France were declared open to all Englishmen in 1604. From 1627 to 1629 there was also war with France and one of the reasons for relatively little progress being made at sea in this period were the losses suffered in the 1620s – perhaps 300 ships, including over one hundred ships exceeding 100 tons – losses which were probably not counterbalanced in these wars, as they were both earlier and later on, by prizes captured from the enemy.[29] In times of peace French trade remained important.

Partly in consequence of privateering the Moroccan trade languished in the early years of the 17th century, and it was not helped in 1603 by the deaths of both Elizabeth and the Moroccan ruler Muley Ahmed which brought diplomatic links to an end. If Moroccan trade is regarded as one of the stages in the expansion of English trade routes by the chartered companies, with the routes extending gradually from western Europe to Morocco, from Morocco to the Levant and the Guinea coast, and finally round the Cape to the East, the Moroccan phase of this development was already over by the time the eastern route was opened.

In 1615 an Order-in-Council anticipated the later Navigation Acts by prohibiting imports from the Mediterranean unless they were carried in English ships or in the ships of certain Mediterranean ports. However, it was already unusual for any merchant ship from a Mediterranean state to appear in the English Channel. English trade to and from the Mediterranean beyond the Barbary coast was almost exclusively in the hands of the Levant Company whose authority had by this time been extended to Italy and to the Greek islands under Venetian rule. Leghorn and Genoa became increasingly the foci of much of the Mediterranean's trade and the trade with England was revolutionised by the English re-export of pepper brought in by the ships of the East India Company.[30] It was further stimulated in the mid-1620s by the Thirty Years War which closed the overland routes from Italy to north-west Europe. Pepper was sold mainly through Leghorn and there were few homeward cargoes, though after 1620 olive oil was brought from Apulia.[31]

Trade with Asia Minor and Syria continued to flourish, freights on fine goods at £7 per ton being both high and profitable.[32] Levant Company ships traded, in addition to Leghorn and Genoa, to Marseilles, Zante, Cephalonia, Crete, Constantinople, Alexandretta (Iskerandum or Scanderoon, the port of Aleppo), Smyrna, Cyprus, Tripoli, Alexandria and Algiers. They exchanged English woollen cloth, lead, tin and hides for

Turkish or Persian raw silk, cotton, mohair, currants and oak-galls, the latter being used in the manufacture of ink and tannin and for the purpose of dyeing. In 1605, when James I renewed the Levant Company charter 'in perpetuity', Richard Staper claimed that the trade set 100,000 people to work 'by making of fustians' (then a coarse cloth made of cotton and flax) and also produced skilled mariners and nurtured great ships.

In this area the English came into conflict with the French who were busy taking over trade which had formerly been in the hands of the Venetians. The English were also alleged to pirate Venetian and Genoese vessels and sell the booty in the cities along the Barbary coast.[33] In 1600 twenty-nine ships made the voyage on behalf of the Levant Company, seventeen of them chartered and the remaining twelve, ranging from 100 to 350 tons, belonging to the Company itself.[34] English ships were much favoured in the Mediterranean because they were all well-armed, and they would often spend a year or two 'tramping' between Mediterranean ports, operating in what would now be called the cross trades, though usually such trading would be carried on with an eye to bringing oil and currants home in the right season.[35]

Led by the London merchant John Davies, there was continuous trading to West Africa after 1607 and in 1618 James I granted a patent for a joint-stock company to trade to Africa, a similar patent being granted again in 1631. But this Africa Company was never a great success. The East India Company ships used the Guinea factories or trading stations to trade English cloth for gold when outward bound and interlopers were always common on the Gold Coast. As elsewhere, the trade by this time was largely in Dutch hands.

The Levant Company merchants of London were well aware of the threat to their trade which came from Dutch activity in eastern waters and they had therefore been prominent in the formation of the East India Company. By 1618 the latter had organised a number of voyages to the Spice Islands and Captain William Keeling, who commanded James Lancaster's ship *Red Dragon* on the voyage of 1615–17, has left in his journal a first-hand picture of the trade as it was in his time.

It was said that both *Hamlet* and *Richard II* were performed aboard *Red Dragon*. If this were so, such performances appear to have been unique in merchant shipping history. Not until 1972 were classic plays produced again aboard a merchant ship for crew entertainment, and they were then the lighter fare of *She Stoops to Conquer* and *The Importance of Being Earnest*.[36]

Life on board *Red Dragon,* however, was not all beer and skittles. In March 1615 Captain Keeling ordered a sailor to be given thirty lashes for stealing a piece of fresh beef, though he commented that this was the first man he had punished. The punishment seems to have served its purpose for it was not until the following October that he had to punish a man again, this time ducking him for striking another while they were both ashore. On this same day he records that 7000 small shot and 400 pounds of lead had been stolen and sold for toddy or palm wine. That he was no martinet is indicated by the fact that upon the discovery of this considerable theft he merely made it known in each ship of the expedition that anyone caught stealing so much as a bullet in future would be given forty lashes on the bare back.

Like Lancaster, under whom he had served, Keeling knew the value of lemon juice as an antiscorbutic and, in the Comoro Islands outward bound, he bought 300 lemons for two penny knives. Although he lost sixty-two men, only one death was attributed to scurvy.

But not all ships were run so well as *Red Dragon*. One of the other ships sailing with him ran out of beer quite early in the voyage when Keeling himself had used but little. A couple of months later the *Expedition,* also in his company, had consumed all her fish and Keeling spared her '300 couple backalew' or 600 dried cod. This latter ship was also short of sailcloth, her master writing: '. . . the original cause whereof proceedeth from the innumerable many rats which we have had in our ships all this voyage, for by them both sails and other provisions of the ships (besides private men's particulars) have been excessively spoiled . . . It is almost incredible the noisesomeness of that vermin, who have been ready to eat us living (for they have bitten us in our sleeps), but some men that died this voyage in the nights, before morning have had their toes eaten quite off, and other parts of their bodies gnawed. . . .'

By reason of the distance from England at which it operated, and the particular dangers of armed conflict whenever a foreign ship from Europe was sighted in the Indian Ocean, the East India Company was already in a category of its own. The Company was a permanent body with a Governor and Council, which ensured a continuity of management, and it was the sole seller of the goods which it imported, having rules which prohibited private trading, though such rules were being breached by 1635.[37] To join the Company a merchant had to pay a considerable sum.

At this time, however, each voyage was run as a separate syndicate, the accounts being wound up when it was completed and the profit distributed as soon as the homeward cargo was disposed of. Profits on the voyages between 1601 and 1612 averaged 155 per cent, but fell to less than one-third of this in the thirty years which followed, being as low as 12 per cent in the years 1617–1632.[38]

At first the ships used were bought outright, largely from merchants of the Levant Company because the ships had to be large and well-armed. Considerable capital expenditure was involved and the first syndicate invested £45,000 in ships and their equipment, apart from the £27,000 invested in outward cargo. In real terms this total expenditure is nearly six times that invested in Willoughby and Chancellor's voyage to discover a north-east passage in 1553, and at 1988 prices would represent an investment of nearly £6 million.

Subsequently, ships were built for the trade on the Thames and in Ireland, and in 1607 the Company began to build its own ships and to repair them at Deptford and Blackwall, the first and largest being *The Trade's Increase,* a vessel of nearly 1000 tons which proved difficult to handle and was wrecked off Java on her first voyage. Although the ships had to be big enough to ward off enemies, trade had not yet increased enough for the English to fill so large a vessel and the name, for the time being, proved unwarranted. In 1615 the directors declared that 'ships of 300 tons at least and so forth to 600 or 700 tons were fittest',[39] and settled in the main to use ships of between 300 and 350 tons. Although the Company's were among the finest English ships of their time, of the 168 ships (totalling 77,175 tons) sent east between 1601 and 1640, only 104 (totalling 54,318 tons) returned home. In other words, 60 per cent of the number of ships despatched came back, though these were on the whole the larger ships, and not all of those that failed to return were casualties. Some remained to fight in the east and to inaugurate that 'country' or regional trade which became so profitable in the Company's later years.[40]

After 1629 the East India Company preferred to hire ships and in 1654 the Blackwall yard was sold, part of the Deptford yard being kept as a store and repair depot. Eventually, a narrow group of people specialised in building East Indiamen and hiring them out, one such family at the end of the 18th century being the Borradailes, who built their ships at Deptford and owned an estate adjacent to the one owned by the brewer Thrale, Dr Johnson's friend, at Streatham. (In a house built on this estate, in Balham, the Seafarers Education Service was to make its home for thirty years after the Second World War.) Leading figures in the East India Company, whose Company house was always in the Leadenhall Street–Bishopsgate area of the City of London, an area which was long to remain the main centre for British shipping, were often part-owners of the ships. After the system became thus formalised, the ships were commonly employed for sixteen years.

The East India Company's trade in pepper and other spices from the

Indonesian Archipelago was savagely contested by the Dutch and, a weak foothold at Bantam in Java apart, the English had been driven out of all this area by 1623, the year in which English interlopers were massacred by the Dutch at Amboina. The weakness of the Stuart government at home did not help.

A more secure start, and one of the utmost importance for the future, was made on the Indian coast. After initial approaches in 1607, a trading station was established in 1614 at Surat, near Bombay in the territory of the Mogul emperor, after Captain Thomas Best, sailing in command of two of the Company ships, one of them the *Red Dragon,* had defeated Portuguese ships lying in the roadstead. Factories were subsequently set up at ports down the coast and a fleet of ten ships, known as the Indian Marine and manned by British seamen, was based on Surat. On the other side of India the Company established a base at Masulipatam in 1611, and in 1639 a further trading station was established at Madras.[41] The Company's days of grandeur, however, were not to arrive until after the Restoration.

In England the East India Company was not without its critics. Although in the last decades of the 16th century silver flowed from Acapulco across the Pacific to Manila, it was still much scarcer in Asia than it was in Europe. Asians could not therefore afford to buy most European goods and demanded bullion instead. In its first twenty-three years the Company exported £753,336 in bullion and only £351,236 in commodities.[42] Purchasing power parity between east and west had not been established.

According to accepted dogma, the export of bullion was against the country's interests. It was also argued that the capital employed to establish the trade could have been better utilised in England. Imports of spices and drugs, it was suggested, did nothing to help English industry, and all that did help such industry from the cargoes brought from the East were the relatively minor imports of saltpetre and raw silk. This controversy led to some advance in economic doctrine, the advance to mercantilism, for in a *Discourse of Trade from England unto the East Indies,* published in 1621, Sir Thomas Mun argued that the export to India of gold and silver could be justified if there were a sound balance of trade after the re-sale abroad of goods brought from India; in other words, if goods from India were sold in Europe for gold or silver, as was happening in consequence of the sale of spices to Italy.

Although the 1000-ton Portuguese caravel in the Far East trade was twice the size of the biggest English merchant ships, and although Dutch ships were roomier, more hygienic and more economically manned,

English ships by this time were unexcelled in durability, handiness and general efficiency. English gun-power was greater and English gunnery better than that of any of her rivals, and improvement in the ship's rig, to increase manoeuvrability and sail-power, had continued. The area of the foresail was now roughly two-thirds that of the mainsail, with topsails in about the same proportion, though there was considerable variety. The spritsail came to be nearly as big as the fore topsail and was on a longer yard. Because ships were being built higher aft, the mizen mast diminished in size but sometimes carried a square mizen topsail. Topgallant sails were little used and lateen mizen topsails still less, though studding sails of some kind had come into use.[43] Reefing was also little used at this time, the seamen of the early 17th century favouring the addition of bonnets to their sails in light winds.

Many trading voyages followed standard patterns, like the triangular trade to Newfoundland and thence to Spain or the Mediterranean and thus back to England. Most American and West Indies operators regarded a round voyage as a year's operation, though occasionally two voyages from Bristol to Barbados might be made in a year. Ships bound for the Levant usually sailed in the early autumn and returned the following midsummer. Five voyages a year might now be made between Hull and Oslo, two between London and Riga, and two or three between London and Portugal. The Norwegian trade was from March to December because of winter ice, but ships in this trade might thus fit in a winter visit to Spain. Many trades – oranges, raisins, oil and wine, for example – were seasonal; the first ships home, as in the later tea trade from China, benefited from high prices, and there was a risk of cargo deterioration if cargoes were delayed. The coal trade did not suffer unduly from the passing seasons though there was a slowing down in winter: in the 17th century even the Thames, wider and shallower than it now is, froze over occasionally.

Some records of ship operation have survived. In the 1630s, for instance, the 200-ton *Abraham* had a crew of 28–30, 17–19 of these being 'hands' or ratings. Under the master were two mates. There were also a boatswain, gunner and carpenter, each of whom had a mate, and a cook and a surgeon. In this same decade, the 250-ton *Diamond* had a crew of 40 and cost £1150, being one-eighth owned by Thomas Soame, later knighted, and one-sixteenth owned by her master, William Peers. In 1634 she was fitted out, stores and repairs costing £840, nine months victualling (mainly beef, biscuit, beer and cheese) costing £340, and new guns and other items costing £247. She was then hired out on time charter for a voyage to the Mediterranean at £170 a month, the owners paying running expenses and the charterers paying two-thirds of the port charges. She sailed in November to Yarmouth to load red herrings or kippers, sold them in Venice in January, sailed in ballast to Ancona three weeks later and there loaded corn for Lisbon, which she sold in June. In Lisbon the crew were paid three months wages. Partly on a sub-charter she then carried a cargo of salt to the Azores, buying sugar there which she brought to the Thames in September. For a little over ten months' hire the owners received £1757 against which was set master's outlays of £706. Among themselves the owners divided £378.13s – perhaps a dividend of 14.5 per cent.[44]

It is difficult to make any accurate estimate but, from this and other voyages, it does not appear that deepsea voyaging at this time was particularly profitable. The ships were not run with any great efficiency and repairs and replacements were expensive. Coasters were more cheaply built and repaired and perhaps paid better.

While James I did not approve of smoking, he liked pineapples. It is related of him that when, by a speedy voyage, a pineapple was brought from America in perfect condition and he tasted it, he observed that it was 'a fruit too delicious for a subject to taste of'. His accession had certainly not helped the sailor. Although the East India Company did something on behalf of the widows of those lost in its service, the Crown took no care of the disabled seafarer or of the dependants of dead ones. Ever since 1590, when Sir John Hawkins had set it up, the seaman had been paying his monthly sixpence into the Chatham Chest (a new chest ordered in 1625 may be seen today in the National Maritime Museum). But the seaman never saw any of his money back. Despite its five locks, of which the five different keys were supposed to be kept by five representative officers of different grades, Sir Robert Mansel, the thoroughly corrupt Treasurer of the Navy under James I, regarded the Chatham Chest as his own petty-cash box. In 1636 Sir Henry Mervyn complained to the Board of Admiralty that sailors in the King's service were, for the most part, barefooted with 'scarcely rags to hide their skin'. For want of clothing, he wrote, they 'fall down daily into desperate sickness, in as much as I am forced to discharge more men by reason of their weakness than we can again supply ourselves withal from ships passing by'.[45]

These were the pressed men. But it was also suggested that the English sailor brought troubles upon himself: 'Our over-much feeding upon these salt meats at sea cannot but procure much unhealthiness and infection'. Other nations were more sensible. Spanish and Italian sailors, it was said, lived mostly 'upon rice, oatmeal, biscuits, figs, olives, oil and the like'.

And if the English could not be expected to be as eccentric as that, they might at least emulate 'our neighbours the French and Dutch, who content themselves with a far less portion of flesh and fish than we do, and instead thereof do make up their meals with peas, beans, wheat, flour, butter, cheese, and those white meats (as they are called).'[46]

It was not that sensible seamen did not exist, nor that good advice was lacking. Captain Luke Fox and Captain Thomas James, who both sailed for Hudson Bay in 1631, were as chalk and cheese.

James carried, among his many and elaborate instruments, two watches, six meridian compasses, two quadrants and 'a table, every day calculated, correspondent to the latitude, according to Master Gunter's directions in his book; the better to keep our time and our compass, to judge of our course'. Along with these went 'A Chest full of the best and choicest Mathematicall bookes'.[47] James also arranged with Henry Gellibrand, a mathematician, for them both to observe the same eclipse of the moon to determine James's longitude at the time, which they succeeded in doing to within 15 minutes.[48]

Fox, like Conrad's Captain McWhirr, was a common enough type of shipmaster until well into the 1960s. He had no time for reading or for 'mathematical' officers. But he was a good practical seaman and made sure that his ship was sound and that he employed experienced men. 'I had excellent fat beef', he relates, 'strong beer, good wheaten bread, good Iceland ling, butter and cheese of the best, admirable sack and *aqua-vitae,* peas, oatmeal, wheatmeal, oil, spice, sugar, fruit and rice; with "chyrurgerie" [medicines], as syrups, juleps, condits [preserves], "trechissis", antidotes, balsams, gums, unguents, plasters, oils, potions, suppositories, and purging pills.'[49]

Ever since John Cabot, and no doubt before, leaders of expeditions had laid down rules for their conduct. Discussion on what makes a happy ship has ancient origins and, after Cabot, Hawkins and Sir Hugh Willoughby had had their say, Captain John Smith, one-time 'governor' of the Jamestown colony, distilled the wisdom of the age in his book *A Sea Grammar* which was published in 1627. He went further than Captain Fox and recommended the following as ship's stores:

> Fine wheat flour, close and well-packed; rice, currants, sugar, prunes, cinnamon, ginger, pepper, cloves, green ginger; oil, butter, Holland cheese, or old cheese; wine vinegar, Canary sack, *aqua vitae,* the best wines, the best waters, the juice of lemons for the scurvy; white biscuit, oatmeal, gammons of bacon, dried neats' tongues; beef packed up in vinegar; legs of mutton minced and stewed and close packed up with boiled suet or butter in earthen pots. To entertain strangers, marmalade, suckets [fruit preserves], almonds, comfits [sugar-

preserved fruits or roots] and such like. [He went on:] Some it may be will say I would have men rather to feast than to fight; but I say, the want of those necessaries occasions the loss of more men than in any English fleet hath been slain since [15]88. For when a man is ill or on the point of death, I would know whether a dish of buttered rice with a little cinnamon, ginger and sugar, a little minced meat or roast beef, a few stewed prunes, a root of green ginger, a flapjack, a can of fresh water brewed with a little cinnamon, ginger and sugar – be not better than a little poor John (hard dried cod), or salt fish with oil and mustard; or biscuit, butter, cheese or oatmeal pottage on fish days; or on flesh days, salt beef, pork and peas with six shillings beer.[50]

Many read, though few paid heed, to what John Smith wrote. Seamen went on suffering and continued to be ill-fed though the amount of shipping went on growing. Between 1582 and 1629 the total English tonnage increased by more than 70 per cent, to at least 115,000 tons, and the number of ships over 200 tons grew from a mere 18 to more than 145.[51]

A national spirit had arisen in many of the countries of Europe in the 16th century and the strategic importance of the sea had become more fully realised, not least in England. The failure of the Armada had proved that it was not possible for an enemy, however powerful, to transport and land troops in the face of an effective fleet, and this discovery was of special significance to Britain. In the 16th century English sentiment had favoured the growth of maritime power because invasion from Spain was feared. In the 17th century this sentiment was further stimulated by Dutch rivalry and a desire to secure command of the sea for the purposes of trade.

In 1604 the sale abroad of ships capable of bearing ordnance was banned in England. In 1622 English northern traders were required, in the name of legislation passed in 1563 which closed the English coasting trade to foreign ships (a restriction which lasted, with small gaps, for close on 300 years), to ship their imports other than corn in English ships. In 1624 it was ordered that tobacco should not be imported in foreign ships. In 1625 a bounty was given for ships built over 200 tons. In 1626 it was complained that traders to France employed foreign ships 'contrary to divers proclamations'.[52] Rivalry with the Dutch was driving the English inexorably towards the Navigation Act of 1651 and the Dutch wars.

But it was in the first half of the 17th century that, despite the ineffectiveness of government, the indifference of monarchs and a waste of wars at sea, the seeds of empire were sown, not by conquistadors, but by sailors and traders and by political and religious dissidents. By 1649 over £5 million had been spent in overseas ventures and more than 60,000 people, or one in every 100 of the population, had left Great Britain for America.

Nearly 5000 people – one in every 500 of the male population of England – had invested abroad,[53] though the major thrust came from rich merchants like Sir Thomas Smith, the outstanding Governor of the East India Company for most of its first twenty years and Treasurer of the Virginia Company for the first nine; that is, the impetus derived from those merchants who had made fortunes from the chartered companies and from privateering. By 1649 the seeds of empire were sprouting both in India and America.

Notes

1. A. Tawney and E. Power, *Tudor Economic Documents,* Vol. II (1924), London, p. 125.
2. G. S. Graham, *Empire of the North Atlantic: The Maritime Struggle for North America* (1958), London, p. 24.
3. A. McGowan, *Tiller and Whipstaff: The Development of the Sailing Ship, 1400–1700* (1981), London, pp. 37–9; R. W. Unger, *The Ship in the Medieval Economy, 600–1600* (1980), London, pp. 252 and 262–4.
4. E. M. Carus-Wilson (ed). *Essays in Economic History* (1954), London, p. 228: 'Dutch and English Merchant Shipping in the Seventeenth Century' by V. Barbour.
5. Graham, *op. cit.*, p. 25 and p. 46.
6. M. Bogucka, 'Amsterdam and the Baltic in the First Half of the Seventeenth Century' (1973), EHR, 2nd Series, Vol. XXVI, No. 3, pp. 446–7; *also* R. W. Unger, 'Integration of Baltic and Low Countries grain markets, 1400–1800', p. 1, included in *The Interactions of Amsterdam and Antwerp with the Baltic Region, 1400–1800* (1983), Leiden.
7. R. Davis, *The Rise of the English Shipping Industry in the Seventeenth and Eighteenth Centuries* (1962), London, p. 311.
8. J. H. Parry, *The Age of Reconnaissance* (1963), London, pp. 186–9.
9. G. V. Scammell, *The World Encompassed* (1981), London, p. 290.
10. *P.L.A. Monthly,* September and December, 1964, pp. 297 and 409–12.
11. M. W. Thomas (ed). *A Survey of English Economic History,* 3rd ed. (1967), London, p. 153.
12. H. Taylor, 'Trade, Neutrality and the "English Road",' (1972) EHR, Vol. XXV, p. 237.
13. J. S. Kepler, 'Fiscal Aspects of the English Carrying Trade during the Thirty Years War' (1972), EHR, Vol. XXV, pp. 261 ff.
14. P. Croft, 'English Mariners Trading to Spain and Portugal, 1558–1625' (1983), MM, Vol. 69, No. 2, pp. 264.
15. D. B. Quinn and A. N. Ryan, *England's Sea Empire, 1550–1642* (1983), London, pp. 182–3.
16. T. Willan, *Studies in Elizabethan Foreign Trade* (1939), Manchester, p. 193; G. T. Cell, *English Enterprise in Newfoundland 1577–1660* (1969), Toronto, p. 126.
17. J. Nef, *The Rise of the British Coal Industry,* Vol. II (1932), London, App. D, p. 380.
18. Davis, *op. cit.*, p. 311.
19. W. Cunningham, *The Growth of English Industry and Commerce,* Vol. II (1882), Cambridge, p. 247.

20. T. Willan, *The English Coasting Trade 1600–1750* (1967), Manchester, p. 11.
21. Willan (1939), *op. cit.*, p. 68.
22. *Ib.*, pp. 69–74.
23. Cell, *op. cit.*, p. 21.
24. Captain S. Algar, Shell Tankers, in correspondence with the author.
25. K. R. Andrews, *Trade, Plunder and Settlement* (1984), Cambridge, pp. 341–3.
26. *Ib.*, p. 295.
27. *Ib.*, p. 325.
28. Scammell (1981), *op. cit.*, p. 486.
29. Davis, *op. cit.*, p. 315.
30. Willan (1939), *op. cit.*, p. 193.
31. *Ib.*, p. 68.
32. *Ib.*, pp. 69–74.
33. G. Ramsay, *English Overseas Trade during the Centuries of Emergence* (1957), London, p. 43.
34. M. Epstein, *The Early History of the Levant Company* (1908), London, p. 8.
35. Davis, *op. cit.*, p. 196.
36. Aboard the New Zealand Shipping Company training ship *Otaio*, see *The Seafarer* (1973), p. 3.
37. K. N. Chaudhuri, *The English East India Company: The Study of an Early Joint-Stock Company 1600–1640* (1965), London, p. 88.
38. *Ib.*, p. 22.
39. *Ib.*, p. 96.
40. *Ib.*, p. 91.
41. Andrews, *op. cit.*, pp. 269–70.
42. Chaudhuri, *op. cit.*, pp. 114–18.
43. A. Moore, 'Rig in Northern Europe' (1956), MM, Vol. 42, pp. 15–17.
44. Davis, *op. cit.*, pp. 338–40.
45. C. Lloyd, *The British Seaman* (1968), London, p. 64.
46. W. Perrin (ed), *Boteler's Dialogues* (1929), London, p. 65.
47. M. Christy (ed). *The Voyages of Captain Luke Fox . . . and Captain Thomas James* (1894), London, pp. 604–6.
48. D. Waters, *The Art of Navigation in England in Elizabethan and Early Stuart Times* (1958), London, pp. 499–500.
49. Christy (ed), *op. cit.*, p. 265.
50. K. Grell (ed), Captain John Smith, *A Sea Grammar* (1970), London, pp. 96–7.
51. Davis, *op. cit.*, p. 7.
52. *Ib.*, p. 303.
53. T. K. Rabb, 'Investment in English Overseas Enterprise, 1575–1630' (1966), EHR, 2nd Series, Vol. XIX, No. 1, pp. 70–75; *also* C. Shammas, 'English commercial development and American colonization 1560–1620', in K. R. Andrews, N. P. Canny and P. E. H. Hair, *The Westward Enterprise* (1978), Liverpool, pp. 172–4.

11

Defeat of the Dutch

(1649–1689)

Charles I was executed in 1649. Two years later the Commonwealth government provoked the first war between the English and Dutch of 1652–4 by passing a Navigation Act. Although this Act marked no major change of policy, it was more comprehensive than anything that had gone before and most of its basic decrees were to remain in force for nearly 200 years.

The Navigation Act of 1651 ordered that English imports should be brought direct from the country of production or the first port from which they were normally shipped either in English ships or in ships of the country of origin or first shipment. From outside Europe all goods were to be brought to England in English ships.

In 1660, very shortly after the restoration of Charles II, a still more detailed Act was passed. The coasting trade was completely reserved to English ships and, to be considered English, ships had to have an English master and crews three-quarters English. Nearly all the principal products of the Mediterranean and the Baltic, and all Turkish and Russian products, were to be imported either in English ships or in ships of the country of origin or place of first shipment. Foreign goods imported by English ships were to be brought only from their places of origin or usual first shipment. Imports from places outside Europe were to be carried in English, Welsh or Irish ships or in ships belonging to the country of origin. Tobacco, sugar, corn, indigo, ginger, fustic and other dyewoods produced in English possessions outside Europe were to be exported to England, Ireland or other English possessions only. Exports to the colonies were to be sent only on English, Welsh, Irish or colonial ships.

In 1662 a new Act was designed to limit the use of foreign-built ships other than prizes of war, as well as of foreign-owned ships, and bounties for large ships were revived though the definition of large ships was changed.[1] In 1674 duties were placed on goods sent from one colony to another.

As is usual with political acts designed to achieve particular ends, there were side effects which were not foreseen. Scandinavian shipping was given a boost since, to meet the requirements of the Acts, Scandinavian nationals bought Dutch ships which could still prove more economic than expensive English vessels. There were also many pretended naturalisations of Dutch flyboats whereby these vessels were flagged inconspicuously into the privileges of the Navigation Acts.[2]

Nevertheless, the English navy grew from about 130 ships in 1652 to 173 in 1688 and the foreign merchantmen proved of little avail against such warships as the *Sovereign of the Seas*.[3] The final break between warships and merchant vessels had been made and after the First Dutch War no merchant ship was again hired to stand in the battle line.[4]

At the same time the tonnage of English merchant shipping grew, as did the size of English ships. Hull was a port which ranked behind Bristol and Newcastle, behind Yarmouth, and perhaps even behind Ipswich in the tonnage of ships owned. It was also a port which had no connection with the new trades to east and west. But a detailed study of its trade has shown that after the English Civil War its coastwise traffic expanded considerably. To London and elsewhere Hull ships carried textiles and the products of the growing iron and brass industries and brought back tobacco and East Anglian wool. The Navigation Acts halted the growth of the Dutch share in Hull's trade and Hull ships began to voyage more extensively in the Baltic. Between 1600 and 1692 the number of vessels entering Hull in the coastal trade increased from 293 to 339 and, whereas in 1600 225 vessels of the total were colliers, by 1692 the number of colliers, though of a larger size, had fallen to 194. From abroad 154 ships came into Hull in 1687, compared with 129 in 1567. Of the latter number only 61 were English. Of the former number 135 were English. In the course of the 17th century Hull's exports of cloths alone more than doubled.[5]

In the meantime the Dutch continued to enjoy many of their advantages, though some of their trades declined. From about 1650 onwards the average size of Dutch ships carrying grain from the Baltic fell because the Polish surplus of rye diminished and western and southern Europe became more self-supporting in food grains.[6] As late as 1666, however, it was estimated that three-quarters of the capital active on the Amsterdam bourse was still engaged in the Baltic trade.[7] Customs duties on timber imports were low and much labour-saving machinery was used in shipbuilding, so that a flyboat which would cost £1300 in England could be built for £800 in Holland, though the difference in price was less than it had been and the English ship would be more stoutly built. In 1676 an English merchantman of 250 tons would cost £7.2s.6d. a ton, while a 200-ton fluyt built in Holland would cost £4.10s. a ton.[8] The Dutch still sent 700–800 ships a year into the Baltic and employed over 1000 herring busses in the North Sea, 600 of them large vessels.[9] These, however, were lower numbers than they had been in the previous half-century. In the whaling industry the Dutch were by this time the undisputed masters. In the Atlantic they continued to harry Spanish trade, for the Dutch Admiral Maarten Tromp had destroyed the last Spanish Armada to be sent north in 1639, and they carried on a lively trade with the Spanish colonists. In the trade to the East they planted a permanent colony at the Cape of Good Hope in 1652, Dutch possessions and spheres of influence extended from Persia to the Malay Archipelago and the Dutch had opened a trade with Japan. In Ceylon the pearl fisheries and the cinnamon trade were wholly in Dutch hands.

The seas so burgeoned with Dutch-built ships, many of them owned by the nationals of other states, that when they were at war, Dutchmen could often masquerade as innocent Lübeckers or Genoese, and in 1662 the Scots complained that they were being debarred from trade by the English because they used ships which had been built in Holland.[10] Sir William Petty, who had abandoned a life at sea to study in Holland and who had become the most distinguished political economist of his day, could still write in the 1670s, after the three Dutch wars, of 'the Hollanders undermasting and sailing such of their shipping as carry cheap and gross goods, and whose sale doth depend much upon season'.[11] Petty pointed out the cost advantages of cheaply-built ships which were cheaply run, advantages which have remained with bulk carriers down the ages.

The English won the three Dutch wars in the second half of the 17th century by reason of better guns and gunnery and better seamanship in stronger and more manoeuvrable ships, all factors in the defeat of the Armada in 1588. But the appointment during the Commonwealth of soldiers like Robert Blake, who became Generals-at-Sea rather than Admirals, also established stricter discipline, better pay and higher rewards for prizes. Iron guns on wheeled carriages, which could be brought inboard for safer loading, were fired together as 'broadsides', and such gunfire was made more effectual because the ships fought in line ahead. In the first Dutch War of 1652–4 prizes captured by the English are estimated to have numbered between 1000 and 1700 ships. In the second Dutch War of 1664–7, a war said to have cost about £5 million,[12] over 500 prizes were taken. In the third Dutch War of 1672–4 a further 500 prizes were secured, while in the war with Spain from 1655–60, 400 more prizes were captured. In the war against Spain there was a net loss of ships, since the Spaniards captured or destroyed between 1000 and 1500 English ships. To the Dutch, however, the English only lost some 500 ships in all three wars.[13] If these figures can be relied upon it would appear that at the end of the 22 years from 1652 to 1674 the English were many hundreds of ships to the good. Indeed, it has been estimated that for most of these years foreign-built ships taken as prizes were never less than one-third of the total tonnage in English ownership and that by 1675 they accounted for something like one-half of it. By the end of these wars the English possessed not only a larger fleet by reason of these prizes but a better balanced one as well. As Sir Josiah Child wrote in 1669, the English would have been wholly beaten out of the bulk trades 'had we been necessitated to build English ships, and not been requited at moderate prices by flyboats (being ships proper for this trade) taken in the late Dutch war.' 'The Act of Navigation', he went on, 'is now of seventeen or eighteen years' standing, yet in all these years not one English ship has been built for this trade.'[14]

Despite such benefits the wars themselves could not but affect trade adversely. Set back by the Civil War, English trade revived after 1646 only to be checked again in some measure in 1649 by a growth of anti-Commonwealth privateering and a loss of officers after the execution of Charles I. Subsequent recovery was quenched by the first Dutch War and the war with Spain. After the Restoration there was initially a large-scale purchase of ships from abroad and this was followed by a sharp recovery of English shipbuilding after the passing of the Act of 1662. Growth was then checked again by the further Dutch wars.

England's chance came when, after the third Dutch War of 1672–4, the rest of Europe remained at war when England had made peace. As the only neutral among the leading maritime powers England was able, between 1674 and 1678, not only to expand her trade by supplying the warring states, but also to steal the Dutch trade carried on between the Baltic and the Iberian peninsula, particularly the trade in salt. Many ships which now sailed from England to Portugal with corn, carried salt back to Riga or Petersburg and brought hemp, flax and iron back to England.

In these later decades of the 17th century the Iceland fishery declined and the growth in coastal trade was limited. Coal shipments from Newcastle, which had nearly doubled between 1598 and 1634, increased by only one-third, from 409,000 to 560,000 tons, between 1634 and 1698, although after the Restoration the foreign ships involved were driven almost entirely from the trade. It was the more spectacular side of shipping that now progressed rapidly, the large ships, above all the London ships, Dutch in origin though some of them might be, which were bound, on the one hand for Norway and the Baltic on behalf of the big timber traders, and on the other for North America and the West Indies for tobaccco and sugar. In 1664 26 ships cleared London for Norway and 22 for the Baltic; by 1686 these numbers had increased to 111 and 65 respectively. In these same years the number of ships clearing for the West Indies were respectively 45 and 133, and for North America 43 and 114.[15]

To some extent the growth of shipping itself increased the demand for shipbuilding materials since there was an increasing shortage of English oak and elm which had to be replaced by imported fir, pine and spruce. But stimulated by the Great Fire of London in 1666 and the growth of other towns there was also an increased demand for timber for house-building. This expansion of timber and allied imports from the Baltic, which led to a brief prosperity for the Eastland Company, was financed not only by a developing export of woollen goods, but also by the re-export of Indian textiles brought home in the ships of the East India Company and of sugar and tobacco imported from the American colonies. The Eastland Company had died of attrition by the early 18th century but the trade to the Baltic had not. Between 200 and 300 ships a year were bound for England from the Baltic between 1673 and 1700 and by the end of the century half of them were English ships.[16]

The colonies in the New World had by this time developed into two types. From Pennsylvania northwards they became small farming and lumbering communities with a large degree of self-sufficiency and as yet little to export. To the far north the Hudson Bay Company operated after 1670 on a joint-stock basis to import furs, and it enjoyed favour at Court because it checked the expansion of French influence in the north of Canada. Two Frenchmen, in fact, contributed to its inception. By this time the English had ended Dutch dominion on the north American continent and they enjoyed two advantages over the French in the Canadian trade. First, the crossing from England was shorter. Second, in these waters they now had command of the seas. The Hudson Bay Company's business, however, was small-scale and, at this time, politically insecure, and it never despatched across the Atlantic in any one year more than two or three modestly-sized vessels.[17]

South of Pennsylvania the colonies had become plantation colonies, very much dependent upon the export of a single staple crop. By the treaty of 1670 the Spanish government had at last recognised as English those territories which were occupied and Virginia and Maryland were already dependent on tobacco exports, the lightness of this cargo being particularly suited to carriage in the Dutch flyboat.

Further south, Jamaica had been seized in 1655 and the heyday of the buccaneers began. All the islands of the Greater Antilles supported great herds of feral pigs and horned cattle, animals that had bred from those which had escaped from Spanish farms and ranches. Originally making a living from hunting these animals and selling the smoked meat and the hides to passing ships, the *boucaniers* or buccaneers (from *boucon*: smoked meat) had turned to piracy. Their principal bases were Port Royal and Tortuga and their principal patrons were the English governors of Jamaica and the French governors of St Domingue. Under Henry Morgan the Port Royal buccaneers plundered Puerto Bello (Portobelo) on the isthmus of Panama and massacred its garrisons in 1668. The following year they sacked Maracaibo and in 1670 burned Santa Marta, Rio de la Hacha, Panama and other Spanish settlements. Morgan then retired from active buccaneering but was arrested and transported to London. However, a year or two later he was knighted and sent out as lieutenant-governor of Jamaica,[18] a colony in which plantation sugar had been largely financed by Spanish silver earned in a lucrative illicit trade based on plunder and contraband.[19] By 1660 the English trade in both tobacco and sugar from the New World had become of increasing significance.

Ships developed with the trades. Before 1640 only a tiny group of English ships exceeded 350 tons. In the 1640s some 600–700-ton ships were built, the largest finding their employment in the East or on the route to the Levant. A few followed the short-lived fashion of the larger warships of the time in having a fourth mast, the bonaventure mizen, but they were mostly three-masted. Most of these big ships were two-decked, occasionally three-decked, heavily gunned and strongly manned. In wartime they proved the navy's chief reserve. Variations in type, as distinct from variations in size, were important only in ships of less than 50 tons. Among these smaller vessels, vessels which traded with France, Flanders, Holland, Ireland and round the English coast, there was a variety of two-masted rigs. By the middle of the 17th century an alternative fore and aft sail developed in an early form of the gaffsail, and there are the first indications of schooner rig. The terms sloop and ketch come into use, though they were not necessarily what they became in the 19th century, and by the end of the century there is the first mention of a brigantine, synonymous at this time with the brig.[20] The one-masted English hoy grew bigger, varying from 25 to 80 tons, and the rig was modified to become a fore and aft mainsail with a triangular headsail. As there was only one mast the headsail had to be triangular and was set from a stay. By this time English hoys did not generally rig a bowsprit. Hoys continued to be employed in the short sea trades, as coasters and as lighters until the middle of the 19th century.[21] Other one-masted vessels included the doggers and the shallops.

English shipping had found in the Mediterranean the first region in which it could play a significant part in the cross-trades. The ships were well-armed and England was often neutral when other countries were at war. After 1655 the English were usually protected by treaty from Moorish corsairs and in these waters English ships moved grain, rice and salt, rice being transported, for example, from Venice to Leghorn. Freight rates at £5 to £5.10s. a ton were good, though there were heavy charges which had to be borne by the Levant Company. Thus, while the French monarch stood the charge of a consular establishment on behalf of French traders, the British government did not follow suit until 1813. Nevertheless, by 1660 the Levant Company was chartering more ships than it had done fifty years earlier. In consequence of the activities of the East India Company, however, its trade had changed character to some extent for, instead of bringing spices and other eastern luxuries to England from the Mediterranean, it was now supplying them to the Mediterranean after their procurement by way of the Cape of Good Hope.[22]

During part of the Interregnum trade to the East was practically open to all. In 1657, however, the East India company was re-established on a more permanent basis and the capital then raised was treated as a permanent fund. Upon the restoration of Charles II the company was given a new charter and soon developed into a political and judicial power as well as being a trading company.[23] The names of the ships employed in the last decade of the century give a fair idea of where the money came from: *Berkeley Castle*, *Bedford*, *Tavistock*, *Streatham*, *Howland*, *Josiah*, *Martha*, the *Russell* frigate, *Wentworth*, *Beaufort* and *Massingbird*. The aristocracy had decided that shipping was a good investment.[24]

From this time on the Company was allowed to export bullion without a licence and trade increased considerably. Further stations were established in India, at Hooghly near Calcutta in 1650, at Bombay in 1662, and at Calcutta itself in 1686. Disputes with the Dutch continued at Bantam in Java and in 1682 the English were forced to withdraw and established themselves instead at Bencoolen. Spices had by this time lost their pre-eminence among the homeward cargoes, between 70 and 80 per cent of the value of such cargoes now being attributable to cotton textiles. Silks from Persia and Bengal and indigo from Lahore were also valuable cargoes, while pepper from the East Indies and the Malabar Coast and saltpetre and sugar from Bengal provided the bulk. When she sailed for England in 1681 the *Berkeley Castle* was 'reputed for cargo the richest ship which ever went out of Madras Road,' its cargo worth some £80,000 (over £5 million at 1988 prices); but well over half the tonnage on board consisted of saltpetre, which contributed little to the total value. Exports to India were limited. Apart from cloth, ironware, brassware and beer, lead and iron were carried, usually as ballast and often with much of it coming home again.[25] By the late 1680s the East India Company was bringing in about 14 per cent of the country's imports by value and paying annual dividends of 20 per cent.[26]

Edward Coxere is among those who have left us their memoirs of life at sea in this period. Born in Dover in 1633, he died at Scarborough in 1694. He went to sea at the age of 14 and spent some time in Dutch ships, even fighting for the Dutch. Coming ashore in Deal from a Dutch vessel captured by the English about 1650, he pretended to be Dutch and thus escaped from the press while he made his way home.[27] A couple of years later he shipped out as mate for the good wages of 43s a month in the ship *Christopher*, laden with kippers. The ship was driven on to the French coast near Guernsey, the master being drunk, and a French man-of-war commanded them to put out a boat. 'That done, the master, myself, and one more went on board, where we were presently stripped of our clothes.' Even though they were bound for France, and at this time England was at peace with that country, the French then boarded the *Christopher* and stole cloves from the cargo and clothes from the crew.[28]

Two years after his marriage in 1655 Coxere, aboard a vessel laden with currants and muscatel, was captured by Turks from Tunis. Put to work in Tunis, he was imprisoned in Portofarino Castle at night, chained to a fellow seaman and a prey to bugs and lice. Rescued at last, his troubles were still not over, but he succeeded in reaching home in 1658.

> This voyage, I had been from England a year and a half, in which time I had been a slave to the Turks, a prisoner of the Spaniards, as being taken by them, and came home only my clothes to my back to my poor wife, but poor and penniless yet glad to see each other in health again after these troubles. My son Robert died whilst I was a slave, and Elizabeth was born. I was pitied by many, but counted fortunate. At this time my wife did begin to keep shop, there being a necessity for something to be done for a livelihood.[29]

The following spring Coxere sailed again as chief mate to Newfoundland to load 'poor Jack', borrowing £15 to 'fit myself with books, instruments, clothes and a venture'. Having bought cod, the ship sailed for the Mediterranean, where Coxere sold the fish he had bought on his own account and 'bought raisins cheap for eleven shillings a hundred. . . .' 'We got well to London. We had been seven months or eight on the voyage. I had three pounds ten shillings per month, and with the returns of my venture this voyage proved very profitable for me, in which the Lord blessed my endeavours, though through much difficulty. I gained between fifty or sixty pounds. I soon paid my debts and had stock against the next voyage of my own.'[30]

John Baltharpe wrote an account of a voyage of this period in narrative verse. Although his poem describes an expedition against Algiers in 1669–71, when his ship *St David*, of about 685 tons, was part of the Mediterranean fleet, many of his experiences are not unlike those of the ordinary merchant seaman at this time, or at any time in the three centuries which follow. In Spain, he suggests, the seaman ashore is likely to spend 'three months' short-allowance money' in a day's leave and, if there is nothing to pick from his pocket, the Spaniard is likely to take his jacket. On the way to Leghorn:

> Great talk there's now of Leghorn ladies –
> Some swore that they would get them babies
> But 'stead of babies they did get
> What they have hardly clawed off yet.

At Messina the bumboatmen come off to the ship every day except Sunday, when the Admiral does not allow it:

> All sorts of trade they brought aboard:
> Silk stockings, brandy, wine they afford;
> Some cabbages, some nuts, some figs,
> Some Syracuse wine, some eggs.

They are willing to take anything in exchange. At Naples it is the same and everything is very cheap – 'a quarter of a sheep a shilling'. These are the good times, but at sea it can be very different:

> For want of victuals we are now grown faint.
> Our beef and pork is very scant –
> I'm sure of weight one half it want.
> Our bread is black and maggots in it crawl –
> That's all the fresh meat we are fed withal.[31]

In 1659, the year in which Edward Coxere reached home blessed in his endeavours, Edward Barlow, who was to become another professional sailor, went to sea as an apprentice. Born in 1642, he did not come from a seaport for his home was in Prestwich near Manchester but, like thousands of boys after him, he had a yearning for high adventure. After he had learned to read and write, he commented contemptuously in his journal, 'Some of my neighbours would not venture a day's journey from out of the smoke of their chimneys or the taste of their mother's milk'. He was soon to be involved in transporting Charles II back to England, and the year after that he made this typical but not unjustified comment: 'Neither are ships and we poor seamen out of great danger of our lives in calm and fairest weather', for there was always danger from fire and from leaky ships: 'So that I always said how happy were those men above us that lived at home in England and had pleasures of the world to walk when and where they pleased; and all things at their wills, eating and drinking of the best, whilst we were suffering all manner of misery and extremities and only to keep them safe at home from foreign invasions and enemies.'[32] Nevertheless, after a good pay-off he liked to swagger before the girls in his new clothes and talk of his adventures. And, like Coxere, he both stayed and survived at sea, briefly commanding an East Indiaman at the end of his career and retiring at the age of sixty-one.

One of Barlow's ships, *Cadiz Merchant* of 270 tons, was probably built in 1675 for about £1200 and armed with 24 guns. In that year she brought coal from Newcastle to London and, since the Dutch and the French were at war, obtained a 'Sea Brief' or Safe Conduct from the Admiralty. She then picked up more coal at Newcastle for sale in Copenhagen before proceeding to Riga to which port she had been chartered to bring a cargo to Amsterdam. From Amsterdam she went to Hamburg to load cargo for Cadiz and Malaga, adding four more guns to counter the added danger from Moorish pirates, the treaties made with their rulers notwithstanding. She then crossed to the Humber, and made calls at Deal and Plymouth, before arriving in Malaga five months after leaving Amsterdam. All summer she then lay at either Malaga or Cadiz waiting for the season's oil and wine. A year or so after she sailed, the ship discharged in Hamburg, the owners suffering a small loss on the voyage.

Cadiz Merchant then laid up in Hamburg all winter, sailing to London in March 1677 and thence to Norway to load timber for Portugal. On returning to Norway with a cargo of salt, the master experienced such bad weather in the North Sea that he wintered in Hull, not completing the voyage to Norway until March 1678. He then brought a cargo of timber to the Thames, where he arrived in June.

That summer peace was being made in Europe and Dutch competition revived so, after repairs, *Cadiz Merchant* turned south on a tonnage charter to load goods in Turkey and Greece at £6.10s. a ton. In Cadiz she joined a convoy and went to Mahon, Leghorn, Messina and Smyrna. After three months in Smyrna she returned home in convoy by way of Athens, Zante, Messina, Leghorn, Alicante and Cadiz, arriving in London, fifteen months after setting out, in December 1679.

The following spring she was sent to Jamaica by the owners. This was a new trade and she carried both goods and passengers. The sixty-nine passengers each paid £5–£6 a head. Twelve of them were free citizens, but the rest were indentured servants who were expected to serve for four years in return for their passage money. For the benefit of the indentured servants, a chaplain was engaged at 30s a month. The ship was convoyed part of the way, since the English were now at war with the Turks. From Jamaica she brought back a cargo of sugar, cotton and hides, arriving in England in February 1681. Unsurprisingly, *Cadiz Merchant* was not a very profitable ship.[33]

The *Cadiz Merchant*'s normal crew numbered 21. In 1672 the *Falcon*, trading to the Baltic, carried a crew of 17: master, mate, boatswain, gunner, carpenter, surgeon and 11 men and boys; in peacetime the gunner could be dispensed with. When such ships laid up, the crew would be paid off and the master and perhaps one other would look after her.

To be master of any but the smallest ship was a worthwhile and usually profitable profession. Such men tended to be the sons of shipmasters or minor merchants. Masters in the East Indian and Levant trades in the 1660s earned £10 a month; other masters might earn £6 a month, or rather less if they were employed in the provinces. All masters and many seafarers would make additional money on the side, chiefly by trading on their own account, though the master might also make something on charter parties made abroad or on the master's 'bond', that is by selling clothes and spirits to the crew. In the East India Company five per cent of the chartered tonnage was now available for private trading and this privilege mainly benefited the master. On the other hand master and crew might be subject to charges where cargo was damaged.

Barlow as chief mate earned 80s a month, and as second mate 55s. From the 1630s a carpenter's pay was about 40s and an AB's about 20s or 24s a month, though this might nearly double in wartime[34] and tended to rise in any case as the century progressed. A ship's boy of 13 might earn 8s a month and he would normally act as watchman in port.

Wages were normally paid at the end of a voyage, though as early as 1663 East India Company seamen received two months' pay in advance. 'Subs' or advances of pay might also be made during the voyage, and these were common in the Mediterranean trade. If a ship was lost the law did not require that wages be paid even to surviving crew.[35] 'Freight is the mother of wages', it was argued, and as late as World War II wages ceased to be paid in many companies on the day on which a ship sank.

Although in the 1660s – and long after in small vessels – it was possible for the master to be illiterate, and there was a general lack of theoretical understanding, it was a knowledge of navigation which distinguished the master and the mate from the rest of the crew. Barlow's pay when he first went to sea was forfeit to a master he never saw, but he was technically apprenticed to this master for seven years and it was presumably arranged that he receive some instruction in navigation. The navigator's guides, as heretofore, were the compass and log, used together for dead reckoning, with the cross-staff and quadrant to measure the angles of sun and stars to determine latitude. To brush up his knowledge and to remind him of navigational dangers on the coast the master would carry his rutter or pilot-book, and by the middle of the 17th century most masters carried a *Waggoner*, a primitive nautical almanac. In 1673, a century after Hakluyt had urged the necessity for a sound nautical education, a school was established at Christ's Hospital to instruct forty boys in mathematics and navigation. It had no influence, however, upon the majority of ships' officers.

Immense trust had to be put in the masters and hence it was likely that the master was related to at least some of the owners. Policy decisions which could be taken at home would normally require the concurrence of the owners of a majority of the shares in a ship. Such decisions would include the appointment of the master and whether the ship operated when times were bad. Owners might even hire crew, and they would seek cargo, collect freight money and arrange repairs. At the end of a long voyage they would probably meet to hear what dividend was being declared. When accepting cargo the master was sometimes instructed to follow the orders given by the travelling factor, cape merchant or agent appointed to the ship by the owners or charterers, the term 'supercargo' replacing these names in the late 17th century.[36] But in the Baltic, at least, the master would be responsible for loading the ship as well as for navigation since the supercargo, whose responsibility this had been previously, was being dispensed with in established trades. In the Mediterranean the master was often, in effect, the managing owner, the master's responsibilities tending to increase with the length of the voyage.

Broking and other services were beginning to emerge, and many of London's commercial deals were made at the Royal Exchange, which opened three hours a day, or in the streets behind the Royal Exchange. Samuel Pepys would often resort to the Exchange to charter or insure ships. When the old Exchange was burnt down in the Great Fire of 1666 it was not rebuilt for some years and business then began to be transacted in taverns and coffee-houses. In consequence the importance of the Exchange declined and meeting-places tended to specialise in particular kinds of business. After the Civil War in England it became possible to advertise in news sheets.

One important decision which needed to be taken by managing owners was whether to charter ships for their purposes. Nearly all time charters were taken up with a particular voyage but, with a growing capacity among ship operators to estimate the likely progress of a voyage, time

The Humber keel. These sailing barges sometimes carried cargoes to London. Though in recent centuries they might be fore-and-aft rigged for this purpose, the single square sail rig also persisted well into the 20th century. Early keels could carry 30–40 tons of cargo, 19th-century ones up to 100 tons.

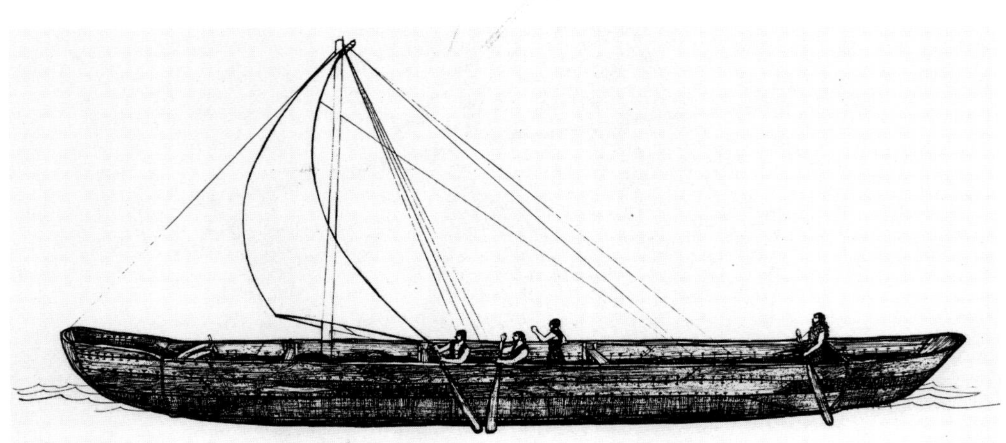

The North Ferriby boat. As indicated, a sail may have been fitted in this earliest known British boat which dates from about 1500 BC. It is the oldest known plank-built boat in the world other than those of similar date found in Egypt.

The curragh or Celtic skin boat. In use from 500 BC or earlier, it had a wicker-work frame covered with hides, perhaps with a double bottom, and up to 20 oarsmen. Such craft ventured well into the North Atlantic.

The Veneti ships. These vessels operated in the English Channel in the 1st century BC and the illustration has been recreated from Julius Caesar's graphic description.

The Blackfriars barge. A British ship dating from the 2nd century AD, this vessel seems to have much in common with the Thames barge of modern times. Peter Knox has suggested Roman influence in indicating the two steering oars aft, the cabin and a woven sail, but one authority sees in it a distinct Celtic tradition.

Cinque Port ship of the 13th century. This representation is devised from the Bayeux tapestry and from drawings on seals and manuscripts. Viking inspiration is clear in the clinker build and hull shape.

14th-century single-masted cog. Based largely on a window in Bourges Cathedral, the seal of Ipswich and a woodcarving from King's Lynn, this merchantman is considerably more sophisticated than the Cinque port ship. The main new feature, the stern rudder, appears to have been of local origin and was a major breakthrough in ship design. The vessel has a crow's nest and rope ladders or ratlines. The bowsprit is retained.

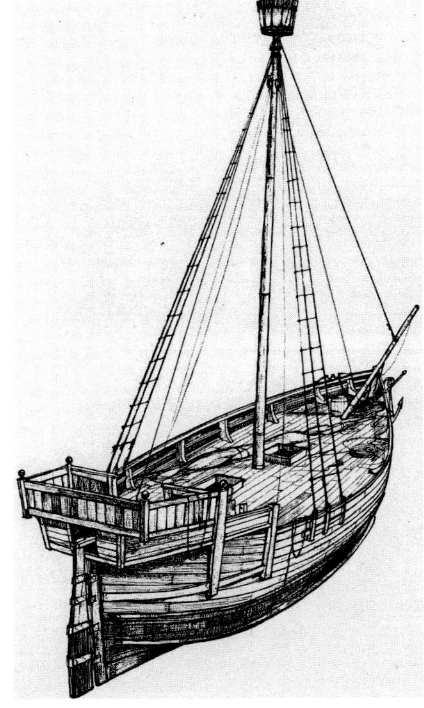

15th-century Carrack. Here is a three-masted ship with a lateen mizen. The accommodation has become an integral part of the structure, with a well-deck amidships. The ship is still round-bottomed, with a round bow, but is a highly sophisticated vessel that could sail across the Atlantic.

This is the acme of Elizabethan shipbuilding, a *Mayflower*-like merchantman, with two sails on main and foremast, a bowsprit which carries a sail, and a beakhead which in the next century developed into a sail-handling platform. Note the bonnet method of shortening sail.

(*Above*) The *Beatty*. A 350-ton merchantman built in Liverpool about 1760, when the slave trade was at its height. Too narrow and too deep, poorly armed and a slow sailer, *Beatty* would have been comfortable nevertheless. Renamed *The Marine Society* in 1786 and, as a hulk, this vessel became the world's first training ship.

A brig used as a collier. The two-masted brig, perhaps 60–70 feet long, and from 100 to 150 tons in capacity, was common from the second half of the 18th century to the second half of the 19th century. Conditions aboard were primitive and the vessels were highly vulnerable.

The barge would have had a simple square sail originally. By the second half of the 17th century more complicated rigs had been developed. This early 19th-century barge also has a jigger mast with a lug-sail at the stern.

Described in 1802 as a yacht, *Speedwell* (*below*) transported passengers and their baggage from London to Ramsgate and Broadstairs. The best cabin cost 7s. (£10 at 1988 prices).

(*Left*) The East Indiaman *Buckinghamshire*. This great ship, of 1369 tons, is arriving home after a voyage to China in 1823. She has been painted by the ship's poulterer, Edward Coverly.

The iron paddle-steamer *Ripon*. Built in 1846 at Blackwall for P&O, *Ripon* was originally 1508 tons gross. In 1850 she brought the first hippopotamus to England. Four years later she was requisitioned for service in the Crimean War, and in 1864 she brought General Garibaldi to Southampton. In 1870 she was sold, her engines were removed and she was reduced to a brig.

Agamemnon, first of Alfred Holt's revolutionary Blue Funnel ships, designed for the China trade in 1865, was of 2280 tons gross. Built by Scott's of Greenock, she could carry coal enough to travel 8500 miles, and managed the journey from Foochow to London comfortably in 65 days.

charters tended to be replaced by tonnage charters or agreements to load so much wine, sugar, oil or some other cargo. Thus after 1650 time charters were rarely used in the tobacco trade and after 1680 rarely used for importing sugar. Although inordinately long by modern standards, loading times were limited in extent and there was a daily payment of demurrage to the shipowner by the charterer for failure to load the ships within the time allowed.[37] After 1660 the hiring and paying of a crew were normally the duties of owners and not charterers.

With better established governments there was a growing respect for law throughout Europe and some process of law could be set in motion to recover a pirated ship or to punish an absconder. A growing network of agents was established abroad and, if his ship were not on charter, the typical managing owner would send his ship to places where he knew factors and agents who were likely to secure cargo. Although owners had to meet some proportion of losses, insurance was becoming widespread, the peacetime rate being 3 per cent or even less and the war risk rate from 6 to 14 per cent, occasionally rising to as much as 35 per cent. Even in wartime there was normally a less than one in ten chance of capture, and during the 17th century the oceans were practically cleared of pirates, with a consequent beneficial effect on insurance rates.[38]

One effect of the wars of this time was to increase the navy's peacetime establishment of between 3000 and 5000 officers and men to a peak in the Second and Third Dutch Wars of 35,000. Impressment was mainly confined to seamen and shipyard workers, the seamen being taken as often as not from incoming ships. Some 'landmen' or volunteers were recruited in wartime, the chief attraction being high wartime wages which were better than the wages ashore of unskilled or even skilled men.

Shipping had begun to grow quite rapidly after 1580 and between 1660 and 1689 it emerged from its earlier insignificance to become one of the fastest-growing English industries. In the century from 1582 to 1686 tonnage multiplied more than fivefold, increasing from 67,000 to at least 340,000 tons and probably more in a period in which population perhaps doubled. As an industry, shipping now came fourth after agriculture, clothmaking and building. The value of English exports and re-exports trebled, and shipping contributed much to the growth of London. By 1689, of a population of 1.5 million men, 50,000 or one in thirty were serving in merchant shipping, but in the following generation the pace of this development slowed down.

Notes

1. R. Davis, *The Rise of the English Shipping Industry in the Seventeenth and Eighteenth Centuries* (1962), London, p. 312.
2. V. Barbour, 'Dutch and English Merchant Shipping in the Seventeenth Century', *contained in* E. M. Carus-Wilson, *Essays in Economic History* (1954), London, pp. 232–6.
3. G. S. Graham, *Empire of the North Atlantic: The Maritime Struggle for North America* (1958), London, pp. 43–7.
4. A. McGowan, *Tiller and Whipstaff: The Development of the Sailing Ship, 1400–1700* (1981), London, p. 50.
5. R. Davis, *The Trade and Shipping of Hull, 1500–1700* (1964), EY Local History Series, No. 17, East Yorkshire Local History Society, pp. 15–24.
6. R. W. Unger, 'Integration of Baltic and Low Countries grain markets, 1400–1800', p. 9, included in *The Interactions of Amsterdam and Antwerp with the Baltic Region, 1400–1800* (1983), Leiden.
7. C. R. Boxer, *The Dutch Seaborne Empire* (1965), London, p. 43.
8. V. Barbour, *op. cit.*, pp. 237–40.
9. *Ib.*, p. 232.
10. *Ib.*, p. 250.
11. C. H. Hull (ed), *The Economic Writings of Sir William Petty* (1899), Cambridge, p. 261.
12. M. W. Thomas, *A Survey of English Economic History*, 3rd ed. (1967), London, p. 195.
13. Davis (1962), *op. cit.*, p. 316.
14. *Ib.*, pp. 52–3.
15. *Ib.*, p. 18.
16. R. W. K. Hinton, *The Eastland Trade and the Common Weal in the Seventeenth Century* (1959), Cambridge, p. 107 and pp. 161–3.
17. E. E. Rich, *The History of the Hudson's Bay Company, 1670–1870*, Vol. I, 1670–1763 (1958), London, pp. 47–55 and p. 105.
18. J. H. Parry, *The Spanish Seaborne Empire* (1966), London, pp. 263–4.
19. N. Zahedieh, 'Trade, Plunder and Economic Development in Early English Jamaica 1655–89' (1986), EHR, 2nd Series, Vol. XXXIX, No. 2, pp. 205 ff.
20. McGowan, *op. cit.*, p. 50.
21. *Ib.*, pp. 35–6.
22. K. N. Chaudhuri, *The English East India Company: The Study of an Early Joint-Stock Company 1600–1640* (1965), London, p. 45.
23. W. Cunningham, *The Growth of English Industry and Commerce*, Vol. II (1882), Cambridge, p. 262.
24. J. Sutton, *Lords of the East: the East India Company and Its Ships* (1981), Greenwich, p. 17.
25. Davis (1962), *op. cit.*, pp. 257–8.
26. G. V. Scammell, *The English Chartered Trading Companies and the Sea* (1983), National Maritime Museum, p. 13.
27. E. Myerstein (ed), *Adventures by Sea of Edward Coxere* (1946), New York, pp. 26–8.
28. *Ib.*, pp. 41–2.
29. *Ib.*, pp. 119–20.
30. *Ib.*, pp. 126–7.
31. J. Baltharpe, *The Straights Voyage or St Davids Poem* (1959), Oxford.

32. B. Lubbock (ed), *Barlow's Journal*, 2 vols. (1934), London, pp. 60–1.
33. Davis (1962), *op. cit.*, pp. 346–57.
34. *Ib.*, p. 135; *see also* M. Oppenheim, *History of the Administration of the Royal Navy . . .* (1896, reprinted 1988), London, p. 243 and p. 314.
35. *De Jure Maritimo et Navali* (1676), London, p. 211.
36. P. Croft, 'English Mariners Trading to Spain and Portugal 1558–1625' (1983), MM, Vol. 69, No. 2, p. 251.
37. Davis (1962), *op. cit.*, p. 167.
38. *Ib.*, p. 318.

12

Rise of the Slave Trade (1689–1739)

The development of shipping between 1500 and 1815 did not have wholly beneficent consequences. New discovery and new ideas were undoubtedly stimulating, and it can be argued that capital acquired from the new trades financed the industrial revolution. New foods like potatoes, maize, cassava and tomatoes arrived in Europe and Africa from America, as did new raw materials like mahogany, and these contributed to the general welfare of those who acquired them. The transfer of horses from Europe to America, on the other hand, contributed greatly to the near annihiliation of the native inhabitants, as did the transfer of the plague, smallpox and measles. Syphilis, brought to Spain by the Taino Indians who accompanied Columbus, was equally unwelcome in the West.[1]

The great new trades themselves were at best unnecessary and at worst positively harmful. The drugs and spices from the East did not cure any illnesses nor preserve any foods. Tea was less healthy than English small beer, as Jonas Hanway averred, and was paid for in part by forcing opium upon the Chinese peoples. Rum and sack made people drunk, sugar rotted their teeth, and tobacco was and remains a killer of powerful proportions.

To gain these useless products many thousands of seafarers met a premature death, not merely from the normal dangers attendant upon their profession but from the effects of piracy and war, which were themselves consequences of the new discoveries. On top of all this was imposed the horror of the slave trade, the legacy of which is still very much with us.

It has been estimated that before the English became much involved, which was not until after 1680, some two million slaves had been transported across the Atlantic.[2] By this time the state of Massachusetts had forbidden slavery in the colony and, according to one authority, 'almost everyone who had not been corrupted by the trade felt that it was wrong in principle'.[3] Nevertheless, the trade had acquired an air of legality. The slaves were sold largely by black merchants and caboceers or village headmen under the supervision of the coastal kings of West Africa, most of whom were slave-traders themselves. Slaves were capital and it was sensible not to squander capital. Proportionately fewer slaves than sailors died on the notorious 'middle passage' to America though there were, of course, many more slaves involved. A dead slave was money lost: from £2. 10s. to £3. 10s. was the customary purchase price for a male slave at this time and he would sell in the West Indies for £18.[4] Dead sailors drew no pay.

Among those who did not consider the trade wrong in principle was the Duke of York, brother of Charles II and subsequently King James II. In tribute to him for providing their charter in 1660, the Company of Royal Adventurers of England trading to Africa branded its slaves with the letters DY. The company had contracted to supply a minimum of 3000 slaves a year to the new sugar- and tobacco-producing colonies. The King himself invested in the company and, to advertise it, issued a new coin called a 'guinea' which was minted from gold imported from the Guinea Coast. As it turned out the King and his fellow investors lost most of their investment on this occasion since, despite the outcome of the Dutch Wars, the trade remained largely in Dutch hands. In 1672, however, the Royal African Company was founded and things began to look up.[5]

Between 1680 and 1688 the Royal African Company seems to have organised some 250 slaving voyages, embarking 60,783 slaves of whom 46,396, or 3 in 4, survived the voyage. Almost from the first the Company had to contend with English interlopers. Between 1680 and 1700 it has been estimated that some 300,000 slaves, worth £3 million or more in the New World market, were shipped in English vessels, including both interlopers and Company ships. To the beginning of the 18th century the English contribution to the slave trade had been less than 10 per cent of the total, the rest of the slaves having been carried largely in Spanish, Portuguese, Dutch and French ships.

Both Captain Nathaniel Uring and Captain Thomas Phillips have left records of English slaving in this period. In his journal for 1693 the latter wrote: 'We spent in our passage from St Thomas to Barbados two months eleven days in which time there happened much sickness and mortality among my poor men and negroes, that of the first we buried 14, and of the last 320 whereby the loss in all amounted to near 6560 pounds sterling. The distemper which my men as well as the blacks mostly die of was the white flux, which was so violent and inveterate that no medicine would in the least check it, so that when any of our men were seized with it we esteemed him a dead man, as he generally proved.'[6] Captain Phillips presumably wrote of the probable sale price of his negroes and there were obviously high profits to be made in the trade to Barbados.

In 1698 the slave trade was thrown open to all English merchants who agreed to pay a 10 per cent tax on their cargoes for the benefit of the Royal African Company. The War of the Spanish Succession, waged from 1701 to 1713, greatly reduced the influence of France and Spain and established England as the dominant power in Europe. In the treaty that ended this war, the Treaty of Utrecht, England gained effective control of the Guinea Coast from Gambia to the Congo (as well as effective control of Canada) and, at the same time, the infamous *Asiento* or contract with Spain authorising the supply of 4800 slaves each year to the Spanish colonies by the South Sea Company, a right which it relinquished in 1739.[7]

London was the headquarters of the Royal African Company and hence, until the end of the 17th century, the principal port from which the slavers sailed. After the trade was thrown open, Bristol soon began to outdistance London, and Liverpool began its rise to eminence. Remote from French privateers in the wars which raged from 1689 to 1713, with easy access to a developing textile industry and, particularly after 1700, benefiting from the exploitation of Cheshire rock-salt deposits, Liverpool enjoyed many advantages in this period, and the first docks in Liverpool were built as early as 1709. After 1713 English slave-trading boomed, soon averaging 70,000 slaves a year, most of them being sold in the West Indies at about £30 a head, with Jamaica as the principal market, but with more reaching the American mainland every year.[8] Much of this latter trade, however, came to be handled by American ships.

Until very recent times the carriage of people by ships has been an important function of merchant shipping and it was a particularly important function of British shipping in the 18th and 19th centuries. Black slaves and white overlords were not the only people carried to the New World. Until well into the 18th century indentured servants, many of them offered for sale, were carried from England. After Monmouth's rebellion in 1685, hundreds of rebels were sold into slavery in America and the West Indies, the King giving favourite courtiers the gift of a hundred or two rebels for disposal.[9] Some convicts continued to be sent to the New World until, towards the end of the 18th century, the first convicts were despatched to Australia. Indentured servants were often cheaper than slaves and they had the advantage of speaking the language of their masters. Because of this, however, and because they enjoyed a similar cultural background, white slavery was never sustained in the way that black slavery was.

Slaves, ivory, gold and redwood (used to produce a dye) were bought in West Africa with guns, brassware, spirits and textiles. In addition to indentured servants and slaves, textiles, wine, iron goods and other manufactures were carried to America, including quantities of meat and dairy produce loaded in Ireland for the West Indies. But such outward freight was rarely considerable.

Back to England from the West Indies – from Barbados, the Leeward Islands and Jamaica – came sugar, and a cargo of slaves would buy more sugar than could fill a slave-ship. There was therefore homeward cargo for those ships which sailed direct from England with manufactures and foodstuffs. Since the crop varied from year to year this trade could be speculative. The sugar cane was cut in summer and then partly processed to produce the muscovado or unrefined sugar which was exported. Before the middle of the 18th century molasses and rum, which were other products of the sugar cane, went mainly to the North American colonies. Shipment was made between January and July, before the hurricane season. Because of the danger of attack by Spaniards or corsairs the ships used tended to be 300 tons or more, the freight rate being £3–£4 a ton in peacetime and perhaps treble this amount in wartime. From the 1720s it became customary to pay the ships' crews some part of their wages in the colonies and this was usually worthwhile to the owners because of the frequent debasement of colonial currencies.

From Virginia and Maryland came tobacco. From a total crop of no more than 300 tons in 1635, exports had grown to 70–80,000 tons a year by 1735. As time went on the tobacco was compressed more and more. Since the ship's 'ton' was represented by a fixed cubic space rather than by weight carried, this meant that each ship carried more tobacco and the freight rate gradually rose from £5 to £7 a ton, though this figure too might treble in wartime. In this trade the ships were more likely to be 150–250 tons. They sailed from England in the autumn and sailed for home again in the spring, over 200 of them loading each year by the beginning of the 18th century.

After England's Act of Union with Scotland in 1707 Scotland, treated hitherto as a foreign country, came within the terms of the Navigation Acts and there was a consequent upsurge in Scottish trade with the British North American colonies. Before the middle of the century half the tobacco imported was going through Glasgow and other Scottish ports. From the south-west, through Plymouth, Exeter, Bideford, Cowes and other ports, tobacco was re-exported to the Continent. However, the years of war and the illegal sale of Newfoundland fish to Spain by ships from New England led to some decline in the ports of the south-west. While in the 1640s several hundred vessels had sailed from these ports to Newfoundland each year, only a few dozen were making the voyage by the beginning of the 18th century.

After 1700 rice, the production of which was concentrated round

Charleston,[10] became an important export from North America, proving in volume to be one of England's principal imports by the middle of the century. From the mainland colonies further north pitch, tar, resin and even ships were beginning to be exported to Britain, bounties being paid to anyone importing naval stores in English ships.[11] Even as early as this the colonies were violating the Navigation Acts where they could and a spirit of opposition was growing to the exactions of the mother country. An Act of 1726, which allowed Pennsylvania to import salt for the curing of fish direct from Europe provided it was imported in British owned and manned vessels, expressed the essence of England's policy toward the colonies: they were expected to become buyers on an increasing scale of British manufactures, and were to be encouraged to establish their own industries only where the products did not compete directly with British goods.[12]

In the years following 1688 there appears to have been a fall in British trade and a decline in the British merchant fleet, though there was some recovery before the middle of the 18th century. The impressment of merchant seamen for service in the navy had serious effects; in some years as many as 30,000 of a total workforce of 50,000 were pressed into the royal service. There were also heavy losses of ships in the early period, perhaps as many as 4000 being lost between 1689 and 1697, during the war of the League of Augsburg. Between 1686 and 1702 English tonnage seems to have fallen by 20,000 tons to a total of 323,000 tons. Subsequent ship losses in the later wars of 1702–1712 seem to have been compensated for by the taking of prizes,[13] but great delays, with a consequent deleterious effect upon trade, resulted from ships assembling to travel in convoy.

After 1680 the East India Company suffered from the competition of interlopers, some of them no more than pirates, and from 1698 to 1708 the Company's monopoly was temporarily suspended. The ensuing competition made the Company put defence second to profit and the great ships, by this time of 700–800 tons, were replaced by ships of 400–600 tons. It was during this difficult period that English trade was first extended to China, though initially only 150–200 ton ships were used in the China tea trade. Hitherto large quantities of coffee had been imported from Mocha on the Arabian Red Sea coast in the Company's ships, but by 1736 tea was becoming more popular than coffee, though high taxes induced smuggling and did nothing to help the Company's trade.[14] Silks and porcelain were also imported from China but the most valuable cargoes from the East remained the fine silk and cotton manufactures from the Bay of Bengal, which were highly fashionable in well-to-do circles. Freight rates on these cargoes were £20 or more a ton.

The kernel of the protectionist view at this time was that, if raw materials were imported and resulted in the export of manufactures, this was good for the country because it created more employment at home. From this point of view there was not much to be said for the trade of the East India Company. But the Company had powerful apologists. Sir Josiah Child, in his *New Discourse of Trade* published in 1690, and Dr Charles Davenant in *The Essay* (1697) and *The Discourse* (1699) argued in favour of the company's monopoly, both of them believing in 'free' trade in so far as it served the company's interests, while Davenant argued for the international division of labour.[15] Much money was spent by the directors for political purposes and, after lengthy negotiations, the 'United Company of Merchants of England trading to the East Indies' was established in 1708 with exclusive rights guaranteed by Act of Parliament until 1726, a period which was subsequently extended. Although the trade increased gradually, the increase in the first third of the 18th century was no more than modest.

The population of England and Wales, which may have declined in the second half of the 17th century, was about 5.5 million in 1700.[16] National income per head of population has been estimated to be rather more than double that of a modern underdeveloped country. Trade was expanding faster than net income was growing, some 10 per cent of the net national product being exported and balanced by imports of equivalent value, the net national product being of the order of £500 million. As much as one-half of England's woollen goods were exported and one-quarter of English manufactures, with a corresponding amount of manufactures being imported.[17] The demands made upon the revenue to finance the wars of this period, even more than the protection given by the Navigation Acts, had created a high tariff wall round the economy which sheltered domestic industry.[18] At the same time the needs of the colonies stimulated development in that industry, and the supply of goods to the colonies made shipping one of the most important areas of investment. The Navigation Acts reserved for Liverpool, Bristol, London, Whitehaven and, after 1707, Glasgow – the most rapidly growing cities in Britain – all the profit and all the employment opportunities arising from the new colonial trades.

The most influential voices on trade policy became those of the slave-owning sugar planters and tobacco growers, and enormous capital was piling up from these trades. In annual value British exports rose from £4.1 million in the 1660s to £6.4 million in 1700 and more than half this rise came from re-exports made largely to Europe. Woollens, which had represented some 85 per cent of the total value of exports, now represented no more than 50 per cent. The re-exports, which now accounted for nearly one-third of total exports, were principally tobacco, linens and calicoes, and sugar, together with some coffee and spices.[19] By 1700 English merchants handled almost all of the country's overseas trade.

The bulk of Britain's trade, of course, remained with the Continent of Europe or was carried round the coast. The greatest market for British goods, with the cloth-trade still pre-eminent, was to be found in ports from Hamburg to the Bay of Biscay and in Ireland, as it had been for centuries, and these places were also the principal suppliers of goods to Britain. In volume, the coal trade exceeded all others. From about 120,000 tons in 1685, cargoes increased to a total of 328,000 tons by the middle of the 18th century.[20] English colliers, now numbering more than 1500,[21] continued to take over more of the trade that had once been in foreign hands, and round the coast and in the trade from Whitehaven and Workington to Ireland, the carriage of coal was entirely in English hands. The volume was so vast that it always employed a high proportion of the nation's total tonnage of shipping. With the continued growth of the trade after 1700, the ownership of the colliers tended to pass to the north and their building was based largely on Whitby and Scarborough.

One triangular trade that existed at this time was coal shipped from Newcastle to Holland, a voyage made in ballast from Holland to Norway, with a cargo of timber brought back from Norway. Three out of five ships entering the Baltic from England in this period were in ballast for it was from this area that the heavy cargoes of timber came. Timber was imported from the eastern Baltic and the White Sea as well as from Norway. Also from the eastern Baltic and the White Sea came hemp and flax, together now with a little iron, though the bulk of the iron imports still came from Sweden.

In 1697 Peter the Great visited London and conceded a tobacco monopoly in Russia to English merchants. At the same time the fee on admission to the Russia Company was reduced from £60 to a mere £5 and the Company ceased any longer to have a monopoly of the trade. Even so, shipowners operating from the outports were still often stigmatised as interlopers. The Baltic remained an important market for English cloth and to a lesser extent for lead, coal, salt and malt.[22] Slowly England drew to an equality with the Dutch in the Baltic, the consequent stagnation of Dutch trade proving disastrous for Holland. The ships which carried timber to London were large vessels of 300–350 tons and the London trade was handled by a few large merchants, though an increasing number of the ships were owned on the north-east coast. Vessels used by the outports tended to be smaller than those that sailed from London.

Next to coal in volume among the British exports of the first half of the 18th century was wheat, which went mainly to Spain and Portugal. If shipped in British ships an export bounty was payable and this effectively excluded Dutch ships from the trade. Exports rose from about 120,000 quarters at the turn of the century to nearly four times this figure by 1720, continuing to rise for thirty years thereafter.[23] In addition to wheat, small amounts of coal were exported to Iberia from South Wales, salt pilchards from Cornwall, red herring from Yarmouth, and miscellaneous brass and iron manufactures from various places. Small vessels returned with oranges and lemons and, after 1689, the fortified wine port began to come in from Oporto. Given preference by the Customs after the Methuen Treaty was made with Portugal in 1703, port became a popular drink and the sales of both claret and sack declined.

Trade with the Mediterranean and the cross-trades within the Mediterranean continued to grow, despite keen French competition in the Turkey trade and disastrous losses suffered at the hands of the French off southern Portugal in 1693.[24] After 1719, when Trieste was established as a free port, a new traffic developed and the import of raw silk and yarn from Italy increased. It was still not uncommon for English ships to spend two or even three years trading in the Mediterranean without returning home. Freight rates from the Mediterranean continued normally to be £5–£5.10s. a ton, which compared with a £2 a ton peacetime rate from Lisbon, but like other rates, these might treble in the years of war.

Trade with France was prohibited in wartime and the duties imposed on such trade in peacetime were very high even after 1713. In consequence smuggling across the Channel was rampant. After their failure in 1692 to establish naval supremacy the French, who had by this time replaced the Dutch as Britain's principal trade rivals, gave support to privateering. Outside the fortified harbours, the Channel was a place of great danger for unescorted English vessels and losses in this area were high. French privateers were also active in the West Indies. This era – from 1690 to 1720, the classical age of the French corsairs – witnessed a resurgence of buccaneering, a threat to the legitimate trader which was exacerbated by such ill-treatment of seafarers that they were sometimes driven to piracy. Unemployment after the end of the war in 1715 gave a further spur to piracy.[25]

In wartime, when trade was in the doldrums, the English owner of large ships could either put his ship to government service, where payment was slow, or, if the vessel were suitable, he might use it for privateering. This is the time, therefore, of such privateersmen as Captain Woodes Rogers who explained in his bestselling memoirs, *A Cruising Voyage round the World*, that:

> Most of us, the chief officers, embraced this trip of privateering round the world, to retrieve the losses we had sustained by the enemy. Our complement of sailors in both ships was 333, of which about one-third were foreigners from most nations; several of Her Majesty's subjects on board were tinkers, tailors, haymakers, pedlars, fiddlers, etc, one negro, and about ten boys. With this mixed gang we hoped to be well-manned, as soon as they had learned the use of arms, and got their sea-legs, which we doubted not soon to teach 'em and bring them to discipline.[26]

In 1708 Queen Anne's government sanctioned privateering solely for the benefit which it was hoped to derive from injury inflicted on the enemy, and the privateers were no longer expected to make over to the Crown one-fifth of the value of prizes taken, as had been the practice hitherto. The whole corporation of the City of Bristol, including a Sir John Hawkins, sometime mayor, seem to have invested in Woodes Rogers' voyage of 1708–1711, and it was clearly designed, as some voyages a century and more earlier had been, to help open the South Seas to British shipping.[27]

Having rounded Cape Horn, Woodes Rogers refreshed his men with green vegetables and fresh water on the island of Juan Fernandez off the coast of Chile, thus rescuing Alexander Selkirk who had been marooned there in 1703 by another English captain operating in the South Seas. Subsequently, Selkirk's story provided Daniel Defoe with material for *Robinson Crusoe*.

The dream of every sailor who entered the Pacific Ocean was to emulate Thomas Cavendish who in 1587 had captured the 'Manila ship', one of the treasure-filled galleons that sailed every year from Acapulco to Manila. Woodes Rogers and his company hit the jackpot when, at the end of 1709, they captured the *Nostra Seniora de la Incarnacion Disenganio*, although in the engagement Woodes Rogers was shot through the left cheek. 'The bullet struck away great part of my upper jaw and several of my teeth', he remarks nonchalantly, 'part of which dropped down upon the deck where I fell.' It was bad luck since only one other of his men was wounded.[28]

To fit out his ships, the 320-ton *Duke*, armed with 30 guns, and the 260-ton *Duchess*, armed with 26 guns, had cost Woodes Rogers £14,000. His net profits amounted to at least £800,000,[29] perhaps nearly £43 million at 1988 prices. He opened a door to the South Seas which was never closed again and in 1711 the South Sea Company, to which the *Asiento* was made over two years later, was incorporated to develop trade in this area.

One who studied Woodes Rogers' book and followed in his wake was

Captain George Shelvocke, who circumnavigated the world between 1719 and 1722 and also published his memoirs. His second captain had been third mate to Woodes Rogers, and Shelvocke's men, like their predecessors, were much concerned with their shares of the booty. In the end this was shared by only 33 of them, Shelvocke included, since 83 more had died, deserted or been captured on the voyage. In 1720 Shelvocke captured off Peru a vessel which was already engaged in the guano trade – 'cormorants' dung' loaded from the offshore islands to be used as fertiliser. Shelvocke is also interesting for the light he sheds on aspects of privateering. At first he sailed under Austrian colours with Flemings among the crew because at that time Austria was at war with Spain. Later in the year, when Britain entered the war, the Flemings were paid off and the ships reverted to English names and colours. An incident in 1719 involving a Portuguese ship resulted in a charge of piracy being brought against him. Later that same year, off Chile, he considered it politic to fly French colours.[30]

Captain Nathaniel Uring was a privateer for only part of his sea career. Son of a sailor turned shopkeeper, he spent six months in London at the age of 14 studying the rudiments of navigation. He started at sea in the coal trade, but soon transferred to a 'galley' which sailed to Ireland and Barbados. Captured by the French on this voyage, he was landed at Penzance and had to walk to London. Joining a 130-ton ship, he then sailed to Malaga and again to Barbados where the ship loaded rum and molasses for Newfoundland. From Newfoundland they took cod to Virginia to load tobacco but the ship caught fire in Chesapeake Bay. Uring then shipped out in a sloop, only to catch smallpox and to be put ashore destitute. This was in 1699 and he was still only 17 years of age. He recovered from the smallpox and managed to obtain a berth on a ship bound for England where he joined a vessel bound for the Levant, but he left this vessel at Deal to join the Navy.

After seeing action in Copenhagen Uring joined another merchantman as second mate and sailed to the Guinea Coast for slaves who were sold at Nevis, sugar being bought with the proceeds. On his return home in 1702, at the start of the War of the Spanish Succession, he was impressed by the Navy before he had set foot on shore, and this time he saw action at Cadiz and Vigo.

The customary method of communication overseas at this time was by way of the shipmaster's mailbag. This mailbag hung on a hook in a popular tavern in the port until a ship was due to sail when the mail was collected. To provide a more regular and predictable postal system, for official mail in particular, a packet service to the West Indies was established in 1702, though the initiative was not sustained in the post-war years.[31]

With help from his kinsman, Admiral Sir Clowdisley Shovell, Uring was now appointed master in this service. To the West Indies these packets operated from Falmouth, which was sufficiently down-Channel to speed escape from the Channel if the south-westerly wind prevailed. Five years later Uring was again captured by the French but, after nine months in captivity, he was allowed to return home on parole to be exchanged for a French prisoner-of-war. In 1709 he took command of a 150-ton ship with 16 guns and sailed to New England and Antigua, but was captured by the French once more, being permitted this time to ransom his ship for its owner for £400. After a further incursion in the slave trade, he was given command of a privateer and had many more adventures in the West Indies and in the Mediterranean.

In 1670, nearly 200 years after the papal bull which divided the world between Portugal and Spain and nearly 100 years after the defeat of the Armada, England and Spain had at last signed a treaty which recognised the right of each country to whatever territory it possessed at the time. Although possession might still be disputed, this treaty officially allowed of English settlement in parts of central America and thus the development of mahogany exports. After the War of the Spanish Succession Uring pioneered the English logwood trade from central America – from Belize and Honduras – and this trade marked the beginning of the mahogany era in English furniture. The freight in Jamaican pounds was £5 a ton. Uring retired from the sea in 1721 but died in sound financial circumstances 22 years later at the age of 61.[32]

During the War of the Spanish Succession 1622 letters of marque were issued and 1343 vessels engaged in privateering. Their overall 'take' was not spectacular and few had the power or the luck of Woodes Rogers.[33] As well as being well-armed, the two vessels commanded by Woodes Rogers were more intensively manned even than the East Indiamen of the period. Woodes Rogers had a crew of 117 in his 320-ton *Duke*. By comparison, the 450-ton East Indiaman *Colchester* was manned in 1703 by a crew of only 89. In the latter vessel there were, under the master, 5 mates and 3 midshipmen, a boatswain with 2 mates, a gunner with 3 mates, a carpenter with 4 mates, a cook, a cooper and a caulker each with a mate, a steward, a captain's steward and 2 assistants, a purser, a joiner, 2 tailors, a surgeon with 2 mates, and 51 men and boys, a few of whom were quartermasters.

Except in East Indiamen and the Levant ships a third mate was never carried before 1700 but, in spite of a continuing fall in crew numbers in relation to ship's tonnage, a third mate now became increasingly common even in ships of quite moderate size because of the refinement of navigational skills. On the other hand, the purser was disappearing from most ships and the surgeon was often dropped in the transatlantic trades. Except in East Indiamen, the gunner too began to disappear in peacetime.

In wartime the wages of an able-seaman might be pushed up to £4 a month but the norm on long voyages was from a guinea to 27s a month. Aboard the Newcastle-to-London colliers he was paid 30–35s a voyage according to season, and in the timber trade to Norway about £3.5s for the round voyage. In fishing, privateering and some coastal trades the crew were paid on a 'shares' basis, the owners taking the customary one-third of the earnings, the other two-thirds being shared between the crew according to an established formula. After 1696 seamen paid a levy of 6d a month for the support of the Greenwich Hospital. In 1729 an Act was passed for the Better Regulation and Government of Seamen in the Merchants' Service and this instituted written contracts between seamen and owners, the beginning of the practice known as 'signing on'.[34]

By 1720 there were several schools of navigation of the kind attended by Nathaniel Uring, both in London and in provincial ports, among them Sir Joseph Williamson's Mathematical School at Rochester, established in 1701, Neale's Mathematical School in Fleet Street, established in 1715, and the Royal Hospital School at Greenwich, established in 1716. Some instrument makers also taught the use of their instruments.

Advancement from chief mate to master often trebled an officer's income, established him in a different social class, and possibly put him on the path to becoming a merchant. In the coastal and short sea trades, where vessels might be of 50 tons or less, the master would usually be a part-owner and others holding shares were likely to be relatives, friends and business acquaintances. In this way risks were spread, for ship insurance developed later than cargo insurance, after the beginning of the 18th century. In the deepsea trades much more capital was involved and ownership was in the hands of merchants who had connections with fellow merchants and the well-to-do and who might be represented abroad by factors and agents. Shipowning might then become the minor function of entrepreneurs whose important interests were in being a 'Turkey merchant' or a 'Russia merchant' or, indeed, in having several irons in the fire.[35]

With the exception of the years 1690 to 1720, the latter being the year in which the South Sea Bubble burst and the South Sea Company collapsed, the joint-stock company method of business organisation was uncommon. The normal shipowning group was also very different from the ordinary partnership of the day. Property in a ship was customarily divided into equal parts or shares – eighths, sixteenths, thirty-seconds or

Fig. 2. THE NUMBER OF MERCHANT SEAMEN SERVING ON BRITISH SHIPS (UK REGISTRY), 1550–1987

Seafarers on leave are included, and fishermen and naval men excluded. 'Others' include Lascars, other Commonwealth seafarers, and foreigners. Lascars numbered some 45,000 before World War I, nearer 50,000 between the wars, and about 40,000 between 1948 and 1964, when numbers began to fall. Foreigners numbered as many as 30,000 in some years before World War I, about 10,000 between the wars, and 5000 or fewer since. Accuracy in these statistics, even today, is difficult to obtain.

YEAR	UK-RESIDENT	OTHERS	TOTAL
1550			25,000
1700			50,000
1800			150,000
1850			200,000
1870			200,000
1890	200,000	50,000	250,000
1910	200,000	50,000	250,000
1920	170,000	70,000	240,000
1930	140,000	60,000	200,000
1950	140,000	50,000	190,000
1960	140,000	50,000	190,000
1970	100,000	30,000	130,000
1975	87,000	20,000	107,000
1980	65,000	14,000	79,000
1985	42,000	3000	45,000
1987	27,000	1300	28,300

(*Sources:* R. Davis, *The Rise of the English Shipping Industry*; G. V. Scammell, 'Manning the English Merchant Service in the Sixteenth Century'; V. C. Burton, 'Counting Seafarers: The Published Records of the Registry of British Seamen, 1849–1913'; the Quinquennial Census figures; the Registrar-General of Shipping and Seamen's figures; and those issued since 1973 by the General Council of British Shipping.)

sixty-fourths – a pattern which was international and of great antiquity, and investors would take up so many shares. Thus, in 1686, Sir Henry Johnson, an exceptionally large investor in shipping, owned parts of 38 ships, nearly all East Indiamen, his total holdings amounting to 88/32nds.[36] The 80-ton *Diligence*, bought for fourteen owners at a public sale in 1728 for £525, was owned five-sixteenths by Daniel Dixon, the principal owner, the rest being shared between the others. Although this was a relatively small ship, the master owned no part of her.[37] Each ship was a separate venture and the originator 'laid off' all but a small part of his commitment as a bookmaker hedges his bets. A given amount of capital could thus be spread over a number of ships in the expectation that at least some would come home and yield a handsome profit.

The Royal Exchange in London and Tolsey in Bristol were well-established markets for shipping services before 1700, and even the shipbroker was becoming recognised as distinct from other brokers or middlemen, who had been at work at least since the Middle Ages. Ship sales took place at the Ship and Castle in London which, presumably to indicate its function, had changed its name from the Castle Tavern in 1654. In 1692 Lloyd's Coffee House, the centre for arranging ship and cargo insurance, moved into Lombard Street, and the shipping newspaper *Lloyd's List* was first published in 1734. By the 1720s virtually all prospective losses could be covered by insurance and interest rates had fallen to 5 per cent, a sign of stability and well-organised markets for this was half the normal rate of a century earlier.[38] On the other hand, as the collapse of the South Sea Company in 1720 indicated, unwarranted speculation could induce uncertainty and slump.

Although London remained pre-eminent as a builder of East Indiamen, West Indiamen and most ships designed for the Levant, shipbuilding was beginning to decline in London and East Anglia and was increasing on the north-east coast. Significantly, Ambrose Cowley's great iron works, which had been particularly concerned in London with ships' fittings, moved to Sunderland in 1682. In 1694 bounties were given on the building of merchant ships of 450 tons and over if they were so equipped as to be of immediate use for service in the navy. Where appropriate, Dutch hull forms were being adopted for merchantmen and English shipbuilders gradually evolved merchant ships in which fewer crew needed to be employed, thus increasing operational efficiency. Shipping tons served per man rose from 9 to 10 or even 11 between 1686 and 1736.[39] In ships intended for northern waters, where competition was keen and the seas safer, one crew member per 20 tons of ship capacity became the norm. It is at this time, at the very beginning of the 18th century, that the steering wheel first appears. The long-standing problem of how to guide large ships with increasingly heavy rudders was satisfactorily solved at last.[40]

Notes

1. S. E. Morison, *Christopher Columbus, Mariner* (1956), London, p. 104.
2. D. P. Mannix & M. Cowley, *Black Cargoes* (1963), London, p. 171. *Also* P. E. Lovejoy, *Transformations in Slavery: A History of Slavery in Africa* (1983), Cambridge, p. 36 and p. 45.
3. Mannix *op. cit.*, p. xiii.
4. A. Dewer (ed), *The Voyages and Travels of Captain Nathaniel Uring* (1726, reprinted 1928), London, p. 41; Lovejoy, *op. cit.*, p. 51; and D. Galenson, 'The Slave Trade to the English West Indies 1673–1724' (1979), EHR, 2nd Series, Vol. XXXII, No. 2, pp. 241 ff.
5. K. G. Davies, *The Royal African Company* (1957), London, pp. 41 ff.
6. T. Phillips, *A Journal of a Voyage made in the Hannibal of London* (*1693–1694*). See A. & J. Churchill, *A Collection of Voyages and Travels . . .*, Vol. VI (1704), London.
7. J. H. Parry, *The Spanish Seaborne Empire* (1966), London, pp. 292–300.
8. Mannix, *op. cit.*, p. 67.
9. *Ib.*, pp. 251–2.
10. R. Davis, *The Rise of the English Shipping Industry in the Seventeenth and Eighteenth Centuries* (1962), London, p. 290.
11. M. Hunter, *How England got Its Merchant Marine, 1066–1776* (1935), New York, p. 211.
12. *Ib.*, pp. 251–2.
13. Davis, *op. cit.*, pp. 316–17; also p. 68.
14. J. Sutton, *Lords of the East: the East India Company and Its Ships* (1981), Greenwich, p. 14.
15. P. J. Thomas, *Mercantilism and East India Trade* (1926, reprinted 1963), London, pp. 70–79.
16. M. W. Thomas (ed), *A Survey of English Economic History*, 3rd ed. (1967), p. 215.
17. R. Davis, *English Overseas Trade 1500–1700* (1973), London (published by Macmillan for the Economic History Society).
18. P. Mathias, *The First Industrial Nation: An Economic History of Britain 1700–1914*, 2nd ed. (1969), London, pp. 10–14 and p. 29.
19. *Ib.*, p. 84.
20. Davis (1962), *op. cit.*, p. 203.
21. G. S. Graham, *Empire of the North Atlantic: The Maritime Struggle for North America* (1958), London, p. 56.
22. Davis (1962), *op. cit.*, p. 219.
23. *Ib.*, p. 203.
24. G. V. Scammell, *The English chartered trading companies and the sea* (1983), National Maritime Museum, p. 25.
25. D. J. Starkey, 'The economic and military significance of British privateering, 1702–83' (1988), *The Journal of Transport History*, 3rd Series, Vol. 9, No. 1, pp. 50–59; J. S. Bromley, *Corsairs and Navies 1660–1760* (1987), London.

26. W. Rogers, *A Cruising Voyage round the World, 1712* (1928), London, p. 6.
27. *Ib.*, pp. ix–x.
28. *Ib.*, p. 215.
29. *Ib.*, p. xxv.
30. G. Shelvocke, *A Voyage Round the World* (1726, reprinted 1928), London.
31. I.K. Steele, *The English Atlantic 1675–1740: An Exploration of Communication and Community* (1986), Oxford, pp. 113–14 and pp. 168 ff.
32. A. Dewar (ed), *op. cit.*
33. D.J. Starkey, *op. cit.*, p. 52; W.R. Meyer, 'English privateering in the War of the Spanish Succession 1702–1713', (1983) MM, Vol. 69, No. 4, pp. 435–45.
34. C. Dixon, 'Signing-On' (1984), MM, Vol. 70, No. 3.
35. Davis (1962), *op. cit.*, p. 81.
36. *Ib.*, p. 83.
37. *Ib.*, p. 357.
38. *Ib.*, p. 29.
39. *Ib.*, p. 58.
40. A. McGowan, *Tiller and Whipstaff: The Development of the Sailing Ship 1400–1700* (1981), London, p. 43; J. H. Harland, 'The Early History of the Steering Wheel' (1972), MM, Vol. 58, No. 1, p. 47.

13

Colonial Prosperity
(1739–1775)

The fivefold increase in the tonnage of English shipping which took place in the century prior to 1686 was not repeated in the century that followed. Between 1686 and the American Declaration of Independence in 1776 the tonnage of the English fleet less than doubled, increasing from 340,000 tons to about 608,000 tons, though if, as one authority argues, the latter figure excludes a large section of the coasting fleet, it may have been as high in 1776 as 1,125,600 tons – a three-fold increase.[1] During the wars of King William III and Queen Anne the increase was very modest, and war continued to take its toll in the years thereafter. Between 1739 and 1748 (the War of Jenkins' Ear) 3000 ships were probably lost to Spain and France,[2] losses which were only compensated for in part by the 1500 foreign prizes taken. Lack of comment on losses in the Seven Years War (1756–1763), however, suggests that the 1855 foreign prizes then taken[3] represented some net gain to British merchant shipping. The prizes were mostly French and probably proved to be a well-balanced addition to the British fleet. However this may be, the pace of growth in the peaceful years of this era was so fast that rapid advance was made despite the ravages of war, and a great new expansion of the British merchant fleet began in the middle of the 18th century.

It was at this time that the maximum size of merchantmen increased again. East Indiamen, which had declined from a peak size of 700–800 tons in the 1690s, passed the 700-ton level once more in 1764 with *Speke*, and increased further to 860–870 tons five years later. In 1787 the first 1000-ton English merchant ship, *Ceres*, entered the East India Company's service.

In the Baltic trade the size of the ships grew from 300–350 tons to 400–500 tons, and in the transatlantic trade the size grew from around 200 to 350 tons. These trades had expanded and, since there was now less danger of the under-utilisation of cargo space, advantage was taken of the economies of scale. East Indiamen alone maintained very heavy manning. Other ships, particularly the larger ships, were by this time carrying much more in relation to their dimensions than they had been a century earlier.

Warships were now built like greyhounds, for speed and manoeuvrability. But merchant vessels were built like boxes, to carry as much as possible. 'Most ships', said one commentator in 1748, 'are now built in such a manner as to take the ground loaded'; that is, they were flat-bottomed and full built.[4] Before 1700 ships carried less than their measured tonnage. By 1775 most ships carried more.

The complexity of the three-masted rig grew steadily, with the result that it became possible to sail closer to the wind, a development of particular importance to sailing down the English Channel where the prevailing south-westerlies could often keep outward-bound ships trapped for weeks on end. By mid-century the typical ship carried from two to three staysails, triangular sails running on stays between the masts or from a mast to a bowsprit. One might be set up on the mainmast, one on the foremast and perhaps one on the mizen. The use of studding sails spread slowly, and the jib was adopted in the 1720s. After 1700 bonnets disappeared and it became the practice to reef sails instead.

These developments notwithstanding, the great majority of ships were still under 200 tons, and in the coasting trade to Ireland and across the Channel they were mostly 20–50 tons.

A ship with fewer masts can be operated by fewer crew. For this reason the dividing line between two- and three-masted ships changed in the second quarter of the 18th century. In 1700 it had commonly been at 50–60 tons, vessels below this size having two masts and those above this size having three. By the 1740s the dividing line was 100 tons or more, and by the 1760s, 140–150 tons. The large brig, used mainly in the North Sea, and the large snow, used more commonly on ocean voyages, both two-masted vessels which differed only in the way one sail was set, were common by the end of the century.[5]

The practice of classifying ships by rig began to appear in the second half of the century. The name bark or barque, for example, came to be applied to the three-masted vessel which was square-rigged on the fore and main masts and fore-and-aft rigged on the mizen. Other vessels built, each indicative of a particular rig, included brigs and ketches, a handful of schooners, and many such one-masted vessels as hoys, doggers, bilanders and sloops, each of which had its special use.

The growth of shipbuilding in the north-east continued. In the early 18th century the building of larger ships had been concentrated on the Thames, at Shadwell, Rotherhithe and Blackwall, and on the estuarine creeks of East Anglia, but none of this business was large scale. In the second half of the century Ipswich and other East Anglian shipbuilding communities suffered some decline because prize ships were meeting part of the demand. But shipbuilding on the north-east coast began to develop further, particularly in Whitby and Scarborough, and by the time the North American colonies declared their independence the north-east coast towns, from Newcastle to Hull, were in aggregate by far the largest producers of British ships. By this time ships were being built all along the river Tyne from Newcastle to South Shields and in Stockton and Sunderland as well as in Scarborough and Whitby. Captain Cook's ship *Endeavour*, selected for his purpose in 1768, was built in Whitby as the 369-ton collier *Earl of Pembroke* and, although it is likely that the famous East End public house 'The Prospect of Whitby' was so named by a retired shipmaster who had commanded a Whitby-built vessel called the *Prospect*, tradition has it that the name was inspired by the view from its windows – a never-ending stream of Whitby colliers making their way to the City of London.

London remained by far the greatest of English ports and most of Newcastle's coal came to London. Having pioneered the Mediterranean and East Indian trades, London largely kept them. Before 1776 most cargo was carried for merchants other than the owners of the ship, such merchants either chartering the ship or hiring cargo space within it. This was not true, however, of the great London timber merchants trading to the Baltic. These drew widely on London business circles to take shares in these ships but such part-owners had no participation in the ships' cargoes. In volume the timber trade was the largest of the foreign trades and transport costs made up one-third of the cost of timber.[6]

Although with over half the total trade London maintained its pre-eminence, the north-east and west coast ports began to develop in the 18th century as total trade increased. The tonnage of ships entering and leaving Liverpool rose from 27,000 tons in 1710 to 100,000 tons in 1760,[7] and in 1739 a second Liverpool dock followed the one which had been built thirty years earlier. While London stood still, Liverpool, the major coal ports and the corn-shipping centres of East Anglia made great strides forward. Ipswich, Hull, Newcastle and Bristol were all important ports. Hull developed particularly after 1730 in consequence of its timber imports and the import of Swedish iron for the growing industries of Sheffield and Birmingham. By 1774, when its first dock was built, Hull's overseas trade equalled that of Bristol.[8] After the Act of Union, Scotland's industrial development was greatly fostered by profits made from the colonial trades, trades largely channelled through Glasgow.[9]

The Seven Years War increased the importance of such north-west coast ports as Liverpool and Glasgow because ships sailing from these ports were less likely to be attacked and less likely to be caught smuggling.

The contemporary development of the cotton and linen industries helped further, since these provided goods for export; and business men in these areas entered the slave trade with zeal, developing in consequence into independent carriers of tobacco and sugar. It was said that Liverpool merchants allowed their masters few perquisites and it is probable that wages were lower in the north-west than than they were in London.[10] After the Seven Years War Liverpool's business was further enhanced as its river and canal connections extended into the Midlands and it then became, as it remained for nearly 200 years, the second port after London.

Commercial acumen was developing throughout this period. The Baltic Mercantile and Shipping Exchange, known in shipping circles as the Baltic, has as its primary function the provision of facilities for securing cargoes for merchant ships. It originated in one of the 17th-century coffee houses, the Virginia and Maryland Coffee House, which changed its name in 1744 to the Virginia and Baltic because it was from these two areas that most of the merchandise dealt in came. Ships became more cost effective, profits increased, and some felt that something had been lost along the way. Calling for seamen to fight the King's wars and to man a bigger fleet, Jonas Hanway, founder of The Marine Society and a Russia Company merchant, commented ruefully: 'There was a time, *in my memory*, when merchants prided themselves in charming gallies they sent to sea; they saw and admired them with a lover's eye, and did not reckon on *much gain* on them, merely as a *ship-account*; but those days are gone.'[11] The bulk-carriers of his day did not charm Hanway for they were built to make money. Others, wearing the fashionable beaver hat made from the felt obtained from the beaver furs imported in their tens of thousands by the Hudson Bay Company, were not so sentimental.

Although checked by the war of 1739–48, English trade doubled both in value and tonnage in the first half of the 18th century. Much of the increase in tonnage was due to the exports of coal and corn, the latter peaking in mid-century. Textiles accounted for 70 per cent of the value, miscellaneous metal goods and hardware coming next.[12] Imports had multiplied ten or twelve-fold in 150 years and by this time totalled 560,000 tons a year, half the total being timber from Norway and the Baltic, cargoes which represented less than 5 per cent of the total value of imports but which nevertheless employed a great many ships and seamen. The trade was badly balanced for only 30,000 tons of goods were exported to northern Europe. On the other hand, 510,000 tons of exports, mostly coal, went to the ports of nearby continental Europe while only some 44,000 tons of goods were imported from these ports.

To southern Europe 90,000 tons were exported and 39,000 tons imported, this imbalance being reversed in the trades to Africa and the West Indies, on the one hand, and to North America, on the other. From Africa and the West Indies, mainly from the latter, 70,000 tons were imported and only 10,000 tons exported. From North America 88,000 tons were imported and 20,000 tons exported.

Colonial Americans were already killing sperm whales in the South Seas, a business which the British South Sea Company had not made a success. Government bounties were offered to whalers, and the demand for whale oil was growing fast, so after 1749 the British became more involved in 'Greenland' whaling in Arctic waters. Leith was first off the mark, but British whaling did not flourish greatly until near the end of the 18th century.[13]

By the middle of the 18th century, after a century of development, the American colonies were prospering and the import to Britain of timber from North America, foreseen by the colonial pioneers, was developing rapidly. By the time of the American War of Independence the northern colonies – New Hampshire, Maine, Nova Scotia and those on the banks of the St Lawrence river – were the principal source of masts for British ships and the cessation of their supply in 1776 caused a crisis in English naval dockyards. New England, in particular, had also become an important supplier of ships to English owners. By the terms of the Navigation Acts such ships were regarded as English built and, because of the abundance of local timber, they could be built more cheaply in New England than they could be in England. By 1730 one in six of English ships was American built; by 1774 it was one in three. These colonies were still envisaged in Britain as markets for the export industries and in 1750 they were prohibited from making steel, refining iron and manufacturing finished iron products.[14]

By this time the industrial revolution was under way in England and new national industries were coming into existence. Foremost among these was to be the manufacture of cotton cloth. There is evidence that some kind of cotton cloth was being made in England before the 18th century, and to protect the woollen weavers it was made illegal to wear such cloth, but this legislation proved ineffective. By the middle of the century the quality of imported Indian calicoes had declined and English printers had become skilled in the art of printing on cotton. In 1774 a statute legalised 'the new manufacture made entirely of cotton spun in the Kingdom'.[15] However, wool remained more important for the moment and West Riding worsteds were developed considerably round about the middle of the century, for there was a growing American market for worsteds. But the textile industry, inclusive of linen manufactures, was not the only industry that was expanding. The metal-using industries were also well to the fore, and there were rapid developments in the production of leather goods, hats and cordage.[16]

Growing most rapidly was the shipping that traded to America. By 1763, when they were annexed by the Crown, British settlements had been made in St Vincent, Dominica, St Lucia and Tobago, and by 1775 the plantation colonies in the West Indies, plus Georgia, the Carolinas, Virginia and Maryland in North America, were the biggest customers of British ships.[17] After the middle of the 18th century nearly half of all English shipping was engaged in transatlantic traffic.

English manufactures apart, ships bound for the West Indies carried great quantities of beef, pork, butter and cheese from Ireland, and pipe-staves for wine and barrels and hogsheads for oil and sugar which were largely produced in Hamburg. Sugar and tropical timber came back. Mahogany was increasingly exported after 1740 and Mr Gillow, whose name was later incorporated in that of the firm of Waring and Gillow, made his fortune by designing furniture in this popular new material. After mid-century rum also began to reach England in significant quantity.

Although the absolute amount of tobacco exported continued to increase, compression decreased still further the amount of hold space it required. The weight of the hogshead content trebled between 1660 and 1774[18] and by the latter date tobacco was so tightly packed that it was as heavy as water.

The freight rate was £4–5 a ton and before American independence four-fifths of the imports were re-exported to the continent; thereafter it was shipped direct. To provide stability to the ships iron was also exported from Virginia and Maryland after 1730, the freight rate being a mere 10s a ton. Other exports were rice, pitch and tar, raw cotton exports at this time being of much smaller importance. By 1750 tobacco imports topped 50 million pounds of which total perhaps one-quarter was smoked in Britain. At least one-third of that smoked, however, did not pay duty and smuggling was rife, not least in Scotland.[19]

With increased efficiency, including a reduction in loading times, came a lowering of costs. The cost of carrying a ton of sugar across the Atlantic was at least one-third lower in 1770 than it had been in 1670 and the fall in the cost of carrying tobacco was greater still. Increasingly agents in England became managing owners of ships or small fleets, with planters in the colonies among the part owners. The substantial sugar agent Richard Lascelles, for example, owned shares in 21 ships in 1753.[20] Increasingly, too, ships from London were ordered to give priority to the cargoes of particular planters, who in their turn were expected to give preference to particular shipmasters. However, slave-traders carrying sugar back to England after having sold their slaves ensured that the market remained largely free, and considerable seasonal fluctuations in the sugar crop made it impossible to exercise any real control over prices. In Virginia growing wealth led to more stockholding of tobacco and this tended to modify price fluctuations in this market.

Between 1750 and 1752 the Royal African Company was dissolved, and after this time the forts along the West African coast were maintained by a committee of English merchants with the help of government subsidies.[21] After 1713 between 40,000 and 100,000 slaves a year were transported from Africa, the annual average being about 70,000, most of them being sold in the West Indies but an increasing number being sold in North America. The plantation owners in the Carolinas, for example, bought 2800 slaves in 1738. In 1714 the total slave population in the British colonies of North America was 59,000. By 1754 this number had grown to 298,000 and it increased rapidly thereafter though in some measure this was due to an excess of births over deaths.[22]

From 1750 to 1754 John Newton – later to become a clergyman and the abolitionist largely responsible for bringing Wilberforce into the anti-slavery campaign – was a master of slave ships and he kept a journal, not published at the time, which covers three voyages from England to the West Indies by way of West Africa. After over four years in the trade he thanked God for leading him into 'an easy and creditable way of life'.[23] His ships, like others, sailed up and down the Guinea Coast selling by barter the goods they had brought – ironmongery, textiles, guns, gunpowder, beads, kettles, cider and spirits. The denominator used in barter was called in Sierra Leone a 'bar' and elsewhere on the West African coast a 'piece', an 'ackey', a 'pawn' or a 'copper'. Originally the bar was a piece of iron brought from England which, in 1710, cost 3s 6d in London and 5s when delivered in Africa. All other goods were valued in bars. A slave would be bought for a certain number of bars and the bars so acquired were then exchanged for goods. A gun might be ten bars, a length of cotton eight bars and a gallon of brandy three bars. The value of the bar varied from time to time and place to place and there was sometimes a difference in value between 'country bars' and 'ship's bars'. Much of the trading was done in boats which plied between the ship and the many rivers and creeks, and this trading often took six or eight months.

The second side of the triangle, the middle passage, was between Africa and the West Indies or North America, where the slaves were sold, usually by auction, to plantation owners, the captain receiving a 'prime' (primage) of about four per cent on the selling price of every slave landed alive.

The triangle was completed by the homeward passage to Britain with plantation produce.

When they visited England plantation owners brought slaves with them, as some Arab diplomats do today. To the Quakers slavery was a sin and George Fox had condemned it as early as 1671, only eight years after the future James II had launched the Company of Royal Adventurers of England trading to Africa, and some years before the British slave trade really got under way. In the reign of William and Mary Lord Chief Justice Holt had declared that 'as soon as a negro comes to England, he becomes free', but this was an expression of opinion and not a court decision. In 1761 English Quakers decided to exclude from their membership anyone who should be 'concerned in the unchristian traffic of negroes', and two years later they extended this ban to anyone who should aid or abet or in any shape give encouragement to the trade.[24] However, it was through the instrumentality of Granville Sharp, a man who was not himself a Quaker though he had associated with Quakers and came from a clerical background, that the timid Lord Chief Justice Mansfield was driven to declare in court in 1772 that no man in England could be a slave, though this declaration had no immediate effect upon the slave trade.

As happened in the slave trade, the trade with Asia Minor and Syria, hitherto the monopoly of the Levant Company, was thrown open in 1753. This trade had continued much as in the past and English factors were still to be found in Aleppo, Smyrna and Constantinople. Outward and homeward the ships called at Cadiz, the hub of the Spanish trade. Speedier loading could mean three voyages a year to and from Cadiz instead of two and as shipping grew more efficient freight rates fell. A regular trader, the *Ceres* of 120 tons, came into London two or three times every year from 1751 to 1768 and she was typical of her kind.

By mid-century Madeira wine was becoming popular in England and, since Madeira, a Portuguese colony, was also a frequent call for ships bound for America, the wine became a convenient cargo to carry to the West Indies and the southern colonies of North America.[25] The figures for a ship which carried butts of port to England from 1754 to 1766 – the 150-ton *Caroline* which cost £950 and a further £569 to fit out – indicate, however, that profits in the wine trade were low.

The Peace of Paris, which concluded the Seven Years' War in 1763, left Britain the paramount western power in the East and, although the French disputed control of these seas for a short time during the American War of Independence and Mauritius was not seized by the British until 1810, the French were never again to occupy the strong position they had held at the middle of the 18th century. The contest between Britain and

France for predominance in India brought about a complete metamorphosis of the East India Company. Large cities had developed from its simple trading stations and by 1764 the company was the undisputed ruler of Bengal.[26] In 1744 it had again given assistance to the government and its exclusive powers, which had been extended to 1766, were further extended to 1780 though the Company was reconstructed in 1773.

In the trade to the East Indies at this period a mere 8000 tons of goods were imported annually, but these were particularly valuable cargoes, silk above all. Precious metals apart, exports on this route were negligible and in consequence outward freight rates were low. For homeward cargoes freight rates in 1772 were £30–£35 a ton, being higher for such 'fine' goods as silks, calicoes and indigo than for 'gross' or 'gruff' goods like saltpetre, sugar and pepper, the general principle being, as always, to charge what the goods would bear. By 1760 2.5 million pounds of China tea were being imported.[27]

Since the East India Company's ships were heavily armed, the freight rates rose little in wartime by comparison with rates on other routes. Shipmasters in this trade were the most privileged of their profession and usually paid heavily for their commands. To avoid the monsoon season they had to leave the Indian coast before the end of January or otherwise in June or July. In China they had to arrive in August or September to secure the new tea harvest. By the time the Americans fought their War of Independence the East India Company was the only chartered company which still preserved a trading monopoly. The prohibition by the home government of their direct participation in this trade was one of the grievances nurtured by the North American colonists and one consequence was some American piracy on the route, Madagascar being used as a base.[28]

Life in an East Indiaman could be agreeable and civilised. Captain Waddell, who was in command of *Plassey* in 1768–9, was described by William Hickey, one of his passengers, as a man of about forty, 'naturally grave, with an appearance of shyness or reserve, [and] possessed [of] one of the mildest and most equal tempers that ever man was blessed with'. Hickey sailed with him to India and returned home again with him and never once, he says, did he see the captain angry, nor 'hear him utter a single oath or hasty expression'. Throughout these voyages, he kept an excellent table.

Captain Waddell's mate had a coarse tongue but was as pleasant a fellow, and both men were superbly fit. The third officer in this ship, Mr Douglas, was also noteworthy. He was remarkably dressy, so much so as to be distinguished in the service by the title of 'Count Douglas'. But, 'although he laid out more money upon his person than was usual with men in his station, no one kept a stricter look out after the main chance than he did, well knowing how to make the most of every shilling', and he let pass no opportunity of doing so. His cabin was as neat and elegant as his person. 'It was painted,' Hickey tells us, 'a light pea-green with gold beading.' The bed and curtains were of the richest Madras chintz and the dressing tables held every possible article of use. A beautiful bureau and book-case, stored with the best books, and three neat mahogany chairs completed the furnishings. Hickey was invited to help himself to the books.[29]

Although shipmasters and officers in East Indiamen would have been the best-trained navigators there were at sea, deepsea navigation was still a clumsy business. Harrison produced his chronometer in 1759 and it was tested by Captain Cook but it had no immediate application in merchant ships. For their longitude most captains still depended entirely on their dead reckoning. The quadrant and the log had been further refined. By the second half of the 18th century the best logs consisted of a piece of wood usually in the form of a quadrant of a circle five or six inches in radius and a quarter of an inch thick and so balanced by a leaden weight as to float perpendicularly almost immersed in the water. This was called the 'ship' and was fastened to one end of a long line called the log line, the other end being wound on a reel placed in the stern of the vessel. The 'ship', on being heaved or thrown into the water, theoretically kept its place while the line ran off the reel as the ship moved, the length unwinding in a given time thus giving the rate of sailing. This rate was calculated by knots made on the line at regular intervals and a sandglass which ran a certain number of seconds. To avoid calculation the length between these knots was so proportional to the time of the glass that the number of knots unwound while the glass ran down should be the number of miles the vessel would sail in an hour, hence the origin of the knot or nautical mile. The log was not an accurate instrument and allowance had also to be made for the effect of wind and currents, so the reckoning was frequently wrong and when at sea out of sight of land a captain seldom knew exactly where he was.

In wartime privateers still sailed the seas in large numbers, 1191 licences being issued in the War of Jenkins' Ear and 1679 in the Seven Years' War.[30] One of the most notable during the War of Jenkins' Ear was Commodore George Walker. Since his crew numbered only 32, he carried marine clothes which he arranged like scarecrows in order to deceive the enemy, and sometimes he rigged his ship with wooden guns to the same end. For his entertainment he carried a small orchestra – two horn players who could double on the trumpet, two flautists who could also play the hautboys, a black drummer, a harpist and a violinist. He had two other violinists among the crew. On a cruise with a fleet of four private ships which ended in 1747 he took four prizes valued at more than £220,000, but he appears to have been cheated by both agents and managers and finished in a debtors' prison.[31]

Commodore George Anson's voyage round the world, from 1740 to 1744, was no commercial enterprise but a naval expedition. Nevertheless, like Cavendish and Woodes Rogers before him, he hit the jackpot with his capture of the great Manila galleon, *Nuestra Señora de Covadonga*, with its fabulous prize of 1,313,843 pieces of eight plus 35,682 ounces of virgin silver, said to be the biggest booty that ever returned to England in a single vessel. The survivors returned rich men, but of the 961 who left England in the three ships under Anson's command 626 died during the first twelve months alone, most of them from scurvy.[32] It was not sufficient that Anson's men were aware that fresh fruit and vegetables would cure scurvy if the complaint were not too far advanced: they were too far away from the opportunity to eat any. It was Anson's experience which stimulated Dr James Lind to make a series of experiments and observations which showed that scurvy was essentially a dietary disease. His *Treatise of the Scurvy* was published in 1753 though it was nearly another century before the issue of citrus fruit juices became standard practice in merchant ships.

Anson had been promised 300 able sailors and was provided with 170 men, some of them sick. He had been promised a further 300 able soldiers, and he was supplied with 259 invalid Chelsea pensioners, some of them over 70 years of age. But it was difficult to get good men, particularly in wartime. Of slaver crews Captain John Newton reported in a letter to Dr David Jennings in 1752: 'We are for the most part supplied with the refuse and dregs of the nation. The prisons and glass houses furnish us with large quotas and boys impatient of their parents or masters, or already ruined by some untimely vice and for the most part devoid of all good principles.'[33] He had trouble with his crews and without strict discipline, he averred, the common sailors would be unmanageable.

Thomas Clarkson, the abolitionist, prepared a table of comparative mortality for nine slaving voyages made between 1766 and 1780, for which there were complete figures, and found that of 203 sailors 22 or 11 per cent died; of 2362 slaves, 154 or 6.5 per cent died.[34] Slaves, of course, made their crossing once whereas the professional sailor was always at risk.

Bad food, disease and brutality, and the hazards of shipwreck, fire and accident were common to most ships, particularly to those which pursued ocean voyages. Falls from rigging were frequent and drunkenness was rife. One mate, John Cramer, gave his captain two black eyes, thinking he was the member of the crew who was last to appear when all hands were called out on deck. In August 1775 armed seamen with a wage grievance held Liverpool for three days and during this time several people were killed.[35]

In 1753 the seaman's wages were 23s a month and this was typical of peacetime rates. The seaman was better off than the agricultural labourer and, if the value of his food was included, his pay approximated to that of a London labourer who earned 10s–12s a week. On the other hand he had to keep himself while ashore and he had to work a seven-day week at sea. From 1747 a tax on merchant seamen's wages went in part to merchant seamen's hospitals and pensions but there is still no evidence that merchant seamen benefited greatly. Until this date Greenwich Hospital was used exclusively for naval pensioners and even after this date the old or unemployed merchant seaman had to rely largely on the Poor Law, though a few almshouses existed in ports like Whitby.

The glamour which had attached to seafaring in Elizabethan times had largely disappeared and by the middle of the 18th century a seaman had little chance of rising to high naval rank. Apprenticeship became less common and an apprentice might be hired out as an able seamen. One Liverpool master shipwright had fifteen apprentices at sea, each of them earning for him something between 15s and 30s a month. As the merchant fleet grew, seamen became scarce, particularly in wartime. At the outbreak of the Seven Years' War seamen's monthly wages touched 70s, treble what they had been three years earlier.

The Navigation Acts required that English ships should have crews which in number were three-quarters English. Had such clauses been rigorously enforced in wartime, few English ships could have continued to operate. In fact, these clauses were sometimes suspended to enable more foreigners to be employed. There were also attempts to limit sailors' pay.[36] These conditions gave rise to the operations of crimps, agents who supplied seamen, whose activities became notorious in the 19th century. This is the era in which Dr Johnson pronounced that 'no man will be a sailor who has contrivance enough to get himself into a jail; for being in a ship is being in a jail, with the chance of being drowned. . . . A man in a jail has more room, better food, and commonly better company.'[37]

Officers and petty officers did not gain proportionately as much as seamen in wartime, when there was always a narrowing of differentials. On the other hand, they were freer from the activities of the press gangs.

Shipmasters and first mates were exempt and so very often was some proportion of the crew of an East coast collier. The English Channel and the approaches to western ports were the favourite lurking places of the press gangs, together with the ports themselves, and Commodore Walker was not perhaps alone in refitting his ships abroad in order to avoid the press.[38] Impressment was not inexpensive. During the Seven Years' War it cost on average more than a year's wages to impress each seaman retained in the king's service – over £900 per head at 1988 prices.[39]

On his second slaving voyage of 1752–3, which lasted just over a year, Captain John Newton's share of the profits amounted to £257.3s.11d. At this time the master of an East Indiaman was still receiving a basic £10 a month and other masters £6 a month, rates which were much what they had been a century earlier. But if his 'perquisites' were included, the master of an East Indiaman might well make as much as or more than Newton, perhaps £300 a year. The pay of other crew in an East Indiaman had risen as follows: chief mate £5 a month, second mate £4, third mate £3, fourth mate £2, fifth mate 30s, purser £2, surgeon £3, bosun 55s, gunner 55s, carpenter 70s, surgeon's mate 30s and carpenter's mate 50s.[40]

The peacetime establishment of officers and men in the navy rose to 16,000 after 1763, twice the number a quarter of a century earlier and perhaps four times the number a century before.[41] The number of merchant seamen and fishermen grew from an estimated 50,000 in 1688 to 80,000 in 1756, the year of the outbreak of the Seven Years' War, but most of these seamen were pressed into the service of the Crown in wartime – 30,000 in 1688 and 60,000 in 1756 – so that the peak wartime strength of the navy rose from 35,000 in the Second and Third Dutch Wars to 52,000 in 1747 and 84,770 at the end of the Seven Years' War.

Of the extra men and boys needed by the King's ships for the prosecution at sea of the Seven Years' War no fewer than 10,625, or more than 15 per cent, were supplied by The Marine Society, founded for this purpose in 1756 by the remarkable Jonas Hanway.[42] These volunteers came from poor families and had not been to sea previously. Hanway tried to arrange for them to have a modicum of training and efforts to this end were made by The Marine Society from this time on.

Notes

1. R. Davis, *The Rise of the English Shipping Industry in the Seventeenth and Eighteenth Centuries* (1962), London, p. 27: *see also* D. E. Robinson, 'Secret of British Power in the Age of Sail: Admiralty Records of the Coasting Fleet' (1987), *American Neptune*, Vol. XVIII, No. 1. pp. 6 ff.

2. Davis, *op. cit.*, p. 317.
3. *Ib.*, p. 68.
4. *Ib.*, p. 74.
5. *Ib.*, p. 76.
6. *Ib.*, p. 95.
7. M. W. Thomas (ed), *A Survey of English Economic History*, 3rd ed. (1967), London, p. 203; *see also* P. G. E. Clemens, 'The Rise of Liverpool, 1665–1750' (1976), EHR, Vol. XXIX, No. 2, pp. 211 ff.
8. Davis, *op. cit.*, p. 39.
9. T. M. Devine, 'The Colonial Trade and Investment in Scotland, c. 1700–1815' (1976), EHR. Vol. XXIX, No. 1, pp. 1 ff.
10. G. Williams, *History of Liverpool Privateers* (1897), London, p. 471.
11. J. Hanway, *Reasons for an Augmentation of at least Twelve Thousand Mariners, to be Employed in the Merchants' Service and Coasting Trade* (1759), London, p. 56.
12. Thomas, *op. cit.*, pp. 202–3.
13. G. Jackson, *The British Whaling Trade* (1978), London, pp. 48 ff.
14. P. Mathias, *The First Industrial Nation: An Economic History of Britain 1700–1914*, 2nd edn. (1969), London, p. 79.
15. P. J. Thomas, *Mercantilism and East India Trade* (1963), (1st edn. 1926), London, p. 165.
16. Davis, *op. cit.*, p. 23.
17. *Ib.*, p. 268.
18. *Ib.*, p. 288.
19. R. C. Nash, 'The English and Scottish Tobacco Trades in the 17th and 18th Centuries: Legal and Illegal Trade' (1982), EHR 2nd Series, Vol. XXXV, No. 3, pp. 354 ff.
20. Davis, *op. cit.*, p. 272.
21. D. P. Mannix & M. Cowley, *Black Cargoes* (1963), London, p. 30.
22. *Ib.*, pp. 67–8.
23. J. Newton (ed. B. Martin & M. Spurrell), *The Journal of a Slave Trader 1750–1754* (1962), London, p. xiii.
24. O. A. Sherrard, *Freedom from Fear: The Slave and his Emancipation* (1959), London, p. 102.
25. Davis, *op. cit.*, p. 242.
26. J. Sutton, *Lords of the East: the East India Company and its Ships* (1981), Greenwich, p. 14.
27. G. V. Scammell, *The English chartered trading companies and the sea* (1983), National Maritime Museum, p. 30.
28. W. Cunningham, *The Growth of English Industry and Commerce* (1896), Cambridge, pp. 270–1.
29. A. Spencer (ed), *Memoirs of William Hickey (1749–1775)* (1913), London, pp. 142–4, p. 121.
30. D. J. Starkey, 'The economic and military significance of British privateering, 1702–83' (1988), *The Journal of Transport History*, 3rd Series, Vol. 9, No. 1, p. 52.
31. G. Walker, *Voyages and Cruises* (1760), (reprinted 1926), London.
32. G. Anson, *A Voyage Round the World* (1974), London.
33. Newton, *op. cit.*, p. xiv.
34. Mannix, *op. cit.*, pp. 150–1.
35. Davis, *op. cit.*, pp. 154–5.

36. M. Hunter, *How England got its Merchant Marine, 1066–1776*, (1935), New York, p. 264.
37. J. Boswell, *Life of Johnson* (16 March 1759).
38. Walker, *op. cit.*, p. 198.
39. Estimated from L. Neal, 'The Cost of Impressment during the Seven Years' War' (1978), MM., Vol. 64, No. 1, p. 53.
40. Newton, *op. cit.*, p. 87.
41. Davis, *op. cit.*, p. 321.
42. See J. S. Taylor, *Jonas Hanway: Founder of The Marine Society* (1985), London.

14

War and Expansion (1775–1815)

Ironically, the British defeat of France in the Seven Years War made it possible for the American colonists to oppose the British government in the years that followed, for by defeating the French the British had removed the danger of French expansion beyond Canada. In 1775 the differences between the colonists and the British over taxation, trade and self-government came to a head and led to an outbreak of hostilities. In the following year the Americans declared their independence. In 1778 the French joined in the war against Britain, and Spain joined a year later still. Peace was made in 1783, but ten years later France again declared war against Britain and, the short peace of 1802–3 apart, this war continued until 1815, with Spain at war with Britain from 1796 to 1802 and from 1804 to 1808, and with the United States also at war with Britain from 1812 to 1814. For nearly thirty of the forty years between 1775 and 1815, therefore, Britain was at war, with much of these wars being fought at sea.

At the outset of this period Britain lost its most notable colonies, those on the American mainland, and this loss should have proved disastrous to its shipping and its trade had the prevailing theory of mercantilism proved right in practice. In his book on *The Wealth of Nations,* published as the colonies declared their independence, Adam Smith attacked mercantilism and sowed the seed of the new theory of *laissez-faire,* or government abstention from interference in commerce, which was to dominate the economic thinking of the 19th century. In the forty years which followed the loss of the American colonies and the publication of *The Wealth of Nations,* the British merchant fleet, far from declining, at least doubled in size. Estimates of tonnage in 1776 vary from 608,000 tons to 1,125,600 tons, the latter figure being said to take account of coastal vessels excluded from the former. The Navigation Act of 1786, however, decreed that all vessels of over 15 tons had to be registered and so the tonnage of 1,187,000 tons recorded in 1792, on the eve of the French wars, is likely to be more reliable. By 1815 this figure had increased to some 2,600,000 tons, a figure not surpassed for a further twenty-five years.[1]

The American War of Independence, however, did disrupt trade with the former colonists, and after Spain's entry into the war, trade with the Mediterranean was also affected adversely. The years preceding 1783 were years of stagnation. Throughout this first war of the period the British suffered a grave geographical disadvantage. They had to maintain over 70,000 troops in North America, and most of these troops had to be carried more than 2,000 miles across the Atlantic and supplied in America with food, ammunition and other provisions. In 1776 alone more than 27,000 troops were shipped to North America, as many as Julius Caesar had shipped across the Channel in 54 BC to conquer England. In the further course of the American War of Independence more than 29,000 German mercenaries were among those who crossed the Atlantic.

All these troop movements and the movement of stores associated with war made demands upon shipping. To carry 100 soldiers a 200-ton ship was required. Although the same ship might have been used to transport four times as many slaves, the troops were still said to be packed like sardines, lying 'in what boys might call "spoon fashion" ... when they tired on one side, the men on the right would call "about face", and the whole file would turn over at once; then, when they tired again, the man on the left would turn back to the first side'.[2]

For the carriage of troops and stores to the West Indies or to India the government could ordinarily charter space in merchant ships which were going about their normal business because there was relatively little outward cargo carried by such ships and military stores and many military men did not return. But to take troops and stores to North America the Navy Board needed to charter some 300 ships a year.[3] For this purpose a Transport Board was established by the Admiralty, as it had been for the wars between 1690 and 1724 and was to be again in 1794 for the French wars.[4] For each of the war years 1776–83 this transport service cost between £500,000 and £1,000,000 and it employed about 80,000 tons of shipping, thus raising freight rates on the open market. Most of these ships were hired in London and the Navy Board undertook to compensate the owners of ships under charter for damage sustained from hostile action. Despite this undertaking, there were many bankruptcies among shipowners at this time, and freight rates fixed by the Board were among the causes.[5]

Ship losses during the American War of Independence were no more in number than they had been a century earlier in the wars in which William III engaged, a time when the merchant fleet was considerably smaller than it was in 1776. Even so, 3386 British merchant vessels were captured and, although 495 of these were recaptured and a further 507 ransomed,[6] this still left over one-third of the total number of British ships at the outbreak of the war lost to British service. At the beginning of the war a large number of Dutch vessels were hired. By the end of the war the lack of shipping had brought the transport service to such a point that only peace could save it.

When the war ended in 1783 there was a wave of pessimism in Britain. The loss of the North American colonies appeared to some to be the eclipse of Britain's greatness, though others saw reason for hope in the prospective exclusion after independence of New England shipowners from those trades protected by the Navigation Acts. It certainly proved true that much of the entrepôt trade attributable to North America, principally in tobacco, was lost, since American ships now began to trade directly to Europe and to the Far East. Glasgow's tobacco imports, for example, fell from 45 million pounds in 1775 to 0.3 million pounds in 1777 and Glasgow's place in the international tobacco trade was gone for good.[7]

American vessels also began to trade increasingly direct to Britain since, by the terms of the peace settlement, American produce was admitted at the same customs rates as those charged on imports from the remaining British colonies. Such goods could enter in American vessels without paying the 'alien duty' charged on other foreign ships. Tobacco and dressed timber were admitted duty free and American dressed timber thus enjoyed an advantage over similar imports from the Baltic.[8] The demand for American timber increased in any case since trade with the Baltic became difficult during the French Wars. Between 1801 and 1811 the amount of timber imported from Europe into Britain fell from 159,000 to 125,000 loads, while in the same period imports from America increased from a mere 3000 to 154,000 loads. The combined effect of the preferential treatment of American imports, difficulties in trading to the Baltic and American neutrality until 1812 favoured American shipping and greatly helped the American balance of payments. After the outbreak of the French Wars trade between Britain and the United States was conducted increasingly in American ships.

Britain at this time took two-fifths of North American tobacco exports and one-fifth of the exports of rice and indigo. After 1790 exports of potash and pearl ash – used in the bleaching of fabrics and in the production of soap – were worth as much as rice, and wheat and flour also entered the trade. There were modest shipments of furs, maize, iron in the form of pigs or bars, tar, turpentine and fish oil, and greater exports of timber, chiefly as staves and headpieces.

From Great Britain and Ireland to the United States went nearly 90 per cent of the manufactured goods sold there – cloth and clothes, shoes, pottery, metalware, sheet glass, paint, white lead, books, guns, beer, salt, coal, nails and cheese.[9] Independence notwithstanding, the United States had become the most important single market for British products. The trade in both directions increased in value between 1783 and 1801 and, although it decreased between 1801 and 1807, British exports to the former colonies for this quarter of a century averaged about £5 million a year, with exports being more than three times the value of the imports.[10]

Trade with the United States was of particular importance to Ireland. In growing flax the grower has to choose between growing for seed and growing for fibre. Partly because of the climate but also because American ships used cotton sails, the Americans grew for seed. The Irish grew for fibre. The seed was shipped to Ireland from New York in winter, and the cargoes included flour and potash. In return the Irish sent linen, cheese and people – the latter being one reason why so many New York policemen are of Irish origin and why American funds still finance the Irish Republican Army.

In England American ships docked mostly in Liverpool. The cotton industry was growing fast and the northern stretch of the Irish Sea was safer during the French Wars than was the English Channel. The route across the Atlantic was shorter from Liverpool and by this time canal connections to the Midlands and the south of England were fully developed. For most of these reasons Liverpool also became relatively more important during this period in trade with Newfoundland and in trade with other parts of North America.

Until this time west country merchants had monopolised Newfoundland's staple industry, the cod fishery, but changes were taking place. Although the colony remained a tough and turbulent place – in 1804 over sixty ships were lost in a single gale-stricken day – the rough justice of the 'fishing admirals' was replaced in 1791 by a court of civil jurisdiction and the government was given over to a naval Commander-in-Chief.

As they had done in Elizabethan times and ever since, merchants trading to Newfoundland and others engaged in fishing off Newfoundland still fitted out their vessels in the spring and caught, cured and exported the fish in the summer. But by this time a quarter of the cod caught went to the West Indies where it was exchanged for sugar, rum and molasses. One-half of it went to Spain, Portugal and the Mediterranean and bought salt, fruit, wine and olive oil. The rest, together with fish-oils and the products of the seal fishery, was shipped mainly to Britain. In the seal fishery the vessels started for the ice on St Patrick's Day, 17th March, each year and over 100,000 seals would be caught to produce both skins and 1500 tons of seal oil.[11] Cod oil was also imported as a lubricant and an illuminant, the price of £40 a ton being halved at the beginning of the 19th century when gaslighting was developed. From the United Kingdom to Newfoundland went salt, bread, flour, beef, pork, cheese, woollens, fine goods and hardware. The west country supplied serges among the woollens, ropes, nets and twines. Fine goods and continental wares were shipped from London, salt, coal and manufactures from Liverpool, and foodstuffs and emigrants from Waterford, Cork and other Irish ports. Altogether the cod fishery employed 20,000 men and the trade was worth £2 million a year at the end of the Napoleonic Wars, exports having doubled over the previous ten years.[12] The number of vessels entering St John's increased from 400 in 1794 to 852 in 1815.

For Britain the trade to the West Indies at this time was second only to that carried on in European waters, and it remained the most important of all colonial commerce. It was worth more than other colonial trade and, since most of the money made in sugar was spent in Great Britain, it conformed to mercantilist ideas.

Whereas the regular traders to North America now arrived twice a year, in April or May and again in September or October, in the West Indian trade the ships still made only one voyage a year. They left Britain in the autumn, picked up the sugar harvest in the following May or June, and arrived home in time for the cargoes to be transhipped to the Baltic before ice formed in the Baltic ports. Insurance rates doubled if they delayed sailing from the West Indies into the hurricane season.

In 1774 234 ships carrying 76,600 casks of muscovado or unrefined sugar and 12,257 casks of rum, which was made from the sugar by-product molasses, entered British ports from the West Indies. The total tonnage of British vessels then sailing to the Caribbean was five times greater than that of vessels trading to Asia, twenty-eight times greater than that of vessels trading to Africa, and nine times the tonnage of both British and foreign vessels going to the United States. Since West Indiamen were permitted to carry out goods for both the Spanish and the colonial markets, they returned laden with the produce of the Spanish possessions as well as that of the British islands. In 1804 London despatched 326 ships to the West Indies, the English outports a further 188 and Scotland 84, two-and-a-half times as many as a quarter of a century earlier. Four years later still a further 200 ships were trading with the colonies which had been taken from other European powers.[13]

Except by the Royal Navy, rum was never greatly appreciated in England. Nor, despite reductions in the duty paid, did the West Indians have great success in England with coffee. Nine-tenths of the 51 million pounds of coffee imported in 1814 (40 million pounds of it coming from the West Indies, with Jamaica being the greatest producer) was re-exported. Of the other West Indian exports, cotton was by now the most important, though indigo, dyewoods, pimento and ginger also entered into the trade, with mahogany still being shipped from Honduras. Carolina indigo and, after 1790, Bengal indigo competed with the West Indian product. At the outbreak of the French wars exports of cotton from the United States to Liverpool were modest. By 1807, however, the original British West Indian islands were contributing 5 million pounds of a total of 74 million pounds of cotton imported into England, the newly conquered colonies were sending nearly 10 million pounds, and the rest was coming from the United States. But West Indian cotton – what is now called 'Sea Island' cotton – was of particularly high quality in consequence of its long staple and this cotton went mostly to Lancashire.

Spain, France, Holland, Denmark and Sweden all had trading outposts in the West Indies at the beginning of the French wars but most of the foreign islands were captured by the British in the years that followed. A great many British soldiers and sailors died in the West Indies – 40,000 by 1796 – but by 1814 their sacrifice had secured for the British Crown, at least temporarily, the islands of St Lucia, Trinidad, Tobago, Martinique, Guadaloupe, St Thomas, Curaçao and St Eustatius, together with the mainland colonies of Surinam, Demerara, Essequibo and Berbice. After the wartime destruction of the French plantations in St Dominique, the British West Indies accounted for a large proportion of all the sugar consumed in Europe. New kinds of sugar were introduced and from 1793 onwards yields increased. Eventually, this led to over-production and contributed to a surplus of sugar on the British market after 1799 and a halving of the price in the next seven years. As sugar revenues fell, bullion from the Caribbean and South America took their place for the purchase of imported manufactures, the bullion being required by Britain to finance the East Indian trade.

Both 'established ships' and 'seekers' traded to the West Indies, the latter being vessels which went out looking for homeward cargoes. The most important of the seekers were those engaged in the slave trade. Both types of vessel might pick up Madeíra wine on their way south for, usually drunk as sangaree, Madeira was by this time the only wine drunk in large quantities in the West Indies.

It was during the later years of this period that the British trade in slaves was abolished, not much more than a century after it had become a significant British activity. The Quakers petitioned Parliament to end it in 1783, and in 1788 John Newton wrote his effective pamphlet *Thoughts upon the African Slave Trade*. In the latter year Parliament passed a regulative act which did something to ameliorate the lot of the slaves on the middle passage, requiring African ships, for example, to carry qualified surgeons. In 1789 John Newton was among those who gave evidence against the trade to the Privy Council. The Privy Council concluded that by this time only one in eight of the slaves carried died on passage to America, instead of one in four, as had been the case a century earlier.[14] By the end of the century mortality rates were even lower, perhaps one in 18.[15] One reason for their better care was that slaves had become more expensive in West Africa, the price having more than trebled in 100 years from about £3 to £10 or more. The Bristol Society of Merchant Adventurers petitioned Parliament against the abolition of the trade in 1792 but the House of Commons resolved that it should cease by 1796. When war broke out again the matter was left in abeyance and in 1796 Liverpool, where the interest in slaving now much exceeded that in other ports, petitioned against abolition. Another Bill for Abolition was presented in 1799 and again Liverpool petitioned against it.

In the course of the 18th century the English had carried 2.5 million slaves out of some 6 million transported across the Atlantic, one-third of the English total being carried in the quarter of a century preceding the abolition of the trade in 1807.[16] By this time there were over 700,000 slaves in the former British colonies of North America, mostly south of the Mason and Dixon Line, but demand increased in the West Indies after the capture by Britain of the French and Dutch islands shortly after the turn of the century. In these last years the English traffic was virtually monopolised by Liverpool, slave ships despatched from Liverpool averaging 100 a year in the fifteen years preceding abolition. In the peak year of 1798 149 Liverpool ships, totalling about 50,000 tons, carried 52,557 slaves across the Atlantic. The ships, which had previously averaged about 160 tons, were now between 300 and 500 tons.

By the end of the era slaves were bought for goods worth about £25, though the price varied with quality. They were then branded on the breast. Women and children were not fettered but the men were fettered in pairs until the ships were away from the coast. There were some inhumane captains and occasional slave mutinies, but in three successive voyages one master, a Captain Crow, lost no slaves on the crossing.[17] The food he provided was said to consist of a broth made from dried shrimps, yams, beans and rice; bread and coconuts were also provided and the sick were given special food. In America the slaves sold for sums varying between £50 and £80.

The trade was undeniably profitable, and contributed much to the wealth of Liverpool at this time as it had done earlier to the wealth of

Bristol and London, but it was not perhaps as profitable as has been suggested by one work of repute. The *Enterprize* of Liverpool, after an unusually short and successful voyage of 1803–4, is said to have made a 'profit' of £24,430. 8s. 11d, which would appear to be about the sale price of her 412 slaves. Against this, however, must be set expenses of £17,045. 2s. 5½d, which would suggest that the return on capital invested was of the order of 40 per cent.[18] Some light on public attitudes at the time is shed by an advertisement for the sale of goods valuable in the trade – guns, shackles, thumb screws, gold-laced hats, knives, 'diamond necklaces at 3s per Pound', linen, looking glasses and horse beans. It was stated that specimens of the whole were on view 'except the Thumb Screws, the sight of which it is thought would too deeply wound the feelings of those not inclined to purchase'.[19] It compares, perhaps, with the modern attitude towards battery hens.

With the merchants demanding compensation for losses suffered, Samuel Wilberforce at last succeeded in his efforts to abolish the trade in 1807, the last English slaver, *Kitty's Amelia,* leaving the Mersey on 27th July in that year.[20] Abolition was built into the peace treaty in 1815, for the British not only abolished their own trade but initiated a seventy-five-year campaign against the traffic of other countries. The transatlantic trade dropped off rapidly after 1849, but in some degree it was replaced by contract labour, often little short of slavery, particularly by the French and Portuguese.[21]

The end of the slave trade was not the sole factor in diminishing the economic importance of the West Indies. Increasing competition in sugar production came from Brazil and the East Indies, and French and German chemists were discovering that sugar beet was a substitute for sugar cane. The heyday of the West Indies was over.

Among the deepsea trades at this time, particularly between 1783 and 1808, whaling, both in the Arctic Ocean and in the South Seas, took second place to that of the West Indian sugar trade. Subsidies to whalers had cost nearly £2 million between 1733 and 1800 but not until the 1780s did the cost to the state of a ton of whale oil fall below its market value.[22] Whale oil was used for domestic lighting, streetlighting, as a softening fluid for coarse hard fabrics, as a lubricant and for other purposes, and the captains and officers of the whaling vessels were paid by shares in the results of a voyage. Between 1800 and 1804 whalers totalling some 25,000 tons and averaging about 80 tons in size were bringing back 7000 tons of oil and more than 7000 hundredweight of whalebone a year. As demand grew and inflation pushed up prices the price of the oil crept up to £60 a ton by the end of the French wars.[23] For Arctic whalers Hull was the most important port, while London was particularly interested in the new venture of hunting the sperm whale in the South Seas, a trade which first became of importance during the American War of Independence, with cachalot hunting beginning by the outbreak of the French Wars.

Robert Eastwick's first voyage, begun in 1784, was made aboard a whaler. He started his apprenticeship at the age of 12 and was away for 16 months aboard the *Friendship*, which returned with a full cargo of spermaceti. While the captain was kind, he believed in throwing a boy in at the deep end and the mate, in the young Eastwick's view, was 'a savage'. However, Eastwick was befriended by an old seaman of 65 who had seen service in the King's ships and he told Eastwick: 'There is no justice or injustice on board a ship, my lad. There are only two things. Duty and Mutiny – mind that. All that you are ordered to do is duty. All that you refuse to do is mutiny. And the punishment for mutiny on a king's frigate is the yard arm. In the merchant service you only get rope's-ended.'[24]

Despite the growth of cotton in the New World and the machine manufacture of it in Lancashire, the trade to the Far East remained important. Adam Smith had attacked the East India Company's sovereign powers in India and in 1784 these powers were brought under governmental scrutiny by the establishment of a Board of Control.[25] Dual control of the Indian spheres of influence had begun with the Regulating Act of 1773, but in 1789 the government virtually took over in the sub-continent, appointing Warren Hastings first Governor-General. By 1818 the British government was the dominant power in India. From 1793 the East India Company was forced to relinquish its trade monopoly with India and this trade was thrown open completely in 1813. During the French wars the company's income from tax collection in Bengal was largely swallowed up by the costs of defence. It has been estimated that one-tenth of the number of soldiers despatched to India each year in the Company's ships had to be replaced.[26] In addition to troops and government goods, the ships took bullion, iron and woollens, the latter under statutory obligation. Imports from India still included cotton goods, along with silks, saltpetre, indigo, sugar and rice, most of these goods coming from Bengal. Madras, Bombay and, after 1790, Penang were all held mainly for strategic reasons and, in the course of the French wars, the Cape of Good Hope and Ceylon were taken from the Dutch. The East Indies proper, however, remained a Dutch preserve.

Ships sailing to the East loaded up-river on the Thames, passengers joining at Gravesend. The voyage, which was normally a tedious one, really began at Deal or, when Britain was at war, at Portsmouth. The average China voyage lasted about 18 months and sailing dates were so arranged that these vessels could catch the south-west monsoon up the China coast and the north-east monsoon back.

Commercial profits now came largely from the China tea trade, with woollens, tin and other goods being sent from Britain in part exchange, and raw cotton and opium being carried from India to China in the local or so-called 'country ships'. The Commutation Act of 1784 virtually removed the tax on tea which had so incensed the American colonists and which had greatly increased smuggling. In return the East India Company agreed to sell tea at home at a reasonable price. In the two years that followed imports jumped from 6 to 20 million pounds.[27]

Of the 'country ships' 70 or 80 operated from Calcutta and a further 25 or so from Bombay. These ships were built of teak in India and, like the 1406-ton *Earl of Balcarres* built in Bombay in 1810, could be large. The still existing *Foudroyant,* built in Bombay in 1817 as the warship *Trincomalee,* would not be greatly different from such a ship. Each year the country vessels exported goods to the value of some £5 million and this 'country trade' could be assigned by the East India Company to its servants and protégés in India.

Those ships operating in the Far East trade from Britain were built in the main by a ring of capitalists who chartered them to the East India Company for a stated number of voyages, and the operation had become rather more formalised and sophisticated with the passage of time. The owners, known collectively as 'The Shipping Interest', were also shareholders in the Company. They still built their ships in the Thames, their 'regular' ships being in the trade all the time, with 'extra' ships being added when required. With English oak in shorter and shorter supply, the Company used increasing quantities of iron, and the use of Indian-built teak ships increased as the 18th century drew to a close. When the China trade had been first established the ships engaged in it were much smaller than those bound for India. Now, furnished with 36–38 guns and carrying a crew of 125, they cost £50,000 to £70,000 to build and, at 1200 tons, were considerably larger than the Indiamen. At their destination, by decree of the Chinese government, they were allowed to lie only at the Whampoa anchorage off Canton.

The size of the ships trading to India was determined in part by the depth of water in the Hooghly river. For the more valuable of the Indian trades, for piece-goods and silks, 800-ton ships were used carrying a crew of about 100 and 26–32 guns. For the 'gruff' goods – saltpetre, sugar and rice – ships of about 500 tons sufficed, and these carried 12–20 guns.[28] The 'extra' ships were usually of the smallest class and, inclusive of such vessels, the East India fleet consisted of about 100 sail, totalling some 90,000 tons,[29] with 30 in each of the top two classes.

Arising in consequence of the voyages of Captain Cook and from the American War of Independence, a new 'trade' which was to have tremendous significance for the future was opened up in 1787. This was the transport of convicts to Port Jackson on Botany Bay in 'New Holland' or Australia and also to the remote Pacific island of Norfolk. Before 1775, many convicts had been shipped to America, over 40,000 of them in the preceding sixty years.[30] In that trade the contractors who worked on behalf of the government had some interest in the welfare of their charges because the sums paid in America for the services of the prisoners for the term of their sentences were assigned to the contractors. The American outlet for felons was closed by the War of Independence and they were crowded instead into old hulks. The Transportation Act of 1784 established the machinery for despatching them to Norfolk Island and to Botany Bay. The Australian contractors responsible for their transport had no such proprietary interest as those who had shipped felons to America because as yet there was no demand in Australia for indentured servants. Initially, on this new run, a dead convict was more profitable than a live one since the contractor received £17. 7s. 6d. either way.

In the early years of transportation to Australia conditions on board ship were often bad and disease was rife. The first fleet of 1787–8 consisted of six transports chartered for the convict service plus three store-ships and two warships. The ships ranged from 200 to 400 tons and on this occasion carried 584 men and 192 women convicts. The death rate was highest in the second fleet despatched, with 267 prisoners dying at sea and a further 150 dying after landing out of a total of 1006. In this case the contractors – Camden, Calvert and King – had been slaving contractors. After the third voyage payment to the contractor was deferred until the convict was landed in decent health. After 1815 the death rate averaged one in 122.[31] Although there were exceptions, the sexes were normally segregated after 1811, the women being carried in one ship and the men in another. The contingent of 1798, at least, was representative of all ranks of society since this batch included the 'Croppies' who had been sent out for complicity in the Irish rebellion of that year. John Nicol, whose *Life and Adventures* was published in 1822, had served aboard a convict ship and he observed no ill treatment; he recorded that the women were allowed to choose a temporary husband from among the members of the crew.

Captain Robert Eastwick, who brought tea and sugar from India in a 'country ship' to both Port Jackson and Norfolk Island at about the turn of the century, reported that in general the convicts were well reconciled to their lot. Although mutton cost 2s 6d a pound[32] (perhaps £2.80 a pound in 1988), in Port Jackson a theatre had been built and Eastwick saw *The Recruiting Officer* and *The Virgin Unmasked*, 'both affording very excellent amusement'.[33] At the opening of this theatre a celebrated pickpocket was said to have recited in the prologue:

> From distant climes o'er widespread seas we come
> (Though not with much éclat, or beat of drum),
> True patriots all; for be it understood,
> We left our country for our country's good.[34]

Altogether, between 1787 and 1868, the date of the last convict ship, 825 shiploads of prisoners were sent to Australia and 160,023 male and female prisoners were landed.[35] The first influx of free immigrants did not travel until the 1820s.

It was in no way unusual for ships to sail together as the first convict fleet sailed to Australia, even in peacetime, and wartime convoys have an ancient history. The convoy system for the protection of merchant ships was adopted during the American War of Independence and again when war broke out in 1793. With certain exceptions sailing in convoy was made compulsory by an Act in 1798 and the financial cost was largely offset by a reduction in war insurance premiums, though the prices of such imports as sugar tended to fluctuate more because convoys took time to assemble and delivery to the home market came all at once or not at all. The number of ships in a convoy was often between 60 and 100, though in 1798 160 vessels left England together for Jamaica and on another occasion at least 300 ships sailed together out of Spithead.

In certain conditions West Indiamen could obtain a licence to proceed alone in wartime, but the vessels which regularly sailed alone were the Post Office packets, vessels carrying official and other mail which by this time were indispensable to British trade. A packet service had started in Harwich as early as 1661 and a packet sailed to Hellvoetsluys every Wednesday and Saturday at about 2 p.m. so as to be 'on neither shore in ye night time.'[36] The Falmouth service, at first to Corunna, started in 1689 and extended its service in the course of the following century.[37] Other packet stations were to be found in London, Dover, Holyhead and Milford.

The importance of Falmouth lay in its position, which was clear of the English Channel and its headwinds. The first mail coach service from London to Falmouth started in 1785. Thirty regular packets were stationed there, speedy and elegant vessels of between 150 and 200 tons, costing

£4000 to £4500 each, and armed as 'runners' with up to 18 guns according to size and with crews of from 18 to 40 men who were immune from the activities of the press gang. Standing orders obliged them to sail immediately on receipt of government mail provided they could carry a double-reefed topsail. Although his nominal annual salary was only £104, a captain in the packet service could earn up to £1000 a year and command was often passed from father to son. Even crew members earned relatively good money, though there were unsuccessful strikes for more pay in 1810 and again in 1814.

The packet boats were hired by the Post Office, usually being on contract for a period of seven years, expressly for their speed in delivering mail, though they also moved specie, carried the news, and were a valuable source of naval and military intelligence. There were regular and frequent services to Ireland, the Continent, Lisbon (weekly), Gibraltar, the West Indies (monthly), Brazil and Halifax, and in 1806 the packet service was extended from Gibraltar to Malta. If the ships suffered attack the mail carried was thrown overboard and sunk. A letter to Spain cost 2s 2d and to America 3s 7d.[38] Unofficial bags of mail were also collected through coffee houses and despatched by way of other merchant vessels. In an attempt to regularise this system the Post Office established the Ship Letter Office in 1799, and an Act of 1814 allowed the Post Office to use for the carriage of mail either men-of-war or other merchant ships.

On the whole the packets gave good service, but the cargo apart from mail and specie was the province of the master and crew and sometimes their private interests were in conflict with those of the Post Office. In wartime they were prone to attack weaker vessels to secure prizes and thus delay official communications. The crews sometimes engaged in smuggling, and it was not unknown for these ships to harbour spies. The ships carried passengers, mostly army officers, government officials, and merchants and their families, and the fares ranged from 35 guineas to Gibraltar to 54 guineas to Jamaica.[39] Some were captured in wartime by privateers, nineteen of the Falmouth packets being so taken in the French wars.

In wartime privateers were still active. Over 7000 letters of marque were issued to commanders of British vessels between 1777 and 1783 and, according to the Earl of Derby in 1778, Liverpool would have been ruined at this time had it not been for the success of the privateers. Privateering represented an alternative wartime investment opportunity for merchants and shipowners, as it had done in earlier wars.[40] Other nations, too, authorised privateering in wartime. Captain Eastwick tells us that in the East, probably in 1797, French privateers captured or sank some £2 million of British shipping in a single year. One of the fortunes that Eastwick lost, when his ship was uninsured because he could not afford the insurance premium, was when he was taken in his own ship, *Endeavour,* by a French privateer, a frigate of 50 guns. He found discipline slack and the privateer was subsequently taken by a British man-of-war.

Privateers were particularly numerous in the approaches to the English Channel and the Irish Sea, off Cuba, and off the Coromandel Coast or in the Malacca Strait (where pirates were still to be met with in the 1980s). Based on places like St Malo and Mauritius, they relied on speed, disguise and a knowledge of the trade routes. Convoys were not always an adequate protection against them since many merchant ships were slow, ill-armed and undermanned. Losses grew in the War of 1812 when American privateers were also at sea raiding the Newfoundland Banks fishing fleet and British shipping trading to Canada and the West Indies. Overall, however, losses were more than made good by new building and by the absorption of prizes and total British tonnage increased rapidly after 1783 in consequence of the marked growth in foreign trade.

The number of seamen also increased. Seafaring at the end of the 18th century was far more significant as a national industry than it is today. In a population of 12 million there were by this time nearly 300,000 seamen of all descriptions, excluding 33,000 foreigners who also served the British at sea. The employment of Asian seafarers went back to the earliest days of the East India Company, when the crews of homeward-bound Indiamen, seriously depleted by death and desertion, were brought up to strength with Indians (lascars) and, later, Chinese. The employment of such seafarers in British ships persisted into the 1980s. Returning home in an Indiaman in 1808 William Hickey commented on the 'strange motley crew, consisting of natives of almost every nation in Europe, besides nine Americans and eighteen Chinese'. He reckoned that there were not more than ten Englishmen on board. The 'country ships' carried only a few Europeans, and Asian seamen came at half their price.[41] During the Napoleonic Wars there were 126,000 seamen and marines in the Royal Navy and a further 145,000 in registered merchant ships. In addition to these there were fishermen, watermen and seamen who served in unregistered ships.[42] In Britain one family in six may well have been directly dependent on the sea.

Officers in the East India Company, the Hudson Bay Company and the packet service wore uniform, though most merchant service officers did not. However, the distinctive blue serge trousers and jacket and the hair tied in a queue readily identified the sailor who, as 'Honest Jack' and 'the True British Tar', was a national character. The queue did not outlast the French wars, and seaman William Richardson recorded an early appearance in 1785: 'Up to this time our captain, as was the custom, had worn his hair in curls, and loose behind the ears; but one of these days he came on board with his hair tied in a queue, and looked so strange that he did not seem like the same person; this was the first time that tails came into fashion.'[43]

In 1783 Jonas Hanway, founder of The Marine Society, published a book in which he advocated the establishment of a sea school in every county. In the year of Hanway's death, 1786, The Marine Society established the first training ship for ratings, converting an old merchantman to this purpose, and the following year Hull Trinity House established a marine school on shore, perhaps because John Thornton, Treasurer to The Marine Society, was from a Hull family and able to spread the Hanway gospel in that port. For the time being not much more was done to train seamen, though there existed already a number of small establishments for the teaching of navigation to potential officers, at least in Bristol, Whitby, Newcastle and London. William Wales, headmaster of Christ's Hospital from 1775 to 1798, was a mathematician who had been to sea and served with Captain Cook. Thomas Lynn retired at this time from the East India Company's service to set up as a teacher in Leadenhall Street where the Company itself had its offices and sale-rooms. In 1772 John Hamilton Moore of Tower Hill published his *New Practical Navigator,* and round about 1800 J. W. Norie, still known for his *Nautical Tables* and his *Seamanship,* was also to be found in Leadenhall Street.[44]

Officers in the East India Company apart, everyone rose from the forecastle, for even apprentices messed in the forecastle with the crew and not aft with the officers. Captain Eastwick was apprenticed and premiums paid for apprenticeship ranged from £10 to £20. Captain Samuel Kelly, whose memoirs have also been preserved, was not apprenticed when he went to sea in 1779, though he received favourable treatment and was master at 23. At the end of the 18th century a regular scale for carrying apprentices was laid down and during the last three years of their apprenticeship apprentices were protected from impressment. In the lucrative trades influential connections were often the key to a young man's success.

Every potential officer in the East India Company, like every candidate for a commission in the Royal Navy, had to pass an examination in navigation, but most merchant service officers were still very much rule-of-thumb navigators, knowing only their 3 Ls–log, lead and latitude. In East Indiamen, as Hickey had found, the Commander might be a gentleman of good education who wore uniform and held a service at sea on a

Sunday, but the ordinary merchant service master was invariably tough, sometimes cruel and usually a heavy drinker. According to Captain Frederick Marryat drink accounted for more than half the number of shipwrecks and sea tragedies.

Generalisation about so diverse an industry as shipping is seldom easy. By the end of the 18th century, if not earlier, it was the practice in the East India Company for the managing owner of an East Indiaman, the 'ship's husband', to 'sell his ship' to the captain to whom he offered a command and he often obtained £8000 or even £10,000 for the appointment. If he so wished the commander thus appointed could sell his command to the highest bidder thereafter. Clearly, whoever paid such high sums would expect high returns in addition to normal merchant service pay. In addition to his pay of £10 a month and allowances for his table and expenses in port, the commander had a right to free outward freight to the extent of 50 tons, though he could not on his own account export woollens, metals or military stores. On the homeward voyage he was allotted 20 tons of free freight, limited to certain scheduled goods. On these he might hope to earn £25 a ton. He also earned primage, a percentage of the total earnings, and in a 1200-ton ship primage for the voyage might amount to £100. In addition he made money from carrying passengers, outward fares ranging from £95 for a subaltern to £235 for a general officer, and even more for exalted passengers. Return fares were higher still. Fees were paid to him, too, for midshipmen's places. It has been estimated that the gains made by a prudent commander might average £4000 a voyage[45] or even more, though at least a quarter of this would represent interest on capital invested. Prices in general trebled in the last half of the 18th century but, even after every allowance is made for inflation and his own heavy investment in his command, the East India Company commander towards the end of the Company's existence and in wartime seems to have been earning more in real terms – probably over £50,000 a year at 1988 prices – than ever shipmasters earned before or since. These were the nabobs of the merchant service.

East India Company commanders were in a class of their own. Most masters, and sometimes officers and crew, could make something above their pay by way of permitted perquisites or private trading, and yet Captain Kelly claimed that in all his time at sea he only once cleared more than £75 a year in salary and perquisites combined. The usual rate for an AB in the merchant service was only about 30s a month though it could be much more in special circumstances. As always, wages rose in wartime and in the West Indies in 1795 Kelly, short of men, had to pay each seaman 45 guineas for the run home – three times his own earnings.[46] In the packet service seamen were said to earn only 22s 6d a month but they might make a profit on an 'adventure' of their own. In the East India Company service the AB's normal pay was now 35s a month, and in the transport service 60s. But in wartime aboard a slaving vessel Captain Crow paid ABs 6 guineas a month plus £3–£4 given as 'crimpage' or fee to their suppliers. The carpenter received 10 guineas a month. In the West India trade a Bristol seaman received three months pay in advance and half the balance due to him while he was in the West Indies. Working conditions for seamen were best organised in the coal trade on the north-east coast and it was in this area that the first unions were established[47] though they were purely local and of short duration. Seamen on the north-east coast, at least, were expected to pass a stiff *viva voce* examination in practical seamanship before being rated AB. According to Nicol, Greenlandmen – that is, Arctic whaling men – had the reputation of being the roughest of British seamen and such 'toughies' did not hesitate to fight off the press-gangs.

It was not in the whalers, of course, but in the East Indiamen that the best conditions were found. The *Royal George,* 1200 tons, for example, sailed from Plymouth for Madras in 1807 with over 500 soldiers and 160 crew on board. In a five-month voyage her commander, Captain Timmins, meted out no punishments, there was very little illness, and only one death.[48] Some years earlier, in 1792, Robert Eastwick had sailed on the East Indiaman *Barwell* as fifth mate. *Barwell* was commanded by the appropriately named Captain John Welladvice, 'a good seaman and a kind gentleman of whom I always retained the most friendly recollection'. There were seven officers on board and 'they were one and all gentlemen by education and family'.[49]

Joining the country service in India, Eastwick was given command of the *Rebecca* when he was 21, a ship which was 'equal to at least £4000 a year' in the opium and cotton trade to China. However, in an uncertain world it was as easy to lose money as it was to make it and, in an adventurous life which was not confined to the East India Company's service, Eastwick made and lost three modest fortunes before he made £10,000 – only half of one of his earlier fortunes and worth perhaps £230,000 at 1988 prices – in 13 months' active employment in the new trade to South America. On this sum, in 1814, he retired, at least for some years.

British trade to South America had been accelerated enormously during the French wars in consequence of the enforced isolation of the Spanish colonies. In 1806 the British captured Buenos Aires and from 1808 there began those wars of independence to which Britain ultimately became

Fig. 3. DEATH RATES AMONG BRITISH SEAFARERS, FROM ALL CAUSES, 1590–1986

YEAR(S)	ERA	NUMBER OF DEATHS PER ANNUM PER 1000 SEAMEN AT RISK
1590	The privateering years	100
1800	The Napoleonic Wars	50
1835		25
1870		20
1900		10
1914–18	First World War	25
1919–23		6.34
1931–35		4.22
1939–45	Second World War	50
1948–57		2.85
1958–67		2.11
1968–77		1.87
1978–86		1.27

(*Sources:* General Council of British Shipping and Registrar-General of Shipping and Seamen, allowance being made for changes in base used; official estimates of war casualties for the two World Wars; earlier figures are estimated from sources indicated in the text.)

committed.[50] When Captain Eastwick took command of the *Anna* to exploit the new opportunities he observed that he had no personal knowledge of what kind of goods were best suited to such a market. He concluded that 'where there are British troops and fighting, there is always drinking, and where there is victory there is toasting, and so amongst other things I laid in eighty pipes of Spanish wine and forty casks of brandy'.

In the East the opium trade could seem legitimate since the use of opium was legal in Britain. William Jardine, opium-trader and joint founder of the illustrious firm of China merchants, Jardine, Matheson and Company, started his sea-life in 1802 as surgeon's mate in the 1200–ton East Indiaman *Brunswick* and thus became familiar with the trade in opium and cotton to China in which both *Brunswick* and Eastwick's *Rebecca* were engaged.

Jardine's pay was £2. 10s. a month but he was allowed 2.5 tons of 'privilege' cargo. Promoted to surgeon in 1804, his pay went up to £3 a month and he was allowed 7 tons of cargo.[51]

Both East Indiamen and Greenlandmen carried a surgeon, as did the slavers after 1789 and passenger ships after 1803. Nevertheless, sickness and death at sea reached a high point in this period. The price of victory at sea in the French wars was 100,000 dead[52] and the number of maimed seamen begging in the streets was a national scandal. No infectious diseases other than smallpox could be controlled; scurvy was still rife since oranges and lemons were expensive; no one noticed the contagious character of cholera; and malaria, dysentery, consumption and, in the West Indies, yellow fever were all common. Casualties as well as disease were frequent – deaths from drowning, falls from masts, suffocation from foul air in the holds, burns, wounds, poisoning, and much more. Accommodation on board ship was often insanitary, ventilation poor, food – salt pork and biscuits – usually bad, and water often undrinkable. Aboard slavers the death-rate among crew was comparable to that of British soldiers in Flanders in the First World War. More than one-fifth of all seamen on Liverpool and Bristol slave-ships died on board during the voyage, and there were additional deaths among those who deserted or who had been discharged. The average slaver sailed with a crew of thirty-five. Of these seven or eight died on the ship and eleven more were left behind, usually sick, either on the Guinea Coast or in the West Indies; less than half of the original crew returned home. According to Clarkson, of those who stayed on these vessels, a great number were permanently crippled, went blind or died in the Liverpool and Bristol infirmaries. He estimated that the English slave trade at this time employed 5000 seamen and that each year deaths numbered 2000 or 40 per cent.[53]

The seaman also had to live with the press. During the French wars The Marine Society supplied an average of 1000 landmen a year to the Navy – 22,973 in 22 years – recruits who were so undernourished that they were no bigger than the hill tribesmen of New Guinea.[54] Many more sailors, however, were required and apprentices were of value in merchant shipping since they were exempt from impressment and provided cheap labour at a time of labour shortages and high wages.[55] In 1812 the mode of entry to the average warship was: 8 per cent boy volunteers, 15 per cent adult volunteers (each receiving a bounty of £5), 12 per cent quota men (where bounties might be as much as £70), 15 per cent foreigners, and 50 per cent British pressed men.[56] Every successfully pressed man cost about £27, though the pressed men received no part of this money.[57]

Between 1775 and 1815 impressment was the main recruiting instrument, and these were the last wars in which the system operated. Merchant seamen were pressed in India, where half-manned ships were forced to enlist native seamen. Seamen were also pressed in America, which sometimes resulted in victualling ships on government service being immobilised overseas.[58] But, most of all, seamen were pressed in British waters, frequently when homeward bound. Where they could, pressed men often deserted – one in three according to one authority[59] – and Nelson calculated that 42,000 seamen had deserted the fleet in the French war before 1803.

Impressment was one of the two major causes of the War of 1812. By the Decrees of Berlin and Milan in 1806 Napoleon established the 'Continental System' whereby the Continent was forbidden to trade with Great Britain. Britain retaliated with 'Orders in Council', blockading Continental ports. This action infringed the rights of neutrals and, since the United States had considerable trade with the Continent, her interests were thus affected.

At the same time the British impressed British seamen, or suspected British seamen, found in American ships, for the British held that a merchant ship was not part of a nation's sovereign territory although the Americans held that it was. Americans admitted the right of wartime search, but only for contraband and 'persons in the military service of the enemy'. Great Britain adhered to a doctrine of the 'indefeasible allegiance' of the British subject, whereas the United States advanced a doctrine of 'voluntary expatriation'.

The consequence was that British naval officers boarded American ships and removed from them, illegally according to the Americans, British seamen on board. In the process they also removed perhaps 8000 American seamen.[60] In *Frank Mildmay* Captain Marryat illustrates the problem. A British officer is talking to the master of an American privateer in 1812. 'Some of them, I suspect, are English', he says, referring to the crew. 'It is not for me to peach', replies the wary American. 'It is always difficult to know if a man who has been in both countries is a native of Boston in Lincolnshire, or Boston in Massachusetts; and perhaps they don't always know themselves. We never ask questions when a seaman ships for us.'

Throughout these long years of war British trade was developing fast. Of the chartered companies only the East India Company still enjoyed exclusive privileges, and these had been breached. The Hudson Bay Company still traded and owned its own ships but it had long since lost its legal monopoly. After 1750 the Royal African Company had become a very loose association. The Russia Company still had some interest in the trade to Archangel; but the Levant Company, which had suffered seriously from French competition, was kept alive only by government subsidy. The oldest of all the regular companies, the Company of Merchant Adventurers, came to an end in 1806, by which time it was maintaining a staple only in Hamburg.

The great bulk of British trade was now carried on by private firms in a stubbornly individualistic and fiercely competitive manner. Partnership was the main form of business structure, though many coasters were under sole ownership. The trading interest and the shipping interest were becoming differentiated, a process encouraged by the establishment of the Transport Board in 1794,[61] and, at the beginning of the 19th century, the General Shipowners' Society, established in 1802, boasted that its membership was confined to shipowners pure and simple. These members, however, were to be found mainly in London and the society was not particularly influential. Other shipowners' clubs were to be found on the north-east coast, foreshadowing the protection and indemnity societies of today. In the sugar trade the relationship between planter and merchant was close, but most firms were fairly small. The Society of West India Merchants in London dealt with the Admiralty, but there were other West India associations in Glasgow, Liverpool and Bristol.

In the long-distance trades it was becoming unusual for the master to have a financial interest in his ship. He had become a salaried servant, though he still held great responsibilities and might arrange to take up cargo or fix a charter.

The specialised coffee-house remained a feature of the shipping industry. The Jerusalem Coffee House was the resort of East India merchants; the Jamaica was a rendezvous for merchants and shipmasters in the West India trade; and the volume of business at the Virginia and Baltic was such that a move was made in 1810 to the larger Antwerp Tavern in Threadneedle Street which was then renamed the Baltic. In 'Sam's next the Custom House' captains met prospective shippers and passengers, and Lloyd's Coffee House was so much a favourite resort of shipmasters that by 1812 it had already begun to be referred to as 'The Captain's Room' and there is 'The Captain's Room' at Lloyd's to this day.

The 'New Lloyd's' was established in the Royal Exchange in 1774. It withstood the strains of war and by 1810 there were 1400 to 1500 subscribers of whom two-thirds were underwriters. One of them, 'Dicky' Thornton, eldest son of John Thornton, anti-slaver and first Treasurer of The Marine Society, was said to be 'good for three millions' and he once 'wrote' £250,000 on a shipment of gold to St Petersburg and offered to deposit Exchequer Bonds as security until the risk was run off.[62] By 1810 risks covered in London exceeded £100 million and Lloyd's was by far the greatest centre of marine insurance in the world. A Liverpool

Underwriters' Association was formed in 1802, and private underwriting was also carried on in other ports.

In coastal trading losses were comparatively small, but marine losses from other causes were at least as numerous as losses resulting from enemy action and there were more of the former in the coastal and short sea trades. In foreign trade one ship in sixteen was lost each year between 1793 and 1801; in 1795 the French admiral Richery captured thirty ships, mostly laden with silk, out of a convoy in the Levant, and in 1810 there was a wholesale seizure of British ships in Baltic ports. Insurance rates fluctuated according to these wartime risks. Only 1.5 per cent for coastal voyages, they rose to 20 per cent in high risk war zones, and averaged about 6 per cent. Without insurance the great expansion of tonnage during the war could not have taken place. Lloyd's enjoyed good relations with the Admiralty, receiving particularly warm praise from Nelson, and underwriters raised money for the relief of the wounded and for the dependants of those killed in action. From 1802 Lloyd's established lifeboats round the coast.

Although Parliament cared little or nothing for the welfare of seafarers, being concerned only with their supply, investors in shipping were given some limited protection after 1786 by an extension of the Navigation Act of 1696 which required the general registration of all British Empire ships of more than 15 tons. The Act was intended to distinguish British shipping, entitled to the privileges of the Navigation Acts, from American shipping after the War of Independence. This register, which became the first foundation for reliable statistics, was to record the names of the owners at the time of first registration though not the size of their shares. Two distinct types of certificate were granted: for ships eligible for colonial trade there was the 'British Plantation Registry'; for others there was the 'Foreign Ships Registry for the European Trade, British Property'.

In 1797 a Manifest Act made compulsory for British ships the carriage of a full manifest of cargo. By this time the Navigation Acts were proving too restrictive and the exigencies of war forced some relaxation. Because seamen were in short supply, an Act of 1794 allowed up to three-quarters of the crew of a British ship to be foreigners instead of one-quarter as hitherto. In certain trades – the re-export of colonial goods to European ports, for example – foreign ships were now granted licences for what had previously been reserved to British ships. American vessels were also given permission to trade between the West Indies and the United States. Trade could expand more quickly where it was free of restriction, especially in the circumstances of the time.

By the outbreak of war with France in 1793 some 5500 British vessels were engaged in foreign trade, excluding the Asiatic 'country trade', and a further 12,000 were engaged in 'foreign coasting' and British coastal traffic, the inshore fisheries and the local traffic between the West Indies and North America. During the French wars direct trade with France, Flanders and Holland ceased, but the Continent was hungry for British goods and Napoleon's 'Continental System' largely failed because of the corruption of French officials. Traffic with the Channel Islands and Ireland increased throughout the war, the Channel Islands providing links with France and Ireland being a source of food supplies. Trade also increased with both the East and the West Indies, and before the end of the war to South American ports.

From the major Scottish ports 692 ships totalling 52,225 tons were engaged in foreign trade by 1774, and a similar number of ships but totalling only half the tonnage were engaged in the coastal trade, including the trade to Ireland, incomparably chief of Scotland's trading partners. Port Patrick was opened in 1778 as a packet port for Anglo-Irish mail and, in the years thereafter, the coal ports of Alloa and Kirkcaldy on the east coast and of Ayr and Irvine on the west coast grew rapidly.[63]

By 1805 the English canal system had linked the river Severn with the river Trent, the Trent with the Mersey, and all these with London. Larger ships had led to the decline of many ports which could not provide them with suitable facilities, but larger ships in no way diminished the importance of London, Liverpool, Glasgow, Newcastle, Hull and Bristol. Bristol merchants and shipowners owned about 300 vessels, many of them trading with the West Indies and with Ireland. They were not as specialised as the ship operators in London. During the French wars they sent sixty-three privateers to sea. Liverpool developed greatly during the wars and by the turn of the century Liverpool shipowners were operating some 800 ships totalling 140,000 tons and manned by about 10,000 seamen. Of the more than 4000 vessels entering and clearing the port each year, 2300 were for Ireland. After 1793 a large number of Liverpool vessels were commissioned as privateers and, although in the later years of the French wars trade was adversely affected by the Continental blockade and troubles with the United States, Liverpool's recovery was swift once peace came. It was at this time that, to take advantage of the new opportunities, families later to be well known in the shipping world moved to Liverpool: Swires, Brocklebanks, Ismays, Inmans, Harrisons and Holts.[64]

London remained by far the most important centre for trade. About 14,000 vessels cleared the port each year, 10,000 of them coasting and 3700 of them engaged in foreign trade, 2200 of the latter being British vessels. Congestion was appalling between May and October and, before the river police were established in 1798, pilfering from cargoes was estimated to cost £350,000 a year. The ships included over 400 West Indiamen bringing some 122,000 hogsheads of sugar a year, over 400 timber ships of which 250 discharged their cargoes in the river, some 300 colliers, each of them surrounded by a dozen barges, and 50 East Indiamen. In addition to the ships there were more than 3500 barges, lighters, hoys, punts and other craft.[65] The only wet docks were Brunswick Dock at Blackwall and Greenland Dock at Rotherhithe. The West India Dock opened in 1802, the East India Docks in 1806, while the London Docks were developed after 1800, the St Katharine's Dock being completed in 1828. The Greenland Dock was extended by the Commercial Dock Company from 1807 onwards. The first fifteen years of the 19th century was a period of enormous activity which established a dock pattern for London which lasted 150 years. Most congested of all the London areas was the Pool of London.

By 1776 nearly 40 per cent of British tonnage was built in the colonies and, if foreign-built vessels are added, less than half the vessels in the Register of that year were built in Britain.[66] With the loss of the American colonies more Canadian ships were bought and increasing quantities of timber were imported from Canada, the West Indies, Africa and India. At the same time there was a growing use of iron to enable timber to be conserved.[67]

As a shipbuilding centre London continued to decline. The north-east coast now produced 40 per cent of new British tonnage, much of it for the coal trade, by this time maintained by a fleet totalling 120,000 tons and employing 6000 men. London, the south coast and the north-west coast each produced about 15 per cent of new tonnage, with the Bristol Channel and Wales taken together and the East Anglian ports each producing about 7.5 per cent of the total. In 1790 some 50,000 tons of shipping was built, a total of 600 ships, but only 75 of these exceeded 200 tons.[68] At the turn of the century there were 14,363 British ships but the average capacity was still only 113 tons.

The largest ships were East Indiamen like the *Royal Charlotte* of 1282 tons and the *Marquis of Cornwallis,* built in 1804, of 1360 tons. Such a ship might be 130 feet long and 40 feet in the beam. A flush deck had been introduced and, to replace wood, iron knees and standards had been evolved. The traditional 'tumble-home' side, where the ship was wider at the waterline than at deck level, was tending to disappear. Not until 1810 did the East India Company begin to use metal nails and bolts in place of wooden pegs. In the building of these ships there was a temptation to sacrifice breadth in favour of depth because of a faulty system of tonnage measurement. By rules laid down in 1773 the depth of ships was not used in computing the cubic capacity of ships for tonnage measurement purposes. Depth was assumed to be half the breadth. In consequence, ships were often built with smaller breadth and greater depth to 'reduce' the tonnage and such charges as were paid on it. The result was the narrow, deep 'coffin' ship which was vulnerable in bad weather.[69] This irrational method of tonnage measurement hampered progress in hull design until the middle of the 19th century.

West Indiamen were similarly too narrow and too deep. They ranged from 200 to 500 tons and their average size in the first decade of the 19th century was 300 tons. As a protection against worms the hulls were sheathed in copper. They were poorly armed and mostly slow sailers but they were often comfortable. Men among the five to ten passengers normally carried could even take a plunge in a bath erected on the deck. As they sailed down the 'trades' in balmy weather the crew would paint the sides yellow or black and occasionally red. There was still much variety in the colours of all classes of ship. The black and white chequer design typical of the 'wooden wall' in popular imagination did not materialise until the 19th century.

Vessels trading to North America included barques of 150–250 tons, but the ships ranged up to 400 or even 500 tons. The whaler was much like the ordinary merchantman except that the clews or lower corners of the foresail were made fast to a light boom to make the ship more manoeuvrable. Southseamen differed from Greenlandmen in that they were fitted with brick tryworks which were necessary to boil oil out of the blubber. The average size of colliers at the turn of the century was 220 tons.

Even 150-ton ships were ship-rigged by 1800, and the barque and barquentine were rarer than they were to become by 1850. Two-masters were common, and most of the colliers and Baltic traders were brigs or snows. The fruiters racing from Smyrna and Greek ports with oranges and raisins were topsail schooners. The fore-and-aft schooner had made its appearance in the cod fishery. Most of the cross-Channel traffic and coastal passenger traffic was carried on in smart cutters specially developed by the English.

By 1793 most British ships had replaced the lateen sails on the mizen mast with a fore-and-aft sail called the 'driver' or 'spanker'. The whole of the sail was now abaft the mast, extended at the head by a gaff in place of the old yard, and towards the end of the century carried over the stern by a boom. On each mast sail area was increased by the addition of new sails. Studding sails were set on foremast and mainmast; a topgallant sail appeared on the mizen which was prolonged by a topgallant mast in order to carry it; and similarly the bowsprit was lengthened by the addition of a jib-boom to carry the new triangular jib. Staysails appeared on every stay, and by 1800 the full-rigged ship was complete, carrying as many as 37 sails.[70] The days of elaborate decoration, on the other hand, had gone and the figurehead had become the chief attempt at embellishment. The average vessel might last up to 40 years and cost ranged from £5 to £20 a ton at the end of the 18th century, the peacetime price being nearer £5.[71]

The first steam engine had been perfected to provide pumps against flooding in coalmines, and the first steam railway was to be built from Stockton to Darlington to carry coal to the river jetties. Of the greatest significance for the future of shipping was the appearance, before the end of the French wars, of the steamboat. William Symington's first boat steamed successfully on Dalswinton Lake in Dumfries in 1789, and his *Charlotte Dundas* drew barges on the Forth-Clyde Canal in 1802. While Britain was still at war the United States forged ahead with regular steamboat services on rivers and lakes, but in 1812 Henry Bell built the *Comet* – the 'stinkboat' as it was dubbed disdainfully by the Clyde boatmen – which steamed from Greenock to Glasgow and became an immediate success. By 1815 steamships on rivers and inland waterways were no longer a nine-day wonder and in that year the *Thames* steamed from Glasgow to London by way of Dublin and Land's End and then started a service from London to Margate,[72] a service which was still familiar to Londoners for some years after the end of World War II.

Notes

1. R. Davis, *The Rise of the English Shipping Industry in the Seventeenth and Eighteenth Centuries* (1962), London, p. 27; D. E. Robinson, 'Secret of British Power in the Age of Sail: Admiralty Reports of the Coasting Fleet' (1987), *American Neptune*, Vol. XVIII, No. 1, pp. 6 ff; S. Ville, *English Shipowning during the Industrial Revolution: 1770–1830* (1987), Manchester, p. 11.
2. E. J. Lowell, *The Hessians and other German Auxiliaries of Great Britain in the Revolutionary Wars* (1884), New York, p. 56.
3. D. Syrrett, *Shipping and the American War 1775–83* (1970), London, p. 249.
4. M. E. Condon, 'The Establishment of the Transport Board – a subdivision of the Admiralty – 4 July 1794' (1972), MM, Vol. 58, No. 1, pp. 69–84.
5. Syrrett, *op. cit.*, p. 78 and p. 103.
6. *Ib.*, p. 77.
7. G. Jackson, 'Scottish Shipping, 1775–1805', in P. L. Cottrell and D. H. Aldcroft (eds),

Shipping, Trade and Commerce: Essays in Memory of Ralph Davis (1981), Leicester, p. 125.

8. C. N. Parkinson (ed), *The Trade Winds: A Study of British Overseas Trade during the French Wars 1793–1815* (1948), London, p. 195.
9. *Ib.*, pp. 196–7.
10. *Ib.*, p. 201.
11. *Ib.*, p, 233.
12. *Ib.*, p. 232.
13. *Ib.*, p. 182.
14. D. P. Mannix and M. Cowley, *Black Cargoes* (1963), London, pp. 150–151; K. G. Davies, *The Royal African Company* (1957), London, p. 293.
15. H. S. Klein, 'The English Slave Trade to Jamaica, 1782–1808' (1978), EHR, 2nd series, Vol. XXXI, No. 1, p. 38.
16. P. E. Lovejoy, *Transformations in Slavery: A history of slavery in Africa* (1983), Cambridge, p. 48; D. Eltis, 'The British Contribution to the 19th Century Trans-atlantic Slave trade' (1979), EHR, 2nd series, Vol. XXXII, No. 2, pp. 211 ff.
17. Parkinson, *op. cit.*, p. 267.
18. *Cf.* Parkinson, *op. cit.*, p. 271.
19. *Ib.*, p. 262.
20. P. N. Davies, *Henry Tyrer: A Liverpool Shipping Agent and his Enterprise 1879–1979* (1979), London, p. 36.
21. D. Eltis, *op. cit.*; Lovejoy, *op. cit.*, pp. 140–6.
22. G. Jackson, *The British Whaling Trade* (1978), London, p. 76.
23. *Ib.*, p. 82.
24. H. Compton (ed), *A Master Mariner, being the Life and Adventures of Captain Robert William Eastwick* (c. 1891), London, p. 25.
25. H. T. Fry, *Alexander Dalrymple and the Expansion of British Trade* (1970), London, p. 148.
26. Parkinson, *op. cit.*, p. 142.
27. J. Sutton, *Lords of the East: the East India Company and Its Ships* (1981), Greenwich, p. 14; Moh-Cheung and L. H. Mui, 'The Commutation Act and the Tea Trade in Britain 1784–1793' (1963), EHR, 2nd Series, Vol. XVI, No. 2, pp. 234 ff.
28. Parkinson, *op. cit.*, p. 144.
29. G. V. Scammell, *The English Chartered Trading Companies and the Sea* (1983), National Maritime Museum, p. 37.
30. R. Hughes, *The Fatal Shore* (1987), London, p. 41.
31. *Ib.*, pp. 145–51.
32. Compton, *op. cit.*, p. 188.
33. *Ib.*, p. 196.
34. C. Bateson, *The Convict Ships 1787–1868* (1959), Glasgow, p. 3.
35. Parkinson, *op. cit*, p. 286; Hughes, *op. cit.*, p. 143.
36. A. W. R. M. Greenham, 'Packet Boats' (1958), Harwich, privately distributed.
37. J. W. Beck, 'Tercentenary of the Falmouth Post Office Packet Service' (1988), *Newsletter of the Maritime Economic History Group*, Vol. II, No. 2, pp. 8–10.
38. Parkinson, *op. cit.*, p. 286.
39. *Ib.*, p. 285.
40. D. J. Starkey, 'British Privateering against the Dutch in the American Revolutionary War, 1780–1783' in S. Fisher (ed), *Studies in British Privateering, Trading Enterprise and*

Seamen's Welfare, 1775–1900 (1987), Exeter, p. 5; D.J. Starkey, 'The economic and military significance of British privateering, 1702–1783' (1988), *The Journal of Transport History,* 3rd Series, Vol. 9, No. 1, p. 54.
41. A. D. Blue, 'Asian Seafarers' (privately circulated).
42. M. Lewis, *A Social History of the Navy 1792–1815* (1960), London, p. 121.
43. H. Moyse-Bartlett, *A History of the Merchant Navy* (1937), London, p. 198.
44. E. C. Millington, *Seamen in the Making* (1935), London, pp. 31–8.
45. Compton, *op. cit.*, pp. 43–4.
46. C. E. Fayle, *A Short History of the World's Shipping History* (1933), London, p. 214.
47. Parkinson, *op. cit.*, p. 111.
48. *Ib.*, p. 88.
49. Compton, *op. cit.*, p. 60.
50. G. S. Graham, *The Politics of Naval Supremacy* (1965), Cambridge, p. 99.
51. A. D. Blue, 'The Iron-headed Old Rat' (Chinese nickname for William Jardine), *Nautical Magazine* (August 1988).
52. Lewis, *op. cit.*, p. 441.
53. Mannix and Cowley, *op. cit.*, p. 151.
54. R. Floud, 'A Tall Story? The Standard of Living Debate' (1983), *History Today,* Vol. 33, p. 39.
55. S. Ville, *English Shipowning during the Industrial Revolution: 1770–1830* (1987), Manchester, p. 109.
56. Lewis, *op. cit.*, p. 139.
57. J. R. Hutchison, *The Press-Gang Afloat and Ashore* (1913), London, p. 327.
58. Syrett, *op. cit.*, p. 166.
59. Hutchison, *op. cit.*, p. 326.
60. Lewis, *op. cit.*, p. 438.
61. Ville, *op. cit.*, pp. 2–5.
62. Parkinson, *op. cit.*, p. 41.
63. G. Jackson (1981), *op. cit.*, p. 118 and p. 124.
64. S. Marinner and F. E. Hyde, *The Senior: John Samuel Swire 1825–98* (1967), Liverpool, p. 10.
65. Parkinson, *op. cit.*, pp. 50–51.
66. J. A. Goldenberg, 'An Analysis of Shipbuilding Sites in Lloyd's Register of 1776' (1973), MM, Vol. 59, No. 4, p. 422.
67. R. MacGregor, *Merchant Sailing Ships 1775–1815. Their Design and Construction* (1980), Watford, Herts, p. 5.
68. R. Davis, *op. cit.*, p. 70.
69. A. G. Course, *The Merchant Navy: A Social History* (1963), London, p. 201.
70. Moyse-Bartlett, *op. cit.*, pp. 202–4.
71. Ville, *op. cit.*, p. 47.
72. A. Deeson, *An Illustrated History of Steamships* (1976), London, pp. 47–8.

15

The Birth of Steam
(1815–1850)

For twenty years after the Napoleonic Wars the shipping industry suffered from depression and tonnage on the British register did not increase beyond the 2.6 million tons in existence at the time of the Treaty of Paris. As had happened before, and as was to happen a century later, the end of the war brought slump, a sharp fall in freight rates and a reduction in seamen's wages. Seamen on the Tyne and on the Wear went on strike, demanding a rise in wages and reversion to pre-war manning scales. Foreign seamen taken into employment during the war had been kept on, leaving native 'Geordie' seamen unemployed. The strike collapsed when its leaders were imprisoned for six months. In the country at large many thousands of seamen were unemployed and there was much distress among them.[1]

Such distress, and the miserable condition of many seamen even when in work, occasioned some social concern and, in particular, inspired the activities of the Baptist minister George Charles Smith, better known at the time as 'Boatswain' Smith, and of the Anglican minister Richard Marks. Marks had been a naval lieutenant who fought at Trafalgar. Smith had been apprenticed to the master of an American schooner but had been pressed into the Royal Navy.

Although the crimp flourished most in prosperous times,[2] he was an integral part of the system of recruiting seamen for long voyages. Commonly a lodging-house keeper, the crimp specialised in providing these crews and discounted for cash the 'advance notes' or pay promised to them after they had worked for an agreed period at sea. The crimp and his accomplices then often helped the seaman to spend this pay, giving poor value for money, and produced him on board at sailing time. It was not uncommon to see such men taken to their ship in cartloads, too drunk to walk on board.[3]

Both Smith and Marks understood the sailor and both were deeply concerned that 'poor Jack' should prove so frequently the victim of the crimp and the brothel-keeper. From their work on the sailor's behalf arose much of that evangelical activity which, later in the 19th century, led to the foundation of such societies as the British Sailors' Society and The Missions to Seamen.[4] In 1818 Smith arranged for one of Nelson's ships, the sloop *Speedy*, to be moored at Wapping Stairs to serve as a floating church for sailors and soon – in Liverpool, Glasgow, Hull, Bristol and other ports – many similar institutions were established.

The aims extended beyond the saving of sailors' souls. What is now the Sailors' Children's Society began as a floating chapel in Hull in 1821 but it soon turned its attention to sailors' orphans. In the same year the Seamen's Hospital Society put an old hulk on the Thames to other uses than the conduct of church services. Nor was it long before specialised seafaring institutions came into existence ashore. The National Institution for the Preservation of Life from Shipwreck (now the Royal National Lifeboat Institution) was set up in 1824, and the Merchant Seamen's Orphan Asylum (now the Royal Merchant Navy School) and the Destitute Sailors' Asylum (subsequently the Sailors' Home and Red Ensign Club in London's Dock Street) both date from 1827. In the course of time the latter was to house the first Mercantile Marine Office, help in the drafting of a major Merchant Shipping Act, found a seamen's bank, establish a pioneer navigation school with a branch at Gravesend which developed into the shipping industry's sea school for ratings, become the London examination centre for navigating officers, set up the first School of Nautical Cookery, and include Joseph Conrad among the thousands of seafarers who lodged on its premises. In 1974, when the closure of the London and St Katharine Docks indicated that its useful days were over, the Club became part of The Marine Society. The part which seamen's charities have played in improving the sailor's lot needs to be acknowledged. Voluntary action normally precedes government action and usually points the way.

For the moment the government was not concerned. Indeed, in the spirit of *laissez-faire,* it was trying not to be involved.

In 1824 the government bounty on whaling was discontinued and within forty years Hull, where more whalers had been owned than in any other port, had none. As the whales became scarcer, the whaling grounds in the north moved westwards towards the Davis Strait and new grounds were opened up in the southern hemisphere, the 160-ton whaler *Weddell* of Leith discovering and giving its name to the Weddell Sea. It was the Americans, however, who reaped most of the southern harvest. Steam whalers began to operate from Dundee in 1858 and the slaughter of whales was greatly boosted after 1865 by the development of an efficient harpoon gun, but whaling was never a substantial British industry. By the middle of the 19th century gas had largely displaced whale oil as an illuminant, though whale oil continued to be used in other ways until the 1950s, and Christian Salvesen of Leith were still whaling after World War II.[5]

The initiative in shipping in these post-Napoleonic War years rested with the Americans, who had continued to prosper in their Atlantic coast states and who had been stimulated in their development both by whaling and by the wars. It has been remarked that a thorough investigation of all letters patent relating to improvements in ships between the years 1618 and 1810 has disclosed no improvement worthy of record.[6] If the implications of this statement are too sweeping, it is nevertheless true that in their efforts to beat the British blockade of the Continent during the Napoleonic Wars – whether inspired, as some have supposed, by the French lugger or, as others aver, by the Bermudian sloop[7] – the Americans made great improvements in ship design which did not yet extend to Britain. In the Atlantic trade the average British merchantman was still only 250 tons. Between 1815 and 1840 the Americans built for this trade a fleet of packet ships whose size increased steadily from 500 to 1200 tons. These ships were cheap to build, since they were built from abundant supplies of American softwoods, and their lines were fined down until the proportion of length to beam was 5.5:1, as compared with 4:1 in the British East Indiaman. This meant that they could carry a greater spread of sail and outsail any rival.

Most famous of these American vessels were the ships of the Black Ball Line, which in 1816 began a fortnightly service between New York and England, thus becoming the first line to start regular scheduled sailings. Full or empty, in fair weather or foul, a Black Ball Line packet left its New York pier for Liverpool on the first of every month.[8] This was the beginning of a new era in shipping, for by such regular scheduling the Americans had invented the liner, a ship which gives reliable and regular service. No earlier vessels could claim anything like six transatlantic crossings a year, but by 1825 the Black Ball Line had achieved average crossings of 23 days eastwards and 40 days westwards over a period of nine years, perhaps two-thirds of the time taken by British ships. The Black Ball Line was rapidly followed by others – Red Star, Swallow Tail and Black X – but they were all American and the transatlantic mail and passenger services fell very largely into American hands.

This decline in British competitive efficiency extended to other areas. Speedy little Yankee brigs and schooners became favourites in the Mediterranean fruit trade[9] and in the Far Eastern opium trade, and American vessels proved able to carry cargo from the Far East to Boston and from Boston back to Europe more cheaply than the East India Company carried it on the direct route.

Although it proved no more than a flash in the pan, the Americans were also the first to despatch a sailing vessel with auxiliary steam power across the Atlantic. However, in a passage which lasted 29 days, the vessel was under steam for only 85 hours. This ship, *Savannah*, was built of wood in New York and fitted with collapsible paddle wheels. Despite the few hours she spent under steam when she made the crossing in 1819, she had to pick up coal in Kinsale in Ireland before sailing on. After Tsar Alexander I, to whom she was offered, had declined to buy her, the ship returned to the United States where her engines were taken out. The Americans produced no further ocean-going steamships until well after the British had established themselves as leaders in this field.

By 1819 the use of steam in Britain had extended well beyond the river estuaries. The voyage of the paddle-steamer *Thames* from Glasgow to London in 1815 has been recorded already. In 1816, the *Elise*, formerly *Margery*, sailed in heavy seas from Newhaven to become the first steam packet to cross the English Channel.[10] The *Rob Roy*, built in 1818, maintained a regular steamship service between Greenock and Belfast until, in 1821, she transferred to the Dover–Calais run. In 1819 Messrs Langtry of Belfast, owners of a fleet of smacks which traded regularly to Liverpool, added a schooner-rigged paddle-steamer, *Waterloo*, to their fleet at a cost of £10,000, a vessel which was scheduled to perform two round voyages between Belfast and Liverpool each week.[11]

With good timber at a premium, more iron was being used in shipbuilding. In 1818 the Scottish-built *Vulcan* was constructed entirely of iron; and three years later the *Aaron Manby*, built by an ironmaster of that name, became the first iron steamboat. When she voyaged across the Channel to Paris many of those who saw her thought that she must be a fake because it was well-known that iron did not float.[12]

In 1818 an Englishman, John Allen, inaugurated a regular steamship service between Trieste and Venice,[13] and in 1821–2 a British steam warship, *Rising Star*, crossed the Atlantic from east to west, mostly under sail, and voyaged on to Valparaiso, thus becoming the first steamer to enter the Pacific ocean. In 1825 a British-built steamboat, *Enterprise*, made a voyage to India under steam and sail, steaming for 64 days out of a total passage time of 113 days. Like other ocean-going steamships at this time, she had to steam on sea water and, like all the engines of this period, her engines were grossly inefficient.[14] The normal safe boiler pressure was no more than 5 pounds per square inch and the consumption of coal was 10 pounds per horse-power per hour.

Its inefficiency notwithstanding, the steam engine had undeniably created new short-range services which were popular with passengers while, incorporated in a tug, it began rapidly to assist the sailing vessel in and out of harbour. The disadvantages of steam were least apparent in the coastal and short-sea trades where coal was readily to hand. Some packet lines turned to steam, and many new companies, all of them fiercely competitive, were established. By 1825 forty-five steamship companies had been registered in London alone,[15] and two rival steamships plying between Belfast and Glasgow were carrying first-class passengers for 2s a head and deck passengers for nothing.

Pleasure steamers plying on the Thames and extending their trips to coastal resorts beyond the river mouth inspired the formation, in 1824, of one of the most vigorous and long-lived of companies in the short sea trades, the General Steam Navigation Company, since absorbed by P & O. Between 1824 and 1828 the General Steam Navigation Company purchased 12 wooden steam packets. Another long-lived and vigorous company founded in the same year was the City of Dublin Steam Packet Company, which fought its two competing companies in the Liverpool–Dublin trade by reducing its fares to 6d a head. It also fought the Postmaster-General who, in 1826, established a government steam-packet service in direct opposition to it, emerging triumphant in 1850 as the sole authorised instrument for the carriage of Her Majesty's mails across the Irish Sea.[16]

The great advantage of the steamship was its independence of wind and its consequently reliable schedule. For passengers and the carriage of mail this advantage proved overwhelming. Its disadvantages were the high cost of construction, the volume of freight-earning space which had to be sacrificed to the stowage of coal, and its total dependence on any but the shortest routes on conveniently-spaced coaling depôts. It was uneconomic in the normal cargo-carrying trades, and for the carriage of bulk cargoes on long routes the steamer did not become economic for another fifty years.

Because it was the only industrial nation, Britain alone made a sustained effort to develop the ocean-going steamship. Coal production, which in 1790 had been 7.6 million tons, had grown by 1816 to about 16 million tons, and by 1854 was 54.7 million tons. Iron production, which had been 125,000 tons in 1796, grew to 2.5 million tons in 1854, and as production rose, the price fell.[17] Gradually, the British coasting companies operating steamships extended their services and, since the time taken to beat down the Channel was always one of the most unpredictable items in a voyage under sail, it is not surprising that within two years of its formation the General Steam Navigation Company, which was well managed and had a strong capital base,[18] put steamers into the trade between London and Portugal. Two years later still the Dublin Steam Packet Company announced a steamship service between Dublin and Bordeaux. Some enlightened support to the idea of communication by steamer was given by government, both in Britain and in India, where coastal steamers were also rapidly established; and gradual improvements were made not only in engines but in the lines of the ships themselves, the bows being fined down, the stern made less stumpy and the mid-section less square.[19]

Although the paddle-steamer *Cape Breton* crossed the Atlantic from east to west and arrived in Nova Scotia a fortnight before *Royal William* sailed in 1833, it is not known whether she used her engines on the crossing.[20] It is *Royal William*, therefore, which is credited with the second crossing of the Atlantic under steam by a merchant vessel. Inspired by Samuel Cunard, a shipowner of Halifax, Nova Scotia, *Royal William* crossed from west to east entirely under steam except when her boilers were shut down for the descaling of salt, an operation which took place roughly every fourth day. The crossing, from Quebec to the Isle of Wight, was made in seventeen days, six days less than the average time taken by the Black Ball sailing ships.

It was in this same year of 1833 that the East India Company's monopoly finally came to an end. The charter had been renewed for the last time in 1813 but even at that time the Company's powers had been heavily restricted. While it had retained an exclusive right to trade between England and China, a door had been opened for other operators. British, Americans and Indians were all engaged in ferrying opium from India to China against the wishes of the Chinese government and, to elude both Chinese warships and Far East pirates, they operated smart little clippers, mostly built on the Hooghly river and often commanded by officers who had been in the East India Company's service. William Jardine, by this time a major operator of opium clippers, had led the fight against the East India Company's monopoly of the China trade and in 1832 had established his partnership with Matheson. In 1834 Jardine, Matheson sent home to London the first China cargo to be free of the East India Company's monopoly.

All Chinese trade was supposed to be conducted through Whampoa at Canton but, as the Chinese tried to exercise more control over the opium trade, opium entered illicitly through Lintin island, further down-river, where a number of hulks were moored to store the drug. After the Opium War of 1840 the Chinese were forced to make further concessions. Hong Kong became a free port and in 1843 Shanghai was opened to foreign trade. Over the next seventeen years the Yang-tze-Kiang river was opened up as far as Hankow. A treaty made with Japan in 1858 extended eastern trade to the whole area.

The Act of 1833, in removing what remained of the East India Company's monopoly, gave shareholders a guaranteed annuity of £63,000 a year (£2·2 million at 1988 prices) for a minimum of forty years; but in 1858, well before this time was up, the remaining powers and duties of the Company were transferred to a new Secretary of State and in 1873 the shareholders were paid off, the Company being dissolved in the following year. In its latter years Thomas Love Peacock, novelist and head of the Company Examiners' Department, is said to have written of his working day:

> From ten to eleven, ate a breakfast for seven;
> From eleven to noon, to begin 't was too soon;
> From twelve to one asked, 'What's to be done?'
> From one to two found nothing to do;
> From two to three began to foresee
> That from three to four would be a damned bore.[21]

The East India Company had flourished for nearly 250 years and had added the vast Indian sub-continent to the British Crown. In 1825 26 of its regular ships (20 of them in the 1200-ton class) and 11 'extra' ships sailed east on behalf of the Company, but in the same year 170 other ships, averaging 530 tons, cleared for the East. By the time the Act of 1833 was passed many good quality ships built specifically for passengers and seldom less than 500 tons had entered this trade. Dubbed 'Blackwall frigates' by 20th-century writers, they were owned by such firms as Richard & Henry Green, Money Wigram & Sons, Thomas & William Smith and Duncan Dunbar, all household names in their day.[22]

With the dispersal of the East India Company's sailing fleet came the gradual rise of a government-subsidised steamship fleet, which began to make progress after *Royal William* had crossed the Atlantic under steam in 1833. It was the granting to steamships at this time of government subsidies for the carriage of mail which clinched Britain's position as the world's greatest maritime power. P & O, Cunard, Royal Mail, Pacific Steam and other companies which themselves became household names, all owed their establishment and survival to mail subsidies, though these subsidies imposed no overall cost upon the government, for what the government paid to the new shipping companies it saved on the packet service. It was not exactly *laissez-faire*, but the proponents of *laissez-faire* might suggest that it at least bore some semblance to 'privatisation'.

The leading figure in the campaign which persuaded the British government to abandon its packet service and put the carriage of mails out to tender was James MacQueen. For ten years this policy remained unique to Britain and it gave British ocean steam shipping a start that it did not lose for 100 years, a new impetus at a time when there was not much else to be said for British merchant shipping or for those who served it.

James MacQueen was born in 1778 and was manager of a sugar estate in Grenada by the time he was 19. In 1821, the year in which the Post Office established its first steam packets at Holyhead[23], he settled in Glasgow, an acknowledged authority on imperial subjects. In 1837 he laid before Her Majesty's Government – Queen Victoria had just come to the throne – his first plan for a steam packet service between England and the Caribbean. He was highly critical of the service then in operation, which he castigated as a disgrace to the country, and he followed this first polemic with a much more ambitious 'General Plan for a Mail Communication between Great Britain and the Eastern and Western Parts of the World; also to Canton and Sydney westward to the Pacific'. 'Steamboats carrying mails', he averred, 'should be the mail coaches of the ocean.' He even envisaged a Panama Canal.[24]

By this time the Post Office packet service had been taken over by the Admiralty, and the government had already yielded to pressure to the extent of awarding, in 1834, a first mail contract to the General Steam Navigation Company for a service to Rotterdam and Hamburg. This was followed by promises of subsidy to the East India Company for a mail service by steam between Bombay and Suez, and to what was to become P & O to take a first step from Britain towards Alexandria.[25]

The Peninsular Campaign of the Napoleonic Wars had increased British traffic to Spain and Portugal and a captain's clerk named Arthur Anderson, who had seen service during the war, arrived in London in 1815 looking for a job. An uncle secured one for him with a shipbroker named Brodie Willcox and the two, who became partners, specialised in the peninsular trade. By 1835, Anderson, who spoke and wrote Spanish, was known in government circles and, when the Spanish minister in London urged that there should be a steamship connection between his country and Britain, the organisation of this service was put into the hands of Willcox and Anderson. Anderson believed in steam and by 1837 the firm was able to advertise a fortnightly service from London via Falmouth to Oporto, Lisbon, Gibraltar and Malaga with 'new, powerful, large and splendidly fitted up steamships'. Although by this time some steamers were operating in the Mediterranean, the Falmouth packets to Lisbon were still sailing vessels. They took up to three weeks to get there while Anderson's steamers could make the voyage in less than one-quarter of the time.[26]

Anderson argued that he could provide a cheaper service than the Falmouth packets and, with a government already open to suggestion in consequence of MacQueen's pamphleteering, he won the day.

Anderson's contract, made in August 1837, to carry Her Majesty's mails on a regular weekly basis to and from the peninsular ports between Vigo and Gibraltar for an annual payment of £29,600 saved his firm from bankruptcy, for at this time it was operating at a loss. The service for which he had contracted proved to be an unqualified success and, after a period of lobbying by Lord Bentinck, Governor-General of India, the government sought tenders for a regular service to convey the Indian mail as far as Alexandria. Messrs Willcox and Anderson's tender of £34,200 was accepted.

With this extension of its service the company, incorporated by Royal Charter and with a capital of £1,000,000, became, in 1840, seven years after the East India Company had lost its monopoly, the Peninsular and Oriental Steam Navigation Company or P & O. It was agreed that within two years a complementary service would be started between Calcutta and Suez,[27] but P & O did not wrest the mail service on this passage from the East India Company until 1854.

It was at this same time, between 1837 and 1840, that the British counter-attack was launched on American domination of the Atlantic. As early as 1819 Parliament had voted in favour of emigration as a way of relieving national distress, and by 1840 it was widely agreed that 'shovelling out the paupers', as William Cobbett put it, from both Scotland and Ireland had everything to commend it. The greatest passenger trade the world had ever known was under way, soon to be extended to Australia as well as to America.

Once again, it was mail contracts awarded by the British government which launched the steamship companies across the Atlantic and beyond, Cunard and Royal Mail Line in 1839 and the Pacific Steam Navigation Company of Liverpool in the following year.[28] Indeed, 1840 – the year in which Rowland Hill's Penny Post was introduced – saw the fulfilment of much of MacQueen's grand plan, for contracts had been entered into for the carriage of mails by private enterprise to the West Indies, to North America, to the Pacific coast of South America and to the eastern part of Her Majesty's Empire.

It is noteworthy that the American packet-owners, who lost out in consequence of these developments, never sought any subsidy. Nor, despite the fact that they were developing the steamship on lakes and rivers and seized readily upon the new invention of the propeller in the 1840s, did the Americans start rival steamship companies on the crossing from Europe. The leaders of the rapidly progressing science of marine engineering were to be found, not in America, but in Scotland and England.

The subsidies given by the British government were not negligible. As a percentage of operating cost they amounted to 20 per cent, and in the case of P & O to about 40 per cent, in the years from 1840 to 1895, dropping thereafter to about 11 per cent in the period up to the First World War. Considerable prestige was also attached to being a 'Royal Mail steamer' and mail ships had priority in port. It was inherent in the subsidy scheme that large and powerful companies would be the beneficiaries, and by 1853 it was possible for a parliamentary inquiry to comment that 'the ocean has been traversed with a precision and regularity hitherto deemed impossible, commerce and civilisation have been extended, the colonies have been brought more closely into connection with the Home Government, and steamships have been constructed of a size and power that, without Government aid, could hardly, at least for many years, have been produced'.[29]

All this lay in the future. In the meantime it was an engineer of genius, Isambard Kingdom Brunel, chief engineer to the Great Western Railway, who inspired the building in 1837 of the *Great Western*, a paddle-steamer of 1320 tons. His purpose was to carry the link between London and Bristol on across the Atlantic. A London company with a similar aim had been formed and, when its engine-builders went bankrupt, this company chartered an Irish Channel steamer of 703 tons, the *Sirius*, to cross the Atlantic. Not to be outdone, a Liverpool company decided, at short notice, to charter another *Royal William* – not the vessel which had crossed from west to east in 1833 but a small cross-Channel steam packet – and despatch her to New York as well.

Sirius left London on 28th March 1838 and sailed from Cork, with 94 passengers, on 4th April. *Great Western* sailed from Bristol four days later.[30] *Sirius* arrived in New York, with only 15 tons of coal left, on 23rd April and *Great Western*, with 200 tons of coal left, arrived a few hours afterwards. *Royal William,* which did not sail until July, was so overloaded with coal that her sponsons were submerged and her passengers enjoyed the doubtful convenience of being able, by leaning over the bulwarks, to wash their hands in the water.[31] That the steamship could operate on the north Atlantic route had been proven.

Later that year Samuel Cunard crossed to England in the *Liverpool*, a new ship despatched in the wake of *Royal William*. With George Burns and David McIver, Cunard had formed the British and North American Mail Packet Company, a company which developed into the Cunard

Line, and, to the fury of the owners of the *Great Western*, he secured the mail contract for the north Atlantic route. In 1840 his *Britannia* sailed from Liverpool for Halifax and Boston, the first of four ships each of about 1100 tons built specially for the new venture. Only five years earlier a regular transatlantic steamer service had been pronounced as impossible as a voyage to the moon.[32]

By the 1830s it was becoming more usual for owners to express profits as a return on capital. Before this time profits were either 'good' or 'bad' – between £500 and £1000, for example, was a 'good' profit for a venture to the West Indies, while £50 to £100 was a 'good' profit on a coal voyage to London. In the 1830s the view is expressed that 10 or 15 per cent is a fair remuneration as a rate of return on the original fixed capital cost of a vessel.[33] Economics was still a young science and the economics of the early steamship voyages was fraught with problems.

Although one steamship could make the voyages of two sailing ships, ton for ton they cost three times as much to build – £45 a ton for the first Cunarders against £15 a ton for the American sailing packets. Moreover, coal cost money and took freight space. *Britannia* had to allot 640 tons out of 865 tons of weightlifting capacity to coal, leaving only 225 tons for cargo. Very nearly half the total space was occupied by the engine department. The table on p. 274[34] indicates the deficit on operating the first Cunard steamers when compared with a sailing vessel. The mail subsidy of £2300 almost balanced the steamer deficit of £2550.

At this stage of its development the steamer could not compete with the sailing vessel as a cargo-carrier, but economies in labour and coal costs were to be realised as efficiency increased. Once the sails, which were essential to the early deepsea steamer, could be dispensed with, some seafarers would become redundant; and once engines were improved, coal would be saved and cargo space increased. In 1848 a 1400-ton liner burned 60 tons of coal a day to maintain about 10 knots; by 1948 a tramp steamer three times the size could maintain the same speed on 26 tons of coal a day.[35] But even in the 1840s the government was said to be saving money in paying out £400,000 a year in mail subsidies, and passengers were saving time. The best American packets had averaged 40 days westward and 23 days eastward; the *Great Western* reached New York in 15 days and returned in 14.

Although Lloyd's had at first refused to classify iron ships for insurance purposes, iron steamboats for short haulage were fairly common by the 1830s.[36] This new use of iron for shipbuilding cut right across traditional techniques, but Britain had been deforested, the price of imported timber had risen and the price of iron plate was falling. In 1843, Brunel's second

Fig. 4. THE ECONOMICS OF STEAM IN 1840

COSTS	CREDIT £S	DEFICIT £S
225 tons of cargo at £2 extra, earned twice	900	
70 first-class passengers at £13 extra, earned twice, say	1800	
300 emigrants at £1.50 extra, one way	450	
Coal consumed, 900 tons at average 15s. say		700
Loss of freight on 750 tons weight of coal and machinery at £3 each way		4500
Depreciation on higher capital cost over sailing ship		275
Wages, engine-room and stokehold		100
Repairs, engine-room and stokehold		125
	3150	5700
Deficit, compared with sailing ship		2550

great ship, *Great Britain*, was not only built of iron but incorporated the new screw propeller. On her maiden voyage from Liverpool to New York in 1846 she carried 60 passengers and 600 tons of cargo, crossing in just under, and returning in just over, 15 days, but she went aground in Ireland the following year and this disaster ruined the company so that both she and the *Great Western* were sold. The latter continued to operate from Bristol to New York and then from Southampton to the West Indies until 1857, when the ship was broken up at Vauxhall.[37] The former was used on the Liverpool–Melbourne route until 1882, then as a sailing vessel until 1886. After this *Great Britain* was used as a coal-hulk until 1937, in which year she was beached near Port Stanley in the Falklands. Restored, the ship is now a museum piece in Bristol.

The first engineers at sea, seamen of a new breed, enjoyed a relatively privileged position, the first engineer being paid more than the mate and the fireman being paid more than the able-seaman.[38] As early as 1847 the first engineer of the P & O steamer *Hindostan* was found guilty of using 'exceedingly disrespectful language' to the second officer, and immediately afterwards he insulted the chief officer grossly by saying to his men while at a distance from the chief officer of only three or four feet, 'God damn the officers, I am the head man here!' As reported in the ship's log, the chief officer had requested him, civilly, to leave a clear space for hooking on the fore topsail sheets while the chief engineer was organising the stowage of his empty coal bags.[39] It is the first intimation that oil and water did not mix. A year or two later P & O officers are reported to prefer 'lascar' or Indian crews, who kept vessels 'in magnificent order', to European crews, who were forever 'growling and quarrelling' among themselves,[40] a preference which was to endure.

By 1847 P & O had been operating a steamer service to India for four years, a service carried on by ships of about 2000 tons. *Great Liverpool* and *Oriental* carried mail and passengers from London to Alexandria. From Alexandria they travelled overland to Suez, where *Hindostan* and *Bentinck* carried them on to Calcutta.[41] Round the Cape of Good Hope the East India Company was still operating a number of sailing ships, as were many shipping partnerships. Until the early 1860s P & O was the only regular steamship company operating to the East.

P & O officers inherited the style of the officers in the service of the East India Company – their captains were called 'Commander' – though there are indications that in its years of decline the latter's officers were not all thorough gentlemen. One or two, perhaps, 'came up through the hawsepipe', that is, rose from the ranks. In 1823, before the East India Company's monopoly of the China trade was abolished, a rating named Edward Coverly kept a journal of a voyage made to China aboard the East Indiaman *Buckinghamshire*. Coverly was the poulterer on board and, although he seems to have worked as crew in exceptional conditions, he was somewhat incensed when hailed early in the voyage by one he describes as a 'hog stye' officer. 'Hallo, sir, who are you?' sang out the officer. 'Me sir, I am the poulterer', replied Coverly. 'Oh, very well, Mr. Jimmie Ducks', replied the officer, 'if you are the poulterer, sign your hand to this cable.' The poulterer lent a hand and contented himself with the reflection that he need put up with such behaviour only for the duration of the voyage, after which it would be 'farewell to such puppies'.[42]

The poulterer had a full-time job for, on a previous voyage, the captain's and third mate's stock alone had consisted of 840 poultry, 20 pigs, 24 sheep and a cow, and such quantities of livestock were still common in steamships forty years later. Aboard the P & O steamship *Pottinger*, which was operating from Suez to Bombay in 1858, there was reported to be 'a regular farmyard on board', including about 40 sheep in addition to cows, a gazelle, a goat and a kid.[43]

Given the general conditions of the time, life aboard these prestigious ships, whether under steam or sail, was not always bad. But such ships were in a tiny minority. If it is difficult to imagine the 'farmyard' that such ships carried before the days of refrigeration, or the conditions under which some emigrants voyaged, it is even more difficult to imagine just how many ships there were before the steamship became established. On the occasion of a favourable change of wind in the Downs, Edward Coverly wrote: 'Immediately we weighed anchor, the band playing "Rule Britannia". The scene was now grand beyond description, about 100 sail of all description were under sail in less than 15 minutes, the sun shining with splendour upon their white canvas had a most imposing effect.'

By 1836 there were 25,864 British vessels totalling 2.8 million tons, these figures being much what they had been in 1816. One-fifth of this total belonged to the colonies. Seafarers on the General Register of merchant seamen, established in 1835, numbered 170,637. Only 100 of the 25,864 vessels were over 1000 tons and 8000 of them were under 50 tons.[44] By 1851 the number of vessels had increased to 34,244, the tonnage to 4.3 million tons, and the number of seafarers to 240,928.[45]

The significance of shipping to local communities and the nature of shipping may both be illustrated by reference to two areas. In Llanelli and Carmarthen 89 vessels totalling 6106 tons were owned. They comprised 24 sloops, 21 smacks, 26 schooners, 3 brigantines, 11 brigs, 1 barque (of 454 tons) and 3 paddle-steamers. Most of these vessels were engaged in mundane coastal activity.[46]

At Dumfries 75 vessels were registered and they totalled 4781 tons. Ten vessels were engaged in foreign trade and these included the ship *Elizabeth* (374 tons), the snow *Adeona* (256 tons) and the brig *William and George* (83 tons). Two further vessels normally coasted but sailed occasionally to foreign parts. The remaining 63, all small, were engaged in the coastal trade and in the trade to Ireland. In the neighbouring ports of Kirkcudbright, Wigtown and Stranraer a further 135 vessels were registered. The small vessels engaged in regional trade imported coal and lime and exported farm produce and copper ore, the latter to Swansea. The foreign traders went to the Baltic or carried emigrants to Canada, bringing timber back. Some of the Scottish emigrants were building ships in the St Lawrence estuary and Canada by this time provided one-sixth of the tonnage owned in the United Kingdom. One or two Dumfries firms probably had offices in Canada. By about 1830 steamboat services were established between the Solway ports and Glasgow, Whitehaven and Liverpool.[47]

As many as 2000 vessels, totalling 300,000 tons, were engaged in the British North American timber trade alone.[48] Nearly 1000 more vessels were carrying coal to London, and other colliers traded round the British coastline, across to the Continent, and still further afield. Altogether the coal trade employed a greater volume of British shipping than any other trade, and the average collier size had increased from 200 tons in the middle of the 18th century to 300 tons in the middle of the 19th. Turn-round was speedier and the number of voyages made from Newcastle to London each year had increased to eight or nine.[49] Overseas coal was shipped increasingly as ballast and for this reason shipowners could offer lower outgoing freights and bring back bulk commodities more cheaply than the Dutch, Britain's nearest rival as an oceanic carrier. By 1850 coal exports were worth £46 million and it was quite normal for ships carrying coal outward to bring home hides from Argentina, nitrates from Chile and guano from the Pacific islands. All this was the work at this time of sailing vessels, though the demand for coal by steam vessels added to the work-load.

In addition to the fully-rigged three-masted ships and the two-masted brigs and snows, the latter now carrying as much canvas as the former if they were of similar tonnage, the schooner was to be seen more frequently in Britain from the 1830s onwards. The fine lines of these fast British sailing vessels are thought to have derived from the 18th-century cutter rather than from American models,[50] but the schooner's fore-and-aft rig was adopted first in America. Schooners were cheaper to build and rig than brigs and required fewer crew. By the middle of the 19th century 240 schooners were employed in the Mediterranean fruit trade, and other schooners sailed to the Azores, across the Atlantic to the West Indies and to Newfoundland, and even round Cape Horn to Chile for copper ore. The schooner was not a standardised vessel and might have two or three masts. It did much of the work round the coasts and remained in business until after the First World War. The early steamers were often schooner-rigged, the *Great Britain* being the world's first six-master.[51]

The average monthly wages of able-seamen on sailing vessels in the middle of the 19th century were 50s, with perhaps 65s being paid in the mail packets and as much as 84s to a fireman. A master in one of the better ocean-going vessels earned from £280 to £400 a year, and the mate from £6 to £15 a month.[52]

The nature of the deepsea crew is indicated by Coverly, though it must be remembered that he himself, even if unusual, was of their number. His ship, outward bound, had been moored to the East India Company buoy at North Fleet, and the boatswain had piped hands to dinner. 'In the ship's galley', wrote Coverly, 'were more than a dozen men, swearing and fighting for the frying pans to cook their beefsteaks, while others, who had their wives and companions on board, were devouring their steaks which their wives had cooked while the ship was going down [river]. At one end of the deck might be seen clusters of lumpers [dockers], drinking down the table beer by gallons, and devouring the beef as though they had not had a dinner for a month. The scene was grotesque in the extreme and might well have employed the pencil of an Hogarth.'

The leisurely style of life still to be found in the service of the East India Company is indicated by the fact that it was a full month later, after the ship had loaded 'iron, quicksilver and bales of blue cloth' for the east, that the *Buckinghamshire* anchored in the Lower Hope at the mouth of the Thames. Here it was customary to pay the ship's company two months' advance of wages and 'two hours were allowed to lay out their money with the boat alongside, and to take leave of their wives and companions'.

> And here [continues Coverly] a scene revolting to human nature commenced. The crimps and other plunderers had provided a good supply of liquor, which they freely gave to those whom they intended to plunder, and then, when nearly dead drunk, made out a bill for certain articles, which no doubt the poor fellow never had. But Jack is an easy fellow, and easy parts with his money, which he sets little value on, and satisfies himself that money will be no use at sea, and when the voyage is over he will have plenty more; therefore, what is the use of grumbling.
>
> The two hours allowed as just stated was spent in the most disgusting manner, men and women inflamed with liquor, pouring the most abusive language on one another; some fighting, others lamenting the period of parting. Indeed such a scene can be compared to nothing but a floating Hell.

Crew aboard the emigrant ships which plied across the Atlantic were little different, though they were not away from home for as long as the East Indiamen. Conditions for the passengers – 'ignorant, ill-fed, verminous peasants', to quote one description of them – were not as good as they were on the ships which went East. The one-way passage in the sailing packets in the 1840s cost £3. 10s, or even less from Ireland, and the emigrants were crowded, 300 to 500 at a time, into the 'tweendeck of a vessel 150 feet long, with no more than 16 square feet allowed per passenger and the height between decks barely 6 feet. The bunks were wooden shelves three deep and the alleyways were crowded with personal belongings and food, for the ship provided only water and, on deck, a galley in which passengers were allowed to cook. The Irish emigrant carried a sack of potatoes for his provisions. Ventilation could come only if the hatches were open and in bad weather the hatches would be battened down. 'When the hatchways were opened . . .', commented one contemporary, 'the steam rose and the stench was like that from a pen of pigs.'[53]

American vessels enjoyed the highest reputation for seamanship, though some proportion of the crew was often British. In British ships the standard of seamanship appears to have declined. In the 18th century the East India

Company had lost only 91 ships in 98 years. During the first 18 years of the 19th century the Company lost 33 ships. In 1816 343 British ships were stranded or wrecked, in 1817 362, and in 1818 409.

In these three years an average of 763 seamen were lost at sea each year. By 1830–5 the number had risen to 894. According to W. S. Lindsay, shipowner and historian of shipping, a shipowner in the 1830s received the insured value of the ship even if this exceeded its true value, unless fraud could be proved. In his *Metropolitan Magazine* Captain Marryat averred that the system of marine insurance was 'murder for gain', and in the second quarter of the 19th century the average annual loss of ships by storm, bad navigation, piracy, fire and other hazards was estimated to be five per cent.[54]

Despite the prevalence of the *laissez-faire* philosophy the government was gradually forced to intervene in shipping as it was in other fields. An Act of 1817 forbade more than one person on board, including crew, for every 1.5 tons of registered tonnage, and laid down that there should be 5.5 feet of headroom in the hold for passengers. In 1835 masters of emigrant ships were instructed to carry 'a sufficient supply of medicines', and in the 1850s this measure was followed by Acts which decreed that such ships had to conform to certain minimum standards, provide cooked food and carry a doctor where there were more than 100 people on board.[55]

It was not until 1834 that merchant seamen stopped paying contributions to Greenwich Hospital, an institution whose facilities they could use only if they had spent at least half their time in the Royal Navy. After 1834 they paid instead a shilling a month to a Merchant Seamen's Fund for hospitals and institutions, an imposition which continued until 1851 when the scheme was wound up. Pensions from this fund were finally stabilised four years later when a disabled or 'worn out' seaman was given £3. 8s a year pension and a widow with three children £5. 10s.[56] The Greenwich Hospital was closed in 1869, being converted into the Royal Naval College in 1873. As a trust the Hospital still exists, funds being used for the support of elderly seamen and their widows, the payment of maintenance grants to orphaned children, and the education of the sons and grandsons of seafarers at the Royal Hospital School, Holbrook.

In 1835, at the annual dinner of the Royal Humane Society, a Captain Hyland referred to the great loss of life at sea caused by shipmasters who were 'entirely ignorant of the use of the sextant or chronometer' and who did not use the best instruments for taking soundings, and Parliament was petitioned to inquire into the causes. The following year the Government appointed a Select Committee of the House of Commons to 'inquire into the causes of the increased number of shipwrecks, with a view to ascertain whether such improvements might not be made in the construction, equipment and navigation of merchant vessels as would greatly diminish the annual loss of life and property at sea'.

With admirable comprehensiveness and impartiality, the Committee in its report[57] listed ten principal causes of shipwreck: defective construction; inadequate equipment; imperfect state of repair; improper and excessive loading; inappropriate design resulting from a system of tonnage measurement which induced shipowners to build ships which would combine small tonnage with large capacity; incompetency of masters and officers; drunkenness among officers and crew; marine insurance which inclined owners to take less care in construction and to neglect equipment and disregard safety; lack of harbours; and faultiness of charts. Safety regulations, the Committee pointed out, were virtually non-existent.

'Coffin' ships – ships too narrow and too deep – continued to be built, although in 1836 depth was taken into account for the first time when measuring tonnage. The 'new measurement' (nm) superseded the 'old measurement' (om) and the new practice had some beneficial effect on the depth of ships. From 1798 the system of classification at Lloyd's Register of Shipping had been based on age and port of construction, a system which led to the building of cheap ships which were sold after 6–12 years when they lapsed into second class.

The Select Committee suggested that a decline in navigational competence among shipmasters might be attributed to their sailing in convoy during the Napoleonic Wars, in which circumstances naval escorts took responsibility for navigation. A law dating from the reign of Queen Anne, which required masters to carry a given number of apprentices, was largely ignored and so young men received no proper training. It was recognised that American shipmasters were better educated than the British, and it seemed obvious that good teaching and the examination of officers paid dividends. George Coleman, a former East India Company officer turned teacher of navigation and astronomy, was among those who gave evidence to the Committee, and it was noted that in the ships of the East India Company, where officers underwent examination, standards were higher than they were in many other ships. The better companies insisted that their officers attend classes conducted by Coleman or the remarkable Mrs Janet Taylor, who wrote textbooks as well as running a navigation school, or others of their ilk, and subsequently pass examinations. In Sunderland shipowners and masters instituted their own examinations.[58] In London the shipowners Messrs Daniel & Company of Mincing Lane insisted that their officers pass examinations and in over twenty years they had lost only one ship.

The Select Committee which reported in 1836 put forward a comprehensive plan of reform and recommended the establishment of a 'Mercantile Marine Board to direct, superintend and regulate the affairs of the Mercantile Marine of the United Kingdom', but the only immediate outcome was an Act of 1839 which prohibited the carriage of deck cargoes on ships sailing from British North America. For the moment other problems were left to private enterprise and 1839 witnessed the establishment of the Shipwrecked Mariners' Society.

Four years later, however, in 1843, Parliament was forced to appoint another Select Committee to enquire into shipwrecks, for in January of that year 240 ships had been wrecked and 500 lives lost, all within the space of three days. In the same year the Foreign Office, which had become alarmed at the bad name abroad of British ships and seamen, issued a circular letter to all British consuls asking them a series of leading questions on the quality of British masters. The consul in Riga replied: 'I am sorry to state that, in my opinion, the British Commercial Marine is at present in a worse condition than that of any other nation. Foreign shipmasters are generally a more respectable class of men than the British.' The consul in Danzig commented: 'Taken as a whole, there is not – and I say it with regret – a more troublesome and thoughtless set of men, to use the mildest term, to be met with than British merchant seamen.' The consul in Odessa reported: 'Some shipmasters are shamefully illiterate and are not qualified to do justice to the interests of owners in common transactions that occur in this port.' The consul in Paraguay stated: 'Shippers now give such a decided preference to the merchant vessels of Sweden, Denmark, Sardinia, Hamburg and Austria that they are rapidly engrossing the carrying trade of Brazil.'[59] The consul in Pernambuco reported that hardly a British ship arrived without the seamen complaining of brutality, starvation and insulting language, and of their ship being shorthanded, and that in nine cases out of ten he was obliged to decide in favour of the men.[60]

The Select Committee of 1843 endorsed the views of its 1836 predecessor and added further recommendations for government supervision of all steamships carrying passengers. It also made recommendations concerning lighthouses, lightships, beacons and various other aids to navigation and safety. An Act of 1844 laid down the quantity of provisions, including limejuice, to be issued to crews, though this was not the end of scurvy for an Act of 1851 permitted the substitution of citric acid crystals for limejuice. Not until a further Act was passed in 1867 did the incidence of scurvy decline.[61] The Act of 1844 also introduced provisions for agreements with crews, the proper payment of wages, a supply of medicines, the punishment of deserters, the registry of seamen, and the compulsory carriage of apprentices according to tonnage, though this compulsory apprenticeship was abandoned in 1849. In 1845 the Board of Trade established voluntary examinations for masters and mates in two classes,[62] and two years later set up a Commission to enquire once more into the condition of the Merchant Service.

The Whig government which came into power in 1848 had a strong mandate for free trade and, except where they restricted coastal traffic, swept away what remained of the Navigation Acts in 1849. Many shipowners of the day were opposed to these changes but five years later the coastal trade too was opened to ships of all nations.

These Acts, followed as they were by an unprecedented growth of British tonnage, have persuaded some that the abolition of the Navigation Acts was the cause of such growth. In the very different circumstances of a century and a half later, this 19th-century growth of shipping is still produced as an argument for free trade and an argument in favour of governments that do not interfere with shipping.

The truth is more complex. The Navigation Acts had been considerably eroded in the quarter of a century which preceded the Act of 1849. From 1824 to 1849 William Huskisson had pursued his reciprocity policy, making a series of treaties that removed preferential duties and similar limitations on trade with those countries which agreed to act in a similar manner. In 1830 it was agreed that American ships could carry American produce direct to any British possession and could carry exports from any British possession to any foreign country. American ships were even allowed to trade from the United Kingdom to India. In South America the Napoleonic Wars were followed by a revolt of the Spanish and Portuguese colonies, which were then allowed to bring their products to Britain and, since these products rivalled those of the West Indies, the British West Indian possessions had the restrictions on their choice of shipping partially removed. By 1845 half of British trade was governed by exceptions to the Navigation Acts.

During the same period there was much evasion of the terms of the Acts. Smuggling was commonplace, and coffee, timber and silk imports which were supposedly subject to the Acts found means of ingress which evaded them. Some South American coffee came to the United Kingdom by way of South Africa; some Scandinavian timber arrived by way of North America; and some Indian silk reached Britain in American ships.[63]

After the Napoleonic Wars it can scarcely be argued that the Navigation Acts were a curb on British enterprise. During the long depression that followed those wars British shipping declined by 12 per cent, though this was only half the decline suffered by other European countries. During Huskisson's reciprocity period, when trade had been partially freed, the yearly tonnage entering British ports increased fast, but not as fast as the corresponding increase in foreign entries.[64] Contrary to the received view, even after the complete repeal of the Navigation Acts, British shipping failed to maintain its relative position. Although by 1861 British tonnage was 50 per cent higher than that of 1849, American tonnage had almost doubled in the same period and the advance of Norway, by then England's most dangerous rival in Europe, was just as marked.[65]

English shipwrights could not build wooden sailing ships as cheaply as their principal competitors. They could not build as cheaply as the Dutch because Dutch shipbuilders could borrow money more cheaply. And they could not build as cheaply as the Americans, the Scandinavians and the Germans because the raw materials they required had largely to be imported from these peoples. It can be argued, therefore, that British shipwrights required the protection of the Navigation Acts until iron began to replace timber, though it is possible that, by harming the Dutch, the Acts increased the price of Baltic timber and, overall, restricted the growth of trade. Whatever the strength of these arguments, what eventually put British shipping ahead of that of the rest of the world was building with iron, the development of the steam engine, and Britain's abundant coal. Growth was compounded by the demands that arose from the Crimean War, the American Civil War, and the Australian gold rush. Contributory in the early stages was the government's provision of mail contracts.

Between 1750 and 1850 the population of Britain had increased from 6.5 million to 18 million and it was still increasing rapidly. Textiles were pre-eminent among Britain's exports, as they had been since the later Middle Ages, but cottons had become more important than woollens. By value, woollens contributed half and cottons one-quarter at the end of the 18th century. By 1850 cottons contributed 65 per cent and woollens only 20 per cent, the rest being made up of other manufactured goods – notably those of iron and steel – and coal. Imports of raw cotton had increased in 50 years from 54 to 775 million pounds. Wool imports in the same period had increased from 7 to 74 million pounds. The price of cotton yarn had fallen to one-tenth of what it had been at the turn of the century.[66] As Sydney Smith remarked, 'The great object for which the Anglo-Saxon race appears to have been created is the making of calico.' Britain had become the 'workshop of the world' and 'King Cotton' ruled.

Trade had multiplied twelve-fold in a century. Cotton came from across the Atlantic, as did tobacco, sugar and timber. Although grain as yet averaged only 9 per cent of imports by volume, some came from the Black Sea. Long hauls and more business meant more ships. At the same time, overseas territories were developing rapidly and thousands of Europeans were emigrating to the New World, 32,000 a year on average between 1825 and 1834, and 71,000, more than double the earlier figure, between 1835 and 1844.[67] With the coming of British transatlantic steamers, the British share of this traffic increased rapidly.

Notes

1. S. Ville, *English Shipowning during the Industrial Revolution: 1770–1830* (1987), Manchester, p. 99 and p. 164; A. G. Course, *The Merchant Navy: A Social History* (1963), London, p. 198.
2. C. Dixon, 'The Rise and Fall of the Crimp, 1840–1914', in S. Fisher (ed), *British Shipping and Seamen, 1630–1960* (1984), Exeter, p. 51.
3. Anon, *Seafarers and Their Ships* (1955), London, pp. 10–11.
4. R. C. Blake, *The Missionary Century in the Royal Navy,* unpublished.
5. G. Jackson, *The British Whaling Trade* (1978), London, passim: J. A. Troup (ed), *The Ice-bound Whalers* (1987), Kirkwall, Orkney.
6. Anon, *Two Centuries of Shipbuilding by the Scotts of Greenock* (1920), London.
7. B. Lubbock, *The China Clippers* (1914), Glasgow, p. 185; D. R. MacGregor, *Fast Sailing Ships, 1775–1875* (1973), London.
8. R. H. Thornton, *British Shipping* (1939), Cambridge, p. 7.
9. C. E. Fayle, *A Short History of the World's Shipping Industry* (1933), London, p. 228.
10. A. F. L. Deeson, *An Illustrated History of Steamships* (1976), Bourne End, p. 47.
11. Thornton, *op. cit.*, pp. 11–12.
12. Deeson, *op. cit.*, p. 76.
13. Thornton, *op. cit.*, p. 35.
14. Deeson, *op. cit.*, p. 58.
15. Thornton, *op. cit.*, p. 11.
16. *Ib.*, p. 12.
17. M. W. Thomas, *A Survey of English Economic History,* 3rd edn (1967), p. 247.
18. S. Palmer, '"The most indefatigable activity." The General Steam Navigation Company 1824–50' (1982), *The Journal of Transport History,* 3rd Series, Vol. 3, No. 2, pp. 19–20.
19. Deeson, *op. cit.*, p. 35.
20. See *Shipbuilding and Shipping Record,* 28th November, 1963.
21. W. Foster, *The East India House* (1924), London, p. 229.
22. D. R. MacGregor, *Merchant Sailing Ships, 1815–1850: Supremacy of Sail* (1984), London, p. 161.
23. P. Bagwell, 'The Post Office Steam Packets, 1821–36, and the Development of Shipping in the Irish Sea' (1971), *Maritime History,* Vol. 1, No. 1, pp. 4–25.

24. T. A. Bushell, '*Royal Mail*': *A Centenary History of the Royal Mail Line, 1839–1939* (1939?) London.
25. F. Harcourt, 'British oceanic mail contracts in the age of steam, 1838–1914' (1988), *The Journal of Transport History*, 3rd Series, Vol. 9, No. 1, p. 1.
26. B. Cable, *A Hundred Year History of the P & O* (1937), London, pp. 30–31.
27. *Ib*., p. 43.
28. R. E. Duncan, 'Captain George Peacock: The Pioneer Commander of Pacific Steamers' (1980), MM, Vol. 66, No. 1, pp. 17 ff.
29. Harcourt, *op. cit*., p. 2.
30. Deeson, *op. cit*., p. 68.
31. Thornton, *op. cit*., p. 12.
32. Fayle, *op. cit*., p. 230.
33. Ville, *op. cit*., p. 120.
34. Thornton, *op. cit*., p. 27.
35. Fayle, *op. cit*., p. 231.
36. Deeson, *op. cit*., p. 77.
37. *Ib*., p. 69.
38. H. C. McMurray, 'Ships' engineers: their status and position on board, c. 1830–65,' in S. Fisher (ed), *West Country Maritime and Social History: Some Essays* (1980), Exeter, pp. 90–94.
39. P. Padfield, *Beneath the House Flag of the P & O* (1981), London, pp. 16–17.
40. *Ib*., p. 39.
41. D. & S. Howarth, *The Story of P & O* (1986), London, p. 35.
42. Unpublished manuscript written by an ancestor of Captain J. de Coverley and in the latter's hands; an extract appeared in *The Seafarer*, Autumn 1983.
43. Padfield, *op. cit*., p. 18.
44. Anon, *Seafarers and Their Ships* (1955), London, p. 54.
45. S. Jones, 'Blood Red Roses: The Supply of Merchant Seamen in the Nineteenth Century' (1972), MM, VOl. 58, No. 4, p. 442.
46. R. Craig, 'Carmarthenshire Shipping in the 1840s' (1985), *The Carmarthenshire Antiquary*, Vol. XXI, p. 50.
47. *Shipping in Dumfries and Galloway in 1820* (1973), Scottish Local History Texts, No. 1, Glasgow, pp. 4–6.
48. F. W. Wallace, *Under Sail in the Last of the Clippers* (1936), Glasgow, p. 139.
49. S. Ville, 'Total Factor Productivity in the English Shipping Industry: The North-east Coal trade, 1700–1850' (1986), EHR, 2nd Series, Vol. XXXIX, No. 3, pp. 355 ff.
50. D. R. MacGregor, *Fast Sailing Ships, 1775–1875* (1983), London.
51. B. Greenhill, *The Merchant Schooners* (1988), London, pp. 9–11, p. 24; D. R. MacGregor, *Schooners in Four Centuries* (1982), Hemel Hempstead, pp. 10–11, pp. 68–72.
52. J. Press, 'Wages in the merchant navy, 1815–54' (1981), *The Journal of Transport History*, 3rd series, Vol. 2, No. 2, pp. 37–52; H. C. McMurray, *op. cit*., p. 90.
53. W. S. Lindsay, *History of Merchant Shipping and Ancient Commerce*, Vol. III (1876), London, p. 330.
54. *Ib*., pp. 465–9.
55. *Seafarers and Their Ships*, p. 64.
56. *Ib*., p. 55.
57. *Report from the Select Committee appointed to inquire into the causes of Shipwrecks* (1836).

58. Course, *op. cit.*, p. 202.
59. *Seafarers and Their Ships*, pp. 22–3.
60. Course, *op. cit.*, pp. 202.
61. C. Dixon, 'Pound and Pint: Diet in the Merchant Service, 1750–1980', in S. Palmer & G. Williams (eds), *Charted and Uncharted Waters: Proceedings of a conference on the Study of British Maritime History* (1982), London, p. 168.
62. Course, *op. cit.*, pp. 202, 214, 217.
63. P.L. Cottrell & D.H. Aldcroft, *Shipping Trade and Commerce* (1981), Leicester, pp. 99–112.
64. L.A. Harper, *The English Navigation Laws* (1964), New York, pp. 350–1.
65. *Ib.*, p. 356.
66. Thomas, *op. cit.*, p. 253; p. 325.
67. Fayle, *op. cit.*, p. 227.

16

Clippers and Steamships (1850–1870)

Ironically, it was the *laissez faire* Government of 1848, the Government which abolished the Navigation Acts, which found itself impelled in 1850 to pass an 'Act for improving the condition of Masters, Mates and Seamen and maintaining discipline in the Merchant Service'.[1] A Parliament nominally committed to non-interference thus laid the foundations for a sizeable edifice of paternal legislation.

By the Act of 1850, which called into being the Marine Department of the Board of Trade, the Board was given a definite responsibility for the welfare of those employed in shipping and of those entrusting their goods or persons to British ships. Provision was made for the first time for the compulsory examination of masters and mates and the issue of certificates of competency. The Board was given power to cancel certificates in cases of incompetency or other unsuitability.

By this same Act the keeping of an official log (that is, a record of all the events occurring in a ship's voyage) was rendered obligatory; regulations were laid down for the disciplining of merchant seamen; a scale of accommodation, food and medical supplies was established; and local Marine Boards were constituted at the principal ports to supervise the engagement and discharge of seamen and the administration of the Act. Each seaman was to have nine superficial feet of space in the forecastle or deckhouse, well ventilated, allocated to him, space which was increased to twelve superficial feet in 1867. Local Marine Boards were to establish shipping officers; and shipping masters were appointed to give a proper 'discharge' to a seaman when he paid off or left his ship, a system which evolved later into a book of continuous discharges which was used for well over a hundred years. 'VG' and 'G' entered in the seaman's discharge book by the master signified 'very good' and 'good'. The entries 'M' for 'middling' and 'I' for indifferent, replaced in 1894 by the single comment 'DR' or 'decline to report', were tantamount to saying, 'This man is no good'.

In a measure to combat the crimps, the Act made it illegal for private persons to board inbound ships until a certain time after their arrival at their berths. Crimps now waited instead at the dock gates.

Strikes by collier seamen had not been uncommon,[2] but one outcome of the 1850 Act was the formation by seamen on the north-east coast of 'The Penny Union'. Many seamen were opposed to the disciplinary regulations of the Act, and also to the shilling charge which was to be made for engagement or 'signing on', and demanded higher wages. In January 1851 a strike was ably organised by Thomas Moore and a large protest meeting was held in Sunderland. Concessions were made, including the suspension of twenty-two disciplinary regulations, but the Union received its death blow two years later when a Bill was presented to Parliament to repeal the manning clause in ships: in the interests of free trade it was no longer to be mandatory that three-quarters of the crew of a British ship should be British.

By this time British tonnage had risen to 4.3 million tons and the number of seafarers was more than 200,000. At least 14,000 new seafarers were required each year, to replace the 7000 or more who left the sea, the 3000 who died of disease and the 1300 who drowned, and to allow of some increase.[3] In consequence of their new freedom shipowners nearly doubled the number of foreign seamen in British ships in the space of a year, the number increasing from 7321 to 13,230. At the same time, because gold was discovered in Australia in 1851, there were plenty of men willing to work a passage out for £5 even though it was not so easy initially to find men willing to work a passage home. After 1850, too, the steam train began to make an impact on the collier fleet and the amount of coal sent to London by rail began to increase rapidly. Seamen's wages fell and the Penny Union folded up in 1858.[4]

Further state interference came in 1851 when the Steam Navigation Act gave the Board of Trade power to appoint surveyors of steamships instead of the power to approve such appointments, as had been the case previously. After this date duties relating to the safety of ships were carried out through the Marine Survey Offices opened in the principal United Kingdom ports. The following year a further Act tightened earlier provisions relating to tonnage and the number of passengers who could be carried and laid down a dietary scale for passengers.[5]

All this and earlier legislation was consolidated and further extended in the first great Merchant Shipping Act of 1854, an Act with no fewer than 548 clauses. The Board of Trade was given yet more powers and the Act compelled shipmasters to specify in the Agreement with crew the kinds and amounts of food which they proposed to provide on the voyage and made provision for weigh-scales to be at hand so that the crew could check their 'whack'.

Since it was customary to auction on board the possessions of a sailor who died at sea so that the proceeds could be sent to his nearest relative, records of such possessions exist. James Thomson, a 20-year-old Shetlander drowned in Canada in 1857, possessed a seaman's chest, a clothes bag, a reefing jacket, 2 woollen coats, a pair of woollen and a pair of cotton trousers, 2 cloth caps, a southwester, 2 flannel shirts, 2 cotton shirts, 2 woollen vests, a pair of socks, 2 cravats, a silk handkerchief, 2 pairs of boots, a pair of shoes, a towel, a looking-glass, 2 brushes, a razor, a spoon and a needle case, together with a blanket and a bed cover. It is more than many seafarers carried a century later and Thomson was better equipped than many of his contemporaries. John Giles, a Londoner who fell to his death from the fore-topgallant yard on a voyage from Liverpool to Quebec in 1863 left: 1 pair of blue trousers, 1 blue shirt, 1 white shirt, 1 old Guernsey frock, 1 singlet, 1 pair of flannel drawers, 1 set of oilskin coat and trousers, 2 blankets, 1 bag and 1 mattress.

To make it easier to work in unison on heavy tasks sailors chanted together from early times, but the sea shanty as it is remembered today does not pre-date the end of the 18th century. Some of these songs are thought to have derived from those sung by negroes met with in the cotton trade. These slaves lived in shanties and were known as shantymen.[7] French-Canadian lumbermen also sang songs when paddling their canoes, and they, too, lived in shanties and used the word 'chanter' to mean 'sing'.[8] The two areas – the cotton-growing areas in the south and the lumbering region of the St Lawrence river – were linked by both British and colonial seamen who worked along the east coast of North America and back to Europe.

Whatever the origin or origins of the first modern shanties, the shanty did not enter into its heyday until well on in the 19th century, in the so-called 'glorious days of sail', particularly when the true sailorman's task grew harder as the owner of his ship reduced the number of crew to compete more successfully with steam. Shanties were not much sung after 1880,[9] by which time steam had largely won.

Within a year or two of the passing of the act of 1854 more than one shanty was devoted to it and topsail yards were being hoisted to a shanty which began:

> You'll do no good by grumbling,
> You know how well you're whacked
> With lime juice and vinegar,

According to the Act. . . .

and ended:

You'll do no good by grumbling,
I'll tell you for a fact,
They can sew you up and dump you
According to the Act.[10]

One consequence of the Acts of 1850 and 1854 was the establishment of schools of navigation. With the help of grants made by the government's Science and Art Department, 17 such schools had been established in 15 different ports (there were 3 in London) by 1862. At the end of the century the Department was merged with the Board of Education and the schools were taken over in 1908 by the local authorities. Since payments were by results they were largely cramming institutions in these fifty years.[11] At the same time further hulks, the first since that established by The Marine Society in 1786, became training ships, the officers' training ships *Conway* and *Worcester* being established, respectively, in the Mersey and in the Thames in 1859 and in 1862.

Arising from these same conditions came the formation in 1857 of the Mercantile Marine Service Association, an organisation designed 'to improve the condition and promote the interests of masters, officers and men of the British Merchant Service' and 'to promote the better education of its members, to provide aid in sickness or death, and to provide legal advice and assistance'. For well over a century, until its amalgamation with other officers' organisations in 1985, the MMSA was the shipmasters' 'trade union'.

The 1850s and 1860s also witnessed a number of other developments which indicated a higher degree of sophistication in the shipping world. With the introduction of continuous service in the navy in 1853 the press-gang, unused since 1815, was no longer required. In 1857, forty years after Captain Marryat had pioneered a code of signals for merchant ships, the Board of Trade introduced a new code of signals which was gradually adopted by most maritime nations. In 1859 the Royal Naval Reserve was established, and in 1860 the Institute (now Royal Institute) of Naval Architects. The Merchant Shipping (Amendment) Act of 1862 confirmed the general regulations then existing for preventing collisions at sea, laid down the rules for carrying navigation lights, and extended the provisions on examinations and certificates to marine engineers. From this time forward foreign-going steamships were required to carry one or more qualified engineers. In 1864 an Order in Council reserved the Red Ensign for the sole use of British merchant ships. In 1867 the first edition of the *Ships' Captains' Medical Guide* appeared, a work which in revised form is still giving yeoman service.

None of these measures turned seafaring into a salubrious profession, for life at sea remained cramped and confined. W. S. Lindsay served his apprenticeship at sea in the 1860s and he has left a description of life in his 420-ton vessel. The crew numbered 21, and the master, first and second mates and the steward messed in the cabin. The steward, together with the carpenter, cooper and cook, helped in the seamen's duties where necessary, as the poulterer Edward Coverly had done. In addition to these there were ten seamen and four apprentices. One of the latter, presumably the senior one, lived with the carpenter and cooper in the 'steerage', a small space temporarily separated by some rough stanchions and boards from the cargo in the square of the after hatch. Here their tools were kept, together with various stores of ropes and sails. The cook, the seamen and the other three apprentices – 14 in all – lived under the forecastle, a triangular space perhaps 21 feet wide at the after end or widest part, tapering gradually to the narrow point of the stem, the length amidships being about 20 feet. The height from deck to beam was about five feet.

Despite the terms of the 1850 Act, there was no light or ventilation in bad weather and little enough in good. It was damp. The crew slept in hammocks, and the tops of sea chests served for table and chair, meals being taken sitting astride the chests. At all times, wrote Lindsay, 'it was a foulsome and suffocating abode, and in bad weather the water and filth washed about the deck and among the chests and casks created the most intolerable and loathsome stench'. Food consisted almost entirely of inferior salted pork, beef which was sometimes nearly as hard and unpalatable as the kids or wooden mess-tubs in which it was served, and brown biscuits or hard tack, too often mouldy and full of maggots. The forecastle was full of rats.[12]

Many of the best British seamen in the mid-19th century served in the collier brigs that brought coal from the north-east coast to London, Holland and France. For a round voyage the master would be paid £8 or £9, mates £5 to £6, the cook £5 to £5.10s and ABs £4 to £4.10s, rates of pay which were rather higher than they had been a decade earlier. The four apprentices carried in these ships each received £50 for the five-year apprenticeship, beginning at £8 for the first year and then rising by £1 a year until their 'time' had expired. In the summer months a few of the best colliers were taken off the coast and traded to the Baltic, Archangel, Portugal or Spain. The monthly rates of pay were then the same as or slightly lower than those for a round voyage carrying coal, ABs in these trades in the 1860s earning £3.10s to £3.15s a month.[13]

By this time steamships were going regularly round Cape Horn, the Pacific Mail Steamship Company having been established in the United States with the aid of the American Congress in 1847. Still economically precarious, these steamships were saved from early bankruptcy only by the discovery in that year of gold in California.[14] The most dramatic consequence of this gold rush, and of the subsequent discovery of gold in Australia in 1851, was not the development of the deepsea steamer but the tremendous stimulus that it gave to the production of more efficient sailing vessels. Although they suffered a lingering death thereafter, sailing vessels enjoyed a glamorous twenty years from 1849 to 1869, a time when commercial sail was developed to its ultimate pinnacle of achievement in the oceanic clipper, in the 'golden' days before steam could compete economically in the distant trades. It was a period which until very recent times still aroused in the hearts of thousands a nostalgic love for the glory of things past, most nobly expressed by John Masefield towards the end of the 19th century in the lines:

> I cannot tell their wonder nor make known
> Magic that once thrilled me to the bone. . . .
>
> These splendid ships, each with her grace, her glory,
> Her memory of old song or comrade's story. . . .
>
> They mark our passage as a race of men.
> Earth will not see such ships as those agen.

The genius who improved the clipper and began to build the ships which became legendary was Donald Mackay, a Nova Scotian by birth, who produced the 1783-ton *Flying Cloud* and other vessels of similar size to cope with the Californian gold rush. Despite the difficulties and dangers of the voyage round the Horn, Mackay introduced many gadgets to facilitate the working of the ship which enabled these big clippers to sail with a crew of twenty instead of the thirty employed in a large British vessel. On the Atlantic, where Mackay built the new White Diamond Line of sailing packets for the British shipowner Enoch Train, his ships were as large and spacious as those of his Cunard competitors, who favoured steam, and provided a sweeter, if longer, passage.

In 1849 90,000 people sailed from the Atlantic ports of the United States to San Francisco. But in California there was little other than gold dust to pick up as cargo. It became the practice, therefore, for the new clippers to sail on across the Pacific Ocean to China and there pick up a cargo of tea for Boston or New York or, after the repeal of the Navigation Acts, for London. It was a trade in which speed paid. In August 1850 the

American clipper *Oriental* arrived in Hong Kong and was promptly chartered to load 1600 tons of tea for London at £6 per ton of 40 cubic feet while British ships were finding it difficult to fill their holds at £3.10s per ton of 50 cubic feet. On 3rd December she arrived in London after a record passage of 97 days, securing the highest prices for the new season's tea at the tea sales.[15]

The first shipment of Australian gold reached England in 1852 and from then on there started a flow of emigration to the settlements in Australia which was almost as strong as that across the Atlantic. By reducing the bulk of wool as the bulk of tobacco had been reduced a century earlier, the prosaic wool press made it possible for Australian wool to compete with that from Spain and Germany despite the long haul to England,[16] and the emigrant rush of the 1850s was succeeded by annual races to bring the season's wool clip back to London.

This time British shipowners responded positively to the demand. In London, three of the principal owners in the East India trade, Duncan Dunbar, Richard and Henry Green and Money Wigram, who were looking for alternative outlets to a trade under threat from steam, diverted some existing ships to the new Australian trade and built others. Liverpool men bought secondhand a whole fleet of American Atlantic packets and put them on the run to Australia. The leaders there were Pilkington and Wilson, founders of the White Star Line, James Beagley and the famous James Baines. They also placed orders for new ships with the builders of Boston and New Brunswick. In 1854 Donald Mackay delivered four ships to Baines's new Black Ball Line of Australian packets, *Lightning, Champion of the Seas, James Baines* and *Donald Mackay*. *Lightning* made a passage of 63 days from Melbourne to England, a passage which was never equalled under sail. *James Baines*, a ship of 2275 tons, was generally considered to be Mackay's masterpiece.

These big Liverpool ships, all of them over 2000 tons, almost monopolised the Australian emigrant traffic and their speed was such that Baines could contract with the Postmaster-General to deliver the mails to Australia in 68 days with a penalty of £100 for every day's delay. In a single decade the sailing ship on the long distance runs had been revolutionised, for in 1845 the *Rossendale*, of only 296 tons, had been considered a 'splendid first-class ship' in the Australian trade. The 'dash' of the new Liverpool owners was in marked contrast to that of the 'gentlemanly' London owners of the Blackwall frigates and, in the view of one Liverpool owner of a later generation,[17] the new Australian trade moulded professional deepsea shipowning for a hundred years.

Britain's first New Zealand contacts of any consequence came after

1840, when that country was formally annexed to the British Crown. 'Paddy' Henderson of Glasgow, a firm founded in 1834, and Willis, Gann of London pioneered this trade, but it was not until Robert Shaw and Walter Savill, one-time employees of Willis, Gann, formed their partnership Shaw, Savill in 1858 that development began in earnest, development which was greatly accelerated by the discovery of gold in Otago in 1861 and the receipt by Shaw, Savill of a Government contract to carry emigrants in 1862. Between 1858 and 1882, in 1310 ship voyages, the firm carried over 100,000 passengers to the new colony, but they sailed in ships which were generally well under 1200 tons, ships considerably smaller than those in the Australian trade.[18]

In these years the voyage to Australia or to New Zealand was suited to the sailing ship. There were few suitable refuelling stations for the steamer and the Cape of Good Hope to Melbourne crossing was more than twice the distance across the Atlantic. Moreover, the winds of the extreme southern hemisphere are consistent and westerly. Five hundred miles west of Tristan da Cunha a sailing ship can turn almost at a right angle and 'run her easting down' with a favouring westerly wind for the whole 8000 miles to Melbourne. The route could be both shortened and quickened by dipping south on a Great Circle track, and the publication round about 1830 of wind and current charts and the statistical compilations made from them in 1850 by Lieutenant Maury of the US Navy also helped.[19] Homeward, the westerlies were still employed by returning round Cape Horn.

At the height of the Australian goldrush in 1852 many ships laid up in Melbourne for want of crews, one ship advertising unsuccessfully for sailors at £30 a month. The notorious Captain 'Bully' Forbes of the *Marco Polo*, who lost men, spars and his temper on every voyage, solved the problem by having his crew thrown into prison until the ship sailed. But not all masters were like Forbes. William Stewart as master of *The Tweed* and *Loch Etive* never lost a man or a spar in 43 years. In Baines's *Lightning* Anthony Enright was a born hotelier as well as a shipmaster. He carried a full export cargo, 50 saloon passengers, 370 emigrants and 85 crew, with several bullocks, 70 sheep, 70 pigs and 1000 head of poultry at the outset of the voyage. The ships frequently carried a band; deck games were played; there might be a ship's library; and aboard the *Lightning* a ship's magazine was printed daily.

In these ships there was a demand for speed. According to her master, Captain W. Crockett, his ship *Annandale* logged 381 miles in a day on one occasion in 1855, averaging nearly 16 knots and thus making better speed than ever did *Thermopylae*, built a decade later. In their pursuit of speed masters sometimes took risks, and the ships could be uncomfortable. When the ship was logging 16 or even 18 knots the decks would be almost continuously awash, with the passengers battened down in suffocating misery. The log of the *Thomas Stephens* in 1869 suggests how advantage was taken of a gale to make up a little lost time, but not without expense:

> Sunday, Dec. 10th, A.M. heavy gale, high cross sea: ship labouring, decks at times completely flooded fore and aft. 1 a.m. main topgallant staysail carried away: 7 a.m. gale continues, logging 16 knots. Heavy sea carried away starboard lifeboat, completely flooding main deck and washing away main hatch-house. 9.30 a.m. gale moderating, made all plain sail, still logging 16 knots. P.M. moderate with high cross sea, decks completely flooded.

After which the master, the same Captain Enright who had commanded *Lightning*, would write a circular letter to his passengers informing them of the ship's remarkable speed and ending, 'I hope this information will in some degree compensate you for the inconvenience which the heavy weather has occasioned you.'[20]

Whatever Britain's advantages in steam, in the freely competitive trades the Americans were still supreme. So much was this so that in the early 1860s the young Walter Runciman, founder of the shipping company of that name, could feel that his youthful egotism made him long 'for the notoriety of being able to say that I had served on board an American ship and, when the opportunity offered, I jumped at it.'[21] But the challenge of the post-repeal era, when Navigation Acts offered no protection, applied to shipbuilders as well as shipowners, and it was taken up by the builders Hall and Hood of Aberdeen, by Robert Steele of Greenock, and by Richard Green, an hereditary builder and owner in the Indian trade, in London. In 1851, at a large City dinner, Green announced his intention of trying to beat the Americans at their own game and in the following year he put his new ship *Challenger* into the China tea trade where, by two days, she beat the American clipper *Challenge* from Anjer on the homeward run. In command was James Killick, co-founder of Killick Martin, a firm which turned from shipowning to shipbroking in 1886 but which still survives.[22]

The large East Indiamen apart, probably only two wooden merchant sailing ships over 1500 tons were ever built in the United Kingdom. It was cheaper to buy or charter American or Canadian ships.[23] But the ships from North America, being built of softwoods, became waterlogged after a voyage or two and their qualities deteriorated. The Merchant Shipping Act of 1854 had established more rational British rules for tonnage measurement whereby tonnage was based on the cubic capacity of the hull,[24] and hardwood ships and composite ships, where iron frames were used with teak and oak sheathing, proved better when built according to these new rules than the American softwood ships, even though they were smaller. From 1863 to 1869 British yards turned out an unimpeachable series of 800-ton ships, like *Taeping, Serica, Ariel, Sir Lancelot, Thermopylae* and *Cutty Sark*, ships in which the crews were well fed and in which, as in P & O, the officers were similar in quality to those who had worked for the East India Company. These were the ships of those 'glorious days of sail' which featured in the great tea races of the 1860s and early 1870s.

Fig. 5. THE RISE OF BRITISH SHIPPING, 1558–1921

Between 1558 and 1921 the carrying capacity of the British merchant fleet probably increased 1000-fold. In the same time-span the population increased 6-fold. The figures usually given for tonnage prior to 1776 do not apparently allow for coastal shipping. The upper figure in these years makes such allowance. 3 tons of sail are taken to be equivalent to 1 ton of steam.

YEAR	SAIL (NET TONS)	STEAM (GROSS TONS)	STEAM EQUIVALENT (GROSS TONS)
1558	50–90,000	—	17–30,000
1581	67–120,000	—	22–40,000
1629	115–200,000	—	38–67,000
1686	340–630,000	—	113–210,000
1702	323–600,000	—	108–200,000
1736	391–700,000	—	130–233,000
1776	1,125,600	—	375,000
1792	1,187,000	—	396,000
1814	2,329,000	—	776,300
1835	2,750,000	—	833,000
1850	3,618,000	275,000	1,481,000
1870	4,876,000	1,819,000	3,444,000
1890	3,127,000	8,240,000	9,448,000
1910	1,205,000	17,264,000	17,666,000
1921	—	19,320,000	19,320,000

(*Sources:* The post-1835 figures are derived from the Statistical Abstracts of the UK; the sources of earlier figures are indicated in the text.)

After 1861 the British benefited greatly from the fortuitous circumstances that a civil war removed their leading rival from the shipping scene. By 1865 United States shipowners had sold over 730,000 tons of shipping to foreign competitors and American participation in the English carrying trade had diminished by over one million tons.[25] The effects of the American Civil War could have been temporary but by the time that war was over American energies and American capital were largely diverted to internal recovery and to the development of the west and middle west. Before Britain's European competitors had any opportunity to substitute for America, the opening of the Suez Canal and the development of trade with the British colonies of India, Australia, New Zealand and, later, those in Africa, all offered new opportunities specifically for British shipping.

By 1853 steam packet companies with mail subsidies owned 91 steamships which together made up half the 275,000 tons of British steamships on the register.[26] In 1851 the newly-formed African Steam Ship Company secured a ten-year mail contract with a substantial subsidy to maintain a monthly service to the West African colonies and in consequence commissioned five steamships with the new screw propellers.[27] The following year P & O established the first mail service to Australia. Singapore was used as a transhipment base and the mail was sent on by the *Chusan*, another iron steamer with a screw propeller, though she was barque-rigged and depended a good deal on her sails.[28] In 1856, also with a mail contract, the Allan Line of sailing ships turned over to steam on the service to Quebec. In 1857 the Union Steamship Company, precursor of the Union-Castle Line, was awarded a monthly mail contract to South Africa. By 1860 the British government was disbursing £1 million a year on mail contracts.

Mail contracts helped the British ocean steamer to make progress, but for some years after 1853 it was a change in the methods of ship construction which was the most important single factor in the further development of British shipping, for it was in these years that iron came rapidly into favour. The hull of an iron ship grew foul more rapidly than that of a wooden ship and under sail it could rarely equal the speed of the wooden ship on long-distance voyages.[29] But the iron ship weighed less and it could carry more cargo. Most importantly, iron ships could be much bigger. The limit to the size of wooden vessels was a length of about 300 feet, and few sailing vessels were ever built to exceed 2000 tons. After 1865 the majority of square-rigged ships of over 500 tons built in Great Britain were of iron.[30] Iron was also used for the rigging. Wire rigging was to be found increasingly in large British ships from this time on, though the 'bottle screw', used to make wire rope taut, was not perfected until about 1875.[31] There proved to be a practical limit to the size of sailing vessels even when they were built of iron. A handful of 5000-ton sailing vessels – five-masted barques and schooners – were built at the very end of the days of sail, but still bigger ones would have proved too difficult to handle.

Such a limitation did not apply to the steamship. *Great Eastern*, the last of Brunel's great ships, launched in 1857, was 680 feet long and her gross tonnage was no less than 18,914 tons. Big enough to go to Australia and back without coaling, *Great Eastern* proved to be well before her time, for trade had not yet expanded enough for the ship and the ship was not yet economic enough for the trade. But by 1862, the year in which Harland & Wolff built their first yard on Queen's Island, Belfast, steamers of between 3000 and 5000 tons were already a paying proposition. By this time the combined tonnage of iron sailing ships and steamers built in Great Britain equalled those built of wood.[32]

Although the victory was not yet assured, the steamship had to win. In addition to the limitations on size, even the best sailing ships were hopelessly irregular. The passage from Foochow to Liverpool in a sailing ship could be 90 days one year and 120 the next. Thompson's *Thermopylae* claimed a ten-year average of 69 days from England to Melbourne, but only from the Lizard, after the journey down-Channel had been completed.[33] Although most of the early steamers – the Cunarders of the 1840s for example – steamed at no more than 10 knots, and even less into the wind on the outward passages, while Mackay's *Daniel Webster* could be described, apologetically, as only an 11-knot ship, the steamer offered a regularity which appealed to passengers and sail was relegated to the carriage of cargoes where time was of little importance. The largest tonnage of sailing ships ever built in Great Britain in a single year was the 272,500 tons of 1864, a year in which 159,400 tons of steamers were built.[34] The sailing fleet's peak tonnage came in 1865 at 4.9 million net tons, a year by which steam tonnage was still only 0.8 million net tons. In the bulk trades the sailing ship continued to remain competitive until the mid-1880s.

Small sailing vessels were still at work round the coast in their thousands. A photograph taken in 1850 shows 300 merchant sailing vessels sheltering, windbound, in Plymouth Sound. They were mostly humble coasters or short-sea traders, owned or part-owned by their masters: brigs, brigantines, sloops, small barques and schooners,[35] the latter a term not yet as strictly defined as it was to be by 1880. In the 1850s the term often embraced barquentines and occasionally brigantines; later it meant a vessel which was fore-and-aft rigged on all masts, with some additional square canvas on the foremast. In the 1850s the average size of vessels in the home trade was still only 80 tons, a craft crewed by only 4 men, and the average size of sailing ships employed in foreign trade was only 350 tons, with vast numbers below 150 tons. During these middle years of the 19th century the design of the sailing cargo-carrier was modified and sharpened to bring about a fusion with the design of the medium clipper.[36]

Both sailing vessels and steamships were operated by many shipowners in these years and Thomas and James Harrison, brothers who established the still privately owned company of T. & J. Harrison, were not unique in not seeing eye to eye on the question of their relative merits. They first experimented with steam in 1860, ran both in the 1860s and 70s, and finally abandoned sail in 1880.[37] One historian has expressed surprise that the full-rigged sailing ship with a small auxiliary engine, by which speed could be maintained in calms, was not developed as a longer-term commercial proposition, and such vessels have also been proposed and developed experimentally as a means of saving fuel in recent times. The early steamships were, of course, fully rigged. They needed to be in case the engines broke down. And the steamship with auxiliary sails really had quite a run for its money.

But as engines became more reliable and economical and ships grew bigger, it became too expensive to pay for the extra crew and for the extra maintenance required where sail was carried. The prospective economies in coal did not cover the other costs. With a view to competing successfully with the full-powered steam vessel, the American R. B. Forbes in 1845 promoted the *Massachusetts*. This ship ws a medium-sized and fully-rigged sailing vessel with a small auxiliary engine and a retractable propeller.[38] Although the *Massachusetts* did not prove commercially viable, such ships were still being built for the Australian trade in 1871.

In the decade following 1845 2.5 million people sailed for North America from British ports alone, more than three times the number who emigrated from Europe as a whole in the previous decade.[39] For the moment there was room for everyone in the passenger-carrying business across the Atlantic, but the steamer had begun to encroach upon other trades, and the Government now found the steamer indispensable in another field beside the carriage of mail. P & O, a company which had 'invented' Mediterranean cruising as early as 1844 when it offered the novelist W. M. Thackeray a free voyage,[40] had also been used to carry troops on certain occasions from about that time. During the Crimean War of 1854–6, when other companies, like T. & J. Harrison, also hired out ships for trooping, no fewer than 11 of P & O's ships, amounting to one-third of its total tonnage, were used for this purpose.[41] Thereafter the company developed fast. By the end of the decade, it employed 55 regular ocean-going liners on its routes to the East, extended by this time to Hong Kong and Sydney, and shortly to be extended further to Yokohama. Also by this time the Company had established a monopoly in the opium trade from Bombay to China, a position it maintained into the 20th century, and had cornered the market in China silk.[42]

Over these years coaling stations, served by sailing ships, had become more numerous and steamships themselves had been much improved. Cunard ordered its first iron ship, *Persia*, in 1855, though it remained true to the paddle-steamer until the early 1860s. Even so the *Persia*, which could accommodate 250 passengers, made the crossing in 1856 in nine days and claimed the Blue Riband for the fastest passage.

Despite Cunard's caution, the screw propeller had proved its worth in other vessels, like those of the African Steam Ship Company, and John Penn's application in this decade of lignum vitae provided the propeller with a watertight sleeve.[43] Subsequently, the steamship was made even more economical by the use of the two-stage expansion or compound engine with surface condensers.

Samuel Hall had introduced marine surface condensers in the 1830s, thus making it possible for steamers to steam on fresh water even when at sea. In this way the encrustation of brine was eliminated and the boiler's efficiency was greatly improved. Not until about 1860, however, did better manufacturing techniques make these condensers more generally applicable.[44] At the same time the introduction of the compound engine reduced fuel consumption. This revolutionary engine, designed by John Elder and Charles Randolph, was fitted in 1856 in two new ships, *Inca* and *Valparaiso*, which the Pacific Steam Navigation Company added to their fleet on the coal-less Pacific coast of South America. In 1861 P & O fitted a compound engine in their new ship *Mooltan*.

The secret of John Elder's invention, an invention which brought about a revolution in the economics of marine transport, was that he made better use of the steam generated by first admitting it to a small cylinder, where some of its energy was expended, and then by passing it on to a second and larger cylinder where its expansion was completed. By this process a second piston was operated. The result was that much more horsepower was obtained from a pound of steam and therefore from a pound of coal. Elder's invention made the long-haul steamship an economic proposition. The refinements made subsequently to this compound engine were all British.

Alfred Holt, railway engineer and son of a Liverpool cotton broker and banker, had joined the unrelated shipping company of Lamport & Holt in 1851 at a time when the firm was replacing their sailing ships engaged in the Mediterranean trade with small steamships. The following year Holt set himself up as a consulting engineer in India Buildings, a property that his father, George Holt, had financed in 1834. In 1853 Alfred Holt was asked by Thomas Ainsworth of Cleator to advise him on the reconstruction of a small steamer, and subsequently George Holt and Ainsworth bought a steamer, *Dumbarton Youth*, which Alfred managed and provided with a blue funnel. Alfred saw possibilities in the screw propeller and the iron ship and he persuaded his father and Ainsworth to put up capital for *Cleator*, a ship built for the iron ore and coal trades but hired to the French government during the Crimean War. He then laid down a larger ship which he and his brother put into the West Indian trade. In 1862 he produced a more economical version of Elder and Randolph's compound engine and ran it experimentally in *Cleator*. Convinced that the compound engine fitted in an iron ship with a screw propeller had a rôle to play in the Far East, he registered the Ocean Steam Ship Company in 1865 and ordered his first three ships, *Agamemnon, Ajax* and *Achilles*.[45] Thus was born the Blue Funnel Line of Homeric heroes. By 1877 Holt was able to tell the civil engineers that fuel consumption in steamships had been halved in the preceding twenty-five years.[46]

It thus came about that the elegant clippers built in this period were destined for a trade that was already as good as lost. In the year in which Robert Steele of Greenock was building *Ariel* and *Sir Lancelot*, Scott's, next door, were building Holt's new steamships. Each of 2280 tons gross, fitted with a single crank compound tandem engine and with a length about eight times the beam, a higher ratio than had hitherto been considered practicable except by Messrs. Bibby of Liverpool, *Agamemnon, Ajax* and *Achilles* could carry enough coal to travel 8500 miles, more than the distance from South Africa to Melbourne. They achieved a boiler pressure of up to 60 pounds and coal consumption as low as 2.25 pounds per horse-power per hour. The fastest tea clipper, carrying not much more than a quarter of the cargo of Holt's new liners, took 90 days from Foochow to London. The Holt ships managed the journey comfortably in 65 days and operated profitably without any mail contract.[47] In 1867 P & O suffered its first loss, though by this time it was experiencing competition from the heavily subsidised Messageries Impériales of France as well as from Holt.

By the 1860s twin screws were being fitted to some small vessels, and screw propulsion won its final victory over the paddle wheel in 1867. It was in that year that *City of Paris* captured the Blue Riband from *Scotia*,

Fig. 6. THE GROWTH OF STEAM

Steam tonnage as a percentage of total tonnage: vessels entered and cleared in the foreign trade at United Kingdom ports.

	1860	1870	1880	1890	1900
All ships	20.1	41.1	63.4	83.0	91.7
British ships only	30.1	53.2	74.9	90.8	94.7
Foreign ships only	7.2	15.0	35.9	62.3	83.8

(*Source:* C. E. Fayle, *A Short History of the World's Shipping Industry* (1933), London, p. 247.)

the last and finest of the paddle-steamers, which had been built for Cunard in 1861. *City of Paris* was also one of the first steamships to be built of steel, a technical advance almost as significant as the change from wood to iron, for steel was less vulnerable to corrosion and fouling. At this time it was very expensive, but the price fell progressively in the years that followed.

In the 1840s the Continent of Europe was too disordered to offer any rivalry and it was difficult to raise capital there. Moreover, the Continental powers had no considerable navies and no extensive empires so that the new British policy concerning the maintenance of communications, which resulted in steamship subsidisation, had no application on the Continent. In 1847, largely with German financial help, an American company established a steamship service to Bremen via Southampton, but this line lasted only ten years. The professional American shipowner was inclined to boycott steam and it was only under pressure from Congress that E. K. Collins went into steam in 1850, when he put four great steamships on the Atlantic run. It was the Collins Line which started the fashion for the fastest run, the battle for the Blue Riband, and also for decorative vulgarity, but it accumulated ruinous losses in the process and collapsed when Congress withdrew its subsidy.[48] Another seventeen years passed before the Americans started a monthly subsidised mail service across the Pacific to Japan, three years after P & O's mail service had been extended to Yokohama.

It was in 1851 that the French Government decided to subsidise mail contracts and turned to the Messageries Nationales which established the Messageries Maritimes, but it was another six years before the French subsidised a steam packet service on the Atlantic. The Hamburg-America Line was founded in 1856, but the Germans turned to British yards for their ships and were still buying British in 1870. By that time the Dutch were just beginning to build their own deepsea steamships.

On the Continent most progress had been made in Trieste, where the screw propeller had been pioneered as early as 1826. Austrian Lloyd was established in 1836 and started to build a great shipyard in 1853, by which time it was operating 47 steamships in various Mediterranean and Black Sea services. From 1855 Austrian ships were subsidised to meet subsidised competition from the French, but it was not until 1866 that Lloyd Arsenal launched the first steam vessel which could claim to be a native product. No until 1877 did Lloyd Triestino (the former Austrian Lloyd) venture outside the Mediterranean to establish, with government assistance, a service to Bombay.

In Britain company development was fostered by the liberalisation between 1855 and 1862 of company law. The new Acts conferred full legal power and limited liability on all joint-stock companies on their registration and thus offered new ways of mobilising capital. By 1865 the United Kingdom had stopped building enough new sailing ships to replace those lost or sold. By 1868 the tonnage of steam-propelled vessels being built exceeded that of sail tonnage built. In the following year, 1869, a further blow to sail was struck by the opening of the Suez Canal. The Canal offered the steamer a shorter through route to the East, a route which was very shortly studded with coal-bunkering stations at convenient intervals.

By this time London was fast losing its shipbuilding business to the northern ports of Glasgow, Greenock, Newcastle, Sunderland and Liverpool, all of which had coal close at hand. The steamship was clearly indicating its great advantage of size and speed, and already had a better safety record than sail. Plumbing on board was more liberal than it was in the sailing ship, more fresh water was available to crew and passengers, cabins were fully furnished, and saloon accommodation had vastly improved.

By 1870 British shipbuilders and British shipowners were pre-eminent. In steam-equivalent terms the British merchant fleet represented some 45 per cent of the world total, and its carrying power was four times that of the American foreign-going fleet, five times that of the French fleet, and six times that of the German or Italian fleets. Of the ships being built in Britain, three-quarters of the tonnage under construction was steamers, and five-sixths of these ships were being built of iron.[49]

Notes

1. *Collection of the Public General Statutes* (1850), London, pp. 805ff.
2. S. Jones, 'Community and Organisation – Early Seamen's Trade Unionism on the North-East Coast, 1768–1844' (1973), *Maritime History*, Vol. 3, No. 1, p. 42.
3. S. Jones, 'Blood Red Roses: The Supply of Merchant Seamen in the Nineteenth Century' (1972). MM, Vol. 58, No. 4, p. 442; A. P. Ryder, *6th Report of the Science and Art Department*, Appendix I (1858).
4. A. G. Course, *The Merchant Navy: A Social History* (1963), London, pp. 222–5; derived from an unpublished MS by Matthew Swainston.
5. Anon, *Seafarers and Their Ships* (1955), London, pp. 26–7.
6. J. Fingard, *Jack in Port: Sailortowns of Eastern Canada* (1982), Toronto, pp. 79–80.
7. S. Hugill, *Shanties from the Seven Seas* (1961), London, pp. 1–23.
8. F. W. Wallace, *Under Sail in the Last of the Clippers* (1936), Glasgow, pp. 136–9.
9. *Ib.*, p. 136.
10. *Seafarers and Their Ships*, p. 28.
11. E. C. Millington, *Seamen in the Making* (1935), London.
12. *Seafarers and Their Ships*, pp. 70–1.
13. W. Runciman, *Before the Mast – and After* (1924), London, pp. 85–7.
14. R. H. Thornton, *British Shipping* (1939), Cambridge, p. 30.
15. C. E. Fayle, *A Short History of the World's Shipping Industry* (1933), London, pp. 234–5.
16. F. J. A. Breeze. 'The Cost of Distance: Shipping and the Early Australian Economy, 1788–1850' (1975), EHR, 2nd Series, Vol. XXVII, No. 4, p. 597.
17. R. H. Thornton.
18. D. Savill, *Sail to New Zealand* (1986), London, pp. 17, 47 and 69.
19. G. S. Graham, 'The Ascendency of the Sailing Ship 1850–1875' (1973). EHR, Vol. IX, No. 1, pp. 77–8.
20. Thornton, *op. cit.*, pp. 47–9.
21. Runciman, *op. cit.*, p. 104.
22. D. R. MacGregor, *The China Bird* (*Killick Martin & Company*), 2nd edn (1986), London; B. Lubbock, *The China Clippers* (1914), Glasgow, pp. 77–8.
23. D. R. MacGregor, *Merchant Sailing Ships 1850–1875* (1984), London, p. 52.
24. F. C. Lane, 'Tonnages, Medieval and Modern' (1964), EHR, 2nd series, Vol. XVII, No. 1, pp. 213ff; Graham, *op. cit.*, pp. 77–8.
25. L. A. Harper, *The English Navigation Laws* (1964), New York, p. 357.
26. *Fairplay*, 10.5.1984, p. 14.
27. J. R. Harris (ed), *Liverpool & Merseyside* (1967), London, p. 214.
28. W. Girvan, 'The First Mail Service to Australia', *British Shipping*, No. 21.
29. Graham, *op. cit.*, p. 76.
30. D. R. MacGregor, *Merchant Sailing Ships 1850–1875*, p. 113.
31. D. R. MacGregor, *Merchant Sailing Ships 1815–1850* (1984), London, p. 150.
32. *Ib.*, p. 15.

33. Thornton, *op. cit.*, p. 52.
34. D. R. MacGregor, *Merchant Sailing Ships 1850–1875*, p. 16.
35. M. Langley & E. Small, *Port of Plymouth Series: Merchant Shipping* (1988), Devon, p. 1.
36. D. R. MacGregor, *Merchant Sailing Ships 1850–1875*, pp. 19, 72–3 and 87.
37. F. E. Hyde, *Shipping Enterprise and Management, 1830–1939: Harrisons of Liverpool* (1967), Liverpool, pp. xix, 11 and 45.
38. W. S. Lindsay, *History of Merchant Shipping and Ancient Commerce*, Vol. IV (1876), London, pp. 190–4.
39. Thornton, *op. cit.*, p. 29.
40. D. & S. Howarth, *The Story of P & O* (1986), London, p. 47.
41. *Ib.*, p. 92.
42. F. Harcourt, 'The P & O Company: Flagships of Imperialism', in S. Palmer and G. Williams (eds), *Charted and Uncharted Waters: Proceedings of a Conference on the Study of British Maritime History* (1982), London, pp. 15–18.
43. *Fairplay*, 10.5.1984.
44. A. F. L. Deeson, *An Illustrated History of Steamships* (1976), Bourne End, pp. 84–5.
45. F. E. Hyde, *Blue Funnel: A History of Alfred Holt and Company of Liverpool from 1865 to 1914* (1956), Liverpool, pp. 1–19.
46. *Fairplay*, 10.5.1984.
47. Thornton, *op. cit.*, p. 57.
48. *Ib.*, pp. 30–3.
49. Fayle, *op. cit.*, p. 242.

17

Crest of the Wave

(1870–1890)

In 1887 Queen Victoria celebrated her Golden Jubilee – fifty years upon the British throne. Prime Minister Benjamin Disraeli added the jewel of India to her Crown, and British merchant shipping reached its peak, its unique position as a carrier of world trade. Never before and never since has one country so dominated the world economy.

The symbolic cities of the new industrial Britain were Manchester, Birmingham and Glasgow. The total quantities of cotton goods manufactured continued to increase up to World War I, but their share in British exports was shrinking as the share of metal and engineering goods grew. The British economy became dependent on its ability to sell cheap cloth, cheap iron, machinery and coal, and to buy from abroad much of its basic food and many of its raw materials. Fundamental to this exchange was Britain's ability to provide ships to carry the cargoes, not merely from and to Britain, but to and from many other nations. The world of today was born of improvements made in British transport and the concomitant growth of Britain's foreign trade.[1]

A patriotic inhabitant of Birmingham boasted at this time:

> The Arab sheik eats his pilaf with a spoon from Birmingham. The Egyptian pasha takes his cup of sherbert on a Birmingham waiter, lights his harem with candelabra and crystals from Birmingham, and nails to the wood partitions of his yacht knick-knacks from Birmingham on mashy paper also from Birmingham. To feed and defend himself the Redskin uses a gun from Birmingham, the luxurious Hindu orders plate and lamps for table and drawing-room. To the plains of South America, for the swift-riding horsemen, Birmingham despatches spurs, stirrup-leathers and burnished buttons; to the Colonies, for native planters, hatchets for cutting sugar cane, vats and presses. The musing German needs a Birmingham strike-a-light for his eternal pipe, and the emigrant cooks his humble repast in a Birmingham saucepan on a stove from Birmingham. The name of a Birmingham manufacturer is even graven on the tin boxes which conserve his luxuries.[2]

What was true of Birmingham was only less true for Britain's other major cities, and more significant than the items mentioned by the

Birmingham enthusiast were the railway equipment, cloth and ships. In the years to the end of the 19th century over 40 per cent of the £4000 million which the British invested abroad went into railway building alone.[3]

After 1887 the tonnage of the British merchant fleet continued to increase, and for some 75 years, until well after World War II, Britain remained the world's principal maritime nation, but as a maritime carrier of goods and people the British were never again to come near to carrying 60 per cent of the world total of ocean-going trade.

If the statistics are accurate, the British Empire in 1870 possessed on its register 5,947,000 net tons of sailing vessels and a further 1,202,000 net tons of steam ships, Britain itself possessing 4.5 million net tons of sail and 1.1 million tons of steam. To suggest that in lifting power one ton of steam was equivalent to three tons of sail may be an exaggeration in these relatively early days of the steam engine, but it is a widely accepted approximation. On this basis, in 1870 the British Empire possessed a total of 3,184,000 tons of 'steam equivalent' shipping. The other chief maritime countries – the United States (counting only those ships registered for foreign trade), France, Germany, Norway, Sweden, Denmark, Italy and Austria-Hungary – possessed 6,295,000 tons of sail and 554,000 tons of steam, making a total in terms of steam of 2,652,000 tons. Of the combined tonnage, the British Empire possessed 54 per cent.

By 1880 the British Empire sailing fleet had declined to 5,498,000 net tons and the steamship fleet had more than doubled to 2,949,000 tons, making a total in steamship terms of 4,782,000 tons. In this year the other maritime countries possessed 6,380,000 tons of sail plus 1,037,000 tons of steam, making a total in steamship terms of 3,164,000 tons. Of the combined total tonnage in steam terms the British Empire now possessed 60 per cent.

If similar calculations are made for 1890, by which time the British Empire's sailing fleet had declined still further to 4,274,000 tons and the steamship fleet had increased to 5,414,000 tons, while the sailing fleet of other maritime countries had fallen to 4,865,000 tons and the steamship fleet had more than doubled to 2,293,000 tons, then the British Empire possessed 63 per cent in steam terms of the combined tonnage.[4]

By the time another ten years had passed the British share was only 61 per cent and Britain had passed the peak, though it must be said that at this time the British fleet was qualitatively superior to that of the rest of the world and so the difference between 1890 and 1900 was not very marked. Throughout this period maritime Britain was on the crest of its wave. The carriage of goods was becoming progressively cheaper, and

Fig. 7. THE MARITIME NATIONS, 1870–1910 (IN ORDER OF SIZE AS IN 1910)

Net tonnage (million net tons), with sail expressed in steam-equivalent terms (3 tons sail = 1 ton steam), both the world and US figures excluding tonnage enrolled for US rivers and lakes. Prior to 1897 tonnage was given in net tons only. Conversion factors normally used are: (a) sailing vessels, 1 net ton = 1.065 gross tons; (b) steam and motor vessels, 1 net ton = 1.634 gross tons. The results are approximate only; see text for further information on tonnage.

	1870	1880	1890	1900	1910
World	5.9	8.6	12.0	16.6	23.9
UK	2.6	4.0	6.0	7.9	10.8
Germany	0.4	0.5	1.0	1.4	2.6
Japan	—	—	0.1	0.7	1.4
Norway	0.3	0.5	0.7	0.8	1.1
France	0.5	0.5	0.6	0.7	1.0
Italy	0.4	0.4	0.3	0.5	0.8
Spain	na	0.3	0.5	0.7	0.8
Sweden	na	0.2	0.3	0.4	0.7
US foreign trade	0.6	0.5	0.4	0.5	0.6
Netherlands	0.1	0.2	0.2	0.3	0.5
Austria–Hungary	0.1	0.1	0.1	0.3	0.5
UK as % of world	45	46	50	48	46

na = not available

(*Source:* Adapted from *Progress of Merchant Shipping in the United Kingdom and Principal Maritime Countries* (1912), Cmd. 6180.)

the culminating factor in this cheapening process, reinforcing the achievement of steam, was the installation throughout the world of the submarine telegraph. In this business of laying cable Brunel's *Great Eastern* had played a valiant part, and by the time of Queen Victoria's Golden Jubilee the mileage exceeded 100,000 miles. The world-wide telegraphic network revolutionised the techniques of buying and selling and steadied and regulated the flow of trade, thus enabling every moment of a ship's life to be usefully employed.

The reasons for Britain's supreme position at this time have been largely indicated already. Industrialisation, stimulated by both colonisation and trade to the East, had come first to Britain and was firmly based on native sources of power, notably coal. In consequence of industrialisation, together with agricultural and medical advances, and despite extensive emigration to the colonies, population in the United Kingdom was increasing rapidly, doubling in the first half of the 19th century and almost doubling again in the second half. All these factors reacted upon one another. As the United Kingdom population grew and became increasingly urbanised, so the demand grew for food, tobacco and industrial raw materials. Many of these imports could be supplied by the emigrants who were developing the colonies and the former colonial territories and these imports were paid for by the export of manufactured goods and coal. Between 1865 and 1894 British emigrants to the United States alone averaged 119,000 each year and Germany supplied a further 107,000 each year.[5] All this – imports, exports and emigrants – required ships, shipbuilding yards, ship-repairing facilities and the development of ports, and in consequence of these activities industry and trade grew still further. In 1889 Britain built for foreign account alone 182,331 tons of iron or steel merchant vessels.[6]

The British Empire was also greatly enlarged during this period, growing from 4.5 million square miles, with a population of 160 million, in 1850 to 11.5 million square miles, and a population of 420 million, by 1911. Chartered companies established between 1884 and 1889 – the British North Borneo Company, the Royal Niger Company, the Imperial British East Africa Company and the British South Africa Company – all ended in the assumption by the Crown of responsibility for large new territories. Just under 4 million square miles of territory were added to Britain's possessions between 1884 and 1899, and many other places became 'spheres of influence.'

Britain was not alone at this time in carving out for herself new colonies and spheres of influence. France sought new outlets after her defeat in Europe by Germany. The Germans themselves looked abroad in the 1880s, and Russia, Japan, Italy and the United States followed these leads.[7] Each new assumption of territory by these other powers raised a barrier to British exports and sowed the seeds of competition, but the barriers only proved effective, and the seeds grew mainly, after 1890. Until then only the Americans might have proved rivals of any significance but, although in 1870 the total of American steam shipping was no more than 20 per cent short of the British total, less than 200,000 tons was registered for foreign trade. The Americans had committed themselves to a high tariff policy and thus could not afford to buy British iron or steel plate and their own metallurgical industry could not produce such plate as cheaply. By 1890 the American steam tonnage registered for foreign trade had not increased beyond the 1870 figure. In the 1830s some 90 per cent of United States foreign trade had been carried in American vessels; by 1890 this figure had fallen to a mere 9 per cent.[8] By the 1870s, too, the American softwood sailing vessels were at a disadvantage because the British iron sailing vessel had a higher cargo capacity and a more economical sail plan. Wherever speed was unimportant it was a formidable competitor.

The period from 1870 to the outbreak of World War I has been described as the era of the merchant schooner, but the schooner was becoming increasingly a coastal workhorse. A few schooners continued to make a living, albeit an increasingly poor one, in such mundane tasks as lifting bricks, gravel, coal and clay along the coast and into dozens of small ports until World War II.[10] Indeed, Westcotts of Plymouth maintained a fleet of schooners and ketches which were engaged in both trade overseas and trade at home from the 1880s to the 1930s,[11] and F. T. Everard, a company founded in 1880 which prospers still, built 250-ton steel sailing barges until 1927. Everard, however, was also running both steamers and motor ships after 1913[12] and, in the coastal trade overall, the steam coaster romped away after 1880, and the steam collier had by this time replaced the greater number of 'Geordie' brigs.[13]

Just as sail round the coast lingered longest carrying bricks, clay and gravel, so sail deepsea lingered on carrying such bulky commodities as iron, coal, jute, rice, grain, wool and nitrates, all of them expanding trades. The transition from the sailing ship to the iron and steel cargo steamer was not completed until 1885, and even in the 1890s there was a small boom in the building of large steel sailing vessels. In years of depression sailing ships tended to return to favour because they could wait inexpensively for cargo. The early 1870s were years of slump and after 1873 there was a brief but spectacular revival in the building of large sailing ships. Composite shipbuilding was at an end so far as British square-rigged vessels were concerned, and wooden shipbuilding was confined to barquentines, brigantines, schooners and smaller vessels. The new and lofty ships were iron-hulled and fitted with steel masts and rigging and the latest labour-saving machinery which halved the number of seamen carried.[14] Nine of these new vessels, built in 1873–4 and each exceeding 1500 tons, proved to be overmasted. They lost masts on their maiden voyages, perhaps as the result of the injudicious stowage of iron too low in these vessels, which made them too laboursome.[15]

The opening of the Suez Canal had cut the China voyage by 3000 miles and steaming time by 10 or 12 days. By 1875 the China clippers were suffering badly from the competition of steam and round about 1880 most of them went into other trades. On the other hand, rice and jute unlike tea, could not afford steamer freight rates, which were increased by the dues paid for transit through the Canal, and one shipowner could still comment in 1876: 'Steam-boats, even though largely subsidised, especially to India by way of the Cape, have found it impossible to compete successfully with the sailing ships of Messrs Green of Blackwall, Messrs T. and W. Smith, and other private shipowners long engaged in the trade.'[16] Where steam had established itself successfully – as in the case of P & O and other long-distance steamer services – it was still maintained by the aid of sail. For P & O alone 170 sailing vessels carried coal to bunker stations in the Mediterranean, India and the Far East.[17] The few voyages of full-powered steamers to Australia prior to 1875 are of merely historical interest and sail continued to predominate in the trade to the Antipodes into the 1890s.

After 1870 British imports of grain came chiefly from Russia and the United States. The shipment of grain, which became significant in these years, was almost a monopoly of sail and such shipment from the west coast of North America reached its climax in 1882 when 550 sailing vessels, mostly British or American, cleared from Californian and Oregon ports with cargoes amounting to about 1.25 million tons of wheat and barley. Carrying low-grade cargoes, sail remained competitive down to the opening years of the 20th century, especially on long voyages and in the service of ports where loading and discharge were slow and uncertain. Many a once famous member of the tea or wool fleet ended her days carrying wheat from Australia or round the Horn from San Francisco to the United Kingdom, nitrate from Chile to Europe, timber from Quebec across the Atlantic, or coal from Newcastle, New South Wales, to South America.[18]

It was in the Australian trade that the development of a liner service under sail reached its furthest point. James Baines's Black Ball Line, the White Star Line, founded by Messrs Pilkington and Wilson, George Thompson's Aberdeen White Star Line, pioneers of the wool traffic, and Bethel, Gwyn & Company's Line of Australian packets all provided monthly sailings from Great Britain to Australian ports.

The provision of such a service demanded a fleet of more than 12 ships and, since a colonial clipper might cost £30–40,000, few owners could provide this service from their own resources. Some of them chartered vessels to fill the gaps in such service as they could provide themselves. Others, like James Baines, who were shipbrokers as well as shipowners, could arrange for vessels entrusted to them for loading to carry their houseflag and fill the vacant dates. Some managing owners, like Bethel, Gwyn & Company, were shipbrokers first and foremost, and most of the ships which carried their flag were separately owned. Messrs Devitt and Moore, who carried much of the Blackwall tradition into the Australian passenger trade, started as shipbrokers, loading on commission, but later acquired an interest in or bought outright many of the ships on their list. Many successful owners were retired shipmasters who gave much personal supervision to the running of their ships.

Some of the later fleets, however, were large. Duncan Dunbar, for intance, owned 40,000 tons of shipping – perhaps fifty ships. Even as late as the 1890s, after steamers had acquired the bulk of the passenger traffic in these trades and it no longer paid sailing ship owners to arrange regular monthly sailings, the bulk of the wool clippers were regular traders belonging to big fleets.[19]

With well-established firms of shipbrokers now acting as intermediaries between shipowners and shippers, with brokers and agents at most of the leading foreign and colonial ports, and with some big firms of regular shippers, all of them able to communicate with one another by wireless telegraphy, the securing of the cargo became less and less the concern of the shipmaster. Where the sailing-ship master now came into his own was not in the securing of cargo but in its economical stowage, and in the keeping of passengers happy. Captain Enright of *Lightning* was particularly good at pleasing passengers and could thus demand and receive £1000 a year.

The careful stowage of cargo on board could have a beneficial effect on the speed of a clipper ship as well as increasing her cargo capacity. By minute attention to the screwing into her holds of wool cargoes Captain Woodget of the 963-ton *Cutty Sark* gradually increased her cargoes from 4289 to 5304 bales. *Mermerus*, 1651 tons, managed to carry 10,000 bales, the fleeces of a million sheep, worth up to £130,000. Such a cargo would bring her owners £5000 in freight money. Since, to keep his ship running at the end of the days of sail, the sailing-ship master had to economise wherever he could, his responsibilities were greater than those of the steamer captain. It was important to bring out a ship's 'ghosting' qualities in light winds; and iron nerve was needed to 'carry sail' in high winds as Bully Waterman did, or to take short cuts through the reefs and islets of treacherous eastern seas in the manner of Captain Robinson of *Sir Lancelot*.

Although the attempt to combine sail and steam in vessels with auxiliary engines had not proved successful in other areas, it was tried in the emigrant trade to Australia and Joseph Sams has left an account of his voyage in 1874, made aboard the iron ship *Northumberland*, a vessel built in 1871 and owned by Money, Wigram & Sons of Blackwall, London.[20] The ship, which was of 2170 tons and fitted with 300 horse-power engines, was capable of 10.5 knots when sailing. The sails were set whenever the wind was right and the ship's screw would be hoisted up and her telescopic funnel lowered if she was sailing well at anything over 8 knots. The ship was much more comfortable when under sail except in bad weather. In bad weather she was a 'wet' ship, with the sea sweeping across the decks and sometimes entering the accommodation. In the cold South Seas, where the ship kept no lookout and carried no lights and was nearly run down on one occasion, the passengers were much warmer when the engines were working since, as in all sailing ships, there was no other heat.

In bad weather the third-class passengers up forward, of whom there were up to 200, were battened down and had a very uncomfortable time. These passengers were issued with rations and prepared their own food which they took to the 'cookhouse' for cooking. Sams, with 76 others, travelled second-class and was accommodated amidships and dined in the saloon. In the after part of the ship travelled 85 first-class passengers who, according to Sams, lived like 'fighting cocks'. The third-class passengers on this voyage were mainly 'low class' Germans and the second-class mainly middle-class English who supplemented the ship's food by taking a few luxuries of their own, like marmalade. The forecastle was the customary farmyard, for the ship carried two cows, several pigs, and ducks, geese, poultry and sheep 'in abundance'.

Like his fellow-passengers, Sams occupied a berth which measured 2 by 6 feet and the berths were in three tiers with one on the deck and two above. In hot weather Sams slept on deck. He ate at a table for five, and smoking was not allowed between decks. The smoking-room to which he had access was one of the casualties – thoroughly smashed up – in a storm. The officers had no jurisdiction over quarrels between passengers and boredom promoted a fair amount of 'skylarking' and practical joking, though amateur concerts and other simple entertainments were also arranged.

The ship provided some equipment for each 'mess' of six passengers, along with the basic diet, but emigrants, some of whom had received government bounties, were recommended to take, as necessities, a knife, fork, teaspoon, tablespoon, pewter plate, pint mug, hook pot, meat dish, water can, washbasin, scrubbing-brush, flour bag, Bath brick, two sheets of sandpaper, two coarse canvas aprons, a hammer and a bag of mixed nails, a 'gimblet' (for boring small holes), three pounds of 'marine soap', and a long leather strap and buckles with which to secure the 'bed' on deck when twice a week it was exposed to sun and air. In addition, half a gallon of sand was recommended which, after it had been heated up, was used to dry out the berth, after which the sand was swept up for further use. The carriage of two cabbage nets was also suggested, for in these washed clothes could be hung in the rigging to dry. In the early days of emigration a shortage of water had not permitted the washing of clothes on board. If it was like most other ships, the *Northumberland* would have been infested with bed-bugs and rats, though Sams makes no mention of them.

In the 1880s the *Northumberland*, by then owned by Shaw, Savill & Company, reverted to sail only.

Throughout this time further advances were being made in steam. The introduction of Siemen's steel made it possible, after about 1878, to construct boilers that would operate without difficulty or danger at high pressures, and the main stream of development was towards increased thermal efficiencies and consequently lower fuel consumption. The traditional box-like form of Elder's boiler, dating from 1862, was replaced by cylindrical shells and flues designed to withstand the higher pressures and this 'Scotch' boiler became the most popular boiler in merchant ships. Sturdy and reliable and suitable for pressures of up to 80 pounds per square inch, it was, when used in conjunction with the compound engine, ideal for the long-haul cargo steamers which were beginning to displace the last generation of sailing vessels.[21]

In 1881 George Thompson & Company of Aberdeen commissioned from Robert Napier & Sons of Glasgow a vessel of 3616 gross tons for the Australian emigrant trade and this was fitted with Alexander Kirk's triple expansion engine. The steam, generated in a Siemen's steel boiler at the hitherto impracticable pressure of 125 pounds per square inch was to be used now in three stages of expansion, in high pressure, intermediate and low pressure cylinders. The *Aberdeen* was a great success and the prototype of thousands of steamers built over the next half-century. Coal consumption on her maiden voyage proved to be no more than 1.25 pounds per horse-power per hour and, with the development of this engine, the building of ships of 15,000 tons and more became an economic proposition. The launching of this steamer spelled the end for the large sailing vessel. Sail's replacement by steam had taken some twenty years longer than, in the 20th century, did the passenger liner's replacement by air transport. So far as shipbuilding was concerned it proved to be the last nail in London's coffin for the Thames was unsuitable for the building of such large vessels.[22]

William Denny of Dumbarton was the man most responsible for the introduction of steel for the hulls of large merchant ships, and in 1879 he built a steel hull for *Rotomahana* ordered by the Union Steamship Company of New Zealand.[23] Two years later Cunard introduced a steel liner, the *Servia*, into their fleet, and this ship was the first to be provided with electric light. The Royal Mail *Orinoco*, built of steel by Caird of Greenock and launched in 1886, was one of the early passenger liners to be fitted with a triple expansion engine, and Thomas Ismay's White Star Line built two more such ships on Clydebank for the Atlantic trade in 1888. These ships, *City of New York* and *City of Paris*, each of more than 10,000 tons, were also fitted with twin screws and achieved speeds of 19 knots. In ships fitted with triple expansion engines pressures of 192 pounds to the square inch were now being achieved.

Engines and propellers were by this time becoming so safe that auxiliary sails and their rigging were abandoned and steamer design began to move away from that of the sailing ship. The installation of twin screws meant that even the breakdown of some machinery could be faced with equanimity.

In an increasingly prosperous age Thomas Ismay realised that on the Liverpool–New York run, at least, a profit could be made from increasingly luxurious passenger ships. Hitherto, following sailing ship practice, those passengers paying the highest fares had been berthed aft, but it was not particularly comfortable over the screw and the best accommodation in passenger ships now began to be provided amidships.

Money could be made at sea in many ways at this time. James and John Denholm of Glasgow, a company which lives on, established and developed their business in Greenock from 1872 by buying secondhand wooden sailing ships when other owners in sail were going into iron.[24] R. W. Leyland of Liverpool bought his first sailing ship in 1875 and his company owned 21 of them by 1888, but in this case the company did not long survive a belated move into steam.[25] Andrew Weir did not found the Bank Line until 1885 but within a decade he had built up the largest sailing ship fleet under the British flag. It was not until 1896 that he bought his first steamer, but the company survived nevertheless.[26]

The opening of the Suez Canal, the rapid development of the New World and the Antipodes, and the improvement of the marine engine: all these were factors which contributed to the rapid growth of the British tramp-steamer. Its activity increased at a rate of 7 per cent per annum compound from 1870 up to World War I.[27] To fuel it Welsh steamcoal was much in demand and from the 1870s Cardiff shipowners began to purchase tramp steamers on an increasing scale, taking coal out and bringing grain home, either from the Black Sea or from across the Atlantic, in a trade that was to remain for 60 years the backbone of British tramping. The age-old method of raising capital by selling ships in 64 parts was now supplemented, under the terms of the new joint-stock legislation, by establishing one-ship joint stock companies, a number of such companies often being jointly managed. The advantage of this was that it reduced the management's liability to maritime claims in such eventualities as collision, particularly where a cheap ship inflicted costly damage on an expensive one. Evans Thomas, Radcliffe & Company of Cardiff raised capital by way of 64ths to begin with, but subsequently financed each ship on a joint-stock basis, as did many other owners. This company was also one of the first to cut down the rigging of their steamers, thus reducing top hamper and the tendency for the ship to roll.[28]

This was an age of shipping entrepreneurs – Holt, Cayzer, Runciman, Mackay, Swire, Booth, and many more. Some came from families with capital and connections. Others had had experience of the East in the service of the East India company and were aware of opportunities there. Many came from Scotland. Some rose from among the poor. One of the latter was Alfred Jones, later knighted, who went to sea as a cabin boy aged 14 in 1859, employed by the African Steam Ship Company. By 1884 he was senior partner in Elder Dempster & Company, where he transformed a relatively small firm of shipping agents into a great monopoly which controlled not only the shipping of West Africa but many aspects of its trade and economy.[29] Another was Donald Currie, also knighted, the son of a barber who was first employed as a shipping clerk in Greenock. In the 1860s he entered the trade to Calcutta with iron-hulled sailing vessels and, in 1872, transferred to the South African trade with two steamers to become, with the aid of mail contracts and the carriage of troops, official cargoes and sponsored emigrants, architect of the Castle Line. Like his rival Union Company, he adopted the triple expansion engine after 1883, and amalgamated with that company to form Union-Castle in 1900. Currie, like others of his kind, lined his own pockets in ways that were not always ethical. As his biographer has written, his career can stand either as 'the full bloom of individual merit rooted strongly in the soil of laissez-faire' or as 'a monument to the loopholes in the law, the gullibility of shareholders, the power of combinations and the imperial connection.'[30]

Nor were imperial and Scottish connections lacking in the families which built up what has become the Inchcape Group, the Mackays, Mackinnons and others who established the British India Steam Navigation Company and its associated agencies. They took over much of the trade to Bombay, Calcutta and other Indian ports, expanded into the

Arabian Gulf and out to Australia and, when the expeditions of Livingstone, Burton and Speke drew attention to the possibilities on the mainland of East Africa, secured in 1872 a contract for BI to establish a mail service between Aden and Zanzibar.[31]

One of BI's employees was Charles Cayzer who, though born in London of Devonian stock, went to Glasgow, where much of the action was and, with the help of local businessmen like John Muir of Finlay & Company and shipbuilder Alexander Stephen, launched the steamship *Clan Alpine* in 1878. When Sir Charles died in 1916 the Clan Line owned sixty ships, and by the late 1930s the company ran the largest purely cargo-carrying fleet in the world.[32]

In the trade to the Far East the Suez Canal limited the size of ships using the route and the number of passengers did not in any case warrant the building of liners of Atlantic dimensions. When, in 1872, P & O first offered a continuous passage through the Suez Canal to China four new ships of about 3500 tons were used, the first ships of such a size to be used on the route since the *Himalaya* of 1853. The opening of the Canal had affected P & O adversely. With increased competition both passenger receipts and freight rates fell, the latter from about £20 to £3 a ton. The company also lost capital since transhipment, and hence the use of hotels and overland carriage, was no longer necessary. In the first decade of the Canal's operation P & O's freight revenue fell by £700,000 and the eastern trades were overtonnaged for the rest of the century.[33]

Never again enjoying its earlier primacy, P & O was nevertheless gradually restored to a dominating position in the eastern trades by Thomas Sutherland, though P & O and the other companies involved were less innovative than were those operating on the Atlantic. P & O, for example, did not fit twin screws in their ships until after the turn of the century. During the 1870s the ships continued to be lit largely by candlelight and not until 1878, when the *Kaisar-i-Hind* (*Empress of India*), a ship of rather more than 4000 tons, was built, did P & O take their first step towards greater luxury with the introduction of electric bells in cabins, refrigerating machines and swinging oil lamps.[34] In the 1880s further improvements in passenger accommodation were made and music and smoking rooms were introduced. Not until 1881 did P & O build ships of more than 5000 tons. Three years later electric light was installed in the *Chusan*, and in 1887, the year of both Queen Victoria's and the Company's Golden Jubilee, P & O built four steamers each of about 6500 tons.

There were slumps and booms in shipping between 1870 and 1890 as there were in other eras, but overall trade routes in the east were extended and trade increased rapidly. Cunard, White Star, Anchor Line, P & O, Royal Mail, British India and Pacific Steam, which had established rail links across the isthmus of Panama, were all flourishing passenger-line companies which together offered world-wide services. By 1875 Alfred Holt's Blue Funnel Line was operating 14 ships which made passages to China through the Canal, taking 55 days outward bound and 60 days home. Within ten years Blue Funnel had extended its routes to Jeddah and Japan and greatly increased the number of its ports of call.[35] Holt's had also developed two subsidiary shipping ventures, one to pick up North Sumatran tobacco and the other to load rice in Bangkok.[36] Among the original subscribers to Holt's Ocean Steam Ship Company was John Swire, who had established a merchanting firm which acquired the agency for managing Holt's ships. In 1872 John Swire formed the China Navigation Company and began to send small steamers up the Yangtze river, subsequently extending his trading to Australia.[37] In Singapore, Blue Funnel's agents were Walter Mansfield, a firm which gradually extended its business throughout the Malay peninsula and the East Indies. Just as the British India Steam Navigation Company and P & O worked closely and developed together with such agencies as Mackinnon, Mackenzie in India, so Ocean Steam Ship, Butterfield & Swire and Mansfield worked closely and developed together in the Far East.

During these years teas from India and Ceylon began to be preferred in Britain to those from China, a trade in which Harrisons of Liverpool had been a pioneer. T. & J. Harrison had worked outwards from the European coastline, where they had traded in wine and brandy, to establish transoceanic services which extended from New Orleans and the West Indies to China, India and Ceylon. To provide labour in the West Indies they carried 'coolies' from Calcutta in sailing ships.[38]

As early as 1850 some steamship companies had agreed on minimum freight rates. In 1869 a steamship conference was held which involved all the north Atlantic companies, and two years later a similar conference was held by those involved in the South American trade.[39] Keener competition in India inspired in 1875 the first liner conference to regulate the trade to Calcutta and shortly afterwards the companies engaged in this trade established common freight rates and introduced the deferred rebate system to tie shippers to their use of the conference lines. The 1870s were difficult years in shipping, with falling freight rates, severe financial stringency and many bankruptcies and failures. John Samuel Swire was a keen observer of the outcome of the Calcutta conference and chief instigator of the first China conference in 1879 which brought agreement between Ocean Steam Ship, P & O, their French rival Messageries Maritimes, and the Glasgow companies, Glen Line and Castle Line, which had introduced faster and more modern ships to the Far Eastern route.[40] By 1886 the conference system, a target for critics of shipping ever since, had been extended to the trades to Australia and South Africa.

By this time the new steamers had a cargo capacity little, if at all, inferior to that of the big sailing vessels and it was a sign of the times that two of the new P & O steamers were described as cargo vessels pure and simple. In the Mediterranean trade there were some very fine vessels of this type. One of these vessels could carry 4800 tons of cargo exclusive of bunkers on a gross tonnage of only 3052 tons.[41]

In 1879 the *Circassian*, owned by J. & A. Allan of Glasgow, brought the first cargo of mechanically chilled or refrigerated meat to Britain from the United States, a consequence of the commercial development of electricity. Australia's first consignment arrived in London aboard *Strathleven* in 1880. Two years later the Albion Line, which amalgamated in that year with Shaw Savill, to form Shaw, Savill & Albion, brought back the first New Zealand refrigerated cargo aboard its sailing vessel *Dunedin*, and the New Zealand Shipping Company took out to New Zealand frozen fish, poultry and game aboard the sailing ship *Mataura*. In 1884 the first frozen meat from the River Plate arrived in Houlder Brothers' steamship *Meath*. By 1890 South Africa's export trade in fresh fruit had begun.[42] Shaw, Savill & Albion took advantage of a substantial subsidy for direct steam communication between England and New Zealand, but did not abandon its fine fleet of sailing vessels. Its last, the *Hinemoa* of 2283 tons, was not sold until 1913.

The coming to sea of electricity greatly reduced the risk of fire aboard ship, and made possible the use of electric fans as well as electric light in cabins and public places. The introduction of refrigeration also gave to livestock a quite different significance. Not only did it do away with the 'farmyard' on board passenger ships, but it meant that long-distance trade in this field was no longer just a matter of skins, fleeces, horns and tinned meat. The cost of refrigeration proved to be very low, though considerable cargo space had to be sacrificed to provide for the necessary insulation.

After a few experiments with composite ships, the 1880s also witnessed the first specially constructed tank steamer or tanker, the *Glückauf* of 2300 tons, built at Newcastle upon Tyne in 1886 and capable of carrying 2600 tons of oil. At first oil had been carried in 40-gallon barrels – the paraffin cask – but this was not an economic shape because one-third of the vessel's cargo space was lost in stowage. The 4-gallon square tin was then introduced and the tins were popular because they could be put to all kinds of other uses. Steamers to carry them were still being built right up to the First World War. But there were obvious economies to be made if oil could be carried in bulk. At an oil depot like Thameshaven it would take four days to discharge 1700 tons of oil in cans, whereas if carried in bulk discharge would take only six hours. However, bulk carriage raised problems. A rise in temperature causes oil to expand and this expansion must be allowed for in tanker design. To avoid spillage tanks had to be very carefully rivetted and caulked. There was also an ever-present danger of fire and this led to the placing of the engines and boiler aft with a double bulkhead between boiler space and hold.[43] To minimise the use of naked lights the *Glückauf* was fitted with electric light. She was also fitted with a triple expansion engine.

In the long run the tanker was destined to become more important than the passenger liner, but in the shorter term it was the cargo steamer which proved of greater significance. As soon as bunker ports for the loading of coal had become widely established round the world, the cargo steamer began to gain ground over the sailing ship, with tramp steamers competing for such seasonal cargoes as wheat and cotton and offering their services to ports not important enough to warrant a liner service. The tramp steamship owner carrying bulk cargoes, like iron ore, coal and timber needed no elaborate organisation and could operate as a one-ship firm. The chartering of ships had been well organised at the Baltic Coffee House before 1883 but in that year the Baltic Exchange was established as the world's chief centre for the chartering of tramp tonnage and the sale of bulk cargoes, and the tramp owner, who could now reach the shipmaster by electric cable at every port, came into his own. Goods that had been luxuries became thought of as necessities, the standard of living rose in all countries, and it was by courtesy of the cargo steamer that urban civilisation as it is lived today became possible.

The steamer had proved safer and more seaworthy than the sailing ship, and a Royal Commission which examined the loss of British ships of all kinds between 1856 and 1872 concluded that unseaworthiness was no longer a major cause of loss. According to the Royal Commission, 65 per cent of all ship losses were due to drunkenness, ignorance or incompetence on the part of seafarers, a further 30.5 per cent were caused by adverse weather and other uncontrollable forces, and only 4.5 per cent could be attributed to the unseaworthiness of ships or poor equipment.[44] But although the steamer was more seaworthy than the sailing ship, the number of lives lost at sea had increased. Indeed, the number of deaths from drowning and accident had more than doubled in the fifty years prior to 1870, and an agitation began for the suppression of the overloaded or so-called 'coffin' ship by the introduction of a compulsory load line.

Between 1872 and 1884 an average of 3000 seamen a year lost their lives from drowning and accidents. In 1865 2259 seafarers also died from disease, the principal killers being cholera, dysentery, yellow fever and other unspecified 'fevers'.[45] These figures exclude those who came ashore to die, and many seafarers serving in foreign-going ships were sick men by the time they were 40. Scurvy was still to be met with in merchant ships and even increased in the decade after 1873.[46]

In 1870 the number of seafarers serving in the British merchant marine is estimated to have been rather more than 200,000.[47] In 1891 the number given by the quinquennial census was 173,000, and of these 21,000 were lascars and 24,000 foreigners.[48] These latter figures exclude seafarers on leave. If we put such figures together with the mortality figures the annual death-rate per 1000 seafarers at risk would appear to have been about 11 in consequence of drowning and accidents, and above 23 if all causes are taken into account. Such figures are more than 18 times what they are a century later.

Not all shipowners, of course, ran 'coffin' ships. In the year in which Samuel Plimsoll was uttering his wildest denunciations of them, Cunard could claim that they had not lost a life by mishap in thirty-four years of North Atlantic crossings,[49] and in 1873, when Plimsoll's influential book *Our Seamen* was published, the Aberdeen White Star Line named its fine new wool clipper *Samuel Plimsoll* in his honour and installed his sculptured portrait as the figurehead. Indeed, it was a shipowner on Tyneside, James Hall, who was the instigator of the legal suppression of overloaded ships, and it was Hall who, in 1870, inspired Plimsoll to take up the seaman's cause.[50]

Plimsoll, who made money out of carrying coal to London by rail, had become a Radical member of Parliament in 1868, and in 1870 he moved a resolution in general terms for legislation to diminish shipping losses demanding, in particular, a compulsory loadline and a survey for all ships. The Merchant Shipping Act of 1871 proposed that a scale showing the draught of water should be marked on the stem and stern of every ship and in 1872 the Board of Trade was given statutory powers to make and enforce detention orders in cases of overloading or improper loading.

One consequence of this legislation seems to have been the imprisonment between 1870 and 1872 of 2287 seamen for periods ranging from 14 days to 3 months for reporting their ships unseaworthy and demanding Board of Trade surveys.[51] However, the publication of *Our Seamen* had its effect and in 1876 a new Merchant Shipping Act made it compulsory for the owner of every foreign-going British ship to mark upon her sides a maximum loadline. Unfortunately, this legislation was not particularly effective because it was left to the shipowner or his agent to decide the point where the loadline was marked.

In 1882 Lloyd's Register of Shipping published a series of reserve buoyancy tables which helped to establish the loadline on a scientific basis and in 1890, subject to approval by the Board of Trade, the two classification societies (Lloyd's Register had been incorporated in 1870, and in 1890 the British Corporation for the Survey and Registry of Shipping was founded in Glasgow) were entrusted with the task of assigning load lines to British ships.[52] Problems of ships carrying excessive deckloads, however, were to remain into the early years of the 20th century.

Good crews were still not easy to come by. In giving evidence to the

Fig. 8. THE MERCHANT SEAMAN'S 'PRODUCTIVITY', 1550–1987

These figures are obtained by dividing total British tonnage by the number of seafarers in the Merchant Navy; tonnage before 1776 is assumed to be the lower of the two figures given in *Fig. 6*. These are average figures (a crew of 25 might work a 200,000-ton tanker). In the sense defined, the merchant seaman's productivity has increased about 1000-fold since Elizabethan times.

YEAR	TONS PER SEAFARER		IN 16TH-CENTURY EQUIVALENTS
	SAIL	STEAM/OIL EQUIVALENT	
1550	1.7	0.5	1
1700	6.5	2.2	4
1800	15.5	5.2	10
1850	—	7.5	15
1870	—	15.7	31
1890	—	40.0	80
1910	—	61.6	123
1938	—	111.2	222
1951	—	121.2	242
1969	—	243.3	487
1979	—	388.2	776
1987	—	467.0	934

Royal Commission on Unseaworthy Ships in 1874, Mr Lamport of Lamport & Holt said even of steamships: 'My firm and many of the large steamship owners in Liverpool are compelled to send their ships into the river and lie at anchor for twenty-four hours to let the crews become sober'. In the large sailing ships a crew might well desert in San Francisco and the master then had to seek a 'hard case' crew from the crimps. Such a crew was not easily managed, not even by a mate who, when a sailor put inedible food before him and said, 'Look at this', replied by planting his fist between the sailor's eyes and saying, 'Look at that.'[53] Competition was forcing many sailing ship owners to reduce the number of crew. In 1867, for example, the 2131-ton *Sobraon*, a three-masted, full-rigged ship, carried a crew of 69. Still with the same rig the ship carried a crew of 59 in 1890.[54] Working such a vessel was extremely hazardous and has been described by one who experienced it in the following manner:

> Assume that a stout pole is thrust out of a fourteenth floor window for a length of 30 feet. The pole has an iron rod running along the top of it and a loose wire suspended below it. From the street level, without using the elevator, a man climbs the stairs to the fourteenth floor and creeps out on the spar, his feet on the loose wire rope, his hands on the iron rod.... But instead of the security of the flight of stairs, the climbing is done up a series of iron rods or ropes stretched across wire ropes in the form of a ladder. The higher up one travels, the ladder narrows and becomes almost perpendicular. Envisage the conditions on a dark night, the wind blowing, the rain driving. And when one finally reaches the yard one finds a great sail thrashing and ballooning over the spar, threatening to knock you off.

According to this seafarer, boys were expendable, for a master was not likely to turn round if a boy fell overboard. Such British sailing ships were also invariably bad feeders.[55]

Along with government efforts to improve the lot of the seaman came the seamen's efforts to improve their own lot. Other port unions had come and gone since the days of the Penny Union of 1851, and in 1879 in Sunderland the North of England Sailors' and Sea-going Firemen's Friendly Association or Sunderland Seamen's Union was formed. By this time firemen in steamships comprised nearly half the workforce.

Among the members of the new union was James Havelock Wilson who, on going to sea at an early age, had had experience of the activities of crimps in San Francisco and had come into contact with a seamen's union on the Australian coast. By the time he was 20 Wilson had become the driving spirit of the Sunderland Seamen's Union and, when he married and came ashore to run a restaurant, he established branches of the union in other northern ports. In 1887 he formed the national Amalgamated

Sailors' & Firemen's Union of Great Britain and Ireland and by 1889, no doubt with some exaggeration, could claim 65,000 members and branches in 60 ports.[56]

At this time the British able-seaman earned from 45–55s a month and the fireman from 50–60s a month. For most seamen the working week was one of 84 hours, accommodation on board ship was poor and, despite a growing number of Sailors' Homes, the crimps remained active. Joseph Chamberlain, as President of the Board of Trade, abolished the sailor's 'advance note' in 1880 but its abolition proved impracticable. Sams records in this period that aboard the *Northumberland*, as in most deepsea ships, the sailors 'burned the dead horse',[57] that is to say they celebrated, when they had worked off their advance of wages and were working for pay once more.

In P & O and other companies trading in the Far East the officers continued to work happily with lascar crews, as they still did a century later. This was largely because they did not have to communicate with these seafarers, for orders were given through a 'serang' or petty officer who spoke a little English. For the shipowner, lascars were cheap labour. At first, many engine-room ratings in such ships were East African negroes known as 'Seedies', but these too became lascars, working under a petty officer known as a 'tindal'. A main line steamer of 1875 was likely to carry 35 coal trimmers and firemen plus 2 serangs and 2 tindals, 3 greasers, a lamptrimmer, a native cook and a general servant. These would be supervised by 5 British engineer officers, though the number of engineer officers was tending to increase.[58]

P & O ships, in particular, were generously officered. The early ships of under 2000 tons carried on deck a chief, second, third, fourth and fifth officer and to these were added a supernumerary second officer for the 4000-ton ships of the 1870s.[59] By the 1880s the three-watch system still applicable a century later had become standard practice in P & O.

A shipmaster in this trade earned £25 a month and might still make something more by trading on his own account, but the days of the maritime 'nabob' who worked for the East India Company were long since over. In a steamer trading to the Black Sea a master earned £20 a month, and in a foreign-going sailing ship £15 a month.[60] For victualling purposes the master was allowed 3s a day for officers and 1s 9d for crew.

Since sufficient numbers of seafarers were hard to come by hulks for the training of ratings began to proliferate at this time, some of them being established for delinquent youngsters. Between 1856 and 1895 19 such training vessels were established, 3 as 'reformatory' ships to which boys were sent by the order of magistrates, 11 as 'industrial' training ships and 5 more for destitute boys and poor volunteers. But such training ships supplied no more than 1000 boys a year for the sea at a time when more than 10,000 new ratings were required. Since seafaring was uncongenial, the quality of seafarers was low. According to Sams, aboard the *Northumberland* the officers led the way up the rigging to reef the sails, and one sailor caught smoking between decks, against the ship's rules, had a fight with the second mate when he was told to stop.[61] Yet the *Northumberland* seems to have been a well-run and well-manned ship. Her crew consisted of 38 seamen, plus a carpenter, baker, butcher and poultryman, and she carried several midshipmen, apart from the officers. Her sailors are likely to have been above average.

On the crest of the shipping wave many shipowners were making great personal fortunes and establishing dynasties that would still be ruling British shipping a century later. However, they were spending little or nothing on the training or welfare of the men who manned their ships, and they fought bitterly against the new seafarers' union.

Notes

1. P. Mathias, *The First Industrial Nation: An Economic History of Britain 1700–1914*, 2nd edn (1969), London, p. 231.
2. G. S. Graham, *The Politics of Naval Supremacy* (1965), Cambridge, p. 100, from V. Bernard, *L'Angleterre et L'Imperialisme* (1900), Paris, pp. 74–5.
3. Mathias, *op. cit.*, p. 232.
4. Estimated from C. E. Fayle, *A Short History of the World's Shipping Industry* (1933), London, p. 246.
5. S. G. Sturmey, *British Shipping and World Competition* (1962), London, p. 17.
6. L. A. Harper, *The English Navigation Laws* (1964), New York, p. 363.
7. M. W. Thomas (ed), *A Survey of English Economic History*, 3rd edn (1967), pp. 447–9.
8. R. H. Thornton, *British Shipping* (1939), Cambridge, p. 65.
9. Fayle, *op. cit.*, p. 242.
10. B. Greenhill, *The Merchant Schooners* (1988), London, p. 25; p. 254.
11. M. Langley & E. Small, *Port of Plymouth Series: Merchant Shipping* (1988), Devon, p. 2.
12. *Port of London* (1980), 4th edn.
13. Fayle, *op. cit.*, p. 243.
14. Graham, *op. cit.*, p. 85.
15. D. R. MacGregor, *Merchant Sailing Ships 1850–1875* (1984), London, pp. 167 and 176.
16. Fayle, *op. cit.*, p. 244.
17. *Ib.*, p. 244.
18. *Ib.*, pp. 245–6.
19. *Ib.*, pp. 254–5.

20. S. Braydon & R. Songhurst (eds), *The Diary of Joseph Sams* (1982), London.
21. A. F. L. Deeson, *An Illustrated History of Steamships* (1976), Bourne End, p. 101.
22. *Ib.*, p. 106.
23. *Ib.*, p. 98.
24. J. R. Hume & M. S. Moss, *A Bed of Nails: The History of P. MacCallum & Sons Ltd of Greenock 1781–1981* (1981), Greenock, p. 42.
25. D. Walker, *Champion of Sail* (1986), London.
26. *Telegraph*, August 1988.
27. H. Gripaios, *Tramp Shipping* (1959), London.
28. R. Craig, 'Trade and Shipping in South Wales – The Radcliffe Company 1882–1921', in C. Baber & L. J. Williams (eds), *Modern South Wales: Essays in Economic History* (1986), Cardiff, pp. 171–86.
29. P. N. Davies, *Sir Alfred Jones: Shipping Entrepreneur Par Excellence* (1978), London.
30. A. Porter, *Victorian Shipping, Business and Imperial Policy. Donald Currie, the Castle Line and Southern Africa* (1986), Woodbridge, Suffolk.
31. S. Jones, *Trade and Shipping: Lord Inchcape 1852–1932* (1989), Manchester; J. F. Munro, 'Scottish Overseas Enterprise & the Lure of London. The Mackinnon Shipping Group, 1847–1893' (1988), *Scottish Economic & Social History*, Vol. VIII, pp. 73–87.
32. N. L. Middlemiss, *Gathering of the Clans: History of the Clan Line Steamers Ltd* (1988), Newcastle upon Tyne.
33. P. Padfield, *Beneath the House Flag of the P & O* (1981), London, pp. 47–8; S. Rabson & K. O'Donoghue, *P & O: A Fleet History* (1988), Kendal, p. 79.
34. Padfield, *op. cit.*, p. 51.
35. F. E. Hyde, *Blue Funnel: A History of Alfred Holt and Company of Liverpool from 1865 to 1914* (1956), Liverpool, p. 27.
36. *Ib.*, p. 50.
37. S. Marriner & F. E. Hyde, *The Senior: John Samuel Swire 1825–98. Management in the Far Eastern Shipping Trades* (1967), Liverpool, pp. 22 ff.
38. F. E. Hyde, *Shipping Enterprise and Management, 1830–1939. Harrisons of Liverpool* (1967), pp. 33–40.
39. B. M. Deakin (in collaboration with T. Seward), *Shipping Conferences: A Study of their Origins, Development and Economic Practices* (1973), Cambridge.
40. Hyde (1956) *op. cit.*, p. 54; Marriner & Hyde (1967), *op. cit.*, pp. 135–43.
41. Fayle, *op. cit.*, p. 243.
42. PLA Monthly, March 1964; A. W. Kirkaldy, *British Shipping* (1914), London, p. 115.
43. Kirkaldy, *op. cit.*, pp. 120–5.
44. Thornton, *op. cit.*, p. 69.
45. A. G. Course, *The Merchant Navy: A Social History* (1963), London, p. 195.
46. RSA Journal, Vol. XXX (1882).
47. Course, *op. cit.*, p. 258; V. C. Burton, 'Counting Seafarers: The Published Records of the Registry of British Seamen, 1849–1913' (1985), MM, Vol. 71, pp. 305–19.
48. Fayle, *op. cit.*, p. 289; Quinquennial Census, 1891.
49. Thornton, *op. cit.*, p. 72.
50. Course, *op. cit.*, p. 230.
51. *Ib.*, p. 231.
52. Fayle, *op. cit.*, p. 284.
53. G. V. Clark, *The Last of the Whaling Captains* (1987), Glasgow.
54. The late Captain A. G. Course in correspondence with the author.

55. F. W. Wallace, *Under Sail in the Last of the Clippers* (1936, reprinted 1986), Glasgow, p. 78; p. 15.
56. *The Story of the Seamen*, National Union of Seamen (1964), pp. 5–8.
57. Brandon & Songhurst, *op. cit.*, p. 34.
58. Padfield, *op. cit.*, p. 117.
59. *Ib.*, p. 97.
60. Course, *op. cit.*, p. 234.
61. Brandon & Songhurst, *op. cit.*, p. 37.

III

THE DECLINE OF BRITISH SHIPPING

1890–1988

18

The End of an Era
(1890–1914)

From 1850 to 1914 shipping companies based in the United Kingdom alone operated one-half or very nearly one-half of the world's carrying capacity at sea. But if Queen Victoria's Golden Jubilee in 1887 marked high water, the tide had clearly turned by the dawn of the 20th century. Nevertheless, United Kingdom tonnage continued to increase and at the outbreak of the First World War British ships carried 92 per cent of the British Empire's trade, 63 per cent of that between the Empire and foreign countries, and 30 per cent of the trade between countries outside the Empire.[1]

The value of United Kingdom trade, exclusive of shipments of bullion, which had been estimated at £260 million in 1855, had risen by 1912 to £1232 million – a six-fold increase if allowance is made for the fall in prices over this period. Over the same time-span the tonnage of ships entered and cleared in British ports had increased from 18.5 million tons to 139 million tons, a seven-fold increase.[2] World trade as a whole had quadrupled in these same years[3] and such trade was no longer a matter of a few specialised products, most of them luxuries. To pay for the Argentine beef which they ate the British were supplying railway lines and rolling stock. To pay for the Assam tea which they drank they were now exporting cotton shirts to the sub-continent which had once supplied expensive cotton goods itself.

Up to the middle 1880s textiles still accounted for nearly half the value of exports, though cotton had largely usurped the place once held by wool. After 1885 the emphasis in exports shifted significantly to engineering and other capital goods and to coal. By 1913 British exports of coal, which had been 11 million tons in 1870, had grown to 77 million tons, representing 75 per cent of exports by weight and 10 per cent by value. Of this massive total 21 million tons was coal shipped for the use of steamers.[4]

Imports were increasingly dominated by foodstuffs. Imports of frozen mutton, a mere 400 carcases in 1880, had grown to 3.9 million carcases by 1893, 1.9 million coming from New Zealand, 1.4 from Argentina and 0.6 million from Australia.[5] By 1910 more than 4 million carcases of beef were being imported, together with 13 million carcases of sheep and lambs. Rabbits, dairy produce and fruit had all been added to these refrigerated cargoes, the first load of bananas coming from Jamaica in 1896. By 1914 over 200 steamers were operating in the refrigerated trade alone and the food thus imported represented 20 pounds per head of the United Kingdom population per year.[6] Exports of cocoa from Gambia rose from 536 tons in 1900 to 53,888 tons in 1914.[7] Since the coming of steam the national income had risen ten-fold and the per capita income of those living in the United Kingdom had increased more than four-fold.[8]

As the sailing ship was superseded, a process which was virtually completed by 1914, the number of ships began to fall. The peak for the United Kingdom for ships of all sizes was reached in 1866 when there were 26,140 sailing vessels totalling 4,904,000 net tons and 2831 steamers totalling 876,000 net tons, making a total of 28,971 vessels. By 1914 the number of sailing vessels had dropped dramatically, to 8203 vessels totalling 865,000 tons, while the number of steamships had risen to 12,862 – of which number 1300 were liners and 7000 tramps[9] – totalling 19,145,000 gross tons. Despite the enormous increase in trade in the half century prior to World War I, the number of vessels carrying it had fallen by more than 20 per cent.[10] In 1870 the carrying power of steam in the British fleet had been only two-thirds that of sail. By 1890 it was five times that of sail. And while only 20 per cent of the tonnage entered and cleared in the foreign trade at United Kingdom ports was steam powered in 1860, over 90 per cent was in this category by 1900. In 1860 a vessel over 1000 tons was considered large. By 1914 Atlantic passenger liners exceeding 40,000 tons were being built.

Freight rates had fallen enormously in consequence of the increase in shipping's efficiency and a fall in shipbuilding costs. Tea which the clippers of the 1870s had brought home for £6 a ton was being carried for £2 10s a ton by the outbreak of the First World War, and in the same period the cost of sending a ton of cotton goods from Lancashire to Shanghai had fallen from £6 to £2. Atlantic grain freights fell from 8s 3d a quarter in 1856 to 2s 3d in 1900, and Minnesota wheat could come to Liverpool for only about 5s a ton more than could Yorkshire wheat. The cost of importing wheat, rice and sugar was less than a farthing a pound.[11] For twice the capital cost of a typical clipper of the 1860s a 10-knot cargo steamer could, by 1900, carry four times as much cargo and cover three times the mileage in a year's work. It was clearly a sound economic proposition to operate steamers even though freight rates had fallen to one-third or less of what they had been thirty years earlier.

The steamship had changed the quality of life and new and increased trading opportunities were now available throughout the world. More frequent contact between peoples resulted in an enlargement and diffusion of ideas and the growth of new requirements. The steamship also greatly accelerated the peopling of the world's undeveloped territories and an annual trickle of 32,000 emigrants from Europe to the United States in the 1830s grew to a flood of more than 1,000,000 in the decade before World War I.[12] The general approach of shipowners operating in the north Atlantic was that the emigrant trade should pay for the running of the ship and that anything earned from first and second class passengers was a bonus. The emigrant fare was about £5 10s.[13]

From this deepsea transport revolution the United States, concerned with the absorption of these millions of new citizens and with the development of a sub-continent, had opted out. When the First World War broke out the United States might still claim to be second among maritime nations in terms of tonnage operated but this was in consequence of the continued growth of its river and lake trade, particularly on the Great Lakes. In American domestic trade even sail continued to grow, reaching a peak of 2,450,405 tons in 1907, not far short of twice the 1850 figure of 1,418,550 tons. In the same period in the domestic trade steam had multiplied ninefold, from 481,005 tons in 1850 to 4,343,384 tons in 1910. By contrast, sail in US foreign trade had declined from 1,540,709 tons to 234,848 tons between these same dates. In steam-equivalent terms the United States operated 22 per cent of total world tonnage of 29 million tons in 1910, a figure which compared with the United Kingdom's 37 per cent. But if US domestic tonnage is removed from the figures, the United Kingdom operated 46 per cent of the world total and the United States only 2.5 per cent.

By 1890 the territorial claims that had been staked in Africa and elsewhere by the maritime powers were being backed up by the establishment of national shipping lines. Although still a long way behind, Germany had become Britain's closest rival in the maritime field. After the unification of the country in the 1870s the German economy grew rapidly to maturity and its shipping development was stimulated by European emigration across the Atlantic. The new Germany commanded the continental hinterland and both Crown and Parliament fostered and encouraged shipping. Through the establishment of preferential railway rates trade was diverted to German ships, and by their management of control stations German shipping companies were able to intimidate emigrants and prevent them from sailing in British ships.[14] In the thirty years that followed 1873 German exports increased at a more rapid rate than did those of Britain.

The Germans competed particularly in the provision of high quality liner tonnage and established a reputation for careful organisation, impeccable discipline and punctilious service. North German Lloyd had been founded as early as 1857, but it was only after J. G. Lohmann became chairman in 1877 that the line established itself as a serious competitor in the Atlantic passenger trade. An express service was inaugurated by the 16-knot *Elbe* in 1880, and in 1886 the German government began to subsidise mail lines. German competition for mail tenders cut the cost of transatlantic postage. A group of Hamburg merchants founded the Hamburg South America Line in 1871 and by 1913 it was a serious rival in its field and possessor of 57 vessels.[15] In 1888 Albert Ballin, son of a small Hamburg broker, joined the board of the Hamburg America Line and under his management the company grew in twelve years to a worldwide organisation possessing the largest fleet of ships in the world under one flag. Until 1880 the German-operated steamships had been built in Britain but Bismarck instigated the Imperial Far East Mail Line, which was a commercial failure in its first ten years, and decreed that it should be operated only with German-built ships.[16]

At his grandmother Queen Victoria's invitation, Kaiser Wilhelm II of Germany took part in her Golden Jubilee celebrations and attended her review of the fleet at Spithead. What impressed him most on that occasion was not the assembled warships but White Star's 9000-ton *Teutonic,* then the largest ship afloat. After his return home, British maritime supremacy was never quite the same. The Hamburg America Line and North German Lloyd were both receptive to the Kaiser's suggestion that they should build bigger and faster passenger ships and Albert Ballin was the impresario.[17] Only a few years after its unification Germany had become the second maritime nation, and by 1910 its 'steam equivalent' fleet was 2,565,679 net tons, as compared with the United Kingdom's 10,814,034 net tons, and amounted to 11 per cent of the world total. By 1914 Germany had built the biggest ships in the world before the *Queen Mary*.

Japan's meteoric rise as a maritime nation was a feature of the opening years of the 20th century. From 1888 both building and operating subsidies were offered to Japanese shipping by the government, and the industry was further stimulated by Japanese emigration to the United States. Virtually without deepsea ships of any description in 1880, the date at which Japan's industrial revolution began, Japan had become the third maritime power by 1910, with 1,371,805 'steam-equivalent' tons – half as much ocean-going tonnage as Germany and twice as much as the United States.

Unique among the maritime nations, Norway maintained a merchant marine far in excess of its own foreign trade requirements, thus becoming the first disinterested professional carrier. Proportionately, sail remained significant for longer than it did in the nations so far considered, sail tonnage peaking in about 1890, some twenty years after it had peaked in Britain. In 1910 Norway was operating a fleet under sail which totalled 628,287 net tons and a steamship fleet totalling 897,440 tons, making a steam-equivalent total of 1,106,869 tons. These figures were close to those of France, where the 1910 figures were 636,081 net tons of sail, 815,567 net tons of steam, and a total fleet in steam-equivalent terms of 1,027,594 tons.

Italy, Spain, Sweden, the United States (in foreign trade) and the Netherlands all had fleets exceeding 500,000 steam-equivalent tons and Austria-Hungary operated a fleet not far short of this figure. The development of Italian shipping, like that of Germany, was helped by emigration. From 1895 to 1914 157,000 Italians a year emigrated to the United States and even more went to South America. Immigration into Argentina and Brazil rose from 109,000 in 1903 to 503,000 in 1912. Italian shipping companies received preferences in the carriage of Italian emigrants.

Direct subsidies to shipping unlinked to postal subsidies had now become common. Initiated by France in 1881, they were also given in subsequent years by Italy, Japan and Austria-Hungary. In France and Italy these subsidies merely prolonged the use of sail, but in the very different conditions in Japan they proved true 'infant-industry' or nurturing subsidies which stimulated the growth of a modern merchant navy.[18] Other incentives were also given to their shipping companies by some countries. France, the United States and Russia were among those which reserved their coastal trades to their own vessels, even extending the definition of 'coastal' to include traffic to distant possessions, as they do still. Voyages from Marseilles to Saigon and from New York to Honolulu were thus regarded by France and the United States respectively as coastal voyages reserved to their own shipping.

In Britain, on the other hand, there was little element of subsidy by this time,[19] the coastal trade was open to anyone, and by 1914 the only British ships receiving any kind of assistance were Cunard's crack liners *Mauretania* and *Lusitania* – the former described by Rudyard Kipling as a 'monstrous nine-decked city' gone 'to sea' – and Elder & Fyffe's West Indian fruit ships which had been granted a subsidy in 1897 in the hope of relieving distress caused by the collapse of the market for cane sugar.[20]

If subsidies now helped Britain's rivals rather than Britain, a long-standing British commercial practice was also tending to boomerang against her as the trade of other nations developed. If a country's exports are sent c.i.f., that is with the cost of insurance and freight paid by the shipper, it saves the shipowner the expense and difficulty of collecting his freight costs on exports at the delivery end of his run. Contrariwise, if goods to be imported are delivered f.o.b. – free on board – he can collect payment for freight at home in his native currency. While Britain remained the world's major exporter of industrial goods and the world's major importer of raw materials and food the desire of importers to purchase f.o.b. and exporters to sell c.i.f. favoured the employment of British ships. As other countries adopted this same practice, their own ships came to be thus favoured.[21]

By the outbreak of the First World War British shipping's pre-eminence had been challenged in the shorter trades. Japan and many countries in Europe were developing their own fleets; and British tramp owners were beginning to feel the effects of Greek and Scandinavian competition, where secondhand tonnage and low-wage labour were often employed. In 1913 about 85 per cent of British coal exports went to Europe and the Mediterranean and less than 40 per cent of this total was carried in British ships. The other 15 per cent went mainly to South America, where German competition was becoming increasingly fierce. In the liner trades on this route Royal Mail had been outpriced by her more vigorous rival.[22] Of the shipping tonnages entered and cleared in British ports 79 per cent was British in 1870 but by 1911 this had reduced to 56 per cent, though the total tonnages had increased nearly six-fold.[23] In shipbuilding Britain remained supreme up to 1914, producing almost 60 per cent of the total world production of ships.[24]

In these years before World War I it was being suggested, in France and the United States as well as in Germany, that rail and ship traffic might be integrated, a notion that the British engineer Brunel had had years earlier. In 1873 the Pennsylvania Railroad board conceived a plan for projecting a service across the Atlantic by launching the American Line. J. Pierpont Morgan amalgamated various railways in Pennsylvania and planned preferential tariffs for his ships. By 1886 he controlled the American Line, the British Inman Line and the Belgian Red Star Line. By 1900 he also controlled the British Leyland and National Lines and planned to buy the Dutch-owned Holland America Line together with Cunard.[25] By 1912 Pierpont Morgan's International Mercantile Marine Company (IMM) comprised the White Star, American, Red Star, Atlantic Transport, Leyland and Dominion Lines, a fleet of 126 ships totalling

1,000,140 tons gross. But although 1912 was a boom year for shipping and 122 different British companies paid dividends that year which averaged 7 per cent,[26] IMM paid no dividend at all. Competition for the Blue Riband on the Atlantic crossing was proving costly, and liner companies were sensitive to the ratecutting which had been taking place in the emigrant traffic.

By this time some other combinations of shipping companies had been achieved, cartels were being established in the industry, and the conference system devised to fix freight rates had been developed further.

The Royal Mail Company headed a combination which included the Pacific Steam Navigation Company, Lamport & Holt, Forwood, Glen Line, Shire, Elder Dempster, Nelson, Union Castle, the British and African Steam Navigation Company, the African Steam Ship Company, the Elder Line and the Imperial Direct West India Mail Service[27] – over 1,400,000 tons in all. By 1914 Cunard included Anchor Line, the Brocklebank Line and the Thomson Line, and P&O had acquired BI, the Australasian United Steam Navigation Company and the Blue Anchor Line.

The Calcutta, China, South African and Australian trades were covered already by the conference system and it was extended before World War I to West Africa and North Brazil (1894), to the River Plate and South Brazil (1896) and to the west coast of South America (1904). By this time, too, the Liverpool Steam Ship Owners' Association, established in 1858, and the Chamber of Shipping of the United Kingdom, which had developed from the General Shipowners' Society and been established in its own right in 1878, were together able to speak for the British shipping industry as a whole, acting jointly through the Shipowners' Parliamentary Committee; but they had to meet criticism of the deferred rebates which were commonly offered to regular customers by the shipping conferences. Shippers who shipped exclusively in conference ships for, say, a six-month period were credited with a refund of 5 or 10 per cent repayable six months later if they remained faithful to the conference lines. Critics claimed that the conferences were monopolistic but shipowners argued that they gave regular and efficient service and offered stability to the shipper. They also pointed out that the monopoly of the conference lines was never complete since it could always be threatened by outside ships and a large proportion of homeward traffic was always free of conference regulation. In 1909 a Royal Commission on Shipping Rings was established but it concluded that there was little or no evidence of unfair burdens on shippers arising from the system.

It was during this period that the tramp steamer, which could always prove a threat to the liners in the conference systems if their profits became excessive, evolved as the cheapest commercial vehicle the world had ever known. As late as 1891 there were seventy-seven sailing vessels in Sydney alone loading wool for the London market, and well into the 1890s the big iron wool clippers and two or three of the later China clippers – *Thermopylae* and *Cutty Sark,* for example – continued to race home from the Australian ports. But by the end of the decade the volume of tramp steamer tonnage had outstripped that of the steam liner fleets and the last stronghold of sail was being increasingly invaded. By 1914 tramp steamers comprised 60 per cent of Britain's tonnage and two-thirds of Britain's ocean-going steamers were tramps.

Of the total United Kingdom tonnage about 40 per cent was employed in the cross-trades – that is, in trade carried on between countries abroad – and 75 per cent of such trade was carried in tramp steamers.[28] Despite the importance of the cross-trades, however, the average British tramp came home fairly frequently because of Britain's own large import and export trade. This gave the British operator some advantage over his competitors because in the United Kingdom repairs could be arranged conveniently and crews changed. The British operator also enjoyed the advantages of the London charter market where further work could be arranged. With large British exports of coal and large imports of grain, sugar, cotton and mineral ores, tramping in this free trade era was pre-eminently a British institution.

However, tramp steamers were a speculative investment. A boom in trade or an increase in demand for shipping transport, as in the South African war, induced existing owners to add to their fleets and new owners to set up in business, and a short-lived boom was likely to be followed by a prolonged slump. Between 1883 and 1913 the shipping magazine *Fairplay*'s index figure of homeward freights varied from 125 to 58 and outward from 119 to 50, and between 1898 and 1913 the price of a new cargo-steamer of 7500 deadweight tons varied from over £60,000 to £36,000.[29] It had no sooner become established than steam-tramping became an increasingly uncertain business.

Round the coast the steam coaster had by now made considerable inroads into the coal, ore, cattle-carrying and other trades which had once been the preserve of merchant schooners. They were of three main types: those with bridge and engines amidships and holds fore and aft, about 230 feet long overall; those with engines aft and bridge amidships between the holds, about 150 feet long overall; and those with both bridge and engines aft and holds forward, 90–140 feet overall. Those with engines aft were most numerous, and could manage up to 9 knots on a fuel consumption of 0.5 ounce of coal per ton-mile steamed.[30]

The triple expansion engine remained common in merchant vessels but as steam pressures rose above 200 pounds to the square inch marine engineers decided to expand yet another stage to achieve still further economies in the use of fuel. In 1894 engineers at the Central Marine Engineering Works in West Hartlepool designed a 5-cylinder 4-stage expansion engine which was fitted to the cargo vessel *Inchmona*. The new engine was a success, with coal consumption reduced to 1.15 pounds per horse-power per hour. By 1912 the typical new cargo steamer was fitted with quadruple expansion engines. Such a vessel by this time would be about 7760 tons gross and it would carry 10,400 tons of cargo. Its length was some 470 feet, its breadth in the beam 54 feet, and its depth of hold 31 feet. With a boiler pressure of 220 pounds to the square inch, it would travel at 13 knots and burn 68 tons of coal a day.[31]

Until the early years of the 20th century quadruple-expansion engines of increasing size and power continued to be built for all the leading shipping companies operating passenger liners on the north Atlantic. The last British ship thus supplied was *Asturias,* built in 1907 by Harland & Wolff of Belfast, by this time the world's leading shipbuilder, building the world's biggest ships in the world's biggest shipyard.[32] But as passenger ships became larger and larger, the turbine proved to be the best power unit for these speedy vessels and in this field the quadruple-expansion engine was rapidly superseded.

At higher speeds the steam turbine or rotary system developed by Sir Charles Parsons enjoyed economic advantages. The experimental *Turbinia,* constructed by the Parsons Marine Steam Turbine Company of Wallsend-on-Tyne in 1894, achieved a speed of 34.5 knots. From 1902 onwards steam turbines began to be installed in passenger vessels. The Midland Railway Company ordered them for the *Londonderry* and the *Manxman,* both built for the Irish Sea service, in the following year. On trials they achieved a speed of 22.3 knots and the vessels were used for many years on the Heysham to Belfast crossing.

In 1901 the White Star *Celtic* became the first ship to exceed the *Great Eastern*'s tonnage of 18,914 tons gross. *Celtic,* of 20,904 tons gross, was a popular ship, with sufficient space for the provision of gymnasia, swimming and Turkish baths, and a verandah café. Five years later, however, the great and glamorous age of transatlantic travel was truly ushered in by the legendary Cunarder, *Mauretania,* first of the 'ocean greyhounds', a vessel which held the Blue Riband for the fastest crossing for more than twenty years.

The *Mauretania* was 790 feet long, 88 feet wide and 31,938 tons gross. She carried 560 first-class, 475 second-class and 1300 third-class passengers, and 812 crew. Her quadruple four-bladed propellers were driven by Parsons turbines of 70,000 shaft horse-power and the ship achieved a speed of 27.4 knots, steam being supplied by 25 Scotch boilers fuelled by the 6000 tons of coal she could carry in her bunkers. Subsequently Parsons developed a hybrid installation which made use of the turbine in conjunction with the reciprocating engine, the idea being to achieve the flexibility of the reciprocating engine with the much greater efficiency of the turbine at low pressures. In 1911 two cross-Channel steamers were fitted with geared turbines.[33]

After the launching of the *Mauretania,* Atlantic liners continued to grow in size and to compete in speed and luxury. In 1911 the White Star *Olympic* of 45,324 gross tons became the biggest ship in the world until she was overtaken briefly in the following year by the ill-fated White Star *Titanic* of 46,329 gross tons. These ships were of such a size that they required lifts. It was, however, symptomatic of Britain's changing place in the world that in 1913 the Hamburg America Line's *Imperator,* 52,117 gross tons (after the war to be taken over by Cunard and renamed *Berengaria*), became the biggest ship in the world, to be superseded the following year by the same Line's *Vaterland* (subsequently renamed *Leviathan*), of 54,282 gross tons.

As in earlier years, change in the trade to the East was less rapid and less spectacular. Seven-course dinners were standard in P&O by 1907, but accommodation was still very cramped, there were no single cabins, ventilation was by punkah, and there was no heating. Cabin doors were covered with canvas whenever the ship was coaled to stop coal dust from penetrating into cabins; otherwise it got everywhere. But the second-class accommodation had become the 'second-saloon' and was good value at half the first-class fare. Even gentlemen might travel second-class provided they did not mind dining in the middle of the day. The second-saloon enjoyed early morning tea or coffee at 6 am, breakfast at 7.30, 'dinner' at 1.30, afternoon tea at 5.30, and supper – 'a substantial meal of cold meat, salad if procurable, and occasionally tinned fish, marmalade and jam, tea and coffee if asked for, but no hot dishes' – at 7.00. The only difference between this programme and that of the first-saloon was that the latter took 'tiffin' at 12.00 and dinner in the evening. Most P&O navigators started as cadets on the training-ship *Worcester* and considered themselves the élite of the merchant service.

By 1890 the new passenger ships to the Far East were fitted with triple-expansion engines capable of a top speed of 18 knots, though schedules were based on 12 knots. Passage times had been halved. India could be reached in fourteen days if the ship were joined at Marseilles or Brindisi;

otherwise it took just over three weeks, while Sydney and Shanghai took forty-two and forty-four days respectively. The large P&O mail steamers left the Royal Albert Dock every Thursday at noon, one week for Bombay and the next week for Sydney.[34] The *Himalaya* and *Australia* which were put into service in 1892 were 7000 tons, and by the end of the century the new ships were nearly 8000 tons and 'posher' than home for most passengers. Indeed by this time travel to the east and to Australia had become a rather grand event and was to remain so for seventy years. The *Maloja* of 1911 was 12,500 tons, 550 feet long, and carried 450 first-class passengers, forty of them in single berth cabins, and 200 second-class passengers, with a crew of 400. In July 1913 the White Star liner *Ceramic,* fitted with triple-expansion engines plus low pressure turbine, made her maiden voyage from Liverpool to Sydney. Of 18,481 gross tons, she was the largest vessel in the trade up to that time.

In 1894 the Admiralty decided that in future the carriage of troops was to be put wholly into the hands of commercial vessels and P&O and BI were the first to take up the offer, building specially designed ships for charter to the Admiralty for the next sixty years.[35] But, trooping apart, two-thirds of P&O's passengers to India were government employees and in large degree the company was an unofficial arm of the Raj, deriving much of its income from the public purse.[36]

Ocean Steam (Blue Funnel) continued to expand though it received no help of the kind that came to P&O. Chinese seamen were employed after 1894 – at this time Chinese coolies were being shipped in large numbers by other companies as indentured labour for the South African gold-mines – and the company cut its costs in other ways. The ships grew to 7000 tons and the cost of working a Holt ship was reduced from 0.514 old pence per ton-mile in 1880 to 0.142 pence per ton-mile in 1900. Profits were ploughed back to finance expansion. For the Indonesian trade Ocean established a Dutch company in 1891 and in 1902 it bought one of its rivals, China Mutual. Its services were extended to the Philippines, to Australia, and across the Pacific to North America, and by 1913 Ocean ran seventy-seven ships totalling nearly 0.5 million tons gross.[37]

Alfred Holt had pioneered the long-distance steamer but the steamer, after a century of existence and a full generation of dominance, was about to be challenged by the internal combustion engine, and the initiative was not with the British. So far coal had been supreme, and in the 1880s oil was nearly twice the price of coal. But by 1902, when the Suez Canal authorities first allowed tankers to pass through, 200 tank steamers were registered at Lloyd's and the price of oil was falling. In 1903 Dr Diesel's new engine was fitted to the 800-ton Russian ship *Wandal* and five years later it was fitted to a 4000-tonner.[38] The motor ship had arrived.

In 1913 tests by Canadian Pacific indicated that oil had become more economical than coal. It was estimated that the fuel costs for an oil-powered ship would be only two-thirds those of coal, and there would also be a considerable saving in labour costs for only six men instead of eighteen would be required in the engine room.[39] The motor ship did not displace steam immediately and the British, with their great resources of coal, were slow in adopting it, but its coming marked the end of the great period of British shipping. By the outbreak of World War I the number of tankers had doubled to 441 and they were carrying annually 2,334,000 tons of oil.[40]

The number of seafarers serving in British ships increased in this period. From 173,000 in 1891 the number grew to 209,000 in 1912, but in these figures the number of lascars had more than doubled, to 47,000, and the number of foreigners, at 31,000, had also risen. At the wages paid it was not possible to staff British ships entirely with British ratings, and the quality continued to be poor.[41]

By 1912 the crew of a typical cargo steamer of 7760 tons numbered seventy-seven, with forty-three on deck and thirty-four in the engine room. If the ship carried emigrants, she would also carry fourteen more seamen and twenty-nine stewards.[42] Such a ship would burn sixty-eight tons of coal a day and all this coal had to be manhandled into the furnaces by the firemen and trimmers. From these figures it would appear that a fireman might shovel two tons of coal into a furnace in every four-hour watch and he kept two such watches a day. The trimmer would bring this amount of coal to him from the bunkers. Theirs was undoubtedly the hardest work and Liverpool firemen were little different from the P&O 'Seedies' who had been described as 'those human salamanders' who 'emerge from time to time, glistening with perspiration from the Hades of the furnace room, and lie with nothing but a scanty loincloth around their middle, cooling their black bodies in the wet refreshment of the scuppers.'[43] Covered in coaldust, the Liverpool Irish were even much the same colour.

In steam coasters seamen and firemen lived either side of a fore-and-aft partition in the cramped forecastle, seamen to starboard, firemen to port, and the forecastle would also accommodate a lamp-room, paint locker and crew's toilet. A coal-fired bogey stove provided the only heating. The deck officers had poky cabins under the bridge and the engineers had similar cabins above the noisy engine-room. There were no refinements. The bridge was usually open with only a shoulder-high canvas 'dodger' to afford shelter against the weather.[44] A coaster of the period, *Robin* of 400 tons, is preserved in the St Katherine's Dock, London.

However much improved the life of passengers at sea, that of seafarers remained hard, hazardous and insalubrious. In 1892, Havelock Wilson, founder of the seamen's union, was elected to Parliament as a member of the Independent Labour Party. Under pressure in Parliament from Wilson better dietary scales for seamen were introduced and schools for ships' cooks were established, the first being the London School of Nautical Cookery, opened at the Red Ensign Club in Dock Street in 1893 and closed by The Marine Society in Lambeth in 1986. In 1904 a Royal Commission reported that conditions in the merchant service would need to be improved if good men were to be attracted to it. Seafarers' quarters were often miserably primitive and desertion was common – over 50,000 men a year at the turn of the century according to one authority.[45] The Merchant Shipping Act of 1906 increased the living space allocated to each seaman to 120 cubic feet (roughly one-half of that provided in prison cells), laid down a minimum scale of provisions, and decreed that all ocean-going vessels should carry a certificated cook, though this latter provision took some years to implement. This Act also applied the bulk of British safety regulations to foreign vessels using United Kingdom ports and created a Merchant Shipping Advisory Committee on which seamen were represented along with shipowners and shipbuilders.

These improvements notwithstanding, the Medical Officer of Health in Newport, Monmouthshire, reported in 1912 that one vessel in six of those inspected was insanitary[46] and this was probably an underestimate. In 1914 the Port of London's Medical Officer of Health commented that the conditions under which seamen lived on many vessels could be compared only with those under which cave-dwellers lived in prehistoric times.[47] And although after 1895 crimping was largely ended in Britain by the employment of many seamen through the Shipping Federation's offices, the crimps in San Francisco could still obtain £28 for supplying a man to a ship.[48] The Reverend James Fell, who went to that port in 1893 to start a Mission to Seamen, is said to have fought some of the crimps personally. Fortunately, he was a boxer of some prowess.

In 1890 a seafarer was said to be twice as likely to die of disease as was a passenger at sea, three times as likely to die from shipwreck, and twenty times more likely to die from accident. By 1913, according to the same source, the seafarer was still twice as likely as the passenger to die from disease, but twenty times more likely to die from shipwreck, and twenty-five times more likely to die from accident.[49] Such figures are probably based on incomplete data and another authority suggests that the deathrate among seamen from disease was double the rate implied.[50] Nevertheless, the risks to seamen of shipwreck and accident were greatly reduced in the quarter of a century before World War I, and fell even more dramatically for passengers.

In the years immediately prior to the war the master of a 4000 ton cargo steamer was paid £22 a month, his chief engineer £20 and the mate £12 10s.[51] Although Captain Smith of the doomed *Titanic* was paid £1250 a year, the highest salary of any man afloat, it was said of officers in the north Atlantic liners generally that 'in no other trade or profession is equal ability so badly paid'.[52] In P&O in 1913 a middle-aged chief officer was paid £24 a month and a junior second officer £10,[53] both salaries being increased after a strike in that year which was supported by the Imperial Merchant Service Guild, a new officers' union which had been formed by Captain Thomas Moore in 1893 because he felt that the Mercantile Marine Service Association collaborated too readily with the shipowners.

For seamen, too, wages rose in the decade that preceded the war. In 1906 an able-seaman in sail received about £3 a month and £4 if he was in a steamship. A strike in 1910 established £5 10s a month minimum on cargo vessels and £6 on passenger liners, with 35s a week on coastwise ships with the men providing their own food.[54]

The improvement in seafarers' wages resulted from successful unionisation. On the officers' side the Mercantile Marine Service Association of 1857 had been followed by a sea-going engineer officers' association in 1871 and a marine engineers' union formed by chief engineer officers in 1887 to try to establish equal status with navigating officers. Two years later a professional society, the Institute of Marine Engineers, was established. On the navigating side, an unsuccessful National Certificated Officers Union of Great Britain and Ireland launched in 1889 was followed by the successful Imperial Merchant Service Guild of 1893.

The real battle, however, was fought between the shipowners and the ratings. The Steamship Owners' Mutual Protecting and Indemnity Association of 1874 was the first of what are now called the P&I Clubs, and in 1885 a Central Association of Shipowners was set up by owners in Sunderland, Newcastle and Glasgow to put their views before the Royal Commission of 1886. It did not prove permanent, however, and its books were left in the charge of the North of England Protecting and Indemnity Association with which the pioneer P&I Club of 1874 had amalgamated.

The Shipping Federation, which was among the earliest employers' organisations in the country, was established in 1890 as a fighting machine to counter Havelock Wilson's National Amalgamated Sailors' and Firemen's Union of 1887. By 1889 the latter claimed to have 40,000 members and had persuaded the reformer Samuel Plimsoll to become its first president.

Liverpool shipowners formed their own Liverpool Employers' Association, but by 1891 the Shipping Federation was employing only those men who held the Federation's 'ticket', and it bought three vessels and an ocean-going tug specifically to provide accommodation and transport for its 'free labour' which was moved from one port to another as the occasion arose to break strikes.[55]

Opposition from the owners apart, Havelock Wilson was bedevilled by the formation or attempted formation of other unions and, after trouble in Cardiff, he was sent to prison for six weeks. In 1893, a year of depression in shipping, one million tons of British steamers were laid up and Wilson's membership collapsed to under 18,000. The following year the National Amalgamated Sailors' and Firemen's Union went into voluntary liquidation and Wilson established a new union, the National Sailors' and Firemen's Union.

By 1895 the Shipping Federation had enrolled 80,000 'ticket' men, but Wilson gradually built up his new union, being helped by the Trade Disputes Act of 1906, which provided certain legal privileges to the unions, and by the general attitude of the new Liberal government. He was also strengthened by his affiliation to the International Transport Workers' Federation (ITF) organised by Tom Mann and Ben Tillett.

In 1910 Joseph Cotter formed a cooks' and stewards' union which won a strike. At this time Wilson was working for the establishment of a Conciliation Board which would help solve industrial problems but the shipowners wanted nothing of it so in June 1911, a boom year, Wilson called a strike even though no more than 20 per cent of British ratings were members of his NSFU.[56] In consequence of ITF affiliation the British dock and road transport workers came out in sympathy, as did seamen in four other countries. The strike led to the recognition by the employers of Wilson's union – that is to say, the shipowners no longer barred its members from employment – and the Federation 'ticket' disappeared in 1912. Improvements in conditions led to some increase in the proportion of British seamen among crews and by 1914 the NSFU was claiming to represent 90 per cent of British ratings.

The government of the day also played its part in improving the lot of the seafarer. In 1890 the government first enforced the rules which determined where the Plimsoll line should be placed – there are, in fact, several different lines for different densities of water or allowing for different weather conditions – and those loadline requirements were applied to foreign vessels in United Kingdom ports by the Merchant Shipping Act of 1906.

In 1892 an Inspectorate of Ships' Provisions for Long Voyages was established. In 1894 a great consolidating Merchant Shipping Act had been added to the statute book and this repealed in whole or in part forty-eight earlier Acts, codifying what remained in 748 clauses and twenty-two schedules. Part V of this Act dealt with safety and provided the Rules of the Road at Sea which were encapsulated in verse by Thomas Gray, head of the Marine Department of the Board of Trade, e.g. for two steamships meeting:

> When both side lights you see ahead
> Port your helm and show your RED;

which has since been revised to:

> Green to green or red to red,
> Perfect safety, go ahead.

The sinking of the *Titanic* in 1912, with the loss of 1489 lives, led to the convening in 1913–14 of the first International Safety Conference. The conference agreed that ocean-going passenger ships must carry lifeboats enough to accommodate all those on board. It agreed further that radio should be installed, and that there should be an established procedure by which a ship in distress could try to obtain help. Because war broke out this convention was never ratified, but nevertheless its proposals were gradually adopted by all maritime nations.[57]

Notes

1. C. E. Fayle, *A Short History of the World's Shipping Industry* (1933), London, p. 275.
2. A. W. Kirkaldy, *British Shipping* (1914), London, p. 337.
3. S. Pollard & P. Robertson, *The British Shipbuilding Industry 1870–1914* (1979), Cambridge, Mass., p. 25.
4. W. E. Minchinton, 'British Ports of Call in the Nineteenth Century' (1976), MM, Vol. 62, No. 2, p. 150; P. Mathias, *The First Industrial Nation: An Economic History of Britain 1700–1914,* 2nd edn (1969), London, p. 231.
5. Kirkaldy, *op. cit.,* p. 581.
6. *Ib.,* p. 114.
7. P. N. Davies, *Sir Alfred Jones: Shipping Entrepreneur Par Excellence* (1978), London, p. 7.
8. Mathias, *op. cit.,* p. 222.
9. Pollard & Robertson, *op. cit.,* p. 20.

10. *Economic Development in the United Kingdom 1850–1950,* Labour Information, MSA Mission to the UK, pp. 41–4.
11. R. H. Thornton, *British Shipping* (1939), London, pp. 74–5.
12. Fayle, *op. cit.,* p. 251.
13. *Shipbuilding & Shipping Record,* 10.4.1958, p. 469.
14. S. G. Sturmey, *British Shipping and World Competition* (1962), London, pp. 24–30.
15. J. Cooper, A. Kludas & J. Pein, *The Hamburg South America Line* (1989), Kendal, p. 7.
16. Thornton, *op. cit.,* pp. 75–6.
17. W. H. Miller, *German Ocean Liners of the 20th Century* (1988), Northants.
18. Sturmey, *op. cit.,* p. 31.
19. F. Harcourt, 'British oceanic mail contracts in the age of steam, 1838–1914' (1988), *The Journal of Transport History,* 3rd series, Vol. 9, No. 1, p. 10; C. R. Parry, 'The General Post Office's Zanzibar Shipping Contracts, 1860–1914' (1982), MM, Vol. 68, No. 1, p. 66.
20. Fayle, *op. cit.,* p. 274.
21. Sturmey, *op. cit.,* p. 34.
22. R. G. Greenhill, 'The Royal Mail Steam Packet Company and the Development of Steamship Links with Latin America' (1973), *Maritime History,* Vol. 3, No. 1, p. 88.
23. Kirkaldy, *op. cit.,* p. 338.
24. Pollard & Robertson, *op. cit.,* p. 8.
25. Thornton, *op. cit.,* p. 78.
26. Kirkaldy, *op. cit.,* p. 79.
27. E. Green & M. Moss, *A Business of National Importance – the Royal Mail Shipping Group, 1902–37* (1982), London, p. 29.
28. Fayle, *op. cit.,* pp. 268–9.
29. *Ib.,* p. 277.
30. M. Langley & E. Small, *Port of Plymouth Series: Merchant Shipping* (1988), Devon, p. 12.
31. Kirkaldy, *op. cit.,* p. 112.
32. M. Moss & J. R. Hume, *Shipbuilders to the World: 125 Years of Harland & Wolff* (1986), Blackstaff Press.
33. A. F. L. Deeson, *An Illustrated History of Steamships* (1976), Bourne End, pp. 112–121.
34. P. Padfield, *Beneath the House Flag of the P&O* (1981), London, pp. 56–86.
35. D. Williams, *Liners in Battledress* (1989), London, p. 21.
36. S. Rabson & K. O'Donoghue, *P&O: A Fleet History* (1988), Kendal, pp. 79–80.
37. F. E. Hyde, *Blue Funnel: A History of Alfred Holt and Company of Liverpool from 1865 to 1914* (1956), Liverpool.
38. Kirkaldy, *op. cit.,* p. 143.
39. *Ib.,* p. 143.
40. Pollard & Robertson, *op. cit.,* p. 23.
41. G. Rawson, *Sea Prelude* (1958), London; A. L. Lloyd, *Folk Song in England* (1975), London, p. 260; and much other evidence.
42. Kirkaldy, *op. cit.,* p. 112.
43. Padfield, *op. cit.,* p. 69.
44. Langley & Small, *op. cit.,* p. 12.
45. A. G. Course, *The Merchant Navy: A Social History* (1963), London, p. 258.
46. Kirkaldy, *op. cit.,* p. 269.

47. *The Times,* 14.7.1914.
48. Course, *op. cit.,* p. 243.
49. W. Abell, 'Sea Casualties and Loss of Life' (1902), London (A paper read before the North-East Coast Institution of Engineers and Shipbuilders); C. Jones, *British Merchant Shipping* (1922), London, pp. 144–5.
50. Fayle, *op. cit.,* p. 287.
51. *Ib.,* pp. 287–8.
52. Course, *op. cit.,* p. 265, quoting *Scribner's Magazine* (May 1891).
53. *Ib.,* p. 266.
54. *Ib.,* p. 262.
55. L. Powell, *The Shipping Federation 1890–1950* (1950), London, pp. 1–12.
56. B. Fletcher, 'The experience of the Shipping Federation, 1906 to 1910' (1984), *Maritime Policy and Management,* Vol. XI, No. 4, pp. 261–8.
57. Anon, *Seafarers and Their Ships* (1955), London, pp. 35–6.

19

First World War
(1914–1920)

The First World War had a profound effect on British shipping. Between 1914 and 1919 the world's tonnage of steam and motor ships increased from 45.4 to 47.9 million gross tons. In this same period the British fleet declined from 18.9 to 16.3 million gross tons, or from 41.6 to 34.2 per cent of the world total.[1] The size of the British fleet had been reduced by more than 1.5 million tons.

During the war 15 million tons of world shipping were lost, and of this total British losses accounted for 9 million tons – nearly one-half of the British pre-war fleet. World losses were more than made good in the war years themselves. British losses were not.

At the outbreak of the war the British government took over many merchant ships to act as armed merchant cruisers, troopships, hospital ships and stores transports. As the war went on, more and more ships were requisitioned. For the movement of troops and other personnel the government Transport Department provided tonnage during the four years from August 1914 to October 1918 for 23,700,000 individual passages, tonnage enough to move half the population of the British Isles. Much else was also moved: 2.2 million animals, 0.5 million guns and vehicles, and little short of 50 million tons of military stores, equivalent to a year's imports in normal conditions. All these figures exclude exports or imports on civilian account.[2]

Ships were requisitioned at what were known as 'Blue Book' charter rates. These rates, determined in 1915, were influenced by the comparatively poor rates prevailing immediately before the war broke out and they were overtaken rapidly in the free market, which was beyond the control of the British government, as shipping tonnage became more difficult to procure. The free market freight for coal carried from Cardiff to Port Said, for example, jumped from under 7s per ton in 1913 to 21s in 1914, 68s in 1915, 80s in 1916 and 120s in 1917. To move 100 pounds of cotton from New Orleans to Liverpool cost 31 cents in 1913 and 625 cents in 1917.[3] In the four years from 1913 to 1917 prices in general doubled.

In 1915 the British government requisitioned all British refrigerated space at Blue Book rates, and later it requisitioned all the grain space in the North Atlantic trades. In 1917 the government appointed a Shipping Controller and in the last twelve months of the war about 96 per cent of cargo handled by British ships was carried at government rates. In some instances these rates were claimed to be unremunerative until they were revised in 1918.[4]

To carry cargo at Blue Book rates made a great difference to profits. Monthly time charter rates for tramp steamers on the free market, which had been 4s a ton in July 1914, had risen to 25s a ton by December 1915.[5] Government requisitioning meant that many British shipowners were unable to profit so much from the wartime shipping shortage as were those foreign competitors who could take full advantage of the greatly inflated wartime rates. The impact of government regulations fell unevenly, too, upon British owners because it was the ship at hand which was requisitioned and it became something of a game of skill for British owners to keep their ships out of British ports so that they could not be taken over. Since the government also preferred fast ships built to good specifications, wherever these were available, the best owners tended to be penalised.[6]

In 1915 an Excess Profits Duty was exacted on British owners, though initially only upon profits earned in excess of the good profits earned in 1912–13. This duty was made more onerous after 1917.

These restrictions and exactions notwithstanding, in the early years of the war British ships on average spent only 25 per cent of their time on requisition and, despite what has been said above, some companies made very high profits. According to Sir Leo Chiozza Money, one-time Parliamentary Secretary to the Ministry of Shipping, British shipowners as a whole amassed net profits of close on £300 millions (over £6500 million at 1988 prices) in the first two years of the war, and in the same two years the capital value of British ships increased by more than £300 million.[7]

In the middle of 1917 Bonar Law, who was Chancellor of the Exchequer at the time, made the following comment in the House of Commons:

> The sum of money I had invested in shipping, spread over different shipping companies, was £8100. Five per cent interest on that, which in ordinary times I should be glad to get, would be £405, but for 1915, instead of £405, I received £2624, and for 1916 I received £3847 after Excess Profits Duty had been paid. One of the steamers had either been sunk or sold. I do not know, either way she had been turned into money for me. In that ship I had £200, and after the very handsome dividend which I received on liquidation I received a cheque for over £1000. There is another shipping company in which I

> invested £350. The other day I received a letter from the Managing Owner saying that because the cost of building ships was so high, they were going to make a division of the surplus capital. For that £350 capital of this division I received a cheque for £1050.[8]

Some of Britain's largest tramp shipowners did so well that they sold their fleets while the going was good.

It was from such profits as those described that Sir William Burrell amassed that Burrell Collection which is now the pride of Glasgow, but lesser men did not possess his public spirit. 'It was', wrote one commentator who was not unsympathetic to the shipping community, 'bad economically' and 'still worse from the social and political standpoint that any section of the community should reap so rich a harvest from the common peril.'[9]

Shipowners also did well in many cases from government compensation for vessels lost. Lord Inchcape (James Mackay), who became chairman of P&O in 1914, minimised the book value of his ships when he did not want to disclose the company's wealth, but maximised this book value for government hand-outs. 'Some particularly old and almost redundant vessels . . .,' his biographer relates, 'brought large sums to the P&O coffers.' The BI ships *Golconda* and *Mombasa,* both vessels of under 5000 tons and over 27 years old when they were torpedoed in 1916, were compensated for to the tune of over £100,000 though for many years they had been written off in the company's books. The fact that Inchcape was closely associated with the government and that shipowners were closely involved in running the Ministry of Shipping did P&O no harm. For the *Ballarat,* lost in 1917 when she was written down to £15,000 in the books, the company received £420,000.[10] During the war P&O added the New Zealand Shipping Company, Federal Steam Navigation Company, William Cory & Son, Union Steam Ship Company of New Zealand, Hain Steamship Company, Nourse Line, Mercantile Steamship Company and Orient Steam Navigation Company to its acquisitions, some of these being tramp ship companies. Despite enormous casualties the P&O group emerged from the war stronger than ever, with nearly 2 million tons of shipping under Inchcape's control.

The high profits of 1915 and 1916 encouraged the entry of speculators into the industry. In 1915 alone ninety-four new shipping companies were formed, increasing the demand for shipping and accentuating the inflation of ship prices. There was considerable speculation in shipping company shares at this time and, in the light of high earnings, many companies were recapitalised at false values. At the same time the price of secondhand ships rose from about £5 a ton to something nearer £50 a ton.[11]

After the sinking of the *Lusitania* in 1915 Cunard suspended their Atlantic passenger services and other United Kingdom liner services were withdrawn as ships were requisitioned for war purposes. Some liner companies fared worse than others. Cargo liner owners, who imposed war surcharges which were often unnecessarily high, did well later in the war, though the opportunities for British ships to earn very high profits were largely gone after 1917.

The vacuum caused by the wartime withdrawal of British shipping services – at least one-quarter of British ocean-going tonnage – was naturally filled by others. Foreign shipowners benefited most from the high wartime freight rates, which were often four times the British Blue Book rates. The shipping of the United States, Japan, France and Italy probably profited most.

In the United States there was spectacular wartime growth. Following the withdrawal of foreign tonnage, the output of American shipyards increased enormously. It increased further to help replace the losses suffered by those fighting the war. It increased further still to supply the ships needed when the Americans themselves entered the war. In 1913 the United States produced only 230,000 tons of ocean shipping. By 1919 this figure had increased to 3 million tons. In 1914 the American sea-going fleet amounted to only 2 million tons, half of which was engaged in providing coastal services. By 1919 this fleet totalled nearly 10 million tons, largely government-owned, though some of this total never saw service at sea at all.

During the war British ships were withdrawn from trades not directly serving the Allied cause. Since the La Follette Act prevented American ships from employing Asiatic crews, the Pacific Ocean became in consequence largely a Japanese preserve and the Japanese entered trades in the Far East which had hitherto been British trades. Able to take advantage of the high free market rates, the Japanese also enjoyed the assistance of subsidies, low labour costs, low building costs and integrated merchanting and shipping organisations. From 1915 to 1918 leading Japanese shipowners netted annually more than ten times the annual average net earnings from 1900 to 1914, and in the single year of 1918 net earnings were more than 30 per cent higher than they were for all the years from 1900 to 1914 put together. In this way extensive reserves were built up.

The French ended the war with a merchant fleet virtually unchanged in size. Two million tons of British shipping requisitioned at Blue Book rates were lent to the French government while a substantial part of the French fleet was free from requisition and able to trade at free market rates. Italian experience was similar. In 1916 400,000 tons of British shipping was chartered at Blue Book rates and lent to the Italians while Italian shipping was free from control as late as 1917. High wartime profits were followed by the post-war acquisition of Trieste and the dissolution of the Austro-Hungarian fleet, most of which went to Italy. Under the reparation arrangements Italy received ton for ton compensation for ships lost.

Norway, Denmark, Sweden and the Netherlands, although neutral during the war, all lost shipping and only the Dutch finished the war with a bigger fleet. However, shipowners in these countries all earned substantial profits. Half the pre-war Norwegian fleet was sunk but Norway's gross freight earnings in foreign trade increased fivefold. On the other hand replacement cost rose, Norwegian government insurance payments for war losses were not generous, and taxation was high, with the consequence that the main expansion in the inter-war period came from new Norwegian ship operators.

On the whole Danish, Swedish and Dutch shipowners benefited from the war, the Dutch proving able to expand their liner services and thus encroach upon British trade. Increases in reserves resulting from wartime profits financed a 60 per cent increase in the size of the Dutch fleet between 1919 and 1924.

Although they lost or sold 500,000 tons of shipping, the Greeks also did well out of the war, as did some minor maritime countries where fleets increased in size, often with government support, to guard against the disruption of trade and to minimise payments to foreigners.[12] Twenty-five new liner services were started during the war by non-British owners to replace suspended British services and much of the British entrepôt trade – 14 per cent of the total trade in 1913 – was lost for good, largely to Japan and the United States. Australian wool now went direct to the United States instead of through London and American cotton which had formerly passed through Liverpool now went direct to the Continent.

No doubt, had the war never been fought, British entrepôt arrangements would not have lasted and competition from foreign liner companies would have increased, but the war undoubtedly hastened these processes. The war speeded the decline of British shipping in many different ways.

Although those who invested in British shipping did well out of World War I, some of them doing very well, the same cannot be said for the crews of British ships. Much ingenuity was employed in efforts to camouflage ships to save them from destruction[13] but they were sunk, and seamen died, nevertheless. Within forty-eight hours of the declaration of war 8000 merchant service officers and men joined the Armed Forces. A few deserted to American ships, where the pay was twice as high. Of the 200,000 or so who remained to give war service in merchant ships, 14,428 lost their lives by enemy action. It may not have mattered much to Bonar Law and other investors whether the ships from which they made money were sunk or sold but no doubt it mattered to the seafarers and to those they left behind them. In addition to the number who died as a result of enemy action, a further 3348 lost their lives in consequence of the ordinary risks of sea life, and over 3000 more lost their lives through illness and disease.

From 1915 onwards the British Admiralty paid the surviving crew of a ship under charter to the government their wages until these survivors reached their homes, provided that they did so within fifteen days of being sunk. The government also refunded rail fares in such cases. Most shipowners running ships not under charter to the government did not follow this example. If a ship not under charter sank, the merchant seaman's pay ceased at the time of the sinking, as it had done in earlier times, and he received no compensation for his lost belongings.[14]

The seaman's pay during the war was scarcely handsome. Seamen were given a rise after the cost of living had risen by 50 per cent. In 1917 an AB's pay rose from £8 10s to £11 a month and a fireman's from £10 to £12.[15] The war brought the inclusion of seamen in the unemployment insurance scheme, from which they had been excluded hitherto, and in the war-built ships accommodation was improved. The accommodation moved aft and wooden bunks against the side of the ship were replaced by iron cots fixed clear of the side. Iron cots harboured fewer bugs and they stood clear of the condensation that ran down the ship's sides. In some instances granulated cork was used to cover the bare metal of the ship's side to moderate condensation and provide insulation. Glass ports were increased in size and skylights fitted. Washing places were provided with cement floors and showers. For sleeping purposes each seaman was allocated thirty-two square feet of floor space in addition to recreation and messroom space. In passenger liners the old 'glory hole' accommodating sixty or seventy stewards was replaced by dormitories for twelve and, later, ten men. Later still these were replaced by four to six berth cabins. Such improvements came only slowly, as old ships were replaced by new ones.

Certain companies were pioneers in the provision of better facilities for the crew, notably the Blue Funnel Line, whose Lawrence Holt helped Albert Mansbridge, founder of the Workers' Educational Association, to establish the Seafarers Education Service in 1919 to provide a library service for merchant seamen. Hitherto, in most cases, the provision of such literature as there was – mostly religious tracts – had been the province of the missionary societies.

Crimps disappeared in Britain with the issue of a port security document which Havelock Wilson tied in with an inspection of union cards when seafarers 'signed on'. Crimps could not secure jobs for men without papers.[16] In 1916 the government established a Ministry of Shipping and in the following year the National Maritime Board was set up to control the supply of seafarers to ships. It was jointly controlled by the Shipping Federation and Wilson's seamen's union, Wilson having proved himself a moderate and patriotic leader. In 1919 the National Maritime Board was reconstituted as a Joint Industrial Council and made permanent, its functions being to supervise the engagement of seamen, to fix wages and conditions, and to avoid costly disputes. Manning scales, accommodation, leave and welfare were all matters for the Board, as well as wage-rates and hours of work, and for nearly fifty years the Board was held up as a model of its kind.

Up to this time different shipping companies had prescribed different liveries for their officers, and sometimes for their ratings. During the war a Captain Fryatt, master of a railway steamer plying between the United Kingdom and the Continent, rammed and sank a German submarine. Captured at a later date by the Germans, Captain Fryatt was shot because he was a 'civilian' wearing a company livery and not a service uniform when he killed Germans. With the intention that in the event of another war the merchant service should automatically become one of the Services, an Order in Council was promulgated in 1918 to prescribe a standard merchant service uniform. This measure was intended to become a protection against incidents such as the one that had cost Captain Fryatt his life. After the uniform was introduced there were several occasions when it was worn improperly and this led to the promulgation of the British Mercantile Marine (Uniform) Order of 1919 and the subsequent Order in Council dated 13th December 1921. By the terms of the latter shipping companies were permitted to retain a distinctive cap badge if such a badge predated 4th September 1918.[17]

The number of ratings in the merchant service by this time was about 120,000 and their average length of service was estimated to be ten years. It was difficult at times during the war years to crew merchant ships and it was recognised that to maintain a steady supply of ratings, even in peacetime, it would be necessary to recruit at least 10,000 young men each year. With this requirement in view, the Gravesend Sea School was opened in 1918 for the training of boys aged 16–17. The school replaced one on the same site previously run by the Sailors' Home and Red Ensign

Club of Dock Street but in its new guise it was financed by the Ministry of Shipping and the Shipping Federation. Since rebuilt on a nearby site, and now financed by the Department of Education and Science and the General Council of British Shipping, it still functions as the National Sea Training College.

Four years after the war, in public recognition of the service rendered during the war by merchant seamen, King George V conferred honour and status on the merchant service or mercantile marine by providing it with the title 'Merchant Navy', the then Prince of Wales being appointed 'Master of the Merchant Navy'.

Notes

1. Lloyd's Register of Shipping.
2. C. E. Fayle, *The War and the Shipping Industry* (1927), London, pp. 319–20.
3. J. Woddis, *Under the Red Duster* (1947), London, p. 13; C. E. Fayle, *The War and the Shipping Industry* (1927), London.
4. S. G. Sturmey, *British Shipping and World Competition* (1962), London, pp. 46–9.
5. H. Gripaios, *Tramp Shipping* (1959), London, p. 122.
6. *Ib.*, p. 123.
7. Woddis, *op. cit.*, p. 12.
8. A. G. Course, *The Merchant Navy: A Social History* (1963), London, p. 274.
9. Fayle, *op. cit.*, p. 192.
10. S. Jones, *Trade and Shipping: Lord Inchcape 1852–1932* (1989), Manchester, pp. 109–110.
11. Sturmey, *op. cit.*, p. 52.
12. *Ib.*, pp. 39–45.
13. D. Williams, *Liners in Battledress* (1989), London, pp. 59–62.
14. Anon (J. Kinahan), *The Story of the Seamen* (1964), London, p. 18.
15. Course, *op. cit.*, pp. 273–5.
16. C. Dixon, 'The Rise and Fall of the Crimp, 1840–1914' (1984), in S. Fisher (ed), *British Shipping and Seamen, 1630–1960: Some Studies*, Exeter, p. 63.
17. *Final Report of the Court of Inquiry into certain matters concerning the Shipping Industry* (the Pearson Report), Cmnd. 3211 (1967), London, pp. 115–16; *Ocean Mail* (journal of Ocean Transport and Trading), July 1971, p. 6.

20

The Long Slump
(1920–1939)

World shipbuilding capacity had increased two-and-a-half times during the First World War. Even so there was a shipping shortage in the immediate post-war period. This shortage was induced by wartime ship losses and the existence of a large pent-up demand for goods which resulted from wartime deprivation. The shortage was exacerbated by port congestion which lengthened the time taken for loading and unloading.

Shipowners as a body have a propensity to take short views and in 1919, in response to the boom conditions of the immediate post-war months, 7 million tons of merchant shipping was launched, 4 million tons of it in the United States and 1.6 million tons in the United Kingdom. In the exceptional year of 1920 the net earnings of British ships in foreign trade, the sea transport balance, amounted to £340 million (£5000 million at 1988 prices) and shipping's 'invisible earnings' comprised the United Kingdom's most valuable export. Thereafter, those earnings ranged from £105 to £140 million until 1930. Dropping to £59 million (£2000 million at 1988 prices) at the bottom of the slump in 1933, they rose again to around £100 million (£3000 million at 1988 prices) in each of the three years prior to the Second World War.[1]

The slump arrived at the end of of 1920. The immediate post-war demand had been satisfied and the price of a 7500-ton cargo-steamer, which had been £45,000 in 1914, fell from £232,500 to £105,000. By the end of 1922 the price had fallen to £70,000.[2] Freight rates fell even more dramatically. Coal carried from the Tyne to Port Said and demanding a freight of up to £10 a ton during the war could get no more than 11s 3d a ton by 1923. All Britain's wartime controls had disappeared, but by this time freight rates were often below the wartime Blue Book rates. Coal shipped from Britain for use in steamers engaged in foreign trade fell from the 1913 peak figure of 21 million tons to just under 11 million tons in 1921.[3]

In these immediate post-war years the British government put on the market nearly 4 million tons of wartime standard shipping, together with old German tonnage which had been handed over as part of the peace settlement. These sales did the British shipbuilding industry no good, and they saddled British shipping with a large block of out-of-date tonnage.

Some help to both shipping and shipbuilding came from the Trade Facilities Act of 1921, which offered loans at approximately 2 per cent below market rates, and from the Revenue Obsolescence Agreement of 1922, by which refunds amounting to some £80 million were made of the wartime Excess Profits Duty. But, as is often the case when government tries to help, these measures may have done as much harm as good, as will be seen below.

Many shipowners had done well out of generous government compensation for lost ships, and many had amassed considerable reserves from inflated wartime profits.[4] But the basic trouble was that the world merchant fleet was expanding faster than world seaborne trade. If 1913 is taken to represent 100, world seaborne trade had fallen to 82 by 1921, by which time over 20 per cent of the British fleet was idle. Thereafter the index rose to a pre-1937 peak of 135 in 1929, falling to 101 – about the 1913 level – in 1932.[5] But by 1932 the volume of tonnage available to carry this trade was 50 per cent higher than it had been in 1913 and by this time 20 per cent of the world fleet was idle. In effective carrying power the world fleet had increased by more than the 50 per cent indicated by the tonnage figures because the new ships were faster and had been improved in other ways by the naval architects. At the same time the passenger trade had been hit by a reduction in the number of emigrants. The persistence in the post-war world of too many ships for the trade available was a new experience for many British owners.

The figures for 1932 – 50 per cent more tonnage for the same volume of trade and only 20 per cent of that tonnage laid up – indicate that those ships which were at sea had to be sailing less than full. Rather than steam home in ballast, tramp ships were willing to accept rates below voyage costs, and their readiness at times to accept cargoes at almost any price passed their problems on to the liner trades. At the same time liners, if they could, began to fill up with part cargoes or 'parcels' of such bulk commodities as grain, sugar, rice and maize, thus doing the tramps out of business. And because liners had to wait longer for cargoes, and had to sail very often with only part cargoes, there was a great temptation for liner companies to undercut the freight rates fixed by their shipping conference. Between 1929 and 1935 only just over 10 per cent of normal depreciation was earned by 913 British tramps, and the average dividend in these years paid by British liner companies owning some 6 million tons of shipping fell from 6.23 per cent in 1929 to 1.56 per cent in 1933.[6] Profits in shipping in 1935 were the lowest of all the profits made by British

Fig. 9. UNITED KINGDOM AND WORLD TONNAGE, 1914–1939 (million gross tons)

YEAR	UK REGISTERED TONNAGE	WORLD TONNAGE	REGISTERED TONNAGE AS PERCENTAGE OF WORLD TONNAGE
1914	19.3	49.1	39.3
1921	19.3	58.8	32.8
1922	19.1	61.3	31.2
1923	19.1	62.3	30.7
1924	19.0	61.5	30.9
1925	19.3	62.4	30.9
1926	19.3	62.7	30.8
1927	19.2	63.3	30.3
1928	19.8	65.2	30.4
1929	20.0	66.4	30.1
1930	20.3	68.0	29.9
1931	20.2	68.7	29.4
1932	19.6	68.4	28.7
1933	18.6	66.6	27.9
1934	17.6	64.4	27.3
1935	17.3	63.7	27.2
1936	17.2	64.0	26.9
1937	17.4	65.3	26.6
1938	17.7	66.9	26.5
1939	17.9	68.5	26.1

(*Source:* Lloyd's Register of Shipping.)

industries, no more than one-seventh of the profits, expressed as a percentage of paid-up capital, made in the motor industry.[7]

Britain's shipping problems were exacerbated by the actions of the United States government. In defiance of purely economic considerations and in reversal of the pre-war trend, the United States was determined to maintain a substantial merchant fleet on the grounds that it was required for the purposes of defence. In 1920 the United States Merchant Marine Act was passed 'to provide for the promotion and maintenance of the American Merchant Marine', and the US Shipping Board was empowered to operate a shipping service wherever no American citizen was prepared to do so. From its sales of ships built for the government in wartime the Board was empowered to spend up to $25 million over a five-year period to build vessels deemed necessary to maintain essential services.[8]

Between 1920 and 1937 the American Congress spent $900 million on the American merchant navy, maintaining thirty-eight separate uneconomic services,[9] and throughout this time the United States kept its second place as a world maritime nation, a place which had been established by its wartime building. Although a new Merchant Marine Act of 1936 terminated all US mail contracts with shipping companies, it replaced them by direct construction and operation subsidies for ships employed on what were deemed essential trade routes.

American policy in the inter-war years had a particularly serious impact on British shipping because a high proportion of American trade, some 20 per cent of world trade by volume, had been carried prior to the war in British ships. The US-subsidised Matson Line now took some of the trade which had previously gone to the British Union Steamship Company of New Zealand. Before this time the Union Steamship Company, a subsidiary of P & O since 1917, had held its own. Furthermore, Union Steamship was unable to share in the lucrative tourist traffic on the San Francisco to Hawaii leg of the transpacific route because this was reserved to American ships as 'coastwise' traffic. This is but one example. Expressed in terms of percentages of entrances and clearances the employment of American ships in American trades nearly doubled, from 14.0 to 26.6 per cent, between 1913 and 1936. Norway and Japan also increased their share of this trade, but British participation halved, from 51.7 to 27.5 per cent.[10] Despite state help, however, the United States fleet fell from 15.7 million tons in 1920 to 11.4 million tons in 1939 and her place among maritime nations at the latter date would be below that of France if what the Americans regarded as coastwise tonnage were excluded from the figures.

All maritime nations suffered from the long slump but the degree to which governments helped their ailing shipping industries differed considerably. Subsidies increased in significance in Japan only after 1932 when a subsidised 'scrap and build' scheme was started. Efficiency and enterprise were not lacking among Japanese shipowners, but nor were some sharp practice and ratecutting.[11] Consolidating upon its wartime achievement, Japan took better advantage than did either Britain or America of the new facility of the Panama Canal, which had opened in 1914. By 1936, for example, 88 per cent of imports from the Far East to the Atlantic seaboard of the United States came by way of the Canal and none of them was carried in British liners. Between 1920 and 1939 Japan's tonnage nearly doubled, from 3.0 to 5.6 million tons, and Japan remained the third maritime power, increasing its relative importance.

The fleets of the Scandinavian countries more than doubled between the two world wars, increasing overall from 3.7 to 7.6 million tons. Shipowners in these countries established liner trades to Canada, East Asia and the Pacific, brought timber from the Baltic to Britain and, above all, developed the refrigerated ship and the tanker trades, much of this development coming not from established shipping companies but from new ones.[12] Among these countries Norway remained pre-eminent and was fourth in place as a world maritime power by 1939. Since it cannot be argued that Scandinavian shipping companies benefited greatly from government measures in these years their success compares interestingly with Britain's relative decline.

Germany and her allies had entered the First World War with 6.5 million tons of shipping and had lost 2 million tons in the course of the war through sinkings and seizure. At the end of the war the remaining fleet was seized by the Allies as reparations and the Austro-Hungarian fleet was never replaced. The 52,000-ton *Imperator* went to Cunard, presumably as compensation for the wartime loss of *Lusitania*, and was renamed *Berengaria*. The 54,000-ton *Vaterland* beame the USS *Leviathan*. The 56,000-ton *Bismarck*, which was not finished until after the war but became, and for nineteen years remained, the world's largest ship, went to White Star, presumably as compensation for the loss of *Britannia*, and was renamed *Majestic*.[13]

By 1920 Germany possessed only 419,438 tons of shipping, with hardly any ship fit for overseas trade. In the post-war reconstruction period the German government paid some compensation to German shipowners for war losses suffered but this compensation did not cover the costs of replacement. Nevertheless, by the end of 1924 the German fleet was restored to 2.8 million tons or rather more than half the pre-war tonnage and this fleet consisted of up-to-date, economic and highly competitive ships. After 1925 cheap building loans helped the fleet to recover to 4.2 million tons by 1931, and by 1932 nearly half the loans to the North German Lloyd and Hamburg America Lines had been written off.

The competition of German ships was keen throughout most of the inter-war years and German liner operators broke the conference rules

Fig. 10. THE MARITIME NATIONS, 1914–1939

(IN ORDER OF SIZE AS IN 1939)
(million gross tons)

	1914	1921	1931	1939
World	49.1	58.8	68.7	68.5
UK	19.3	19.3	20.2	17.9
US	5.4*	15.7	12.8	11.4
Japan	1.7	3.4	4.3	5.6
Norway	2.5	2.4	4.1	4.8
Germany	5.5	0.7	4.2	4.5
Italy	1.7	2.5	3.3	3.4
Netherlands	1.5	2.2	3.1	3.0
France	2.3	3.3	3.5	2.9
Greece		0.6	1.4	1.8
Sweden		1.1	1.7	1.6
UK as % of world	39	33	29	26

* of which 2.4 operating on Great Lakes

(*Source:* Lloyd's Register of Shipping; vessels over 100 gross tons.)

when it suited them. In 1932 the German government established a scrap-and-build scheme with interest-free loans, and in 1933 a general operating bounty of up to 25 per cent of operating costs was introduced though this was, in part, compensation for the over-valuation of the Reichsmark. Other assistance to shipping was forthcoming, and barter deals made by the Nazis gave preference to German companies. By 1939 the German fleet of 4.5 million tons was over ten times what it had been in 1920.

Italian fleet growth in the inter-war period was not so spectacular – a mere 50 per cent increase from 2.1 million tons in 1920 to 3.4 million tons in 1939. In some degree the Italians benefited from taking over Trieste and the former Austro-Hungarian maritime domain. In the fast liner services government subsidies made it possible for Italian shipping to compete with British and other lines, and in the emigrant trades there was flag discrimination in favour of Italian shipping. In other areas currency restrictions hampered shipping development. Some of P & O's trade to the Far East was lost to the Italians between the wars and, although the total number of emigrants – over one million to America in 1913 – tailed off, the average annual emigration of Italians remained high, particularly in the aftermath of World War I. From an annual average of 0.45 million between 1920 and 1923, the number of emigrants fell to an average of 0.16 million between 1924 and 1930, and to 0.03 million between 1931 and 1938.[14]

Following this survey of some of the external competition to which British shipping was subject between the two wars, one may turn to look more closely at the British industry itself.

In this period there were some 300 British shipping companies, but amalgamation and acquisitions had continued. P & O added Khedivial Mail Steamship & Graving Dock Company, the General Steam Navigation Company and Strick Line to its group by 1923, giving it a fleet of 460 ships totalling over 2.5 million tons gross.[15] During the later war years Cunard had acquired Canadian Northern Steamships, the Donaldson Line and the Commonwealth & Dominion Line (later reformed as Port Line), and had bought a substantial holding in Brocklebank Line, which it acquired outright in 1940. Between the wars Sir John Ellerman, who left nearly £37 million when he died in 1933, also developed his fleet, and the Furness Withy group expanded.[16]

By the end of World War I one-quarter of the United Kingdom tonnage was controlled by the 'Big Five' lines – P & O, Royal Mail, Cunard, Ellerman and Furness Withy; and by 1939 the 'Big Five' – now P & O, Furness Withy, Ellerman, Cunard and Ocean Steamship – controlled over one-third of United Kingdom tonnage. The war had accentuated the tendency to combine in the liner trades and many hitherto well-known flags had disappeared while others, though still used, had passed under the financial control of leading groups. Many one-ship companies also disappeared. In 1914 120 different companies maintained offices in Cardiff. By 1939 there were about 20.

For the last quarter of the 19th and the first half of the 20th century British shipping was largely controlled by, or closely associated with dynasties of shipowning families – Inchcapes, Ismays, Roydens, Holts, Brocklebanks, Ellermans and others in the big groups, Bibbys, Cayzers, Runcimans, Denholms, Ropners and many more in smaller but still substantial companies. By way of amalgamation some of these men wielded considerable power and dispensed great patronage. Liner companies like Cunard, P & O, Union-Castle, White Star and Royal Mail were household names, and in consequence of the war some personal fortunes were immense. Many of the wartime mergers, however, had been effected at inflated values and had left the controlling companies saddled with a heavily watered capital structure which handicapped them in the subsequent slump.

Notable among these companies was Royal Mail, a group which had been built up by Owen Phillips, later Lord Kylsant. As early as 1912 Kylsant controlled the Pacific Steam Navigation Company, Union-Castle Line, Nelson Line, Elder Dempster, Shire Line, Glen Line and Lamport & Holt, in addition to the Royal Mail Steam Packet Company. During the war he took over Moss Steamship Company and MacAndrew's and launched Coast Lines. In the heady days of 1919 he bought Bullard King and David MacIver Sons & Company and, through James Moss & Company, J. & P. Hutchinson. The group had accumulated wartime profits of some £20 million and, also in 1919, Kylsant had bought 77 of the government's standard wartime ships and dispersed them among his fleet. Harland & Wolff was a further member of the group and Kylsant now enlarged its shipbuilding capacity with a view to establishing vertical integration in the industry. Total new issues on the stock market in this boom period amounted to £384 million, and of this amount the Royal Mail Group alone raised £11.5 million.

Then came the slump of 1920 and freight rate wars in the liner trades. Kylsant was in no way daunted. Despite his purchase of wartime standard ships he favoured technically advanced tonnage, being among the first British shipowners to invest in the motor ship. He also believed that businessmen had a duty to increase the opportunities for employment. Under the terms of the Trade Facilities Act of 1921 he made application for a government loan and, despite the slump, he continued to raise money through the new issue market. By the end of 1922 the group had raised £25 million since the war ended, most of it being made over in exchange for fixed interest stock paying about 6 per cent. In other words, Kylsant's shipping empire was highly geared, with a high proportion of fixed interest stock in relation to the equity and saddled with interest payments exceeding £1 million a year. To remain in business the group was coming increasingly to rely on borrowed money.

Still undaunted, Kylsant proceeded to buy the White Star Line (Ocean Steam Navigation Company) from the American International Mercantile Marine Company, the old Pierpont Morgan empire, this purchase to become effective from 1st January 1927. He also bought such shares as his Group did not own already in the Shaw, Savill & Albion Line. These companies, too, had received government loans and these loans were due to be redeemed in ten annual instalments starting on 31st December 1928. Kylsant made a further issue of preference shares and, encouraged by an upturn in freight rates in 1926, added more tonnage to his fleets and took a further government loan. The return of the White Star Line to British ownership had been a popular move.

By this time the Royal Mail Group comprised 140 companies – not all of them in shipping – with a fleet tonnage of over 2.6 million tons or nearly 15 per cent of the British merchant navy. Extensive share transfers had been made between members of the group so that Kylsant controlled the whole of this empire through just one of his companies, Elder Dempster, and he alone knew all the ramifications.

By 1928 the viability of the group depended upon a rapid and sustained boom which, unhappily for Kylsant, did not materialise. Instalments for the purchase of the White Star Line, the Shaw, Savill Line and yet another acquisition, the Australian Commonwealth Line, were due, as were the first repayments of the loans negotiated under the terms of the Trade Facilities Act. The government refused to extend the time for repayment under the Act and on 12th November 1928 the liner *Vestris* foundered, thus jeopardising the future of Lamport & Holt, one of the group's members.

The group, which had been inherently unstable in consequence of its cross-shareholdings and its high gearing almost from the time when it had acquired Elder Dempster in 1910, finally collapsed in 1930. The chairman, Lord Kylsant, was found guilty of issuing a false prospectus and sent to prison for twelve months. With particular help from two highly respected shipowners, Sir Frederick Lewis of Furness Withy and Richard Durning Holt (later knighted) of the Blue Funnel Line, a re-organisation scheme for Royal Mail was then instituted and, after proper depreciation of the assets, each fleet was transferred to new management.

Some of Royal Mail's difficulties might be said to lie in the change in trading patterns which arose out of World War I. World tonnage and competition had both increased and the shipping slump lasted for longer than slumps had been wont to do. The memory of losses suffered in the collapse of Royal Mail deterred investors from buying shares in shipping companies and shipping equities were underpriced for the next thirty years. Frightened of the high gearing which Kylsant had engineered, other shipowners became loath to borrow, and this had implications for fleet replacement programmes after World War II and thus for the British shipping industry. The collapse of Royal Mail harmed the industry, and made it possible, ultimately, for foreigners to gain control of a sizeable part of British shipping.[17]

Conditions after World War I had led to the abandonment of Britain's free trade policy. The McKenna Duties of 1915 levied heavy duty on certain luxury imports and protection was extended in 1920 and 1921. In 1931, a year after the collapse of Royal Mail, Britain went off the gold standard and the pound was devalued. The Import Duties Act of 1932 imposed a general duty on all articles imported, excluding foodstuffs and raw materials, and preference was given to articles imported from the Empire. Between 1931 and 1937 the share of imports from Empire countries rose from 25 to 37.5 per cent, but the share of British imports sent to those countries rose only from 33 to 40 per cent.[18]

The effect of all these factors varied from company to company and from trade to trade. Blue Funnel and the Harrison Line, for example, continued to make substantial profits, though to some degree this was in appearance only because their capital structure was very different from that of the public companies.[19] British square-rigged ships and even coastal schooners vanished from the seas. The *Garthpool*, the last four-masted steel barque to operate under the Red Ensign, was wrecked in the Cape Verde Islands in 1930 while still engaged in the Australian grain trade. The *Waterwitch*, a wooden barquentine and last of the British square-rigged merchantmen operating in the home trade, made her last passage with cargo in 1936.[20]

In consequence of the devaluation of the pound sterling British shipping was less affected by the slump years of the 1930s than was the shipping of those countries which did not devalue their currencies,[21] but the difference was marginal. In 1932 only 17 per cent (3.56 million tons) of British shipping was laid up, compared with 20 per cent in the 1920s when the pound sterling was overvalued and British slipping had fared worse than world shipping as a whole.

In 1933 world trade picked up slightly but, to meet this demand ships were taken out of lay-up, so freight rates did not improve until 1934. Operating subsidies for tramp ships had been introduced in Italy in 1932, in Germany and Holland in 1933 and in France in 1934. Not until 1935, however, did the British government pass the British Shipping (Assistance) Act which offered assistance from public funds to tramp ships for voyages undertaken at freight rates lower than the standard rates, provided that the shipping industry established a self-governing organisation designed ultimately to secure those standard rates. This scheme subsidised British tramp operation to the extent of £2 million in 1935 and a further £2 million in 1936. Such assistance to British shipping had no precedent in the 20th century. J. & J. Denholm were among the shipowners who probably owed their survival to this measure.

Also in 1935 a Tramp Shipping Administration Committee was set up in Britain with international support and this Committee proscribed voyages in ballast by unfixed vessels in the administered trades. A successful international agreement in this year to fix minimum freights in the Argentine grain trade led to its extension to the St Lawrence (Canadian) and Australian trades, and the St Lawrence agreement was extended into a general North Atlantic scheme covering grain east and coal west, though some threat to the scheme's success was offered by underemployed liners. These subsidies and limitations went some way towards helping the British tramp industry to survive.

Under the terms of the British Shipping (Assistance) Act the government provided further assistance for tramp ship owners in the form of a plan for scrapping and building modelled on the scheme adopted by Japan. £3.55 million was lent to tramp owners under this scheme, 97 vessels totalling 385,625 tons being scrapped and 50 new vessels totalling 186,000 tons being built. Only six of the 97 vessels scrapped, however, were originally the property of the applicant companies, the rest being old ships which had been bought overseas for the purposes of scrapping under the terms of the Act. The chief beneficiaries of this scheme, therefore, were foreign owners who were thus able to sell these old ships to British owners above scrap prices.[22]

In consequence of Italy's war against Abyssinia (Ethiopia), the Spanish Civil War and a rising volume of world trade – the index rose to an inter-war peak of 141 in 1937 – freight rates began to rise in 1936 and in 1937 Britain's scrap-and-build scheme was abandoned.

In the North Atlantic liner service there was general over-tonnaging in the 1930s because the United States reduced the level of immigration. German and French liner shipping was subsidised but little was done by the British government in this field. Slight help was given to Cunard in 1930 when the government agreed to take up, though only at the commercial rate prevailing, that part of the insurance which the insurance market could not absorb for Job 534, the liner building on the Clyde which was launched in 1934 as the *Queen Mary*. In the latter year the government also agreed to advance up to £3 million so that this liner could be completed, and up to £5 million for a sister ship to be built, but only on condition that the Cunard and White Star lines merged. A further £1.5 million was advanced to the merged companies for working capital.

It has been argued that British shipowners were unenterprising in the inter-war period, and that there was some decline in British shipping efficiency because conference arrangements lessened competition. A new initiative was displayed only in cruising, which attracted 62,500 passengers before World War II. It has also been suggested that second- and third-generation shipowners in families which had built up the British steam fleet lacked the abilities of their progenitors. The principal critic of British shipping has suggested that, after allowing for the irreversible effects of World War I and the pre-war trends in shipping, Britain should have had a fleet of 23.1 million tons in 1939, or 34.5 per cent of the world total, whereas she had only 17.9 million tons, or 26.1 per cent of the world total, a fleet which was smaller than it had been in 1914. In other words the British fleet had declined more than it should have done.[24]

There is some warrant in these criticisms but it can scarcely be imagined that pre-war trend lines would have continued unchanged. Many nations with a seaboard – Australia, South Africa, Canada, Poland – wanted a substantial merchant navy after having had maritime services cut by the war. After 1920 international trade was hampered by tariffs, quotas and exchange restrictions as countries tried to satisfy national ambitions or protect themselves from slump. Subsidies to foreign shipping became increasingly common. Restrictions were placed on international migration and, after 1930, bilateral trade pacts and currency controls imposed further restrictions on trade.

Between the two wars exports from the United Kingdom declined and imports increased. This meant that the practice of selling exports c.i.f. and buying imports f.o.b. continued to work to the detriment of British shipping. In Britain's import trade the shipping of the United States, Germany, Italy and Japan together increased its share. Between 1913 and 1937 the entrances at British ports of British ships declined from 65.8 to 55.8 per cent of the total. The entrances of subsidised foreign ships, on the other hand, increased from 7.5 per cent to 17.2 per cent.[25] In value terms the share of world trade carried in British ships fell from 52 per cent in 1912 to 40 per cent in 1936.

Fundamental to this change in the British position was the very substantial decline in coal exports – from 77 million tons in 1913 to 38 million tons in 1938 – and the growth of oil imports. Coalmines had been developed elsewhere in World War I and oil, the demand for which had been growing fast, had not yet been found in British home territory. To make matters worse for British shipping, a much smaller proportion of the coal exported was being carried to such distant markets as South America so that United Kingdom tramps were particularly hard hit. In 1913 British coal exports provided continuous employment for 5 million tons of tramp shipping of which about 3 million tons was British-owned. In the 'boom' year of 1937, when about 2.5 million tons of shipping was carrying British coal exports, only 1.5 million tons was British owned.[26]

Oil imports, on the other hand, increased from 1.7 million tons (1.1

per cent of British seaborne trade) in 1913 to 11.1 million tons (9.5 per cent of British seaborne trade) in 1938, and accounted for 50 per cent of the increase in import volume.

World crude oil production had increased from less than one million tons in 1870 to 45 million tons in 1914, 95 million tons in 1920 and 276 million tons in 1937. Exports by sea, 14 million tons in 1914, were 60 million tons by 1931 and more than 84 million tons by 1937. Less than 5 per cent of world seaborne trade by tonnage in 1913, oil amounted to 21 per cent by 1937. To carry oil exports the world tanker fleet, which had been 1.5 million tons in 1914, half of it British-owned, had risen to 11.4 million tons by 1939. By 1939, however, only 25 per cent of this tanker fleet was British-owned.

British shipping companies may well be criticised for not building a bigger tanker fleet between the wars. Tankers did not appeal to established British liner operators who, shortsightedly, continued to regard them as floating pieces of pipeline rather than 'real ships' right down to the early 1950s. British tramp owners lacked both the capital and the enterprise to switch to tankers. Coal and coal-burning ships had been basic to their trade for nearly a century and they seemed to turn their backs on oil much as American sailing shipowners in the 19th century had turned their backs on steam.

Many British shipowners preferred steam to motorships, and until 1933 British loadline requirements made British tankers less economic than American or Norwegian tankers. Since in Scandinavia all fuel had to be imported and the tonnage of fuel per horse-power produced was lower for oil than for coal, oil was more competitive with coal in Scandinavia than it was in Britain. Norwegian crews were also cheaper than British crews. For all these reasons the Norwegians gained much of what the British lost. In the inter-war years, and particularly after 1926, a fleet of independent tankers grew up and these ships were chartered on either time or voyage charters to the oil companies. The risks involved in building and operating such ships were accepted by Norwegian owners, most of them new to shipping, and they were also willing to accept a low profit margin. They built diesel ships which were larger and more economical than the steam tankers built for British owners.

Although Britain's trade demanded a considerable fleet of refrigerated vessels and British refrigerated tonnage increased, the Scandinavians took the lead in the development of these ships. Other specialised ships such as ore carriers were also appearing as a threat to the traditional tramp, a process which was to continue after the Second World War.

In the inter-war period the widespread adoption of diesel propulsion in shipping was the major technical innovation. The Royal Navy had been largely converted to oil in World War I and the Scandinavians adopted the new fuel for their merchant shipping almost as soon as it became possible to do so. But oil was slow in coming to British merchant ships. It was European engineers who took the lead in the development of diesel propulsion and Britain's pre-war technological advantages were steadily eroded.

The earliest ocean-going motorship had been the Dutch oil tanker *Vulcanus* built at Amsterdam in 1910. With a service speed of about eight knots, she consumed two tons of oil per 24 hours and remained in service until 1931. The first cargo motorship to cross the Atlantic was the *Toiler*, fitted with a Swedish diesel engine but built in Newcastle in 1911.[27] By 1922 *British General*, built for the British Tanker Company, was typical of the new oil-powered steam turbine tankers. Built by Palmers Shipbuilding & Iron Company at Jarrow, the ship's engines – one high pressure and one low pressure turbine, both connected by double-reduction gearing to a single screw shaft – were fitted aft, largely for reasons of safety. Steam was supplied by three single-ended boilers fired with oil-fuel and normal speed was 11.8 knots. In 1926 a successful motor liner, *Carnarvon Castle*, was built by Harland & Wolff for the mail service to South Africa. She was 636 feet long and was provided with seven large cargo holds and accommodation for 660 passengers. Her normal speed was about 15 knots and, after being partly rebuilt and re-engined in 1938, she served as an armed merchant cruiser in World War II, being broken up in Japan in 1962.[28]

Lord Kylsant of Royal Mail Lines and Sir Frederick Lewis of Furness Withy were early British converts to the motorship, as was Andrew Weir of Bank Line, who began to build a fleet of motor vessels in 1923. Nevertheless, British shipbuilders and British shipowners as a whole were slower than their Continental rivals in recognising the merits of motor ships, and for them these merits were not immediately obvious. Diesel engines were more expensive in first costs and suffered high maintenance charges though, when fully developed, they saved on both weight and space with the result that more cargo could be carried in the completed ship. They were also easier to bunker and required fewer men in the engine room.

The comparative figures below relate to about 1930, after two decades of development of the motor vessel, and detail the costs of running a motorship and an economical steamship, each of about 8000 tons deadweight, at a speed of 10.5 knots for a period of 30 days. The running costs alone of motorships were clearly lower.

Fig. 11. THE ECONOMICS OF OIL-FIRED SHIPS IN 1930

	DIESEL SHIP OIL-FIRED	STEAMSHIP COAL-FIRED
Tons of fuel used	282	1005
Cost of fuel	£916.5	£1256.25
Cost of lubricating oil	£45	£19.5
Number of engine room staff	8	21
Wages and victualling of above	£181	£307.25
Total engine room costs	£1132.5	£1583
Engine-room cost per ton carried	£0.141	£0.198

The diesel engine became increasingly economic for speeds between 12 and 17 knots for those prepared to accept its more exacting standards of technical proficiency. Most British shipbuilders adopted continental designs for internal combustion engines, building the engines under licence, but William Doxford & Sons of Sunderland were in the van in Britain, producing a diesel propulsion unit of their own which was first installed in the 9000 deadweight ton *Yngaren* for Swedish owners as early as 1921.[30]

While Scandinavian shipowners were building diesel-engined tankers, fruit carriers and cargo ships suitable for charter to liner companies, United Kingdom tramp owners continued to favour the traditional 9–10 knot dry cargo steamship. At the same time improvements were being made in the British Parsons steam turbine and, by the introduction of gearing, it was possible to obtain substantially the advantages that it offered to the passenger liner at the more modest speeds of the cargo liner. Liner owners in Britain frequently selected the geared turbine as the most cost effective method of propulsion for fast cargo vessels of the highest quality.

Other improvements continued to be made to the passenger liner and in the Eastern and Australasian trades the slow increase in size was maintained. Turbo- or electrically-driven pumps and compressors replaced reciprocating auxiliaries. The *Mooltan* and *Maloja*, built in 1924 for the Australian service, burned oil instead of coal and thus eliminated a great deal of dirt on board. These ships were of 20,000 tons and carried 650 passengers, all cabins being provided with portholes. In 1925 five smaller but elegant liners – *Ranpura, Ranchi, Rawalpindi* and *Rajputana* of 16,500 tons and *Chitral* of 15,000 tons – were built for the Far East services. The first large British turbo-electric vessel, *Viceroy of India*, entered the P & O service in 1929. The turbo-electric drive provided a smoother passage than piston-engines, and *Viceroy of India* was the first P & O liner to have a built-in swimming pool. All her first-class passengers had single-berth cabins and it was symptomatic of things to come that she went cruising in the off-season.

The final class of main liners built for P & O before World War II were the 'Straths' built for the Australian service, *Strathnaver* in 1931 and *Strathaird* in 1932. The ships had a service speed of 20 knots and all cabins were provided with running water, first-class cabins enjoying both hot and cold. Forced ventilation cooled the air in hot weather and warmed it in cold, though this innovation was still a long way from the air-conditioning which became common after 1950 for the bathrooms in these ships were akin to saunas. By this time the Victorian days of amateur entertainment on board were largely over and passenger activities were becoming more organised in holiday camp fashion.[31]

On the Atlantic there were no particularly innovative features in the post-war liners until the *Empress of Britain* was launched in 1930. She was built for cruising as well as for the Atlantic crossing. Her length was 760 feet and she carried 1180 passengers. Her engines were a 4-shaft arrangement of Parsons single reduction gear turbines, each screw shaft being driven by an independent set. Steam was supplied by eight Yarrow water-tube boilers and one Johnson boiler. Her cruising speed was 24 knots.[32] With the decline in immigrants the shipping lines began to develop a so-called 'tourist third cabin class' designed for those with a desire to travel on limited incomes, mainly students and teachers.[33]

The French liner *Normandie*, an outstanding example of turbo-electric propulsion, was launched in 1932 and was the first transatlantic liner to exceed 1000 feet. She was the most popular ship on the Atlantic run and it was difficult to secure a cabin even at the height of the depression. Renamed USS *Lafayette* in 1941, she was broken up in 1946 after a fire had gutted her in 1942. Her great rival was Cunard's *Queen Mary*, 81,235 gross tons, Britain's first vessel over 1000 feet long. *Queen Mary*'s four shafts were each driven by separate turbines through single reduction gearing, and steam was supplied at 400 pounds per square inch at a temperature of 371°C by 24 Yarrow water-tube boilers. The *Queen Mary* gained the Blue Riband in 1936, lost it to *Normandie* in 1937, and regained it in 1938 at an average speed of 31.7 knots. The ship is now a museum piece in Los Angeles. The *Queen Elizabeth* of 83,673 gross tons, Cunard's other most famous vessel, and at 1031 feet in length the biggest passenger liner ever built, was launched in 1938 but did not sail until March 1940.

In 1919 the International Labour Organisation had been established with the object of improving labour conditions and, in these inter-war years, a few modest steps were taken in the direction of the further safety of ships and seafarers and in the direction of pollution control. The latter arose directly from the growth of the oil industry and the proliferation of the motor ship. The former arose largely from the sinking of the *Titanic*.

The discharge of oil and mixtures of oil and water into British territorial waters was prohibited by the Oil in Navigable Waters Act of 1922, and in 1926 British shipowners and some others entered into a voluntary agreement not to discharge oil into the sea within fifty miles of the coast.[34] In 1929 18 nations – five more than in 1913 – were represented at a second International Safety Conference and it was there agreed that cargo ships of 1600 gross tons or more should keep a radio watch for distress calls, a provision which had been in force in British ships since 1919. A few years later 'wireless operators' were promoted to 'radio officers'. In 1930 an International Loadline Conference agreed a set of rules, and British requirements were modified in 1933 when the Merchant Shipping (Safety and Load Line Convention) Act gave an oil tanker of 450 feet the legal right to load an additional 750 tons of fuel. At about this time British ships were beginning to be fitted with the new 'wireless direction finding sets' as an aid to navigation. At least one British shipmaster felt that he would be insulted if an owner fitted one in his ship.[35]

At the inspiration of Sir Robert Burton-Chadwick, and four years after the mercantile marine had been designated the Merchant Navy, a further step was taken to enhance the status of the Merchant Navy officer. This was the establishment, in 1926, of a Company of Master Mariners as a City livery company, something which one might have thought would have happened, by analogy with the fishmongers and shipwrights, in earlier, even medieval, times. Two years later the Prince of Wales became the first Master and the King bestowed the title 'Honourable' upon the Company.

However, in the year of the General Strike all was not well with shipping and enhanced status did nothing to increase pay. Following the slump of 1920, Havelock Wilson had accepted a reduction by one-third of seamen's wages. From the end of war level of £14.10s a month, the able-seaman's wages had fallen to £9 a month, though when freights improved after 1922 an increase of £1 was given. In such circumstances a moderate trade union leader like Wilson was not likely to go unchallenged.

After the strike of 1911 the Southampton branch of Wilson's union, which did not want its funds controlled from the centre, had broken away from the Sailors' and Firemen's Union to form the British Seafarers' Union and they were subsequently joined by Glasgow's 1000 members. In 1909 Joe Cotter had formed a separate Cooks' and Stewards' Union whose members subsequently joined with the British Seafarers' Union to form the Amalgamated Marine Workers' Union, an organisation which caused disruption among seafarers in 1925. However, Wilson won that battle, renaming his own organisation the National Union of Seamen in 1926, the more militant Amalgamated Marine Workers' Union coming to an end in the following year. In the meantime Wilson's union had refused to back the General Strike and was in consequence expelled in 1928 from the Trades Union Congress, though it was readmitted in 1929, the year of Havelock Wilson's death.[36]

There was dissatisfaction too, among the officers. In 1919 the British Merchant Service League had been formed as an officers' trade union but it was dissolved in 1921. In the latter year, however, Captain W. H. Coombs left the sea to found the Navigators and General Insurance Company, an organisation designed to give officers an opportunity to insure against the loss of their professional certificates following an official inquiry into the loss of a ship, a collision or other accident. In 1925, at his own expense, Coombs published a book which he called *The Nation's Keymen* in which he argued the officers' case. Increasingly he found that he was becoming the spokesman for Merchant Navy officers. In 1928 he inspired the formation of the Officers' (Merchant Navy) Federation, a body through which both British and Commonwealth officers' organisations could work together, and in 1932 he formed The Watch Ashore, an organisation designed to represent officers' wives.

The following year Coombs mounted a demonstration on the Thames and presented a petition carrying 23,000 signatures to Parliament, complaining that there was no control over the entry of apprentices and cadets into the Merchant Navy, that officers enjoyed no legal or customary rights to periods of leave, that officers had no fixed hours of duty, and that they enjoyed no pension rights. Coombs received sufficient support to force through some reforms. The Merchant Navy Officers' Pension Fund was established, the Officers' Federation was admitted to the National Maritime Board, and in 1935 a Central Board for the Training of Officers for the Merchant Navy was established to promote a uniform training scheme at sea for deck apprentices. In this same year Coombs realised that his insurance company could not continue to fill the role of a trade union and he established the Navigators & Engineer Officers Union. In 1936 the two older bodies representing officers, the Mercantile Marine Service Association and the Imperial Merchant Service Guild, amalgamated, under the title of the first-named.

By this time a few enlightened shipping companies concerned for the quality of their officers – the British India Steam Navigation Company, the New Zealand Shipping Company and Brocklebank's – were using cargo liners as school ships for their cadets. But a high proportion of apprentices and over 60 per cent of the deckboys going to sea still had no induction course of any kind.[37]

Between 1929 and 1932 the total of world shipping tonnage laid up increased fourfold, and in the latter year 1,663,000 tons of British shipping were laid up and 40,000 British seafarers were unemployed.[38]

During the slump officers' salaries were reduced and jobs were so few that some qualified master mariners were sailing 'before the mast' as able seamen. As in all slumps, those who remained in employment suited to their qualifications did not suffer unduly, but for others the situation was desperate.

The master of a 10,000-ton cargo ship now received £24 a month. The chief officer received £19 a month, the second officer £14 and the third officer £10. An experienced radio officer was paid £12 a month. Out of their pay officers bought their uniforms, sextants, bedding, towels and soap. Only the radio officer, employed by a radio company and not directly by the shipping company, received bedding and towels free. Engineer officers received salaries similar to those of the navigating officers. Apprentices, of whom there were some 3000 at sea, were frequently sweated labour, often working as seamen, sometimes receiving 1s, sometimes 30s a month, and sixpence an hour overtime. ABs received £10 and firemen £10. 10s a month and were paid overtime. Since they did not have the same expenses, ratings were financially better off than junior officers. Lascars received 30 rupees a month, the equivalent of 45s, and their living conditions in many ships were abominable.

There were many 'two-mate' ships in which the chief and second officers kept alternate watches. Sometimes they were expected to chip, scrape and paint holds or sew canvas. When down the holds at sea, they left a whistle with the man at the wheel and, if another vessel hove in sight, the helmsman blew the whistle and the officer came to the bridge. When such ships reached port, although worn out by lack of sleep, the officers had to keep cargo watches.

By this time officers were entitled to fourteen days leave a year, but often if an officer took his leave it meant that he also lost his job. Most companies kept no relieving officers so anyone taking leave was paid off and his place was filled by one of the unemployed. If leave was not taken, money could be claimed in lieu, but if the money were claimed the officers concerned were sometimes told that their services were no longer required. Thus men living, say, on Tyneside whose ships ran into the Bristol Channel seldom saw their homes. Their wives 'came through', as the expression was, to spend a few days in poky, coaldust-smothered, uncomfortable cabins, and often such visits were allowed only after the ship had been away for a year or more.

An officer's accommodation comprised a small box of a cabin with one tiny porthole. The furniture consisted of a single bunk, a wash-handstand with no running water and a tiny wardrobe. Ratings were still herded into fo'c'sles, wedge-shaped spaces in the ship's bows and, if the ship were in a collision, death and injury among the crew were common. These ratings slept in tiered bunks, ate at a bare deal table between the bunks, and provided their own bed (a straw-filled mattress or 'donkey's breakfast'), bedding, towels, soap, plate, mug, knife and fork. A few portholes, seldom opened, were supposed to ventilate the fo'c'sle. In a large passenger ship 200 stewards might have 15 washbasins between them.

Seldom even for officers was an electric fan or mosquito net provided. On arrival in port it was common practice to shut down the ship's dynamo and then lighting was by 'oil batti' or paraffin oil lamp. The fo'c'sles had coal bogies to heat them in cold weather but with the donkey boiler shut down in port to save coal there might be no heat in the officers' cabins at all, even though the ship were frozen in the river Danube in winter.

Bathrooms were frequently dismal places. 'We sometimes bathed in bare, rusty wash places', one seafarer at sea in the 1930s has reminisced. 'On one ship the cubby-hole for washing, off the engine-room middle platform, was so rusty and unusable that we washed in buckets on deck. Lavatories were often on open decks, dangerous to get to in heavy weather, and wetted inside by seas sloshing up an outlet pipe with a faulty valve. Dhobying, or washing clothes, was done in a bucket on deck and the washing dried on lines strung between cargo derricks.'[39]

The usual manning for an 800-ton coaster between the wars was 14 – 4 ABs, 3 firemen, 1 donkeyman, 2 mates, 2 engineers, 1 cook and a skipper. When the slump came, first of all 2 ABs went, then a fireman and the cook, and finally one of the mates signed on as bosun.[40] The normal crew of an 8000 deadweight-ton tramp numbered 33: master, 3 mates, chief, second, third and fourth engineers, wireless operator, bosun, carpenter, steward, cook, 4 apprentices, 4 seamen, 6 firemen, 3 trimmers, mess-room boy, galley boy and cabin boy. The four apprentices lived, slept and ate in a room which measured 11 feet by 9 feet. On deck they worked watch and watch, four hours on and four hours off day and night seven days a week.[41]

A passenger ship might have several hundred crew, most of them in the catering department. A steward would be called at 0530, start cleaning at 0600, lay up tables from 0645, and shave and change into uniform between 0715 and 0800. From 0800 to 0930 he would serve at table, taking his own breakfast while standing up at slack moments during this time. From 0930 he would clean up, being ready for inspection by the captain and chief steward before 1200. At 1200 he would begin to prepare for lunch and snatch his own before serving lunch between 1300 and 1400. Some stewards would then work from 1430 until 1700 and then be off duty until 1830, finishing serving and clearing dinner by 2045. Those who did not work from 1430 to 1700 would work after dinner until 2300.[42]

On deck seamen had many more jobs than are done today: 'holy stoning' the deck; painting awkward fittings; rubbing brass, and often making the cleaner from bathbrick rubbed to dust with a makeshift grater (made from an old tin) and then mixing the dust with colza oil; stowing anchor cable in the cable locker, a filthy job; oiling the main steel decks; and cleaning holds and bilges, particularly loathsome after a cargo of grain had been carried. Safety was not much thought about; and the only water supply was from a hand-pump outside the galley which would be locked up except for specified times if water was short.

There were no refrigerators on the older cargo ships, though some perishable foods were stored in a large ice-box. Up to 1938 the seaman was entitled to a one-pound tin of condensed milk every three weeks, 1.25 pounds of sugar a week (of which one-quarter was withheld for cooking purposes), and 1.75 ounces of tea a week (less than the civilian ration in wartime). 'Soft bread' was eaten on Sundays, Tuesdays and Thursdays; otherwise it was ship's biscuits, known as 'hard tack' or 'Liverpool pantiles'.[43] Food was usually adequate, though not always appetising. Serving under a master in Denholm's, one officer was told, 'Misterr Shaw, we're a vairy eeconomical company here – and we – I must remind you – always butter our biscuits on the side where there aren't any holes.'[44]

One rating who described his experiences in 1934 said that hundreds of ships were laid up and he himself was 'on the beach' when a former shipmate wrote to say that there was a job going on a tanker in Thameshaven if he could get there in time. His wife pawned a few things to raise his train fare from South Shields in Northumberland to King's Cross in

London. From King's Cross he had to walk across the City of London to Fenchurch Street, carrying his sea-bag and donkey's breakfast, to catch another train to Stanford-le-Hope in Essex where he arrived late at night. It was raining, but again he had to walk some miles until he found the ship lying at a jetty in Shellhaven.

He described the ship – a coal-burning tanker of about 5000 deadweight tons and over 40 years old – as 'a steel workhouse'. The fo'c'sle was under the waterline and nine seamen lived in a space little bigger than the single cabins which were the norm by the 1950s. 'A coal bogey belched out smoke, the stink a conglomeration of smells, coal fumes, hot oil, foul air, human sweat and urine.' A small table was covered with rusty kits, tin mugs, tin plates, beer bottles, hand-rags, sweat-rags, cockroaches, bugs, flies and rats.

A few drunken seamen sprawled in the bunks and, since it was three o'clock in the morning, all was quiet. The new rating had not eaten since he had left home, but he found a few hard biscuits and a piece of salt-junk which belonged to the mess. After sharing this meal with a couple of rats he flopped into a low bunk. 'A drunk got up', he wrote, 'and used a bucket near my head. The bucket was for washing up plates and mugs, but also for slushing down the lavatory and bathing in.'

The following morning he 'signed on' for a voyage to Mexico and back. Homeward bound his elderly watchmate fell sick but was accused of malingering. This man continued to stagger on watch until, a day or two later, he was found dead in his bunk. That morning the body was sewn up in a waste-bag, since there was no canvas on board, and flung into the sea. At the end of the voyage the rating was signed off the ship and, again unemployed, signed back on the dole.[45]

British ships between the wars were often dirtier and less hygienic than foreign ships calling at British ports, and less well provided with water. Lady Astor in 1938 said in the House of Commons that a colleague who had taken a look at the conditions in which seamen lived had said he would not expect ferrets to live in such conditions. Seamen were three times more likely to die from tuberculosis than the average British male and nearly three times more likely to die of an accident than was a coalminer, a notoriously dangerous occupation.[46] Nevertheless deaths from accidents and sinkings were less than one-quarter of what they had been before the war.[47]

Seamen's wages, cut again in 1932, were gradually restored to pre-slump levels by the beginning of 1937. By the outbreak of the Second World War wages in real terms were perhaps 33 per cent above what they had been in 1914. Working hours had also been reduced in these years and, despite the bad conditions in older ships, accommodation had improved in some degree since Edwardian times.[48]

When war broke out again, Britain still remained the world's greatest maritime country. In 1938 the value of all textiles exported – wool, cotton and other materials – amounted to £92 million. Machinery exports were valued at £58 million, vehicles at £45 million, iron and steel manufactures at £42 million and chemicals at £22 million. Exports of coal were worth £37 million. Britain's ocean-going fleet of liners and tramps, ships generally of more than 3000 tons, was as follows.[49]

Fig. 12. BRITISH SHIPS EXCEEDING 3000 TONS GROSS, 1939

	NUMBER OF SHIPS	TOTAL GROSS TONNAGE	OWNED BY
Liners	1170	8,744,469	68 companies
Tramps	577	2,708,443	50 companies, each with 5 or more ships
	36	168,751	9 companies, each with 4 ships
	48	222,121	16 companies, each with 3 ships
	48	205,109	24 companies, each with 2 ships
	30	142,027	30 companies, each with 1 ship
Tramp total	739	3,449,401	129 companies
Grand total	1869	12,233,920	197 companies

At this time, when airmail had still not crossed the Atlantic, the United Kingdom possessed one-third of the world's deepsea tonnage and, in tonnage terms, nearly half of its large passenger ships, more than half of its refrigerated ships, and one-quarter of its tankers.

However, impressive though these figures are, decline had set in. The gross tonnage of the fleet was less than it had been in 1914 and from operating half the world fleet, as she had done in 1890, Britain was by this time operating little more than one-quarter.

Notes

1. P. Duff, *British Ships and Shipping* (1949), London, pp. 14–15.
2. S. G. Sturmey, *British Shipping and World Competition* (1962), London, p. 59; J. Woddis, *Under the Red Duster* (1947), London, p. 13.
3. W. E. Minchinton, 'British Ports of Call in the Nineteenth Century' (1976), MM, Vol. 62, No. 2, p. 150.
4. S. Jones, *Trade and Shipping: Lord Inchcape 1852–1932* (1989), Manchester, pp. 119–120.
5. Sturmey, *op. cit.*, p. 65.
6. H. Gripaios, *Tramp Shipping* (1959), London, p. 3.
7. R. Hope, *Profits in British Industry 1924–1935* (1948), Oxford University, unpublished thesis.
8. Sturmey, *op. cit.*, pp. 38–9.
9. R. H. Thornton, *British Shipping* (1959), Cambridge, p. 85.
10. Sturmey, *op. cit.*, pp. 130–1.
11. *Ib.*, pp. 120–2.
12. *Ib.*, p. 91.
13. W. H. Miller, *German Ocean Liners of the 20th Century* (1988), Northants.
14. Sturmey, *op. cit.*, pp. 115–17.
15. S. Rabson & K. O'Donoghue, *P & O: A Fleet History* (1988), Kendal, pp. 170–1.
16. Woddis, *op. cit.*, p. 15.
17. E. Green & M. Moss, *A Business of National Importance* (1982), London, *passim.*
18. M. W. Thomas, *A Survey of English Economic History*, 3rd edn (1967), London, pp. 494–7.
19. F. E. Hyde, *Shipping Enterprise and Management 1830–1939: Harrisons of Liverpool* (1967), Liverpool, pp. 174–5.
20. B. Greenhill, 'The Death of Mercantile Sail' (28.6.1979), *Fairplay.*
21. Sturmey, *op. cit.*, p. 66.
22. *Ib.*, p. 109.
23. M. Langley & E. Small, *Port of Plymouth Series: Merchant Shipping* (1988), Devon, p. 30.
24. Sturmey, *op. cit., passim*, particularly pp. 66, 96, 127 and 134.
25. *Ib.*, p. 127.
26. *Ib.*, pp. 73–4.
27. J. Guthrie, *A History of Marine Engineering* (1971), London, p. 200.
28. A. F. L. Deeson, *An Illustrated History of Steamships* (1976), Bourne End, Bucks, pp. 125–7.
29. Sturmey, *op. cit.*, p. 83 (from Brassey, 1935, p. 337).
30. R. Craig, *Steam Tramps and Cargo Liners 1850–1950* (1980), London, p. 54.
31. P. Padfield, *Beneath the House Flag of P & O* (1981), London, pp. 124–8.
32. Deeson, *op. cit.*, p. 129.
33. F. Bustard (10.4.1958) in *Shipbuilding & Shipping Record*, p. 469.
34. Anon, *Seafarers and Their Ships* (1955), London, p. 88.
35. Captain C. Colburn in correspondence with the author about a master under whom he served.
36. A. Marsh & V. Ryan, *The Seamen: A History of the National Union of Seamen* (1989), Oxford, pp. 105ff.

37. *The Seafarer* (January 1944), p. 11.
38. Woddis, *op. cit.*, pp. 65–8 and p. 84.
39. R. Hope (ed), *Sea Pie* (1984), London, pp. 104–5.
40. Woddis, *op. cit.*, p. 74.
41. R. F. McBrearly, *Seafaring in the 30s* (1989), Lewes, pp. 15–17.
42. Woddis, *op. cit.*, p. 71; *The Seafarer* (July 1935), p. 29.
43. McBrearly, *op. cit.* pp. 55–61.
44. F. Greenhalgh-Shaw, *Stories from Eighty Years of Travel and Adventure* (1988), Ilfracombe.
45. Hope (1984), *op. cit.*, pp. 1–2.
46. Woddis, *op. cit.*, pp. 44ff.
47. *The Marine Observer* (July 1955).
48. Marsh & Ryan, *op. cit.*, pp. 140–2.
49. P. Duff, *op. cit.*, p. 37.

21

Second World War

(1939–1948)

Unrecognised, you put us in your debt;
Unthanked, you enter, or escape, the grave;
Whether your land remember or forget
You saved the land, or died to try to save.

Poet Laureate John Masefield was trained for the Merchant Navy aboard the officers' training ship *Conway* and had been round Cape Horn in sail. He wrote the lines above in tribute to the merchant seaman at war. In World War II the fighting services, in terms of those killed or missing, suffered little more than one-third of the casualties suffered in World War I. In the Merchant Navy, a civil occupation, the figure for World War II was twice as high as that for World War I.[1] More than one-quarter of the men in the Merchant Navy did not survive until the end of the war and, proportionately, casualties in the Merchant Navy were far higher than they were in the armed forces.[2]

The merchant seaman was involved in the war from the beginning. The first British merchant ship sunk, the 13,581-ton *Athenia*, was torpedoed by a German U-boat under the command of Commander Fritz Lemp nine hours after hostilities began on 3rd September 1939. It was the first hostile act of the war. Ironically, Lemp subsequently helped to shorten the war by not destroying his code-books and Enigma machine when another U-boat he commanded was taken by the British. Lemp did not survive the capture but, with his code-books and machine, experts were able to unravel German messages.

Some 60 passenger liners were taken over by the Admiralty at the outbreak of the war for conversion into armed merchant cruisers. Two of these subsequently won places for themselves in the annals of heroic naval actions by fighting, and losing, against overwhelming odds: *Rawalpindi* was sunk in action against the German warships *Scharnhorst* and *Gneisenau*, and *Jervis Bay* was sunk by *Admiral Scheer*.

At Dunkirk in the early summer of 1940 the defeated British Army – 350,000 soldiers – was brought home from Europe and the rescue was largely the work of merchant ships. The sinking of merchant ships rose sharply thereafter and the first heavy attack by the Germans on the docks of London took place in September of that year. By the end of 1940 6000 merchant seamen had been killed. Seven thousand more were killed in 1941, and nearly 8000 in 1942.[3] When Europe was at last invaded, on 6th June 1944, some 2000 merchant ships, aggregating 4 million tons, most of them British, supplied and maintained the Armed Forces. At this time and in the months that followed more than 70,000 merchant seamen served in such ships. By the end of the war 2426 British ships totalling 11,331,933 gross tons had been lost,[4] and 6500 decorations had been given to merchant seamen for specific acts of gallantry.

The census figures of 1938[5] indicate that at the time at which the census was taken 159,313 men were employed at sea on British sea-trading vessels. This figure excluded seafarers on leave. 59,553 served on deck, 54,045 in the engine room and 45,715 were stewards. Of the total, 107,088 were British nationals. A further 45,182 were from the British Commonwealth, 75 per cent of these being Indian and the rest Chinese or from other Commonwealth countries. The remaining 7043 were foreigners.

Some of the foreigners ceased to serve on the outbreak of war. Of the British nationals, 7000 transferred to the Royal Navy since they were members of the Royal Navy Reserve. Despite these losses, the number of British merchant seamen was raised to an average of 145,000 throughout the war years. This number included some boys of 16, an age at which they were not allowed to join the Armed Forces. It also included a few who were younger than 16. These had lied about their age.

Despite fears in the months before May 1941, when seafaring was made an 'essential' occupation, that there would be a drift of seafarers to shore work, there was never any difficulty in securing enough seamen even when the war at sea was at its worst. Morale remained high throughout. Excluding any deaths among the British Commonwealth seafarers who continued to serve, it has been estimated that no fewer than 50,525 British merchant seamen died, either directly or indirectly, as a result of enemy action between 1939 and 1945.[6]

Some merchant ships were capable of only five knots, the speed of the slowest convoys. When in convoy ships had some protection from Royal Navy escorts, but many merchantmen lacked even the most rudimentary means of self-defence and self-preservation. Those men who sailed in these ships through the submarine-infested waters of the 'Western Ocean' or North Atlantic of 1941 and 1942 were at greater risk than ever seamen had been before. Cargoes of oil could turn ships and the surrounding sea into a blazing inferno. Cargoes of iron ore or war materials could cause a damaged ship to sink like a stone. One convoy to Russia which set out with 40 ships arrived in Murmansk with 13. 'The waste of precious cargoes', said Winston Churchill in 1943, 'the destruction of so many noble ships, the loss of heroic crews, all combine to constitute a repulsive and sombre panorama.' He nevertheless allocated to the Royal Air Force bomber aircraft which might have been better deployed protecting convoys.

The official historian of the British Merchant Navy at war pays tribute to the men who manned these ships by quoting A. E. Housman.[7]

> What God abandoned, these defended –
> And saved the sum of things for pay.

So far as pay is concerned, on 15th September 1939 a 'war risk' payment of £3 was added to the able-seaman's basic monthly pay of £9 12s 6d. This sum was labelled 'war risk' money so that other industrial workers would not make matching wage demands. In 1942 the war risk money was raised to £10. By February 1943, inclusive of war risk money, an able-seaman's monthly pay had risen to £24. In these same years the government instituted a war pensions scheme for seafarers,[8] and it was agreed that, if sunk, the merchant seaman who survived would receive his full wages, inclusive of war risk money, until his return to the United Kingdom or until he was offered another job.[9] If his ship was sunk, he also received compensation for the loss of his effects and fourteen days special shipwreck leave with full pay in addition to any leave that was due to him. When the seaman was ashore the government bore the cost.

In some degree, however, the merchant seaman remained a second-class citizen. When the *King City* was sunk her surviving crew were landed in Italian Somaliland from where they were rescued by the Army in 1941. They were sick, emaciated and mentally drained, but they were not greeted like heroes. While there appeared to be an excellent standard procedure for dealing with ex-prisoners from the Armed Forces, merchant seamen were said to be 'treated like lepers'.[10] A ship's carpenter who survived the torpedoing of the Harrison Line *Wayfarer* in 1944 came ashore in East Africa and after great privation was repatriated from Port Said on the *Queen of Bermuda*, which was trooping. 'Aboard the *Queen of Bermuda*', he recalled later, 'we were treated like criminals and our official reception in Liverpool was in no way welcoming.'[11]

Early in the War, in February 1940, the victualling scale aboard ship was revised to provide the seaman with more food, particularly fresh food. To reduce delays in ships sailing, a 'Merchant Navy Reserve Pool' of labour was established in December 1940 and one consequence of its establishment was that seamen were now offered continuous instead of casual employment. The Pool was also supposed to accept only new recruits who had undertaken a course of training,[12] but this did not always prove to be the case. After the war, in March 1947, a Merchant Navy Established Service Scheme replaced this wartime arrangement and those seafarers who so chose could henceforward be assured of two-year contracts of work.

When, in May 1941, seamen's work was made the subject of an Essential Works Order, seamen had to register their names. A new Central Register of seamen was then compiled by the Registrar General of Shipping and Seamen and in 1942 a special form of identity card was introduced.

In addition to the change in the victualling scale, the seaman's lot was made better in other modest ways in the war years. Accommodation was better aboard the newly-built American 'Liberty' ships and, not surprisingly, life-saving apparatus was improved. The Ministry of Shipping and its successor, the Ministry of War Transport, authorised the supply of libraries by the Seafarers Education Service to merchant ships taken over by the government. Inspired by Ernest Bevin, a former dockers' leader who had been appointed Minister of Labour and National Service, the government took a new interest in the welfare of seamen when in port, appointing welfare officers in the main British ports and in New York, a measure which led in 1948 to the establishment of a Merchant Navy Welfare Board. In 1942 a Merchant Navy Training Board was established and the Shipping Federation developed some further training schemes for deck ratings and firemen. By 1943 a 56-hour working week was becoming the norm at sea.

The trade unions tried to extend some of these improvements to the international field. Because Allied merchant shipping was controlled largely from London union officials from different countries were able to meet together and in 1944 they produced an International Seafarers' Charter. This document formed the basis for discussion at the International Labour Conference which was held at Seattle in 1946 and conventions were there agreed that dealt with wages, manning scales, hours of work, the certification of able seamen, food and catering, social security and medical care.[13] However, this did not result in any international ratification of the Seafarers' Charter. In the manner of international conferences it led merely to some minor advances and prepared the ground for further discussion.

In the first months of the Second World War there was a shortage of ships, though no Allied ships that were at sea when the Germans attacked in the west returned to enemy-occupied territory. After the invasion of

Norway and the fall of France the British were able to use much Norwegian and French shipping. By this time the war at sea was beginning in earnest and the English Channel and the North Sea became particularly dangerous with the result that shipping was diverted, wherever possible, to the safer areas of the Clyde, the Mersey and the Bristol Channel. Regional Port Directors were appointed in the spring of 1941.

British repair yards were already more than full. Damaged ships needed repair, and old American ships which had been made over to the British required repair and modification. To protect them from magnetic mines ships had to be fitted with degaussing apparatus, which neutralised the ship's magnetisation with an encircling current-carrying conductor. Throughout the war about one-eighth of the British fleet was under repair at any one time.[14]

Initially Britain suffered an acute foreign exchange problem and Erling Naess, a Norwegian who ran ships under the Panamanian flag, told of how he 'bought' his way out of Britain in 1940 and went to the United States by making over $1 million available to the British government.[15] The foreign exchange problems largely disappeared with the passing of the American Lend-Lease Act in March 1941. From that time on repairs to damaged ships could also be carried out abroad. At the same time the Americans were authorised to make available to the British any American shipping which was surplus to United States requirements.

To organise this large fleet for the effective prosecution of the war a Ministry of Shipping had been established within six weeks of the war starting. In May 1941 this Ministry was amalgamated with the Ministry of Transport to form a Ministry of War Transport which had complete control of all means of transport inclusive of shipping. In consequence of German territorial aggression, however, it became increasingly difficult for British ships to enter the Mediterranean and, to cope with Middle East requirements, a Middle East Supply Centre was established in Egypt to which supplies could be delivered by way of the Red Sea. By this time other passenger liners had been converted to carry troops and by the second half of 1941 the *Queen Mary* and the *Queen Elizabeth* were busy ferrying Australian troops to the Middle East. Between them these two ships alone transported 1,250,000 troops safely across the ocean between the spring of 1940 and the summer of 1945.

The problems of the early war years were manifold. At the end of 1941 the Americans were aiming to provide 1.5 million tons of shipping to carry lend-lease cargoes, and it was intended that American shipbuilding yards would provide 7 million tons of new shipping in 1942. These plans were put in jeopardy by the Japanese attack on Pearl Harbor in December

1941 and from that time until the victory over the German forces in North Africa a year later was a period of acute difficulty. In retrospect it can be seen that for the Allies 1942 was the worst year of the war.

During 1942 Britain was trying to supply nitrates to Egypt, coal to East Africa, Arabia and Ceylon, phosphates to South Africa, Australia and New Zealand, armaments and other equipment to Russia, and food grains to East Africa, India and Ceylon. Burmese supplies of rice to India had been cut off by the Japanese invasion of that country. All these cargoes, which make heavy demands on shipping, needed to be moved at a time when ship losses were at their peak. British losses in the first quarter of 1942 were double what they had been in the last quarter of 1941 and went on rising throughout the year. A thousand British and British-controlled ships were lost in 1942 and for the first time in the war the British-controlled merchant fleet began to fall steadily.

Through its control of all merchant ships the Ministry of War Transport was able to make effective use of space by loading both military and civil cargoes in the same ships, and it economised in the use of space by devising new stowage techniques. By March 1943 the Ministry had organised the transport of over a quarter of a million British troops and their equipment to North Africa alone. But there were conflicts over the use of shipping, both in European waters and in the Far East. There were many narrow squeaks and some failures. Many people throughout the world, including of course the United Kingdom, went without things to which they were accustomed. The United Kingdom was forced to run down its capital equipment because proper maintenance was impossible. In India there was starvation: severe food shortage in Southern India and famine in Bengal led in the summer of 1943 to the deaths of 1.5 million people.[16]

By this time, however, the tide was on the turn and new ranges of standardised ships were being built. In British yards various 'Empire' types of vessel were launched. In the United States a design evolved from the *Dorington Court*, a British 7000-ton oil-fired steamer capable of 11 knots and built in Sunderland in 1939, became the model for the American 'Liberty' ships, the first of which had been delivered at the end of 1941. These, together with the American-built T2 tankers, played a large part in ensuring victory for the Allied forces. The output of such ships amounted to no less than 12 million gross tons in each of the peak years of 1943 and 1944.

The Ministry of Shipping had been established with the specific purpose of enabling the Government to secure the vessels it required. Within a few weeks of the outbreak of war freight rates were controlled, a licensing system was introduced and, early in 1940, a full requisitioning scheme was enforced. All British-owned vessels were taken on charter by the Government, freight rates being so determined as to allow the owners a profit of 5 per cent on the agreed value of the ship, together with a 5 per cent allowance for depreciation. Except when requisitioned for use by the Royal Navy, liner tonnage remained under the control of the owners who were paid a management fee based on average costs. Most tramp ships were also placed by the Government under the management of liner companies.[17] Management fees were not intended to yield a profit.

The consequence of these measures was that British shipowners did not do so well out of World War II as they had done out of World War I. They were unable to profit from the high freight rates ruling in neutral trades, and the rates paid by the Government for British-owned tonnage were well below the rates paid for neutral tonnage. The neutral rate in the River Plate to United Kingdom trade was 55s a ton, while the British rate was 32s 6d. In the Montreal–United Kingdom trade the rates were 11s and 4s 6d respectively.[18] Naess ships, registered in Panama but chartered to the British government, earned high returns. In 1941 Naess paid his shareholders a dividend of 25 per cent and also put considerable sums to reserve. However, he did even better from American charters once the Americans entered the war.[19]

From 1942 onwards a scheme existed to sell Government-owned ships to private owners at the end of the war for the replacement of their fleets, the ships being sold at cost less depreciation. Under a Government Tonnage Replacement Scheme for privately-owned ships which were lost about 25 per cent of the original cost of the ship was added to that cost figure to cover wartime increases in insurance values. But when a ship was lost only the basic element of the insurance, or the original cost of the ship, was paid to the owners in cash, the remainder being credited to the owners but withheld until the ship was replaced.[20]

These wartime financial arrangements were generally considered to be fair and reasonable. The liner companies held their own in the face of shipping losses and rising building costs but did not make great gains. For tramp shipowners the financial results of the war were no better than those in a good pre-war year and less good than they had been in 1937.

Initially shipowners in neutral countries were able to make large profits. This may help to explain the sudden emergence in shipping after 1946 of certain Greek entrepreneurs like Aristotle Onassis and Stavros Niarchos. But as the war went on the gap between British and foreign freight rates narrowed and after the American entry into the war there was not much neutral tonnage left. In the second half of the war considerably less than 10 per cent of world tonnage was operated by neutrals.[21]

During World War I Britain had lost 9 million gross tons of shipping or half its merchant fleet. During World War II, 11 million tons of shipping or 60 per cent of the fleet were lost. But much of this loss was made up by wartime building, purchases from the United States, enemy prize tonnage and ships allocated to the United Kingdom by the Inter-Allied Reparations Agency. As a result, between 1939 and 1946 the United Kingdom fleet declined by only 3·6 million tons or 21 per cent.

Many other nations suffered proportionately greater losses. The enemy countries of Italy, Germany and Japan lost 91, 90 and 78 per cent of their fleets respectively. In Greece, France, the Netherlands, Belgium and Norway the losses were, in the same order, 70, 56, 44, 43 and 40 per cent. Altogether all countries other than Britain lost 21 million gross tons of shipping, as against 6 million tons in World War I, and these losses were divided almost evenly between the enemy countries and the Allied and neutral countries other than the United Kingdom. Of the pre-war world fleet of 61.4 million tons, 32 million tons or just over half the total were lost. In the same period, however, by way of new building, the British Dominions increased their fleets by 72 per cent and the United States increased its fleet by no less than 369 per cent.

At the end of the war the United States, the British Dominions and neutral Sweden were better placed in the shipping world than they had been at its beginning. In Britain, tramp owners displayed a lack of initiative at the end of the war when compared with the Greeks and the Norwegians. Their attitude probably owed something to the expectation of many that a slump of the 1920 kind would follow a short post-war boom. British liner owners were no better off as a result of the war, as they had been after World War I, and the prices of replacement ships continued to rise. Since at this time British shipyards were fully employed, all owners seeking new ships had to join a queue and some deferment of replacement was inevitable.

These reservations notwithstanding, British shipowners were in a better position when the war ended than owners in most other maritime countries. However, they made no attempt to raise new capital for the purpose of building new fleets, as they might well have done. On the contrary, they tended to repay old loans and thus lose capital. In 1946 British shipowners as a whole did not seem very willing to consider fleet expansion. They did not expect the boom years to last.

Notes

1. R. H. Thornton, *British Shipping* (1959), Cambridge, p. 93.
2. C. B. A. Behrens, *Merchant Shipping and the Demands of War* (1955), p. 172.
3. *Ib.*, pp. 154–5 and p. 172.
4. J. Slader, *The Red Duster at War: A History of the Merchant Navy during the Second World War* (1988), London.
5. HMSO, *Census of Seamen 1938* (1939).
6. Behrens, *op. cit.*, p. 185; lower figures are given by other authors, e.g. 38,000 by A. Marsh & V. Ryan, *The Seamen: A History of the National Union of Seamen* (1989), Oxford, p. 149.
7. Behrens, *op. cit.*, p. 156.
8. *Ib.*, p. 174.
9. Anon, *The Story of the Seamen* (1964), London, p. 31.
10. B. Edwards, *The Fighting Tramps* (1989), London, p. 38.
11. R. Hope (ed), *Sea Pie* (1984), London, p. 43.
12. *The Seafarer* (January, 1944), p. 11.
13. A. G. Course, *The Merchant Navy: A Social History* (1963), London, p. 291.
14. Behrens, *op. cit.*, p. 144.
15. E. D. Naess, *Autobiography of a Shipping Man* (1977), Colchester, p. 91.
16. Behrens, *op. cit.*, p. 343.
17. S. G. Sturmey, *British Shipping and World Competition* (1962), London, p. 143.
18. *Ib.*, p. 142.
19. Naess, *op. cit.*, p. 78.
20. Sturmey, *op. cit.*, p. 144.
21. *1970 Committee of Inquiry into Shipping* ('Rochdale Report'), London, p. 10.

22

Halcyon Years
(1948–1957)

For British seafarers the dozen years which followed the end of World War II were halcyon years. The superstructure of a ship could be painted something other than a dreary grey. Ships sailed no more in convoy and the nightmare of station-keeping was over. Lights were switched on and portholes opened. Careless talk no longer cost lives. The watchkeeper on the bridge at night could light a cigarette without fear that the glow would bring a torpedo to sink the ship. And more of the world's ports were open for a run ashore. Gradually the wartime developments of radar and a new positioning aid, the Decca Navigator, came into use in merchant ships and, despite learned discussion on 'radar-assisted' collisions, navigation became safer.

In 1954, the year in which films began to be supplied in addition to libraries as a means of entertaining crews at sea, new regulations for improved crew accommodation were adopted in Britain; and three years later salt meat and ship's biscuits vanished officially from the dietary scales.[1] But many shipping companies had improved food and accommodation already. Writing in 1954 one seafarer was lyrical in his description of post-war conditions of work:

> I had just finished a five-month trip and, after twenty-seven days' leave with pay, I reported to the Pool to ship out again. With two shipmates, I travelled from Shields to Lancaster, already on pay again and with a free railway warrant. A car at the station took us and our suitcases to the agent's offices at Heysham. The ship was at anchor in the bay. 'She's not coming alongside till three o'clock,' the agent said. 'Leave your baggage here. The car will take you to a hotel at Morecambe for lunch, pick you up at three, and take you down to the ship.'
>
> We looked around to see what we were joining. Bathing-pool, smokeroom, library, recreation room, showers, single rooms for everyone on board, bed lights, and so on. We signed on her. That night I took a shower all by myself. Here was something I had dreamed of. Back in the old days, I washed in the heads, three to a bucket, and so overcrowded I was never quite sure whose leg I was washing. Then I turned in, my head on yielding pillows, stretched my

> legs under white linen sheets, soft and smooth, switched on my bed light and read the shipping reports in the *Evening News*. Next morning I went to the messroom to a breakfast of cereals, curry and rice, eggs and bacon, hot rolls and marmalade, with cups of tea. I had been a long time thinking of this kind of berth.[2]

The census of 1951 indicated that the number of seafarers had fallen slightly since 1938. Of the total of 152,707 – those serving at sea on the day of the census – 105,080 were United Kingdom residents, some 2000 fewer than just before the war. 'Lascars' and other Commonwealth seafarers numbered 41,957, and there were still 5670 foreigners serving in British ships. Of the 105,080 British seafarers, 22,500 officers and 35,000 ratings – over half the total – were by this time serving under the terms of two-year contracts of service which were renewable.[3] Seafarers were not compelled to be on a two-year contract, but the casual labour system of pre-war days had been very considerably modified.

These improvements by shipowners were reflected in the attitudes of both government and seamen's charities. In 1948 thirty countries participated in an International Conference on the Safety of Life at Sea which was held in London, and revised regulations for preventing collisions at sea came into force in 1954. Also in 1948 the Merchant Navy Welfare Board was established as a 'permanent' organisation for the monitoring of seamen's welfare. Government departments were represented on the Board in addition to shipping employers, seafarers' organisations and maritime charities. The Board proceeded to run a number of hotels for seafarers and established new high standards of accommodation which the voluntary societies strove to match. Unfortunately, it was arranged that the Board's income should derive from payments made by shipping companies to the Ministry of National Insurance on behalf of non-domiciled seafarers. Such seafarers did not benefit from the British social services, which were financed in part from such payments, and it was therefore argued that these particular payments should be used to benefit seafarers generally. What was unfortunate was that these payments did not prove a permanent source of income. For the time being, however, the money helped to improve the amenities provided for seafarers, particularly when they were at leisure in port.

With peace restored, the war risk or 'danger money' which had been added to seamen's wages throughout the war disappeared and in 1947 the able-seaman's basic pay was reduced from £24 to £20 a month. However, this basic pay was increased to £24 where the seaman had given four years' 'efficient service' and for most seamen pay remained the same. Compensation was also given at this time for Sundays spent at sea. In real

Cutty Sark. Built at Dumbarton in 1869 and of composite (wood and iron) construction, *Cutty Sark* was 963 tons gross and 224 feet long. Her sail area totalled three-quarters of an acre. Although one of the fastest sailing ships ever built, her best passage from China was 107 days.

SS *Tregenna*. Built at South Shields for Edward Hain & Son of St Ives in 1880, *Tregenna* was a tramp steamer of 1332 tons gross, 247 feet long, engaged mainly in the Black Sea grain trade.

Glückauf. Built in Newcastle upon Tyne in 1886, this first specially constructed tanker carried 2600 tons of oil and embodied many long-lasting tanker features.

Royal Mail liner SS *Briton*. Built by Harland and Wolff for the Union-Castle Line in 1897, she ran between Southampton and South African ports. Of 10,248 tons gross, she was 530 feet long. The ship was broken up in 1926.

In 1905, 40 years after the steamer *Agamemnon*, Scott's of Greenock built *Archibald Russell*, a four-masted barque of 2385 tons and 291 feet long. She was built to the order of J. Hardie & Company of Glasgow, the last ever placed by a British shipowner for deepsea sailing tonnage.

Four-funnelled steamer. In 1910, only five years after the building of *Archibald Russell*, Harland and Wolff built *Olympic* for White Star Line. At 45,324 gross tons and 883 feet long, she was then the world's largest ship with a speed of 21 knots. She was not withdrawn from service until 1935.

SS *Aeneas*. Another Homeric hero, this cargo-liner of 10,085 gross tons, built for the Ocean Steam Ship Company in 1910 became in 1920 the first ship to carry a crew library supplied by the Seafarers Education Service. She was bombed and sank 21 miles south-east of Start Point, with the loss of 19 lives, in 1940.

Jervis Bay became an armed merchant cruiser at the outbreak of the Second World War. She was sunk by the German battleship *Admiral Scheer* while bravely defending a convoy in mid-Atlantic. Of her crew, 187 died.

Liberty ships, British and American, may be said to have won the Second World War. These standardised vessels also remained the basis of many post-war fleets. *Empire Liberty*, of 7157 tons gross, was built by J. L. Thompson of Sunderland for the Ministry of War Transport and managed by R. Chapman & Son.

MV *Clan MacNab* off Cape Town, one of the last of the traditional British cargo-liners, carrying mixed dry cargoes, 9169 tons gross and 468 feet long, built in Greenock in 1961 for Cayzer, Irvine (the British and Commonwealth Shipping Company). She was equipped with diesel engines and had a service speed of 15 knots. Her crew numbered 46, the ratings being Indian.

One of the best-loved of all ships, SS *Uganda*, after being built for the East Africa mail service for the British India Steam Navigation Company in 1952, was converted in 1967 to a school-cruise ship. In the Falklands War she served as hospital ship, being laid up shortly thereafter.

Modern coaster. Small ships still operate: MV *Faience*, belonging to Crescent Shipping of Rochester, was photographed in 1984.

Cruise-ship *Pacific Princess.* Built in Germany in 1971 for a Norwegian Company, *Pacific Princess* joined the P&O fleet in 1975. She carries 644 passengers and operates mainly on the west coast of the United States up to Alaska and through the Panama Canal into the Caribbean.

Container ship *Cardigan Bay*. Built in Germany in 1972 and originally powered by steam turbines, she was converted to diesel engines in 1981, her service speed being reduced from 27·5 to 23 knots. Her capacity is 2961 TEUs (20-foot containers), 95 of them refrigerated. She is now part of the P&O Containers fleet and voyages to the Far East.

Of 280,000 tons deadweight, *British Respect* was a very large crude-carrier built for the BP Tanker Company in Japan in 1974.

LPG *Garinda*. A liquefied petroleum gas-carrier – a ship built in Germany for P&O in 1977 for a new trade. On commissioning she carried a crew of 41: 12 British officers and 29 Asian ratings.

terms the pre-war rate of £10 a month had not been much improved on and, indeed, over the next ten years additions to seamen's wages lagged behind those achieved in comparable industry ashore if overtime is not taken into account.

Tom Yates, fourth in line of succession from Havelock Wilson, became general secretary of the National Union of Seamen in 1947. He proved to be an able union leader in the moderate mould of Wilson's later years. He worked well with the employers and secured a modest wage increase for his members almost every year. The industry proclaimed its good labour relations and it was suggested that, in working together on the Welfare Board and the National Maritime Board, employers and unions grew to understand one another better. The industry remained strike-free until 1955 and the unofficial strike of that year involved only 1700 seamen and was confined to liner shipping in two ports. In essence this strike was a protest by catering ratings against their working conditions in passenger liners for, although a 56-hour working week was now the norm at sea, stewards could still be expected to work a 63-hour week on cargo vessels and a 70-hour week on passenger ships. Following the strike an eight-hour day for all catering ratings was established. In 1959, the year before his retirement, Tom Yates, who had served as chairman of the Trades Union Congress, was knighted, the only seamen's leader to be thus honoured.

Although some men made the Merchant Navy a lifelong career, seafaring remained, as it had been always, a young man's job. The average sea life of the seaman was under ten years, one-third of new recruits leaving the industry within a year of joining it. More than 60 per cent of seafarers were under 35 years of age, the average age in deepsea ships being younger still, and from 10,000 to 15,000 new recruits were required each year.

For ratings training was still a cursory business. No entry qualifications were demanded by the industry though literacy was commonly expected. Firemen and greasers had to be 18 years of age and spent two weeks under training. Stewards and seamen had to be 16 and were trained for 10 to 12 weeks. Such training was a means whereby the Shipping Federation could control entry, and its officials had no interest in education.

Two years of 'national service' was demanded of young men for some years after World War II but merchant seamen were exempt from this conscription. At a time of full employment this exemption made it easier to recruit for shipping, though labour shortages were experienced from time to time.[4] The source of marine engineer officers remained the shipyard-trained apprentice, and one out of four navigating apprentices went to sea with no form of pre-sea training. However, changes were under way. In 1956 the Navigators and Engineer Officers Union amalgamated with the Marine Engineers Association to form the Merchant Navy and Airline Officers Association. Private crammers for the Board of Trade examinations had disappeared and local education authority colleges provided most of the training received by apprentices and officers. The view that a boy should finish his normal education to the age of 16 before aiming to become a seafarer was becoming widely accepted in the industry, and The Marine Society began to demand four passes at ordinary level in the General Certificate of Education before it would make a grant to apprentices for the purchase of uniform. A new pattern of residential training for the school-leaver was introduced at the School of Navigation in Warsash, Southampton, and the *Worcester-Conway* system of recruiting officer cadets at the age of thirteen began to lose its appeal. The training ship, generally, was yielding to state education and after the war The Marine Society did not resume training in the way that it had pioneered in 1786. Class distinctions at sea remained rigid. Although a few ratings rose to officer rank, often with the help of the Seafarers Education Service and its 'College of the Sea', established just prior to the war and maintained by correspondence, shipping companies commonly forbade any social contact between officers and crew.[5]

If these were halcyon years for the British seafarer, they were even better years for the British shipowner. In the words of one former director of P & O: 'The whole process of shipowning was a delightful profession. Ships were beautiful artefacts. The chairman's wife could design the curtains for the captain's cabin. Champagne bottles were smashed against the ship's side when she was launched. All in all it was a charming existence and a very comfortable one and there seemed no good reason for it to change.'[6] By 1948 the post-war transition period was more or less over and Britain, with 27 per cent of the effective world tonnage (that is, excluding the American reserve fleet), seemed as clearly established as the world's major maritime power as she had been in 1939.

By 1948 the effective world fleet, excluding the 13 million tons of American shipping which had been laid up as a 'reserve fleet', was only marginally less in tonnage than it had been immediately before the war. The United Kingdom had preserved its pre-eminence and the British dominions, with 3.2 million tons or nearly twice their pre-war tonnage, had increased their relative importance. Of course, American trading power had grown considerably, as it had in similar circumstances in World War I, and American ships again filled the vacuum created by the disappearance of the German fleet and the considerable reduction in Japanese and Italian shipping. The defeated powers had suffered dramatically but, broadly speaking, Norway, France and the Netherlands had each maintained their relative positions in the world shipping league. The chief anomaly in the post-war figures was a marked improvement in the position of Panama. Although a few foreign shipowners had registered ships in Panama before the war, it was not until 1948 that this 'flag of convenience' appeared on the shipping horizon as a cloud the size of a man's hand. This storm had yet to gather.

Fig. 13. THE MARITIME NATIONS, 1939–1957

(IN ORDER OF SIZE AS IN 1948)
(MILLION GROSS TONS)

	1939	1948	1957
World	68.5	80.3*	110.2
US	11.4	29.2*	25.9
UK	17.9	18.0	19.9
Norway	4.8	4.3	8.5
France	2.9	2.8	4.0
Netherlands	3.0	2.7	4.3
Panama	0.7	2.7	4.1
Italy	3.4	2.1	4.6
USSR	1.3	2.1	2.7
Sweden	1.6	2.0	3.0
Canada	1.2	2.0	1.5
Greece	1.8	1.3	1.5
Denmark	1.2	1.1	1.9
Spain	0.9	1.1	1.5
Japan	5.6	1.0	4.4
UK as % of world	26	22	18

* includes US reserve fleet of 13.1 million tons

(*Source:* Lloyd's Register of Shipping; vessels over 100 gross tons.)

In the meantime British shipping sailed on storm-free seas and on his way to the East the seafarer still saw evidence of the power of the British raj – as he steamed past Gibraltar, as he picked up his sun helmet in Port Said from 'George Robey' and was piloted through the Suez Canal by a British pilot, as he refuelled in Aden, as he drank a Singapore Sling in the Raffles Hotel or beer in any of the similar hotels in Bombay, Colombo and Penang, and as everywhere along the route to Hong Kong he saw the palatial buildings which housed British governors, British banks and British business houses.[7]

But the old imperial trade preferences had disappeared and the British Empire was beginning to disintegrate. When India achieved independence in 1947 she reserved her coastal trade for Indian ships and nurtured her deepsea fleet. Since much of the British merchant fleet had grown to serve the Empire which it had created, Indian independence severely affected the fortunes of the Anchor Line, Bibby Line, the British India Steam Navigation Company, Brocklebank's, the Clan Line, Ellerman's, T. & J. Harrison, 'Paddy' Henderson's of Glasgow and P & O. With the decline of the Indian trade went the virtual disappearance, in consequence of political changes, of trade to Burma and to mainland China. India apart, other members of the British Empire (or Commonwealth, as it had become after 1931) soon fretted to achieve independence, and when they did they also aspired to build merchant fleets of their own. In 1949 the South African Marine Corporation was established. A decade later came Ghana's Black Star Line and the Nigerian National Shipping Line.

In these same years there was an upsurge of national consciousness in other countries, big and small, while United States tramping interests were aided by that country's 50:50 legislation of 1948, legislation which proved to serve as a model elsewhere.

The US Foreign Assistance Act of 1948 decreed that 50 per cent of all American aid cargoes should be carried in American vessels. Further Acts in 1949 decreed that this 50 per cent was computed separately for different trades and areas so that it became more like 60:40 than 50:50.[8] From the beginning this legislation enabled the ships used to offer lower rates for return cargoes. This was the thin edge of a discriminatory wedge and some other countries, having no desire to distinguish between aid and trade, began to apply the 50:50 principle to all shipments. The countries of South America in particular, countries which had built up their fleets during the war, modelled themselves upon the United States and embarked upon a thorough policy of maritime protection. Brazilian import preferences halved the service given by British ships, and by the end of the 1950s the Royal Mail Line was using only three passenger ships on the South American run where in 1939 the company had found trade enough for nine passenger ships and numerous cargo ships.[9]

The most favoured discriminatory device, however, was a bilateral trade treaty containing a restrictive shipping clause, a device favoured by some 30 different countries. The British government refused to execute trade treaties containing such restrictive clauses, but it could have little or no effect upon the behaviour of other governments. Discrimination in favour of the national flag was practised and continued to be practised by the Soviet bloc, the United States, the major South American republics, certain Middle Eastern countries, Spain, Portugal and France, to name only the principal countries concerned. Many governments also gave preference to their native shipping lines through their control of the foreign exchanges.

In the 1950s the British government made 74 formal protests to 31 countries in respect of flag discrimination but achieved little by way of result.[10] British diplomacy proved ineffective in tackling this problem and, rightly or wrongly, it was felt that retaliatory action would affect adversely the British cross trades, those cargoes carried by British ships between two foreign ports. Such indirect trade, an important area of British commerce, was affected particularly by discrimination. It has been suggested that more British companies might have been established behind such discriminatory barriers in the way in which the British and Commonwealth Shipping Company set up the Springbok Company in South Africa in 1958, but such action was not widely possibly because foreign-owned or foreign-controlled companies were often banned.

Post-war British shipping was affected adversely in other ways. A general move outside Britain for importers to puchase f.o.b. and for exporters to try to sell c.i.f. made it more likely that the carriage of the goods concerned would be diverted to nationally-owned vessels. In America subsidies to shipbuilding and shipping operation enabled United States shipping companies to maintain an active fleet under the American flag which was about 15 per cent greater than it had been in 1939. Communist country fleets were also subsidised, and the growth of fleets in Italy, Spain, France and West Germany all owed something to government subsidy.

American support and the use of United States aid funds also helped to reconstruct the fleets of Italy, West Germany and Japan. In the late 1940s 20 per cent of the world merchant fleet was engaged in delivering American aid to Europe under the conditions described above, and from 1948 onwards this 'Marshall Aid' (which derived its name from the US secretary of state and one-time Army chief of staff) laid the foundation for the great West German recovery, the 'German miracle'. The initial step in shipping was an American gift in 1949 of $42 million to German shipping companies. This was followed in 1951 by a loan to these companies by the West German government of some £40 million at extremely low rates of interest to enable them to order new ships. At the same time the German government introduced an income tax provision which was calculated to foster German shipping. By 1957 the West Germans possessed a modern fleet comprising more than 2000 cargo ships and 100 tankers totalling 3.6 million gross tons.

In Japan the American General MacArthur had decreed that the country should be self-supporting in both shipping and shipbuilding by 1952. Large sums of American money were invested in Japanese shipyards, which had been virtually undamaged in the war, and ten years after the war ended Japan became the world's leading shipbuilder. By 1957 her merchant fleet exceeded 4.4 million tons.

By this date, although Britain's tonnage had increased by more than one million tons since 1948, the British fleet had fallen to 18 per cent of the world total. A notable critic of the British shipping industry writing in the early 1960s[11] suggested that this proportionate decline – from 45 per cent at the beginning of the century – could not be explained by high crew costs, foreign shipping policies, war, taxation or government restrictions. He concluded that the explanation must be sought in what he called 'internal restraints', among which he listed complacency, less internal competition, and a growing remoteness of shipowners from their ships. He drew attention to what he saw as a neglect of the tanker and of the diesel engine, a disinclination to standardise the form of ships and to increase their speed, and an obtuse avoidance in these years of the opportunity to buy ships cheaply abroad. There was also, he considered, a lack in the industry of self-criticism.

Certainly, British shipowners generally – and in this they are not untypical of managers everywhere – thought that they knew their own business best. They were slow to employ university graduates, other than members of the families which had established many of the major companies, and slow to promote able people to directorships. They neglected some fast-growing and profitable sectors of the industry, like the supply of coal, iron ore, oil and potash to Japan.[12] They even appeared to neglect traditional liner trades, for the Shaw, Savill Line gave up trading between South and East Africa and Australia and New Zealand in 1956 because it was not worth chartering ships to carry it on, while the Orient Line gave up cruising in 1957 because of the heavy demand for travel on the Line's Australia, New Zealand and North American services. At the same time Italian ships were bringing West Indians to the United Kingdom by way of Genoa.[13] Although they could have financed expansion from reserves and from loan capital in these halcyon years from 1948 to 1957, mindful perhaps of the Royal Mail collapse between the two wars, they made no attempt to do so. None of the liner companies listed in the Stock Exchange Year Book raised any new capital between 1945 and 1960.

However, all of the factors listed above – war, foreign shipping policies, taxation, government restrictions, even crew costs – were marginally effective to the detriment of British shipping and, as economists are aware, it is at the margin that decisions are effected. Further reference will be made to these factors. Here, in the area of government restrictions, it may be noted that in the immediate post-war period any British shipowner wishing to build a ship abroad needed to obtain permission and, because of currency problems, permission was usually refused. If an expenditure of dollars was involved, shipowners could be refused permission to purchase secondhand ships abroad, though restrictions on expenditure in 'soft' currencies were lifted in 1951. Licences for the import of ships from Japan were not issued until 1956, and until 1959 owners required Treasury permission before they could accept loans from abroad.[14]

If they had not done so well in World War II as they had in World War I, British shipping companies had certainly not suffered in monetary terms in consequence of the war. They had built up reserves and they had received adequate compensation for war losses. They met with problems only if they delayed decisions, as many did, at a time of continuous inflation. Sir John Denholm wrote of the family shipping company, J. & J. Denholm:[15] 'When the second war was over, my brother and I decided we had either to get out, or go right for it. We'd have done nicely if we had sold out then, but we made the decision, and we went ahead while other firms waited for the slump that never came . . . It seemed unfair to inflict the whole gamble on our shareholders. So we reduced our capital by repaying 10s in the £ . . . By 1951 we had seven ships, all of them built or bought at prices we could never have hoped for if we had waited to see what would happen.'

J. & J. Denholm expanded, but many other tramp owners held off replacing their war losses because they thought that shipbuilding prices would slump as they had after 1920, whereas shipbuilding prices continued to rise for some sixteen years. They were also, no doubt, influenced by the decline of coal exports and the increase in protective preferences established in South America, at one time an important route for tramps. British coal exports declined from 38 million tons in 1938 to 7 million tons in 1960 and while much of these exports had been carried by foreign ships the long-distance trade had been largely in British hands. British tramp shipowners did not take readily to operating tramps in the alternative oil trade although long-term charters and adequate finance were available. This dilatoriness provided opportunities for many overseas owners.

In the field of cargo liners it was suggested that the liner conferences, which established freight rates, inhibited expansion, partly by fixing freight rates too low, and that foreign companies operating outside the conferences were able to provide cheaper or faster services which eventually forced British owners to accept them into the conference thus reducing British profits.[16] This is a weakness inherent in the conference system. The conference will always tend to give way to the aggressive outsider determined to push in and, while the British invented the rules and tended to 'play the game', their rivals did not always do so. Despite the critics of conferences, however, both shippers and shipowners have found the system preferable to any proposed alternative for more than a century though, as in some other maritime fields, it might behove the British to think again.

Opportunities may well have been missed by British shipowners in the cosy decade which followed World War II, when it was relatively easy to make money in shipping. But trade routes were changing, the British Commonwealth was disintegrating, and there was a new economic nationalism abroad which included the subsidy of foreign shipping, overseas discrimination against British shipping, and American support of the recovery and expansion of rival shipping powers while still subsidising its own shipping industry. In the circumstances it was not easy to buck the long-term trend and it may not seem surprising if there proved to be more profitable outlets for British capital in the immediate post war years than in the further expansion of the British merchant fleet.

One of the ways in which the Americans helped other nations, including the British, after the war was by passing the United States Merchant Ship Sales Act of 1946. This allowed the sale of American war-built vessels which were surplus to government requirements, those vessels not sold being placed in the American reserve fleet. Among these ships were the Liberty ships, the later 'Victory' class of cargo motor-ships and the 16,000-ton T2 tankers. The two latter types were more economical than the Liberty ship in their use of fuel. These vessels became the backbone of many post-war fleets. American shipowners had first choice of the better ships sold and between 1945 and 1953 3·5 million gross tons were transferred by private American owners to flags of convenience.[17] In the same period a further 7.5 million tons were transferred to other foreign registries, United Kingdom owners buying one million tons, mostly by the end of 1948. They could have bought more but, as has been noted above, tramp owners were not optimistic at this time. Many British owners were also wary of welded, as distinct from riveted, ships and the American war-built ships had been welded.

As it turned out there continued to be an absolute shortage of shipping in relation to trading requirements. In the years 1946–1948 voyage profits of over 60 per cent of paid up capital were enjoyed by many British shipping companies[18] and post-war freights continued at generally profitable levels until 1957. From 1950 to 1952 there was war in Korea and from 1956 to 1957 the Suez Canal was closed, since it had been blocked by the Franco-British military expedition which followed the nationalisation of the Canal by Egypt's President Nasser. During the Korean War a division of American troops transported across the Pacific required 250,000 deadweight tons of shipping for eighty days. To maintain a division in the field required 135,000 deadweight tons of shipping each month. While the Suez Canal was closed more shipping was required to maintain services on the longer sea routes round the Cape of Good Hope. Inflation was endemic at this time and a Liberty ship which had cost £40,000 in 1949 might have been sold for as much as £620,000 in 1956.[19] During this period freight rates seemed to have less and less significance for importers. Coal was shipped, on the one hand from Poland to Pakistan and, on the other, from India to Copenhagen. Grain moved from Australia to northern Europe and from the United States to India.[20] This could not but be good for shipowners everywhere.

By 1948 world seaborne trade already exceeded that of 1938 in volume. By 1959 it was twice the pre-war volume. In value terms world trade, worth $US 21 billion in 1938, was worth $45 billion at 1938 prices by 1953. Dry cargo shipments, however, did not double. Between 1938 and 1959 dry cargo shipments increased by only 50 per cent in volume and British dry-cargo trade was actually smaller in volume in 1960 than it had been in 1938.[21] From 1945 to 1956 the tonnage of United Kingdom tramp ships declined despite the Korean War and Suez Canal boom periods and British tramp owners remained both cautious and conservative. Many of the wartime-built ships had engines converted to oil-burning, and steel hatch covers, designed by Joseph and Robert MacGregor, replaced the old wooden hatch boards covered with tarpaulins since they offered increased security, saved time in port, could be closed more quickly in bad weather and made the provision of larger hatchways possible. Ships' electric and hydraulic deck cranes also replaced steam-driven winches serving cargo derricks, though some vessels dispensed with cargo gear and relied solely on loading and discharging facilities in the ports.[22] Despite such innovations, in the late 1950s some British tramp operators were still building tramps which were traditional in style and of a size too small in a world where the multiple handling of cargo was becoming increasingly expensive, though they could argue that one reason was that many British ports were unable to handle larger ships. It had been the primary function of British shipowners to service British trade and the small ships which had been suitable for that trade could no longer compete with similar ships operated from low-wage countries.

It is new entrants to an industry who are likely to initiate change and many of the innovators of the 1950s proved to be foreign. In 1951 the International Cargo Handling Co-ordination Association (ICHCA) was formed and subsequently efforts were made to simplify stevedoring work, for example by the use of the forklift truck and pallets, and thus reduce the number of days spent in port loading and unloading cargo. The economic incentives to make such improvements are indicated by the increase in handling costs for cargo liners. In the 1930s these costs had been about 13 per cent of normal freight earnings, but by 1955 they had risen to 40 per cent of such earnings. In the second half of the 1950s the bulk or specialised dry-cargo carrier began to appear, a single-decked vessel with engine and superstructure aft, as in tankers. At the same time there was a move to bigger and faster tramps. Initially, the British played little part in these developments.

If the traditional British tramp was under threat so, increasingly, was the passenger liner.

In 1939 United Kingdom owners had possessed 3.5 million gross tons of deepsea passenger vessels and they lost 1.5 million tons in World War II. Between 1946 and 1962 they built 1.5 million tons of new vessels. Few fundamental advances in steamship design had been made in the war years,

Fig. 14. PASSENGERS BY SEA AND AIR, 1950–1959 (TO AND FROM BRITAIN FROM AND TO NON-EUROPEAN COUNTRIES)

	1950	1956	1959
Arrivals by sea	269,000	325,000	312,000
Departures by sea	333,000	386,000	334,000
Total	602,000	711,000	646,000
Arrivals by air	125,000	250,000	428,000
Departures by air	130,000	260,000	414,000
Total	255,000	510,000	842,000

(*Source:* S. G. Sturmey, *British Shipping and World Competition* (1962), London, p. 164.)

but boilers had become more efficient and new and improved steels were brought into service for turbine rotors, while similar progress was made in other machinery components.[23] The first British post-war liners proved to be speedier and more graceful than their predecessors but otherwise they remained traditional. Owners like Cunard, Shaw, Savill and Blue Star opted for medium-sized passenger-cargo liners with accommodation for 30 to 290 first-class passengers. Typical of the earlier post-war ships was Shaw, Savill's twin screw geared turbine steamship *Athenic* of nearly 16,000 tons completed in 1947, a vessel which carried 85 first-class passengers and had a service speed of 17 knots. P & O post-war rebuilding started with the company's third *Himalaya*, some 28,000 tons, completed in 1949 and costing £110 a ton to build, which compared with a pre-war figure of £48 a ton. The *Himalaya* was followed in the early 1950s by the *Chusan*, for the China run, and two other liners, *Arcadia* and *Iberia*, each of almost 30,000 tons and designed to carry 679 first-class and 735 tourist-class passengers. These ships were fitted with stabilisers to modify rolling in a rough sea. The use of aluminium alloy in the superstructure reduced topweight and allowed of more accommodation, and all public rooms and several first-class cabins were air-conditioned, many cabins having their own bathroom or shower and lavatory. Life on board was becoming somewhat less formal than it had been in pre-war days.[24]

On the north Atlantic the economic limits of speed and size had been reached in pre-war days. In 1952 the United States Line ship *United States*, a 53,000-ton vessel, came into service and won the Blue Riband for an American-built passenger liner for the first time in a hundred years. Her average speed eastbound was over 35 knots. But she could not have been built without government subsidy. Having cost $70 million, she was 'sold' to the United States Line for $32 million.

In 1955 the Shaw, Savill Line introduced a new concept into passenger travel by building *Southern Cross*, a 20,200-ton, 20-knot geared turbine ship for the carriage of passengers only. The machinery was placed well aft and the ship carried 1160 one-class passengers in fully air-conditioned accommodation. In 1962 she was joined by her sister ship *Northern Star* and these ships went round the world in opposite directions.

But by this time passenger services deepsea were doomed. The peak year for sea travel proved to be 1957, a year in which one million passengers crossed the north Atlantic by sea. Before World War II no scheduled passenger air service crossed the Atlantic and there was no more than a very limited air service to other areas. At that time, Sir William Currie, chairman of P & O, gave it as his opinion that there was little likelihood of P & O passenger ships becoming 'either obsolete or redundant through the attraction of air.'[25] In the immediate post-war years passenger ships remained the basic means of international passenger transport, and as late as 1946 a critic of British shipping still considered that, while aircraft might take some passenger traffic, the number of people travelling would grow and compensate for such loss.[26] By 1952, however, aircraft were taking one-third of the Atlantic passengers and by 1958 this proportion had grown to one-half. After the war aircraft development had been heavily subsidised by many governments, and British government controls prevented shipping companies from expanding into this new mode of transport, as some wished to do. Liner owners made a desperate bid to compete by providing largely 'tourist-class' accommodation, but competition with air travel in terms of price was no longer possible.

As aircraft took over from passenger ships so road and rail transport also tended to erode sea trade round the coast. The capacity of the coasting and home-trade dry-cargo fleet had declined from 1.75 million deadweight tons in 1939 to 1.1 million deadweight tons in 1957. In the latter year the Atlantic Steam Navigation Company, pioneers after the war in the development of transport ferry services, launched *Bardic Ferry* for service in the Irish Sea. She was the first specially-built ro-ro, or roll-on, roll-off vessel.

In only one branch of British shipping was growth the order of the day.

Between 1937 and 1957 the tonnage of oil moving in international seaborne trade quadrupled. The world tanker fleet, which had been 11 million tons in 1939, had grown to a vast 38 million tons by 1960. British imports of oil had increased in the same proportion, by 350 per cent.[27] The British tanker fleet had increased by 130 per cent.

Why did British shipping companies or British entrepreneurs not respond more positively and more quickly to the need for increased tanker tonnage? Part of the answer seems to be that liner operators had no experience in this field and considered that the carriage of oil had little to do with the business of shipping because there was no 'skill' in it, while a number of the remaining tramp owners were being spoiled at this time by the offer of lucrative charters for the carriage of iron ore by the British Iron and Steel Corporation. It was not until 1955 that P & O ordered twenty-five tankers, ships which came into operation too late to benefit from the boom for which they had been designed.

The oil companies themselves owned two-fifths of the tankers in operation, but over the years the proportion owned by these companies had declined and there was room for an increase in the number of independent operators. After 1948 there was also a move to refine oil not in the oilfields

Fig. 15. NUMBERS OF PASSENGERS CROSSING THE NORTH ATLANTIC, 1955–1970

YEAR	BY SEA*	BY AIR† (THOUSANDS)	TOTAL	AIR TRAFFIC AS % OF TOTAL
1955	964	652	1616	40
1956	1018	785	1803	44
1957	1036	968	2004	48
1958	957	1193	2150	55
1959	880	1367	2247	61
1960	865	1760	2625	67
1961	782	1919	2701	71
1962	814	2272	3086	74
1963	788	2422	3210	75
1964	712	3069	3781	81
1965	649	3611	4260	85
1966	606	4198	4804	87
1967	506	4987	5493	91
1968	375	5258	5633	93
1969	335	5996	6331	95
1970	249	7202	7451	97

* Excludes traffic by non-conference lines

† In addition IATA members carried the following numbers of passengers on charter flights: 1962 – 315,000; 1963 – 414,000; 1964 – 482,000; 1966 – 503,000; 1967 – 517,000; 1968 – 435,000; 1969 – 780,000; 1970 – 817,000.

(*Source:* Maritime Transport 1971 (OECD).)

but in the importing countries. The reasons for this were partly political and partly economic. In 1951 the Persian (Iranian) government nationalised the Anglo-Iranian refinery at Abadan and action of this kind was always possible if capital were invested in the exporting country. At the same time, since skilled labour was available, it was cheaper to build refineries in the industrialised countries and then to move the oil products in these areas where there was a ready market for the refined oils as well as for the chemical by-products obtained from the refining process.

For these reasons there was scope deepsea for economies of scale. Bigger tankers moved crude oil more cheaply. The pre-war tanker of 12,000 deadweight tons had grown in size to 16,000 tons by 1949, and in 1951 the term 'super-tanker' was coined for ships above 26,000 deadweight tons. The BP tanker *British Sailor*, a ship of 37,000 deadweight tons, was a new and sensational 'monster' at the Coronation Review of shipping at Spithead in 1953. It was not difficult for the owners of such economical tankers to find employment for them.

One other development that took place in the 1950s was the foundation in the United Kingdom by American oil interests of tanker companies to carry their products. Overseas Tankships (UK), Mobil and Standard Vacuum companies were set up and it may be argued that in these instances the Red Ensign was being used as a flag of convenience. Other overseas entrepreneurs also established companies in Britain at this time. One of these was the Greek shipowner Niarchos who, along with his compatriot Onassis and the American shipowner Daniel K. Ludwig, had by this time realised that the larger the ship for the carriage of bulk commodities, the lower the unit transport costs. Other foreign entrepreneurs who established British companies included a number of Norwegians and Greeks, many of them borrowing funds from British institutions. The Ship Mortgage Finance Company, established in 1951 to make loans available on the security of new ships being built in United Kingdom yards, encouraged this process. Until their loans had been repaid these owners registered their ships under the British flag. After the loans had been repaid the ships were usually transferred abroad. Also perceiving the advantages of bulk carriers, several British industrial companies, like the sugar manufacturers Tate & Lyle, now set up companies to ship their own products.

Such developments go a long way to suggest that there were opportunities in these years which the traditional British shipping companies and other British investors missed. This is also indicated by the figures for the entrances of foreign tonnage into British ports. From 43 per cent of the total entrances in 1938, foreign entrances had fallen to 34 per cent by 1949, but by 1960 they had risen to 51 per cent.[28] Missed opportunities are indicated too by the low rate of growth in refrigerating capacity in British ships, a mere 4 per cent increase between 1953 and 1958 compared with an increase of 120 per cent in the Norwegian fleet.[29] In 1952 the net earnings of British shipping were £360 million (£3400 million at 1988 prices) and contributed 12.2 per cent of the total import bill. By 1960 these earnings had fallen to £249 million (£2100 million at 1988 prices), a fall of nearly 40 per cent if one allows for inflation, and the contribution to the import bill was only 6.1 per cent or half the figure of eight years earlier.[30]

The Norwegians did not seem to suffer such 'internal restraints' as were said to inhibit British shipping and the Norwegian flag fleet doubled in tonnage between 1948 and 1957. During the war years the Norwegian fleet had earned enormous sums for free Norway. In 1940–1, for example, Norwegian ships carried 40 per cent of British oil imports. In the spring of 1944 Norwegian owners turned away from ordering ships in Britain, where delay in delivery was likely, and placed large orders in Sweden, a neutral country in which some credit was made available.[31] By the end of the war 83 ships totalling 760,000 deadweight tons were on order from Sweden. In the immediate post-war years the Norwegians also proved freer from controls than the British, had readier access to finance,[32] and Norwegian taxation was so framed as to encourage shipbuilding and to discourage selling out.

Some Norwegians and many Greeks now transferred their operations to the 'true' flags of convenience, like Panama. The United Kingdom flag was not thought of as a true flag of convenience because British registered ships were subject to strict regulations. A true flag of convenience was the flag of a state where registration was not a way of imposing control over that state's own shipping but was a service which could be sold to foreign shipowners who wished to escape the fiscal or other consequences of registration under their own flags.[33]

The attractions of a flag of convenience were freedom from taxation and freedom from national regulations concerning standards of equipment, manning scales, the qualifications expected of crew, wage rates and social service payments. Cheap seafarers could be employed; crew conditions could be bad; crew numbers could be cut; and operators under flags of convenience did not need to pay training costs. As Erling D. Naess, by this time an American and the chief apologist for what he described as 'flags of necessity', said at this time,[34] under a flag of convenience the operator could cut 'red tape'. In other words, he could sail a ship undermanned and without proper equipment.

For these reasons flag of convenience tonnage increased from 3 million gross tons in 1948 to 12 million gross tons in 1957 and continued to increase rapidly thereafter.

In these years the main flag of convenience countries were Panama, Liberia and Honduras – hence the contemporary terms 'Panlibhon' and 'Panholib' – and Liberia was (and remained) chief of them. The owners of the tonnage registered under these flags were largely Messrs Niarchos, Onassis and Livanos (45 per cent), various American companies (40 per cent) and Italians (5 per cent).[35] The Americans adopted these flags because of high American wage costs and because American tramps, bulkships and tankers were not subsidised by the state. The Greeks adopted them because of political conditions in Greece in the years immediately after the war. Such registration of ships in Liberia or Panama rather than in a politically uncertain Greece cleared the way for the sale of American ships to Greek operators who were financed, at least in part, by loans advanced by American or international banks.

As indicated already, in the early and mid-1950s the British Iron and Steel Corporation (Ore) Ltd offered the British owners of some seventy ships lucrative time charters for up to fifteen years to bring iron ore to the United Kingdom. By the end of the decade it had become increasingly common to order vessels to execute previously contracted long-term transport commissions of this kind. In the tanker and bulkship field, if the prospective operator could arrange for a ship to be chartered for the carriage of oil or of some other commodity for from seven to fifteen years, he needed to find no more than 5 per cent of the cost of building the ship himself. The other 95 per cent could be raised from American banks on the security of the time charter.[36] With this high degree of gearing – that is, with fixed interest payments on 95 per cent of the capital – very high profits could be and were earned in periods of high demand for shipping. Following the Korean War and Suez shipping booms the prospect of such profits attracted many speculators who adopted flag of convenience registration.

Because conditions generally were so good British shipowners ignored the competition from such ships until the middle 1950s, but at that time complaints and threats began to be voiced.

The complaints related mostly to British taxation. Before profits were taxed ship depreciation could be deducted, but depreciation was allowed only on what the ship cost originally – its historic cost. The allowance for depreciation could be calculated in one of two ways. Either the owner could set off against profits a fixed amount each year, 5 per cent of the original cost in the case of liners, which were estimated to last twenty years, and 6.25 per cent for tankers, whose life was reckoned to be sixteen years. Alternatively 'accelerated' depreciation was allowed: this permitted a higher percentage of earnings to be tax-free in the early years of a ship's life and a smaller percentage in later years. After these deductions, profits, if earned, were all taxed. In an inflationary age this did not allow for full ship replacement from untaxed earnings. Under a flag of convenience profits, if kept abroad, would be free of tax.

The threats made concerned the removal of ships from the British register. The transfer of ships abroad had been prohibited in 1939, but these restrictions were eased in the 1950s though they were not entirely removed until after 1959. The Bermudian registration of ships – the establishment of a British flag of convenience in Bermuda – was first mooted in 1954 and Shell transferred sixteen tankers to Bermuda after the establishment of Shell Bermuda (Overseas) in the following year. One of the 'London' Greeks, London & Overseas Freighters, also formed a company in Bermuda.

It was not a simple matter for British shipowners to follow in the footsteps of Anglo-Dutch Shell and Greek London & Overseas Freighters. Under British law a non-British shipowner could establish a shipping company in Bermuda and then operate ships flying the Red Ensign and having a home port in the United Kingdom provided the master, chief engineer and radio officer in each of the ships were UK citizens. This arrangement was available to British owners to a limited degree only. A British owner could not transfer existing ships to the Bermudian (or any other Commonwealth) registry, and could not register new ships in Bermuda if they were of the same kind as the ships the British operator owned already in his UK company. Unless his Bermudian venture were entirely new, in no way similar to his UK one, the door was closed.[37] Since P & O had never operated tankers before, they could set up a tanker business in Bermuda.

The threatened exodus of British shipping did not occur at this time because United Kingdom fiscal arrangements were changed in 1954. Hitherto the government had so far recognised the deleterious effect of inflation on capital replacement as to allow in all industry 'accelerated' depreciation by way of an 'initial allowance' of 20 per cent. This meant that the owner of a new factory, machine or ship could write off 20 per cent of its total cost in the year of acquisition, although overall he could still not set aside tax-free more than the historic or original cost.

In 1954 this initial allowance was replaced by an 'investment allowance' of 20 per cent. This allowed the owner to write off 120 per cent of the original cost. On a ship costing £1,000,000 the owner could now write off £1,200,000 before tax was due on profits earned. This meant that there was an eventual remission of income and profits tax of £20 in every £100 spent on capital plant. At the then rates of income and profits tax the investment allowance amounted to a subsidy of roughly 10 per cent on investment in new ships or other capital goods.[38] Henceforward, Bermudian registration did not, according to the shipowner Lord Runciman, offer any great advantage in the first ten years of a ship's life. Over that period the gain from the investment allowance just about balanced the taxes which were paid in the United Kingdom but not in Bermuda.[39]

The investment allowance was suspended for most other industry in

1956 but not for shipping, and the industry's 'unique position' was officially underlined in 1957 when the investment allowance for shipping was increased to 40 per cent. From 1957 British shipowners were allowed to write off 140 per cent of the cost of vessels newly ordered for British registration. A ship which cost £250,000 in 1937 cost about £1,250,000 in 1957. To replace the 1937 ship an untaxed £250,000 could have been set aside. With a 40 per cent investment allowance a further £500,000 could be contributed untaxed to the 1957 cost, leaving only £500,000 to be found from taxed earnings. The advantage of going to Bermuda had virtually disappeared.

Shipping profits fell generally after 1957 and for a time the advantages of flags of convenience no longer loomed so large. If profits are not earned there is no point in their being tax-free. For the years immediately ahead British shipping remained British and British shipowners gave no genuine support to the International Transport Workers' Federation in its fight against flags of convenience on social grounds – the low wages paid to many of these seafarers, the conditions under which they served in some of these ships, and their non-unionisation.

By this time the net earnings of British liners and tramps were falling, and shipping profits were coming under examination. In the relatively good year of 1956 the net profit after tax of the P & O group was only 5.2 per cent of paid-up capital and only 2.7 per cent of assets. Unilever at this time enjoyed a consolidated net profit of more than 10 per cent. One shipping paper asked if British shipowners were in the wrong business.[40] Should they not be selling margarine or developing electronics instead?

To the directors of Clan Line it still seemed worth while taking over the Union-Castle Line, despite the uncertain future of passenger liners. In 1956 the two companies merged to form the British and Commonwealth Shipping Company and thus became one of eight large liner groups which between them now owned over 80 per cent of all British liner tonnage as well as some tramp and tanker tonnage. The largest of these groups remained P & O, with Furness Withy, Cunard, the new British and Commonwealth Group, Ellerman, Blue Funnel, the Vestey Group and the Weir Group following on in order of tonnage owned. The ownership of such British tramps as still existed was otherwise well diffused. Of the British tanker fleet, 4 million tons was owned by oil companies, with independent companies operating just over 1.25 million tons. But the bulk of this tanker fleet was now operated by companies which, although technically British, were themselves owned by non-British interests. In 1957 J. & J. Denholm were asked to manage a 9000-ton ore carrier, *Naess Trader*, which the American Naess had built specifically for British registration to take advantage of the British Iron and Steel Corporation (Ore) charters. A few years later Denholm had become the largest British firm of professional ship managers.

By the end of these halcyon years, although British tonnage had risen from 18 to 20 million gross tons in less than a decade, a significant part of this fleet was not owned by Britons. With this foreign-owned tonnage removed, the British fleet had diminished to a size which had been unknown since before World War I.

Notes

1. C. Dixon, 'Pound and Pint: Diet in the Merchant Service, 1750–1980', in S. Palmer & G. Williams (eds), *Charted and Uncharted Waters: Proceedings of a Conference on the Study of British Maritime History*, p. 170.
2. Report to the author.
3. L. H. Powell, *The Shipping Federation, 1890–1950* (1950), London, p. 42; A. Marshall & V. Ryan, *The Seamen* (1989), Oxford, pp. 156–7.
4. See, e.g., *Shipbuilding & Shipping Record* (10.11.1955; 11.4.1957; 13.6.1957).
5. For social conditions at sea at this time see T. Lane, *Grey Dawn Breaking: British Seafarers in the Late Twentieth Century* (1986), Manchester; S. R. Green, *Whither O Ship: Adventures in a Tramp Steamer* (1989), London; and R. Hope (ed), *The Seaman's World* (1982), London.
6. J. G. Davis; see M. B. F. Ranken (ed), *Britain and the Sea: Future Dependence, Future Opportunities* (1984), Edinburgh, p. 84.
7. For a description of this seafaring life, albeit relating to the early 1960s, see R. Woodman, *Voyage East* (1988), London.
8. *Shipbuilding & Shipping Record* (29.5.1958).
9. S. G. Sturmey, *British Shipping and World Competition* (1962), London, pp. 206–7.
10. *Ib.*, pp. 195–9.
11. Sturmey, *op. cit.*
12. D. H. Aldcroft, 'Reflections on the Rochdale Inquiry into Shipping: A Review Article' (1971), *Maritime History*, Vol. I, No. 2, pp. 207–8; E. D. Naess, *Autobiography of a Shipping Man* (1977), Colchester, p. 175.
13. 'Lost Opportunities' (5.7.1956), *Shipbuilding & Shipping Record.*
14. Sturmey, *op. cit.*, p. 172.
15. *Denholm News* (company magazine), 'The Denholm Story'.
16. Sturmey, *op. cit.*, pp. 351–8.
17. *Ib.*, p. 155.
18. *Ib.*, p. 156.
19. *Shipbroker* (May 1972), p. 109.
20. T. Rinman & R. Brodefors, *The Commerical History of Shipping* (1983), Gothenburg, p. 110.
21. Sturmey, *op. cit.*, pp. 161–2.
22. W. G. D. Ropner, 'A Century of British Tramping' (19.5.1983), *Fairplay Centenary Issue.*

23. A. F. L. Deeson, *An Illustrated History of Steamships* (1976), Bourne End, Bucks, p. 137.
24. P. Padfield, *Beneath the House Flag of P & O* (1981), London, pp. 134–5.
25. S. Rabson & K. O'Donoghue, *P & O: A Fleet History* (1988), Kendal, p. 176.
26. J. Woddis, *Under the Red Duster* (1947), London, pp. 28–9.
27. Sturmey, *op. cit.*, p. 169.
28. *Ib.*, p. 170.
29. *Ib.*, p. 165.
30. *Ib.*, pp. 155–6.
31. Rinman, *op. cit.*, pp. 97–99.
32. Sturmey, *op. cit.*, pp. 174–6.
33. Cf. S. J. Bergstrand, *Buy the Flag* (1983), Polytechnic of Central London, p. 2.
34. To the author.
35. Sturmey, *op. cit.*, p. 214.
36. See Naess, *op. cit.*, p. 116.
37. *Ib.*, p. 175.
38. *Financial Times* (8.4.1959).
39. *Shipbuilding & Shipping Record* (14.2.1957).
40. *Ib.* (31.5.1956).

23

The Great Revolution
(1957–1973)

In 1957, when the Suez Canal re-opened after its closure in 1956, the dream world of the first dozen post-war years ended. Although in the twelve years that followed much seemed to go on as usual, and a sense of euphoria was maintained in some areas by government financial support, a revolution took place in shipping which was as dramatic and far-reaching as the change from sail to steam.

It all happened very quickly. Passenger services on ocean routes virtually disappeared, and along with them disappeared the livelihoods of thousands of stewards. Large bulk carriers of dry goods replaced most of the old tramp ships. The short-sea trades were revolutionised by the introduction of the ro-ro, and road transport made further encroachment upon the traditional work of coasters. The size of the largest tankers escalated to exceed a fantastic 300,000 tons deadweight. And, towards the end of this period, a great many cargo-liners began to be replaced by a small number of box-carriers or container ships. Fewer and fewer ships could carry more and more cargo.

The number of passengers crossing the Atlantic by air exceeded the number crossing by sea in 1958, the year in which the first commercial jet aircraft reduced a six-day journey to a matter of six hours. By 1965 more passengers came by air than by sea from South Africa. By 1968 this was also true of the traffic to and from Australia and New Zealand.[1] Once the large jet aircraft – the Boeing 707 and then the Jumbo jet – were introduced, the passenger fleet declined rapidly.

In the years from 1957 to 1970 passengers travelling by air across the north Atlantic increased from 1 million to no fewer than 8 million, while passengers crossing by sea declined from 1 million to one-quarter of a million. By 1967 90 per cent of long-distance passenger journeys to and from the United Kingdom were made by air, and by the following year no major passenger liners were operating on the north Atlantic route in the winter months. In the 1960s passenger traffic by sea declined on all deepsea routes except to Australasia. In 1962 the government decided to fly all troops abroad, making the *Oxfordshire*, the last troopship built, redundant in that rôle only five years after she was first commissioned.[2] By 1967, the year in which peak passenger traffic by sea was reached on the Australasian route, the Suez Canal had been closed for a second time in consequence of the Israeli-Egyptian Seven Day war and was this time to remain closed for eight years. This closure ended much of the passenger trade by sea to the Far East.

Although there was talk in America in 1959 of two very large transatlantic liners being built to compete with air travel[3] – the ships were to have cafeteria messing and low-priced berths – nothing came of it, and in the British industry, for reasons of economy, the Orient Line amalgamated fully with P & O the following year. Suitable vessels were henceforward diverted to cruising, including *Nevasa*, the penultimate troopship, which thus participated in P & O's imaginative 21-year experiment of school-cruising, which introduced nearly 800,000 schoolchildren to such far-flung places as Trabzon and Leningrad in the years from 1961 to the Falklands War. Between 1961 and 1967 the number of passengers cruising from United Kingdom ports increased by 17 per cent,[4] but such an increase could do little to modify the general decline. Many passenger ships went to the breakers, while others were sold to Greek owners who operated them under flags of convenience and competed on a number of routes for such passenger traffic as was still available. The return on capital invested in the liner trades fell rapidly and by 1964 was only marginally more than 2 per cent for the seven major liner groups – a net profit of £12 million on a capital employed of £568 million. This compared with 20 per cent for such stores groups as Marks & Spencer and an average of 10–15 per cent for top companies.[5] The 125-year-old Royal Mail Line had suffered losses for four years and was soon to disappear. By the end of 1968 the British deepsea passenger fleet had declined to less than one-third of what it had been thirty years earlier.[6]

In such circumstances few new passenger liners were ordered. In 1960 shipyards at Birkenhead, Barrow-in-Furness and Belfast were at work on the three largest British liners to be built since the *Queen Elizabeth* had been completed in 1940, and these ships were almost the last to be built in Britain. Union-Castle was adding the 37,600-ton *Windsor Castle* to its fleet, the biggest ship ever built for the South African trade. P & O-Orient were building the 41,900 ton *Oriana* and the 45,700-ton *Canberra*, the greatest team ever intended for service beyond the north Atlantic. *Canberra* came into service in 1961, with engines and funnel right aft. Her turbo-electric propulsion gave rise to serious initial problems, but she was fitted with a bow thruster to facilitate berthing and established new high standards for passengers. The ship was fully air-conditioned and had a relatively new AC electrical system. She was also fitted with an internal television service and the first real cinema aboard ship. There was continuous organised activity for the 548 first-class and 1690 tourist-class passengers.[7]

The 66,800-ton *QE2*, completed in 1969, was designed for the dual purpose of crossing the Atlantic and cruising, and in that year the Cunard chairman announced the 'phased withdrawal' of her two great predecessors, *Queen Mary* and *Queen Elizabeth*. In 1972 the much smaller *Cunard Adventurer* and *Cunard Ambassador* joined the Cunard fleet, the first new Cunard ships apart from the *QE2* since the 1950s. At the same time P & O acquired the Italian-built *Spirit of London* (renamed *Sun Princess* two years later), a ship of a mere 17,000 tons and the Company's first liner since *Canberra*. These last three ships were designed as short-range cruise liners.

By this time Cunard had been taken over by Trafalgar House, basically a property company, and the P & O group had been reorganised into five operating divisions. The names of well-known companies like New Zealand Shipping and General Steam disappeared in the reorganisation. Coast Lines was acquired and disappeared with General Steam into P & O's new General Cargo division. When there was disagreement among the directors on the terms on which the building firm of Bovis should be acquired, Lord Inchcape took over as chairman. From 1965 the government had allowed a shipping company to write off the cost of a ship as fast as profits would allow and, since this permission was given to the company, there was point in merging a property company which was earning high profits with small tax remissions with a shipping company which had low profits and high tax remissions. Also in 1972 Ocean Transport and Trading (the reorganised Ocean group which had become a public company in 1970 and included the Blue Funnel Line and Elder Dempster) acquired William Cory, a company with considerable road haulage interests.

In the light of changed conditions these venerable shipping groups were reorganising or being reorganised and diversifying their interests, as too was the British and Commonwealth Shipping Company. Union-Castle, British and Commonwealth's passenger-liner constituent, ended its famous weekly sailing for South Africa from Southampton at 4 o'clock on a Thursday afternoon on 8th July 1965. A week later the new *Windsor Castle* inaugurated an $11\frac{1}{2}$-day service to Cape Town. In 1977 the South-African flagged *S A Vaal*, formerly the Union-Castle *Transvaal Castle* and a ship in which British and Commonwealth still had a financial interest, was taken off the Cape route, thus ending a 120-year-old passenger and cargo liner service. By this time the passenger liner was finished and the cargo liner was vanishing rapidly.

Such United Kingdom sea passenger traffic as remained by 1970 was carried largely on the short sea routes, where ferries could still compete with aircraft, and some two-fifths of these passengers were carried in British ships. There were suggestions at this time that the newly developed hydrofoil and hovercraft would affect this traffic but in the event the impact was minimal. More important was the ro-ro, a vessel which, in addition to passengers, can carry fully-loaded vehicles which drive on and off the vessel by way of doors fore and/or aft which are lowered in port to become ramps. The ro-ro was introduced on the North Sea route in the mid-1950s and soon replaced many traditional cross-Channel steamers. By 1970 the use of ro-ros had extended to more distant waters where they replaced many cargo-liners.

The main threat to the cargo liner, however, was the container-ship. The bulk-carrier also played its part, though the major rôle it was to play was in the downfall of the traditional tramp.

In a lecture given in 1968 a British shipowner[8] outlined the economics of the bulk-carrier. Whereas a 5000-ton deadweight ship might cost £85 a ton to build, the cost of a 20,000-tonner would fall to £35 a ton. The bigger the ship the less the unit cost of propulsion: the horse-power required might rise 10 times if the deadweight tonnage (the weight of cargo lifted) increased 40 times. A further saving was to be found in daily costs apart from fuel. Above 65,000 tons deadweight crew costs were static. Overall, running costs fell dramatically with size, the advantages being the greater the longer the vessel could be kept at sea. The larger the ship the less relative need was there for gear to move its own cargo, for such equipment could then be provided ashore. There were only two limitations on size: the draft of ports and canals, and the amount of cargo to be shifted.

At this time the maximum draft of the St Lawrence Seaway was 27.75 feet, of the Panama Canal 37 feet, and of the Suez Canal 38 feet. In the latter case there were plans to increase the draft first to 48 feet and eventually to 62 feet.

Bulk dry cargo consists largely of iron ore, ores like bauxite, alumina and manganese, phosphate rock, potash and other fertilisers, grain, sugar, wood products, soya beans, salt, scrap iron, sulphur and coal. Up to the 1950s most of these products had been carried by tramps, general-purpose multi-deck vessels of between 6000 and 15,000 deadweight tons which included the wartime Liberty ships. In 1966 the standardised SD14 built in Britain and the Freedom ship built in Japan, each of them vessels of

14,000 tons deadweight with enclosed weatherdecks, were introduced in the belief that they were suitably modern replacements for such ships. The SD14, powered by a Sulzer engine, had a service speed of 14 knots on a daily fuel consumption of 19.5 tons of oil. These 'shelter-deckers', with their enclosed top deck, evaded the tonnage regulations which otherwise excluded this deck from the carriage of cargo because technically it was not enclosed. Water could flow right through the deck and escape into the sea.

In the meantime, however, the bulk-carrier commonly called the OBO, because it was designed to carry *o*il, *b*ulk cargoes of other kinds or *o*re, had been developed from an idea pioneered by the Swedes in the 1930s. Up to this time the largest such carrier had been Bethlehem's *Venore* class of 24,500 tons deadweight. Now, in consequence of tanker development, the construction problems of large single-deck ships had been overcome, and the slump in freight rates which followed the reopening of the Suez Canal in 1957 made a large OBO carrier economic. By 1959 the older type of tramp, such as the Liberty ship, could operate profitably no longer whereas bulk carriers, even if they were tankers converted for the carriage of grain, could pay their way despite the disadvantage, inherent in the bulk-carrier, that it has to spend much of its time at sea in ballast without a cargo.

Dry bulk cargoes moved at no more than one-third to one-half of the volume of oil, the total of such cargoes in the 1960s being some 400 million tons a year. It followed that dry-bulk ships were not likely to reach the contemporary size of tankers. Since iron ore moved in annual quantities of about 150 million tons it was suggested that this trade might accommodate ships of 120,000 tons deadweight. Annual grain shipments were about 80 million tons, coal shipments about 60 million tons, sugar and fertiliser shipments from 20 to 30 million tons, much of the remaining 20 million tons being timber. Economic bulk carriers for many of these cargoes were likely to be smaller than 120,000 tons deadweight.

Since heavy capital expenditure was required even for ships of these sizes, consortia to carry bulk commodities were established, notably Seabridge, a consortium formed by a group of British owners in 1965. By 1969 this consortium embraced Bibby Line, C. T. Bowring, M. Clarkson & Company, Dene Shipping, Hunting Group, Houlder Brothers and Furness Withy, and individual members had already taken delivery of 21 bulk carriers and had 13 more on order.[9] P & O had placed orders for four OBOs each of 74,000 deadweight tons in 1964 but even a group with P & O's resources did not 'go it alone', for it had already established Associated Bulk Carriers in conjunction with the Anglo-Norness Shipping

Company, a company inspired by Erling Naess, using American finance, and working with J. & J. Denholm.[10] From 1966, when the Suez Canal was closed for the second time, large tonnages of dry-bulk carriers were ordered and by 1970 some 100,000-tonners were in service.

Still bigger ships were being built for the carriage of oil alone. Oil shipments in this era filled 40 per cent of the world's fleet, and by the 1960s oil was moving on the oceans at ten times the 1948 quantity, at a prodigious 900 to 1000 million tons a year. It was in this area that the economies of very large ships seemed most likely to be realised and there were those who foresaw the building of 1,000,000-ton tankers.

But it was not all easy going. The reopening of the Suez Canal in 1957 created a temporary surplus of tanker capacity and provided an inauspicious start for the growth in British tanker ownership which had followed the orders of the liner companies, like P & O, after 1955. The years from 1964 to 1966, in particular, were years of slump in the tanker market. The boom years followed the second closure of the Suez Canal at the end of 1966. This eight-year closure brought with it the most prosperous period for tankers in tanker history.

The first tanker to carry 100,000 tons of crude oil, the American Daniel K. Ludwig's *Universe Apollo*, had appeared in 1959. Six years later the first British tanker of this size, BP's *British Admiral*, 917 feet long, went into service. She was Britain's first VLCC or very large crude carrier. In 1966, a few months after the first British 100,000-tonner, came *Indemitsu Maru*, the world's first 200,000-tonner, a ship which could carry sixteen times the cargo of the T2s of the Second World War. Nor was this the end. Soon after the second closure of the Suez Canal Ludwig commissioned the first of six 312,000-ton deadweight tankers, and in 1973 *Globtik Tokyo* (493,664 tons) and *Globtik London* (483,939 tons) were commissioned to become the largest ships the world had ever seen, though a 'jumboised' or extended tanker was to exceed 560,000 deadweight tons. These ULCCs (ultra-large crude carriers), however, were not destined for the British flag.

By this time traffic through the Dover Straits was having to follow prescribed routes, and inflatable rubber liferafts had been introduced to supplement lifeboats. Navigational instruments had been refined further and Loran C, an improved method of fixing the ship's position by way of radio transmissions from land stations, was being installed in some ships, the name being derived from '*lo*ng *ra*nge *n*avigation'. Satellite-based navigation systems like the Navstar/Global Positioning System, which provide an accurate ship's position anywhere in the world, were also coming into use after 1964.

But the development of enormous ships created some problems and the members of the Honourable Company of Master Mariners discussed the difficulties of conning such ships in restricted waters, since there was something like 1000 feet of ship forward of the bridge. One of its members also complained that 'like all large turbine tankers the stern power leaves much to be desired and when coming to an anchor the last two miles seems never ending'.[11] More importantly, round about 1960, there was a series of explosions in combination carriers in ballast which led to the subsequent practice of feeding inert gases from the funnel into the tanks when cleaning them so that sparks cannot arise in the cleaning process.

Another problem was highlighted when the fully-loaded *Torrey Canyon*, of 120,890 deadweight tons, ran aground in 1967 off Land's End with an estimated spillage of 100,000 tons of oil. An International Convention for the Prevention of Pollution of the Sea by Oil, drawn up in 1954, had come into force in 1958, its supervision to be administered by a new United Nations organisation, the Inter-Governmental Maritime Consultative Organisation. IMCO (which became the International Maritime Organisation or IMO in 1980) had held its first assembly in 1951 and came formally into existence, with a London headquarters, in 1962 when a further conference to review the Convention was held. The purpose of this new body was to secure the widest possible cooperation in maintaining the highest practicable standards in matters concerning maritime safety and the efficiency of navigation. It was also concerned to prevent and combat marine pollution from ships.

The United Kingdom had put the 1954 Convention into effect in the Oil in Navigable Waters Act, 1955, and made even more stringent requirements in the Oil in Navigable Waters Act, 1963, which came into force in the year of *Torrey Canyon*'s grounding. After the *Torrey Canyon* disaster a new international Convention was signed by twenty countries in 1969 and by its terms the human victims of oil pollution damage could claim compensation from shipowners and from insurers up to higher monetary limits. It was not clear that the Convention proved effective when the Onassis tanker *Olympic Bravery* (275,000 tons), sailing under the Liberian flag, went aground off Ushant in 1976.

In the meantime pollution on a lesser scale was ameliorated by the 'load on top' system devised for dealing with oil residue from dirty ballast and cleaning water. Instead of being discharged into the sea, as hitherto, this oily water was now transferred to special tanks and allowed to settle. After the oil had settled on top, the water was run off from below and oil was loaded on top of the oil residue. The days were largely ended when seamen had had to descend into the tanks to load buckets with oily waste which were then hauled up to the ship's side and the sludge dumped into the sea. It was mildly ironic that, as their job became cleaner, seafarers no longer had any problem in obtaining fresh water, for it was beginning to be distilled on board from sea water in sufficient quantity to satisfy all purposes, even for that of flushing toilets.

Another disagreeable activity which disappeared in this era from British shipping was the slaughter of whales. If one is concerned with the welfare of the earth and those who occupy its surface, there is, perhaps, no clearer indication that unrestricted competition is basically flawed than the whaling industry. Erling Naess, who like the unscrupulous Greek Onassis made large sums from whaling, wrote that it was 'an illustration of how the human race will continue to proceed along a path which is bound to result in destruction'. Those involved in whaling knew well that they were exterminating the animals from which they derived a livelihood but they nevertheless continued to do so. Naess consoled himself with the thought that 'if I had desisted somebody else would have taken my place.'[12] It is not, of course, inevitable that the human race should destroy itself or anything else. When hydrogenation made whale oil suitable for soap and margarine manufacture in the first years of the 20th century and new whaling areas were established in the Antarctic, demand seemed unlimited and Christian Salvesen of Leith was first among those who re-established British whaling. Between the wars and after World War II many attempts were made to cull and not destroy the stock of whales, but in the period dealt with here the business became increasingly unprofitable because these attempts failed. The British, Norwegians, Germans and Dutch all withdrew from whaling, leaving only the Japanese and Russians to pursue it. Salvesen's had withdrawn completely by 1964. The company has prospered since in other and wholesome fields.

In 1962 the 12,000-ton nuclear-powered American ship *Savannah*, named after the first steam ship to use steam power in crossing the Atlantic, became operational, but the vessel was clearly uneconomic and made no impact on the history of merchant shipping. More important for the commercial ship operator were improvements made in ships' engines, which grew in size and efficiency, improvements made to the screw propeller by the use of new materials and in other ways, and improvements made in hull design, for example, by way of a bulbous bow which reduced wave formation and water resistance. In consequence of these and other advances in ship construction another international agreement inspired the passing in 1967 of the Merchant Shipping (Loadline) Act.

This Act made it legal to load ships more deeply than was previously allowed and in consequence some large tankers had their deadweight tonnage increased by 4 per cent. At the stroke of a pen the deadweight tonnage of the United Kingdom fleet was thus increased by 5 per cent and its gross tonnage by 1.75 per cent.[13]

With the decline at this time of the tramp, the dry-cargo liner and the passenger ship, and the growing importance of the bulk-carrier, it was becoming more usual to express shipping statistics in deadweight rather than gross tons – in other words to express them in terms of the weight of cargo the ships can carry rather than in terms of their cubic capacity. The measure of cubic capacity is more appropriate to mixed cargoes and deadweight to bulk cargoes. The difficulties of comparison may be indicated by the fact that the gross tonnage of passenger ships can be more than four times the deadweight tonnage, while for a few dry-cargo ships and tankers the deadweight tonnage can be more than double the gross tonnage.

The different tonnage measurements may be set out as follows:

1. Gross registered tonnage (used after 1870 to express total enclosed space).
2. Net registered tonnage (used after 1870 to express income-yielding enclosed space).
3. Deadweight tonnage (used to express the weight of maximum cargo).
4. Measurement freight tonnage (used to express the cubic volume of maximum cargo).
5. Displacement tonnage (used after 1870 to express the weight of the ship itself).
6. Old registered tonnage (used before 1870 as the official expression for the size of the ship).

G. Moorson and others between 1860 and 1870 established the relation between the various tonnages then in use and a typical merchant sailing vessel of that time would have had tonnages in these proportions: old registered tonnage of between 90 and 120 tons was equivalent to 100 gross registered tons, 96 net registered tons, 150 deadweight tons, 187.5 freight tons and 150 displacement tons. The proportions for a Liberty ship of World War II are rather different, namely: 7185 gross registered tons, 4380 net registered tons, 10,500 deadweight tons, 11,700 freight tons (which equals a bale capacity of 468,000 cubic feet divided by 40, since 40 cubic feet represents 'one ton' in this measurement), and 3600 displacement tons.[14] It is roughly true for comprehensive and recent statistics, as distinct from those for a particular vessel, that 1 gross ton equals 1.63 deadweight tons. To make matters still more difficult, some published statistics exclude vessels of below 500 or even 1000 gross tons while others include all vessels above 100 gross tons. Only the small print in the published tables is likely to solve the latter problem. So far as is possible, gross tons are used in tables in these pages and all vessels above 100 gross tons are included in comprehensive statistics.

Some of the new bulk carriers of this period were highly specialised, certain ships being built exclusively for the carriage of particular chemicals, cars, timber or liquefied gas. The transport of liquid natural gas was a new trade pioneered in 1959 by the North Thames Gas Board in conjunction with the American Constock Liquid Methane Corporation. Shell joined in and Constock became the Conch International Methane Marine Company which, together with the British Gas Council, ordered the first purpose-built LNG carriers, the 27,400 cubic metre *Methane Pioneer* and *Methane Progress* (which thus used yet another measurement of ship capacity) which were delivered by British shipyards in 1962 to carry liquid gas from Algeria to France and Britain.

Much more importantly, Britain was also a pioneer on a world scale of the process of containerisation, the most dramatic change in sea transport in a century and a half. Containerisation was about to change everything connected with the transport of all goods other than those carried in bulk.

Although by 1965 long-distance passengers travelled almost wholly by air, aircraft had made little impact on the carriage of cargo. Only mail and the most valuable cargoes were carried in this way because air freight rates were twenty times those applicable at sea. Nevertheless, as the passenger liners disappeared so too did many cargo-liners and tramps, some because their cargoes were being carried in bulk in the new bulk carriers, others because their cargoes had been containerised.

United States Lines had used containers of a kind since 1949, particularly in the trades to Puerto Rico and Hawaii. But it was not until 1965 that the vast and capital-intensive operation which today offers a world-wide service began to develop. The great breakthrough for containerised cargo came when it was accepted that the box which was 8 feet square at the end and 20 feet long should be the standard. It is true that boxes 40 feet long are also carried, and that slightly higher boxes are used and longer boxes planned. These, however, do not break the basic rules of standardised handling.

With a standardised box, ships, trucks, railway wagons and handling equipment could all be specially built to carry and move such containers. Indeed, to complicate still further what has been written above about ship measurement, container ships are defined not by their deadweight or gross tonnage, as other merchantmen are, but by the number of standard boxes, the TEUs or twenty-foot-equivalent units, that they carry. Thus the

Harrison Line mv *Author*, delivered in 1981 for the West Indian run, is a 1412 TEU container ship. The P & OCL (formerly OCL) mv *Kowloon Bay*, delivered in 1972 and re-engined in 1982 to operate in the Far Eastern service, is a 3000 TEU container ship. To provide extra speed, the new gas turbine, first fitted as an alternative to the steam turbine in the Shell tanker *Auris* in 1951, was adopted for a few of the early British container ships but proved unsatisfactory and was removed. Others were fitted with steam turbines but the improved diesel engine, though slower, was found to be more economical when keen competition developed. Fitted with a diesel engine, *Kowloon Bay* operates at 22 or 23 knots. This ship is 290 metres (950 feet) long, 32 metres in breadth and has a depth of 24.6 metres. The gross tonnage is 56,822 and the deadweight tonnage 47,342.

The first purpose-built fully-cellular container vessel in the world was the Australian *Kooringa*, which began a two-weekly service between Melbourne and Fremantle in January 1964.[15] In the following year the concept took off in a big way. In the United Kingdom–West African trade, where Nigerian oil had just begun to flow, Elder Dempster lines, Palm Line (at that time owned by Unilever) and the Nigerian National Shipping company (in which Elder Dempster and Palm had taken shares when it was established in 1958, two years before Nigerian independence, acting then as managing agents) began to operate their African Container Express (ACE) service. This initial service, however, used containers which were smaller than the standard which was shortly to be established.[16]

Also in 1965 the American trucking company Sea-Land announced that it intended to start a container line carrying cargo across the north Atlantic, and a little later Wallenius, Transatlantic and Swedish American Lines combined with Holland-America and Cunard to form the Atlantic Container Line (ACL).

Of greater significance than these, from the point of view of world trade, was the announcement in 1965 that four of Britain's largest liner companies – P & O, Blue Funnel (later Ocean Transport and Trading), British and Commonwealth and Furness Withy – had formed a team to develop container traffic and proposed to establish a new company, Overseas Containers Limited (OCL), formed with an initial share capital of £100,000 split equally between the four groups. A director of P & O was appointed first chairman and in 1986, two chairmen later, P & O took over OCL. A further consortium, in which Cunard, Blue Star, Ben Line and Ellerman joined to establish Associated Container Transportation (ACT), followed shortly afterwards. The first cargoes were carried the following year.

In March 1969 OCL's *Encounter Bay*, the world's first fully purpose-built container ship for international trades, completed her maiden voyage from Rotterdam to Fremantle, thus inaugurating the first fully cellular container service in the Europe to Australia trade. She beat ACT's *Act 1* by less than a month. By 1971 the Australian and New Zealand trades were fully containerised, and the Far East trade was containerised shortly afterwards.

These were brave decisions and it is doubtful whether, at the time, anyone could cost accurately the potential savings implicit in the new operation. Certain possibilities were, however, clear. First, containerisation made it possible to offer a through service. Containers could be filled or 'stuffed' at a factory, an agricultural centre or an inland depot, put on a lorry, trailer or train, taken to the docks and transferred to a ship, transferred again at the port of destination to a lorry, trailer or train, and taken to the final point of delivery to be 'unstuffed'.

The container still required labour to fill it and empty it and, if it were to cross international boundaries, it still required customs clearance. But once filled and cleared, it was more secure than its contents would have been otherwise and, given the proper equipment by way of specially built cranes and straddle carriers and plenty of space on the quayside in which to move the containers about, the process of shifting cargo from shore to ship and ship to shore became very quick indeed. No longer was it likely that Australian dockers would walk off a ship demanding 'temptation money' for unloading cases of whisky or 'embarrassment money' for unloading lavatory pans.

Something could certainly be saved, but there were also costs. Even in the early days the container itself cost anything from £300 to £1400. Although containerisation stopped much pilferage, whole containers are sometimes stolen. They can also be damaged; and in many trades there is a problem of returning the 'empties' if the trade does not offer opportunities for filling them with return cargoes. Trade rarely balances nicely in any physical sense.

Containers are very suitable for the carriage of cargo where they can be fully packed with a particular cargo, like whisky or wool. In the case of wool, containerisation has even led to more economical packaging since it has induced exporters to compress the wool still further in order to waste no container space. But some containers have to be filled with part-cargoes and unpacked in more than one place, and some cargoes, like timber, have to be specially prepared for the container.

Another problem which arises is that of so filling the ship that it remains stable, both at sea and while unloading a mixed cargo in different ports, a problem largely, but not always ideally, solved with the aid of computers.

In the event containers have been adapted to a multitude of purposes. Horses and even giraffes have been carried in containers. Of particular importance is the carriage of cargoes at different temperatures. Fish, for example, is carried at a temperature of −18°C, while indoor plants travel at 14°C, and containers filled with potatoes may start off at 12°C, with the temperature rising gradually to 22°C. These temperatures must be maintained both ashore and afloat.

Because of the size and complexity of this operation it required from the start more capital than could be subscribed by even the largest shipping companies and it was even more important than in bulk-shipping to establish consortia. Many of these consortia were, from the beginning, international in their composition. A north Atlantic pool agreement came into force in 1971 and has been followed by similar agreements in other areas.

In the through service that containers make possible – the 'development of intermodal services by facilitating interchange between carriers', as one writer has put it[17] – the other advantages and disadvantages of containerisation are implicit. In the docks in post-war years dock labour had become increasingly expensive and dockers were prone to strike. Even without strikes deepsea liners operating break-bulk services – that is, loading and unloading cargoes in the old labour-intensive way – spent 200 or more days in port each year. Increased efficiency in port offsets the poorer use of space in the ship which containerisation involves. But new costs have been involved in ports too. Specially equipped container depots have to be established and require much space, space which was not available in many ports. In consequence many ports have died following the introduction of containerisation and new ones have been developed. Through the development of bigger ships and containerisation all the docks in London from Tower Bridge to Tilbury have closed or largely closed – St Katharine, London, Surrey Commercial, East India, West India and the Royal Docks. A similar list of closures could be compiled for Liverpool, once the second port in Britain, and Liverpool has declined dramatically. New ports like Felixstowe have developed in their place. The social costs involved in these changes do not fall upon the container companies alone.

The container ship greatly increases vessel utilisation by reducing the time spent in port. Whereas the cargo liner often spent more time in port than it spent at sea (thus making it possible for a man to join the merchant navy to see the world) the container ship ratio of port-to-sea is more like one in four or even less. The turn-round time is measured in hours, from four to perhaps twenty-four, and these hours can be wholly night-time hours. The container ship of 1400 TEUs can do the work of about seven conventional cargo-liners of the old kind, and it is automated to a much greater degree. It is operated by a crew of twenty-nine at most and the 3000 TEU ship requires no more than two more crew. It follows that, with the decline of the deepsea cargo fleet, there was a marked reduction in the requirement for seafarers.

If the idea of containerisation was hardly noted in the press before 1965, it was possible by 1967 for a trade paper to indicate some of the savings in time.

> On a typical general cargo import berth today, a good rate of unloading is 20 tons per hatch per hour, using a gang of twenty-six men. Five hatches and gangs mean 100 freight tons per hour from 130 men. With double-shift working for a five-day week, 250 men unload 8000 tons. Output per man per week – not allowing for lost time between ships, etc. – is thus about 30 freight tons. In the case of loading, with no allowance for lost time, the average labour output is about 32 tons per man per week.
>
> With containers, each crane will be able to handle 450 containers each way per day. With four gangs of 36 men handling cranes and containers over three shifts the theoretical weekly output of the 144 men is 9540 containers each way on one berth.
>
> The output per man-week would be 600 freight tons, compared with the 30 or so tons at present. It is estimated that the current average 100,000–150,000 tons per year handled on a general cargo berth today could increase to two million tons a year.

In general these figures, with 20–22 containers handled per hour, were soon realised on fully equipped berths, though in poorly equipped ports the number might be as low as 8. By 1988 64 containers per hour could be handled in Singapore.

The article referred to added that inland clearance depots would be set up at strategic points to handle both import and export cargoes and to provide customs clearance facilities. It also pointed out that important to the success of the new enterprise were the internationally agreed standards for containers.[18] By 1974 another shipping journal was able to report that the speed with which containerisation had got under way had enabled shipowners to 'at least keep some check on the increases made in freight rates'.[19]

The process of containerisation, like the building of big bulk carriers, was helped by government fiscal policy, a policy which sowed the seeds of subsequent disaster in some areas of shipping though no one foresaw this at the time. Between 1948 and 1957 the British merchant fleet grew in tonnage by some 10 per cent, from 18 to 20 million gross tons. Between

1957 and 1973 it grew by more than 50 per cent, from 20 to 30 million gross tons, peaking at 33 million gross tons in 1975, a figure never approached hitherto. The rate of growth was most rapid in the years following the second closure of the Suez Canal, years which coincided with generous government help to the industry, not all of which was well-conceived.

In 1961 the British government had provided £24 million by way of a loan for the building of *QE2*. Three years later the Shipbuilding Credit Act made it possible for any shipping company established in the United Kingdom to obtain credit for 80 per cent of the cost of a new ship, interest being paid at 5.5 per cent, the loan to be repaid over a period of from 8 to 10 years.

In 1965 the government allowed a shipping company to write off the cost of a ship as fast as profits would permit before any tax was paid on those profits, The following year the 40 per cent investment allowance which had been available to shipping companies since 1957 was abolished. In its place the government provided a cash subsidy of 20 per cent for any new ship built. In 1967 this cash subsidy for new vessels was increased to 25 per cent. To qualify for the subsidy the ship had to remain on the British register for five years, but the subsidy was given no matter where in the world the ship was built.

This combination of cheap credit and cash subsidy meant that a company needed to put up very little of its own money to invest in new ships and, if profits were earned when the ship traded no tax would need to be paid because the ship could be written off. This was a government licence to build without great immediate risk and when the Suez Canal was closed at the end of 1966, thus increasing the demand for shipping, both British and foreign companies grabbed at the subsidies. Many more foreign interests established companies in Britain simply to take advantage of the cash subsidies.

Nearly 1000 grant-assisted vessels were built in consequence of this policy and the subsidies given amounted to £620 million. By the time the cash subsidy was abolished, in 1970, the British merchant fleet had grown to an unprecedented size and over half the new tonnage – some 5 million gross tons – was owned by foreigners. Many of the new ships were built in Japan, the world's leading shipbuilder after 1957, and, since these ships could be built abroad and the foreign owners could remit profits abroad, once they had paid tax if any were due, the British balance of payments was affected adversely by measures which had been intended to benefit British shipping, British shipbuilders and the country as a whole.[20]

Fig. 16. GROSS AND DEADWEIGHT TONNAGES OF WORLD AND UK FLEETS, 1973–1988

YEAR	WORLD FLEET		UK FLEET	
	GROSS TONNAGE	DEADWEIGHT TONNAGE	GROSS TONNAGE	DEADWEIGHT TONNAGE
	(MILLION TONS)			
1973	290	452	30	47
1974	311	494	32	50
1975	342	553	33	53
1976	372	608	33	54
1977	394	649	32	52
1978	406	670	31	50
1979	413	681	28	45
1980	420	691	27	44
1981	421	697	25	41
1982	425	702	23	36
1983	423	695	19	30
1984	419	683	16	24
1985	416	674	14	22
1986	405	639	12	16
1987	403	637	9	11
1988	403	637	8	11

(*Source:* Lloyd's Register of Shipping; vessels over 100 gross ton.)

Britain did not stand alone in providing cheap money for ships. In 1970 the shipbuilding countries of Europe and Japan all agreed on standard credit terms: where a ship was built credit would be given for 80 per cent of the cost and this amount would be repayable over eight years at an interest rate of 6 per cent.[21] Nevertheless, the shipyards of some countries were giving credit for periods of up to ten years.

General operating subsidies continued to be paid to shipping operators in the United States and Japan and subsidies for specific purposes were given to operators in Italy, France and Spain. The United States continued to subsidise shipbuilding, and in 1963–4 the Japanese government gave subsidies to its shipping industry to induce it to concentrate in a few large groups.[22] After 1968 the Greek government made considerable tax concessions to Greek shipowners which induced many of them to transfer ships back to the Greek flag.

In 1967 Japanese shipping companies, which were finding Japanese seamen increasingly expensive, found a way to circumvent Japanese currency and credit regulations by making so-called 'shikumisen' deals with shipowners in Hong Kong. Hong Kong vessels registered under flags of convenience are exempt from all tax on income earned and such vessels transferred from the Japanese flag could be chartered back to Japanese companies with benefit to both parties.

One other way in which money became easily available for ships at this time was in consequence of the large supply of Eurodollars. Eurodollars were earnings on American post-war investments in Europe. After 1957 large amounts of Eurodollars were earned and, for tax purposes, not repatriated. They thus became available for short term loans many of which were invested in flag of convenience shipping.

In 1960 a shipping paper wrote of Erling Naess: 'Mr Naess has evolved the ultimate in triumph in operating ships at the most economic advantage. Finance them from sources where money is readily available, build them where costs are relatively low and delivery relatively quick, register them where taxes are negligible and man them with British seamen and have a British company operate them in order to knock the feet from under the bulk of the opposition.'[23] Naess was not the only man in the game.

Following the Cuban blockade of 1962 the Soviet Union began an extensive programme of rebuilding to become independent of the western world. By 1969 it was estimated that one-half of USSR shipping requirements was met by her own fleet.[24] Between 1970 and 1977 Russian ships took a growing part in the cross-trades and the USSR established itself in a large number of liner trades.[25] Economic considerations played little part in this expansion.

By 1968 the communist countries and some thirty other countries imposed flag discrimination. Although it has been argued that flag discrimination did not inhibit the growth of flag of convenience fleets,[26] it does not follow that such discrimination had no deleterious influence upon the British fleet. In the years immediately prior to 1968 flag discrimination had nearly halved the proportion of liner traffic carried by United Kingdom operators to Uruguay and seriously affected the trades to Brazil and India.[27] A new United Nations organisation, the United Nations Conference on Trade and Development (UNCTAD), was established in 1964 and, since all countries were given an equal voice in its deliberations,

Fig. 17. THE MARITIME NATIONS, 1957–1988 (IN ORDER OF SIZE AS IN 1988)

FOR BENEFICIAL OWNERSHIP SEE TEXT

(MILLION GROSS TONS)

	1957	1972	1982	1988
World	110.2	268.3	424.7	403.4
Liberia	7.5	44.4	70.7	49.7
Panama	4.1	7.8	32.6	44.6
Japan	4.4	34.9	40.8	32.1
USSR	2.7	16.7	23.8	25.8
Greece	1.5	15.3	40.0	22.0
US*	25.9	15.0	19.1	20.8
Cyprus	0.0	2.0	2.1	18.4
China (People's Republic)	0.5	1.2	8.1	12.9
Norway	8.5	23.5	21.9	9.4
Philippines	0.1	0.9	2.8	9.3
Bahamas	†	0.2	0.4	9.0
UK	19.9	28.6	22.5	8.3
Italy	4.6	8.2	10.4	7.8
South Korea	0.1	1.1	5.5	7.3
Hong Kong	0.4	0.5	3.5	7.3
Singapore	†	0.9	7.2	7.2
India	0.6	2.6	6.2	6.2
Brazil	0.9	1.9	5.7	6.1
Taiwan	†	1.5	2.2	4.6
UK as % of world	18	11	5	2

* includes in 1988 1,324,210 gross tons for service on Great Lakes; the US Reserve Fleet is estimated at 3.3 million gross tons

† not separately recorded

(*Source:* Lloyd's Register of Shipping; vessels over 100 gross ton.)

it was dominated by the less developed nations. By 1968 UNCTAD was pressing for still further discrimination, and discrimination had been developed by countries like Brazil to become a sophisticated instrument of cargo control.[28] It is small wonder that a British government report on shipping in 1970 suggested that the prevalent *laisser-faire* and free trade attitude of both the British government and British shipowners might require some reappraisal.[29]

Flag discrimination results in the uneconomic loading of ships and so, too, can the 'open' conference. The open conference is one which has to admit any ship operator who wants to join and, with its anti-trust bias, the United States insists on the open conference where it can. Because of the open conference on the north Atlantic at this time, there was substantial overtonnaging, with cargo liners sailing from one-half to two-thirds empty.

Over 300 conferences operated in the world as a whole, with memberships ranging from 2 to 40 different lines. Some two-thirds of these conferences encouraged the loyalty of shippers either by deferred rebate or the dual-rate contract method. Unlike that of the United States, the Australian government considered that 'closed' conferences operating rationalised services were in the best interests of shippers[30] and most conferences were, in fact, closed. From shipping company accounts of this period it would not appear that the closed conference led to excessive profits. On the other hand, although the level of freight rates agreed might operate in this direction, there was no specific mechanism within conference agreements which allowed the efficient member to expand or forced the inefficient member to contract or improve performance.

The factors considered above – cheap money, government support and discrimination, together with the operation of some conferences – led to too many ships being built and the world fleet began to grow faster than world trade. During the hectic years of 1972 and 1973 ship finance became a wide open field in which numerous US provincial banks and finance companies became heavily involved. The risk of ship finance without the security of first-class charters was largely disregarded and these banks and finance companies knocked on the doors of shipowners to offer them credit on speculative new building contracts, especially for tankers.[31] By 1973 both the United Kingdom and the United States fleets were 70 per cent above their pre-war levels, but these increases were nothing when compared with the increases in the fleets of other countries. West Germany, Italy and the Netherlands had all doubled their fleets, while other west European nations had at least trebled or quadrupled theirs. The Japanese fleet had multiplied sixfold, the Greek fleet tenfold, and the Russian fleet thirteenfold. But the most striking growth of all, of course, was in the flag of convenience fleet, much of which was owned by citizens of the United States, Greece and Japan, with hardly any of it owned by Britons. Almost non-existent in pre-war days, the flag of convenience fleet had grown to almost 20 per cent of the world total by 1973. As an entity it was twice the tonnage of the United Kingdom fleet and it was growing at rates more than twice those of the world fleet as a whole.

Criticism of such fleets continued, and not without reason. The proportionate losses of Liberian ships were twice as high as the losses suffered by OECD member countries.[32] The International Transport Workers' Federation (ITF) had developed the ITF Collective Agreement, which aimed to establish wages, hours of work, the manning scale and other working conditions in flag of convenience ships. If the operators agreed to ITF conditions the vessel was issued with a 'Blue Certificate' of ITF approval which exempted the vessel from boycott or 'blackings' by transport workers in its ports of call. The International Law Commission had recommended as early as 1958 that there should be a 'genuine link' between a ship and the state whose flag it flew, and this recommendation was also supported by the ITF. But neither the ITF nor the International Law Commission received any practical support from shipowners or governments, British or otherwise, and no Samuel Plimsoll appeared on the world scene to condemn unseaworthy ships or unqualified seafarers.

In 1959 a prominent British shipowner asserted that the British mercantile marine occupied a position of unrivalled supremacy in the maritime world, 'not merely in its size but in the variety of its ships and the noticeably high general standard of its direction and management'.[33] Seven years later, another prominent British shipowner said that British shipping still led the world, 'not necessarily in size of fleet' – for Liberia had just taken the statistical lead – 'but in efficiency and competitiveness'.[34] As late as 1969, after enormous subsidised investment in the container fleet, comparable to the support given to the early ocean-going steamers by mail contracts, it was claimed that in terms of value the United Kingdom fleet was still the largest. But by 1973 the days of British shipping supremacy, however measured, were definitely over. In the ten years prior to 1973 the world merchant fleet had doubled, to a total of 290 million tons gross. By this time the fleet sailing under the Liberian flag had increased to a massive 62 million tons and Japan had usurped second place with nearly 37 million tons. The United Kingdom came third with 30 million tons, while Norway, in fourth place with nearly 24 million tons, still had a fleet larger than Greece's 19 million tons. The USSR came sixth with 17 million tons and the United States seventh with 15 million tons.

In the first twelve years after the Second World War it had been difficult to make losses in shipping, and British companies needed to raise no new capital. In the years thereafter it was not easy to make profits in the western world despite easy credit terms and a favourable fiscal regime, and by

Fig. 18. UNITED KINGDOM TONNAGE AS A PERCENTAGE OF WORLD TONNAGE, 1948–1988

(MILLION GROSS TONS)

YEAR	REGISTERED TONNAGE*	BRITISH OWNED†	REGISTERED TONNAGE AS PERCENTAGE OF WORLD TONNAGE	BRITISH-OWNED TONNAGE AS PERCENTAGE OF WORLD TONNAGE
1948	18.0	18.0	22.4	22.4
1949	18.1	18.1	21.9	21.9
1950	18.2	18.2	21.5	21.5
1951	18.6	17.5	21.3	20.1
1952	18.6	17.4	20.7	19.3
1953	18.6	17.3	19.9	18.5
1954	19.0	17.1	19.5	17.6
1955	19.4	16.8	19.2	16.7
1956	19.5	16.5	18.6	15.7
1957	19.9	16.9	18.0	15.3
1958	20.3	17.2	17.2	14.6
1959	20.8	17.0	16.6	13.6
1960	21.1	17.1	16.3	13.2
1961	21.5	17.3	15.8	12.7
1962	21.7	16.8	15.5	12.0
1963	21.6	16.6	14.8	11.4
1964	21.5	16.5	14.0	10.8
1965	21.5	16.5	13.4	10.3
1966	21.5	16.6	12.6	9.7
1967	21.7	16.8	11.9	9.2
1968	21.9	16.9	11.3	8.7
1969	23.8	18.0	11.3	8.5
1970	25.8	18.9	11.4	8.3
1971	27.3	19.3	11.1	7.8
1972	28.6	19.6	10.7	7.3

Continued on next page.

(MILLION GROSS TONS)

YEAR	REGISTERED TONNAGE*	BRITISH OWNED†	REGISTERED TONNAGE AS PERCENTAGE OF WORLD TONNAGE	BRITISH-OWNED TONNAGE AS PERCENTAGE OF WORLD TONNAGE
1973	30.2	20.3	10.4	7.0
1974	31.6	21.5	10.1	6.9
1975	33.2	22.2	9.7	6.5
1976	32.9	21.9	8.9	5.9
1977	31.6	20.5	8.0	5.2
1978	30.9	20.3	7.6	5.0
1979	28.0	19.8	6.8	4.8
1980	27.1	20.2	6.5	4.8
1981	25.4	20.2	6.0	4.8
1982	22.5	20.0	5.3	4.7
1983	19.1	19.0	4.5	4.5
1984	15.9	15.9	3.8	3.8
1985	14.3	14.3	3.4	3.4
1986	11.6	10.9	2.8	2.7
1987	8.5	‡	2.1	‡
1988	8.3	‡	2.0	‡

* Lloyd's Register of Shipping
† estimated
‡ not available

1973 nearly half the total capital employed by twenty British shipping companies was borrowed money.[35] Britain was in the forefront with containerisation and had pioneered the gas-carrier, but Britain was not a front-runner in the development of bulk-carriers.

Although world shipments of dry cargo of all kinds increased from 375 million tons in 1937 to 720 million tons in 1965, the trade in mixed dry cargoes did not grow proportionately, and Britain's main bulk export of the past – coal – scarcely featured in the figures by the 1970s. These trades had moved eastwards and Europe was relinquishing the initiative to Japan and south-east Asia. Two-thirds of all the maritime transport of coal and iron was now to Japan, and by 1970 the Japanese need for imported raw materials employed 40 per cent of the world's bulk carrier fleet. What British ships had been doing for Britain a century earlier Japanese and flag of convenience ships were by this time doing for Japan. Operation under flags of convenience was cheaper than it was under the traditional maritime flags. Easy credit had led to both excess shipbuilding capacity and too many ships. Rapid technological change, stimulated by the closure of the Suez Canal, rendered some vessels, like tankers built in the 1950s, obsolete before their cost had been written off. The net earnings of British shipping in the 'invisible' trade of the United Kingdom, which had contributed positively to the balance of payments in the first two decades after the war, had become a net loss by 1970.

In an increasingly complex industry many ships acquired a distinctly international flavour. In 1972 a British chief engineer officer reported that his ship carried American coal to Japan and Japanese cars to America. The ship had been built in Scotland and the generators, pumps and steering gear were British. The main engine, however, was a Japanese-built engine of Danish origin – Burmeister and Wain – with Swiss turbochargers and a United States governor. Most of the electric motors were French. The car decks of Finnish steel were built and fitted in Norway, while the deck cranes were Swedish. The crew were Indian, the catering staff coming from Goa, and the officers were British. Nominally owned by the Cardigan Shipping Company of Cardiff, the vessel was chartered by Godager of Norway, who owned Cardigan, and managed by Harrison's of Glasgow.[36] As contemporary shipping went this was relatively uncomplicated.

For some seafarers new long sea passages of a kind unknown since the days of sail had become the norm. One regular bulkship trade in iron ore was round the world. The ship loaded at Dampier in Western Australia in 10 hours, discharged this cargo after a 33-day passage at sea in Taranto, Italy, in 20 hours, sailed in ballast to Port Cartier in Canada in 11 days and there, in 10 hours, loaded iron ore for Tobata in Japan, a 32-day passage via the Panama Canal. The cargo would then be discharged in Tobata in 20 hours, and the ship would proceed to Dampier in ballast, a passage of 10 days, to load again. The ship thus almost equalled the time allowed by Jules Verne – round the world in 86 days, with a total of 60 hours in port and a chance for the crew of no more than an hour or two ashore in some not very attractive place. Such seafarers no longer went to sea to see the world.

Seafaring remained a dangerous occupation, though the death-rate per 1000 British seamen at risk had fallen from 5.10 between the world wars to 2.36 between 1948 and 1973 – less than half the pre-war figure.[37] The accident rate remained the highest in British industry, with 7420 accidents reported in 1972, 1091 of them occurring when seamen were off duty. Seafarers, too, suffered a much higher than average rate of gastro-intestinal, respiratory and skin diseases. Conditions on board, however, continued to improve. Of 11,000 ships inspected in 1972 in the Port of London, only 196 were found to be verminous, few of them British. Videocassettes were added to films, libraries, crew bars and swimming pools for crew entertainment, diet became healthier and more varied and, to encourage fitness among seafarers, some employers even experimented with rowing and cycling machines on board ship. But, by reason of the quicker turn-round of ships in port and the falling number of crew on board, seafaring was fast becoming a less attractive profession, and its image ashore was not a glamorous one.

With the decline in the number of passenger ships, with bigger and fewer cargo ships, and with increasing automation, the number of British seafarers began to fall dramatically. In 1951 18 million tons gross of British shipping had been crewed (using the census figures of those actually at sea on the day) by 105,000 seamen signed on British articles, plus 48,000 non-Europeans. By 1971 the fleet totalled 27 million tons, an increase of 50 per cent, but the number of seafarers had halved, to 54,000 British and fewer than 20,000 non-Europeans.[38] In 1958 there had been 36,000 British catering ratings in the merchant navy. By 1968 the number was only 22,000. In this latter year the crew of a 200,000-ton tanker numbered 40, no more than the crew of a 20,000-ton ship twenty years earlier.

Despite these reduced requirements it was not easy to recruit seafarers. The Shipping Federation maintained 25 local offices, conducted 'how to go to sea courses' for educationists, arranged some 1200 visits to schools each year and employed eight full-time selection officers. The bigger shipping companies maintained their own recruiting organisations. Between them they had to find over 8000 new entrants each year because ratings stayed at sea, on average, only six or seven years. Officers stayed, perhaps, twice as long.[39]

The Shipping Federation recruited and trained over 80 per cent of the ratings – 2400 stewards, 1600 deckboys and 750 greasers in 1960 – the remaining recruits coming from charitable training schools or, in one case, being trained by an employer. Since the war the Shipping Federation had run the training-ship *Vindicatrix* at Sharpness as well as the World War I establishment at Gravesend, but *Vindicatrix* was closed in 1968 because by that date the annual entry had fallen to 1700 stewards and 800 deckboys. The Gravesend school was rebuilt and promoted to a 'college' but the training remained much the same.

In the early 1960s the industry still required over 1000 newly certificated navigating officers each year and 400 newly qualified radio officers. The radio officers had to arrange for their own college education but the trainee navigators, now become 'cadets' rather than 'apprentices', were trained at nautical colleges run by local education authorities, partly at the expense of the shipping companies. The traditional navigating officer training establishments, *Worcester* and *Conway*, were both near their end, and it soon became apparent that there were far too many nautical colleges as well.

After the abolition of conscription, which was finally phased out in 1963, the shortage of engineer officers became ever more apparent. In the 1960s a new engineer cadet scheme had to be introduced to add to the supply. The aim was to provide a new source of engineer officers by training suitable school-leavers at college and at sea rather than relying entirely on recruits from the engineering industry ashore.

The new marine engineering cadets, like engineers apprenticed ashore, could aspire to an ordinary national certificate or diploma, a qualification of a generally recognised standard. By analogy, the Merchant Navy and Airline Officers Association now demanded the establishment of a similar qualification for navigators. The usefulness of such a qualification in obtaining jobs ashore – a reason advanced for its introduction – remained somewhat doubtful. However, ordinary national certificates and diplomas for navigating officers were duly established.

In 1965, under pressure from the educationists, the Merchant Navy Training Board, an organisation that had been largely moribund hitherto, announced that the minimum academic entry qualification for cadets would henceforth be three ordinary-level passes in the General Certificate of Education. The industry thus accepted in large measure, albeit reluctantly, the minimum entry qualification demanded by The Marine Society shortly after World War II. In 1968 1200 deck and 800 engineer cadets were accepted by the industry, over half of them recruited by the Shipping Federation, the rest being recruited by the larger shipping companies. The owners were complaining already of the cost of training. This was said to be about £11 million a year, though the shipping companies subscribed only 40 per cent of this total, the rest coming from public funds and from seafarers themselves.[40]

For 150 years Britain had been the world's major maritime power. In all this time most shipping companies had taken little or no interest in the training of seafarers and none in man management on board ship. Nor, if shipbuilding be excluded, had maritime matters interested anyone in the academic world. The British Empire had been built upon British ships but the well-being of seafarers and the nature of their science had interested only a handful of charitable persons and the odd clock-maker. Suddenly, with the industry on the eve of rapid decline, the Merchant Navy Training Board established short courses in personnel relations for senior merchant navy officers, thus endorsing pioneer work which had been carried on since 1961 by the Seafarers Education Service and the Honourable Company of Master Mariners. At the same time, two universities and two polytechnics established four new degree courses in nautical science – at least two too many from the start – for which the new ordinary national diploma for navigating officers was one entry qualification.

In the meantime, industrial relations, described as 'admirable' by one shipowner in 1959,[41] had turned sour. In the halcyon years following World War II the catering ratings employed by Cunard, predominantly Liverpool men, were known by their peers as Cunard Cowboys or Cunard Yanks. They sported 'superior' American working clothes, enjoyed high overtime earnings and tips despite their low basic pay, and tended to be at the centre of any industrial trouble. In 1960 a minor disciplinary incident aboard a liner led to a substantial unofficial strike which lasted, with one intermission, from July to September and affected both liners and cargo vessels in British ports.

'The truth is', reported one journal,[42] 'that most of this month's strikers have come not from hardened seadogs acutely conscious of the justice of a cause but from young people just paid off with perhaps £60 after a voyage, who while vaguely feeling that they deserve a better deal, have no objection to spending a week or two and a pocketful of banknotes in the sunny leisure of a strike.' It was not quite as simple as this. Under the leadership of Sir Tom Yates, National Union of Seamen officials had become somewhat distanced from their members. The dissident seamen, aiming to make the Union take a more militant line, now created the National Seamen's Reform Movement.[43]

The fact was that, although for them the writing was on the wall, the white stewards still had the upper hand. When P & O absorbed the Orient Line, the National Union of Seamen was forced to agree that the traditionally white-crew Orient Line should take on a proportion of Goanese stewards because the industry could not find competent white ones. 'In the catering department of Orient ships', reported the official union journal, 'the changes at the end of each voyage have never been less than 40 per cent, and have sometimes been as high as 60 per cent.'[44]

The immediate result of the 1960 unofficial strike was the introduction of a $5\frac{1}{2}$ day working week at sea, a 44-hour week in port, and a rise in pay. By 1962 an engine-room greaser was receiving a basic £44 a month while an able-seaman with seniority pay received £44.10s. A chief engineer officer's pay at this time was £136 a month and a chief officer's £107.5s a month.[45]

Shortly after the unofficial strike the leaders of the Reform Movement were elected to the NUS executive committee. By 1965 the Union had secured a pension scheme for ratings and a form of shipboard representation new to the industry and it established an educational programme to train those who were to become shipboard representatives. Neither was much of a success. The pension scheme did not last and shipboard representatives seldom proved dedicated. The predominantly young members of the Union were too apathetic. However, the militant element scored a further victory when in 1965 a 40-hour week in port was accepted, though the working week at sea could still be extended to 56 hours if the work were deemed essential.

Discontent arising from this 'essential work' clause of the agreement led in May 1966 to the first official strike in the industry since 1911. The oil companies avoided the effects of the strike by rerouteing their ships, but the strike continued for some 47 days and at the end nearly 900 ships were said to be immobilised.[46] The socialist prime minister, Harold Wilson, denounced the strike on television and radio, describing eight of the Union's militant members as communists, but set up a Court of Inquiry into the dispute, chaired by Lord Pearson. This Court reported the following year, concluding that the major cause for complaint was the inferior status conferred upon the rating by the Shipping Acts and all that followed from them. The Report proposed that these Acts be brought up to date and that more use be made of the law of contract and less of the criminal law. It recommended more flexible manning systems on board ship in place of the rigid division between seamen, greasers and stewards, and considered that reports on conduct need be entered in a seaman's discharge book no longer. More effective personnel policies were required, and conditions on some ships should be improved. Although stewards were only four to a cabin in new passenger ships, 6, 8 and even 10-berth cabins existed in older ships. The Court was critical of the 'paternalistic' attitude to seamen commonly displayed.[47]

A settlement of the 1966 strike was reached eventually but the strike marked the beginning of the end of the Shipping Federation because the cross-Channel ferry companies and the oil companies had been willing to make separate agreements with the Union. The Union was a closed shop, a situation which suited both employers and union officials, but its membership had declined from 80,000 in 1948 and over 97,000 in 1957 to 56,000 in 1968.[48] Nevertheless it remained powerful because seafarers of quality were not easy to recruit or to retain, powerful enough at this juncture to secure the passage of two Merchant Shipping Acts which aimed to put seafarers on a legal footing similar to that of other workers, in accordance with the recommendations of the Pearson Report. The Merchant Shipping Acts of 1970 and 1974 removed the old disciplinary curbs, the system of fines imposed by the shipmaster which had been introduced in 1854, replacing them with a 'code of conduct' and inquiry by a shore tribunal where the code was breached seriously. The seaman's discharge book no longer reported on conduct and ability. Nor was it necessary any longer to sign on and off articles in the presence of a government official.[49] These new procedures did not have the dire effects on the maintenance of discipline that some officers had predicted though this may have been, in part, because the state of the merchant navy was soon to change startlingly.

For the moment the 'never had it so good' conditions prevailed. Although there had been initial difficulty in commissioning *Southern Cross* in 1955 because the crew accommodation was air-conditioned, the Officers' Association demanded air-conditioning in tankers trading to the Persian Gulf in 1958,[50] and gradually it became normal in all new deepsea ships. From the end of the 1950s some companies had allowed senior officers to take their wives to sea with them, if they wished to do so, and gradually in deepsea ships this privilege was extended to all British seafarers. The officers, too, concluded closed shop agreements with the shipping companies, as the ratings had done, and under the inspiration of The Marine Society a Nautical Institute, strenuously opposed at the time by the Shipping Federation and the MNAOA, was established in 1968. For the first time navigating officers had a professional body distinct from a trade union through which they could educate their members and make representations to government. Seafarers, like the young ashore, now grew their hair long, and old-fashioned marine superintendents had to put up with shoulder-length hair, a style familiar to Drake, Cook and Nelson but one not approved by senior officers in the 1960s. In some companies officers had even given up wearing uniform at sea. In 1973 the National Maritime Board agreed to a new Established Service Scheme which gave greater security and increased benefits to the registered seafarer, but it was not to protect many seafarers for long.

To solve some of their problems shipping companies were pressing by this time for the establishment of a basic watchkeeping certificate for navigators of lower standard than the established second mate's certificate which the educationists had succeeded in making more difficult of achievement. For the first time they were also willing to recruit women as deck cadets and radio officers, though nothing much came of this because, on the whole, women did not like these jobs.

More importantly, there were moves, following extensive engine-room automation and other rationalisation on board ship, towards 'interdepartmental flexibility' and 'general purpose' manning. For the first time it was suggested that ratings might be trained to work both on deck and in the engine room. In 1967 Esso concluded a productivity deal with the NUS which incorporated some of these ideas, and this was followed in 1968 by sixteen similar agreements with other shipping companies.

The National Union of Seamen, which by 1969 was suffering an average weekly deficit of £1000, cooperated in the proposals for general purpose manning, with its saving in manpower, despite its falling membership. There was no Luddite reaction and the reason is not perhaps hard to seek. General purpose manning was most practicable in bulkships and the most important bulkships were tankers. The wages of Indian seafarers were not much more than one-third those of British seafarers, and some other Third World seafarers were cheaper still. Pushed too far, the multi-national oil companies and foreigners operating under the British flag could easily 'ship out' to cheaper national flags and cheaper crews. Indeed, when the Suez Canal reopened and it finally became even clearer that there were too many ships in the world, they proceeded to do so.

Whatever the consequent effects on British shipping and seafarers, the economic effects on Britain of all these changes were less dramatic than they might have been because in 1963 American technological advance had opened up new possibilities. Up to this time oil wells in the sea had been limited to water less than 180 feet deep. Now it was possible to drill oil wells in the open sea in deep water and in 1964 oil and gas were discovered in the North Sea. The first oil platform was constructed in 1966 and large oil strikes were made in 1970. The North Thames and South Eastern Gas Boards, which had together operated fifty-six colliers in 1956, disposed of their last collier in 1971 because by that time they were using North Sea gas. The Central Electricity Generating Board also began to dispose of colliers, thus dealing a further blow at British coastal shipping. However, new opportunities for small ships in coastal or near-coastal waters arose from the need to service oil-rigs and new fleets of oil-rig supply vessels, some of them vessels which had become redundant in such trades as fishing and ferrying, came into existence.

Notes

1. *Committee of Inquiry into Shipping* ('Rochdale Report') (1970), London, p. 90.
2. H.C.B. Rogers, *Troopships and their History* (1963), London, pp. 212–14.
3. *The Times* (22.8.1959).
4. Rochdale Report, p. 93.
5. *Shipbuilding & Shipping Record* (8.7.1965).
6. Rochdale Report, p. 84.
7. P. Padfield, *Beneath the House Flag of P & O* (1981), London, p. 138.
8. F. B. Bolton.
9. *Shipbuilding & Shipping Record* (6.3.1969).
10. E. D. Naess, *Autobiography of a Shipping Man* (1977), Colchester, p. 120 and pp. 181–191.
11. Honourable Company of Master Mariners *Journal* (Autumn, 1974).
12. Naess, *op. cit.*, p. 63 and p. 48.
13. Rochdale Report, p. 28.
14. F. C. Lane, 'Tonnages, Medieval and Modern' (1964–5), EHR, 2nd Series, Vol. XVII, No. 1, pp. 217–18.
15. *Australian Sea Trader* (March/May 1979).
16. *Sunday Times* (9.1.1966); *Ocean Mail* (December 1985).
17. J. McConville, *The Shipping Industry in the United Kingdom* (1977), Geneva, p. 21.
18. *Docks* (September/October 1967).
19. *Fairplay* (24.10.1974).
20. Rochdale Report, p. 347.
21. *The Shipbroker* (November 1970).
22. T. Rinman and R. Brodefors, *The Commercial History of Shipping* (1983), Gothenburg, p. 119.
23. *Liverpool Journal of Commerce* (5.9.1960).
24. Rochdale Report, p. 54.
25. Rinman, *op. cit.*, p. 120.
26. E.g. by R. O. Goss, *The Decline of UK-registered Merchant Shipping*, a memorandum submitted to the House of Commons Transport Committee in October, 1986.
27. Rochdale Report, p. 45.
28. See *Maritime Policy & Management*, Vol. 13, No. 4 (1986), pp. 277–90: 'Protectionism in practice', by S. Farrell.
29. Rochdale Report, p. 380.
30. *Ib.*, pp. 118–26.
31. Naess, *op. cit.*, p. 218.
32. *Nautical Magazine* (September 1972).
33. R. H. Thornton, *British Shipping* (1959), Cambridge, p. 106.
34. See G. J. Bonwick, *British Shipping: an independent study* (1980), Henley-on-Thames, p. 11.
35. S. D. Kumana, 'Financial analysis of UK shipping companies' (9.1.1975), *Fairplay*.
36. Letter to the author.
37. Calculated by the author from the returns of *Casualties to Vessels and Accidents to Men* published annually by the Department of Transport and its predecessors, making allowance for changes in the manner in which seafarers have been counted.

38. Census of Seamen.
39. See: J. M. M. Hill, *The Seafaring Career* (1972), London.
40. McConville, *op. cit.*, p. 46.
41. Thornton, *op. cit.*, p. 106.
42. *The Economist* (20.8.1960).
43. A. Marsh & V. Ryan, *The Seamen* (1989), Oxford, pp. 166–7.
44. *The Seaman* (March–April 1962).
45. A. G. Course, *The Merchant Navy* (1963), London, pp. 304–5.
46. Marsh & Ryan, *op. cit.*, p. 180.
47. *Final Report of the Court of Inquiry into certain matters concerning the Shipping Industry*, Cmnd 3211 (1967), London. (The Pearson Report).
48. Marsh & Ryan, *op. cit.*, p. 307.
49. See: J. Sadler, *Discipline at Sea* (1983), Glasgow.
50. *Shipbuilding & Shipping Record* (6.2.1958).

24

Downhill all the Way

(1973–1988)

In 1973 the Organisation of Petroleum Exporting Countries (OPEC) reduced oil production and quadrupled prices. In doing this they triggered off a world-wide slump in shipping. Five years later the slump was prolonged when oil prices doubled again.

In the years before 1973 the world's appetite for energy, and for oil in particular, had seemed insatiable. This increased the demand for tankers, and political events like the closure of the Suez Canal added further to overall demand for shipping tonnage. Since underwriters were by this time proving reluctant to re-insure wartime Liberty ships, the capacity of these ships had also to be replaced. Massive strides in the technological development of ship construction promised ever bigger vessels. Orders rolled in for new tankers, new bulkers and new cellular or container ships. In the first twenty years after World War II the tonnage of the world merchant fleet had doubled. In the next decade, between 1965 and 1975, it more than doubled again. By 1973 the world's shipbuilding industry had an order book which would have provided work for four years. The orders for ships between 1968 and 1972 averaged about 30 million gross tons a year, but in 1973 a massive 70 million gross tons of ships were ordered. Such orders allowed for no upheaval like the quadrupling of oil prices and after this price increase orders for new ships tumbled. By 1978 new orders amounted to only 8 million gross tons. Over-optimistic forecasting, the mismatching of capacity to volumes of traffic, government subsidies made to shipbuilding, and foolish optimism on the part of banks: all these factors combined to produce an unprecedented slump.

Plans made cannot always be abandoned. The size of the world merchant fleet continued to increase between 1973 and 1982, when it reached the all-time peak of 425 million gross tons (702 million tons deadweight). By this time world trade had long ceased to grow, reaching a peak of 3679 million tons of cargo carried in 1979. Of this total, 2038 million tons had been oil. Less than 60 per cent of this amount was being shipped by 1985.

When the slump came much more shipbuilding capacity existed in the world than was required, particularly in the Far East, and too much of it

Fig. 19. WORLD FLEET AND WORLD SEABORNE TRADE, 1970–1987

YEAR	FLEET (MILLION DEADWEIGHT TONS)	FLEET 1970 = 100	SEABORNE TRADE (MILLION METRIC TONS)	TRADE 1970 = 100
1970	383	100	2482	100
1975	553	144	3047	123
1980	691	180	3606	145
1983	695	181	3090	124
1985	674	176	3293	133
1986	639	167	3362	135
1987	637	166	3418	138

was still being subsidised into use. Japanese shipyards alone, with more than half the world's shipbuilding capacity, could build three times the amount of new shipping that was in demand. South Korea, the fourth most indebted nation in the world and a nation of no shipbuilding significance until 1974, possessed 14 per cent of the world's shipbuilding capacity by 1983. A 'low-tech' or labour-intensive industry, shipbuilding was regarded in South Korea as an activity which, like the building of roads and sewers, was essential to industrial development. In consequence, foreign aid, which might have been differently deployed, went to subsidise the building of ships which had often been ordered by citizens of those western countries which supplied the foreign aid. The shipyards of the western countries declined in consequence. By 1977, when the United Kingdom shipyards were nationalised as British Shipbuilders, Britain, which before World War I had built 60 per cent of the world's ships, built less than 4 per cent. In the eight years that followed some £2 billion was spent in support of British Shipbuilders but output continued to decline, for South Korean prices were often below the raw material element of a British Shipbuilders bid. By 1988, with a labour force by then of under 7000, it would have saved money if British Shipbuilders had paid each worker £30,000 to stay at home.

The consequences of OPEC's quadrupling of oil prices was reinforced in other ways. Between 1967 and 1973 the British government withdrew its military and naval commitment east of Suez, and between 1973 and 1975 the United States withdrew from its involvement in Vietnam. In 1975 the Suez Canal was reopened, and in that same year Britain joined the European Community. In 1978 there was revolution in Iran. All these events were factors in reducing the demand for shipping, though none was as significant as the massive rise in the price of oil.

The quadrupling of oil prices had three major effects. First, it reduced the demand for oil and hence the demand for the carriage of oil across the sea in tankers. The reopening of the Suez Canal two years later reduced further the need for VLCCs, the very large crude-oil carriers which could not transit the Canal. Second, the rise in oil prices raised the cost of running ships: this reduced the profitability of all ships but of older ships particularly, and it stimulated research in both ship design and ship operation with a view to saving fuel. Third, the rise in oil prices stimulated the development of other sources of oil and energy, making some hitherto uneconomic exploitation suddenly worthwhile.

In consequence of the first effect freight rates became severely depressed. The basic freight rate on a typical VLCC voyage from the Arabian Gulf to north-west Europe fell from US $45 a ton in 1973 to US $3.60 a ton in 1978.[1] Since the supply of shipping far exceeded the demand for it, the European shipbuilding industry collapsed and there was a steady and persistent rise in laid-up shipping. The excess of tankers inspired the formation in 1975, the year in which the delivery of new tankers reached its peak, of the International Maritime Industries Forum (IMIF). A 'representative body' of shipowners, shipyards, bankers and oil companies, its object was somehow to reduce the number of tankers, but the Forum enjoyed little success. By 1982, when there were 577 VLCCs in the world, it was found that 326 of them were surplus to requirements. By this time, indeed, there was excess tonnage in every direction and the number of ships on the British register began to fall rapidly.

For the eight years before 1973 world oil consumption had been growing at 7.5 per cent per annum and world tanker demand had grown at around 12 per cent per annum. By 1983, in consequence of the rise in oil prices, the industrialised countries were using only two-thirds as much oil per unit of national income as in 1973 and the demand for OPEC oil had nearly halved, The world demand for VLCCs was similarly reduced by a half and, of the 27 million deadweight tons of combined or OBO tonnage, 10 million tons was changed to carry dry bulk cargo instead of oil.

In these years new ships carrying heavy capital charges were often laid up as soon as they had been completed. Owners of others tried to solve some of their problems by operating at slower and more economical speeds, while many large tankers sailed with part cargoes. In Japan and elsewhere some tankers were used as floating storage tanks.

One of the problems in a free market is that decisions are made by many different people, often operating in very different circumstances, who for their own good reasons see an opportunity of making money. This is both a strength and a weakness of the free market. It leads to innovation and development. It also leads to waste. In implementing new decisions those responsible may render unprofitable expensive capital equipment belonging to others well before that equipment is worn out and perhaps before it has repaid its cost. In shipping this problem was exacerbated in a period of rapid technological change by the possibility of building more economic ships operated by fewer men and burning less fuel per ton-mile. After the reopening of the Suez Canal in 1975 the 100,000 deadweight ton tanker, which could transit the Canal, seemed attractive to some operators who ordered more ships of this size. The consequence was that this sector of the market as well as that sector concerned with VLCCs became depressed.[2]

The transfer of OBO tonnage from the oil to the dry-cargo market spread the slump to this sector of shipping. Many operators who had changed from break-bulk tramps to large specialised bulkers now found that they could not repay the banks which had given them loans and ships were sold or companies were forced into liquidation.[3] By 1978 tween-deck tramps had almost disappeared from the British fleet, and between 1978 and 1983 United Kingdom shipping companies sold without replacing them 178 dry bulk cargo carriers totalling about 9.5 million deadweight tons. It was no longer profitable to operate these ships. The reduced demand for oil thus led to a slump not only in tankers but in all cargo carriers. A further factor in this decline was a contraction in United Kingdom imports of sugar and cereals in consequence of EEC agricultural policy.

The increased cost of fuel raised the running cost of ships, thus reducing their profitability still further. To economise in fuel, the owners of many large ships, both container ships and cruise liners, replaced their steam turbine machinery by diesel engines since the latter used oil much more economically. Indeed, the low fuel consumption of the new turbo-charged diesel engine had put steam plant beyond the realm of practicability[4] and by 1980 the era of steam propulsion machinery at sea was all but over. In consequence, container ships began to operate at slower speeds, and ships generally began to travel at slower speeds so that fuel could be conserved. At the same time, considerable advances were made in waste heat recovery, special boilers being installed for this purpose, and in the development of engines with low fuel requirements and the ability to use fuels of lower grade. This latter development brought no gratification to engineer officers who found that their own problems were thereby exacerbated. Higher costs of all kinds also led to the installation of unmanned engine rooms, more automated bridge equipment and, to reduce ship maintenance, the further development of anticorrosive paints.

For Britain the third effect of the sharp rise in oil prices, namely the development of other sources of energy, was particularly important. The exploitation of North Sea oil and gas became immediately more profitable, and by 1978 drilling rigs could be established in depths of up to 305 metres. Initially Britain had to rely heavily on Americans from Houston, Texas, where these techniques had been pioneered and British companies were thought by some to be slow off the mark. However, their competitive advantage led within a few years to the development of offshore service work for drilling, particularly in Aberdeen and other small east coast ports. The construction of oil-rigs, both in the shape of fixed platforms and as semi-submersible vessels, developed as a new British enterprise.

Oil production on the United Kingdom continental shelf began in 1975 and, boosted by the further surge in oil prices in 1979, the offshore industry enjoyed a boom until oil prices began to fall again, from $35 to $16 a barrel, in the mid-1980s and the shipping slump was extended to the offshore industry. Britain, formerly an importer of all her oil, became not merely self-sufficient but, like the similarly situated Norway, an exporter of oil. Prior even to oil production had been the use of North Sea gas. Between 1973 and 1983 the annual rate of gas production was 35–40 billion cubic metres, making the United Kingdom the second largest producer of gas in the world, second only to the United States. By 1983 oil production was 100 million tons a year and Britain had become the fifth largest producer in the world. From being an importer of long-haul oil, Britain became an exporter of short-haul oil, her oil exports going mainly to other European countries. Britain's trade with the European Community increased rapidly and distant trade decreased. By 1986 only 28 per cent of British trade tonnage operated deepsea. In 1971 the figure had been 59 per cent.

In this period a number of seafarers who, in consequence of the slump, had been made redundant in the deepsea areas of shipping found new jobs in the offshore oil and gas industry. The offshore supply sector grew from 97 ships, totalling 171,000 gross tons, in 1973 to 292 ships, totalling 270,000 gross tons, in 1986, though by the latter year 101 of these ships were laid up. However, oil-rig servicing did little for merchant shipping tonnage. The ships were small and often secondhand. Deepsea the United Kingdom tanker fleet was reduced by nearly 50 per cent between 1978 and 1983 and, although the decline was worldwide, only the reduction by 30 per cent of the Scandinavian tanker fleet approached the scale of the decline in Britain.

Nearly two-thirds of United Kingdom tanker capacity had been under the control of the seven oil 'majors', only one of them a British company. Texaco, Exxon, Socal/Chevron, Gulf (which acquired Socal in 1983) and Mobil were primarily American. Shell was 60 per cent Dutch. BP was British. To cut costs, Texaco, Exxon, and Socal/Chevron placed all new tonnage after 1980 under flags of convenience, while Shell, BP and Mobil brought very few new ships to the British flag. By this time it had become cheaper to charter tankers than to own them, and the oil majors were also losing their control of free-world oil. Their two-thirds control of this oil in 1973 had been reduced to one-third by 1979. As the majors withdrew from the tanker business, the number of independent oil-traders increased and many oil producers began to make direct deals with consumer countries.[5]

In 1974 BP had owned a fleet of 93 ships – by no means the peak fleet – and chartered more than this number. Even at that late date it was experiencing difficulties in maintaining a seagoing staff of 7000 men and an assistant general manager complained that for the British seafaring seemed to have lost its charm. In 1984 BP Shipping was established as an independent business and by the beginning of 1986 – by which time the British government was selling its shares in the parent company – BP Shipping owned only 30 ships, all of them flagged out to Bermuda, Gibraltar and the Bahamas, and it chartered fewer than this number. Without consulting the seafaring unions, the company, which was losing money on its ships, then dismissed its entire seagoing force, by this time reduced to 970 officers and 720 ratings, to save a further £10–£12 million a year. The company suggested that if they wanted further employment at sea with BP Shipping these seafarers would have to come to an agreement with one of three foreign manning agencies.

One minor factor which contributed to the decline in British tanker tonnage after 1973 arose from the International Convention for the Prevention of Pollution from Ships (Marpol) which was agreed in that year and from the Protocol agreed in 1978. These agreements resulted in new international rules relating to crude oil tank-washing which came into force in 1981. The system for tank-washing which was being widely adopted – COW or crude oil washing – was expensive. So, it appeared, would be other measures which needed to be taken and which arose from the Safety of Life at Sea Convention (SOLAS) of 1974. British-flag VLCCs were older, on the whole, than were many other of the world's tankers and to convert them to meet these new International Maritime

Organisation requirements was not worthwhile in the prevailing economic conditions. They were therefore dispensed with.

Since tanker operation had become so unremunerative, United Kingdom liner operators pulled out of the tanker sector, which they had entered only twenty years earlier, and did not re-invest. So, too, did a number of foreign owners who had operated under the British flag.

Another victim of the slump was the new trade, pioneered by the British, of carrying liquid gas. An anticipated increase in demand never materialised and by 1982 most of the large LNG or Liquefied Natural Gas tankers were laid up, as were the LPG or Liquefied Petroleum Gas tankers. Only a year or two before, the latter, which carried ethylene at −104°C. had seemed the bright spot of Britain's high technology fleet.[6]

The investment grants or cash subsidies given by the United Kingdom government to shipping companies which built new ships had been available from 1966 to 1970. In practice, since ships take time to build, they did not peter out entirely until 1973. As we have seen, provided that they sailed their ships under the United Kingdom flag for five years these grants had been available to foreign owners. Before the exploitation of North Sea oil raised its value, sterling was also a cheap currency. For these reasons the foreign-owned element of the United Kingdom fleet increased from 5 to 10.5 million gross tons between 1969 and 1978. By 1983, however, the Red Ensign had ceased to be an attractive flag for foreigners. The cost advantage had been eroded and by this time those foreigners who had received subsidies for the building of their ships had fulfilled their flag obligations. They therefore sold up or flagged out. Inclusive of the multi-national oil companies, 54 per cent of the United Kingdom ships sold between 1978 and 1983 belonged to foreign owners. Most had been attracted to the British flag by government grants and a favourable exchange rate.[7]

Oil-price increases, although the major factor, were not alone in producing the great shipping slump of the 1980s. Bulkers, ro-ros and container ships continued to make inroads into the traffic carried by the cargo-liners of an earlier era and by 1983 only 23 of these 'break-bulk' liners were left in the British merchant fleet.[8] Some 200 of these ships had disappeared in the previous seven years, most of them scrapped. In one British port, West Hartlepool, where there had been 43 companies in 1913, there was now only one.[9] At the same time the British distant-water fishing fleet disappeared because in 1977 many countries had extended their fishing zone to 200 miles from the national coast. No more than a few of these fishing vessels found employment in the oil-rig service industry.

The only relatively cheerful areas in the whole of British shipping were container ships, cruising and the ro-ro ferries. So far as cruising was concerned, in 1988 12 British cruise ships, 7 of them registered in the United Kingdom, were operated by P & O and Cunard. They cruised in North America, largely up the west coast and in the Caribbean, and to a lesser extent in Australian and European waters, and sometimes round the world.

There was a significant level of new investment in ferries, and in the short-sea trades the ferries, together with road transport and the single-deck hatched mini-bulk vessel, effectively replaced the old short-sea dry cargo vessel. At the same time ro-ros were also encroaching upon liner markets in the North Sea and to the Middle East, while the short-sea tanker was being largely replaced by the pipeline, the rationalisation of oil supply and economy in the use of oil.

By 1980 the Trans-Siberian railway was carrying 25 per cent of the traffic between Japan and western Europe and Britain had become one of its major users. The tonnage of container ships outside Britain was increasing and the United Kingdom share of the market was falling. Nevertheless, in the early 1980s British ships were still carrying 10 per cent of world container freight though the British share of world sea-borne trade was only 4 per cent.[10]

In the West African trade the last passenger ship, *Aureol*, had been withdrawn in 1974. Henceforward this trade was served exclusively by new 'combo' containerships which carried both containers and other 'parcels' of cargo. Significantly, the members of the conference, once predominantly British, were now Elder Dempster Lines, Palm Line, Guinea Gulf Line, Black Star Line, Nigerian National Shipping Line, Nigerian Green Lines, Compagnie Maritime Zairoise and Société Ivoirienne de Transport Maritime. In 1989 Ocean Transport and Trading sold the goodwill and assets of the first three – the remaining British contingent – to a British subsidiary of a French group.[11] Keen competition, fragile conferences and leaky rate structures were, by this latter date, removing some of the glitter from the container business generally.

The emerging nations seemed to have won their battle in UNCTAD. In 1974 UNCTAD agreed on the United Nations Code of Conduct for Liner Conferences which recommended that each nation carry 40 per cent of its liner trade in its own ships, leaving 40 per cent for its trading partner and 20 per cent for cross-traders, who might, of course, include the nations directly involved. This Code, including the cargo-sharing provision of '40:40:20', came into force in 1983. Subsequent agreement between member states of the EEC and between EEC and OECD countries – the so-called 'Brussels package' – effectively limited the operation of the

UNCTAD Code to some 25 per cent of the world liner traffic,[12] and the Code did not apply to liners operating outside conferences.

In the event the UNCTAD Code seems to have achieved little of benefit and it has been argued cogently that, instead of developing their merchant fleets, the emerging nations would have been wiser to invest in their export businesses. The Code, developed in the days of break-bulk shipping, is not suited to the container age and leads merely, as proponents of free trade have always argued, to more costly and less efficient transport, inhibiting development by raising the domestic costs of imports and reducing the competitive position of exports.[13]

In 1978, however, orders for ships from the emerging nations provided welcome work for western shipyards and these nations believed that they could increase the merchant fleets under their own flags further if the flag of convenience ships could be phased out, for they, too, could supply cheap seamen.

In an era of slump and rapid change it became increasingly difficult to keep abreast of who owned what in British shipping. In 1960 eight large liner groups – P & O, Furness Withy, Cunard, British and Commonwealth, Ellerman, Blue Funnel, Vestey and Weir – had owned over 80 per cent of British liner tonnage and many other ships as well. By 1980 the situation was vastly different. In that year C. Y. Tung of Hong Kong, shortly to be in economic difficulty itself, took over the entire Furness Withy fleet. Cunard, already part of Trafalgar House, sold its 24-ship Offshore Marine fleet, established only a few years before, to the American Zapata Corporation. The Ellerman group, owners of 130 ships in 1960, now owned only four ships though, since these were container ships, they represented capital which in earlier times might have been invested in upwards of thirty ships. A little later this group changed hands and lost all contact with the trust originally established by Sir John Ellerman.

In so far as these companies survived and owned container ships, they became part of or acted with international consortia which operated over many of the world's trade routes. Ellerman, for example, despite their few ships, had interests in ACT(A), a container ship consortium which traded to Australia and the United States, Ben Line Containers, a company which operated a container service to the Far East within the Trio international grouping, and the Ellerman-Harrison Container Line, which provided a service to South Africa within another international grouping.

Some British family groups remained in business. The Everards were still operating coasters and short-sea traders successfully. The Harrison Line, still family controlled, had moved into the container age by associating itself with international consortia, though by 1986 it had only one container ship sailing under its own colours. The Denholms were still managing other people's ships and operating one or two of their own. The Bibby, Ropner, Runciman, Salvesen, Swire, Thompson, Vestey and Weir families were all still involved with ships, though most had other interests that were more extensive than their shipping interests. The family links in most of the old liner groups, where they existed at all, were tenuous.

After nearly a century of separate existence, the Shipping Federation (by this time the British Shipping Federation) and the Chamber of Shipping had amalgamated in 1975 to form the General Council of British Shipping. Ten years later the decline of British shipping was marked further by the transfer of the new organisation's annual dinner from the Great Hall of Grosvenor House, where 2000 members and their guests could be accommodated, to much smaller premises in the London Hilton. In the same year, 1985, economic pressures forced the amalgamation of the officers' unions into the National Union of Marine, Air and Sea Transport Officers or NUMAST.

Among the traditional British liner groups still further rationalisation, internationalisation, retrenchment and diversification took place. The change from port-to-port operations to fully-integrated transport systems, in which the ship is but one link in the chain, had created a few modern companies which, in addition to operating ships of various kinds, controlled road vehicles, barges, tugs, warehouses, inland and port terminals, and a host of related services. One such survivor was P & O, a company whose sea traditions could be traced back to the East India Company of 1601, but which by 1983 was chaired not by a 'shipping family' director but by a City financier who almost immediately moved the company headquarters from the City of London to Westminster. In 1984, after scrapping *Oriana* and laying up the veteran *Uganda*, P & O launched the Finnish-built cruise-liner *Royal Princess*, still manned by British officers but with the catering franchised to a foreigner. Two years later the company launched the 31,000-ton ro-ro cruise ferry *Norsea*, the largest passenger-carrying vessel built in the United Kingdom since the *QE2*, launched 19 years earlier. The ship could carry 1250 passengers (with 746 in cabin accommodation), 180 freight trailers and 850 cars. Also in 1986 P & O took over a rival ferry operator, European Ferries, and from Ocean Transport and Trading and from British and Commonwealth all those companies' shares in Overseas Containers Limited, thus bringing under one ownership, as P & OCL, 21 container ships, making P & O, in addition to its many other activities, one of the world's largest container ship operators. This was no mean achievement on the eve of the company's

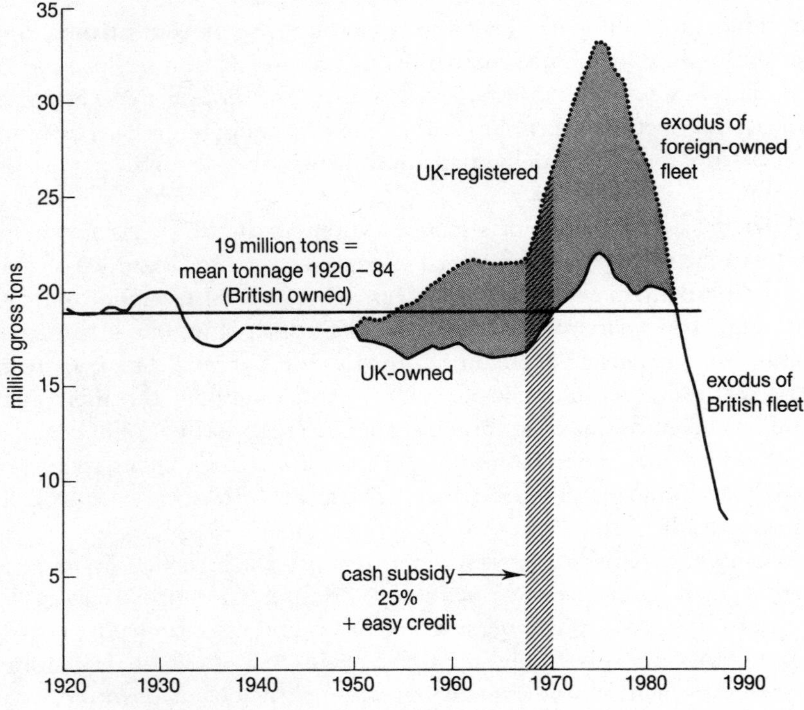

Fig. 20. BRITISH SHIPPING TONNAGE, 1920–1988

150th anniversary. Trafalgar House, owners of Cunard, now owned the second largest container business in the United Kingdom. By 1989 British and Commonwealth and Ocean Transport had diversified out of shipping entirely into other and presumably more profitable businesses.

The slump in shipping continued to be worldwide. Between 1980 and 1985 the world's shipyards delivered 139 million tons deadweight of shipping in a period in which world trade decreased by 313 million tons. Throughout the world debts owed on ships to banks were estimated to amount to $50 billion[14] and the price of a ship in 1985 was less than it had been ten years earlier.[15] Although too much tonnage had been chasing too little traffic at uneconomic rates for far too long, attractive terms were still available to Far Eastern shipowners provided they built in Far Eastern shipyards. In Europe the Norwegian flag fleet declined from 45 million deadweight tons in 1975 to 11 million deadweight tons in 1986, and the West German fleet declined from 13 to 6 million deadweight tons, both countries' shipowners operating nearly one-half of their tonnage under foreign flags by the latter year. In this same period the French fleet declined from 18 to 11 million deadweight tons and the Swedish fleet declined from 12 to 4 million deadweight tons. In the United Kingdom numbers employed in the ports had fallen from 90,000 to under 30,000 and, although Felixstowe had grown considerably, London and the once-great west coast ports of Liverpool, Glasgow and Bristol had declined mightily.

When a depressed market forces shipping profits to zero, or losses are suffered, crew costs suddenly assume a high significance. They become particularly significant in the case of smaller, older and slower ships. The discovery of British oil had strengthened the pound sterling and made it more expensive to employ British seafarers, since costs in shipping are normally reckoned in US dollars. It was also possible to run ships with fewer crew under foreign flags and to evade some of the safety and manning requirements of the Department of Transport.

A 24-hour strike organised by the National Union of Seamen in 1980 laid bare the growing labour crisis. The strike was in protest at Cunard's plans to sail two cruise liners under a flag of convenience. The average weekly income of manual workers at this time was £111.10 for a 45-hour week. The seaman received far more annual leave than the manual worker ashore and he paid for no food at sea. His average wage packet, however, by NUS calculation was £111.97 for a 66-hour week.[16] At these wages shipowners accused the NUS of causing the decline of the merchant navy's tonnage by making excessive wage demands.[17] Although the NUS was opposed to the employment of Asian ratings in British ships, the Union's finances were by this time being propped up by a payment from British shipowners of nearly £200,000 a year so that owners could continue to employ Asian labour at less than a third of the wages of NUS members.[18]

Two years before, in 1978, it had been recognised by the government for the first time that many seafarers worked largely abroad and in consequence they were exempted from income tax where they were absent from the United Kingdom 'for a qualifying period of 365 days or more in the course of which the duties of employment are performed'. This provision allowed for leave to be spent in the United Kingdom provided it did not exceed one-sixth of the total period or 62 consecutive days.

On the face of it, in the late 1970s British officers' pay was not much different in many foreign flag ships from what it was in British ships. Indeed before 1980, when a master's pay under a foreign flag was reported to be £20,000 a year and a third officer's £10,000 a year,[19] many British officers 'flagged out' for higher pay. Three years later it appeared that the average earnings of a master under the British flag were only £19,000 a year, though by this time it was not so easy to earn high salaries under a flag of convenience.

In addition to basic salaries, however, British companies were committed to pension and social insurance costs, whereas under a flag of convenience jobs were not pensionable and continuity was in no way guaranteed. Moreover, the conditions under a flag of convenience were more rigorous and the structure autocratic. As one officer reported, 'You don't argue or comment on any aspect of shipboard life'. Hard work and long hours were demanded in ships registered under a flag of convenience, the ships were usually undermanned by British standards and, in the conditions of the time, it was difficult to rejoin a British flag company once you had flagged out.

There was one further difference between British and flag of convenience ships. British cruise ships, bulkers and tankers made most of their voyages between foreign ports, and a crew change was more likely to take place in New York or New Orleans than in Liverpool or London. By union negotiation, tours of duty had come down to 4–5 months or less and were less than half the time of a tour expected of those under foreign flags. To allow for leave the deepsea ship required 1.8 crews, allowing roughly one month ashore for two spent at sea. Expenses of this kind – air fares and leave pay – were not commonly borne by the flag of convenience operator. Indeed after 1981 an officer (for British ratings were rarely employed in flag of convenience ships) might be expected to pay his own fare to Hong Kong or elsewhere if he wanted a job. To secure jobs in foreign flag ships seafarers made redundant by British shipowners often had by this time to pay fees to manning agents, though it had been agreed by the International Labour Organisation as long ago as 1920 that the charging of such fees to seafarers should be abolished. It was not uncommon for these seafarers to make in excess of 50 applications before work was secured.

British officers, though well qualified and well considered, were expensive by third world standards. Third world ratings could be found at one-quarter of the cost or less of British ratings. Third world officers might cost from one-half to one-third of the cost of British officers.[20] In 1980 the president of the General Council of British Shipping said that a 25,000-ton bulker operated by a Far Eastern crew rather than by a British crew could save £200,000 a year. To make such savings some United Kingdom ships were leaving the British shipping register – being 'flagged out' – already. Britain's foreign exchange controls had been abolished in 1979 and there were no longer any restrictions on transfers abroad of capital of any kind.

Hong Kong and Greece were the chief beneficiaries of flagging out. During the time of the 'Gang of Four' rule in China a British chief engineer officer working for a Hong Kong Chinese company reported:[21] 'All the ships in our fleet – and there are now over 60 of them – are registered under a flag of convenience. A few of us older hands are properly qualified but several of the masters, mates, chief engineers and other officers have no recognised qualification. Chinese fitters and firemen rise very rapidly without any knowledge of engineering in theory or practice. Our ships are old and slow. Authority and discipline are non-existent and it is really amazing how we ever get by. Of course a lot of accidents take place and one just prays not to be in the wrong place at the wrong time.' These young Chinese crews with 'Red Guard' fervour were particularly ill-disciplined. Elsewhere in flag of convenience ships discipline of a kind was easily maintained by 'hire and fire' methods but competence and experience were often lacking and communication was sometimes difficult between members of a crew which could almost be representative of the United Nations.

Fig. 21. PERCENTAGE OF UK-REGISTERED FLEET LOST PER ANNUM

YEARS	PERCENTAGE OF UK-REGISTERED FLEET LOST PER ANNUM
1924–38	0.40
1948–57	0.20
1958–73	0.10
1974–86	0.07

(*Source:* 'Casualties to Vessels and Accidents to Men: Vessels registered in the United Kingdom'. Annual returns from the Department of Transport.)

In 1980 it was reported that the Greek merchant fleet had increased by more than 50 per cent and, if Greek flag of convenience tonnage were added to the Greek flag fleet, Greek owners could claim to have the largest fleet in the world. At the same time it was said that such Hong Kong owners as Sir Y. K. Pao, C. Y. Tung and Frank Chao had steadily increased the Hong Kong fleet until 'they now overshadow even the legendary Greeks'. In 1972 the fleet controlled from Hong Kong had totalled 12.5 million deadweight tons. It probably peaked at about 61 million deadweight tons in 1983 and was still 57 million deadweight tons in 1986.[22] Of the 197 million deadweight tons of shipping registered under flags of convenience by 1982, 30 per cent was beneficially owned in the United States, 21 per cent in Hong Kong, 12 per cent in Greece, 11 per cent in

Japan, and 3 per cent in each of Norway, West Germany and Switzerland. The United Kingdom owned 2 per cent of this tonnage and managed 6 per cent. Smaller interests still were held by China, Italy, the Netherlands and South Korea.[23]

Between 1959 and 1979 the annual total losses of ships as a proportion of those in world-wide service doubled from 0.28 to 0.56 per cent. There can be no doubt that this increase was due to the rise in the flag of convenience and Greek fleets. In 1978, a peak year, 473 ships totalling 1.7 million tons were lost – 0.42 per cent of the world total. Of these ships, Cyprus lost 31, or 3.21 per cent of its tonnage, Greece lost 87, or 2.3 per cent of its tonnage, and Panama lost 62, or 1 per cent of its tonnage.[24] The British casualty record over the five years from 1975 to 1979 was less than one-quarter of the world average.[25] One of the most careful analysts of such figures reported that the probability of total loss varies with the age, size and type of vessel. Allowing for such factors, he found that over the years 1975–80 losses in certain fleets were much higher or lower than anticipated. Of ten countries examined, the results for Sweden, Italy and the United Kingdom were better than expected, Singapore's losses were as expected, while the other six flags he examined suffered losses worse than expected. He commented, 'The losses of Greece, Panama, South Korea and Cyprus were more than twice as bad as could reasonably be allowed for on grounds of fleet composition.'[26]

More than one commentator thought that the difference in insurance premiums paid by a ship operator with a bad record was nowhere near enough to create any incentive to improve performance.[27] In defence of the insurance underwriters it was said that they relied upon the owner's track record and the reports made by the classification societies. So far as the latter were concerned, the critics pointed out that the societies were in competition with one another and unlikely to rush to higher standards for fear of losing business. In the view of many senior officers at sea some surveyors abroad who acted on behalf of the classification societies were lazy, incompetent and corrupt.[28] The British Captain Philip Cheek, appointed to command the Greek-owned *Tiger Bay*, was not unique in finding a ship full of faults, in his case rusted lifeboat davits, winches in need of repair, radio transmitters underpowered, a non-working gyro compass, broken down automatic steering, a damaged sextant, corroded ballast tanks and engines which broke down constantly. This experienced seafarer was unique, however, in swearing an affidavit that his ship was unseaworthy, in consequence of which he was relieved of his command.[29] The 10,000-ton *Pacific Charger*, owned by Hong Kong, Taiwan and Japanese interests and flying the Liberian flag, ran ashore in New Zealand on her maiden voyage. Her master held a Taiwanese master's certificate awarded without examination and on the strength of this plus a $20 fee he had obtained a Liberian master's certificate. No one on board had any radar qualification.

Off the coast of Trinidad the giant supertankers *Atlantic Express* and *Aegean Captain* collided in a rainstorm with the loss of 27 men. On the bridge of the *Aegean Captain* was an uncertificated chief officer, and the officer of the watch on the *Atlantic Express* was a 47-year-old radio officer who was allegedly drunk. Both ships were Greek manned, the *Atlantic Express* sailing under the Greek flag and the *Aegean Captain* being registered in Liberia.[30] The biggest fraud in maritime history was perpetrated by an uncertificated Greek national, Dimitrious Georgoulis, who, in 1980, in command of the Liberian-flagged *Salem*, illicitly unloaded and sold the ship's cargo of 200,000 tons of crude oil in Durban before scuttling his ship off Dakar.[31]

Ships only four years old which carried no corrected charts were reported, and in one case a ship tried to navigate to Bermuda with no more than an ordinary atlas.[32] One writer argued that, with practices and consequences of the kind illustrated above, the use of flags of convenience actually raised transport costs, since the prices determined by the market did not cover such costs as nullifying the effects of pollution or offering compensation for the loss of life or injury at sea.[33] However, as a self-confessed 'realist' pointed out, a ship could be financed internationally, built anywhere in the world by the shipbuilder quoting the best terms, owned by a group who for their own reasons, including tax avoidance, might wish to remain unidentified, managed by people located wherever it was convenient, operated by others at any other suitable location, supervised by a classification society of the owner's choice, and insured on the international market.[34] Under such circumstances the colour of the flag was merely a matter of convenience and the nationality or nationalities of the crew a question of 'cost efficiency' or cheapness.

The International Maritime Organisation sought to improve matters in some degree but obtaining international agreement is a slow business and, even if agreement is reached, implementation is by no means certain. However, higher volumes of traffic in many congested shipping lanes did lead to new regulations, special routeing and traffic separation, as well as to greater intervention by some governments in enforcing higher standards, in surveillance and policing, and in providing better navigational information. The Safety of Life at Sea (SOLAS) Convention was supplemented and modified in 1974 and 1978. In 1977 the International Association of Lighthouse Authorities (IALA) introduced a standard system of maritime buoyage. In 1976 the International Maritime Satellite System (INMARSAT) was initiated and, provided the satellites remained in place, accurate oceanic navigation became independent of the stars. By 1999 it is expected that the Global Maritime Distress and Safety System (GMDSS), which is based on communication by satellite, will have phased out morse radiotelegraphy and it will then be for individual governments to decide whether the employment of radio officers is any longer necessary.

Such aids to safe navigation are one thing, but they do not necessarily produce properly equipped ships or properly qualified seafarers. In 1978 an international convention on Standards of Training, Certification and Watchkeeping for Seafarers (STCW) was agreed by the International Maritime Organisation and ratified by member governments in 1984, but many new commercial 'flags' pay only lip service to IMO requirements.[35] Since training costs money such suggestions for minimum qualifications could have the effect of bringing training in the advanced nations down to the agreed international minimum without necessarily forcing other nations to achieve this minimum. In the United Kingdom it was said in 1980 that training costs were £37 million a year, £23 million for cadets, £11 million for officers and £3 million for ratings. In 1981 a new class 5 certificate was introduced for officers in the short-sea trades and a class 4 certificate as a watchkeeping certificate deepsea. The class 5 certificate was a basic watchkeeping certificate for the majority of home and continental trade vessels between 80 and 4999 gross registered tons. Both these certificates were of a lower level than the old deepsea second mate's certificate which was equivalent to the new class 3 certificate. The class 2 and class 1 certificates corresponded to the old mate's and master's certificates. At the same time the engineers' certificates were increased in number to four, no written examination being necessary to achieve the lowest certificate.

Despite such changes, it remained cheaper, of course, for shipping operators in Britain and the rest of the western world to 'flag out' and to employ seafarers from countries where the standard of living was lower than it was in western Europe. In these circumstances shipping tonnage under the British flag continued to decline fast. 'In most cases', commented a president of the General Council of British Shipping, 'a ship registered abroad must be assumed to be a permanent loss to the United Kingdom register.' Nevertheless, British shipowners remained opposed to any interference, national or international, with their freedom of choice. The use of a flag of convenience, they argued, often made sense.[36]

The changes occurring in the shipping industry were not without their effect on the charitable societies which worked on behalf of seafarers. The religious charities began to close clubs and to work more closely together

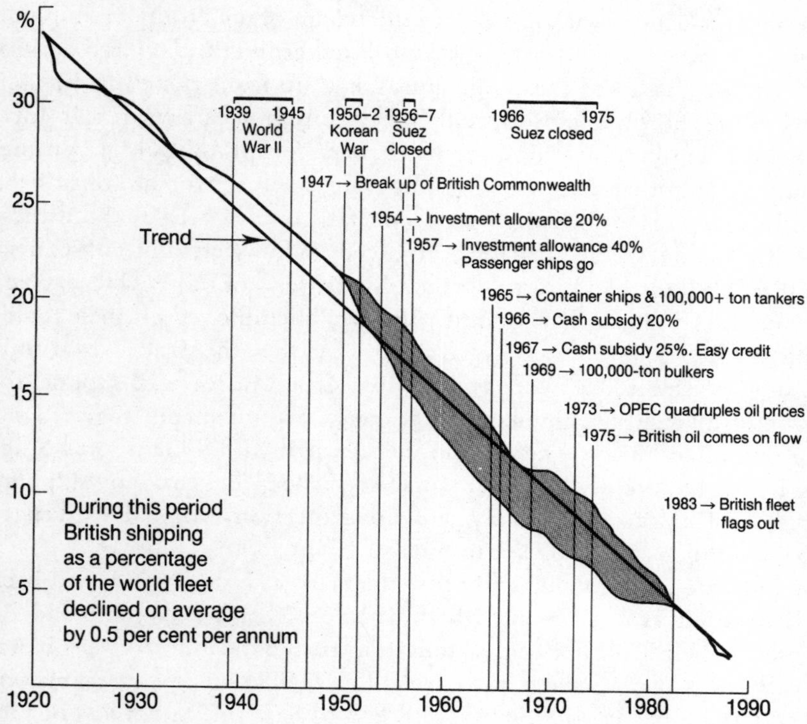

Fig. 22. THE DECLINE OF BRITISH SHIPPING, 1920–1988

(The dark area indicates tonnage which was UK-registered but foreign-owned)

in those clubs which survived. The Seafarers Education Service and The Marine Society amalgamated and absorbed what was left of the work of some other societies, including the Thames Nautical Training College (H.M.S. *Worcester*), the Sailors' Home and Red Ensign Club, and the British Ship Adoption Society, which latter had been established in 1936 to link schools and ships.

When the original source of funds for the Merchant Navy Welfare Board disappeared, the Minister for Shipping (at that time Norman Tebbit) decided that seamen's welfare was the business of the shipping industry and not government and withdrew the government representatives from the Board. H.M.S. *Worcester* had closed in 1968, and even Merchant Navy College, built on the estate subsequently and administered by the Inner London Education Authority, was closed in 1989. H.M.S. *Conway* closed in 1974. In 1988, after 474 years of existence, the Trinity House pilotage service was made over to 'new diversified services'.

In the Falklands war of 1982 54 merchant ships from 33 shipping companies were taken over by the British government (the Civil Service acronym was STUFT, meaning 'ships taken up from trade') to be used as troopships, hospital ships, aircraft and ammunition carriers, repair ships, minesweepers, support ships, despatch vessels and tugs. Many more, including some that were not British, were taken up for use out of the Falklands area. The campaign could not have been waged without these ships and some of the seafarers involved, who were not, of course, members of the armed forces, lost their lives. Many of those who survived were made redundant and found themselves unemployed on their return to the United Kingdom. It was in this year that the British Maritime League was established to act as a pressure group or focus of support for naval and mercantile shipping, but to every argument put forward the government and its civil servants in the Department of Transport's Shipping Policy Division, where there was very little evidence of any shipping policy, replied that no subsidy and no protection would be given to shipping, which was to be left to 'sink or swim'.

In 1984 the government withdrew the tax concession which had been made to seafarers in 1978 and which had been worth between 5 and 7.5 per cent of their income.[37] This action exacerbated the industry's problems since, in consequence, seafarers had to suffer a fall in income or employers had to pay higher salaries or the ships had to flag out with a loss of jobs for British seafarers.

At the same time the government gave the quietus to the shipping companies' ability to write off the cost of ships quickly. Before the Finance Act of 1984, if profits enough were made, British shipowners were able to write off the cost of a new ship in the first year or years of operation. Only after such 'depreciation' had been set aside were profits subject to a corporation tax of 52 per cent. This 'free' depreciation was available only for new tonnage and the system favoured the established owner, who was more likely to be earning the necessary income, and encouraged mergers and the leasing of ships.[38] The 1984 Act substituted a 25 per cent reducing balance depreciation allowance for the previous 100 per cent allowance in the first year, at the same time reducing corporation tax after 1986 to 35 per cent. The 25 per cent reducing balance, which could be claimed back if the ship were sold, offered fewer cash-flow advantages in the first years of a ship's operation than did the earlier arrangement. In consequence, ships on order for the UK registry plummeted to almost nothing. In the ten years from 1975 to 1984, while the fleet was declining by 30 million deadweight tons, only 12 million deadweight tons of new ships had been bought.[39] The government's Business Expansion Scheme, launched in

1982, was of such modest dimensions that it was not initially favourable to the flotation of shipping companies at all, but in 1986 it was enlarged to encompass chartered ships and foreign-going voyages. This scheme enabled the investor to achieve tax relief on his investment and in 1987 it led to the establishment of three small shipping companies, though these were no cure for the industry's ills.

When, at the end of 1985, the Ocean Association of Retired Masters and Chief Engineers – former employees of Ocean Transport and Trading – joined in the protests against the decline in British shipping by writing to the Prime Minister, the Department of Transport reply said that the United Kingdom container, liner and passenger fleets were stable and that these sectors of Britain's merchant fleet, although only 12.5 per cent of the fleet's tonnage, produced 60 per cent of the country's international shipping earnings.[40] The implication was that there was little to worry about. No reference was made to job losses. No reference was made to the fact that the United Kingdom was by this time carrying only 23 per cent by weight of its imports and exports in its own flag ships,[41] and that the UNCTAD proportions of 40:40:20 had become something of a dream so far as Britain was concerned. No reference was made to the fact that Britain's sea transport balance was over £1 billion in deficit whereas it had shown a positive balance only five years earlier.[42]

Two years after his former employees protested to the Prime Minister the chairman of Ocean Transport and Trading shrugged off the decline and commented that flagging out and non-national manning were facts of life and he regretted that much time and energy had been wasted in 'sterile debate' of the matter.[43] By this time the International Shipping Federation had issued an *ISF Guide to International Ship Registers* which divided flags of convenience into three categories: (1) *Independent open registers* like Liberia, Panama and Cyprus (which together covered 30 per cent of the world fleet), along with the Bahamas and Singapore in the middle ranks, and Malta, Sri Lanka, Vanuata and Honduras in the smaller league; (2) *Dependency registers*, which were governed by the laws of a parent state and included Hong Kong, Bermuda, Gibraltar and the Netherlands Antilles; and (3) *Offshore registers* which were secondary registers deliberately established or allowed to evolve by traditional maritime states, primarily to provide a basis for operating for national shipowners who were unable to stay in business under the national flag because of high labour costs. The Norwegian International Register was an example of those created for this purpose, and the Isle of Man of those which had evolved.

By the end of 1986 over one-quarter of the tonnage on the British register was registered in the Isle of Man. The Manx Register of Shipping had been in existence for 200 years but only in 1984 was an Act passed specifically to promote an offshore register. Registration costs and annual fees for a VLCC over a two-year period were said to amount to a mere $300, compared with $111,700 if the same ship were registered in Liberia.[44] Direct taxation on the island was only 20 pence in the pound, with no other direct demands upon companies. Companies set up on the island could either take advantage of the Income Tax (Exempt Companies) Act, which might apply to earnings outside the island, or they could elect to pay income tax in the normal way and take advantage of the capital allowances available, the Manx government having refrained from following the British lead in severely reducing capital allowances. Offshore manning agreements also made it possible to save something on crew costs even if the crews were British. Vessels transferred to the Isle of Man continued to fly the Red Ensign and were included on the United Kingdom register and British officers, at least, continued to be employed. In 1986–7 the 23 vessels of the British fleet run by Shell were transferred to the Isle of Man, along with ships managed by Denholm and the ships of some other owners.

By 1987 3 million more tons deadweight of UK-owned carrying capacity was under foreign or dependent registries than was registered in mainland UK. By this time the number of seafarers on the General Council of British Shipping register, that is the number registered with the Merchant Navy Establishment for employment on UK-registered vessels entered in the GCBS and covered by National Maritime Board agreements, together with non-UK-registered vessels covered by GCBS manning policy, was only 27,000, some 11,000 of these being officers. By 1989 many companies had withdrawn from NMB agreements and fewer than 23,000 British seafarers were covered by GCBS policy. Altogether, including an estimated 9000 officers serving in foreign flag ships, there were, perhaps, 35,000 British seafarers, excluding some 5000 non-UK nationals still serving in British ships, though largely not under the British flag. The number of merchant seamen resident in the United Kingdom was no more than one-quarter of what it had been in the immediate post-war years.

The number of crew in a ship continued to decline. The largest British container vessels might still carry a crew of 32, but some such vessels were being operated by foreign companies with a crew of only 22. The 2675-ton deadweight tanker *Brabourne* which entered the UK coastal and short sea trades in 1989 had a crew of only 5 officers and one rating – master, mate, second mate, chief engineer, second engineer and AB – and they worked flexible watches for four weeks on duty and then had two weeks off. Fatigue at work could prove a problem in such circumstances and, in general, owners and managers had become more remote from masters since recruitment was increasingly done by agents. Government involvement had been reduced, the Department of Transport delegating the conduct of examinations to nautical colleges and the issue of load line and certain safety certificates to the classification societies. The master's responsibilities had been further increased by the Merchant Shipping Act of 1988, by the terms of which he could be fined up to £50,000 or gaoled for running an unsafe ship, polluting the atmosphere or ocean, or otherwise neglecting his duty. This legislation was inspired in part by the capsizing in the previous year of the ferry *Herald of Free Enterprise* with a loss of 193 lives, the worst British maritime disaster since the loss of the *Titanic*. The Merchant Shipping (Prevention of Pollution by Garbage) Regulations of 1988 made the disposal of garbage at sea subject to control, the dumping of plastics anywhere being prohibited. It was not government action, however, but only action by the National Union of Seamen that had prevented the dumping at sea of atomic waste.

The average earnings of a deepsea British shipmaster were by this time around £26,000 a year, with 145 days of leave within the year. Deepsea able-seamen (officially described as Seamen Grade 1A since 1980) earned an average of £200 a week (£100 a week basic), with 68 days leave a year, and those in the home trade earned an average of £250 a week. P & O was successful in 1988 in defeating a seamen's strike on the Dover ferries by men who resisted a proposal to reduce the number of crews per vessel from 3.6 to 2.5, work on such ships being more intensive than it is deepsea. The strike was said to have cost the company £25 million, the saving in the first year being £6 million. British crew costs were reported to be the third cheapest of the ten members of the European Community, only Portuguese and Greek crews coming cheaper.[46] The monthly basic wages of a Filipino crew on a Cyprus-flagged bulk carrier were £778 for the master (£9000 for a full year's work) and £100 for a seaman for a 48-hour working week, with a fixed overtime rate of £30 if he worked up to 120 hours a week.[47]

In 1975, the peak year for British-registered tonnage though not the peak for recruitment, 2315 cadets joined the British merchant navy. In 1982 the General Council of British Shipping abolished its Sea Career Advisory Service, and by 1987 entry to the industry was offered to only 93 cadets.[48] These would all need to stay at sea for more than a working lifetime if such ships as existed at that time were to continue to be manned by British officers, unless, that is, the rate of recruitment were raised. As late as 1980 1745 boy ratings had entered the industry but this number had fallen to 274 four years later.

By 1987 the British government was so far persuaded that problems existed for the British merchant navy that it agreed to help further with training costs and, where crews were changed overseas, with repatriation expenses. It also planned to establish a Merchant Navy Reserve from among those who had left the sea but who had the requisite experience to prove useful in a case of emergency.

By this time, from the peak of 33.2 million gross tons in 1975, the tonnage on the British register had fallen to less than 8.3 million gross tons, one quarter of which was registered in the Isle of Man.[49] The world's ten largest fleets now sailed under the flags of Liberia, Panama, Japan, Greece, the United States, the USSR, Cyprus, China, Hong Kong and the Philippines, and of these nations, the United States, Japan and Hong Kong also owned between them nearly 70 per cent of the flag of convenience fleets.[50] By the four-hundredth anniversary of the defeat of the Armada, from which the rise of British shipping might reasonably be dated, the registered fleet of the United Kingdom, which had been one-half of the world's tonnage just a century previously when Queen Victoria had celebrated her Golden Jubilee, had fallen to less than 2 per cent of the world tonnage. Since the days of Elizabeth I overseas trade had increased a thousandfold and the population perhaps fifteen-fold, but the number of seafarers was about the same as when Drake sailed to face the Armada.

As a percentage of world shipping the British merchant fleet had declined over a period of more than 60 years, from 1921 onwards, with notable consistency, at the rate of about 0.5 per cent of world shipping per year. If the foreign-owned element is removed and the peak war year losses ignored, the tonnage of this fleet remained within 3 million tons of 19 million tons gross throughout the 70 years which followed 1914. During these years the rest of the world's shipping grew from 30 million tons to 400 million tons.

Since 1975 the decline of British shipping has been dramatic but if to the 8.3 million gross tons on the British register at the end of 1988 is added the 4 million gross tons controlled by United Kingdom companies but registered abroad, it can be argued that this fleet is no smaller than the trend lines of earlier years would have indicated. It would not appear that government intervention at any time has had any long-term effect upon the outcome.

Nor would it appear that any action planned by the government in 1988 was likely to have much effect. Britain then took powers to bar foreign shipping from UK cabotage trades – trade between British ports –

unless the European Community agreed to open up other national shipping markets to free competition, but no one expected any great growth in the fleet even if these powers were put into effect. The 1988 Finance Act restored some of the tax reliefs on the foreign earnings of seafarers, reliefs which had been removed by the Act of 1984, but since the government agreed shortly afterwards to accept junior officers from France, Germany, Holland, Denmark and Norway as qualified to serve in British ships, it clearly did not anticipate that there would be any mad rush to sea by the British to benefit from these tax reliefs. Such was the shortage of junior officers that the General Council of British Shipping was pressing the government to accept officers from any country which had ratified the STCW convention.[51]

The Merchant Shipping Act of 1988 established new safety rules, tightened up the regulations which governed the operation of shipping registers in such dependent territories as Gibraltar, Bermuda and Hong Kong, and decreed that the Department of Transport would reimburse to shipowners about half the costs of repatriating seafarers where crews were changed overseas. The Act also made provision for spending up to £3.5 million in 1988–9 and up to £5 million in 1989–90 on merchant navy training, the money being paid to a 'managing agent', perhaps a shipping company, perhaps a training company or perhaps a nautical college. The managing agent would then be responsible for the administration of a trainee's programme. An officer trainee aged 16 would be eligible for assistance during his first two years of training from the Manpower Service Commission's Youth Training Scheme. During his next two years of training assistance would come from the Department of Transport. Junior officers would receive £50 a week during study periods.

Finally, the Merchant Shipping Act of 1988 established the promised Merchant Navy Reserve, offering an annual bounty of £200 to those who, as one shipping paper put it,[52] 'promise to be available when the next war starts.' About one hundred people had volunteered for this Reserve by late 1989.

By 1984 approximately 53 per cent of the world's iron ore cargoes, 40 per cent of the coal, 22 per cent of the grain and 23 per cent of the oil were transported to Japan. Nearly three-quarters of United Kingdom seaborne trade was confined to the near and short-sea trades, largely trade to Europe, whereas ten years earlier more than one-half of British trade had had deepsea destinations. Less than one-third of the United Kingdom's international trade by value was carried in UK-flagged vessels, and only one-fifth by weight. For the time being, at any rate, British oil had freed

Fig. 23. WORLD SEABORNE TRADE BY CARGO, 1986

CARGO	MILLION METRIC TONS	% OF TOTAL
Crude oil	940	28
Oil products	310	9
Iron ore	304	9
Coal	268	8
Grain	160	5
Other bulk cargoes	270	8
Other dry cargoes	1110	33
Total	3362	100

(*Source:* GCBS & First Report of Transport Committee.)

Britain from any reliance on long-haul tankers and was itself providing cargoes for short-haul tankers. More tonnage passed through Sullom Voe oil terminal in the Shetland islands than came through London.

No doubt British shipping managements missed opportunities of profitable activity in these long years of decline, but they also took some of the opportunities that offered themselves. If opportunities in tankers were neglected in the decade before and the decade after World War II, many who had invested in tankers lost huge sums of money after 1973. If opportunities were missed in the carrying trades in the East after the trading pendulum swung in that direction, there were others in a better position to take advantage of them. Britain's place in the world changed with the break-up of the Empire and, if British shipping created that Empire, it could not knit it together when it disintegrated. All the Queen's horses and all the Queen's men could not put Humpty-Dumpty together again. The unbiased judge may well consider unproven the case against British shipping managements that was put forward in the 1960s. More profitable investment opportunities than shipping were available after the war to those with capital in the United Kingdom. The further development of basic industries was no longer appropriate to Britain's post-war position. Much of the decline which took place in British shipping would appear to have been inevitable, and the decline was so managed that there were very few British bankruptcies.

So far as seafarers were concerned there had never been much of a problem. Contrary to legend, the British were never eager seafarers and there was always difficulty in recruiting good British crews, which may not be thought surprising given the conditions in which they were generally expected to serve. Shipping is very much a young man's industry and multitudes went to sea without any intention of staying there for life. The turnover of labour was always high. The well-qualified British officer has seldom had difficulty in securing employment where change has been thrust upon him, whether at sea with foreign employers or at home in a new profession. The British rating has always been unskilled and has fitted easily into unskilled occupations ashore, the more easily for his sea experience. One could imagine an industry differently and more expensively recruited, offering better ladders from bottom to top, but this is so throughout British industry. It is not unique to shipping. British management in shipping has been neither better nor worse than management in other British industries. That it could have been better, everyone who observes its achievement is likely to agree.

Notes

1. G.J. Bonwick, *British Shipping: an independent study (1980)*, Henley-on-Thames, p. 25.
2. H.L. Beth, *et al.*, *25 Years of Shipping* (1984), London, p. 36.
3. British Maritime Charitable Foundation, *Why the Ships Went* (1986), London, p. 36.
4. I. Jung, *The Marine Turbine* (1987), National Maritime Museum, Greenwich.
5. BP *Fleet News*, (August 1980).
6. BMCF, *op. cit.*, p. 61.
7. *Ib.*, pp. 3–4.
8. *Ib.*, p. 16.
9. W.G.D. Ropner, 'A Century of British Tramping' (19.5.1983), *Fairplay* Centenary Issue, p. 93.
10. M.B.F. Ranken (ed), *Britain and the Sea: Future Dependence, Future Opportunities* (1984), Edinburgh, p. 252.
11. *The Telegraph*, April 1989.
12. Ranken, *op. cit.*, pp. 180, 197, 225.
13. U. Alhaji & C.P. Schumaier, 'Why the Unctad Liner Code has outlived its usefulness' (7.9.1989), *Fairplay*, pp. 34–5.
14. *Worldfleets 86*, a conference organised by Lloyd's of London Press (1986), (Boris Nachamkin).
15. *Ib.* (Dennis Stonebridge).
16. *The Times* (13.1.1981).
17. *Daily Telegraph* (19.8.1981).
18. *The Guardian* (25.10.1982).
19. *The Telegraph*, November 1979.
20. I. Chrzanowski, *An Introduction to Shipping Economics* (1985), London, p. 77.
21. To the author.

22. Figures from Helmut Sohmen, *Shipping in Crisis* (1983), Hong Kong, p. 152 and from Kenneth Lo, chairman of the Hong Kong Shipowners Association.
23. UNCTAD, *Beneficial Ownership of Open Registry Ships* (1982).
24. *The Telegraph*, February 1980.
25. Sir R. Swayne, 'Trade by Sea; International Pressures and Problems', paper read to The Nautical Institute and others (15.10.1981).
26. S.J. Bergstrand, *Buy the Flag: Developments in the Open Registry Debate*, Polytechnic of Central London (1983).
27. *Lloyd's Log* as reported in *The Sea* (paper of The Missions to Seamen) (September/October 1985).
28. Reports to the author.
29. P. Cheek, *Legacies of Peril* (1986), Lewes.
30. B. Edwards, *Sunday Express* (16.12.1984).
31. A.J. Klinghoffer, *Fraud of the Century* (1988), London.
32. Ranken, *op. cit.*, pp. 95–6.
33. B.N. Metaxas, *Flags of Convenience* (1985), Aldershot, Hants.
34. J. Whitworth, 'Which Register? Which flag?' A conference organised by Lloyd's of London Press (1987).
35. E.H. Beetham, 'The Changing Role of Command' (March 1989), *Flash* (article originally published by the Nautical Institute).
36. See, for example, Swayne, *op. cit.*, p. 18.
37. *The Seaman* (March 1984).
38. BMCF, *op. cit.*, pp. 87–8.
39. GCBS.
40. *Ocean Mail* (December 1985).
41. GCBS *Statistical Brief* No 17.
42. CSO, *United Kingdom Balance of Payments.*
43. *Nautical Magazine* (August 1987).
44. *Seaways* (September 1987), p. 3.
45. Beetham, *op. cit.*
46. *The Telegraph* (April 1988).
47. *The Telegraph* (July 1988).
48. *Decline in the UK-registered merchant fleet*: First Report from the Transport Committee of the House of Commons (Session 1987–88), London, p. xlii.
49. *Statistical Tables* (1988) Lloyd's Register of Shipping.
50. *Decline in the UK-registered merchant fleet*, p. xxxii.
51. *Fairplay* (15.12.1988).
52. *Fairplay* (25.5.1989).

EPILOGUE

The Great Debate

'If Britain won her Empire ... in a fit of absence of mind,' commented one observer as the British merchant fleet began to disappear, 'the decline of her position in matters connected with the sea has been the result of a similar absence of serious attention.' There was, he suggested, a 'sea-blindness in Whitehall, Westminster, Fleet Street and on television.'[1] In this decline the shipping industry looked to Whitehall for help, but Whitehall and the government of Margaret Thatcher were adamant that, the minor concessions of the Merchant Shipping Act of 1988 apart, shipping was a matter for the shipping industry. The general public was unconcerned. As one writer concluded an account of a voyage to the East made in a Blue Funnel ship of the 1960s: 'The end was anti-climax. We slipped home unnoticed. Britain turned no hair at our arrival, just as she has turned no hair at our extinction.'[2]

A great debate on merchant shipping took place nevertheless, particularly after the ending of the Falklands War in 1982. This debate revolved round two questions: (1) Are merchant ships necessary for the defence and sustenance of the realm? (2) Where British ships are subject to unfair competition, what form, if any, should government support take?

Defence and Sustenance

Defence

Because they nurtured ships and seamen, Adam Smith considered that the Navigation Acts were 'perhaps, the wisest of all the commercial regulations in England' because defence was 'of much more importance than opulence.'[3] Had British ships and British trade remained unprotected, 19th-century industrialism, which endorsed free trade, might never have come into being. On the other hand, had those Acts never been written into the Statute Book, Britain might have been spared many of the wars of the 17th, 18th and early 19th centuries.

When taxed by recent critics on the subject of defence, the British government has replied that the number of merchant ships will remain adequate, especially if considered in conjunction with the resources of the country's allies. It believes that ships registered in British dependencies could be requisitioned or hired along with those on the UK register. It has agreed with the governments of the Bahamas, Liberia and Vanuatu that British-controlled ships registered in these countries will be made available to the United Kingdom in the event of hostilities, and it intends to make further agreements of this kind. It may be supposed that requisitioning of this kind will prove more expensive and less easy than the requisitioning of vessels on the UK register, and that owners may flag out to other registries to avoid such 'conscription'.

For additional manpower in time of emergency the government would appear to rely on Merchant Navy reservists, untrained conscripts or volunteers, and 'mercenaries' or foreigners hired for the purpose. Present indications do not suggest that the Merchant Navy Reserve will provide a sufficient body of skilled seafarers.

Experts in defence often re-fight old wars. In the light of its decisions, the government presumably does not believe that it will need to fight a campaign in the Falklands in the manner in which the last campaign was fought. Defence is currently seen in terms of the reinforcement of Europe from across the Atlantic, the reinforcement of Europe from the United Kingdom, the support of the Royal Navy, and the civil supply of the United Kingdom and European allies. This could be a tall order, and the Defence Committee of the House of Commons concluded in 1988 that the British merchant fleet was inadequate for such purposes.[4]

Preparation for the unknown is difficult, and it will be no new thing if the government is unprepared for the war that comes. Any lengthy conflict would require, as hitherto, the continuous carriage of goods and, perhaps, men by ships, but who can now foretell the length of any conflict? The defence of Britain's offshore oil and gas resources is a new requirement to which little thought seems to have been given. It is possible that continuing research is more important than the maintenance of traditional sea defences.

It takes time to produce ships, shipmasters and chief engineer officers, but fewer ships are required today than were required in the past, and training processes are always speeded up in time of war. As for less skilled manpower, governments have seldom had to give up wars at their beginning for lack of young men willing to lay down their lives. Merchant ships have always been inadequately protected, but no nation ever grieved for long over dead merchant seamen.

Fig. 24. OVERALL BALANCE OF SEA TRANSPORT, 1958–1988, AT 1988 PRICES

YEARS	AVERAGE ANNUAL DEFICIT
1958–67	– £79 million
1979–88	– £476 million

(*Source:* Estimated from UK Balance of Payments.)

Given the imponderables, the 'realist' may well conclude that defence is not a major issue, that traditional merchant shipping can be written off as another sunset industry, and that European integration is the mission of the age. If this is so, the realist may also wonder why Britain still requires the third largest navy in the world. It cannot be for the protection of merchant shipping.

Sustenance of the realm

Shipping's contribution to Britain's balance of payments has fallen dramatically, from 5.7 per cent of all 'invisible' credits in 1975 to 0.9 per cent of such credits in 1985. Nevertheless, the gross earnings of the industry amount to some £3000 million a year and without shipping the country's balance of payments would be that much worse.[5] It is also possible that further decline would mean that shipping generally would call at fewer ports in the United Kingdom, that there would be more transhipment from the Continent, and that transport costs would rise. Employment in ancillary industries like shipbroking, marine insurance and pilotage, which are bolstered by recruitment from the sea, would fall, leading to a further loss of earnings. All this would assume greater significance should earnings abroad from British oil fall and no new exports take its place.[6]

'Shipping', one authority has suggested, 'does not have any special effect on the balance of payments which other industries do not have.'[7] This presumably means that it is best for a nation to specialise in what it is best at (where its comparative cost advantage is greatest) and, if it is no longer best at shipping, it should specialise in something else. It may even be argued[8] that, if other nations choose to subsidise their shipping or shipbuilding, or any other economic activity, one may as well take advantage of the cheap goods or services there on offer and make something else oneself with the resources thus released. The Canadian and Australian economies, for example, do not appear to have suffered because their goods are transported in non-national vessels.

Fig. 25. THE EARNINGS OF UK SHIPPING (£ MILLION)

SECTORS	1970	1975	1980	1983	1985
Tanker	909	1302	1673	1016	749
Liner and container	494	1011	1362	1161	1409
Passenger	106	200	385	589	814
Dry bulk*	140	362	327	228	202
Total	1648	2875	3747	2994	3174
of which:					
owned by UK operators	999	2099	2755	2367	2496
chartered by UK operators	649	766	992	627	677
Total earnings at constant (1988) prices	7465	8634	5950	4437	3911
Sea transport balance	−50	+89	+127	−1013	−1157

* includes combination carriers

Note 1: These earnings are the earnings from ships owned or operated by UK companies. The figures for owned vessels include earnings from some ships registered outside the UK.

Note 2: The sea transport balance is taken from the UK balance of payments. It takes into account not only UK shipping earnings but also earnings of foreign operators on UK trade, disbursements by UK operators overseas, and disbursements by foreign operators in the UK. (Details are given in the CSO publication *United Kingdom Balance of Payments.*)

(*Source: Decline in the UK Registered Fleet* (10.12.1986), House of Commons Transport Committee. Total earnings at constant prices have been expressed at 1988 prices, not 1980 as in the source.)

In a static world of full employment it would be difficult to fault this argument. However, we live in a dynamic world with considerable unemployment and not all redundant seamen or shipbuilders are absorbed rapidly into other and profitable industries. A ship might be built in a foreign shipyard and operated by foreign seamen because it cannot be built in or operated from the United Kingdom so cheaply, but if the men who would otherwise be employed in Britain are, in consequence, receiving substantial social security payments and also deteriorating in quality as a potential workforce for the future, there are high social costs accruing in Britain which have not been taken into account by the ship operator or by the government. And if these British unemployed had been kept in work they would have paid such taxes as might make the cost of setting them to work, and thus maintaining an industry with all its associated skills, comparatively little. If the slump is cyclical and the industry normally pays its way, some support at the bottom of the cycle might prove sound investment.

In 1985–6 a vessel was built for Trinity House, a state institution, in South Korea because the lowest British tender was £5 million above the South Korean tender. Had this vessel been built in Britain it would have provided 500 men with 18 months' work and their total income in employment would have exceeded £6 million. From this the Inland Revenue would probably have taken £1.5 million in taxation and the Department of Health and Social Security would not have paid £2 million in 'dole' money to the unemployed. The British government subsidy to keep this work in Britain might therefore have been as much as £2.5 million but, since the higher expenditure of those in work would have created further employment (through what Keynes called the 'multiplier' effect), further money would have been recovered by the government in taxation and further dole money saved. The continuity of work provided might also have saved one small shipyard from permanent closure, particularly since a second ship for Trinity House was in the pipeline.

Such arguments will not convince those who believe that native shipping is no longer required to sustain the realm. A Channel tunnel and European integration will certainly change the nature of British trade. Even so, however unimportant British shipping may prove to be in the world of the future, it can still be argued that it should not be subject to unfair competition.

Unfair Competition

At least thirty foreign governments help their national shipping companies. This help takes many different forms and many governments give aid in more than one way. The principal kinds of help are: building subsidies, operating subsidies, interest subsidies where capital is borrowed, official loan guarantees, special tax, investment and/or depreciation allowances for shipowners, special tax arrangements for seafarers, cabotage restrictions and cargo preference schemes. Such help apart, shipowners can take advantage of the so-called 'free registries' or flags of convenience, or of such offshore registries as that of the Isle of Man. The latter do not offer all the apparent advantages of the former, largely because they are subject to stricter safety controls of different kinds.

Since 1979 the British government has been opposed to giving help to shipping and a number of British shipowners have stated that they want no subsidies. Nevertheless four ships built in Belfast for the Blue Star Line and the P & O ferry *Norsea*, launched in 1986, received subsidised loans. The government has been persuaded, too, that (a) training costs and (b) crew repatriation costs, where crews are changed overseas, should not fall wholly on shipowners. To some extent the government has also restored the tax reliefs on the foreign earnings of seafarers, though critics believe that the national insurance contributions which employers still have to pay on behalf of British seafarers remain a cost which does not have to be borne by all their competitors.

What else can be done to establish 'fair' or equal ways of operation? This question can be considered under two headings: (a) action which might be taken in conjunction with other governments; and (b) action which might be taken unilaterally. For effective action to be taken on either count it has been suggested that the British government needs to co-ordinate its own expertise.[9] Government responsibility towards shipping in Britain is divided between several government departments. Although there is a Shipping Policy Division in the Department of Transport, there is no powerful shipping focus in government, and shipping ministers – of whom there were seven between 1981 and 1988 – have been in office for brief periods of time, have had little or no experience of the industry, and have sometimes been second-rate. Such weaknesses could be strengthened.

Action in conjunction with other governments

From July 1987 the first stage of a European Community Shipping Policy came into effect. This is intended (i) to co-ordinate action to counteract protectionist activity by other countries; and (ii) to protect European Community liner companies from unfair pricing practices or 'dumping' in shipping by state-owned or state-supported companies. At the same time a timetable was laid down for the removal of cargo reservation measures in member states and of cargo-sharing arrangements in bilateral agreements between member states and third countries.

In the meantime, other member states of the European Community – France and Holland in particular – have been applying more generous fiscal aids to their respective shipping industries than does the United Kingdom. It can be argued, in consequence, that the British government should modify its attitude and become considerably more aggressive than it has proved in the past. Experience, however, does not suggest that this will happen. Action in conjunction with other governments, even closely allied governments, is difficult to bring about where such action does not clearly benefit all parties and injure none of the lobbying interests.

'We will do as we are done by' might be the motto of an organisation even wider than the European Community, an international organisation established to combat flag discrimination and other restrictions on free trade wherever they appear, and to oppose subsidies wherever they are given. In thus aiming to establish free trade, however, it is possible that such an organisation might end up with some kind of universal UNCTAD code in which each nation carries half its trade in its own vessels while its trading partners carry the other half between them. Shipping might thus become as closely regulated as air traffic.[10]

The International Maritime Organisation has agreed on a minimum standard of training which it is desirable that seafarers should achieve. There is no effective monitoring of such programmes, and costs are not allocated to those who benefit. Ideally, the flag country would pay for training in proportion to the number of seafarers engaged under that flag and would recover the costs either from shipping companies or from the general population of the country. Manning levels, safety practices and the provision of adequate equipment on board should be similarly monitored. The International Labour Organisation agrees a minimum wage for seafarers, one which some would think derisory, and agreements have been secured on working conditions and welfare provisions. Again, there is no adequate monitoring process.

Countries could also work jointly towards an internationally accepted system of licensing ship operators. At present anyone with a desk, a telephone and a bank loan is free to operate merchant ships and to select the flag under which they are operated. Other means of transport are controlled. Road hauliers are licensed in the United Kingdom and, no doubt, elsewhere. To operate civilian aircraft an operator has to be licensed, and to obtain a licence he has to show that he has the required expert ground staff to operate aircraft safely. In the International Civil Aviation Authority air transport has an effective regulatory system whereby an immediate inquiry is put in hand after any accident, but no such system exists in shipping. A shipowner requires no licence. He can seek insurance world-wide. And there are no penalties under many flags for undermanning, inadequate maintenance, or even the failure to provide a level of superintendence which ensures that a ship possesses all the charts it may need for an intended voyage.[11] It is felt by some that insurers, including the shipping industries' own protection and indemnity clubs, do not take adequate account of the nature and record of the shipowner when offering insurance, and many serving seafarers, among others, are doubtful whether classification societies always do their job properly. In addition to the ship surveys carried out by such societies, there is a need to assess the competence of managers and crews.

It has been said that there would have been no shipping surplus in the 1970s and 1980s, and therefore no shipping crisis, had every ship been bought for the true cost of building it and had the money lent for building been lent with normal prudence at normal market rates. That is now history; but governments acting together might do something to curtail or control world shipbuilding by fixing production ceilings, by establishing a quota system and by accelerating scrapping. The European Community has certainly not to date exercised the power it possesses jointly to bring about such agreements.

There are those who will believe that all such suggestions are impractical and impossible of achievement. There are those who will believe that any advantages gained will be outweighed by such disadvantages as more governmental regulation, more 'red tape', a loss of 'freedom', and more interference with the competitive process. There are also those who want no measure of control for their own ends: the late Aristotle Onassis was never concerned for the welfare of mankind but only for the accumulation of his personal wealth. However, small advances have been made by joint action, as in the area of port state control mentioned below, and perseverance is desirable.

Unilateral action

Working with others and securing both agreement and effective action takes time, perhaps too much time for the health of British shipping, and involves compromise. What then can the British government do unilaterally to ensure that British shipping companies suffer less from unfair competition?

Research

The surviving British merchant fleet is old and there has been little investment in research to develop a new generation of ships, much less, for instance, than there has been, with government help, in Japan. The British government has not fostered such research.

Charges

If, when going up Channel, a large containership turns left into Southampton, it is said to pay £14,000 in light dues; if it turns right into Le Havre, Antwerp, Rotterdam or Hamburg it pays nothing. Yachtsmen, who most need navigational aid of the kind provided by the lighthouse authorities, pay nothing for their provision in Britain, and nor do fishermen and the Royal Navy. Charges for pilotage and for the maintenance of lights and other navigational aids are met out of general taxation in most European countries. Some governments charge their own ships less than foreigners in the way of harbour dues.

Cabotage: the protection of coastal and offshore operation

Britain has warned the European Community states that it will take unilateral action if no progress is achieved in freeing coastal trade throughout the Community and, after much pressure within the United Kingdom, took powers to do so in 1988. By way of these powers the UK government can prevent ships from engaging in its coastal trade if the companies concerned have not established offices in the United Kingdom (inclusive of the Isle of Man and the Channel Islands). Fifteen years after Britain's entry into the Community some may consider this slow progress.

British coastal trade and the transport of North Sea gas and oil have been open to any vessels. The United States, the Latin American countries, ASEAN countries, Japan, Australia, New Zealand, many European Community countries, the USSR and many more reserve their coastal trade to their own ships and the definition of 'coastal' trade is sometimes very wide. Some 40 per cent of British coastal trade is carried by foreign ships. In 1986 a bumper British grain harvest sold to Spain was all shipped in Spanish vessels at freights 30 per cent above the prevailing rate.[12] In 1984 three-quarters of the oil and gas from Sullom Voe was transported in foreign vessels, and only about half the supply vessels operating in the UK sector of the North Sea flew the Red Ensign. Norwegian vessels only operated in the Norwegian sector.[13] Both German and Dutch investment aid to shipping companies helps their vessels to undercut British ships in the coastal and short sea trades.[14]

Port state control

Nearly a century ago the United Kingdom decreed that all ships entering its ports should conform to its loadline regulations. Through controls exercised by the US Coastguard the United States has long ensured that ships entering American ports conform to certain US practices. This 'port state control' of shipping was extended in a Memorandum of Understanding (MOU) between eight North Sea states, including the United Kingdom, which was signed in 1978 and began to operate in 1982, by which time there were fourteen European members. The target then established was the inspection of 25 per cent of visiting foreign ships each year to see that they reach prescribed standards.

The UN Law of the Sea Convention (UNLOSC), 1982, allows coastal states to claim territorial waters of up to twelve nautical miles and a contiguous zone, for customs, fiscal, immigration and sanitary purposes of up to a further twelve miles offshore.

Port state control, which can ensure that ships are properly equipped and manned, is said to have had some good effect even to the limited extent of its present operation,[15] though outside North Europe and the United States it has been described as 'farcical'.[16] The inspection of foreign ships could be extended beyond 25 per cent unilaterally or in agreement with others, though unilateral action would involve some risk of retaliation from other states, and perhaps the unjustified delay of properly equipped and operated British ships. Marine surveyors in the Department of Transport currently check each year at random some 600 UK-registered vessels and 2300 other vessels. In future they will record the name of the Classification Society and thus ensure that in Britain, at least, no surveys are delegated to societies that do their job inadequately.[17]

Protection and discrimination

'Protectionism in the form of "shares for flags"', an eminent shipping economist has written, 'is likely to be undesirable, uneconomic and fallacious.'[18] It is undesirable, he went on, because it fosters nationalism in a world where the nation state should be obsolete and because it treats developing countries as if they were all alike when they are not. It is uneconomic, in his view, because it does not secure the greatest economic efficiency, which is achieved by unprotected ships moving freely in the service of international trade. And it is fallacious because the benefits obtained from operating ships under a particular flag do not necessarily accrue to the nation whose flag it is.

These arguments may not convince everyone, and the writer himself subsequently modified his views. Nationalism may be undesirable but it shows no sign of going away and has, in fact, increased since the Second World War. Unprotected ships moving freely in competition may be economic if they are fully employed, but what if there are as many again laid up for lack of employment? Is there nothing in the so-called 'infant industry' argument which can give a protected (or subsidised) fleet or shipbuilding industry its first footing in the international field? It would appear to have worked in the case of Japan at the beginning of the 20th century, just as mail subsidies appear to have helped British ocean steamships to establish themselves half a century earlier. Is it fallacious to suppose that Brazil has so organised a protected fleet that the benefits accrue to Brazil,[19] even though some believe that South American protection has reduced South American trade as a whole?[20].

The British government and its civil servants, and indeed some of its shipowners, have argued that protection, for example of the kind known under the British Navigation Laws, is not now in the interest of British shipping, even where state help is admitted to have had its influence in building up the British fleet in the 200 years beteen 1650 and 1850. One argument frequently produced is that protection is not in the interests of British shipping because much of its earnings – 54 per cent in 1988 – come from cross-trading and there would be a risk of retaliation. Gross earnings from the cross-trades (before disbursements overseas are taken away) have halved in real terms in the decade 1978–88, so there is now less to lose.[21] This consideration aside, it is by no means proven that cross-trade earnings would be lost if Britain protected its trade. As an authority quoted above has also written, much of the cross-trade earnings are incidental to a voyage to and from the United Kingdom. 'For example, a ship sailing from New Zealand to the UK via Panama may well carry cargo from New Zealand to Panama; and this will appear in the statistics as cross-trading – i.e. as if similar to voyages mainly between two foreign countries – though it is really only incidental to a direct voyage which would have taken place anyway.'[22]

Less than one-third by value of United Kingdom trade – and even less by weight – is now carried in United Kingdom ships. It is difficult to believe that matters would be worse if United Kingdom shipping were protected. The USSR has had much success in excluding foreign vessels from its trade. Russian vessels dominate the trade between the USSR and the United Kingdom, and the activities of the largest fully-cellular Soviet containerships are almost wholly devoted to cross-trading.[23]

> Let's face it, [wrote a shipping journalist in 1983] for the last ten years at least the most disturbing characteristic of international shipping can be summed up in the single word 'protection', and cabotage has become almost a state of grace in the eyes of many administrations. But goodness me, it has taken long enough for shipowners of countries advocating free trade to publicly advocate that their governments provide a little protection themselves against all this protectionism . . . It does not need an official inquiry to find out that there is a good deal of wrongful discrimination going on in the world. BIMCO, in their publication 'Double taxation of non-residential shipping', can point to a bookful of it. Import taxes – even back dated in the case of some imaginative states – taxes on demurrage. It is all quite unfair, thoroughly discriminatory and is very deserving of retaliatory action. And action *now*, not after ten years of Foreign Office havering have elapsed.[24]

Fig. 26. MEASURES BEING TAKEN IN 1988 BY NON-UK GOVERNMENTS TO SUPPORT THEIR SHIPPING INDUSTRIES. (Between 1976 and 1985 the British merchant fleet declined by 56 per cent.)

COUNTRY	CONSTRUCTION SUBSIDIES	OPERATING SUBSIDIES	INTEREST SUBSIDIES	OFFICIAL LOAN GUARANTEES	CARGO PREFERENCE SCHEME	CABOTAGE RESTRICTIONS	TAX/INVESTMENT/DEPRECIATION ALLOWANCES FOR SHIPOWNERS	SPECIAL TAX ARRANGEMENTS FOR SEAFARERS	INTERNATIONAL OFFSHORE REGISTER	% CHANGE IN FLEET 1976–1985 (100 GRT+)
Argentina	√	√		√	√	√				+67
Australia	√	√		√		√				+67
Belgium			√	√			√		+	+60
Brazil	√	√	√		√	√				+96
Canada						√	√			+27
Chile		√			√	√	√			na
Denmark			√			√	√	√	+	−4
Finland			√	√		√	√	√		−7
France	√		√		√	√			√	−27
Germany FR	√			√		√	√			−33
Greece			√	√		√	√			+24
India	√				√	√	√			+30
Ireland				√			√			na

Italy	√					√					−20
Japan						√	√				−4
Korea, S.	√	√		√	√						+299
Malaysia					√	√	√				na
Mexico	√	√		√	√	√	√				na
Netherlands	√			√			√				−27
Norway				√			√	√	√		−45
Pakistan	√				√	√					na
Philippines	√		√	√	√		√				+351
Poland					√	√					+2
Spain	√		√		√	√			+		+4
Sweden	√					√	√	√			−60
Turkey			√		√	√					+241
US	√	√		√	√		√				+31
USSR					√	√					+20
Yugoslavia					√	√					+39

+ International offshore register proposed.

(*Sources:* British Maritime League, Department of Transport, European Commission, General Council of British Shipping, UN Conference on Trade and Development. *See also* First Report from the Transport Committee (Session 1987–88): *Decline in the UK-Registered Merchant Fleet*, House of Commons.)

Seven of the ten years allowed for Foreign Office havering have elapsed and nothing has been done. A little protection and discrimination might provide the British government with a bargaining counter with which to advocate freer trade. The argument is similar to that in favour of retaining a nuclear deterrent.

Subsidies

In relation to shipping the British government has consistently argued that it believes in free competition and not in subsidy. But where it is implied that this is part of a general policy, the public is misled and perhaps the government misleads itself. The European Community, of which Britain is a member, is highly protectionist, with the consequence that resources are attracted to agriculture and to the protected industries but not to shipping.[25] The British government subsidises farming, the car industry, the coal industry, British Aerospace, and more. But there are few votes in shipping.

Until 1984 British governments gave some support to British shipping, and this support was substantial between 1966 and 1970. There was no reason why the government could not, at any time, have provided shipping companies with many of the advantages of flag of convenience operation. That it went out of its way to stimulate flagging out was, it must be supposed, in line with its general policy of restricting trade union power.

At the end of 1986 the all-party Transport Committee of the House of Commons commented:

> If the political will exists, there is a wide variety of ways that the British government could give real help to the UK-registered merchant fleet. All of them are *now* being applied, somewhere in the world, often by governments which subscribe to the same free trade philosophies as the present British administration. It is a fact that in the real world there are only two alternatives for maritime governments – *either* to promote their country's shipping industry, *or* to see it obey market trends and ebb away to registers which have a competitive advantage even though their advantage may sometimes be artificial. There is no third option.[26]

At 1988 prices the annual balance on sea transport between the two world wars, that is the difference between what British ships earned and what was paid to foreign shipowners or their agents, was roundabout £2500 million. By the decade 1958–67 this considerable positive balance had become a deficit of about £80 million a year. By the decade 1979–88 this deficit had increased six-fold, to an average of £480 million a year. That Britain has suffered little from this loss of foreign earnings is due to the very large earnings from the sale of British oil since exploitation began at the time when OPEC quadrupled oil prices. But the oil is not expected to last and alternative earnings will need to be found. Some would argue that a bigger British merchant fleet would provide some of these earnings, and that a bigger merchant fleet would be encouraged if the government gave help in one form or another, e.g. by increasing money available from its Business Expansion Scheme, and/or by giving 'roll-over relief' on balancing charges. Roll-over relief is relief from taxation exacted on the excess of the sale value of a ship over its written-down value. It is suggested that, to avoid taxation, such receipts should be reinvested within three years in a new or secondhand ship. Ever since the war some of these problems have derived from the fact that the replacement costs of ships have been higher than the untaxed depreciation set aside for that replacement. It should not be beyond the wit of government to solve so universal a problem.

Although what is left of the British merchant fleet is efficient and even innovative, that fleet has been reduced in greater proportion than that of almost any other maritime nation, and the remaining ships are older than the world average. No more than a few years after the establishment in the United Kingdom of the International Maritime Organisation and the subsequent decision that English was to become the world's maritime language, the United Kingdom has declined as a maritime nation to a position where it can carry very little real weight.

'We are a seafaring race and we understand the call of the sea', wrote Winston Churchill in 1941 at the height of the U-boat campaign against British ships. Referring to the merchant seamen of that era, he went on: 'We account you in these hard days worthy successors in a tradition of steadfast courage and high adventure, and we feel confident that the proud tradition of our island will be upheld wherever the ensign of a British merchantman is flown.'

Less than fifty years later the Red Ensign flies at the stern of fewer and fewer ships, ships which are seen in fewer and fewer ports, and the tradition lauded by the wartime Prime Minister is maintained by no more than 30,000 seafarers, one-third of them probably at home, and a high proportion of the rest sailing to and fro across the English Channel and the North Sea. Four hundred years ago the Lord Treasurer of Queen Elizabeth I declared that one small sailing vessel brought in from the Continent as much in one year as ten large merchant ships brought from other places in two years. His modern counterpart in the service of Queen Elizabeth II might make a similar claim for the ro-ro in relation to ten container ships engaged in a world-wide service. But history will not otherwise repeat itself, for British oceanic shipping will not rise again.

Notes

1. M. B. F. Rankin (ed), *Britain and the Sea: Future Dependence, Future Opportunities* (1984), Edinburgh, pp. 217 & 233.
2. R. Woodman, *Voyage East: A Cargo Ship in the 1960s* (1988), London, p. 220.
3. A. Smith, *The Wealth of Nations* (Everyman edn), Vol. I, p. 408.
4. *The Defence Requirement for Merchant Shipping and Civil Aircraft*: Defence Committee, Fourth Report (7.6.1985), House of Commons Paper 476.
5. *Decline in the UK-registered merchant fleet*: Transport Committee, First Report (21.6.1988), House of Commons Paper 303–1, pp. xxix–xxx.
6. P. Shore, 'Decline of UK-registered fleet' (December 1988), *Seaways*.
7. R. O. Goss.
8. F. Eversheim, 'Effects of Shipping Subsidisation' (28.5.1959), *Shipbuilding & Shipping Record*.
9. R. M. Frampton, 'New Ways of Stimulating Shipping Enterprise: A Marine Industries Development Corporation for the UK' (February 1988), *Seaways*.
10. R. Hope, 'The Political Economy of Marine Transportation', in D. M. Johnston (ed), *Marine Policy and the Coastal Community* (1976), London, pp. 103ff.
11. D. B. Foy, *Safety at Sea* (December 1985).
12. *The Times* (13.10.1986).
13. *Seaways* (August 1984).
14. I. Denholm, presidential address to the General Council of British Shipping (1988).
15. F. L. Newby, *World fleets 86* (1986), a conference organised by Lloyd's of London Press; Captain Wickens (Summer 1989), *Journal of the Honourable Company of Master Mariners*.
16. *The Telegraph* (August 1988).
17. *Decline in the UK-registered fleet*, *op. cit.*, p. xlv.
18. R. O. Goss, 'New Challenges for Ships and Ports Symposium' (Haifa, August 1984), Israel Shipping and Aviation Research Institute.
19. S. Farrell, 'Protectionism in Practice' (1986), *Maritime Policy and Management*, Vol. 13, No. 4, pp. 277–90.
20. U. Alhaji & C. P. Schumaier, 'Why the UNCTAD Liner Code has outlived its usefulness' (7.9.1989), *Fairplay*, pp. 34–5.
21. Calculated from *UK Balance of Payments* (1989), London, p. 25, adjusting figures for changes in prices.
22. R. O. Goss, 'The decline of UK-registered merchant shipping', memorandum presented to the House of Commons Transport Committee (October 1986).
23. S. Bergstrand & R. Doganis, *The Impact of Soviet Shipping* (1987), London, pp. 98, 95 and 50.

24. *Fairplay* (22.9.83), p. 3.
25. R. O. Goss, 'Sense and shipping policies' (1986), University of Wales Institute of Science and Technology, p. 10; also R. O. Goss & J. King (January 1986), *Seaways*.
26. *Interim report on the decline of the UK-registered fleet*: Transport Committee (1987), House of Commons.

Bibliography

MM = Mariner's Mirror; EHR = Economic History Review; IJNA = International Journal of Nautical Archaeology and Underwater Exploration

No author attributed:

Casualties to Vessels and Accidents to Men, published annually by the Department of Transport (London).

Committee of Inquiry into Shipping (Rochdale Report) (London, 1970).

Decline in the UK-registered Merchant Fleet: First Report from the Transport Committee of the House of Commons (London, Session 1987–8).

De Jure Maritimo et Navali (London, 1676).

Economic Development in the United Kingdom 1850–1950, Labour Information, MSA Mission to the UK (London, c. 1950).

Final Report of the Court of Inquiry into certain matters concerning the Shipping Industry (Pearson Report), Cmd. 3211 (London, 1967).

Further English Voyages to Spanish America, 1583–1594 (London, 1951).

Interim Report on the Decline of the UK-registered Fleet: Transport Committee, House of Commons (1987).

London in Roman Times: London Museum Catalogue No. 3 (London, 1946).

Report from the Select Committee appointed to inquire into the Causes of Shipwrecks (London, 1836).

Sailing Ships: Their history and development as illustrated by the collection of ship-models in the Science Museum (London, 1932).

Seafarers and Their Ships (London, 1955).

Shipping in Dumfries and Galloway in 1820: Scottish Local History Texts, No. 1 (Glasgow, 1973).

The Defence Requirement for Merchant Shipping and Civil Aircraft: Defence Committee: Fourth Report, House of Commons Paper 476 (7.6.1988).

The Story of the Seamen: National Union of Seamen (London, 1964).

Two Centuries of Shipbuilding by the Scotts of Greenock (London, 1920).

Why the Ships Went & Supplement, British Maritime Charitable Foundation (London, 1986 & 1988).

Abell, W. 'Sea Casualties and Loss of Life': a paper read before the North-East Coast Institution of Engineers and Shipbuilders (London, 1921).

BIBLIOGRAPHY

Aldcroft, D. H. 'Reflections on the Rochdale Inquiry into Shipping: A Review Article' (1971), *Maritime History*, Vol. I, No. 2.

Alexander, D. & Ommer, R. (eds), *Volumes not Values: Canadian Sailing Ships and World Trade* (St John's, 1979).

Alhaji, U. & Schumaier, C. P. 'Why the Unctad Liner Code has outlived its usefulness,' *Fairplay*, 7.9.1989.

Anderson, R. & R. C. *The Sailing Ship: Six Thousand Years of History* (London, 1926).

Andrews, K. R. *English Privateering Voyages to the West Indies, 1588–1595* (Cambridge, 1959).

Andrews, K. R. *The Economic Aspects of Elizabethan Privateering* (Cambridge, 1964).

Andrews, K. R. *The Spanish Caribbean: Trade and Plunder 1530–1630* (New Haven & London, 1978).

Andrews, K. R. *Trade, Plunder and Settlement* (Cambridge, 1984).

Andrews, K. R. 'The Elizabethan Seaman' (1982), MM, Vol. 68, No. 3.

Andrews, K. R., Canny, N. P. & Hair, P. E. H. (eds). *The Westward Enterprise: English activities in Ireland, the Atlantic and America 1480–1650* (Liverpool, 1978).

Anson, G. *A Voyage Round the World* (London, 1974).

Ansted, A. *A Dictionary of Sea Terms* (Glasgow, 1920).

Atkinson, R. *Stonehenge* (London, 1956).

Bagwell, P. 'The Post Office Steam Packets, 1821–36, and the Development of Shipping on the Irish Sea' (1971), *Maritime History*, Vol. I, No. 1.

Baltharpe, J. *The Straights Voyage or St Davids Poem* (Oxford, 1959).

Barbour, V. 'Dutch and English Merchant Shipping in the Seventeenth Century' in Carus-Wilson, E. M. (ed), *Essays in Economic History* (London, 1954).

Bass, G. (ed). *A History of Seafaring based on Underwater Archaeology* (London, 1972).

Bateson, C. *The Convict Ships 1787–1868* (Glasgow, 1959).

Beaglehole, J. C. (ed), *The Journals of Captain Cook on his Voyages of Discovery* (Cambridge, 1955).

Beck, J. W. 'Tercentenary of the Falmouth Post Office Packet Service' (1958), *Newsletter of the Maritime Economic History Group*, Vol. II, No. 2.

Beetham, E. H. 'The Changing Role of Command', *Seaways*, 1988.

Behrens, C. B. A. *Merchant Shipping and the Demands of War* (London, 1955).

Bergstrand, S. J. *Buy the Flag: Developments in the Open Registry Debate* (Polytechnic of Central London, 1983).

Bergstrand, S. J. & Doganis, R. *The Impact of Soviet Shipping* (London, 1987).

Beth, H. L., *et al. 25 Years of Shipping* (London, 1984).

Blake, R. C. *The Missionary Century in the Royal Navy* (unpublished).

Blue, A. D. 'The Iron-headed Old Rat' (Chinese nickname for William Jardine), *Nautical Magazine*, August 1988.

Bogueka, M. 'Amsterdam and the Baltic in the First Half of the Seventeenth Century' (1973), EHR, 2nd Series, Vol. XXVI, No. 3.

Bolton, J. L. *The Medieval English Economy, 1150–1500* (London, 1980).

Bonwick, G. J. *British Shipping: an independent study* (Henley-on-Thames, 1980).

Bosworth, J. *A Description of Europe and the Voyages of Othere and Wulfstan by King Alfred the Great* (London, 1855).

Boxer, C. R. *The Dutch Seaborne Empire* (London, 1965).

Bradford, E. *The Story of the Mary Rose* (London, 1982).

Braydon, S. & Songhurst, R. (eds). *The Diary of Joseph Sams* (London, 1982).

Breeze, F. J. A. 'The Cost of Distance: Shipping and the Early Australian Economy, 1788–1850' (1975), EHR, 2nd series, Vol. XXVII, No. 4.

Brøgger, A. W. & Shetelig, H. *The Viking Ships: Their Ancestry and Evolution* (London, 1951).

Bromley, J. S. 'The British Navy and its Seamen after 1688: Notes for an Unwritten History', in Palmer, S. & Williams, G. (eds), *Charted and Uncharted Waters*: Proceedings of a Conference on the Study of British Maritime History (London, 1982).

Bromley, J. S. *Corsairs and Navies 1660–1760* (London, 1987).

Bruce-Mitford, R. *Recent Archaeological Excavations in Britain* (London, 1956).

Burland, C. 'By Weather to Wineland' (1950), MM, Vol. 36.

Burton, V. C. 'Counting Seafarers: The Published Records of the Registry of British Seamen, 1849–1913' (1985), MM, Vol. 71.

Burwash, D. *English Merchant Shipping 1460–1540* (Toronto, 1947).

Bury, J. *Life of St Patrick* (London, 1905).

Bushell, T. A. *'Royal Mail': A Centenary History of the Royal Mail Line, 1839–1939* (London, 1939).

Buxton, N. & Aldcroft, D. *British Industry between the Wars* (London, 1979).

Cable, B. *A Hundred Year History of the P & O* (London, 1937)

Caesar, J. (trs. Warrington, J.) *War Commentaries* (London, 1953).

Cameron, P. 'Saxons, sea and sail' (1982), IJNA, Vol. II, No. 4.

Carletti, F. *My Voyage Around the World* (London, 1965).

Carson, E. A. 'Customs History and Records of Trade and Shipping' (1972), MM, Vol. 58, No. 4.

Carus-Wilson, E. M. *Medieval Merchant Venturers* (London, 1954).

Carus-Wilson, E. M. (ed) *Essays in Economic History* (London, 1954).

Carus-Wilson, E. M. *The Merchant Adventurers of Bristol in the Fifteenth Century* (Bristol, 1962).

Carus-Wilson, E. M. & Coleman, O. *England's Export Trade 1275–1547* (Oxford, 1963).

Causton, G. & Keene, A. *The Early Chartered Companies* (London, 1896).

Cell, G. T. *English Enterprise in Newfoundland 1577–1660* (Toronto, 1969).

Chaudhuri, K. N. *The English East India Company: The Study of an Early Joint-Stock Company 1600–1640* (London, 1965).

Childe, V. *Prehistoric Communities of the British Isles* (Edinburgh, 1940).
Childs, W. R. *Anglo-Castilian Trade in the Later Middle Ages* (Manchester, 1978).
Christy, M. (ed) *The Voyages of Captain Luke Fox ... and Captain Thomas James* (London, 1894).
Chrzanowski, I. *An Introduction to Shipping Economics* (London, 1985).
Cipolla, C. M. *Guns and Sails* (London, 1965).
Clark, G. 'Traffic in Stone Axe and Adze Blades' (1965), EHR, 2nd Series, Vol. XVIII, No. 1.
Clark, G. V. *The Last of the Whaling Captains* (Glasgow, 1987).
Clark, J. *Prehistoric Europe* (London, 1952).
Clemens, P. G. E. 'The Rise of Liverpool, 1665–1750' (1976), EHR, 2nd Series, Vol. XXIX, No. 2.
Coleman, D. C. *The Economy of England 1450–1750* (Oxford, 1977).
Compton, H. (ed). *A Master Mariner, being the Life and Adventures of Captain Robert William Eastwick* (London, c. 1891).
Condon, M. E. 'The Establishment of the Transport Board – a Subdivision of the Admiralty – 4 July 1794' (1972), MM, Vol. 58, No. 1.
Cooper, J., Kludas, A. & Pein, J. *The Hamburg South America Line* (Kendal, 1989).
Corlett, E. *The Revolution in Merchant Shipping 1950–1980* (London, 1981).
Cottrell, P. L. & Aldcroft, D. H. (eds) *Shipping, Trade and Commerce: Essays in Memory of Ralph Davis* (Leicester, 1981).
Course, A. G. *The Merchant Navy: A Social History* (London, 1963).
Courtauld, A. *From the Ends of the Earth* (Oxford, 1958).
Craig, R. *Steam Tramps and Cargo Liners 1850–1950* (London, 1980).
Craig, R. 'Carmarthenshire Shipping in the 1840s' (1985), *The Carmarthenshire Antiquary*, Vol. XXI.
Craig, R. 'Trade and Shipping in South Wales – The Radcliffe Company 1882–1921' in Baber, C. & Williams, L. J. (eds) *Modern South Wales: Essays in Economic History* (Cardiff, 1986).
Croft, P. 'English Mariners Trading to Spain and Portugal, 1558–1625' (1983), MM, Vol. 69, No. 2.
Crouse, N. *In Quest of the Western Ocean* (London, 1928).
Culican, W. *The First Merchant Venturers* (London, 1966).
Cunliffe, B. 'The First Eight Thousand Years', in Jamieson, A. (ed). *A People of the Sea: The Maritime History of the Channel Islands* (London, 1986).
Cunningham, W. *The Growth of English Industry and Commerce*, Vol. II (Cambridge, 1882).

Daniel, G. *The Megalith Builders of Western Europe* (London, 1958).
Davies, J. C. 'Shipping and Trade in Newcastle upon Tyne, 1294–1296' (1953), *Archaeologia Aeliana*, 4th Series, Vol. XXXI.
Davies, K. G. *The Royal African Company* (London, 1957).

Davies, P. N. *The Trade Makers: Elder Dempster in West Africa 1852–1972* (London, 1973 & 1980).

Davies, P. N. *Sir Alfred Jones: Shipping Entrepreneur Par Excellence* (London, 1978).

Davies, P. N. *Henry Tyrer: A Liverpool Shipping Agent and his Enterprise 1879–1979* (London, 1979).

Davies, P. N. 'The development of the liner trades during the eighteenth and early nineteenth centuries,' in Matthews, K. & Panting, G. (eds), *Ships and Shipbuilding in the North Atlantic Region* (St Johns, 1978).

Davies, P. N. & Marriner, S. 'Recent publications and developments in the study of maritime economic history' (1988), *The Journal of Transport History*, 3rd Series, Vol. 9, No. 1.

Davis, J. *The Voyages and Works of John Davis, The Navigator* (London, 1880).

Davis, R. *The Rise of the English Shipping Industry in the Seventeenth and Eighteenth Centuries* (London, 1962).

Davis, R. *The Trade and Shipping of Hull, 1500–1700*. EY Local History Series: No. 17 (East Yorkshire Local History Society, 1964).

Davis, R. *English Overseas Trade 1500–1700* (London, 1973).

Davis, R. *English Merchant Shipping and Anglo-Dutch Rivalry* (London, 1975).

Deakin, B. M. (with Seward, T.), *Shipping Conferences: A Study of their Origins, Development and Economic Practices* (Cambridge, 1973).

Deeson, A. F. L. *An Illustrated History of Steamships* (Bourne End, 1976).

Devine, T. H. 'The Colonial Trade and Industrial Settlement in Scotland c. 1700–1815' (1976), EHR, Vol. XXIX, No. 1.

Dewer, A. (ed). *The Voyages and Travels of Captain Nathaniel Uring* (London, 1928).

Dixon, C. 'Pound and Pint: Diet in the Merchant Service, 1750–1980', in Palmer, S. & Williams, G. (eds), *Charted and Uncharted Waters*: Proceedings of a Conference on the Study of British Maritime History (London, 1982).

Dixon, C. 'The Rise and Fall of the Crimp, 1840–1914', in Fisher, S. (ed), *British Shipping and Seamen, 1630–1960* (Exeter, 1984).

Dixon, C. 'Signing-On' (1984), MM, Vol. 70, No. 3.

Dodge, E. *Northwest by Sea* (New York, 1961).

Dow, G. *Slave Ships and Slaving* (Salem, Mass., 1927).

Down, W. *On Course Together* (London, 1989).

Drake, F. *The World Encompassed* (London, 1628).

Duff, P. *British Ships and Shipping* (London, 1949).

Duncan, R. E. 'Captain George Peacock: The Pioneer Commander of Pacific Steamers' (1980), MM, Vol. 66, No. 1.

Eames, A. *The Life and Letters of Captain Robert Thomas of Landwrog and Liverpool, 1843–1903* (Denbigh, 1980).

Edwards, B. *The Fighting Tramps* (London, 1989).

Eltis, D. 'The British Contribution to the 19th Century Transatlantic Slave Trade' (1979), EHR, 2nd Series, Vol. XXXII, No. 2.

Epstein, M. *The Early History of the Levant Company* (London, 1908).
Eversheim, F. 'Effects of Shipping Subsidisation' (28.5.1959), *Shipbuilding & Shipping Record.*

Farrell, S. 'Protectionism in practice' (1986), *Maritime Policy & Management*, Vol. 13, No. 4.
Fayle, C. E. *The War and the Shipping Industry* (London, 1927).
Fayle, C. E. *A Short History of the World's Shipping Industry* (London, 1933).
Fenwick, V. 'A new Anglo-Saxon ship' (1983), IJNA, Vol. 12, No.2.
Ferrier, R. W. *The History of the British Petroleum Company, I, The Developing Years, 1901–32* (Cambridge, 1982).
Fingard, J. *Jack in Port: Sailortowns of Eastern Canada* (Toronto, 1982).
Fischer, L. R. & Sager, E. W. 'An approach to the quantitative analysis of British shipping records' (1980), *Business History*, Vol. 22, No. 2.
Fisher, S. (ed). *West Country Maritime and Social History: Some Essays* (Exeter, 1980).
Fisher, S. (ed). *British Shipping and Seamen, 1630–1960* (Exeter, 1984).
Fisher, S. (ed). *Studies in British Privateering, Trading Enterprise and Seamen's Welfare, 1775–1900* (Exeter, 1987).
Fletcher, B. 'The Experience of the Shipping Federation, 1906 to 1910' (1984), *Maritime Policy and Management*, Vol. XI, No. 4.
Fletcher, J. 'The date of the Graveney boat' (1984), IJNA, Vol. 13, No. 2.
Fletcher, M. E. 'From Coal to Oil in British Shipping' (1975), *Journal of Transport History*, Vol. 3, No. 1.
Floud, R. 'A Tall Story? The Standard of Living Debate' (1983), *History Today*, Vol. 33.
Foster, W. *The East India House* (London, 1924).
Foster, W. *The Voyages of Sir James Lancaster to Brazil and the East Indies 1591–1603* (London, 1940).
Frobisher, M. *The Three Voyages* (London, 1847).
Fry, H. T. *Alexander Dalrymple and the Expansion of British Trade* (London, 1970).

Galenson, D. 'The Slave Trade to the English West Indies 1673–1724' (1979), EHR, 2nd Series, Vol. XXXII, No. 2.
Garmonsway, G. (trs.). *The Anglo-Saxon Chronicle* (London, 1953).
Gelsinger, B. E. 'Lodestone and Sunstone in Medieval Iceland' (1970), MM, Vol. 56, No. 2.
Geoffrey of Monmouth, *History of the Kings of Britain* (London, 1963).
Gibb, J. M. *Morels of Cardiff: the History of a Family Shipping Firm* (Cardiff, 1982).
Gibbs-Smith, C. *The Bayeux Tapestry* (London, 1973).
Giggal, K. *Classic Sailing Ships* (Exeter, 1988).
Gilbert, H. *The Voyages and Colonising Enterprises of Sir Humphrey Gilbert* (London, 1940).
Girvan, W. 'The First Mail Service to Australia', *British Shipping*, No. 21.

Glasgow, T. 'Gorga's Seafight' (1973) MM, Vol. 59, No. 2.

Goldenburg, J. A. 'An Analysis of Shipbuilding Sites in *Lloyd's Register* of 1776' (1973), MM, Vol. 59, No. 4.

Golding, G. *Records and Songs of Saxon Times* (London, 1932).

Gordon, R. *Anglo-Saxon Poetry* (London, 1954).

Goss, R. O. 'New Challenges for Ships and Ports Symposium' (Haifa, August 1984).

Goss, R. O. 'Sense and Shipping Policies' (UWIST, 1986).

Goss, R. O. 'The decline of UK-registered merchant shipping': a memorandum submitted to the House of Commons Transport Committee (1986).

Graham, G. S. 'The Ascendancy of the Sailing Ship 1850–1875' (1956), EHR, Vol. IX, No. 1.

Graham, G. S. *The Empire of the North Atlantic: The Maritime Struggle for North America* (London, 1958).

Graham, G. S. *The Politics of Naval Supremacy* (Cambridge, 1965).

Gras, H. S. B. *The Early English Customs System* (Cambridge, 1918).

Grell, K. (ed), *Captain John Smith, A Sea Grammar* (London, 1970).

Green, E. & Moss, M. *A Business of National Importance – the Royal Mail Shipping Group, 1902–37* (London, 1982).

Green, S. R. *Whither O Ship: Adventures in a Tramp Steamer* (London, 1989).

Gripaios, H. *Tramp Shipping* (London, 1959).

Greenham, A. W. R. M. 'Packet Boats' (1958), Harwich.

Greenhalgh-Shaw, F. *Stories from Eighty Years of Travel and Adventure* (Ilfracombe, 1988).

Greenhill, B. (with L. Willis). *The Coastal Trade: Sailing Craft of British Waters 900–1900* (London, 1975).

Greenhill, B. *Archaeology of the Boat* (London, 1976).

Greenhill, B. 'The Death of Mercantile Sail', *Fairplay*, 28.6.1979.

Greenhill, B. (gen. ed.) *The Ship*: see Corlett, E., Craig, R., Greenhill, B., Maber, J., McGowan, A. (London, 1980).

Greenhill, B. *The life and death of Merchant Sailing Ships 1815–1915* (London, 1980).

Greenhill, B. *The Merchant Schooners* (London, 1988).

Greenhill, R. G. 'The Royal Mail Steam Packet Company and the Development of Steamship Links with Latin America' (1973), *Maritime History*, Vol. 3, No. 1.

Guthrie, J. *A History of Marine Engineering* (London, 1971).

Hakluyt, R. *The Principal Navigations, Voyages, Traffiques and Discoveries of the English Nation*. 12 Vols. (London, 1927).

Hanway, J. *Reason for an Augmentation of at least Twelve Thousand Mariners, to be employed in the Merchants' Service and Coasting Trade* (London, 1759).

Harcourt, F. 'The P & O Company: Flagships of Imperialism', in Palmer, S. &

Williams, G. (eds) *Charted and Uncharted Waters*: Proceedings of a Conference on the Study of British Maritime History (London, 1982).

Harcourt, F. 'British oceanic mail contracts in the age of steam, 1838–1914' (1988), *The Journal of Transport History*, 3rd Series, Vol. 9, No. 1.

Harland, J. H. 'The Early History of the Steering Wheel' (1972), MM, Vol. 58, No. 1.

Harper, L. A. *The English Navigation Laws* (New York, 1964).

Harris, J. R. (ed.) *Liverpool & Merseyside* (London, 1969).

Hassall, W. O. *How They Lived 55BC–1485* (Oxford, 1962).

Hawkins, R. *The Observations of Sir Richard Hawkins, Knt, in his voyage into the South Sea in 1593* (London, 1622 and 1847).

Haws, D. *Merchant Ships in Profile*, 4 vols. (Cambridge, 1980).

Hay, D. *Under the Red Ensign: The Merchant Navy 1939–45* (London, 1982).

Hill, J. H. H. *The Seafaring Career* (London, 1972).

Hinton, R. W. K. *The Eastland Trade and the Common Weal in the Seventeenth Century* (Cambridge, 1959).

Hodges, R, 'The Hamwih pottery: the local and imported ware from 30 years' excavations at Middle Saxon Southampton and their European context' (1981), Southampton Archaeological Committee Report 2, CBA Research Report.

Hodges, R. *Dark Age Economics: The Origins of town and trade, AD 600–1000* (London, 1982).

Hoh-Cheung & Mui, L. H. 'The Commutation Act and the Tea Trade in Britain 1784–1793' (1963), EHR, 2nd Series, Vol. XVI, No. 2.

Hope, R. *Profits in British Industry 1924–1935*: unpublished thesis (Oxford, 1948).

Hope, R. (ed). *The Seaman's World* (London, 1982).

Hope, R. (ed). *Sea Pie* (London, 1984).

Hope, R. 'The Political Economy of Marine Transportation', in Johnston, D. M. (ed) *Marine Policy and the Coastal Community* (London, 1976).

Hornell, J. *Water Transport* (Cambridge, 1946).

Hornell, J. 'The Sources of the Clinker and Carvel Systems in British Boat Construction' (1948), MM, Vol. 34.

Howarth, D. & S. *The Story of P & O* (London, 1986).

Hughes, R. *The Fatal Shore* (London, 1987).

Hugill, S. *Shanties of the Seven Seas* (London, 1961).

Hugill, S. *Sailortown* (London, 1967).

Hull, C. H. (ed) *The Economic Writings of Sir William Petty* (Cambridge, 1899).

Hume, J. R. & Moss, M. S. *A Bed of Nails: The History of P. MacCullum & Sons Ltd of Greenock 1781–1981* (Greenock, 1981).

Hunter, H. C. *How England got its Merchant Marine, 1066–1766* (New York, 1935).

Hutchinson, J. K. *The Press-Gang Afloat and Ashore* (London, 1913).

Hyde, F. E. *Blue Funnel: A History of Alfred Holt and Company of Liverpool from 1865 to 1914* (Liverpool, 1956).

Hyde, F. E. *Shipping Enterprise and Management, 1830–1939: Harrisons of Liverpool* (Liverpool, 1967).

Jackson, G. *The British Whaling Trade* (London, 1978).

Jackson, G. *The History and Archaeology of Ports* (Kingswood, Surrey, 1983).

Jackson, G. 'Scottish Shipping, 1775–1805' in Cottrell, P. L. & Aldcroft, D. H. (eds). *Shipping, Trade and Commerce: Essays in Memory of Ralph Davis* (Leicester, 1981).

James, M. K. *Studies in the Medieval Wine Trade* (Oxford, 1971).

Jamieson, A. (ed). *A People of the Sea: The Maritime History of the Channel Islands* (London, 1986).

Jobson, R. *The Golden Trade* (London, 1623; Kingsley, C. (ed), reprinted Teignmouth, no date.).

Johnstone, P. *The Archaeology of Ships* (London, 1974).

Jones, C. *British Merchant Shipping* (London, 1922).

Jones, G. *The Norse Atlantic Saga* (London, 1964).

Jones, S. 'Blood Red Roses: The Supply of Merchant Seamen in the Nineteenth Century' (1972), MM, Vol. 58, No. 4.

Jones, S. 'Community and Organisation – Early Seamen's Trade Unionism on the North-East Coast, 1768–1844' (1973), *Maritime History*, Vol. 3, No. 1.

Jones, S. *Trade and Shipping: Lord Inchcape 1852–1932* (Manchester, 1989).

Jung, I. *The Marine Turbine* (National Maritime Museum, Greenwich, 1987).

Keevil, J. J. *Medicine and the Navy*, Vol. I, 1200–1649 (London, 1957).

Kemp, P. *Oxford Companion to Ships and the Sea* (Oxford, 1976).

Kemp, P. *The Campaign of the Spanish Armada* (Oxford, 1988).

Kepler, J. S. 'Fiscal Aspects of the English Carrying Trade during the Thirty Years War' (1972), EHR, Vol. XXV.

Kerbreck de, R. P. & Williams, D. L. *Cunard White Star Liners of the 1930s* (London, 1988).

Kirk, R. *British Maritime Postal History*, II, The P & O Lines to the Far East (Heathfield, Proud-Bailey, 1982).

Kirkaldy, A. W. *British Shipping* (London, 1914).

Klein, H. S. 'The English Slave Trade to Jamaica, 1782–1808' (1978), EHR, 2nd Series, Vol. XXXI, No. 1.

Klinghoffer, A. J. *Fraud of the Century* (London, 1988).

Knight, R. B. (ed). *Guide to the Manuscripts in the National Maritime Museum*, 2 vols. (London, 1977 & 1980).

Kumana, S. D. 'Financial analysis of UK shipping companies', *Fairplay*, 9.1.1979.

Kverndal, R. *Seamen's Missions* (Pasadena, 1986).

Landström, B. *Sailing Ships* (London, 1969).

Lane, F. C. 'Tonnages, Medieval and Modern' (1964), EHR, 2nd Series, Vol. XVII, No. 1.

Lane, T. *Grey Dawn Breaking: British Seafarers in the Late Twentieth Century* (Manchester, 1986).

Langley, M. & Small, E. *Port of Plymouth Series: Merchant Shipping* (Devon, 1988).

Lewis, A. *The Northern Seas* (Princeton, N.J., 1958).

Lewis, M. *A Social History of the Navy 1792–1815* (London, 1960).

Lindsay, W. S. *History of Merchant Shipping and Ancient Commerce*, 4 vols. (London, 1874–6).

Lloyd, A. L. *Folk Song in England* (London, 1975).

Lloyd, C. *British Seamen* (London, 1968).

Lloyd, T. H. *The English Wool Trade in the Middle Ages* (Cambridge, 1977).

Lloyd, T. H. *Alien Merchants in England in the High Middle Ages* (Brighton, 1982).

Lovejoy, P. E. *Transformations in Slavery: A history of slavery in Africa* (Cambridge, 1983).

Lowell, E. J. *The Hessians and other German Auxiliaries of Great Britain in the Revolutionary Wars* (New York, 1884).

Lubbock, B. *The China Clippers* (Glasgow, 1914; London, 1984).

Lubbock, B. (ed). *Barlow's Journal*, 2 vols. (London, 1934).

Lythe, S. G. E. *Scottish Trade with the Baltic, 1550–1650* (Dundee, 1955).

Maber, J. *Channel Packets & Ocean Liners, 1850–1970* (London, 1980).

MacGregor, D. R. *Schooners in Four Centuries* (Hemel Hempstead, 1982).

MacGregor, D. R. *Merchant Sailing Ships, 1775–1815: Their Design and Construction* (Watford, Herts, 1980).

MacGregor, D. R. *Merchant Sailing Ships, 1815–1850: Supremacy of Sail* (London, 1984).

MacGregor, D. R. *Merchant Sailing Ships, 1850–1875: Heyday of Sail* (London, 1984).

MacGregor, D. R. *The Tea Clippers: Their History and Development, 1833–1875* (London, 1983).

MacGregor, D. R. *The China Bird (Killick Martin & Company)*, 2nd ed. (London, 1986).

MacGregor, D. R. *Fast Sailing Ships, 1775–1875* (London, 1973).

Madox, R. (Donne, E. S., ed). *An Elizabethan in 1582, The Diary of Richard Madox* (London, 1976).

Mallett, A. S. & Bell, A. M. B. *The Pirrie Kylsant Motor Ships, 1915–32* (Cottishall, 1984).

Mannix, D. P. & Cowley, M. *Black Cargoes* (London, 1963).

Maple, J. T. *The Irish Sea Region, 850–1254 AD* (University of Kansas, 1985).

Marcus, G. J. 'The Navigation of the Norsemen' (1953), MM, Vol. 39.

Marcus, G. J. 'The First English Voyages to Iceland' (1956), MM, Vol. 42.

Marinner, S. & Hyde, F. E. *The Senior: John Samuel Swire 1825–98* (Liverpool, 1967).

Markham, C. (ed). *The Voyages of Sir James Lancaster, Kt. to the East Indies* (London, 1877).

Marsden, P. 'The County Hall ship, London' (1974), IJNA, Vol. 3, No. 1.

Marsden, P. 'A boat of the Roman period found at Bruges, Belgium, in 1899 and related types' (1976), IJNA, Vol. 5, No. 1.

Marsden, P. *Roman London* (London, 1980).

Marsden, P. 'The Medieval Ships of London' in McGrail, S. (ed). *The Archaeology of Medieval Ships and Harbours in Northern Europe* (London, 1979).

Marsh, A. & Ryan, V. *The Seamen: A History of the National Union of Seamen* (Oxford, 1989).

Mason, M., Greenhill, B. & Craig, R. *The British Seafarer* (London, undated).

Mathias, P. *The First Industrial Nation: An Economic History of Britain 1700–1914*, 2nd ed. (London, 1969).

Matthews, K. & Panting, G. (eds), *Ships and Shipbuilding in the North Atlantic Region* (St John's, 1978).

Maxwell, I. 'The Location of Ictis' (1972), Journal of the Royal Institution of Cornwall.

McBrearly, R. F. *Seafaring in the 30s* (Lewes, 1989).

McConville, J. *The Shipping Industry in the United Kingdom* (Geneva, 1977).

McGowan, A. *The Century before Steam: the Development of the Sailing Ship, 1700–1820* (London, 1980).

McGowan, A. *Tiller and Whipstaff: The Development of the Sailing Ship, 1400–1700* (London, 1981).

McGrail, S. (ed). *The Archaeology of Medieval Ships and Harbours in Northern Europe*, BAR International Series 66 (London, 1979).

McGrail, S. (ed). *Ancient Boats* (Princes Risborough, 1983).

McGrath, P. 'Bristol and America 1480–1631' in Andrews, K. R., Canny, N. P. & Hair, P. E. H. (eds). *The Westward Enterprise: English activities in Ireland, the Atlantic and America, 1480–1650* (Liverpool, 1978).

McKellar, N. L. *From Derby round to Burketown* (St Lucia, University of Queensland Press, 1977).

McMurray, H. C. 'Ships' engineers: their status and position on board, c. 1830–65' in Fisher, S. (ed). *West Country Maritime and Social History: Some Essays* (Exeter, 1980).

Metaxas, B. N. *Flags of Convenience* (Aldershot, 1985).

Meyer, W. R. 'English Privateering in the War of the Spanish Succession 1702–1713 (1983), MM, Vol. 69, No. 4.

Meyerstein, E. (ed). *Adventures by Sea of Edward Coxere* (New York, 1946).

Middlemiss, N. L. *Gathering of the Clans: History of the Clan Line Steamers Ltd* (Newcastle upon Tyne, 1988).

Miller, L. 'New Fresh Wharf 2, the Saxon and early medieval waterfronts' (1977), *The London Archaeologist*, Vol. 3, No. 2.

Miller, W. H. *Transatlantic Liners, 1945–1980* (Newton Abbot, 1981).

Miller, W. H. *German Ocean Liners of the 20th Century* (Northants, 1988).

Miller, W. H. & Braynard, O. *Fifty Famous Liners* (Cambridge, 1982).

Miller, W. H. & Hutchings, D. F. *Transatlantic Liners at War* (Newton Abbot, 1985).

Millington, E. C. *Seamen in the Making* (London, 1935).

Milsom, C. H. *Blue Funnels in the Mersey in the 1920s* (Liverpool, 1988).

Milsom, C. H. *Blue Funnel: the Later Years, 1925–1982* (Liverpool, 1989).

Minchinton, W. E. 'British Ports of Call in the Nineteenth Century' (1976), MM, Vol. 62, No. 2.

Moody, B. *Merchant Ships in the Solent: Past and Present* (Southampton, 1988).

Moore, A. *The Last Days of Mast and Sail* (Oxford, 1925).

Moore, A. 'Rig in Northern Europe' (1956), MM, Vol. 42.

Morcken, R. 'Longships, Knarrs and Cogs' (1988), MM, Vol. 74, No. 4.

Morison, S. E. *Portuguese Voyages to America in the Fifteenth Century* (Harvard, 1940).

Morison, S. E. *Christopher Columbus, Mariner* (London, 1956).

Moss, M. & Hume, J. R. *Shipbuilders to the World: 125 Years of Harland and Wolff* (Belfast, 1986).

Moyse-Bartlett, H. *A History of the Merchant Navy* (London, 1937).

Muckelroy, K. 'Middle Bronze Age trade between Britain and Europe: a maritime perspective' (1981), *Proceedings of the Prehistoric Society*, Vol. 47.

Munro, J. F. 'Scottish Overseas Enterprise and the Lure of London: The Mackinnon Shipping Group, 1847–1893' (1988), *Scottish Economic & Social History*, Vol. VIII.

Naess, E. D. *Autobiography of a Shipping Man* (Colchester, 1977).

Nash, R. C. 'The English and Scottish Tobacco Trades in the 17th and 18th Centuries: Legal and Illegal Trade' (1982), EHR, 2nd Series, Vol. XXXV, No. 3.

Neal, L. 'The Cost of Impressment during the Seven Years War' (1978), MM, Vol. 64, No. 1.

Nef, J. *The Rise of the British Coal Industry*, Vol. II (London, 1932).

Newton, J. (Martin, B. & Spurrell, M. eds), *The Journal of a Slave Trader 1750–1754* (London, 1962).

O'Donoghue, K. J. & Appleyard, H. S. *Hain of St Ives* (Kendal, 1986).

Oleson, T. *Early Voyages and Northern Approaches* (London, 1964).

O'Meara, J. *The Voyage of St Brendan* (Ireland, 1976).

Oppenheim, M. *A History of the Administration of the Royal Navy and of Merchant Shipping in Relation to the Navy from 1509 to 1660 with an Introduction treating of the Preceding Period* (London 1896 & 1988).

Orbell, J. with Green, E. & Moss, M. *From Cape to Cape: History of Lyles Shipping Company* (Edinburgh, 1978).

Padfield, P. *Beneath the House Flag of the P & O* (London, 1981).

Padfield, P. *Armada* (London, 1988).

Palmer, S. '"The most indefatigable activity." The General Steam Navigation Company 1824–50' (1982), *The Journal of Transport History*, 3rd Series, Vol. 3, No. 2.

Palmer, S. & Williams, G. (eds), *Charted and Uncharted Waters*: Proceedings of a Conference on the Study of British Maritime History (London, 1982).

Parkinson, C. N. (ed). *The Trade Winds: A Study of British Overseas Trade during the French Wars 1793–1815* (London, 1948).

Parry, C. R. 'The General Post Office's Zanzibar Shipping Contracts, 1860–1914' (1982), MM, Vol. 68, No. 1.

Parry, J. H. *The Age of Reconnaissance* (London, 1963).

Parry, J. H. *The Spanish Seaborne Empire* (London, 1966).

Peake, H. & Fleure, H. *The Way of the Sea* (Oxford, 1929).

Perrin, W. (ed) *Boteler's Dialogues* (London, 1929).

Phillips, T. *A Journal of a Voyage made in the Hannibal of London (1693–1694)*.

Phillips-Burt, D. *The History of Seamanship* (London, 1971).

Piggott, S. *Scotland before History* (London, 1958).

Pinkerton, J. *A General Collection of the Best and Most Interesting Voyages and Travels in All Parts of the World* (London, 1808).

Pollard, S. & Robertson, P. *The British Shipbuilding Industry 1870–1914* (Cambridge, Mass., 1979).

Poole, A. L. (ed) *Medieval England* (Oxford, 1958).

Porter, A. *Victorian Shipping, Business and Imperial Policy. Donald Currie, the Castle Line and Southern Africa* (Woodbridge, Suffolk, 1986).

Powell, L. *The Shipping Federation 1890–1950* (London, 1950).

Powell, T. *The Celts* (London, 1958).

Power, E. & Postan, M. (eds). *Studies in English Trade in the Fifteenth Century* (London, 1951).

Press, J. 'Wages in the Merchant Navy, 1815–54' (1981), *The Journal of Transport History*, 3rd Series, Vol. 2, No. 2.

Quinn, D. B. (ed) *The Roanoke Voyages 1584–1590*, 2 vols. (London, 1955).

Quinn, D. B. & Ryan, A. N. *England's Sea Empire, 1550–1642* (London, 1983).

Rabb, T. K. 'Investment in English Overseas Enterprise, 1575–1630' (1966), EHR, 2nd Series, Vol. XIX, No. 1.

Rabson, S. & O'Donoghue, K. *P & O: A Fleet History* (Kendal, 1988).

Raleigh, W. *Works* (Oxford, 1829).

Raleigh, W. *The Discovery of the Large, Rich and Beautiful Empire of Guiana* (London, 1595 & 1848).

Ramsay, G. D. *English Overseas Trade during the Centuries of Emergence* (London, 1957).

Ranken, M. B. F. (ed). *Britain and the Sea: Future Dependence, Future Opportunities* (Edinburgh, 1984).

Rawson, G. *Sea Prelude* (London, 1958).

Rees, H. *British Ports and Shipping* (London, 1958).

Rich, E. E. *The History of the Hudson's Bay Company, 1670–1870*, 2 vols. (London, 1958).

Rinman, T. & Brodefors, R. *The Commercial History of Shipping* (Gothenburg, 1983).

Robertson, A. J. 'Backward British businessmen and the motor ship, 1918–39. The critique reviewed' (1988), *The Journal of Transport History*, 3rd series, Vol. 9, No. 2.

Robinson, C. (trs) *Anskar: The Apostle of the North* (London, 1921).

Robinson, D. E. 'Secret of British Power in the Age of Sail: Admiralty Reports of the Coasting Fleet' (1987), *American Neptune*, Vol. XVIII, No. 1.

Rogers, H. C. B. *Troopships and their History* (London, 1963).

Rogers, W. *A Cruising Voyage round the World, 1712* (London, 1928).

Ropner, W. G. D. 'A Century of British Tramping', *Fairplay*, 19.5.1983.

Rowse, A. L. *The Expansion of Elizabethan England* (London, 1955).

Rule, M. *The Mary Rose: The Excavation and Raising of Henry VIII's Flagship* (London, 1982).

Runciman, W. *Before the Mast – and After* (London, 1924).

Runciman, W. *Collier Brigs and their Sailors* (London, 1926).

Runyan, T. J. 'Ships and Mariners in Later Medieval England' (1977), *Journal of British Studies*, Vol. XVI, No. 2.

Ryder, A. P. *6th Report of the Science and Art Department* (London, 1858).

Sadler, J. *Discipline at Sea* (Glasgow, 1983).

Salway, P. *The Frontier People of Roman Britain* (Cambridge, 1965).

Salzman, A. L. *English Trade in the Middle Ages* (Oxford, 1931).

Savill, D. *Sail to New Zealand* (London, 1986).

Sawyer, P. *The Age of the Vikings* (London, 1962).

Scammell, G. V. *The World Encompassed: The first European marine empires* (London, 1981).

Scammell, G. V. *The English chartered trading companies and the sea* (National Maritime Museum, Greenwich, 1983).

Scammell, G. V. 'English Merchant Shipping at the End of the Middle Ages: some East Coast Evidence' (1961), EHR, 2nd Series, Vol. XIII, No. 3.

Scammell, G. V. 'Shipowning in England circa 1450–1550' (1962), *Transactions of the Royal Historical Society*, 5th Series, Vol. 12.

Scammell, G. V. 'Manning the English Merchant Service in the Sixteenth Century' (1970), MM, Vol. 56, No. 2.

Scammell, G. V. 'Shipowning in the Economy and Politics of Early Modern England' (1972), *The Historical Journal*, Vol. XV.

Scammell, G. V. 'The English in the Atlantic Islands, c. 1450–1650'. (1986), MM, Vol. 72, No. 3.

Schofield, F. *Humber Keels and Keelmen* (Lavenham, 1988).

Shammas, C. 'English commercial development and American colonisation 1500–1620' in Andrews, K. R., Canny, N. P. and Hair, P. E. H., *The Westward Enterprise: English activities in Ireland, the Atlantic and America 1480–1650* (Liverpool, 1978).

Shelvocke, G. *A Voyage Round the World* (London 1726, reprinted 1928).

Sherborne, J. W. 'The English Navy, Shipping and Manpower, 1369–1389' (1967), *Past & Present*, No. 37.

Sherborne, J. W. 'English Barges and Balingers in the late Fourteenth Century' (1977), MM, Vol. 63, No. 2.

Sherrard, O. A. *Freedom from Fear: The Slave and his Emancipation* (London, 1959).

Slader, J. *The Red Duster at War: A History of the Merchant Navy during the Second World War* (London, 1988).

Smyth, H. P. *The B & I Line: a History of the British and Irish Steam Packet Company* (Dublin, 1984).

Sohmen, H. *Shipping in Crisis* (Hong Kong, 1983).

Spencer, A. (ed) *Memoirs of William Hickey (1749–1775)*, 3 vols. (London, 1913).

Stammers, M. *West Coast Shipping* (Anglesey, 1976).

Stammers, M. *The Passage Makers: the History of the Black Ball Line of Australian Packets, 1852–1871* (Brighton, 1978).

Starkey, D. J. 'British Privateering against the Dutch in the American Revolutionary War, 1780–1783', in Fisher, S. (ed), *Studies in British Privateering, Trading Enterprise and Seamen's Welfare, 1775–1900* (Exeter, 1987).

Starkey, D. J. 'The economic and military significance of British privateering, 1702–83' (1988), *The Journal of Transport History*, 3rd Series, Vol. 9, No. 1.

Steele, I. K. *The English Atlantic 1675–1740: An Exploration of Communication and Community* (Oxford, 1986).

Stephenson, M. J. 'Wool yields in the medieval economy' (1988). EHR, 2nd Series, Vol. XLI, No. 3.

Stevens, H. *The Dawn of British Trade to the East Indies* (London, 1886).

Sturmey, S. G. *British Shipping and World Competition* (London, 1962).

Sturmey, S. G. *Shipping Economics* (London, 1975).

Sutton, J. *Lords of the East: the East India Company and Its Ships* (Greenwich, 1981).

Syrrett, D. *Shipping and the American War 1775–83* (London, 1970).

Tawney, A. & Power, E. *The Tudor Economic Documents*, Vol. II (London, 1924).

Taylor, E. *The Haven-Finding Art* (London, 1956).

Taylor, H. 'Trade, Neutrality and the "English Road"' (1972), EHR, Vol. XXV.

Taylor, J. S. *Jonas Hanway: Founder of the Marine Society* (London, 1985).

Thomas, D. A. *The Illustrated Armada Book* (London, 1988).

Thomas, M. W. *A Survey of English Economic History* 3rd edn. (London, 1967).

Thomas, P. J. *Mercantilism and East India Trade* (London, 1926 & 1963).

Thomson, J. *History of Ancient Geography* (Cambridge, 1948).

Thornton, R. H. *British Shipping* (Cambridge, 1939 & 1959).

Thorpe, B. *Ancient Laws and Institutes of England* (London, 1840).

Troup, J. A. (ed) *The Ice-bound Whalers* (Kirkwall, 1987).

Twiss, T. (ed) *The Black Book of the Admiralty*, Vol. I (London, 1871).

Underhill, H. A. *Deep Water Sail* (Glasgow, 1952).

Underhill, H. A. *Sailing Ship Rigs and Riggings* (Glasgow, 1988).

Underwood, D. 'Industrial relations in the shipping industry' (1978), *Personnel Management*, No. 10.

Unger, R. W. *The Ship in the Medieval Economy, 600–1600* (London, 1980).

Unger, R. W. 'Integration of Baltic and Low Countries grain markets, 1400–1800' in *The Interactions of Amsterdam and Antwerp with the Baltic Region, 1400–1800* (Leiden, 1953).

Vamplew, W. *Salvesen of Leith* (Edinburgh, 1975).

Ville, S. *English Shipowning during the Industrial Revolution: 1770–1830* (Manchester, 1987).

Ville, S. 'Wages, prices and profitability in the shipping industry during the Napoleonic wars' (1981), *The Journal of Transport History*, 3rd Series, Vol. 2, No. 1.

Ville, S. 'Total Factor Productivity in the English Shipping Industry: The North-east Coal Trade, 1700–1850' (1986), EHR, 2nd Series, Vol. XXXIX, No. 3.

Waine, C. V. *Steam Coasters and Short Sea Traders* (Albrighton, 1976).

Waites, B. 'The Medieval Ports and Trade of North-East Yorkshire' (1977), MM, Vol. 63, No. 2.

Walker, D. *Champion of Sail* (London, 1986).

Walker, G. *Voyages and Cruises* (London, 1760 & 1928).

Wallace, F. W. *Under Sail in the Last of the Clippers* (Glasgow, 1936).

Ward Jackson, C. H. *Stephens of Fowey: a Portrait of a Cornish Merchant Fleet, 1867–1939* (London, 1980).

Warner, G. (ed) *The Voyage of Robert Dudley afterwards styled Earl of Warwick and Leicester and Duke of Northumberland to the West Indies 1594–5* (London, 1899).

Waters, D. *The Art of Navigation in England in Elizabethan and Early Stuart Times* (London, 1958).

Whitelock, D. *English Historical Documents I* (London, 1955).

Willan, T. *The Early History of the Russia Company* (Manchester, 1956).

Willan, T. *Studies in Elizabethan Foreign Trade* (Manchester, 1959).

Willan, T. *The English Coasting Trade 1600–1750* (Manchester, 1967).

Williams, D. 'Crew size in transatlantic trade in the mid-nineteenth century' in Ommer, R. & Panting, G. (eds) *Working Men Who got Wet* (St John's, 1982).

Williams, D. *Liners in Battledress* (London, 1989).

Williams, G. *History of Liverpool Privateers* (London, 1897).

Williamson, J. *Maritime Enterprise 1485–1558* (Oxford, 1913).

Williamson, J. *Sir John Hawkins, The Time and the Man* (Oxford, 1927).

Williamson, J. *Hawkins of Plymouth* (London, 1949).

Williamson, J. *The Age of Drake* (London, 1952).

Williamson, J. (ed) *The Cabot Voyages and Bristol Discovery under Henry VII* (Cambridge, 1962).

Willis, L. (Introduction and Notes by Greenhill, B.) *The Coastal Trade: Sailing Craft of British Waters 900–1900* (London, 1975).

Willoughby, R. M. *Square Rig Seamanship* (London, 1989).
Woddis, J. *Under the Red Duster* (London, 1947).
Woodman, R. *Voyage East: A Cargo Ship in the 1960s* (London, 1988).

Zahadieh, N. 'Trade, Plunder and Economic Development in Early English Jamaica 1655–89' (1986), EHR, 2nd Series, Vol. XXXIX, No. 2.

Index

Individual ships are to be found under the entry 'Ships'